ROUTLEDGECURZON ENCYCLOPEDIA OF CONFUCIANISM

RoutledgeCurzon Encyclopedias of Religion

Available in the series:

RoutledgeCurzon Encyclopedia of Confucianism
Edited by Xinzhong Yao

Forthcoming in the series:
RoutledgeCurzon Encyclopedia of Taoism
Edited by Fabrizio Pregadio

RoutledgeCurzon Encyclopedia of Islam
Edited by Ian Richard Netton

RoutledgeCurzon Encyclopedia of Hinduism
Edited by Denise Cush, Catherine Robinson and Michael York

RoutledgeCurzon Encyclopedia of Sikhism
Edited by Arvind-pal S. Mandair and Christopher Shackle

ROUTLEDGECURZON ENCYCLOPEDIA OF CONFUCIANISM

Volume 2

O–Z

Edited by

Xinzhong Yao

RoutledgeCurzon
Taylor & Francis Group

LONDON AND NEW YORK

First published 2003
by RoutledgeCurzon
11 New Fetter Lane, London EC4P 4EE

Simultaneously published in the USA and Canada
by Routledge
29 West 35th Street, New York, NY 10001

RoutledgeCurzon is an imprint of the Taylor & Francis Group

Typeset in Baskerville by Graphicraft
Printed and bound in Great Britain by TJ International Ltd, Padstow, Cornwall

British Library Cataloguing in Publication Data
A catalogue record for this book is available from the British Library

Library of Congress Cataloging in Publication Data
RoutledgeCurzon encyclopedia of Confucianism / Edited by Xinzhong Yao.
p. cm. — (RoutledgeCurzon encyclopedias of religion ; 1)
Includes bibliographical references and index.
1. Confucianism–Encyclopedias.   I. Title: Encyclopedia of Confucianism.   II. Yao,
Xinzhong.   III. Series.

BL1840 .R68 2003
181'.112'03–dc21
2002068250

ISBN 0–700–71199–6 (set)
ISBN 0–415–30652–3 (vol. 1)
ISBN 0–415–30653–1 (vol. 2)

Contents

Ogyû Sorai 荻生徂徠

1666–1728

(*na* 名: Sôshô 雙松; *azana* 字: Mokei 茂卿)

Ogyû Sorai is often characterised as one of the three leading figures of the Ancient Learning (*kogaku*) movement in Tokugawa thought, along with **Yamaga Sokô** and **Itô Jinsai**. Sorai's mature Confucian thought is more accurately described, however, as he himself did, as a form of *kobunjigaku* 古文字學 or 'the study of ancient expressions'. The notion that there was an 'Ancient Learning' movement seems to derive from two sources. Firstly, negatively, late eighteenth-century followers of **Zhu Xi** School who opposed the teachings of Sokô, Jinsai and Sorai, and for polemical purposes associated with the Kansei Ban on Heterodox Learning, linked them together as advocates of *kogaku*, or 'Ancient Learning'. Secondly, quite positively, **Inoue Tetsujirô**'s early twentieth-century writings described the *kogaku* movement as a distinctively Japanese development that had attacked and overcome the Zhu Xi philosophy earlier imported from China. One of the early proponents of a nationalistic, imperialistic ethic, Inoue Tetsujirô's interpretations of Tokugawa Confucian thought seem to echo the intensely pro-Japanese sentiments rampant following the Sino-Japanese War, and Japan's astounding defeat of Qing China. Though postwar Japanese scholarship on Sokô, Jinsai and Sorai rarely refers to them in terms of *kogaku*, many western scholars, still following Inoue's dated interpretations, continue to speak of these three thinkers as representative figures in the 'Ancient Learning' movement.

Sorai was born in Edo, in 1666, the second son of a samurai-physician who served Tokugawa Tsunayoshi before the latter became shogun. For reasons that remain unclear, in 1679, Sorai's father was exiled from Edo for just over a decade, to a remote area, Kazusa (in modern Chiba Prefecture). During that time, Sorai, isolated from the distractions of Edo and instructed by a disciplinarian father, had no alternative but to immerse himself in the study of Neo-Confucian works. Shortly after returning to Edo in 1690, Sorai was thus able to initiate his professional life as a Neo-Confucian scholar–teacher. In 1696, he began serving Yanagisawa Yoshiyasu, a favourite of the shogun; this service brought him into close and regular contact with the shogun Tsunayoshi for the next fifteen years. Throughout this period, Sorai remained, officially at least, a Neo-Confucian scholar. Prior to Jinsai's death in 1705, however, Sorai wrote the Kyoto scholar expressing admiration for his *Gomô jigi* (which had been published, without Jinsai's consent, in Edo in 1695). Sorai also made known his desire to establish an academic relationship with Jinsai. But Jinsai never replied, which apparently wounded Sorai's pride and badly soured his respect for the elder scholar. From that point on, Sorai's writings continually criticised Jinsai from one perspective or another.

Following the death of Tsunayoshi in 1709, Yanagisawa retired from public life and relieved Sorai of his official duties, even while continuing to supply him with an ample stipend. Consequently, Sorai was free to pursue scholarship and teaching unhampered by his patron's demands. It was during the next two decades that he produced the works for which he is most often remembered. If Sorai's own testimony is accepted, a crucial influence on his thought had appeared in the form of the writings of Li Panlong (李攀龍 1514–1559) and Wang Shizhen (王世貞 1526–1590), two Ming dynasty literary theorists who had advocated 'the study of ancient expressions'. Though Li and Wang had not applied their ideas to Confucianism, Sorai saw in their literary strategy a basis for pursuing a line of philosophical activity similar to that of Jinsai's *kogigaku* 古義學, or 'the study of ancient meanings', but without having to acknowledge any intellectual debt to Jinsai in doing so. The extent to which Sorai was profoundly influenced by Li and Wang *per se* is questionable, especially since Confucians were traditionally given to returning to the past and engaging in the study of ancient expressions. Moreover, as was true with Sokô and Jinsai earlier, despite Sorai's professed rejection of Zhu Xi's Song Confucianism, Sorai's thought was profoundly influenced in genre, method and content by Neo-Confucians who appeared after Zhu Xi. In particular, Sorai, like Sokô and Jinsai, learned much from the late-Song philosophical lexicon, the **Beixi ziyi** by **Chen Chun**. This is most apparent in Sorai's philosophical magnum opus, the *Benmei* 弁名 (*Discerning the Meanings of Ancient Philosophical Terms*), a lengthy philosophical lexicon modelled after the *Beixi ziyi*,

addressing the meanings of several dozen concepts, including the most distinctive terminology of Neo-Confucian discourse. No doubt Sorai did criticise Zhu Xi and Neo-Confucians, but his willingness to find some acceptable nuances for Neo-Confucian terminology and incorporate the latter into his system of philosophical semantics made him, in certain respects, as much a Neo-Confucian revisionist as anything. In criticising Jinsai, Sorai regularly noted that despite Jinsai's criticisms of Song Confucians, he differed little from them. Surely Sorai must have realised that the same critical judgement could be turned against his writings as well.

Sorai's methodology, philological analysis, was hardly new. Confucians and Neo-Confucians had long engaged in textual analyses and investigations into the original meanings of terms. Most distinctive in Sorai's thought was his consistent willingness to accommodate the political interests of the ruling elite rather than 'the people'. According to Sorai, the way (Jn. *michi* 道) was founded by the early kings of ancient China, all of whom had been sages. Rejecting abstract metaphysical categories, Sorai defined the way concretely, in the form of rites, music and legal and bureaucratic institutions. The ancient sages had founded the way specifically in order to provide for the pacification and stabilisation of the people within a well-ordered state; in doing so they had modelled the way after the patterns they observed in heaven and earth. Later rulers, according to Sorai, did their work best by governing by means of the way as temporal representatives of the early kings. Unlike many Neo-Confucians who claimed that people could attain sagehood through learning and study of the way, Sorai flatly denied that anyone could become a sage. After all, the work which made the sages sages, i.e., founding the way, had been completed once and for all in remote antiquity. Moreover, people were not expected to study the way, or to understand it discursively; rather, they were simply asked to follow it in their behaviour. If they did, then they would gradually realise the particular talents and virtues which made them useful to the state and society. Sorai provided a fundamentalist religious dimension to his political thought by declaring that the ancient sages were divine figures who were rightly worshipped and revered through faith and trust in their way. Moreover, because the ancient sage kings had formulated notions such as 'ghosts and spirits' (*kishin* 鬼神), Sorai insisted that there could be no doubt about their existence. Questioning what the sages had founded revealed, according to Sorai, nothing but irreverence. Though Sorai claimed that his socio-political philosophy was based on a correct exposition of the meanings of ancient words in the Six Classics *Liu jing*, it seems clear that Sorai read those Classics very selectively, highlighting passages which justified or seemed to justify his articulation of an authoritarian and illiberal system meant primarily to enhance the interests of the samurai regime which he still occasionally served. There can be little doubt that Sorai's teachings could have served – although they were never used as such – as ideological means of enhancing state power while weakening that of the private sphere.

References: Koyasu, 1990; Lidin, 1970, 1973; Maruyama, 1974; McEwan, 1962; Minear, 1976; Tahara, 1991; Yamashita, 1994; Yoshikawa, *et al.*, 1987.

JOHN A. TUCKER

Ôjin Tennô 應神天皇

Ôjin Tennô, also called Homuta-wake (or Homuda-wake) no Mikoto 譽田別命, is the fifteenth in the traditional lineage of Yamato sovereigns, but through the work of postwar historians and archaeologists, he came to be widely seen as the founder of a new dynasty – the 'Ôjin dynasty' – that lasted until the end of the fifth century.

According to the *Nihongi*, he was the fourth son of Emperor Chûai 仲哀, who in turn was the son of the legendary conqueror–hero Yamato Takeru no Mikoto 日本武尊. Ôjin's mother, according to both the **Kojiki** and *Nihongi*, was Empress Jingû 神功皇后, who accompanied Chûai on a western expedition to suppress a rebellion by the Kumaso 熊襲 tribe in Tsukushi 筑紫 (northern Kyûshû). While lodging at the Kashihi palace in Tsukushi, Chûai died prematurely (either of illness or an enemy arrow) because he ignored a divine admonition that subjugating the Kumaso was not a worthwhile goal. Jingû, in obedience to oracles from the gods of the Ise 伊勢 and Sumiyoshi 住吉 shrines advising that there was a much better land to conquer across the sea, proceeded to attack and subjugate the eastern Korean kingdom of Shiragi (Silla) 新羅, inspiring the voluntary submission of the other two Korean kingdoms as well – Kudara (Paekche) 百濟 in the West and Kôkuri (Koguryô) 高句麗 in the North. The account of Jingû was modelled partly on the account of the third century CE shaman queen Himiko 卑彌呼 recorded in the *Records of Wei* (*Wei zhi* 魏志), although the historical interaction between the Korean kingdoms and Japan that we get glimpses of in the account appears to have occurred in the fourth century – the 'century of mystery' in Japanese history for which no contemporary Japanese records exist. Interestingly, Jingû is supposed to have been related to the Crown Prince of Shiragi. The account relates that she was pregnant with Ôjin right from the beginning of the campaign, and that he was born in Chikushi upon her return. She governed as Empress Regent until her death, when Ôjin ascended the throne. In the second year of his reign (391 CE), Yamato forces reportedly carried out a campaign from Mimana (Kaya; Imna) 任那, their military base in southern Korea, against Kôkuri, which after its destruction of the Han dynasty Korean commanderies of Lelang 樂浪 and Dafang 大方 in 313 was becoming increasingly powerful and threatening the southern kingdoms. Since Paekche was saved from its enemy by this attack, the king sent envoys and skilled persons to Yamato as an offering of gratitude, reportedly accompanied by large numbers of settlers. One of the group, named Achiki (A-chik-ki) 阿直歧, was reportedly made the Chinese tutor to the Crown Prince, and when asked by Ôjin if there was a man of greater learning, he sent officers to Paekche to summon a learned scholar and scribe named Wani (Wang nim) 王仁, who brought with him copies of the *Lunyu* and the *Thousand Character Classic* as gifts from the Paekche king. This event, believed to have occurred in 405 CE, has traditionally been given great significance as representing the introduction of Confucian Learning into Japan. Aizawa Seishisai's account of the civilising of Japan by the imperial ancestors in his *New Theses* (1825), for instance, states that 'Emperor Ôjin obtained the Confucian Classics and circulated them throughout the realm . . . If only we had adopted Confucius' teachings to make Amaterasu's government and edification more illustrious still!'. While the historicity of Wani's introduction of Confucianism cannot be verified, the account can certainly stand as a symbol of the official adoption of the Chinese written language by the Yamato court for the writing of official records, registers and edicts – an event which was to have profound implications for the development of Japanese culture and political institutions – and of the important role that Koreans played in that adoption. The immigrants (*kikajin* 帰化人) from Paekche founded important clans whose skills contributed much to the consolidation of the authority of the Yamato court, and many more Paekche immigrants arrived in the fifth century. As a result of the new techniques of record-keeping brought in by the Koreans, the accounts of Jingû and Ôjin in the *Kojiki* and *Nihongi* represent the turning-point where the Japanese historical narrative changes from a mixture of myth, fabrication and legend to annalistic history that can frequently be corroborated by other documents or by artifacts. Ôjin, attended by his mother and sometimes his father, later became apotheosised as the Hachiman 八幡 deity, who has been revered particularly by the *bushi* of Japan as the god of warfare (*yumiya no kami* 弓矢の神). The second largest keyhole tumulus still in existence from the Kofun 古墳 period, in Habikino-shi 羽曳野市 southeast of Osaka, is believed to be Ôjin Tennô's tomb.

Tsuda Sôkichi 津田左右吉 (1873–1961) was the first to point out (in 1928–1929) the sharp change in the nature of the historical narrative that occurs in Books Nine and Ten of the *Nihongi* and the first of several historians to argue that Ôjin (or his son Nintoku 仁徳, whose tomb is even larger) was the actual founder of the clan of 'Great Kings' (*daiô* 大王) that accomplished the integration of the 'coalescent core' of Japan around the beginning of the fifth century, the previous fourteen being fictitious. In the postwar period, Egami Namio put forth a famous theory of a foreign Tungusic conquest in the late fourth century, and Mizuno Yû, agreeing that Yamato was conquered by invaders from Kyushu (though not necessarily Tungusic), found compelling evidence that archaic Yamato was ruled by three successive lines of kings. Building on Egami's horserider theory, the Korean scholar Wontack Hong 洪元卓 even contends that it was a group of equestrian Paekche aristocrats who conquered Japan and established the 'Yamato Wa' 大和倭 kingdom. As evidence he argues that only 222 of the 1,182 ruling clans listed in the 'New Compilation of the Register of Families' (*Shinsen shôjiroku* 新撰姓氏録) of 815 were not directly related to Koreans, and that the highest ranking among the clans that claimed imperial descent (*mahito* 真人) were all of Ôjin's line, which, he claims, originated from Paekche royal families. Accepting Kim Sung-ho's 金聖昊 argument that the story of the eastward conquest of Japan by Emperor

Jinmu 神武 in *Nihongi* is nothing but the story of the early experiences of Homuda-wake, a member of the Paekche royal family who decided to extend his rule across the Tsushima Straits to the still uncivilised land of Japan, Hong proceeds to reconstruct Homuda-wake's eastward conquest of Yamato on the basis of the post-Ôjin records in the *Kojiki* and *Nihongi*. The Egami-Hong conquest theory, which completely turns the tables on the hoary tradition of Japanese nationalist historiography, has been rejected by many scholars (including Kirkland and Farris) as incompatible with the archaeological evidence. But the *Kojiki-Nihongi* idea of Yamato's conquest of southern Korea is even more implausible. Recent scholarship has done much to clarify the extent of Wa's cultural debt to Korea (especially Paekche) in this period, a debt that would be even further clarified if the Imperial Household Agency were to relax its Meiji-rooted prohibition on the excavation of the ancient Japanese royal tombs.

BARRY D. STEBEN

Ôshio Heihachirô 大鹽平八郎

Chûsai 中齋, 1793–1837
(*azana*: 子起)

Ôshio Heihachirô was born in a samurai family that held the hereditary position of city police captain (*machi yoriki* 町與力) in the Osaka town-magistrate's office. At fourteen he began his apprentice training as a *yoriki*, a position that carried considerable authority but had a low status ranking. Reading his family genealogy at fifteen, Ôshio discovered that his family's ancestor at the time of the founding of the Tokugawa order was a warrior who in 1590 had impaled an enemy general with his sword before Ieyasu's very eyes. In an 1833 letter to **Satô Issai**, he reminisced, 'On learning all this I was deeply grieved, and felt ashamed at being a petty document writer

in the company of jailers and municipal officials. It seems that my ambition at that time was to fulfil the will of my ancestor by winning fame as a man of great deeds and heroic spirit. Perhaps that is why I constantly felt frustrated and despondent, unable to experience any real enjoyment.' This inner moral confusion led him to take up Neo-Confucian studies. At twenty-four he chanced to read a book of moral maxims by **Lü Kun** that impressed him immensely and convinced him his whole approach to learning – seeking moral principles externally – had been misguided. Searching for the source of Lü's wisdom, he found that he had been deeply influenced by Wang Yangming (see **Wang Shouren**), and began his lifelong study of the teachings of Wang and his followers.

The magistrate who took office in 1820 was impressed by Ôshio's character and abilities, and promoted him to public prosecutor and later public examiner, enabling him to win nationwide fame through his resolute prosecution of three difficult legal cases. In 1830, disturbed over the attention these cases had brought him (and by his patron's retirement), he suddenly resigned his position, hoping to devote himself fully to teaching at his private academy, the Senshindô ('Grotto of Mind-Cleansing'). In 1833, he privately published his most famous philosophical work, *Senshindô sakki* 洗心洞劄記, which focuses on the intertwined practices of 'returning to the Great Vacuity' (*ki Taikyo* 歸太虛) and 'extending the inborn knowledge of the good' while enjoining officials to devote themselves unreservedly wholeheartedly to the welfare of the people. In the same year, the country was struck by severe famine, and in Osaka rumours of riots began to fill the air. Ôshio repeatedly proffered policy advice to the new magistrate through his adopted son, but his advice was angrily rejected. People were starving in the streets of Osaka and in nearby rural districts, but the magistrate's office still issued a decree ordering that Edo be supplied with as much rice as it ordered. Burning with indignation, Chûsai distributed a fiery call-to-arms addressed to 'the village headmen, elders, peasants, and tenant farmers in every village', beginning with a reminder that Heaven's blessings will be withdrawn if the people are driven to desperation. Appealing to the benevolent founding principles of the government established by Ieyasu, he condemns the corruption and immorality that has since spread through officialdom, claiming that the entire populace now burns with rancour against the government. 'Yet since the time of Ashikaga Takauji [1305–58], the Son of Heaven has been removed from participation in government and deprived of the power to distribute rewards and punishments. Therefore the rancor of the people no longer has a place of appeal, and has reached to Heaven itself. In response, Heaven has sent down a long series of calamities . . .'. On 19 February 1837, Ôshio led over twenty of his disciples in a cannon attack on the mansion across the street, after which they set fire to his own residence and sallied forth into the city. The band proceeded to set fire to the entire Tenma district, beginning with the residences of the *yoriki* and their underlings. They then headed for the waterfront area of the city, setting fire to the mansions of rich merchants. By noon the band had grown to over 300 people. The authorities were at first thrown into confusion by the disturbance, but by 4:00 pm they had dispersed the rebels. Within a few days, almost all had either committed suicide, turned themselves in, or been arrested. Over a month later, the police discovered Ôshio's hiding place, at which point he set fire to the house he had been staying in and committed suicide together with his adopted son.

From *Senshindô sakki*:

A: 19. Life is something that can be annihilated. Humanity is the virtue of the Great Vacuity, and it is never annihilated

for all time. It is misguided to throw away what can never be annihilated to protect what is annihilated . . . If the heart has not returned to the Great Vacuity, without fail it will move. Why? Because in an earthquake all things that have form – even the towering mountain peaks and the fathomless ocean – will shake. But no earthquake can ever shake the Great Vacuity. Therefore, only when the heart has returned to the Great Vacuity can one speak of it as 'unmoving'.

A: 162. The sages and worthies not only regard Heaven-and-Earth as everlasting, but also regard their own selves as Heaven-and-Earth. Therefore they are not afraid of the death of the body, but fear the death of the spirit (*kokoro* 心). As long as the spirit does not die, one's unendingness can rival that of Heaven-and-Earth.

B: 20. In studying the Way of the sages, I entrust everything to my innate knowledge of the good. Therefore I am like a madman (*kyôsha* 狂者) in my efforts to realise in the public world what I perceive to be right and wrong. The trouble that this brings upon me from other people is almost too much to calculate. Nevertheless, to end up dimming one's sensitivity to right and wrong just because one is afraid of the trouble it will bring upon one is something that a true man of character (*jôfu* 丈夫) would consider shameful. And what honour would I have to meet the sages in the afterlife? Therefore, I concern myself with nothing but following my resolution.

Sources: *Satô Issai, Ôshio Chûsai*, NST, vol. 46; Miyagi Kimiko, comp., *Ôshio Chûsai, Nihon no meicho*, vol. XXVII (Tokyo: Chûô Kôronsha, 1984). Further reading: Tetsuo Najita, 'Ôshio Heihachirô (1793–1837)', in Albert Craig and Donald Shively, eds., *Personality in Japanese History* (Berkeley: University of California Press, 1970); Barry D. Steben, 'Law Enforcement and Confucian

Idealism in the Late Edo Period – Ôshio Chûsai and the Growth of his Great Aspiration', in *Asian Cultural Studies* 22 (March 1996), pp. 59–90.

BARRY D. STEBEN

Ôta Kinjô 太田(大田) 錦城
1765–1825
(*name* Gensei 元貞, *azana* Kôkan 公幹, *other*, Saisa 才佐)

Ôta Kinjô, a mid-Tokugawa Confucian from Kaga 加賀 domain (now Ishikawa prefecture), is regarded as a forerunner of the *kôshôgaku* 考証學 (School of Evidential Research) in Japan by modern scholars. Influenced by Qing-dynasty philological tradition of evidential research (*kao zheng* 考証), he applied philology, phonetics and textual criticism to the study of the Chinese Classics.

Ôta studied under **Minakawa Kien** and Yamamoto Hokuzan 山本北山 (1752–1812) and was influenced by their eclectic approach in scholarship. Hence, he is also remembered as a major scholar of the eclectic school (*setchûakuha* 折衷學派). Ôta mixed the *kôshôgaku* and *setchûgaku* traditions in his study of Chinese Classics. His representative works include the *Kyûkeidan* 九經談 (*Discourse on the Nine Classics*, 1804) and *Gimonroku* 疑問錄 (*Records of my Doubts*). He was particularly interested in the *Yi jing* (*Book of Changes*) and his writings on the text were primarily historical and philological studies of the main text and the Ten Wings (see *Yi zhuan*). He trained many talented students, including Kaihô Gyoson 海保漁村 (1798–1866) and Tôjô Kindai 東條琴台 (1795–1878), in his private academy, Shunsôdô 春草堂 (Hall of Spring Grass). He served the Yoshida 吉田 and Kaga domains in his later years.

References: Inoue & Karie, 1903: vol. IX; Maruyama, 1974: 140–1; Nakamura, 1986; Ng, 2000: 43–4, 121, 221, 238.

WAI-MING NG

Ouyang Shoudao 歐陽守道
1209–1273?
(*zi* Gongquan 公權, *hao* Xunzhai 巽齋)

Ouyang Shoudao was a native of Jizhou 吉州 (Jiangxi). Actually his name was Xun 巽, but he attended the imperial examinations under the name Shoudao, and was thereafter called by this name. In his youth he was poor and studied diligently without a teacher. In 1241 he achieved the *jinshi* degree. Afterwards he held several positions as a college professor. Later he went to the court, but at an imperial hearing (*zhuan dui* 轉對) he blamed other officials for paying too much attention to their personal advantages, and for this reason soon had to leave his post. In his later years he had no more interest in returning to imperial service.

There is no exact year given for his death, but in a funeral oration by his pupil **Wen Tianxiang** we find the sentence: 'To die at the age of sixty-five is not a premature death' (*nian liu shi wu bu wei yao* 年六十五不為殀). We therefore can conclude that he finished his life in the late years of the Southern Song dynasty (1127–1279).

Although his influence seems to have been rather small during his lifetime, Qing dynasty scholars like **Quan Zuwang** held him in high esteem, especially because among his pupils were patriots like **Wen Tianxiang** and other members of the so-called *Xunzhai xuepai*.

CHRISTIAN SOFFEL

Ouyang Xiu 歐陽修
1007–1072

A major intellectual figure of the Northern Song (960–1127), Ouyang Xiu made a substantial contribution to literature, classical exegesis and historical writing. In literature, he was a leader of the 'ancient style' (*guwen* 古文) movement, opposing the formulaic writing of the Tang (618–907).

In classical exegesis, he was a sceptic who questioned the received reading of the *Spring and Autumn Annals* (**Chunqiu**) and the **Yi jing**. In historical writing, he was the author of two standard histories – *The New History of the Tang* and *The New History of the Five Dynasties* – which shaped later generations' perspective on events from the seventh to the tenth century.

Underlying Ouyang's various endeavours was his drive to reestablish a Confucian socio-political order after the chaos of the Five Dynasties period (907–960). In opposing the Tang style of writing, he reaffirmed the writer's mission for expressing the Confucian Way (**Dao**). By critically rereading the classical tests, he stressed the authority of the Classics in elucidating the Confucian principles of governing. By reinterpreting historical events, he questioned his contemporaries' belief that the Song should model itself on the Tang in every aspect. At times morally didactic, Ouyang stressed Confucian virtue and dynastic legitimacy as the two pillars of a stable and benevolent government.

References: Bol, 1992; Hon, 1999; Liu, James, 1967.

TZE-KI HON

P

Pae Chong-ho 裴宗鎬
1919–1990
(*hao* Ji San 智山)

A philosopher, Pae had studied Chinese Classics before entering elementary school, graduating from high school in 1937 and later from Gyung Sung Imperial University (now Seoul National University) in 1943. He then taught at various levels of schooling, moving to the countryside during the Korean War and staying on for ten years as a teacher and vice-principal. He was fascinated by and well versed in geomancy and geography, which he learnt from Yi Jiong-kyu 李鍾九.

From 1960 to 1984 Pae was a professor of philosophy at Yonsei University as well as the president of various philosophical societies. Later he was a professor at Wŏn'gwang University, president of the Association of Korean History of Thought and head of the Yulgok (**Yi I**) Research Institute. Pae presented many papers on Korean studies and Asian philosophy, presiding at various international academic conferences, especially in Japan, Taiwan and Germany. In 1982 Pae was awarded the National Magnolia Prize, in 1984 the National Peony Prize and in 1986 the Professorial Conference on World Peace Academy Prize. He also published numerous articles including, *An Outline of Philosophy, An Introduction to Philosophy, A History of Korean Confucianism* and *Problems and Developments in Korean Confucianism*. His numerous articles include, *An Investigation into Liqi theory, Hwadam **Sŏ Kyŏng-dŏk**, Yi I's Philosophical Thought, Kwŏn Kŭn's Philosophical Thought*.

References: Pae Jong-ho, 1974, 1985.

NAM-JIN HUH

Pak Chong-hon 朴鐘鴻
1903–1976
(*hao* Yŏlam 洌巖)

A philosopher and educator, Pak became a teacher at the age of eighteen. In 1924 he presented his first philosophical treatise entitled *The Educational Thought of T'oegye* (**Yi Hwang**). In 1929 he entered the philosophy department of Gyung Sung Imperial University (now Seoul National University) and in graduate school studied the philosophy of Kant, Hegel and Heidegger. From 1935 to 1939 he lectured at Ehwa Women's College and after the liberation of Korea in 1945 returned to Seoul National University where he taught until his retirement in 1968. During that time, Pak held various offices, including Head of Department, Dean of the Graduate School, Head of the Korean Philosophy Academy and Head of the Korean Academy of Sciences, among others.

In 1960 he received a Ph.D. from Seoul National University with a dissertation on injustice. Throughout Pak's work, one can often find the word 'exploration', a method of philosophical investigation. Among the pioneering achievements and contributions Pak made, are his research in Korean *Sŏngnihak*, his profound work on the theories of Yi Hwang and **Yi I**, and his investment of such great importance into an independent scholarly tradition that he devoted much of his later years to the modernisation of the Korean education system. Many of Pak's students came to lead the way in Korean philosophical circles as foremost professors of Korea's top universities. He received many awards, including the Korean Academy of Sciences Meritorious Service Award, the March First Independence Movement Cultural Prize, and posthumously the Order of National Service and Grand Order of *Mugunghwa*. His vast works include *General Logic* (1948), *Philosophical Explorations* (1959), *Korean Thought – Buddhism* (1972), *Korean Thought – Confucianism* (1977) and his *Complete Works* in seven volumes.

Reference: Pak Chong-hon, 1998.

NAM-JIN HUH

Pak Ŭn-sik 朴殷植
1859–1926
(*zi* Sŏng Chil 聖七, *hao* Paekam 白巖, Kyumkok 謙谷)

Pak received his early education from the School of the Way (*Tohak* 道學) scholar Pak Mun-il 朴文一. In 1898 he became editor-in-chief of the Hwang Sung (Seoul) Newspaper. In 1908 Pak encouraged educational development by founding various schools and serving as the principal. Along with **Chang Chi-yŏn** in 1909 he helped establish the Great Unity (*da tong*) *Taetonggyo* 大同教 religious movement within the Confucian reformation which led to a patriotic enlightenment movement.

At the start of the Japanese occupation of Korea, Pak fled to Manchuria and later in Shanghai he wrote his indictment of the process of Japanese aggression against Korea in his book *The Painful History of Korea* (Kr. *Hanguk Tongsi* 韓國痛史, 1915). He described the Independence movement in a book entitled *The Bloody History of the Korean Independence Movement* (Kr. *Hanguk Dokrip Untong Jihyulsi* 韓國獨立運動之血史, 1919). As a participant of the provisional government in Shanghai, he was the editor of the Independence Newspaper, becoming the Prime Minister in 1924 and in the following year was elected as the second President of the provisional government, before succumbing to illness in 1926.

In the midst of the social crisis facing Koreans at the time of the occupation, Pak emphasised the need for Confucianism to be established as a modern national religion. In his *A New Treatise on Educational Rules* (*Hakgyu Sinron* 學規新論), he linked the deterioration of the religious function of Confucianism with that of the nation.

Pak's book *Investigations* lists three items for the reform of Korean Confucianism. (1) The emphasis on the King should be switched to the people. (2) Closed-minded Confucianism should be replaced with open-minded Confucianism. (3) The wanderings of the **Zhu Xi** School of thought should be replaced by the simple, immediate Wang Yangming (**Wang Shouren**) School. Pak expressed his intense, confident hopes for the future of Confucianism, and enthusiatically advocated his reform policies for Confucianism.

Pak's fundamental direction for *Taetongkyo* 大同教 was that it must be a doctrine of the virtue of humaneness (*ren*, Kr. *in*) and its aim is to restore humanity and the world to a state of peace, by which he illustrated how a developed *Taetongkyo* could act as a guide for the empowerment of the people.

JANG-TAE KEUM

Pan gong 泮宮

According to the *Records of Rites* (*Li ji*), the school for teaching the feudal lords (*zhu hou*) is called *pan gong*. This is distinct from *bi yong* (which literally means a rounded moat) that is said to be for the king. This was presumably the system of antiquity, although it is an idealised imagination dated perhaps to the second century BCE, if not later. The earliest explanation of the expression, found in **Xu Shen**'s famous *Shuowen* 說文 dictionary, *pan gong* is where nobles 'held archery competition; in the south and west sides there is a pond, and in the north and east sides there is wall (presumably for hanging the targets)'. The word *pan* 泮 carries the meaning of half (*ban* 半) and there have been speculations that the school is named *pan* because the pond takes up only half of the entire compound.

Unlike in the case of *bi yong*, which as an educational institution has been confirmed by archaeological findings, we are not certain whether or not *pan gong* actually existed in antiquity, even though it appears in the *Book of Poetry* (*Shi jing*) and probably refers to an educational institution. The expression has occasionally been used, though informally, to mean higher level schools (and Imperial Academy, *Tai xue*) in later times. Some modern Chinese universities have a pond or lake in the school compound, in keeping with the belief that ancient higher educational institutions had rounded or half-moon lakes.

References: Creel, 1970: 407; Zhu Bin, 1996: vol. I, 5: 176–7.

THOMAS H.C. LEE

Pan'gye Surok 磻溪隨錄
(*Pan'gye's Treatises*)

This work by Practical Learning (*Sirhak*) scholar **Yu Hyŏng-wŏn** outlines his method of social reform, which had a particularly important influence on like-minded move-ments of the nineteenth century. Topics include land redistribution, education and the examination system, royal edicts by government officials, administrative duties and remunerations, local administration, among others. Overall, land reform is most fundamental, the basis on which the tax and military service systems can be reformed. When King Yŏng Cho (r. 1724–1776) read this work in 1770, he praised it highly and ordered it to be published.

JANG-TAE KEUM

Pei xiang 配享
(Correlate or secondary sacrifice)

The Correlate or secondary sacrifice is the practice of offering food to a secondary spirit simultaneously with the sacrifice to the principal god or spirit. The secondary spirit was originally an ancestor of the sacrificer. The classical texts the *Book of Changes* and the *Book of Filial Piety* mention the practice of the Shang and Zhou kings' offering secondary sacrifices to their royal ancestors when offering food to **Shang Di**. By late imperial times sacrifices at all imperial altars and temples included such offerings. Secondary sacrifices were offered to Yan Hui 顏回 in the cult rites to Confucius as early as 241 CE and, beginning in the Song (960–1279), to the **Four Correlates**. This sacrifice is distinguished from enshrine-ment, which refers to offerings to spirits in the temple ranked below Correlate.

THOMAS A. WILSON

Peng Ruli 彭汝礪
1041–1094
(*zi* Qizi 器資)

Peng Ruli was a scholar with a reputation for integrity and a commitment to forthright remonstrance. He qualified for office by passing the *jinshi* examination. **Wang Anshi** was impressed by his *Shi yi* 詩義 (Meanings of the *Poetry*) and saw to his appointment as a Lecturer in the Directorate of Education (*Guozi jian zhijiang* 國子監直講). He then enjoyed a fairly successful career while always being willing to speak his mind. For example, he once confronted Emperor Shenzong (r. 1068–1085) over a plan to give eunuchs military authority (Zhu Xi: 10: 4.2a). He eventually alienated Wang Anshi and endured some periods of provincial service. Nevertheless, he did rise quite high in the ranks, serving as a provisional minister of personnel (*quan Libu shangshu* 權吏部尚書). He died, however, a few months after arriving at his last provincial posting (*Song shi*, 346: 10976).

Peng shared the common Northern-Song interest in returning to and reinterpreting the Classics. He himself had been a student of a certain Ni Tianyin 倪天隱 (?–?) who in turn had been a student of the early Song classicist, **Hu Yuan**. Through this connection, we can also trace Peng's scholarly interests back to Hu. We know, for example, that Peng also composed a commentary to the *Yi jing* under the title *Yi yi* 易義 (Meanings of the *Changes*). Peng's teacher, Ni, had already produced a record of Hu Yuan's oral explanations of the *Yi jing* (*Song–Yuan xuean*: 1.18a).

Only a fraction of Peng's literary collection exists under the title *Poyang ji* 鄱陽集 (*Collection from Poyang* [Jiangxi]). Originally forty chapters, the *Siku quanshu* edition now only preserves twelve.

References: *Song–Yuan xuean*, 1966; Peng Ruli, 1782; *Song shi*, 1977; Zhu Xi, *Sanchao mingchen yanxing lu*.

ANTHONY DEBLASI

Peng Shaosheng 彭紹升
1740–1796
(*zi* Yunchu 允初, *hao* Chimu 尺木, Zhiguizi 知歸子)

A native of Changzhou 常州 (Jiangsu), Peng was first a classicist on the Learning of Principle (*li xue*) and then turned to the Learning of the Heart/Mind (*xin xue*), from which he finally became a pious Buddhist. He obtained his *jinshi* degree in 1769, and in the same year, he gave up the position of the county magistrate and concetrated on the study of Buddhism.

Educated in the classical studies, Peng highly praised the learning of **Lu Jiuyuan** and **Wang Shouren**. He wrote a book on the lives of several Confucian philosophers, entitled *Ruxing xu* 儒行敘; a work about the lives of famous officials of the Qing period (1644–1911), known as *Mingcheng Shizhuang* 名臣事狀, and a collection of biographies of lower officials, entitled *Liangli shu* 良吏述. These works were compiled with his prose writings in a collection entitled *Erlin juji* 二林居集.

Unlike other contemporary scholars, Peng was not so much interested in establishing Buddhism at the expense of Confucianism as to reconcile the two. The underlying theme of his writings is to interpret Confucianism in the light of the Chan doctrine of the mind, arguing that 'the Mandate of Heaven is nothing but human mind, and the Way of Heaven is nothing but human affairs'. In his interpretation of Classical Learning, he proposed that the learning to become a sage was none other than to return to one's own nature (*fu xing* 復性). He also attempted to reconcile the doctrines of Zhu Xi and Lu Jiuyuan, pointing out that their doctrines can not be separated, because both are the way of self-cultivation and governance.

Reference: Hummel, 1943–4.

REBEKAH X. ZHAO

Philosophy East and West

Philosophy East and West is the premier journal in the West devoted to exploring themes central to eastern and western philosophical traditions. Promoting comparative philosophical dialogue remains one of the distinctive characteristics and defining strengths of the journal. It also serves as a venue for scholarship targeting one or more areas of Asian philosophy, including those of India, Tibet, China, Korea and Japan, especially in fields such as Hinduism, Buddhism, Jainism, Islamic thought, Confucianism, Daoism, Legalism, Neo-Confucianism and Shinto. *Philosophy East and West* was founded in 1951, by Professor Charles A. Moore of the Department of Philosophy at the University of Hawaii. It has since been edited by two luminaries in the field of comparative philosophy, Eliot Deutsch (1967–1986) and, currently, Roger Ames (1986–).

JOHN A. TUCKER

Pi Rixiu 皮日休
834?–883?
(*zi* Ximei 襲美 or Yishao 逸少)

Pi Rixiu enjoyed only limited success in his official career. After failing his initial attempt at the *jinshi* examination in 866, he managed to pass at the bottom of the list the next year (Xu Song 1984: 23.854). He then served as a low-ranking assistant to the prefect of Suzhou. It was during this time that he formed a deep friendship with the poet Lu Guimeng 陸龜蒙 (?–881?, *zi* Luwang 魯望). A sizeable corpus of poetry resulted from their collaboration. This poetry is preserved in the ten-chapter *Songling changhe ji* 松陵唱和集. Pi was eventually appointed an academician in the Court of Imperial Sacrifices (*Taichang boshi* 太常博士). Although there is some uncertainty, the consensus is that Pi collaborated with Huang Chao 黃巢 (?–884) during the latter's rebellion against the Tang. He was most probably executed by Huang after insulting the rebel (Nienhauser 1979: 35).

Despite an interest in poetic technique and aesthetic experimentation, Pi's writings reveal a marked social responsibility. His essay 'On the Origin of Transformation' (*Yuan hua* 原化), for example, contrasted the success of Buddhist preachers with the inability of literati to transform society in accordance with the ideals of the sage rulers of antiquity (Pi Rixiu: 3.2a). Much of the poetry in his collection also laments the plight of common people and the evils of corrupt government. Nevertheless, this commitment to political reform never blinded him to the possibility of finding fulfillment in literary pursuits. He seems to have found a genuine camaraderie with other aesthetically inclined poets during his stay in Suzhou.

Pi coupled his desire for political reform with attention to the Classics. He composed an essay explaining doubtful passages in the **Chunqiu Zuo zhuan**, the most important commentary on the **Chunqiu** (*Spring and Autumn Annals*). Pi's writings also suggest an incipient interest in questions of personal moral development. He refers obliquely in several places to the **Yi jing** concepts of 'exhaustively investigating principle' (*qiong li* 窮理) and 'developing one's nature to the utmost' (*jin xing* 盡性).

During his life, Pi was an outspoken champion of **Han Yu**. Thus, he likened Han's opposition to Buddhism to **Mengzi**'s opposition to Yang Zhu 楊朱 and Mo Di 墨翟. Although he recognised that Han Yu was an isolated figure, he shared Han's concern that Buddhism and Daoism threatened the fabric of society. He proposed, for example, changing the civil service examinations by eliminating the *Zhuangzi* 莊子 and the *Liezi* 列子 and requiring the **Mengzi** (Pi Rixiu: 9.6a–7a).

References: Lu and Pi, 1782; Pi Rixiu, 1999; Xu Song, 1984.

ANTHONY DEBLASI

Pi Xirui 皮錫瑞
1850–1908
(*zi* Lumen 鹿門, or Luyun 麓雲)

A native of Hunan province, Pi Xirui was a scholar, classicist and reformer. Gifted in poetry and prose, he passed the provincial civil service examination at the age of twenty-four. Having failed four times at the national level, he finally gave up his examination candidate's career and turned his attention to classical study. Since 1879, he developed a strong interest in the *Book of Documents* (**Shang shu**), and spent the next fifteen years writing a commentary on it. Known as the *Shangshu dazhuan jian* 尚書大傳箋 (*An Annotated Commentary on the Book of Documents*, 1896), Pi's work offered a new interpretation of the classic from the perspective of the New Text School of Former Han Confucianism.

Like many of his contemporaries, Pi was shocked by China's defeat in the Sino-Japanese War (1894–1895). The defeat revealed that China was behind in the global competition for wealth and power. But contrary to the dominant view of the time, he believed that the Chinese should not only reform their political and educational system based on a western model, but also reexamine their own tradition to eradicate its faulty practices.

In 1898, Pi became the president of *Nanxue hui* (The Society of Southern Learning), a public forum for the Hunan elite gentry to discuss public affairs. As part of his duty as president, he regularly gave public lectures on current affairs. In his lectures, he tried to resolve the debate between the New Text scholars and the Old Text scholars by stressing their common roots in Confucianism. Responding to the debate on political reform, he argued that western political institutions of the nineteenth century were originally set up by the 'philosophers' (*zhuzi* 諸子) who left China during the Warring States period (475–221 BCE). With this 'doctrine of the Chinese origin of western learning' (*xixue chu yu zhong xue lun* 西學出于中學論), he attempted to convince the conservatives that in adopting western political institutions they were, in effect, adopting what used to be theirs. Although Pi did not participate in the Hundred Days of Reform (1898), he was saddened by its

abrupt termination due to the Empress Dowager's *coup d'état*. To express his sympathy for the short-lived reform, he wrote poems commemorating the six executed young reformers.

After 1900, Pi was actively involved in the educational reform in Hunan. He taught Confucian Classics at newly established secondary schools and teacher colleges. At one time, he was invited to teach at the prestigious *Jingshi daxue tang* 京師大學堂 (The Imperial University in Beijing), but he turned down the offer to remain in Hunan. For teaching purposes, he wrote two influential textbooks on Confucianism. One was the *Jing xue lishi* (*History of Classical Learning*, 1907) in which he traced the development of Confucian Learning from the sixth century BCE to the late Qing. The other was the *Jing xue tonglun* 經學通論 (*A General Study of Classical Learning*, 1907) in which he critically examined the Five Confucian Classics (**Wu jing**).

References: Pi Xirui, 1959; Zhou Yutong, 1996.

TZE-KI HON

Pictorial hagiographies of Confucius

Although certain episodes in Confucius' life were depicted on carved stones by the Later Han period (25–220 CE), and single-scene narrative paintings of a later date are occasionally recorded in catalogues, the first set of pictures illustrating his entire life appeared in the middle Ming period (1368–1644). Entitled *Shengji Tu* 聖蹟圖 (*Pictures of the Sage's Traces*), it was compiled by the censor Zhang Kai 張楷 (1398–1460; *Jinshi* 1424; *zi* Shizhi 式之), who selected some thirty excerpts from Confucius' biography in the *Shi ji* (47.1905–1947), had pictures made by an anonymous artist, and composed a *zan* 讚 (poetic encomium) for each scene. As an introduction, Zhang transcribed **Zhu Xi**'s preface to the **Lunyu**, itself a slightly bowdlerised biography of Confucius. Completed in 1444, the illustrations offer a humanistic portrayal of events that reveal Confucius' moral character, illuminate his career as a statesman and teacher, and inaugurate his cult. To circulate the compendium, Zhang had it carved onto stone tablets so rubbings could be made.

Although Zhang Kai's *Shengji tu* appears not to survive, it inspired many later compilations, in a variety of media, which repeatedly transformed the configuration of Confucius' life and its significance. Most versions expanded the episodes beyond Zhang's economical core and took a more hagiographical approach, probably reflecting the influence of the flourishing contemporary genre of Buddhist and Daoist pictorial hagiography. Starting with the 1497 woodblock printed edition of He Tingrui 何廷瑞 (*fl.* late fifteenth century), which contained thirty-eight episodes, auspicious omens and demonstrations of preternatural wisdom became standard in depictions of Confucius' life. Among He's additions are three pictures of supernatural events associated with conception and birth: a *qilin* 麒麟 (unicorn) brings Confucius' mother a jade tablet prophesying that her son would become a *su wang* (uncrowned king), gods and dragons appear above the house on the eve of his birth, and heavenly musicians celebrate the arrival of the newborn, whose chest is inscribed, 'Sign [of the one who will] create the regulations to order the world' 製作定世符. Although these marvellous phenomena come from Kong clan lore and also appear in *chen wei* texts of the Later Han era, there are obvious parallels with accounts of the Buddha's birth.

The late Ming period saw the pictures adapted to new uses, as both privately sponsored and commercially printed versions of the *Shengji tu* proliferated, sometimes under that title or variants of it, but also under different ones. An illustrated hagiography might be added to other texts, such as Wu Jiamo's 吳嘉謨 (*jinshi* 1607) 1589

replica of a Song edition of **Kongzi jiayu** (*Sayings of Confucius's Family*), and An Mengsong's 安夢松 1599 popular anthology *Kongsheng quanshu* 孔聖全書 (*Complete Writings of the Sage Confucius*). A suite of pictures even accompanies an early seventeenth-century play, *Xinbian Kongfuzi Zhouyou Lieguo Dacheng Qilin Ji* 新編孔夫子周游列國大成麒麟記 (*Newly Compiled Record of Confucius Travelling around all the States, Great Fulfilment of the Qilin*) by the pseudonymous 'Huanyu Xiansheng Gong' 寰宇顯聖公 (Illustrious Sage-Duke of the World). A few painted sets of annotated pictures, usually closely related to a printed version, also belong to this period. The increased popularity of the subject suggests that by offering direct visual access to the sage, such pictures helped to compensate for the 1530 removal of icons from all Confucian temples save those of the Kong family.

From the many competing illustrated versions, through which various sponsors expressed their values and concerns, one configuration of Confucius' life finally became dominant. In 1592, a monumental 112-scene series was carved on stone tablets and installed in the Shengji dian 聖蹟殿 (Hall of the Sage's Traces), a new building on the main axis of the Qufu Temple of Confucius (**Kong miao**). Organised by the censorial officials He Chuguang 何出光 (*jinshi* 1583) and Zhang Yingdeng 張應鄧 (*jinshi* 1583), the project was intended to create a permanent gallery of pictures showing Confucius 'in action' to inspire present and future generations of officials. Enshrined in the Qufu temple, the 1592 pictorial hagiography was now publicly affiliated with the imperially sponsored cult of Confucius and quickly became the most authoritative representation of his life. It was widely disseminated through rubbings, and, in the Qing, through woodblock-printed reproductions. In late nineteenth- and twentieth-century versions, enframing prefaces and colophons reveal a new desire to popularise and nationalise Confucius by identifying his teachings with Chinese civilisation itself.

Since 1989, another radically different set of stone-carved pictures in Qufu, authorised by the Communist government, presents Confucius as a great man from ancient history, a model of diligence and correct behaviour.

An edition related to He Tingrui's version reached Japan in the late sixteenth century and was much reprinted in the seventeenth, often with substantial modification. The annotated pictures were also reproduced on folding screens, particularly in the Shimazu 島津 domain. Many Qing and Republican editions collected before the Second World War are now in Japanese libraries. In France, twenty-four hand-coloured copperplate prints, copied from an imported early Qing edition, were published to illustrate Helman's 1788 biography of Confucius.

References: An Mengsong, 1599; Baba, 1934; Helman, 1788; Kaji, 1991; Kong Chuan (1134) 1967; Kong Yuancuo (1227) 1967; *Kongzi Shengji Tu c.* 1506; & (1934) 1984/1988; Murray 1996, 1997 & 2002; Sato Kazuyoshi, 1991–2; *Shengji Tu* (1548, 1592) 1988; Shi Ke, 1987; Sima Qian, 1962; Wu Jiamo, 1589; Zheng Zhenduo, 1958.

JULIA K. MURRAY

Ping tianxia 平天下
(Making the world peaceful)

Making the world peaceful is one of the Eight Steps (**ba tiaomu**) in the *Great Learning* (**Daxue**). From the perspective of the ancients, the world (**tian xia**) comprises everything in the four seas, and the ruler of a nation would be a 'son of Heaven' (**tian zi**). In Confucianism, the Son of Heaven is the highest ranking ruler, a representative of the Mandate of Heaven (**tian ming**) itself and in absolute authority, whose primary duty is to bring peace and harmony to the world, through various steps such as cultivating one's self and regulating families.

In the *Great Learning* 10, the following is asserted: 'The making of the whole kingdom peaceful and happy depends on the government of the state.' To govern the state well, the ruler must watch first over his virtue. The feudal lords must be unified for the condition of the entire nation to be safe and tranquil for its citizens. This objective is one of the Three Cardinal Guides (**san gang**), and is related to the practical application of the Eight Steps.

Reference: Legge, 1966.

TODD CAMERON THACKER

Pulssi chappyŏn 佛氏雜辯
(*Miscellany of Mr Buddha*)

This book was written in 1398 by **Chŏng To-jŏn** just prior to his death in the *Tae Jiong* usurpation of the throne. The *Pulssi chappyŏn* remained unpublished until it was discovered in his home by his descendent Han Hyuk 韓奕. Han brought the work to scholars who immediately recognised its merits and had it published. It first appeared in a reprint of Chŏng's *Collected Works*; both **Kwŏn Kŭn** and Sin Suk Ju 申叔周 wrote the preface, and Chŏng's great-grandson Mun Hyŏng 文炯 wrote the epilogue. The core contents of the *Pulssi chappyŏn* brilliantly detail and criticise Buddhist dogma, though it is rather heavily dependent on Chŏng's own Confucian biases and interpretations for its philosophical criticism of Buddhism. However, it does hold an important position in the history of early Chosŏn Confucian thought for its Neo-Confucian based principle (**li**)-vital force (**qi**) critical theories of Buddhist dogma, and as such played a deciding role in later Confucian attitudes to Buddhism in the Chosŏn dynasty.

References: Chŏng To-jŏn, 1977; Song Yŏng-ah, 1995.

NAM-JIN HUH

Q

Qi 氣
(Vital force or material force)

The Chinese term *qi* has become so well known in the West that it is perhaps no longer necessary to translate the expression. It is variously translated as material force, vital force, energy, pneuma, humours, breath, vapour and so on. In its Japanese usages it is usually transliterated as *ki*, as in the term '*akido*', the way (Jn. *do*, Ch. *dao*) of harmonising (Jn. *a*, Ch. *he*) one's *ki* (Ch. *qi*), which is the name of a well-known form of martial art. The precise nature of *qi*, a subtle and enigmatic force, was sometimes thought to exist in multiple valences and was attributed various qualities. *Qi* was understood in various ways and was accorded different levels of importance relative to other elemental components of the universe. *Qi* was a kind of force or energy, but it was at the same time often understood as that which imbued phenomena with materiality, form and substance. Phenomena were suffused with *qi*, and it pervaded the human body. From antiquity to the present-day a wide range of practices have been developed for optimising the movements of *qi* within the human frame, for modulating them relative to the fluxions of other energies external to the corpus, and for calibrating human action and social mores to conform with their operations.

Early texts such as the ***Chunqiu Zuo zhuan*** assert the existence of not one but six *qi*: yin, yang (see **yin–yang**), wind, rain, darkness and light (Year One, Duke Zhao), which are in turn manifested as the four seasons. Hence, the *qi* are here understood as powers of cosmic, meteorological and solar forces. The six *qi* are also described as the products of Heaven and Earth and are manifested as the Five Phases (***wu xing***: earth, water, wood, metal and fire), five flavours, five colours and five sounds; they give rise to human emotions (Duke Zhao, 25th Year). The *qi* thus pervade all phasic operations of the cosmos, all perceptible phenomena, and the subtle expressions of the human body itself.

Warring States thinkers such as **Mengzi** and **Xunzi** elaborated upon the physiological and moral significance of *qi* within the human constitution, and moreover described ways in which one might actively cultivate it. For Mengzi, *qi* suffuses the entire body but is governed by one's will or intentionality, provided the latter is unified and directed. Claiming to be proficient at sustaining his 'flowing *qi*' (***haoran zhi qi***), a powerful but ultimately ineffable force, Mengzi asserted that such *qi* was espoused to righteousness and the Way (*Mengzi* 2A: 9–16). Mengzi thus endowed *qi* with a stronger ethical dimension than was evident in the cosmological systems of the *Chunqiu Zuo zhuan*.

Xunzi spoke of cultivating *qi* in the same breath as cultivating the mind, claiming that one might develop them both through moderation in one's actions, compliance with the Way, attentiveness to others, and adherence to ritual. For Xunzi, then, developing one's *qi* was accomplished within a web of social interactions as well as upon a grounding of cosmic principles such as the Way. For Xunzi, *qi* was a primal form of energy upon which life was based. Fire and water both had *qi*, he asserted, but were not alive; animals were sentient but lacked moral values. Humans, however, had *qi*, life, sentience, and moral values, and were thus, of all life forms, uniquely endowed to develop societies; hence, ritual formulations to regulate and enhance social interaction were of the utmost importance.

Regarding the importance of *qi* in the thought of Han figures such as **Dong Zhongshu**, the physical person of the leader of human society was of greater import than was the more nonpersonal system of ritual formulations espoused by Xunzi. For Dong, the ruler held a unique position almost literally as the head of state: Dong envisioned the state as a social body through which coursed sanguine humours and *qi*. Just as one's own body was governed by the mind (**xin**, which, according also to Xunzi, was the ruler of the body), this corporate society was governed by the ruler. Worthy ministers, who were possessed of the finest *qi*, sustained their responsibilities with the same harmony evidenced in the circulation of sanguine humours and *qi* throughout the body. As the ruler and the ministers maintained states of tranquil vacuity in their own physical persons and developed their own *qi*, so did the state become peaceful and well governed.

Song thinkers such as **Zhang Zai** developed cosmologies in which *qi* was an integral element of a universe where human beings and all other phenomena inhabited a world that was a continually self-renewing process of alternating forces. As Zhang articulated the components of this modulation in his **Zheng meng**, he asserted that *qi* stemmed from, and was even identical with, a formless Supreme Vacuity (**tai xu**) and alternately coalesced into perceptible material phenomena and disintegrated into invisible formlessness. The ethical applications of this ontological vision of interconnectedness were expressed in Zhang's **Xi ming**, where he advocated such values as filial piety (a very expansive filial piety that extended to one's 'father' and 'mother', heaven and earth themselves) and compassion for all human beings. Within the modulations of *qi* was yet a regularity and patterning called principle (**li**), and although Zhang did not develop at great length the relationship of *qi* and principle, it was an important subject to other Song scholars such as **Cheng Yi**, **Cheng Hao**, and **Zhu Xi** (see **li qi**).

The continuity that persists within *qi* despite all its permutations and changes is reflected in beliefs and rituals concerning the reverence of ancestors: within a kinship line, a commonality of *qi* obtains between living sacrificers and the recipients of their offerings, the spirits of the departed. The continuity of *qi* is noted in the writings of the late imperial thinker **Huang Zongxi**, who stated that parents and children share the same *qi* and that the child's body comes from the parents' own. Huang used this metaphor of affinity to explain his notion of the ideal relationship between ruler and minister in the Qing (1644–1911), but the notion of the genealogical continuity of *qi* appeared at least as early as the Han (206 BCE–220 CE). It is a commonly held belief in modern times and is evidenced in present-day ritual practices.

References: de Bary & Bloom, 1999: 297, 684–7; de Bary and Lufrano, 2000: 8–10; Knoblock, 1988–94, vol. I: 143–58, vol. II: 103–5; Legge, 1985a: 704, 708; Loewe & Shaughnessy, 1999; Unschuld, 1985; Zhang Liwen, 1994.

DEBORAH SOMMER

Qi jia 齊家
(Stabilising the family)

This sphere of Confucian self-cultivation set forth in the 'eight specific points' (*ba tiaomu*) in the opening chapter of the *Daxue* marks the transition from the outer and inner dimensions of the individual self: 'cultivating the self' (*xiu shen*) and 'setting straight one's mental faculties' (*zheng xin*), to the broader contexts of one's place in the social and political order. The verb *qi* (齊) occurring in this expression, literally meaning to 'equalise', or to set something on an even keel, is used in this passage as a virtual synonym for the other verbs of ordering that define one's proper function in each of the adjacent spheres of activity. The common word 'family' (*jia* 家) may refer to one's immediate kin or household, or perhaps, in keeping with the hypothetical enactment of the teachings of the *Daxue* by an actual or potential ruler, to the royal house of the ruling clan.

The 'expansion chapter' of the text dedicated to this ideal (chapter 9) brings a series of proof texts and exempla to elucidate the idea of properly ordering one's closest circle of human relations as a precondition of instilling order in the world at large. Here, too, however, the central argument of the *Daxue* revolves around the vital need to find within one's own inner self the moral basis for fulfilling the varying spheres of interaction of the broader human context.

ANDREW PLAKS

Qi jiao 七教
(Seven teachings)

Qi jiao is mentioned in the *Book of Rites* (*Li ji*), *Wangzhi* 王制 chapter where it is stated that 'The minister of education (*si tu* 司徒) establishes six kinds of rites in order to moderate people's nature, illustrate seven teachings in order to make people's virtue flourishing . . .' These seven teachings are explained in *Kongzi jiayu* in terms of the moral influence of the ruler: if the ruler reveres the old, then the people will become more filial; if the ruler respects the elder, then the people below will demonstrate more brotherly love; if the ruler is fond of giving, the people will become more generous; if the ruler has affection towards the worthy, then the people will choose their friends carefully; if the ruler loves virtue, then the people will not hide [wrongdoings]; if the ruler hates greed, then the people will be shameful of contending; if the ruler is honest and yielding, then the people will have a good sense of shame and moderation. These seven teachings are said to be the foundation of governing the people.

Reference: Legge, 1966.

TODD CAMERON THACKER

Qi jing 七經
(Seven Classics)

The term *Qi jing* first appears in *Hou Han shu*, *juan* 35, and the Seven Classics are said to be *Yi jing*, *Shi jing*, *Shang shu*, the three texts of rites (*Li ji*, *Yi li*, *Zhou yi*) and *Lunyu*. When **Liu Chang** of the Northern Song (960–1127) published his *Qi jing xiaozhuan*, he indicated that the Seven Classics were *Shang shu*, *Mao shi*, *Chunqiu Gongyang zhuan*, the three texts of rites and *Lunyu*. Afterwards, there appeared a number of annotations on the Seven Classics, such as *The Royal Compilation of the Seven Classics* (*Yuzuan Qijing* 御纂七經), *The Essential Meanings of the Seven Classics* (*Qijing Jingyi* 七經精義), *The Summary of the Seven Classics* (*Qijing Yaoshuo* 七經要說) and *The Differences and Similarities between the Seven Classics* (*Qijing Tongyi* 七經同異).

References: Fung Yu-lan, 1952; Twitchett & Loewe, 1986.

M.H. KIM

Qi jing xiaozhuan 七經小傳
(*Short Commentaries on the Seven Classics*)

This work, in three chapters, consists of textual notes written by **Liu Chang** on the Seven Classics (**Qi jing**). His style of commentary represented a new type of annotation that was developing in the eleventh century and would take its place within the scope of Neo-Confucian scholarship. The work avoided the literal approach of earlier times and included some penetrating criticism comparable with that of **Wang Anshi**, with whom however Liu Chang had some differences.

M.H. KIM

Qi qing 七情
(Seven Emotions)

The seven inherent and spontaneous emotions are of joy (*xi* 喜), anger (*nu* 怒), sadness (*ai* 哀), fear (*ju* 懼), love (*ai*), hate (*wu* 惡) and desire (*yu* 欲). They are listed in the *Li yun* chapter of the *Book of Rites* (*Li ji*). On the question of the human nature (*xing*), these seven essential qualities are seen as the primary factors in the existence of evil in human action; rites (*li*) are the means of their regulation. Methods of active suppression or elimination of these emotions are explored, because it is believed that when left unchecked Seven Emotions would lead to evil. **Han Yu** and **Wang Anshi** both take emotion to be the movement (*dong* 動) incurred after the mind comes into contact with objects. **Cheng Yi**'s theory of nature ruling emotion (*yi xing zhi qing shuo* 以性制情說) interprets human nature as possessing a disciplining influence on emotion.

TODD CAMERON THACKER

Qi shi 齊詩
(*The Qi tradition of the Book of Poetry*)

The *Qi shi* is one of the three traditions of interpretation and transmission of the *Shi*

jing that were recognised as canonical texts to be taught in the Imperial Academy established during the reign of **Han Wudi**. The '*Rulin zhuan*' 儒林傳 chapter of the *Shi ji* credits its initiation to Yuan Gu 轅固 (*c.* 240–150 BCE), an academician at the court of Han Jingdi (r. 157–141 BCE). The teaching was transmitted through a series of eminent scholars, beginning with **Xiahou Shichang**, and extending through Hou Cang 后倉 (*fl.* ?), Kuang Heng 匡衡 (*fl.* 36–30 BCE), Chancellor under Han Yuandi (r. 49–33) and Chengdi (r. 33–7), and influencing even **Zheng Xuan**, the great Later Han commentator. This tradition is characterised by its use of **yin–yang** and 'Five Phases' (*wu xing*) philosophy to explain the poems and especially their sequence. Its influence is seen particularly among Han apocryphal writings (**chen wei**). Although the '*Yiwen zhi*' 藝文志 chapter of the *Han shu* lists under its section on the *Shi jing* several texts deriving from *Qi* scholars, the tradition seems to have died out by the first half of the third century.

Reference: Lin Yelian, 1993: 95–103.

EDWARD L. SHAUGHNESSY

Qi wei 七緯
(Seven apocryphal texts)

Qi wei refers to the seven apocryphal texts attached to the seven Confucian Classics, including the *Yi wei* 易緯, *Shu wei* 書緯, *Shi wei* 詩緯, *Li wei* 禮緯, *Yue wei* 樂緯, *Chunqiu wei* 春秋緯 and *Xiao jing wei* 孝經緯, which as a term first appears in chapter 82 of the **Hou Han shu**. An early edition of the apocryphal writings was published in the Former Han period (206 BCE–8 CE), and was designed to provide more detailed commentaries on the established Confucian canons. The authors of these texts intended to interpret the classical texts in terms of a new ideology based on yin–yang philosophy and were, however, seriously criticised by later scholars for their distortion of the original meaning of the Classics (see **Chen wei**).

References: Fung Yu-lan, 1952; Twitchett & Loewe, 1986.

M.H. KIM

Qian Daxin 錢大昕
1728–1804
(*zi* Xiaozheng 曉徵, *hao* Zhuding 竹汀)

A native of Jiading 嘉定 in the Shanghai area, Qian was a classicist and historian. He obtained his *jinshi* degree in 1754 and was appointed a compiler of imperial compilations of *Rehe zhi* 熱河志, *Xu wenxian tongkao* 續文獻通考, *Xu tongzhi* 續通志, *Yitong zhi* 一統志, *Tianqiu tu* 天球圖. He retired in 1775 as the director of education in Guangdong province. Thereafter he headed several academies: Zhongshan Shuyuan 鐘山書院 in Nanjing, Loudong Shuyuan 婁東書院 in Songjiang and Ziyang Shuyuan 紫陽書院 in Suzhou.

Qian was a well-known master on the Classics and history, as well as a noted mathematician, geographer and astronomer. In his work on phonetics entitled *Shenglei* 聲類 he discovered the 'unvoiced labials' as recorded in ancient books. Dissatisfied with the ignorance of the Han Learning scholars on history, he examined the Twenty-Two Dynastic Histories and made important critical notes entitled *Nianershi kaoyi* 廿二史考異. Aware of the weakness of the official dynastic history of the Yuan period (1260–1368), he produced the *Yuanshi shizu biao* 元史氏族表, a renewed memorial of the Mongol clan and family, and the *Bu Yuanshi yiwenzhi* 補元史藝文志, a renewed bibliography of the literary works of the Yuan period. He wrote the *Sishi suorun kao* 四史朔閏考 which was to clarify the confusion of the uses of the various reign-titles and conflicting calendars in the writing of history of the four dynasties: Song, Liao, Jin and Yuan. He corrected Hu Sanxing's 胡三省 (1230–1287) commentary on the **Zizhi tongjian** in his

work the *Tongjian zhu bianzheng* 通鑒注辯正. Qian took special interests in recording the dates of birth and death of historical figures and wrote the well-known *Yinian lu* 疑年錄 (*Record of Uncertain Dates*), including some 364 persons, which became the basis of the most important dictionary of dates in China. Most of his important works can be found in two collections, one containing his miscellaneous notes, entitled *Shijiazhai yangxin lu* 十架齋養新錄, and the other his literary works *Qianyantang wenji* 潛犀堂文集.

Reference: Hummel, 1943–4.

REBEKAH X. ZHAO

Qian Dehong 錢德洪
1497–1574
(*zi* Hongfu 洪甫, *hao* Xushan 緒山)

One of the major disciples of **Wang Shouren** (Wang Yangming), Qian Dehong was a native of Wang's home county of Yuyao in Zhejiang. Beginning in 1521, Qian became one of the earliest disciples of Wang at Yuyao. As Wang's popularity grew over the course of the following decade, Qian and another early disciple, **Wang Ji**, were given teaching responsibilities over the many students who came to Yuyao to study under Wang Yangming. In 1526 Qian and Wang Ji travelled together to take the metropolitans examinations in Beijing, but returned before the palace examinations because of public criticism of their teacher. Both proceeded to the examinations a second time in 1529 but returned again, this time due to the death of Wang Yangming. They remained in Zhejiang for three years to mourn their teacher and take care of his estate and family. Qian even negotiated the marriage of Wang Yangming's infant son to the daughter of **Huang Wan**.

Qian and Wang Ji, who became the two primary immediate disciples of Wang Yangming, established the Tianzhen 天真 Academy in Hangzhou in their teacher's honour and both finally received their *jinshi* degrees in 1532. After several years serving as an official, Qian was imprisoned in 1541 for his ruling on the case of the marquis Guo Xun 郭勛 (1475–1542). In prison, Qian focused his energies upon study of the *Yi jing* (*The Book of Changes*). After his release from prison in 1543, Qian travelled for thirty years throughout the provinces of the Lower and Middle Yangtze River valley, propagating Wang Yangming's idea of *liang zhi* 良知 (innate knowledge of the good). He often alternated with Wang Ji in presiding over lectures at famous **shu yuan** (academies) in the region. Finally, at the age of seventy, Qian retired from his travels and died several years later.

Although Qian Dehong and Wang Ji were the two most important immediate disciples of Wang Yangming, their interpretations of their teacher's thought differed. In general, Qian is seen as having stuck more closely to his teacher's thought, while Wang Ji took his philosophy in new directions, emphasising the independence of mind. This difference was centred upon contrasting interpretations of Wang Yangming's Four Dicta (*siju jiao* 四句教): (1) The absence of good and evil characterises the *xin ti* 心體 (the substance of heart/mind), (2) The presence of good and evil characterises the movement of its intentions, (3) The knowledge of good and evil characterises its *liang zhi*, and (4) The doing of good and ridding of evil characterises its **gewu** (investigation of things). Qian takes the first dictum as descriptive of the heart/mind-in-itself in the state of *weifa zhi zhong* 未發之中 (prestirred equilibrium), before the emotions are manifest. Qian interpreted the second through fourth dicta as presenting instructions for practical self-cultivation, the object of which is the recovery of this state of prestirred equilibrium described in the first dictum. Therefore, Qian believes that the distinction between good and evil must be maintained in the first dictum as well as in the following three. Otherwise, self-cultivation makes no sense for Qian if it is simply for the sake of returning to a state in which distinctions between good and evil do not exist.

In contrast to Qian's reading, Wang Ji interpreted the Four Dicta as a comprehensive description of *liang zhi*. The implication of Wang's interpretation is that when one truly understands that the mind is neither good nor evil, then one also recognises that the intentions, knowledge, and things described in the second through fourth dicta are also beyond the category of good and evil. When in 1527 Wang Ji and Qian Dehong consulted Wang Yangming about their disagreement, the teacher proclaimed both interpretations correct, explaining that Wang Ji's interpretation applied to men of superior intelligence while Qian's was more appropriate for the vast majority of people of mediocre or less intelligence. After the death of Wang Yangming in 1529, Qian maintained his notion of gradual self-cultivation through the careful development of *liangzhi*. Qian's interpretation of the Four Dicta came to be known as the Four Positives (*si you* 四有), which affirmed the goodness of the heart/mind, intention, knowledge and things.

Thus Qian was more of a faithful disciple than he was an original thinker. Perhaps his most important contribution to Confucian philosophy lay in his editing of Wang Yangming's works beginning in 1527. He is largely responsible for compiling the second part of Wang's **Chuanxi lu** (*Instructions for Practical Living*), the first part of which had been compiled by **Xu Ai**. In addition, Qian compiled Wang Yangming's chronological biography (*nianpu* 年譜).

Reference: Huang Tsung-hsi, 1987: 111–13.
STEVEN MILES

Qianfu lun 潛夫論
(*The Discourses of a Recluse*)

This work by **Wang Fu** is listed in the *Sui shu* 隋書 as a Confucian text (1973:

998). It is a series of thirty-five essays (*pian*) on aspects of politics, government, society, thought and religion during the author's lifetime, plus a chapter as a summary of the whole book. Fan Ye 范曄 (398–446) judged this work sufficient to give a good picture of the social and political situation of the time; Etienne Balazs considered it the most important eyewitness account of this era. In addition, the work presents a political philosophy of interest in itself. Focusing on the **xian ren** (worthy), Wang Fu argued that such men's strengths and weaknesses were both worthy of recognition and useful employment. While this is hardly a new insight today, his emphasis on the usefulness of imperfections adds an unusual twist to a philosophy based largely on **Xunzi** and Old Text readings of the Classics, although he was as emphatic as **Mengzi** on the importance of dissent and on the scholar's duty to speak truth to power and the ruler's duty to heed it.

The thirty-sixth chapter summarises the main points of the preceding thirty-five chapters. Topics considered include: enlightened ruling and good government (6, 8, 9, 10, 17); the selection of officials (7, 14, 15); the administration of justice (16, 18, 19, 20); social and economic conditions (2, 3, 4, 12, 13); military and border affairs (21, 22, 23, 24); divination (25–9); cosmology (32–4); and genealogy (35). Chapter 1 entitled 'In praise of knowledge' may be his most Confucian essay, in its stress on the primary importance of education, yet even there Wang Fu gives credence to the myth that **Confucius** took Laozi as his teacher. Wang Fu's legalism is more evident in chapters on litigation (18, 19 and others), yet he balances his awareness of the need for the restraints of law with great weight on the primary importance of good character among those chosen as officials. He opposed excessive oversight of local leaders while bitterly attacking corruption and the privileges of the aristocratic and wealthy.

Fan Ye included five chapters of *Qianfu lun* in **Hou Han shu** (1965: 1630 ff). These are substantially the same as the received version. **Han Yu** praised Wang Fu as one of the three worthy men of the Later Han (25–220 CE). Zhou Zhungfu 周中孚 (1768–1831) notes that the *Qianfu lun* was continuously recorded as a work of ten *juan* in all-important bibliographies and library catalogues, beginning with the *Sui shu*. (34, p. 998; under *rujia*). It is also listed in the catalogue of Fujiwara Sukeyo. While some chapters have many textual problems and one is written in a different style, there are no serious questions about the authenticity and authorship. It contains no reference to the *dang gu* 黨錮 incidents (166–184), so it was probably completed before. The four chapters on frontier defence refer to events of 107–118, and were probably composed between 111–118.

The most useful edition of this book is *Qianfu lun jian* 潛夫論箋 (Beijing: Zhunghuashuju, 1979) edited by Peng Duo 彭鐸 It includes modern punctuation and notes by Wang Jipei 汪繼培 (b. 1775) and his preface written in 1814. Its appendices include biographical information, prefaces and assessments of the book. The 1978 Shanghai edition has the same fine notes and punctuation but lacks the appendices.

The English translation of the book by Margaret J. Pearson includes an extended biography of Wang Fu, translations of all six excerpts from the *Qianfu lun* included in the *Hou Han shu* biography of Wang Fu and nine *pian* of the entire work. Most of these are related to Wang's view of contemporary government and politics, these views are analysed and discussed by Pearson in six chapters preceding the translations. Ivan P. Kamenarovic provides a translation of all thirty-six *pian*, with notes identifying textual emendations and providing basic information for non-Sinologists. Anne Behnke Kinney publishes a literary analysis, containing an analysis of the nature of the *lun* as a literary genre and of the *Qianfu lun* compared to other Han discourse, as well as translations of nine chapters, including those on education, divination and cosmology (1, 2, 13, 25–8, 32).

References: Ch'en Ch'i-yun & Pearson, in Loewe, 1993; Kinney, 1990; Pearson, 1989.
MARGARET PEARSON

Qian–Jia xuepai 乾嘉學派
(Qian–Jia School)

The Qian–Jia School refers to those scholars who underscored textual and linguistic evidence in their classical and historical studies in the eighteenth and early nineteenth centuries. Most of the leading scholars who laid the theoretical and methodological foundation lived in the Qianlong reign (1736–1795) and their scholarship provided models through the Jiaqing reign (1796–1820), and hence the name of the Qian–Jia School. Characterised by its stress on philological and textual criticism, their studies were also called *kaozheng xue* 考證學 (evidential research). These classical scholars' heavy reliance on the exegetical works of the Han dynasty (206 BCE–220 CE) also earned them the title of *Han xue* 漢學 (Han Learning) even though some did not exclude post Han scholarship.

The leading scholars of the Qian–Jia period did not undertake academic investigation as an exercise in methodology *per se*. Scholars like **Hui Dong** and **Dai Zhen** formulated methodological doctrines against a clearly targeted exegetical traditions – the Song classical tradition. They were discontented with the Song, Yuan and Ming Confucians whose exegetical scholarship, they argued, had been marred with heterodox ideas from Buddhism and Daoism. These influences had produced skewed readings of the Classics and hence corrupted Confucian teachings. Qian–Jia scholars were committed to cleansing heterodox elements from the exegetical traditions by employing phonological and philological methods.

This Confucian purism was encoded in a methodological doctrine first articulated in Hui Shiqi 惠士奇 (1671–1741). Hui argued that 'the meaning of the Classics are preserved in the exegetical comments; to know its meaning, one needs to understand the meaning and pronunciation of the words. Therefore, ancient exegeses should not be changed.' The 'ancient exegeses' (*gu xun* 古訓) that Hui respected were from scholars of the Han dynasty. This methodological doctrine was further refined by **Dai Zhen** who argued that the meaning of the Six Classics (*Liu jing*) could be known only after the ancient comments on pronunciations and meaning were understood. Only through a thorough study of the phonology of the ancient language in which the Six Classics were written could their meaning be clarified. Dai therefore insisted that knowledge of works on etymology and phonology by Han scholars was a prerequisite for classical studies.

The classical scholars of the Qian–Jia period did not apply their methodology without an ideological stance regarding what moral truth was. They were driven by a 'Confucian ritualism' that underscored a ritualist–institutional approach to ethics. They were critical of the **dao xue** Confucians' discourses on ethics. For them they were abstract reflections on human nature, the mind and their relation with the general order of existence that dominated the exegetical traditions of Song Confucians like the Cheng Brothers, **Zhou Dunyi**, **Zhang Zai** and most importantly, **Zhu Xi**. For Hui Dong and Dai Zhen, the fundamental flaw of these Song Confucians was that their quest for moral truth was not grounded in the Classics, especially the institutions and rites of high antiquity. Following the footsteps of Hui Shiqi, Hui Dong and Dai Zhen, classical scholars of this period assumed that 'moral truths are embodied in rites and institutions'.

The quest for knowledge of rites and institution contributed to better understanding of ancient history in terms of not just objects used in rites and buildings where rites were performed and institutions located.

The methodology and ideological stance encouraged an intellectualism that valorised knowledge of the past, bringing to the foreground the intellectual orientation inherent in Confucian Learning. Many subsidiary branches of learning were deemed crucial to the understanding of the broader social and political conditions in which rites and institutions were created and performed. Knowledge of phonology, paleography, historical geography and astronomy became crucial to the investigation of the historical and material context of ancient rites and institutions. The great achievement in phonology and etymology by scholars like Dai Zhen, **Duan Yucai**, Wang Niansun 王念孫 (1744–1832) and his son Wang Yinzhi 王引之 (1766–1834) marked the high point of the 'evidential scholarship' of the Qian–Jia period.

The extension of the critical and philological methods to the study of history resulted in the rise of an approach that put a premium on the search for 'facts' as the main duty of a historian. The critical works by **Qian Daxin** and **Wang Mingsheng** were representative of this historiographical trend as they hammered away at the minute details and trivialities. While meticulous attention was paid to accuracy of facts and information about 'institution and documents' (*dian zhang* 典章) and 'names and things' (*ming wu* 名物), the larger issue of perspective and the role of the historian as a producer of historical knowledge was neglected or dismissed as obstacles to the quest of truth. The *Ershier shi zaji* 二十二史劄記 (*Notes on the Twenty-Two Histories*) by Qian and the *Shiqi shi shangque* 十七史商榷 (*Critical Study of the Seventeen Histories*) provided the models for historians in the Qian–Jia period. Unlike the work of **Zhang Xuecheng**, they were studies of mistakes and discrepancies rather than the nature, principles and methods of historical writings.

References: Elman, 1984; Chow Kai-wing, 1994.

KAI-WING CHOW

Qian Mu 錢穆
1895–1990
(original name Sirong, 思(鑠) *zi* Binsi 賓四)

Specialising in Chinese history and yet intellectually engaged in the broader cultural questions of twentieth-century China, Qian Mu's life-long support for the inherent value of Chinese traditional culture countered more dominant anti-traditionalist and revolutionary tendencies. Born in the Wuxi 無錫 district of Jiangsu 江蘇 province in 1895, Qian was deeply moved by the questions raised by **Liang Qichao** 梁啟超 about the cultural survival of China in 1910. While teaching in a local elementary school for ten years, Qian read widely in traditional classics, history, philosophy and literature. His early published work in Chinese intellectual history earned him a position at Beijing University, where he taught courses on Chinese history. Achieving a scholarly reputation in 'conservative' works which were criticised by radical intellectuals, as in Guo Moruo's 郭沫若 (1892–1978) *Shi pipan shu* 十批判書, he chose in the face of Communist victories to emigrate to Hong Kong. There in 1949 he established **Xinya xueyuan** or New Asia College with other emigrated scholars including **Tang Junyi**. Retiring later from the post of college principal, Qian in 1967 moved to Taiwan where he lived out the balance of his prolific life as an influential Confucian scholar.

Qian's substantial historical works were influential in several areas. It was his critical historical research in 1930 on the Han scholars **Liu Xiang** and **Liu Xin** which successfully challenged and debunked **Kang Youwei**'s historical justifications for the New Text Confucian school. Ten years later Qian's seminal work, *Guoshi dagang* 國史大綱 (*The Grand Outline of National History*), set new standards and categories for Chinese historical research. There he presented comparative cultural evaluations and an account of the central and distinctive role of Confucian culture in China that were and remain extremely influential. Believing that the Chinese 'national spirit' (*minzu jingshen* 民族精神) was distinctively framed by Confucian virtues, and was also able to be culturally self-renewing through the cultivation of the heart/mind (*xin*), Qian's position necessarily stood in opposition to modern compromises and radical rejections of these cultural resources.

Typical of his thorough research and innovative interpretations which provided comprehensive views of his subject was his multi-volume study of **Zhu Xi** completed after his retirement in 1970, *Zhuzi xin xuean*. Written to reveal the multiform breadth of Zhu's studies and seeking to avoid partisan viewpoints, Qian collected and reorganised quotations from Zhu's major works under topical headings, allowing Zhu's own words to explain his teachings. Ultimately, Qian claimed that Zhu was not a sectarian promoter of Principle-centred Learning (*li xue* 理學), but was in fact a synthetically minded and non-sectarian Confucian scholar rooted in the Learning of Heart/Mind (*xin xue* 心學), the 'school' normally seen as opposing his teaching.

Because of his multifaced scholarship and international reputation, Qian was presented two honorary doctorates from universities in Hong Kong and the United States. Though highly influential among New Confucian scholars and those promoting the inherent value of Chinese traditional culture, his own published works aspired to be non-sectarian, and so he has been called by some the 'modern Zhu Xi'.

Reference: Fang & Zheng, 1995: 150–90.

LAUREN PFISTER

Qian Yiji 錢儀吉
1783–1850
(*zi* Hanshi 衎石, *hao* Xinhu 心壺, Xinwu 新梧)

A native of Jiaxing 嘉興 in Zhejiang province, Qian was a scholar of the Confucian Classics. He passed the *jinshi* examination in 1808. From 1820 to 1830 he held posts in various government ministries. In 1832 he took the post of director in *Xuehai tang* 學海堂 in Guangdong. In 1836 he became the headmaster of the *Daliang shuyuan* 大梁書院 in Kaifeng, where he remained until his death.

Qian compiled a large collection entitled *Guochao beizhuan ji* 國朝碑傳集. This collection consisted of epitaphs, biographical sketches and many other private writings relating to over 800 persons selected from a wide range of occupations. Covering two centuries from the beginning of the Manchu Tianming 天命 reign (1616–1626) to Qian's contemporary Jiaqing 嘉慶 period (1796–1820), the work contained materials drawn from about 560 works and was arranged under 25 categories, 160 sections (*juan*) all together. It was regarded as the most complete collection of its type at that time. While teaching in the *Daliang shuyuan*, Qian collected those scattered works of the Song, Yuan and Ming times on the Classics and compiled them in a collection entitled *Jingyuan* 經苑, including 41 works. Qian wrote a historical book entitled *Sanguo jin Nanbeichao huiyao* 三國晉南北朝會要, on issues of the Three Kingdoms (221–277), Jin (265–420) and Southern and Northern Dynasties (420–589). Being proficient in astronomy, he wrote a book on calendar calculation entitled *Li kao* 歷考.

Reference: Hummel, 1943–4.

REBEKAH X. ZHAO

Qin 親
(To love, intimacy, one's beloved)

Qin means to love, or to be intimate with. For Confucians, *qin* means to love someone like a close kinsman. Hence, *qin* is often contrasted with the word *shu* 疏 (distant). The **Xunzi** states, 'Father and son love each other, but if they are insincere, then their relations will be distant (*shu*)' (*Xunzi*, 3: 9c). The people who one loves (*qin*) the most are usually close relatives, which is why *qin* can also mean 'parents'. One does not indiscriminately love (*qin*) everyone. **Mengzi** makes this explicit: 'As for the people, [the gentleman (*junzi*)] is benevolent (*ren*) towards them, but he does not love (*qin*) them. He loves his beloved (*qin qin*), but he is only benevolent (*ren*) towards the people' (*Mengzi*, 7A: 45). For rulers, loving (*qin*) one's relatives is important because it sets an example of showing kindness to others that will transform the behaviour of ordinary people. Confucius said, 'If a gentleman (*junzi*) is generous to his kin, then the people will flourish in their practice of benevolence (*ren*)' (**Lunyu**, 8: 2).

However, loving someone as close kin is not enough, thus Confucian writers often pair *qin* with the term zun 尊 (to venerate). The two differ in their object: *qin* is directed towards kin, while *zun* is directed towards superiors. A gentleman needs to both love (*qin*) and venerate (*zun*). The *Li ji* states, 'Someone who emphasises benevolence (*ren*) but slights righteousness (*yi*), loves (*qin*) but does not venerate (*zun*); someone who emphasises righteousness but slights benevolence, venerates but does not love' (*Li ji*, 33: 7).

References: Hung, ed., 1972a, 1972b; Lau & Ching, eds., 1992a, 1996a.

KEITH KNAPP

Qin Guan 秦觀

1049–1100

(*zi* Shaoyou 少游 or Tai xu 太虛, *hao* Huaihai jushi 淮海居士)

Despite his early brilliance and literary talent, Qin was unable to pass the demanding *jinshi* examination. He nevertheless caught the attention of the great Northern Song literatus **Su Shi**, who saw in him a talent equal to Qu Yuan 屈原 (332–295 BCE) and Song Yu 宋玉 (fourth century BCE) (*Song shi*: 444.13112). Recommended by Su as worthy and upright (*xianliang fangzheng* 賢良方正), Qin filled a series of academic

appointments including as academician at the Imperial Academy (*Taixue boshi* 太學博士). In that capacity, he edited texts in the palace library and worked as a compiler of the dynastic history. His close connection to Su Shi resulted in his being included in the so-called Yuanyou faction (*Yuanyou dang* 元祐黨). He therefore suffered a series of demotions in the mid to late 1090s.

Qin's collected works, *Huaihai ji* 淮海集 (*Huaihai Collection*) in forty *juan* survives as do a number of other smaller collections. He is best remembered for his literary and artistic abilities. Although he himself was from the southeast (Yangzhou 揚州 in Jiangsu), his literary ability and his relationship with Su Shi made him a recognised member of the so-called Sichuan School (*Shu xue* 蜀學) during the Song.

References: Bol, 1982; Qin Guan, 1782, *Song shi*, 1977.

ANTHONY DEBLASI

Qin qin 親親

(To love one's beloved, nearness of kinship)

Qin qin literally means to love one's beloved, i.e., one's closest kin. It is one of the basic elements of benevolence (*ren*). The *Mengzi* twice states that, 'loving one's beloved is benevolence' (*Mengzi*, 6B: 3, 7A: 15). For Mengzi loving one's beloved (*qin qin*) is so important that it can help establish a perfect social order. Mengzi said, 'If everyone loved their beloved (*qin qi qin* 親其親) and treated their seniors as seniors, the Great Peace (*Tai ping* 太平) would come about' (*Mengzi* 4A: 12). Loving one's beloved creates order through its extension to others. **Liu Xiang**'s *Shuoyuan* 說苑 (*Garden of Persuasions*) says, 'One who loves his or her beloved (*qin qin*) gives first place to his or her intimates and second place to outsiders; first place to benevolence (*ren*) and second place to righteousness (*yi*). These are the traces of the sage–kings' (*Shuoyuan*, 7.42).

Qin qin's other meaning, nearness of kinship, is a technical one that is used to determine to what degree a relative should be mourned. The closer the relative is to oneself, the longer and more severe the mourning rituals would be. For example, since one's parents are closer in kinship to oneself than one's wife, a son mourns them longer (three years as opposed to one) and practices more funerary austerities on their behalf, than he would for her. The *Li ji* states that, 'The mourning rites are determined on six principles: the first is the nearness of kinship (*qin qin*) . . .' (*Li ji*, 16.5).

Reference: Xu & He, 1991: 317–22.

KEITH KNAPP

Qing 情
(Feeling reality)

Standard dictionary entries give two equivalents for *qing*: (1) feelings, emotions and (2) circumstances, reality. In ancient Chinese, the reference to subjective 'feeling' appears to have *grown out* of an original sense: 'reality'.

The character consists of a heart semantic and a phonetic *qing* (life-colour, green/blue, young, growing). We find the phonetic in other characters associated with purity or clarity. The phonetic component also occurs in 'request, please!' with a language semantic.

In early China, the core philosophical dialectic was not between objective reality and subjective appearance but between the natural and the conventional (between *tian* 天, nature or sky and *ren* 人, human). Thinkers treated a *dao* 道 (guide, Way) as either a transmitted *instruction set* or as a pattern in the nature of things (see *dao qi*). To follow social *dao*, one must *correctly* assign names to things in the world (see *shi–fei*). One must also *identify* which of the various competing *dao* to use. The Daoist philosopher, Zhuangzi, used *qing* to talk of those basic roles of *shi–fei* in applying a *dao* to action. He noted that states like fear, anger, sorrow, happiness and joy just 'loom

up before us day and night . . . we know not from whence they arise' but 'without them there would be no "I" and no choosing'.

The Confucian **Xunzi** next used *qing* of the *natural* direction of human motivation (evil) in contrast to the cultivated guidance (good) from a consciously created *dao*. He associated *qing* even more with Zhuangzi's list of states thus giving *qing* a *negative connotation*. Xunzi's attitudes and thought dominated the postphilosophical Han period and when Buddhism reached China, *qing* easily adapted to its doctrine of desire as the root of suffering. It retained the Buddhist meaning in **Neo-Confucianism** but some of the later Confucian thinkers, rejecting Buddhist pessimism, began to view feelings themselves in a more positive and moral light.

References: Graham, 1989, 1990: 7–66; Hansen, 1995: 181–211; Wong, 1991: 31–58; Wu Yi, 1986.

CHAD HANSEN

Qing sanpin 情三品
(The three grades of human emotions)

Within **Han Yu**'s essay *Yuan xing*, he defines human nature (*xing*) and human emotion (*qing*) in three grades or levels: the superior (*shang* 上), the mean or medium (*zhong* 中) and the inferior (*xia* 下). Human nature is composed of the five constant virtues (*wu chang*), i.e., humaneness (*ren*), righteousness (*yi*), propriety (*li*), wisdom (*zhi*) and trustworthiness (*xin*). The nature at the superior grade is entirely good (*shan*), while at the inferior grade it is entirely evil (*e*). So too are the Seven Emotions (*qi qing*), i.e., joy, anger, sadness, fear, love, hate and desire thus classified in three grades: the superior holding to the mean (*zhongyong*) while the inferior is always at an extreme of deficiency or excess. The superior grade can be improved upon by means of education and the inferior must be controlled by laws and sanctions. It is with the medium grade of human nature or emotion that some of the emotions, for example, will be either excessive or deficient, fluctuating between good and evil. Emotions are not innate or inborn, for they arise after birth when a human being comes into contact with the world. Han Yu asserted that **Mengzi**'s theory of innate human goodness and **Xunzi**'s opposite view of its innately evil status addressed only the medium of these three grades. Commenting on this theory, Wing-tsit Chan points out an apparent contradiction between the 'belief in the goodness of human nature and in the ultimate identity of the Sage (*sheng ren*) and the common man' and the 'theory of the three grades, the higher and lower of which are immutable'. Chan sees this seeming contradiction as a result of Buddhist influence that assumed no contradiction between the Buddha nature inherent in all things and the three grades of human nature (Chan, 1963d: 205).

References: Chan, Wing-tsit, 1963d; Fung Yu-lan, 1952, vol. II: 413; Hartman, 1986: 205.

TODD CAMERON THACKER

Qingjiang xuepai 清江學派
(The School of Qingjiang)

The Qingjiang School was established by **Liu Qingzhi** and his older brother **Liu Jingzhi**. Liu Qingzhi was a stronger scholar of the two, and his thought was to be greatly influenced by **Zhu Xi**, **Zhang Shi** and **Lü Zuqian**. Late in his official career when Liu Qingzhi constructed his first scholarly retreat the Linzheng Pavilion 臨蒸精舍 in Jiangxi, his purpose was to 'regulate the mind, regulate the body, regulate the household, and regulate the individual (*zhi xin zhi shen zhi jia zhi ren* 治心治身治家治人)'. At the heart of the Qingjiang School's teachings was the Confucian notion of purpose (*zhi* 志), that is, the purposeful application of oneself in study. Furthermore, the Qingjiang School emphasised the elucidation

of the moral principles in preparation for government service. The Qingjiang School derived teachings from influential thinkers such as Zhang Jiuling 張九齡, **Han Yu**, Kou Jun 寇準, **Zhou Dunyi**, **Hu Anguo**, Liu Yi 劉翼 and Wang Yingzhi 王應之.

Members of the Qingjiang School included Zhao Fan 趙蕃 (1143–1229, *zi* Changwen 昌文, *hao* Zhangquan 章泉), **Huang Gan**, and Zeng Zudao 曾祖道 (?–?, *zi* Zhaizhi 宅之). Both Huang and Zeng would become active participants in the Zhu Xi's *Dao xue* fellowship, and Huang's writings would have a great influence on the eventual acceptance of Zhu Xi's teachings as the basis for the civil service examinations. The Qingjiang School also received strong praise from **Wang Yingchen**, **Yang Wanli**, and the eminent historian Li Tao 李燾 (1115–1184). The school's greatest influence was felt in the southeast.

References: *Song–Yuan xuean*, 1966: *juan* 59, pp. 1939–41; Wu & Song, 1992: 1477–8.

JAMES A. ANDERSON

Qizhi zhi xing 氣質之性
(Physically endowed nature)

As explained by the philosophical school of **Cheng Yi** and **Zhu Xi**, the 'physically endowed nature' of humankind is the opposite of the *benran zhixing* (original nature) or *tiandi zhi xing* (nature of Heaven and Earth). It is that flesh-and-blood, physically concrete nature that, in the case of each person, assumes its form in an 'after-Heaven' (*hou tian* 後天) or *a posteriori* sequence. The original nature is produced from *li* (principle), it is pure and uniform throughout, and it is serenely unmoving. By contrast, the physically endowed nature is produced from *qi* (material force), and its quality is wholly dependent upon the purity or turbidity, the translucence or opaqueness, or the dispersion or viscosity of the *qi* from which it is made. Moreover, there are extreme variations in how the physically endowed nature is manifested in people and all human good and evil, worthiness and foolishness, results from its unequal distribution. For this reason, Zhu Xi seconded **Zhang Zai** in advocating that in order to return to the purity of one's original nature and thus preserve it, one must resist succumbing to one's physically endowed nature at all costs.

Zhu Xi concluded that whenever one is discussing the nature of Heaven and Earth, one's conversation must focus exclusively on principle. But whenever discussing the physically endowed nature, the conversation must centre on the conflation of principle and *qi*. Nevertheless, whenever one addresses the subject of human nature, one must necessarily include the physically endowed nature for such discourse to be complete.

References: Chan, Wing-tsit, 1963: 623–6; Chu, 1922; Fung, 1952: 551–8.

DON J. WYATT

Quan 權
(Weighing the consequences to ascertain the most moral action possible in changing circumstances)

The tension between *jing* (constant principle) and *quan* gave classicism the flexibility it needed to avoid a reduction to mere antiquarianism. An interest in *quan* can be traced back to Confucius, who acknowledged the difficulty of determining the best moral accommodation to changing circumstances (*Lunyu* 9: 30). A semi-playful question put to **Mengzi** (Given ritual segregation by gender within the family, should a man extend his hand to save a female relative on the point of drowning?) shows that the problem of when and how to apply *quan* had not been fully resolved. Yet to Mengzi, 'Holding to the middle without leaving room for weighing moral priorities is like holding onto one extreme' (7A: 26).

It is the *Gongyang* 公羊 interpretative traditions attached to the *Chunqiu* 春秋

(*Chunqiu Gongyang zhuan*), however, which deal most with the interplay of *jing* and *quan*. According to the *Gongyang*, the noble man departs from constant principles, acting in a *quan* manner, only in the hope that his departure may effect a restoration of constant principles; *quan* is not to be confused with mere expediency nor can it be used to justify what is clearly immoral behaviour (harming or killing others to improve one's own circumstances) – what, in the words of **Dong Zhongshu**, master in the *Gongyang* tradition, lay 'clearly outside the realm of propriety'.

In the Northern Song period (960–1127), the political reformers in **Wang Anshi**'s party invoked *quan* to justify their New Policies. The opposition to Wang, which included the Cheng (see **Cheng Hao** and **Cheng Yi**) brothers, then began to deny that *quan* had a valid place in moral thinking. They insisted that 'true *quan* is identical to *jing*'. **Zhu Xi**, slightly less rigid in his views, believed that 'under the usual circumstances, one maintains the constant principle, and under the unusual, one acts to weigh moral priorities', though the need to maintain constant principles was the cornerstone of his teachings.

Reference: Li Xinlin, 1989.

MICHAEL NYLAN

Quan Zuwang 全祖望
1705–1755
(*zi* Shaoyi 紹衣, *hao* Xieshan 謝山)

A native of Yingxian 鄞縣 (Ningbo 寧波) in Zhejiang, Quan was a classicist and historian. Famous as a young intellectual while visiting Beijing, Quan passed his *jinshi* examination in 1736 and was assigned a bachelor 庶吉士 of the Hanlin Academy. He was then recommended for a post as county magistrate. Disgraced by the appointment, he resigned from officialdom and devoted his life to academic studies. From 1737 to 1748 he relied on writing and on patronage for a living. Later, he was the head of Jishan Shuyuan 蕺山書院 and Duanxi Shuyuan 端溪書院 Academies, both for a short time. After 1747 he suffered from chronic insomnia and other diseases until his death.

Quan's great-grandfather was a loyalist to the Ming. In his childhood Quan learnt much from his father about the history of the late Ming period and about the sufferings and the heroism of the Ming Loyalists. This early education resulted in his extreme interest in local history. In a prose collection, Quan recorded the resistance of the Ming loyalists after 1645, with special attention to the part played by the natives of Quan's home district, Ningpo. He gave a plain account of the tragic case of Zhuang Tinglong 莊廷龍 (?–?), which was one of the largest tragic literati inquisitions during the era of Emperors Sunzhi (r. 1644–1662) and Kangxi (r. 1662–1722). He recorded many biographies, life sketches and epitaphs of famous scholars of the early Qing period, such as **Huang Zongxi**, **Gu Yanwu**, **Li Yong**, Liu Xianting 劉獻廷 (1648–1695), **Fang Bao**, Li Fu 李紱 (1674–1750), etc. His writings were fully appreciated, and influenced the anti-Manchu perceptions, in the late Qing and early Republican periods.

Quan admired two local philosophers: **Wan Sida** and Huang Zongxi. He spent over ten years editing and supplementing Huang's famous work on the **Song–Yuan xuean** 宋元學案. On the study of the Confucian Classics and histories he produced the *Jingshi dawen* 經史答問, a collection of dialogues with his students, which was regarded as rivalling **Gu Yanwu**'s *Rizhilu* 日知錄.

He reorganised and annotated the *Shui jing zhu* 水經注 (*Classics of Waterways*) of Li Daoyuan 酈道元 (466? or 472?–527). He compared the texts and notes of at least twenty-nine different scholars of the Ming and Qing periods and discovered that, owing to centuries of faulty transcription, certain passages of Li's commentaries were mixed with the original text of the *Shui jing*. Disentangling those texts, he therefore clarified many puzzles related to the *Shui jing zhu*. His work was entitled *Qijiao Shui jing zhu* 七校水經注 and his method has contributed greatly to textual criticism. His other worthy commentary is the third edition of **Wang Yinglin**'s miscellaneous notes known as the *Kunxue jiwen* 困學紀聞.

Quan's other works include the *Han shu dili zhi jiyi* 漢書地理志輯疑, and *Duyi bielu* 讀易別錄, a bibliography of apocryphal works on the *Book of Changes*.

References: Hummel, 1943–4; *Qing shi gao*, 1970; Zhao & Guo, 1989.

REBEKAH X. ZHAO

R

Rai Sanyô 賴山陽
1781–1832
(*na*: Noboru 襄; *azana*: Shisei 子城; *tsûshô*: Kyûtarô 久太郎)

Since the Meiji period many have regarded Rai Sanyô as the historian who contributed the most to the formation of the historical consciousness that made the Meiji Restoration, and thus the rise of the modern Japanese nation–state, possible. He was the son of Rai Shunsui 賴春水, a well-known Neo-Confucian teacher of Osaka who was enlisted in the service of Aki 安藝 domain (Hiroshima) when Sanyô was four years old. Sanyô's mother was also accomplished in the literary arts, and he had two uncles who were Confucian scholars, assuring that he received an excellent education from an early age. At the age of sixteen (1797), he accompanied his uncle and teacher Kyôhei 杏坪 to Edo, where he studied for a year at the Shôheikô Academy. Here, he is reported to have amazed scholars with his abilities in Chinese poetry and prose. His father had already set out to write a national history and had received the permission of the domainal leaders, but this permission was abruptly withdrawn four years later and his manuscript was destroyed. Hiroshima was a *tozama* 外様 domain (lacking a pre-1600 tradition of loyalty to the Tokugawa), so from the bakufu's point of view its production of a

national history was not to be tolerated. Sanyô was deeply impressed as a child by his father's disappointment, helping to nourish his own aspiration to devote his life to writing history. In order to fulfil his ambition without external pressures, he realised he would have to give up his duties as a vassal in service of a domain and become an unattached private citizen (*sômô no shoshi* 草莽の處士). However, leaving one's domain without permission was a crime under Tokugawa law. At the age of nineteen (1800), after his father was appointed to teach at the Shôheikô, he took the opportunity to flee the domain and hide himself in Kyoto. This led to his father angrily disinheriting him in order to fend off greater punishment, and he was placed under domiciliary confinement for three years. However, he was gradually allowed to have whatever books he needed, and he took it upon himself to read all the Confucian Classics as well as the classical Chinese histories and philosophers. During this period he also began writing the work that made him famous, *Nihon gaishi* 日本外史 (*An Unofficial History of Japan*). In 1809, Sanyô was invited to be headmaster of a private school run by a distinguished poet of Song-style Chinese poetry, Kan Chazan 菅茶山 (1748–1827), in the neighbouring province of Bingo 備後. Although Chazan was hoping to adopt Sanyô as his heir and had arranged a well-paid position for him serving Fukuyama domain, this was hardly a route that would satisfy Sanyô's real ambition, and he carefully explained to Chazan his desire to go to Kyoto. Chazan relented, and in 1811 Sanyô moved to Kyoto, where he opened a small school of his own. Here he lived for twenty years as an independent man of letters, supporting himself by teaching, writing and calligraphy, associating regularly at his school with many of the leading literati of Kyoto in his time – poets, *bunjinga* 文人畫 (literati painting) artists, and unattached Confucian scholars. This was an environment that enabled Sanyô to be quite free about the political views that he wrote into his historical writings. In 1827, he finally completed his *Unofficial History*, and in response to an invitation by the *rôjû* Matsudaira Sadanobu 松平定信 (1758–1829), he presented it to the shogunate. To Sanyô's relief, the work was accepted and even praised by Sadanobu, helping make possible the wide circulation it later enjoyed. This praise also encouraged Sanyô to go on to write two more major historical works, *Nihon seiki* 日本政記 and *Tsûgi* 通議. In his late years, Sanyô presented his *Unofficial History* through his son to the daimyo of Hiroshima, and through his disciples to the daimyo of several other domains. That it truly did present views of a 'dangerous' nature is confirmed by the fact that several domains strictly prohibited the public reading of the book. Famous bakumatsu reformist thinkers like **Yokoi Shônan** 横井小楠 (1809–69) had to get hold of the book surreptitiously and read it in secret. Eventually, however, the book came to be read by virtually everyone who could read classical Chinese and had a concern for the future of the nation, giving an estimated readership of some 300,000 to 400,000 people. Sanyô was not only a historian, but also an accomplished calligrapher and writer of Chinese-style poetry. What helped make his history famous was the elegant, vigorous and highly readable style of Chinese in which it was written, modelled after the **Chunqiu Zuo zhuan** and the **Shi ji**. But it was his philosophy of history that had the greatest impact on his readers. Its first principle was that the name and actuality of ruling authority should properly be united in the sovereign, and not split as had been the case since the actuality was usurped by the military houses. This concept of shogunal rule, influenced by the **Kaitokudô** historians in Osaka, was diametrically opposed to that of **Arai Hakuseki**. According to Sanyô, there is a force or the momentum of affairs (*ikioi* 勢) operating in history independently of human will whereby an original condition where the ruler's will and the people's feelings are in communication decays with the long continuation of peace, producing an alienation between above and below that leads eventually to an overturning of the realm or a change in regime, and these changes are irreversible. As he wrote in *Tsûgi*, although *ikioi* 'is not something that is within the power of human beings to control, when changes are beginning to take place and the change has not yet come to completion, it *is* within human power to act so as to direct the process of change, as long as one relies on that momentum. Even though it is not possible for human beings to go against the momentum of affairs, the momentum of affairs is also sometimes brought to completion by human beings ... *Ikioi* in the realm is like water; it is not possible to stop the water once it has started flowing powerfully in certain direction ... When the momentum reaches its culmination, there will be a change, and once this change has occurred, it is final'. The Meiji Restoration itself can be regarded as a powerful verification of this historical philosophy.

Further reading: Burton Watson, 'Historian and Master of Chinese Verse, Rai San'yô', in Murakami Jyoe and Thomas J. Harper, eds., *Great Historical Figures of Japan* (Tokyo: Japan Culture Institute, 1978), pp. 228–42; Uete Michiari, comp., *Rai Sanyô*, NST, vol. 49 (Iwanami Shoten, 1977); Andô Hideo, comp., *Rai Sanyô Nihon Gaishi* (Kondô Shuppansha, 1984).

BARRY D. STEBEN

Ran Geng 冉耕
544 BCE–?
(*zi* Boniu 伯牛)

Ran Geng was a native of Yuncheng 鄆城 (ninety kilometres west of Qufu), and a prominent disciple of Confucius known especially for his virtue. He received sacrifices in the temple as one of the **Ten Savants** in 712, was ennobled as Marquis of Yun 伯牛鄆侯 in 739, promoted to duke in 1009, given the title of Duke of Pingdong 平東公 in 1113, and called Master Ran Geng 冉子耕 in 1530, when everyone enshrined in the temple was stripped of their noble titles. A shrine 冉伯牛祠 devoted to him was built in Pingdong where sacrifices have been offered to him in the spring and autumn since the Ming.

THOMAS A. WILSON

Ran Qiu 冉求
522–? BCE
(*zi* Ziyou 子有, *aka* Ran You 冉有)

Of the Zhonggong 仲弓 clan of Yanzhou 兗州, Ran Qiu was a prominent disciple of Confucius, and steward in the Ji 季 household. He received sacrifices in the temple as one of the **Ten Savants** in 712, was ennobled as Marquis of Xu 子有徐侯 in 739, promoted to duke in 1009, given the title of Duke of Pengcheng 彭城公 in 1113, and called Master Ran Qiu 冉子求 in 1530, when everyone enshrined in the temple was stripped of their noble titles.

THOMAS A. WILSON

Ran Yong 冉雍
522–? BCE
(*zi* Zhonggong 仲弓)

Ran Yong was of humble origin from the Boniu clan of Yanzhou 兗州 and a prominent disciple of Confucius, and was said by the latter to have the capability to govern as a sovereign. He received sacrifices in the temple as one of the **Ten Savants** in 712, was ennobled as Marquis of Xue 仲弓薛侯 in 739, promoted to duke in 1009, given the title of Duke of Pei 邳公冉雍 in 1113, and called Master Ran Geng 冉子雍 in 1530, when everyone enshrined in the temple was stripped of their noble titles. A shrine 仲弓祠 was built for him in Caoxian 曹縣 (225 kilometres southwest of Qufu) in the late fifteenth century.

THOMAS A. WILSON

Ren 仁
(Humaneness, humanity)

Often translated as 'humaneness', 'humanity' or 'benevolence', *ren* has been one of the most integral virtues of the literati tradition since the time of Confucius. It is an empathy and sense of consideration for others that is the hallmark of the sage (**sheng ren**) and the noble person (**junzi**) but is accessible to all.

The term rarely appears, however, in texts such as the *Book of Poetry* (**Shi jing**) or *Book of Documents* (**Shang shu**), which offer few clues to its early meanings. In the *Book of Poetry*, for example, *ren* occurs in two odes (77 and 103) that laud the virtues of a hunter, and there the concept parallels such qualities as beauty or excellence (*mei* 美), the good (*hao* 好) and martiality (*wu* 武). In the *Book of Documents*, humaneness is a virtue possessed by righteous rulers and their assistants. This leadership quality is accompanied by the companion virtues of frugality, self-control, fairness, generosity, trustworthiness and respect for others. Such rulers are supported by the people and are favoured by Heaven; they conduct punitive expeditions against morally depraved adversaries.

It is only in the *Analects* (**Lunyu**), however, that *ren* becomes one of the most significant qualities of the noble person, and there the term appears with great frequency.

Confucius claimed to transmit the values of the ancient kings rather than create new ones, but he developed a notion of humaneness that far surpassed anything that went before it. Confucius' notion of *ren* still bears some of its earlier connotations of martial self-discipline and upright leadership, but it becomes a much more expansive quality accessible not just to rulers but to anyone who personally and authentically aspires to it. *Ren* consists not just of leading others but of genuinely extending them the same care, consideration, love and understanding one would want for oneself. Humaneness is an inner disposition that is realised through one's interactions with others, and even though its locus is the self, it is a self that is dissolved of selfishness, expanded through reflection and study and cultivated with ritual praxis. *Ren* is moreover manifested as filiality, generosity and respect for others.

In the *Mengzi*, humaneness becomes even more firmly embedded in the human condition. Arguing against those who claim that humaneness is external to the self and must be learned from others, **Mengzi** posits that humaneness is the human mind (*xin*) itself (*Mengzi* 6A: 11). Along with wisdom, rightness and ritual, humaneness is one of the four cardinal virtues internal to the human condition; it is manifested in the empathy and feelings of commiseration one extends spontaneously to others. **Xunzi** also posited that humaneness was potentially accessible to all, although he placed this virtue within the context of ritual and human relationships rather than within the internal workings of the mind itself. It was Mengzi, however, who influenced later notions of *ren*.

Mengzi often paired humaneness with rightness, a tendency continued by some later scholars. The Han thinker **Dong Zhongshu** in his essay *Ren yi fa* 仁義法 (Standards of Humaneness and Rightness, an essay directed primarily at the ruling elite) stated that humaneness consisted not of loving one's own self but loving others; conversely, rightness consisted of rectifying one's own self and not rectifying others. The Tang scholar **Han Yu**, on the other hand, equated humaneness with an expansive notion of love (*bo ai* 博愛) that, when put into practice, was manifested as rightness and the Way. Han Yu contrasted his own notion of humaneness (which was indebted to Confucius) with that of Laozi 老子, Mozi 墨子, and the Buddha, whom he accused of diminishing that virtue.

Song thinkers gave the notion of humaneness a stronger ontological foundation and associated it with cosmological principles such as principle (*li*) or the Five Phases (**Wu xing**). For **Cheng Hao** and **Cheng Yi**, humaneness was the most important of the Five Cardinal Virtues (Mengzi's four virtues, plus trust or faithfulness or *xin* 信), and they associated *ren* with principle (*li*), the Way (**dao**), and impartiality (*gong* 公). The Chengs were profoundly influenced by **Zhang Zai**'s *Xi ming*, which they understood as primarily an explication of the notion of humaneness, even though the concept does not figure largely there. Zhang had proclaimed a consubstantiality of his body (*ti* 體) with that of the entire universe, and for the Chengs, it was humaneness that informed that embodiment.

Zhu Xi's notion of humaneness was highly indebted to the Chengs. He composed a *Ren shuo* 仁說 (*Discourse on Humaneness*), and associated *ren* with the human mind, the principle of Heaven, and the mind of Heaven and Earth, which gives life to things. He also drew from classical sources, however, and the title of his *Reflections on Things at Hand* (**Jinsi lu**) is an allusion to Confucius' comment that humaneness depended simply upon reflecting on what was close at hand (*Lunyu* 19.6).

Zhu's follower **Chen Chun** offered a systematic definition of humaneness in his *Beixi ziyi*, where he equated humaneness with the principle (*li*) of love (*ai*). *Ren* moreover encompassed all the Five Cardinal Virtues (which he correlated with the

Five Phases), but it could be diminished by human desire.

In late imperial times, the reformer **Tan Sitong** interpreted *ren* through the lens of Buddhist philosophy and western learning. Tan's ideals were Confucius, the Buddha, and Christ. In his **Ren xue** 仁學, *An Explanation of Humaneness,* Tan stated that humaneness was interconnectedness (*tong* 通), and he even associated it with the power of electricity. Humaneness connected China with other geographical regions, connected the self with others, and connected such dyads as male and female. Rejecting traditional notions of hierarchy, Tan believed human relationships should be guided by the principle of equality, a virtue of such precision that he calculated it algebraically.

References: Bloom, 1997b; Chan Sin-wai, 1984; Chan, Wing-tsit, 1955 and 1963d: 523–5, 593–7, 1986a: 69–85, 216–27, 1989, 1996: 53–8; Chen Chun, 1986; de Bary & Bloom, 1999: 305–9, 568–73, 693–7, 711–13; Graham, 1992: 96–107.

DEBORAH SOMMER

Ren 人
(Human beings)

In its most common usage, the character *ren* can mean 'person' or 'persons' as well as 'human being' or 'human beings', since Chinese is an uninflected language that does not distinguish singular and plural forms. *Ren* is moreover ungendered: whereas it is often incorrectly translated as 'man' or 'men', the term is gender inclusive and by no means excludes the female sex. In another common usage, the term also means 'others' or 'other human beings' as opposed to oneself. In the *Analects*, for example, 'others' referred to people of high social standing, although in other instances the term referred to 'the people' in the sense of 'the common people'. *Ren* can also simply mean 'someone' in a very generic sense.

Some texts define human beings in terms of what set them apart from other living creatures. In the **Shang shu** humans are said to be the most numinously aware (*ling* 靈) of all the myriad things produced by father heaven and mother earth. For **Xunzi**, humans are possessed of material force (*qi*), life, and intelligence, which distinguished them from fire, plants, and animals, respectively. Moreover, only humans are possessed of a sense of rightness (*yi*), which allowed them to form complex societies. Hence, Xunzi concluded that humans were the noblest of all creatures.

The term 'human being' moreover distinguished the living from the dead. Humans are alive; the dead might become ghosts (*gui*; see **gui shen**), spirits (*shen*), wraiths (*li* 厲) and so on. Confucius, for example, once remarked that those who do not yet know how to serve living human beings need not yet concern themselves with serving ghosts.

In other usages, however, merely being a member of what in modern taxonomy is now called the species *Homo sapiens* does not necessarily exhaust what is truly meant by the term 'human'. Being human meant fulfilling certain moral expectations toward others. In the *Analects*, for example, a text largely concerned with a person's relationships within a social context, what it meant to be human (*ren*) was not infrequently associated with humaneness (**ren**) toward other human beings. Humaneness consisted in part of not acting toward others in ways one did not like oneself; it did not, however, come from others but came from one's own self. Implicit to Confucius' notion of 'being' or 'acting' as a human being (*wei ren* 為人) was the sense that such a person was consistently guided by adherence to moral values and a concern for others and for the larger common good. Such an individual was a 'complete' or 'accomplished' person (*cheng ren* 成人); in contrast, those who acted primarily for personal gain were possessed of a diminished form of humanity and were accordingly called 'little', 'small' or 'petty' people (*xiao ren* 小人). **Mengzi** simply equated 'humaneness' (*ren*) with its homophone 'human being' (*ren*), and he moreover concluded that the conjunction of the two was itself the Way.

What it meant to be human was also based on larger cosmological frameworks in which humans were at once products of, and active participants in, a larger universe. The components of these cosmic formulations were configured in various ways over the centuries. In the **Li ji**, for example, human beings are said to be the inner power (*de*) of Heaven and Earth, the interchange between yin and yang, the commingling of ghosts and spirits and the finest *qi* of the Five Phases. In *Zuo's Commentary on the Spring and Autumn Annals* (**Chungiu Zuo zhuan**), humans are ever-transforming amalgamations of yin and yang, *hun* 魂 and *po* 魄 souls, vital essences (*jing* 精) and spiritual and numinous forces (Duke Zhao, 7th year). The Han thinker **Wang Chong** understood the human frame in terms of the coalescence of *qi*. Song visions of what it meant to be human were based on an ontological grounding of principle (**li**), *qi*, the Supreme Ultimate (**tai ji**), yin and yang, and so on.

Concomitant to each cosmological framework is a path or Way of ethical behaviour one might follow in order to become fully human. These pathways might involve ritual practices, the maintenance of familial and social responsibilities, learning from texts, the cultivation of the body, inquiry into the nature of the world external to the body, the development of the mind or the nature and so on. These paths might ultimately lead one toward a higher, enhanced form of existence as a sage (*sheng ren*).

References: Ames & Rosemont, 1998: 1:5, 2:1, 12:2, 14:42; Knoblock, 1988–94: vol. II: 103–4; Lau, 1984, 7A: 16; Legge, 1985c: 18, 283, 1986, vol. XXVII: 380–1; Nylan, 1994a: 366.

DEBORAH SOMMER

Ren dao 人道
(The Way of humans)

Ren dao is the essence, or Way (*dao*) that comprises human nature. In the *Book of Changes* (**Yi jing**), *Shuogua zhuan* 說卦傳, humaneness (*ren*) and righteousness (*yi*) are deemed to establish the Way of humans. The *Doctrine of the Mean* (**Zhongyong**) 20 states: 'When the way of humans operates, the growth of good government is rapid; when the way of earth operates, the growth of plants is rapid'. It goes on to say that sincerity (**cheng**) is the way of heaven (**tian dao**), and doing that which is sincere is the way of humans. The *Li ji* states: '. . . In affection we have benevolence (*ren*); in nice distinctions, righteousness (*yi*); in defined regulations (*jie*), propriety (*li*); and in the consideration of circumstances (**quan**), knowledge (**zhi**). Benevolence, righteousness, propriety and knowledge – these make up the characteristic attributes of humanity'. For **Xunzi**, 'The rules of proper conduct, standards of justice, and finish and orderliness, together with humaneness, righteousness, obedience to law and uprightness, are what constitute the Way of humans.'

References: Dubs, 1927: 96; Legge, 1966, 1967, 1986.

TODD CAMERON THACKER

Ren lun 人倫
(Human relationships)

Ren lun are the hierarchical social relations that Confucian writers deemed as the moral foundation of society. These relationships were of such import that Confucians believed, if they were not maintained, then social chaos would ensue. The *Analects* states that a duke asked Confucius about governance (*zheng*), Confucius replied that, 'Let the lord be lordly, the retainer loyal, the father fatherly, and the son sonly.' The Duke said, 'Excellent! I believe that if the lord is not lordly, the retainer not loyal, the father not fatherly, and the son not sonly, even if there was grain, how would I be able to obtain it?' (12: 11). Believing that education's primary goal is to promote these relationships, **Mengzi** said, 'Schools are that which all of the Three Dynasties [the Xia, Shang, and Zhou] shared in common. The purpose of all their schools was the same: make clear the human relationships' (*Mengzi*, 3A: 3). As Katherine Carlitz has astutely noted, due to the fact that nearly all Confucian formulations of the human relationships include the lord–retainer relationship, these cardinal relations tie together the public and private worlds, to the extent that actions in one sphere necessarily have ramifications for the other. But for Confucians which relationships were the most important ones?

Different texts give different answers. The *Analects* only places importance on the lord–retainer and father–son relationships. In one place, the **Zuo zhuan** implies that the three most significant relationships are the lord–retainer, father–son, and elder–younger brother (Duke Yin 3rd year). In another place, it singles out the relations between father–son, elder–younger brother, and mother–son (Duke Wen 18th year). In yet another place it emphasises the lord–retainer, father–son, elder–younger brother, husband–wife, and mother-in-law and sister-in-law relationships (Duke Zhao 26th year). The **Xunzi** speaks of four relationships: ruler–retainer, father–son, elder–younger brother, and husband–wife. (*Xunzi*, 27: 41) The *Li ji* posits seven important relationships, which includes that between host and guest. (*Li ji*, 5: 59) The most famous formulation, though, is *Mengzi*'s 'The Five Human Relations' (**Wu lun**): father–son, lord–retainer, senior–junior, husband–wife and friends. What these different formulations indicate is that, among early Confucians, no uniform conception of what the most important human relationships were, existed. Nevertheless, the father–son and lord–retainer are clearly the most cited and significant.

Although most authorities stress the authoritarian impulse behind these almost entirely vertical relationships, **Tu Wei-ming** has pointed out that Mengzi's **Wu lun** (Five Human Relations) emphasises the duties that the members of these relationships owe each other. Mengzi said, 'father and son should share affection, lord and retainer share duties [to each other], husband and wife share distinctions [between their spheres of activity], senior and junior share a respect for ranking, and friends share faithfulness [to each other]' (*Mengzi*, 3A: 4). Rather than exploitative, the relationships are mutually beneficial. Hence, fathers must be kind, while sons must be filial; lords must be righteous, while retainers must be loyal; elder brothers must be loving, while younger brothers must be respectful, and so on. In the same vein, Hsu Dau-lin has pointed out that the concept of **san gang** 'The Three Bonds' (father–son, lord–retainer, and husband–wife), which stresses the subordination that inferiors owe their superiors, was originally a Legalist idea.

Despite these reciprocal obligations, though, one should never forget that these relationships assume a social order that is based on inequality and submission. With the exception of the relationship between friends, all of the cardinal relationships put forth by the Confucian writers were unequal. Moreover, even though the term *san gang* (The Three Bonds) was Legalist in origin, Confucian writers themselves often harp on a triad of hierarchical relationships, whether it be lord–retainer, father–son, husband–wife, or lord–retainer, father–son, and elder–younger brother. The *Mengzi* states, 'Those who are retainers should embrace benevolence (**ren**) and righteousness (**yi**) in serving their lord; those who are sons should embrace benevolence and righteousness in serving their fathers; those who are younger brothers should embrace benevolence and righteousness in serving their elder brothers' (*Mengzi*, 6B: 4). Note here, just as with the *san gang*, the emphasis is on how the inferior serves the superior. It would be fair to say then that even though the human relationships (*ren lun*) were both beneficial to society as a whole and the parties involved, clearly the burden of effort was put on the inferior member of the relationship.

References: Carlitz, 1994: 101–24; Hsu Dau-Lin, 1970–1: 27–37; Tu, 1998: 121–36.

KEITH KNAPP

Ren xin 人心
(Human heart/mind)

Ren xin refers primarily to an individual's human emotions and intentions and the need to pursue the satisfaction of one's desires. An important and subsequently influential reference to the human heart/mind is found in the Old Text version of the *Book of Documents* (**Shang shu**), 'The human heart/mind is restless – prone to err; its affinity for the right way is small'. (*ren xin wei wei, dao xin wei wei* 人心惟危, 道心惟微). The first half of this passage implies that even if people's hearts observe the Way (*dao*), there is a danger of selfish motivations for action emerging, while the second half implies that people's hearts are weak and can fall into ambiguity or confusion, regardless of the clear way forward, i.e. the moral Way. It continues with the following: 'Be discriminating, be undivided, one may sincerely hold fast to the mean (*zhong*)'. **Mengzi** goes on to equate this with humaneness (*ren*).

In Neo-Confucianism of the Song–Ming era, the concepts of the human heart/mind and the heart/mind of the Way became central to the doctrine of self-cultivation. In general the Cheng–Zhu School paid attention to the differentiation of them, equating them respectively with the human desire and the principle of heaven, while the Lu–Wang School insisted that the two heart/minds be the same heart/mind and

therefore opposed any attempt to separate them.

References: Legge, 1985c: 61, 238; *Yugyo Sajon Pyonchan Wiwonhoe*, ed., 1990.

TODD CAMERON THACKER

Ren xue 仁學
(*The Learning of Ren*)

Martyr of the Hundred Days of Reform (11/06/1898–21/09/1898), **Tan Sitong** completed the *Ren xue* in 1897. First published posthumously by **Liang Qichao** in Yokohama and then reprinted in many other publications, the *Ren xue* was a popular reading among the reformists and the revolutionaries for its attack on traditional social customs and the monarchical system.

Tan opened the work with a discussion of *ren* (humaneness, humanity or benevolence). Mixing Song–Ming **Neo-Confucianism** with nineteenth-century western science, Tan argued that all beings in this universe were joined together by a common bond known as *ren*. Because of this common bond, each being in this universe should be treated as an equal and a unique entity. Any barrier separating individual things or human beings from one another was a violation of *ren*.

Applying his understanding of *ren* to the human world, Tan was critical of social and political oppression. In particular, he condemned the Three Cardinal Guides (*san gang*) and Five Human Relationships (**Wu lun**) for privileging the ruler over the ruled, father over son, and husband over wife. For him, the monarchical system epitomised the evils of Confucian hierarchy, in which those in power advanced their private interests at the expense of the public good.

In the final section of the *Ren xue*, Tan looked forward to a perfect society built on equality and the innate rights of the individual. Loosely based on the *Yi jing* and the New Text doctrine of the 'Three Ages', he believed that a perfect society would eventually appear in China after she had gone through cycles of progress, decay and regeneration.

References: Chang Hao, 1997; Fung, 1952; Kwong, 1996; Li Zehou, 1979.

TZE-KI HON

Ren zheng 仁政
(Humane governance)

Ren means humane or benevolent; *zheng* means governance, specifically good governance. Although both humaneness and good governance were elaborated frequently by early thinkers, the particular expression *ren zheng* appears in the **Mengzi** in a passage that outlines the 'well-field' system, which was a method for distributing agricultural land in such a way that the populace was not burdened by heavy taxation (*Mengzi* 3A: 3). The well-field system was so called because its symmetric structure was similar to that of the Chinese character 'well' (*jing* 井), whose graph depicts nine equally spaced squares separated by linear boundaries. Humane governance, the *Mengzi* asserts, is based upon a system whereby a large square measure of land is divided into nine equal squares. Eight families farm the eight outer squares for their own sustenance but maintain the central square in common and remit only the proceeds from that central field to the ruler as taxes. Cruel rulers did not establish such boundaries and their appropriation of taxable commodities from the people knew no bounds. Humane rulers, on the other hand, curbed their desires for wealth and concerned themselves with the welfare of the people.

Later thinkers tried to institute this well-field system. **Zhang Zai**, for example, found in it a model for the equitable distribution of arable acreage and urged its immediate implementation. Extant field boundaries in an area south of his village of Hengqu

橫渠 in Shaanxi province are traditionally attributed to his efforts at land reform in the Song.

References: De Bary, 1953: 98–104; De Bary & Bloom, 1999: 605–9; Jiang, 2001: 248–60; Lau, 1984: 3A: 3; Shun, 1997a; Zhang Shimin & Zhao Junliang, 1999: 31–7.

DEBORAH SOMMER

Renwu zhi 人物志
(*Record of Human Traits*)

The *Renwu zhi* by Liu Shao 劉劭 (?–?), compiled between 240–248, is a systematic treatise on 'knowing men', a subject its author took to be the highest form of practical wisdom instilled in the Five Classics (**Wu jing**) and practised by Confucius. The text therefore classifies humans into twelve different categories (each liable to take up separate vocations), devises guidelines to help ascertain whether the type of person is best suited for any type of public service, and proposes methods by which to interpret external behaviour as an infallible sign of the inner state. As a student of the most advanced theories of his time, Liu Shao approaches humans with the same objectivity that he applies to all other things: 'If a thing possess both form and substance, it is possible to investigate it'. But living in a period of disunion, Liu naturally stresses the sage's capacity to unify the empire. On the model of Liu Bang 劉邦 (256–195 BCE), the Han founder, who was Liu Shao's ideal, the sage must be able to lay far-reaching plans, exude charismatic virtue, live in accordance with the cosmic laws, and, whenever necessary, marshal the forces to restore the peace. Lesser men of lesser talent (*cai*) the sage may usefully employ so long as he anticipates and corrects for their limitations, ever mindful of four general norms (the eternally changing Dao, the penal code, ritual and the complex of human motivations). Only the sage can reliably achieve the ideal Mean in all aspects, and thereby fix constant principles.

Reference: Shryock, 1937.

MICHAEL NYLAN

Ricci, Matteo 利瑪竇
1552–1610

Ricci was an Italian missionary in China. He was responsible for changing the initial missionary policy of accommodation to Buddhist life-style into adaptation to the life-style and etiquette of the Confucian elite of literati and officials. He opted for an openness and tolerance towards Chinese values, but he was of the opinion that the Confucian social doctrine should be complemented with the metaphysical ideas of Christianity. Moreover, he pleaded for a return to original Confucianism which he considered to be a philosophy based on natural law, containing the idea of God. Finally, he adopted a tolerant attitude towards certain Confucian rites, such as ancestral worship and the veneration of Confucius, which he declared to be 'civil rites'. This policy, later identified as the 'Ricci way', determined the basic attitudes of the Jesuits in the seventeenth and eighteenth centuries and were influential on missionary methods until the twentieth century.

Besides some humanistic writings like *Jiaoyou lun* 交友論 (*On Friendship*, 1595), based upon Stoic quotations taken from Andreas Eborensis' (1498–1573) *Sententiae et Exempla*, Ricci's most significant Chinese writing was *Tianzhu shiyi* 天主實義 (*The True Meaning of the Lord of Heaven*, 1603), written in the form of a dialogue between a western and Chinese scholar. It is a typical example of the use of Christian natural theology as a way to approach Chinese literati. As part of his argumentation, Ricci quotes the Chinese Classics to show that in ancient times the Chinese had a natural knowledge of God. His diary, originally written in Italian, became known in the Latin translation by Nicolas Trigault, *De Christiana Expeditione apud Sinas*, Augsburg, 1615 (also translated in French, German, Spanish, Italian and partly in English). It includes one of the first references to 'Confucius' in European publications.

References: Bettray, 1955; Elia, 1942–9; Ricci, 1985.

NICOLAS STANDAERT

Rites of passage

The Confucian tradition identified four rituals associated with the life course: the Rites of Adulthood (**guan li**), Rites of Marriage (**hun li**), Rites of Mourning and Burial (**sang li**), and Ancestral Worship (**ji zu**) as family rituals (*jia li* 家禮). These rituals were an important part of people's lives at all social levels. In the Confucian ritual tradition, the family rituals fall into two opposed categories, auspicious and inauspicious rituals. Cappings, weddings and ancestral rites were auspicious rituals. They all involve communications with ancestors, and require that those officiating be purified. Death, mourning, burial, and the rituals scheduled after a funeral were all inauspicious. Those bereaved by a death could not be purified in order to communicate with ancestors until the completion of the series of rites.

Like rites of passage in other societies, weddings and funerals in China provided structured and dramatic ways for people to work through the social tensions and psychological uncertainties attendant on transitions from one status to another. Heightened emotions – excitement, joy, grief, fear, anger – were intrinsic to these rituals. Performed publicly and often at great expense, these rites involved processions through towns and across the countryside, with some of the participants dressed in highly distinctive costumes. Ancestral rituals were less public, as only descendants of a common ancestor watched a performance.

Their social significance lies less in marking an individual's change in status as in creating bonds among kinsmen. Rites of adulthood may well have been major rites in antiquity, but in later periods are seen as rites called for in the Classics but practised only by those trying to show their commitment to classical forms. Other rites of passage, especially rites associated with birth and infancy, were commonly practised but not treated as formal, Confucian rites, to be modelled on the Classics.

The canonical source for three of these rituals was the *Yi li*, which, however, lacks a chapter on funeral rituals and offers versions of the rituals only for *shi*. As other early texts make clear, in Zhou times each rank of society was expected to perform these rituals in distinctive ways: the Son of Heaven, the feudal lords, the high officials, the *shi* and the ordinary commoners. Thus, besides conveying conceptions of the relationships of the living and the dead, the family rituals described in the Classics clearly expressed principles of hierarchy and organisation among the living, as people of unequal rank did not perform rites the same way. For instance, the size of a coffin, the numbers and quality of the objects buried with it, even the date of burial varied according to the political rank of the deceased. The number of generations of ancestors a man could worship, the number of times a year he would perform sacrifices, and the types of food he could offer similarly varied by rank. Kinship position also mattered. Sons of wives outranked sons of concubines, and the first son of the wife would be his father's chief mourner and later preside at sacrifices to him.

Because the *Yi li* does not describe how those ranked higher than *shi* should perform these rites, Confucian ritual experts from Han times on designed more exalted versions for rulers, nobles and high officials. As ritual experts at court, they emphasised to rulers how important it was for them to perform these rituals in canonically correct ways, and they compiled extensive liturgies for imperial performance. The *Comprehensive Compendium* (*Tong dian* 通典) by **Du You** and later encyclopedic works have voluminous records of the debates of court rituals on how to perform imperial weddings, cappings, funerals and ancestral rites.

The earliest surviving full set of liturgies for the family rituals is found in **Da Tang Kaiyuan li** (*Ritual of the Kaiyuan Period of the Tang dynasty*), which, however, does not provide any instructions for commoners. Comparable works were published in later centuries by the Song, Ming and Qing dynasties did, however, cover commoners. From Song times on, guides to how to conduct these rituals were also privately written and circulated as a way of advancing Confucianism among ordinary people. Particularly influential was **Zhu Xi**'s *Jia li* (*Family Rituals*), which does not draw distinctions of rank. During Ming and Qing times a great many revised, annotated, abbreviated, or expanded versions of this manual were published.

References: Chow, 1994; Ebrey, 1991.

PATRICIA EBREY

Rongo chô 論語微
(*Commentary on the Analects*)

The *Rongo chô* was **Ogyû Sorai**'s masterwork on the *Analects* (**Lunyu**). Although published posthumously in 1740, it dates from around 1720. In it, Sorai expounds his estimation of Confucius while criticising earlier commentaries such as **Zhu Xi**'s *Lunyu jizhu* (see **Si shu zhangju jizhu**) and **Itô Jinsai**'s revisionist study, the *Rongo kogi* (Ancient Meanings of the *Analects*). Yoshikawa Kojiro has suggested that the *Rongo chô* pioneered a view of Confucius as a revolutionary reformer which foreshadowed that expounded by **Kang Youwei**. Undoubtedly the *Rongo chô* was quoted by earlier Qing scholars such as **Liu Baonan** in his *Lunyu zhengyi* (Correct Meanings of the Analects).

References: Lidin, 1973; Yoshikawa, 1983.

JOHN A. TUCKER

Rongo kogi 論語古義
(*Ancient Meanings of the Analects*)

The *Rongo kogi* was **Itô Jinsai**'s masterful commentary on the *Analects* (***Lunyu***). Along with his *Daigaku teihon* 大學定本 (The Original Text of the *Great Learning*), *Môshi kogi* 孟子古義 (Ancient Meanings of the ***Mengzi***), and *Chûyô hakki* 中庸發揮 (Exposition of the *Doctrine of the Mean* (***Zhongyong***), it served as Jinsai's revisionist response to **Zhu Xi**'s *Si shu zhang ju jizhu* (Collected Commentaries on the *Four Books*). Published posthumously in 1712, the *Rongo kogi* conveys Jinsai's quasi-hagiographic assessment of Confucius as the greatest sage in all human history, and the *Analects* as the supreme work of ethical literature for all time.

References: Itô, 1926, 1972; Yoshikawa, 1983.

JOHN A. TUCKER

Ru 儒
(Classicist, Confucian, government official)

It is to Han texts, such as **Sima Tan**'s *Essentials of the Six Groups* (*Liujia zhi yaozhi*), that we look for early definitions of the term *ru*. Unfortunately, those texts use three conceptually distinct definitions of *ru*, each with overlapping applications: (a) 'classicist'; (b) 'Confucian'; and (c) 'government official' (actual or potential). Most often in Han texts a *ru* is simply a 'classicist', one who has mastered the classical precedents stored in ancient texts, in ancient rites, and in ancient music. In the pre-Han period, none of the ancient texts that came to be called the 'Confucian' Classics (and few of the classical practices) had been identified as the exclusive intellectual property of 'Confucians'. Certainly, well into Former Han times, what we now call the 'Confucian Classics' were regarded as the common literary heritage of all well-educated people. That explains why Han writings occasionally identify opponents of ethical Confucians as '*ru*' (e.g., ***Yantie lun*** 1:2:4).

Slightly later, some classical scholars who identify themselves as ethical followers of Confucius (e.g., **Yang Xiong**) tried to reserve the term '*Ru*' for 'Confucians' like themselves, whose conduct was marked by their devotion to ritual and the Five Human Relations (***Wu lun***). Self-conscious adherents of Confucius, with their strong interest in statecraft and in personal relations, tried hardest to distinguish their positions from those of the Logicians, whose theories they saw as 'unworkable', and from those of the Legalists, whose theories they saw as cruel and counterproductive. Han Confucians with far less frequency sought to untangle the connections between their ideas and those put forward by thinkers we now call Monist or 'Daoist', Yin–yang theorist, Legalist or Logician, probably because many of their ideas had been absorbed into the broad stream of Confucian Learning.

Indeed, it makes no sense to think of 'schools' (*jia*) in the pre-Han or Han periods, if the term 'school' implies strict sectarian divisions between well-defined groups. Evidence for the pre-Han period shows that Warring States' thinkers, aided perhaps by the linguistic overlap of key words in Chinese philosophy, borrowed from one another continually in their attempts to devise the most persuasive arguments. That Sima Tan's catalogue divided works in the imperial collection into six main sections did not mean that Han thinkers abandoned their old rhetorical habits. Nor could the '*Essentials*' catalogue alert Han thinkers to the standard distinctions made today. Han works do not typically lump individual thinkers together as members of the same *jia*; instead, thinkers are usually cited as individuals, even with the most self-conscious of the Han Confucian classicists (e.g., in Yang Xiong's ***Fa yan***). It seems, then, that Han thinkers in general were far less preoccupied than many of their late imperial counterparts with the need for ideological purity in the origins, genealogies, and transmissions of specific teaching traditions. In any case, the specific idea of *ru* as 'Confucian' appears always to have been a subset of the general notion of *ru* as 'classicist'. 'Confucian' did not supplant 'classicist' as both meanings of *ru* implied an unusual dedication to the study of antiquity. This dedication, which was sometimes marked by the punctilious performance of prescribed chants, songs, and dances by men in outmoded dress, was easily satirised by utilitarian thinkers as a descent into self-important antiquarianism.

By late Former Han times, however, with *ru* access to the throne dramatically increased, the term *ru* took on a third meaning: it became a near synonym for *shi*, members of the pool of actual or potential government officials. As the poet Zhang Heng 張衡 (79–139) wrote, 'The sashed officials here [at court] gather like clouds; the *Ru shi* 儒士 (*shi* in command of classical knowledge) group to form a forest' (***Hou Han shu*** 59:1906). In similar language, **Wang Chong** described the *shi ru* 世儒 ('worldly *ru*' whose erudition won them high rank at court). With the later Han emperors regularly consulting their *zhong ru* 眾儒 ('many *ru*') employed in an advisory capacity, it is clear that a majority of aspirants and appointees to office were undeniably '*ru*', if only because the standard preparation for most offices above the rank of clerk presupposed some familiarity with, if not wholehearted devotion to, the Five Classics (***Wu jing***). Once increasing numbers of classicists manned key posts in government, the state took it upon itself to assess *ru* mastery in systematic ways: through written and oral examinations, through periodic court debates, through essays, memorials and declamations, through formal recommendations attesting to exemplary ritual practice.

Conservative thinkers in Han times blamed the proliferation of such tests for the rise of *su ru* or 'vulgar *ru*', literati holding the acquisition of factual knowledge or the appointment to high office above adherence to Confucian values. Hence the veiled criticism registered in a Han text: 'One not demeaned by poverty and low rank, not puffed up by riches and high rank, not disgraced by rulers and kings, not bound to elders and superiors, and not distressed by those in office – such a person truly deserves the name of *ru*. These days, [however,] when the masses call someone a *ru*, they habitually, if thoughtlessly, use *ru* as a term of abuse.'

As early as **Sima Qian**, thoughtful men had noted that **Han Wudi**'s decision to favour adherents of *ru* teachings (a decision that was honoured only sporadically by succeeding emperors) increased the likelihood that classical *ru* teachings, originally designed to foster a true nobility of the spirit, would be taken up by ambitious types anxious to make their fortunes at court through conformity to the imperial will. After the *ru* scholar **Gongsun Hong** rapidly advanced from commoner rank to a post as one of the emperor's three chief ministers, 'Scholars throughout the empire, seeing which way the wind was blowing, did all they could to follow his example' (***Shi ji***, 121: 3118). External compliance was so easily mistaken for inner commitment, given the loose equation between *ru* and official. Thus quite disparate ideas, including those of even the Legalists, worked their way into *ru* thinking in the Han, with the result that the *ru* in office, even in the time of Han Wudi, counted among their numbers not only the more traditional 'Confucians' calling for incremental institutional reforms, but also those whose aggressive 'wealth and power' policies revealed the same drives that pre-Han and early Han Confucians had purportedly condemned.

Given overlapping definitions for the single term *ru*, each with a logically distinct relation to the pre-Han Confucian tradition, it is hardly surprising that Han texts, let alone modern historians, furnish wholly contradictory accounts of *ru* thinking. What is perhaps more startling is that even in later imperial China proponents of the state-sponsored Cheng–Zhu Neo-Confucian interpretations of the Classics could never manage to restrict the term *ru* to the dedicated adherents of Confucius' ethical Way, as should be obvious from the title of one famous Ming novel, *Rulin waishi* 儒林外史. Therefore, the reductionist impulse to equate the term *ru* and 'Confucian' must be resisted if we are to devise more accurate accounts of imperial society.

References: Eno, 1989; Fingarette, 1972; *Li ji*, 'Ruxing', in *Shisan jing zhushu*, 1980: 59: 13a-b; Wallacker, 1978: 215–228; Wilson, 1995.

MICHAEL NYLAN

Ru-fo yitong lun 儒佛異同論
(*Discourse on the Differences and Similarities between Confucianism and Buddhism*)

A short exploration by the elderly **Liang Shuming** comparing Confucian and Buddhist teachings, it appeared in Liang's *General Survey of Eastern Scholarship*.

Liang initiates the dialogue by distinguishing the basic orientations of this-worldly Confucianism and other worldly Buddhism. Afterwards he analyses the similarities between them. These similarities appear in their direct analysis of human beings and their concern with practicing body-and-heart/mind cultivation (*shen xin xiuyang* 身心修養) stimulated through interactive learning (*xue wen* 學問). In their latter concern, there is a similarity between Confucius' 'freedom from four personality flaws' (*siwu* 四毋, *Analects* 9: 4) and Buddhists' 'getting rid the self's two attachments' (*po wofa erzhi* 破我法二執). Yet in comparing the *Analects* **Lunyu** and the *Prajnaparamitra Sutra* (or *Heart Sutra*), Liang locates a central difference in the former's orientation toward joy (*le* 樂) and the latter's orientation toward suffering (*ku* 苦). This ultimately relates to a difference in ontology: the Confucian self is cosmo-ontologically united with all things (*tong yuzhou yiti* 通宇宙一體), and practices unselfishness in human relations (**Ren lun** 人倫); the Buddhist selflessness rests on

the emptiness or *sunyata* (*kong* 空) of all phenomena, attaining it through nirvana-oriented meditative yogic practices. While the aspect of restraint is similar, the level of engagement with the present world is different, even in spite of Chinese Mahayana doctrines of non-transcendence and 'no Nirvana'. In the third and final section Liang argues straightforwardly that a main difference is that Buddhism is a religion (*zong jiao* 宗教), while Confucianism may serve a religious function but is not religious.

LAUREN PFISTER

Ruan Ji 阮籍
210–263
(*zi* Sizong 嗣宗)

Son of Ruan Yu 阮瑀 (d. 212) who was one of Cao Cao's intimates during the creation of the Wei dynasty (220–265), Ruan Ji was a great poet who shows himself in his works to have been faithful to the dynasty his father helped create. His poetry in particular shows his anguish at the political immorality he sees around him and the disgust he feels as the usurping Sima clan kill the reigning emperors one after the other. This was a traditional Confucian attitude and, when his works are read correctly, it can be seen that he was at heart a traditional Confucian believer. His 'Essay on Music', *Yue lun* 樂論, is a thoroughly conventional description of the place of music in society as a regulator of the emotions in a strictly hierarchical society ruled by a Confucian sage. In his other prose works and in the historical anecdotes about him he presents himself in a completely different light: he is an anti-ritualist, a free spirit in the Daoist manner who transcends the mundane world. The complete contradiction of these two views can only be explained by the fact that, like **Dongfang Shuo** at the court of **Han Wudi** of the Former Han dynasty, and sickened by the Confucian bigotry propagated by the Sima and their clique, he played the fool to preserve his moral integrity and at the same time escape annihilation for himself and his entire family.

Reference: Holzman, 1976.

DONALD HOLZMAN

Ruan Yuan 阮元
1764–1849
(*zi* Boyuan 伯元, *hao* Yuntai 芸臺)

A native of Yizheng 儀徵 in Jiangsu 江蘇, Ruan was a scholar, bibliographer and enthusiastic patron of letters. Ruan Yuan received his *jin shi* degree in 1789, and subsequently served in the Hanlin Academy and the Imperial Study as Supervisor of Imperial Instruction and other senior editorships. Since 1793 he held provincial posts such as director of education of Shandong and Zhejiang, later as governor-general of Huguang 湖廣, Liangguang 兩廣, and Yungui 云貴.

Ruan was one of the most important advocators of Han Learning in the eighteenth century. As a high official and influential scholar, he had influences at court and his reputation inspired confidence in areas where he held office. He helped many scholars within his official areas to fame either by recommending them to the throne or by employing them in his editing team of the Classics. He founded two academies which became the most distinguished centres of education and classical studies: *Gujing jingshe* 古經精舍 in Hangzhou (1801) and *Xuehai tang* 學海堂 in Guangzhou (1820). Some famous scholars of Han Learning became headmasters at *Gujing jingshe*, such as Wang Chan 王昶 (1725–1806), Sun Xingyan 孫星衍 (1753–1818) and Yu Yue 俞樾 (1821–1907). Students of the two academies included Zhang Tingji 張廷濟 (1768–1848) and Zhang Yanchang 張燕昌 (1738–1814). The writings of the teachers and students of the *Gujing jingshe*, comprising over 2,000 articles, were compiled in a collection entitled *Gujing jingshe wenji* 詁經精舍文集. The publications of *Xuehai tang* include: *Xuehaitang congke* 學海堂叢刻, a collection in two series of six titles each;

and *Xuehai tang ji* 學海堂集, of four collections of poems and short articles in prose.

During the period Ruan Yuan governed Zhejiang, he directed a project of compilation of a major dictionary to the Classics, entitled *Jingji zuangu* 經籍纂詁 in which Ruan employed more than forty scholars, mostly from Zhejiang area. He supervised another large compilation with his own collation notes on the Classics, entitled *Shisanjing Jiaokanji* 十三經校勘集 of 243 *juan*. Among Ruan Yuan's achievements as bibliographer is his vast compilation of the *Huangqing jingjie* 皇清經解, 1,400 *juan*, 366 volumes, of over 180 works, consisting mostly of treatises written on the Classics in the Qing period. However, as Ruan's criterion was influenced by **Hui Dong**, a scholar of Han Learning, works of some famous non-Han Learning scholars such as **Gu Yanwu**, **Huang Zongxi**, Hu Wei 胡渭 (1633–1714) were not included.

Ruan also wrote some philosophical writings based on the Classics: the *Ancient Comments on the Nature and Life (Xingming guxun* 性命古訓), the *Discourses of Ren in the Analects and the Mengzi (Lunyu Mengzi lun ren lun* 論語孟子論仁論), and the *Commentaries on the Ten Chapters of the Zengzi (Zengzi shipian zhu* 曾子十篇注), in which he was concerned with grasping the great meanings (*Dayi* 大義) of the Classics and applying their principles to contemporary problems. Throughout his life Ruan sought moral and intellectual regeneration through classical studies. Ruan's notions presented a philosophical eclecticism which was commonly shared among the scholars of the late eighteenth century, who sought ways to strengthen and rejuvenate the declining imperial state. Ruan submitted reform proposals to, and firmly supported the opium prohibition policy of, Emperor Daoguang (r. 1821–1850) while he governed the Liangguang area.

Besides Ruan's massive works on the Classics, he also contributed to the history of painting, regional history, mathematics and astronomy, epigraphs and poetry. His work on the inscriptions on ancient bronzes, known as *Zhongding kuanshi* 鐘鼎款識 provided a valuable reference on palaeography; Ruan produced a work on history of mathematics and astronomy entitled *Chouren zhuan* 疇人傳, containing biographical memoirs and summaries of the works of 280 astronomers and mathematicians from the commencement of history to the end of the eighteenth century, among them 37 Europeans. Ruan Yuan's interest in mathematics helped to revive the study of ancient Chinese mathematics which had been neglected for centuries.

References: Hummel, 1943–4; *Qing shi gao*, 1970; Zhao & Guo, 1989.

REBEKAH X. ZHAO

Rujia bapai 儒家八派
(The eight Confucian factions)

The term 'Confucianism', coined by western sinology, can be, just as any '-ism', both convenient and misleading in that it may induce one to think of the Confucian heritage as a single integrated whole. One should not forget that, in Chinese terminology, the followers of Confucius were never designated by any other term than that of *ru*, and that according to third-century BCE testimonies, they were far from presenting a united front. The notion that, after Confucius' death, his disciples came to reassemble into no less than eight factions during the Warring States period is to be found in the critical view of the Legalist thinker Han Feizi 韓非子 (*c.* 280–233 BCE), at the beginning of the '*Xian xue* 顯學' (*Eminence in Learning*) chapter (ch. 50) of the *Han Feizi*: 'In the present age, the Confucians and Moists are well known for their learning. The Confucians pay the highest honour to Confucius, the Moists to Mo Di. Since the death of Confucius, the *Zizhang* school, the *Zisi* school, the *Yan* (*Hui*) family school, the *Meng* (Mengzi) family school, the *Qidiao* family school, the *Zhongliang* family school, the *Sun* (Xunzi) family school, and the *Yuezheng* family school have appeared. Since the death of Mozi, the *Xiangli* 相里 family school,

the *Xiangfu* 相夫 family school, and the *Dengling* 鄧陵 family school have appeared. Thus, since the death of its founder, the Confucian school has split into eight factions, and the Moist school into three. Their doctrines and practices are different or even contradictory, and yet each claims to represent the true teaching of Confucius and Mozi. But since we cannot call Confucius and Mozi back to life, who is to decide which of the present versions of the doctrine is the right one?' (see also Watson, 1964: 118).

Heading the first of the eight factions listed by the Han Feizi, the disciple Zizhang 子張 (see **Zhuansun Shi**) features rather prominently in the *Analects* as he is often questioning the Master on various matters, notably methods of government, which seems to indicate that he was after an official career (as will be seen below, **Xunzi** taxes him as a 'base Confucian').

Zisi 子思 (**Kong Ji**), the grandson of Confucius, is usually considered to be the starting-point of a school which included **Mengzi**, described as either his direct or indirect disciple, who in turn had *Yuezheng Ke* 樂正克 as a disciple. This supposedly distinct affiliation leading from Zisi to Mengzi has been traditionally referred to as the 'Zisi–Mengzi School' (*Si–Meng xuepai*).

Yan Hui 顏回 appears in the *Analects* as Confucius' young, poor but nevertheless favourite disciple, the one in whom the Master had placed his highest hopes but whose premature death caused him to weep without restraint.

Qidiao 漆雕 should be identified as yet another disciple of Confucius, Qidiao Kai 漆雕開, whom **Wang Chong** reports in the '*Benxing* 本性' chapter of the *Lun heng* to have defended the opinion that 'there is good as well as evil in human nature' (*xing you shan you e* 性有善有惡), an opinion shared by Mi Zijian 宓子賤, Gongsun Nizi 公孫尼子, Shi Shuo 世碩 and others. The bibliographical chapter of the **Han shu** (ch. 30) records a *Qidiaozi* in 13 pian.

Xunzi is here referred to as the *Sun* 孫 family school because he was also known as Sun Qing 孫卿 'Minister Sun'. The *Han*

Shu records a *Sun Qing zi* in 33 pian, which now bears the title of *Xunzi* in 32 chapters.

As to the *Zhongliang* 仲良 family school, nothing is known about it; some have attempted to refer it to the Chen Liang 陳良 mentioned in the *Mengzi*.

It is interesting to compare Han Feizi's polemical list with his master Xunzi's summary condemnation of what he considers to be the leading schools of the Confucian heritage in his own day in chapter 6 of *Xunzi*, '*Fei shi'er zi* 非十二子' (Contra twelve philosophers). While citing Confucius and Zigong 子貢 (see **Duanmu Si**) as true 'gentlemen' (*junzi*), Xunzi caricatures the schools of Zizhang, Zixia (see **Bu Shang**) and Ziyou (see **Yan Yan**) as 'base Confucians' (*jianru* 賤儒), in a virulent manner reminiscent of Mozi's attack against the Confucians in the '*Fei ru* 非儒' chapter of the *Mozi*:

'Their caps bent and twisted, their robes billowing and flowing, they move to and from as though they were a Yu or a Shun – such are the base *Ru* of Zizhang's school.

Wearing their caps in perfectly correct form, maintaining their expression in perfect equanimity, they sit there all day long as though they were about to gag on a bit, but say nothing – such are the base *Ru* of the school of Zixia.

Evasive and timorous, disliking work, lacking integrity, shameless, interested only in food and drink, they insist that 'a gentleman naturally would not engage in manual labour' – such are the base *Ru* of the school of Ziyou' (Knoblock, vol. I: 229).

The early Han historian **Sima Qian**, in the '*Rulin liezhuan* 儒林列傳' chapter, has yet another story with a different distribution, of a less critical and more historical nature:

'After the death of Confucius, his seventy disciples dispersed and wandered from one feudal lord to another: the most important among the disciples became the lords' masters and ministers, the lesser ones became friends or teachers to the dignitaries, some went into retirement and disappeared. Thus Zilu resided in Wei, Zizhang in Chen, Tantai Ziyu in Chu, Zixia in Xihe, Zigong ended up in Qi. People like Tian Zifang, Duan Ganmu, Wu Qi, Qin Huali all received instruction in the wake of Zixia, and became teachers to kings' (*Shi ji*, 121: 3116).

Sima Qian then goes on to talk about Mengzi and Xunzi as a distinct generation of Confucians in the fourth century BCE: 'During this period, there were armed conflicts everywhere between the warring states, and the Confucian trend of thought dwindled. Only in Qi and Lu did the learned tradition continue. In the reigns of King Wei (357–320) and King Xuan (319–301) of Qi flourished men like Mengzi and Xunzi, who followed the teachings of the Master but extended them, becoming famous among their contemporaries for their wisdom.'

References: Knoblock, 1988; Watson, 1964.

ANNE CHENG

Ruxing jizhuan 儒行集傳

(Collected Biographies of the Conduct of Confucians)

The Collected Biographies is the fifth chapter, in two *juan*, of the Commentaries on the *Li ji* by Huang Daozhou 黃道周 (1585–1646, *zi* You Xuan 幼玄, *hao* Shi Zhai 石齋). Collecting various biographies from a wide source of historical texts, Huang composed this chapter in order to establish criteria for selecting officials, stating in its preface that 'Being worrying that the ignorant of later times do not know that the Way of the Former Kings exists in the conduct of Confucians, Confucius recommended certain personalities as illustrating the Way, in order to enable the Son of Heaven to obtain the worthy for the world by conforming to the name, investigating the actual situation and knowing the people and assigning them with proper positions.' Under different categories such as 'the Self-established' and 'the Courageous', Huang listed those Confucian scholars and officials as examples of worthy and good candidates for government posts.

XINZHONG YAO

S

Sabyŏl-lok 思辨錄
(*Thoughtful Elucidations*)

This is a commentary on the Confucian Classics by Pak Sae-dang 朴世堂 (1629–1703, *zi* Kyekung 季肯, *hao* Sŏkye 西溪). For a period of about fourteen years, from the age of fifty-two, Pak completed this study of the Four Books (*Si shu*). The title he gave to the work derives from the *Doctrine of the Mean* (*Zhong yong*), chapter 20, '... accurate inquiry about it, careful reflection on it...' (Kr. *shinsaji, myŏngbyŏnji* 慎思之, 明辨之). The work did not fall under any of the categories of the time (i.e. the Cheng–Zhu School of thought); it interpreted in a positive and free manner the Four Books and various Classics. It presented a new system of exploration, enabling the original meaning of Confucius to be revealed without resorting to the means of Zhu Xi's system of interpretation, and it played a leading role in promoting later schools of thought which 'find truth in the facts' (Kr. *shilsagushi* 實事求是). However, Pak's method also met with much criticism from many Chosŏn scholars who were inured to Zhu Xi's commentaries.

References: Pak Sae-dang, 1975; Yun Sa-sun, 1982.

NAM-JIN HUH

Sacrifice to Confucius

According to early Chinese sources, Confucius has been the object of cult veneration since the year after his death in 479 BCE. Sacrifices to Confucius were offered by his followers and family descendants, initially at his grave outside his native place of Qufu 曲阜 (Shandong) in the ancient state of Lu 魯, then in a temple at his home in the watchtower district (Queli 闕里).

Expansion of the cult veneration
Confucius received occasional sacrifice in Qufu from imperial entourages beginning in the western Han dynasty (206 BCE–8 CE) and in the imperial capital by the mid third century CE. During the next several centuries the cult of Confucius spread throughout society – primarily among elite and educated sectors of society – and, geographically across the empire through imperial patronage. By the Tang dynasty (618–907), the cult assumed a permanent position in the imperial pantheon of gods and spirits despite the absence of any explicit canonical precedent. From the seventh to the twentieth century, the spirit of Confucius received sacrifices from the emperor and high-ranking court ministers in the capital, from local officials at temples down to the county level, from men educated in the Confucian canon in temples and

altars at schools and private academies, and from his biological descendants at temples maintained by members of the Kong lineage in Qufu and wherever his descendants migrated. At least as early as the Ming dynasty (1368–1644), Confucius received cult veneration by other religious orders in popular temples, although the court proscribed popular sacrifices to Confucius.

Cult veneration of Confucius expanded geographically as far as the imperial bureaucracy's power reached. Sacrifices were also performed beyond China's imperial borders in other parts of East Asia. Sacrifices to Confucius in China were offered by emissaries of the Korean court of Silla as early as the seventh century and at a newly constructed Directorate of Education in Silla by the eighth century. The cult continued under the Koryô kingdom that unified the Korean peninsula in the tenth century and flourished under patronage of the Yi dynasty (1392–1910), which built a large-scale temple in the Chôson capital and smaller temples throughout the kingdom. In Japan sacrifices to Confucius as First Sage, Exalted and Venerable Kong (*sensei Kô senfu*) were offered as early as the Heian period (794–1185) when the court aristocracy was influenced by Tang culture. Cult veneration continued under successive bakufu administrations, and expanded down to the local level in some parts of Japan through patronage of the Tokugawa bakufu (1600–1868). In Vietnam, sacrifices were offered at temples built by the Ly dynasty (1009–1225), which won its independence from China after centuries of colonial rule, and during the Tran dynasty (1225–1400). The later Le dynasty (1428–1788) further expanded cult veneration of Confucius along with Confucian Learning generally.

Unlike most other gods and spirits that received sacrifices at imperial temples and altars, the cult of Confucius was not mentioned in the Classics and thus was not canonical. Classical sources describe in considerable detail the liturgies of sacrifice to Heaven, Earth, royal ancestors, the gods

of soils and grains, etc., whereas they are largely silent on sacrifices to Confucius. In spite of the dearth of canonical precedents, a liturgy for the rites to Confucius was eventually assembled through a series of ritual analogies that situated this cult among the others that constituted the imperial pantheon. The process of locating the cult was not without controversy and disputes over Confucius' ritual status have erupted in every dynasty since the fifth century. To understand the ritual context of the sacrifices to Confucius it is important to look first at the larger domain of the imperial pantheon.

Development of the state cult

The imperial pantheon includes all gods and spirits that received official sacrifices from members of the imperial family (i.e., the emperor, the empress, the heir apparent) or officers of the court and bureaucracy. Sometimes called the 'state cult', the imperial pantheon is distinct from Daoist, Buddhist and popular pantheons maintained by separate managerial bodies, or not at all, particularly in the case of local popular cults. The imperial pantheon comprises gods (e.g., Heaven, Earth, soils and grains, the five sacred peaks, the sun, the moon and stars) and spirits (e.g., royal ancestors) that were mentioned in the ritual canons, the *Book of Rites* and the *Rites of Zhou* (**Zhou li**), or that subsequently received offerings by imperial officers at altars and temples built by the court or bureaucracy. Only imperial officers offered regular sacrifices at most of these ritual spaces, although irregular and unofficial rites were permitted unless explicitly proscribed. All gods and spirits of the imperial pantheon were ranked into three tiers, the great, the middle and the minor sacrifice, marked by posthumous royal and noble titles (e.g., emperor, king, duke, marquis, earl), and by type and amount of offerings, number of ritual vessels, bronze bells and jade chimes, and dancers. Only the emperor was permitted to offer sacrifice to the gods and spirits of the highest tier, called great sacrifice (*da si* 大祀), whose altars and temples were located only in the capital. Eight rows of eight ritual dancers (*ba yi*) were used in such ceremonies, along with four racks of hanging bronze bells and jade chimes, and twelve baskets and twelve jars (*bian dou* 籩豆) of sacrificial foods.

Imperial sacrifices to Confucius did not constitute a regular cult during the early centuries of imperial China. He received very irregular sacrifices from imperial authorities during the western Han. The western Han court conferred a posthumous title of Duke upon Confucius in the year 1 CE, in spite of his humble station during his own lifetime, which made him eligible for higher level rites than some other mortals ranked as middle level sacrifice (*zhong si* 中祀). Imperial sacrifice was offered in Qufu more frequently in the Later Han (25–220), when rites were accompanied by ceremonial music and ritual dance (85 CE), followed a regular annual schedule of sacrifice (170 CE), and used painted portraits to represent the spirit that received the offerings (178 CE). By the end of the Han, therefore, the sacrifices held a relatively stable status among other imperial cults and were performed according to an increasingly elaborated and codified liturgy. The centre of the imperial cult shifted in the Wei (220–265) and Jin (265–420) dynasties to the capital when sacrifices were offered in the Imperial College (**Bi yong**) by the Chamberlain for Ceremonials (241 CE) and eventually by the heir apparent (271 CE) and the emperor himself (357 CE) following lectures on canonical books (e.g., the *Analects*, the *Book of Documents*, the *Book of Rites*). The cult secured more long-standing status in the imperial cult system in the fifth century when a temple devoted exclusively to sacrifice to Confucius was built in the capital.

Many elements of the sacrifice as performed throughout late imperial times had been deployed by various courts before the Tang dynasty, but the rites to Confucius and its status as a middle-level sacrifice were not fixed until the mid seventh century.

For a short period in the first half of the seventh century, primary sacrifices in the imperial temple in Luoyang were offered to the Duke of Zhou (see **Zhou Gong**) as sage rather than to Confucius, who was called teacher and Correlate. The Duke of Zhou was moved to the temple of the Zhou dynasty's founder as Correlate in 657 and Confucius was restored to his position as sage on the grounds that Confucius was the sage of the canonical traditions taught in schools and thus was the proper recipient of the school libation rites (*shi dian* 釋奠) described in the *Book of Rites*. Other changes in the Tang served to permanently structure the internal workings of this cult: temples were ordered to be built in all prefectural and county schools throughout the empire (630), twenty-two masters of the Confucian canon were enshrined as teachers (647), and seventy of Confucius' disciples were enshrined, ten of whom were distinguished as Savants (712). In a series of extraordinary measures, the court used four racks of hanging bells and chimes (732) – previously used in rites for royal personages – then promoted Confucius to Exalted King of Culture (**Wenxuan wang**), seated his temple image facing toward the imperial direction of south, and conferred posthumous noble titles upon all others enshrined in the temple: Correlate Yan Hui was given the title of duke, the Savants the title of marquise, and Zeng Shen of earl (739). These titles effected a ritual hierarchy in the temple that was already implicit with the use of the distinctions of sage, Correlate, savant, teacher, etc. The use of feudal ranks clarified this ritual hierarchy until the Song (960–1279), when the court began to promote some persons above others within the same tier.

Changes in the sacrifices to Confucius were hotly contested and the most far-reaching during the Ming. The first Ming emperor suspended sacrifices in the capital altogether (1369–1382), yet Confucius' ritual status was later elevated by increasing the number of ritual vessels to ten (1455), then later to twelve, when the number of dancers was increased to sixty-four (1477). The latter was again increased to seventy-two in 1496. This seemingly irrevocable trend of ever greater honours ceased in 1530 in a series of the most systematic and fundamental changes of the temple liturgy since the Tang dynasty. Confucius' title of king and the noble titles of all others enshrined were eliminated – bringing this cult into line with the decree of 1370 that eliminated such ranks in all imperial cults – and the number of ritual vessels was reduced to ten and dancers to thirty-six. The sacrificial image of Confucius was replaced by a spirit tablet and a number of canonical exegetes were removed, which served to bring the temple sacrifices in line with the views of Cheng–Zhu orthodoxy. A shrine devoted to Confucius' father was built behind the main hall on canonical grounds that 'a son never eats before his father even if he is a sage' (**Zuo zhuan**, Duke Wen, 2nd year). Sacrifices at this shrine were offered before the main sacrifice to Confucius in imperial liturgies ever since.

The liturgy of the sacrifice to Confucius

The rites to Confucius shared with other upper- and middle-level imperial sacrifices the same basic elements: a preparatory fast; offerings of silk (the canonical precursor to spirit money used in popular sacrifice), libation and food; music and dance; a prayer; and a liturgy that prescribed the rites that served to offer these things to the main recipient and the Correlate. The shared liturgical basis of sacrifices in the cults of the imperial pantheon demonstrates their common purpose of maintaining the cosmic order through serving the gods and spirits who govern various sectors of the cosmos. This liturgy differed from other middle sacrifices in certain respects that underscore its special status in the pantheon as the primary cult of the Confucian literati who constituted the *imperium*'s elite. This classically trained elite not only officiated over the cult of Confucius, it studied and performed (or at least managed) the

sacrifices to all gods and spirits of the pantheon. Even the emperor, who ascended the altar of Heaven alone, required instruction in the Confucian ritual canons and training in the liturgy of the sacrifices to Heaven. The cult of Confucius differed from others in that, with the possible exception of the emperor's sacrifices to the imperial ancestors, it was one of the most hotly contested of the imperial pantheon. Much of the controversy concerned Confucius' posthumous rank, which was often at odds with the cult's status as a middle sacrifice. Confucius alone retained his title of king for one hundred and sixty years in the Ming after all other gods and spirits in the pantheon were stripped of their noble titles in 1370.

Each year the Directorate of Astronomy issued a calendar of sacrifices performed at all levels of the bureaucracy from the court down to the county. By the Ming dynasty it was determined that sacrifices to Confucius were to be performed on the second *ding* day in the spring and autumn (see *Ding* Sacrifice, **Ding ji**). Three days before the sacrifice, the ritual officers observed a two-day 'working fast' (*san zhai* 散齋) when routine duties were carried out while they abstained from consoling the bereaved, inquiring of the ill, passing judgement on convicts, drinking wine, eating meat, contact with wives and listening to music. The purpose of the abstinences and the aim of the fast was to ensure that the consecration officers concentrated on nothing but the spirit that was to receive the sacrifice. The fast was not an expiatory rite to cleanse the sacrificers of sin – a concept that appears to have no place in imperial cult worship of gods and spirits – rather, it served to discipline the sacrificers by unifying body and mind through cultivating authenticity and reverence toward the spirit. On the day before the ceremony the officers reside at the temple to observe the 'strict fast' (*zhi zhai* 致齋) when they attend to this ceremony exclusively and think of nothing other than the spirit that is to receive the sacrifice. When they enter the hall on the morning of the sacrifice, says the *Book of Rites*, they 'almost certainly see him at his tablet'. Only the virtuous man, who devotes his undivided concentration on the service, the *Rites* continues, can commune with the gods and spirits.

The type and number of victims offered in sacrifice was determined by the spirit's place in the pantheon and the rank of the sacrificer. The first recorded sacrifice to Confucius was offered by the founder of the Han dynasty in 195 BCE. Although there was no explicit precedent for such a sacrifice, the emperor offered an ox, goat and pig, or Large Beast Offering (*tai lao*), as sacrifice to Confucius at his grave side. Large Beast Sacrifices were later periodically offered to the spirit of Confucius at the imperial Confucius temple in the capital and smaller beast offerings (*shao lao*) at local temples throughout the empire. According to the regulations of the Ming dynasty, one month before the ceremony the victims are separated from the rest of the herd and kept in a clean pen. On the evening before the sacrifice the consecration officers observe the slaughter of the animals (*xing sheng* 省牲) in the temple kitchen then later bury a portion of the blood and fur outside the main gate to inform the spirits that the whole animal is offered to them. The victims are offered to the gods and spirits of all imperial sacrifices as feasts to be eaten and thus the slaughter of the animals is not part of the main ceremony, although ritual procedures ensure that the slaughter is performed properly.

After the blood and fur are buried in the early hours on the morning of the sacrifice, the celebrants take their positions, a hymn is sung with musical accompaniment while the spirit of Confucius is escorted through the main gate to his tablet on the centre altar in the Hall of Great Consummation (**Dacheng dian**). The principal consecration officer washes his hands in a basin, stands before Confucius' tablet, bows, kneels, or prostrates himself (depending upon circumstances and the rules in effect) three times, then in sequence offers incense, silk and libation. The prayer is read and a sequence of offerings of the wine and feast is performed. Just as the principal consecration officer completes his offering to Confucius, secondary officers perform the same rites to the Correlates and Savants, whose tablets are on altars on the East and West walls inside the main hall, followed by the same rites to the worthies and scholars, whose tablets are in corridors that stretch along the full length of the East and West sides of the temple grounds. The process is repeated a second and final time (see **san xian**), except the incense and silk are not offered, the consecration officer then drinks some of the libation and receives a portion of the sacrificial meat (*zuo* 胙). All celebrants receive a portion of the meat, said to be blessed by its presence in the ceremony, which they share with family members at home within the next day. When the spirit is escorted out of the temple, and the silk and the text of the prayer are burned in an oven – the only two offerings to be so treated, the ceremony is complete.

Music and dance accompany all key parts of the ceremony. This music ensemble requires the eight musical instruments, voice and dance. Each phrase of the hymns (composed of four notes) begins and ends with a drum. Each word of the hymn is initiated by a bronze bell, a yang instrument and consummated by a jade chime, a yin instrument. By the mid fifth century the court systematised the ceremony by applying the specifications for sacrifices to an upper lord found in the *Rites of Zhou*. Thus six rows of six dancers were used and three racks of hanging bells and chimes (*xuan xuan* 軒懸, literally 'chariot hanging instruments,' alluding to a feudal lord's three-sided chariot, in contrast to *gong xuan* 宮懸, or four racks, alluding to the four walls of the royal palace). These numbers were increased in 723, though they were subject to change throughout the course of the imperial era. The hymns praise Confucius as the incomparable one who equalled Heaven and Earth and gave birth to virtue.

The sacrifice to Confucius accomplishes a number of things that vary depending upon who offers sacrifices, the location and circumstances of the ceremony. It is difficult, therefore, to specify what the rites do that apply to everyone and at all times. The principal aim of sacrifice is to feed the gods and spirits of the pantheon who requite the offerings with blessings. The precise nature of the gods' requital is subject to conjecture since the affairs of spirits and ghosts have been largely taboo from the time of Confucius. The blessings the gods and spirits return tend to be specific to the realm of the cosmos they govern. The emperor's sacrifices to Heaven are most general, but they are not exhaustive, for, in the absence of monotheism, Heaven was never construed as omnipotent. Thus the emperor also sacrifices to Earth, to imperial ancestors, gods of soils and grains, sun and moon and stars. Confucius is called the sage of Culture and the temple devoted to him is also known as the *culture* temple (*wen miao* 文廟), which was distinguished since the eighth century from the Taigong temple (*taigong miao* 太公廟) where the spirits of military commanders were venerated. Thus Confucius' domain in the cosmos is 'culture,' a term that eludes precise definition. It includes the civil legacies of what the culture-heros and sage–kings before Confucius taught the people: language and the sacred canonical books concerned with history, ritual, poetic hymns and a way of living governed by rituals that gave perfect expression to human sentiments.

THOMAS A. WILSON

Sakuma Shôzan (Zôzan)
佐久間象山
1811–1864
(*na*: Taisei 大星, Hiraki 啟; *azana*: Shimei 子明; *tsûshô*: Keinosuke 啟之助)

Sakuma Shôzan, the most influential of the late Tokugawa Confucian thinkers involved in the modernisation of Japanese thought, is famous for his advocacy of the principle of 'Eastern morality and western techniques' (*Tôyô dôtoku; Seiyô geijutsu* 東洋道德, 西洋藝術). He was born the eldest son of a low-ranking samurai of Matsushiro 松代 domain in Shinano 信野 province (Nagano prefecture) who was a teacher of swordsmanship. Shôzan was a precocious child who soaked up the early training he received from his father in the Confucian Classics, Chinese poetry, mathematics and military arts. In 1833, the year after his father's death, he was allowed to go to Edo to study, where he pursued **Zhu Xi** learning for over two years at the Shôheikô under **Satô Issai**. Some have claimed that his later activism reflects the influence of Issai's Wang Yangming Learning (see **Wang Shouren**), but Sakuma spoke out strongly against Yangming's intuitionism, especially after Ôshio Heihachirô's rebellion in 1837. A much more important intellectual influence was the *Yi jing*-based philosophy developed by the Song Neo-Confucian **Shao Yong**. In his preface to a collection of Shao's writings published in 1840, Sakuma criticises the impractical nature of the Confucian studies of his day, insisting that no one can attain the sort of broad grasp of moral principles and daily affairs that is necessary to govern wisely unless they have probed into the underlying principles of things (*butsuri* 物理), i.e., the regular laws of change observable in nature and society. He recommends Shao's writings as the best place to start learning how to probe principles, without which human life 'is like riding in a boat with no rudder or standing in a carriage with hubless wheels.' Shao's protoscientific emphasis on probing the regularities of change in the objective world helped steer Sakuma away from abstractions and preoccupation with unchanging moral norms toward the practical study of technology and changing political realities, an emphasis that was apparent in his proposals for educational reform put forth only three months after Ôshio's rebellion.

Returning to Edo in 1839, he opened a private academy to seek practical applications of Confucian Learning in solving the problems besetting the country, the acuteness of which had become painfully apparent through the rebellion and the great famine that precipitated it. In 1841, however, came the even greater shock of the British victories in the Opium War. Sakuma's lord was appointed to the Office of Naval Defence, and Sakuma, appointed as his adviser, enrolled in 1842 in the school of Egawa Tarôzaemon 江川太郎左衛門 (1801–55), a teacher of western gunnery. The next year he submitted a memorial setting out an Eight Point Policy on Naval Defence, suggesting that the failure of the Qing to defend civilisation meant that the burden had now fallen on Japan. The Chinese, as was evident even in **Wei Yuan**'s *Haiguo tuzhi* 海國圖志 (Illustrated Gazetteer of the Maritime Countries) 'had lost the real meaning of true principles and, in place of inquiry and investigation, had substituted conceit and complacency'. The many proposals he put forward for strengthening Japan's coastal defences centred on 'emulating western manufacturing methods in the production of a variety of firearms, and learning about naval science and the equipping of ships'. Though the memorial owes much to Mito formulations of defence and expulsion, it reveals a considerable shift in the ground of argumentation. From this time Sakuma began to repudiate the **Mito School**'s conception of 'inner' and 'outer', which defined Chinese learning as 'ours' but placed western learning in the category of the alien and barbarian. He began to conceive of Japan, rather, as a separate cultural entity from both China and the west and thus in an independent position to draw useful knowledge from all available sources for improving the welfare of the people. All such knowledge could only contribute to 'the Way of the sages'. Sakuma soon realised that assiduous language study was indispensable to mastering western learning, and he took up Dutch in

1844. By 1845 he was able to read Dutch books himself, and he discovered that there were many errors in Egawa's teachings. He studied under other scholars of Western Learning as well, similarly surpassing most of them after a few years of study. He carried out scientific experiments related to techniques of manufacture, and was successful in casting western-style bronze cannon. Acutely conscious of the foreign threat and of the need to 'know one's enemy', he petitioned the bakufu in 1849 and 1850 to be allowed to publish his revised version of a Dutch dictionary, but the petition was rejected (his feudal status was not high enough for his petitions to be taken seriously). He also petitioned for more translations of Dutch technical books. In 1851 he opened his own school of gunnery and Confucianism. 'The method by which you know them', he wrote, 'lies not just in exhausting their skills, but in combining their learning with ours'. This could not be accomplished through an attitude of contempt toward foreigners, such as he found in Wei Yuan and in Japanese diplomatic correspondence, but required serious efforts to understand their thoughts and feelings. Mastery of Western Learning involved not just the study of techniques, but penetration of the universal principles underlying inventions and discoveries. Thus Sakuma insisted that 'basic studies' must precede any attempt at application, seeing mathematics as the ultimate foundation of all learning and investigation. Effective government policies, moreover, depended on the availability and employment of men of talent and ability, which for Sakuma meant men of any social background who were passionately committed to the acquisition of knowledge – including the technical, military, and tactical sort of knowledge that the Chinese literati had always disdained. After the opening of the country, this concern for the practical investigation of social reality and scientific principles took precedence in his writings over the concerns with loyalty and moral rectification that preoccupied most Confucian thinkers and domainal leaders in his time, as epitomised by the Mito School. It was clear to him that no amount of moral rectification of society would enable Japan to stand up militarily to the West, i.e., that *gaikan* 外患 (the threat of external catastrophe) was now a more fundamental problem than *naiyû* 內憂 (putting the natural order into proper adjustment). Dealing with an unprecedented *gaikan* called for a totally new investigation of social reality, not some Mito-style return to the ideal institutions established by sage–kings in ancient times. Moreover, it compelled him to break with the conventional historical awareness in which men imitate moral exemplars in history for a concept that history follows the actions of men. Accordingly, his models of the emperor–hero who could inspire his countrymen to give up 'childish entertainments' and 'construct a Great Plan' – a hero who must come from the lower orders of society so he would truly understand society's problems – were drawn not from Chinese and Japanese history, but from the 'outer' world represented by the modern West: Peter the Great, who had unified his realm, adopted western technology, constructed a navy, prevented colonisation, and elevated Russia to an honourable place among nations; and Napoleon, whose decisive acts based on an understanding of changing conditions had 'smashed contemporary abuses . . . and responded to people's needs.' By 1860, for Sakuma, 'Political culture had replaced ethical culture as the scene of human action . . . A unified political community was essential to a unified defence; and technological change required central political coordination . . . Sakuma was not openly disparaging the usefulness of Neo-Confucian ethics; he was distinguishing realms or modes of experience and action.' That is, the inner realm remained ruled by eastern ethics, which must serve as the firm and unchanging foundation of both the individual and the nation, but the outer realm, 'the world of politics and history,

could only be served after an investigation of contemporary social reality disclosed what needed to be done. Morality was the pledge that such an investigation would be carried out by men of superior talent and ability'. According to **Yokoi Shônan** (who apparently heard it from **Yoshida Shôin**), Sakuma said that in the realm of politics and the tactics of warfare the West is superior to East Asia, and of the Confucian books only the *Book of Changes* is useful in this realm. Echoing the *Yi Jing*, he wrote, 'If we grasp the current and developments of the present, we will be able to foretell disorder.' Rules which were necessary in earlier generations are superseded by 'new facts which crystallise into principles of later generations', and to follow the times and obey change is nothing other than the way of the **Zhongyong**, the way of sincerity.

Famous men who studied under Sakuma include bakumatsu *shishi* 志士 such as Yoshida Shôin, Katsu Kaishû (a Dutch learning scholar who became the first Japanese to navigate the Pacific Ocean in 1860, head of the bakufu's navy, head of the early Meiji navy, and a naval historian), Hashimoto Sanai, Sakamoto Ryôma, and Nakaoka Shintarô, as well as early Meiji thinkers like Katô Hiroyuki, Tsuda Mamichi, and **Nishimura Shigeki**. In 1854 Sakuma was arrested for his encouragement of Shôin's attempt to hitch a ride to America aboard one of Perry's ships, and, after five months of imprisonment in an adjoining cell to Yoshida, he was released to domiciliary confinement in Matsushiro. He took this as an opportunity to devote himself single-mindedly to studying Dutch books, submitting petitions to the authorities, and writing his famous memoirs from prison, *Seikenroku* 省愆錄 (Reflections on My Errors) – which criticises Confucian scholars' ignorance of western science and the shogunate's ineptitude in dealing with Perry's demands. In 1863 he was pardoned, and in 1864 he was summoned to Kyoto, hotbed of the *sonnô jôi* radicals, to serve as an adviser to the shogunate on defence matters. He knew that his life was in danger, but he refused to flinch, convinced that his views would be vindicated by future generations. True to his premonitions, he was assassinated by a radical *rônin* in the seventh month because of his attempts to mediate between the court and the bakufu before the Hamaguri Gate Incident in which radical anti-bakufu forces from Chôshû were defeated in their attempt to reestablish their control over the imperial court.

Further reading: Richard T. Chang, *From Prejudice to Tolerance: A Study of the Japanese Image of the West, 1826–1864* (Tokyo: Sophia University, 1970).

BARRY D. STEBEN

Samguk Sagi 三國史記
(*History of the Three Kingdoms*)

Compiled by Kim Bu-sik 金富軾 (1075–1151, *zi* Ipji 立之, *hao* Noech'ŏn 雷川) and ten others by order of the King in the Koryo dynasty (918–1392), the *Samguk sagi* was finished in 1145. In its introduction, Kim made clear the motivation behind the work, stipulating how Chinese history texts on Korea were often too brief, inaccurate or unable to discriminate proper information from the spurious. The section on politics details government regulations, religious customs, ancestral rites, personnel changes and imperial tours. In the section on natural disasters, comets, eclipses, droughts, floods, earthquakes and the like are all listed and functioned as a means of providing illustrations of how political events could be predicted. In the section on war, 440 wars are listed between the Koguryŏ (*c.* 37 BCE–668 CE) and foreign peoples, as well as with Paekche (*c.* 18 BCE–660CE) and Silla (*c.* 57 BCE–668 CE). Diplomacy, music, clothes, homes, geography are all dealt with.

The contents adhere to Confucian duty and virtuous rule, behaviour of the king and officials. The work is a valuable, though somewhat biased, source of premodern Korean history, influencing latter histories in its understanding of the Three Kingdoms as a complete nation, the king as absolute ruler, viewing national disasters as affecting the people and linked to the King's acts. It considers history to be a source of lessons, emphasising royalty and also the individual in history. The *Samguk sagi* has been reprinted since 1174, and in 1995 it was issued on CD-ROM by Seoul National University professor Hŏ Sŏng-to.

References: *Samguk Sagi*, 1959; Yi Byung-do, 1947.

NAM-JIN HUH

San dai 三代
(Three dynasties)

This expression refers to the Xia, Shang (or Yin) and Zhou ages of high antiquity, which together were understood by Warring States and later thinkers as a golden age when culture heroes and sage rulers walked the earth. In this construction of the past, the three ages were believed to have succeeded one another consecutively and to have followed a moral trajectory through time: good governance prevailed, and when it did not, that sovereignty was replaced by more worthy rulers who augured a new, more righteous age. In the *Analects* 15: 25, for example, Confucius claims that it was the presence of worthy people who made the Three Dynasties move along the straightforward Way. The Three Dynasties were understood as a formative gestational period when specially gifted persons developed and perfected the arts of human civilisation – calendrical systems, governance, rituals, writing systems and so on. The three dynasties were often invoked as an implicit critique of contemporary rulership and social mores, which were seen to have fallen away from the idealised forms of antiquity.

Late nineteenth- and early twentieth-century scholarship revisited the very notion of what constituted a traditional 'dynasty', perceiving the notion more as an historiographic construction, and moreover questioned the very historicity of the Xia dynasty (more recent archeological data, however, has in turn occasioned a revision of the latter critique). The relationships between the Shang and Zhou cultures are now known to have been far more complex and interwoven than the traditional model of conquering-and-succession allowed. (See also **San Tong**.)

References: Ames & Rosemont, 1998, 15: 25; Loewe & Shaughnessy, 1999.

DEBORAH SOMMER

San gang 三綱
(Three Cardinal Guides)

The Three Cardinal Guides in human relations from the Han dynasty (206 BCE–220 CE) onwards were the foundations of the Confucian social order, which specify that a ruler 'guides' the ruled, a father 'guides' his son and a husband 'guides' his wife. The literary meaning of *gang* is a thick guiderope along the edge of a fishing net, to which the mesh is attached and whose weave can be tightened. *Gang* is therefore taken as a metaphor for the nettings which hold society together. The first to use this metaphor was **Dong Zhongshu**. Previously, though not explicitly stated, a similar idea was extant in the early Qin dynasty (221–206 BCE), as for example with the Legalist Han Feizi 韓非子 (?–233 BCE) where in his *Zhong Xiao* (忠孝) chapter it is said that if these three relationships are harmonious, then the world will be ordered, but if not, there will be but chaos.

It is important to note that the Five Human Relations (*wu lun*) contain the Three Cardinal Guides, but when the two are compared, some differences emerge. The former, for example, places the father and son relationship cardinally first. Also, though the five human relationships are the universal and natural expressions of our original nature (*xing*) and the essence of life, the Three Cardinal Guides are more specific to a hierarchy or power relationship denoting the bonds of society. Clearly the two were brought about at different times, and thus under different conditions, historical backgrounds and applications. The *san gang* and *wu lun* are sometimes together termed the *gang chang* 綱常 and clearly provide the essential foundations of a robust Confucian political and moral standard.

Reference: Morohashi, 1960.

TODD CAMERON THACKER

San gangling 三綱領
(Three basic principles)

The three essential spheres of external validation of the 'Way' of Confucian self-cultivation enumerated in the opening line of *The Great Learning* are: 'causing the light of one's inner moral force to shine forth' (*ming mingde*), 'bringing the people to a state of renewal' (*xin min*), and 'coming to rest in the fullest attainment of the good' (*zhi shan*). These ambiguous terms were the subject of unceasing philosophical debate within the Confucian school, but the elucidation of their meaning provided in the 'expansion chapters' assigned to them in the continuation of the text (chapters 1–3) makes clear that the attainment of these ideals rests, on the one hand, in finding and perfecting one's own inborn moral nature, and, on the other, in extending this outward to all human beings through the paradigmatic acts by which one participates in the ordering of the world.

ANDREW PLAKS

San huang wu di 三皇五帝
(Three August Emperors and the Five Lords)

This expression, which dates to Qin and Han times, refers to a pantheon of cosmogonic demigods, mythic culture heroes, and cosmic powers who lived during the primordial dawn of the universe, in the more recent protohistoric past, or in *illo tempore*. The identities of the five and the three varied, but in general the expression refers to a group of unusually gifted or even suprahuman beings who made cultured life possible and brought human beings from a period of unstructured chaos, animal wildness, inchoate disorganisation and illiteracy into a period of cosmic order, civilisation, social organisation and learning.

The Three August Emperors are variously identified as Fu Xi, inventor of divination; Nü Wa, architect of the cosmos; Shen Nong, inventor of agriculture, Zhu Rong, who discovered the use of fire; Huang Di, the Yellow Emperor, inventor of the medical arts; and so on. The three are also identified more generically as Emperor Heaven, Emperor Earth and Emperor Human Being, and in another formulation are the ancient sage rulers Yao, Shun, and Yu (see *Yao Shun*).

The Five Lords were also identified with some of these names, as well as a range of other mythic figures. They were moreover associated and mutually correlated with the powers of the Five Phases, five colours, five directions, and so on.

References: Loewe & Shaughnessy, 1999; Wang Su, 1990: modern pp. 62–6; Watson, 1993a; Yang Jialuo, 1997: 1–48.

DEBORAH SOMMER

San jiao jiu liu 三教九流
(Three religions and nine schools of thought)

San jiao jiu liu is a phrase summing up the totality of human knowledge within Chinese civilisation. It is probably found first in the early thirteenth-century *Yunlu manchao* 雲麓漫鈔 of Zhao Yanwei 趙彥微 (?–?), Section 6, though the two elements from which it is composed go back much further. The 'Three Religions' or 'Three Teachings'

covers Buddhism, Daoism and Confucianism, and appears to have been formulated in the late sixth century as a result of the search of the Emperor Wu (r. 560–578) of the Northern Zhou for the intellectual basis for his intended unification of China. Before this point Confucianism does not seem to have been conceptualised as something equivalent to Buddhism, though in different contexts Confucianism and Daoism or Daoism and Buddhism are compared, the former pair implicitly from Han times, and the latter from the fifth century.

The so-called nine schools of thought, covering Confucians, Daoists, Yin–Yang experts, Legalists, School of 'Names' (Sophists), Moists, Strategists, Miscellaneous and Agriculturalists, go back to the bibliographical categories used in the first century CE in the **Han Shu**, and is the general term used by the author Ban Gu 班固 (39–92) to summarise this list (70B: 4245). Whether they had all constituted self-conscious schools (as the Moists undoubtedly had), or whether their writings were placed together on the grounds of apparent similarities perceived by Han cataloguers is not always clear. In Tang poetry the term would seem to be used already in the late ninth century to mean more loosely 'all sorts of people', and the full phrase 'three religions and nine schools of thought' acquires this meaning also in popular literature of the late imperial period.

TIM H. BARRETT

San tong 三統
(Three Sequences)

Probably first seen in one of the chapters of the *Yi Zhou shu* 逸周書, this term arose in the first instance to denote three sequences whereby the calendar was constructed, and which were later explained as relating to the movements of the three estates of the universe, i.e. Heaven, Earth and Man. In the calendar which was drawn up by **Liu Xin** and named the *San tong li* 三統歷 ('*Triple Concordance System*', or '*Three Sequences Calendar*') time was conceived as a series of cyclical and repetitive stages of being.

In addition the concept of the *San tong* had a profound significance in the formative years of Chinese historiography. It showed that dynastic rule passed legitimately, by way of the three links, through the houses of Xia 夏, Shang 商 (*c*. 1700–*c*. 1045 BCE) and Zhou 周 (*c*. 1045–256 BCE), or possibly Yin, Zhou and Lu 魯. Known collectively as the *San tong*, this process carried with it the acknowledgement that once a ruling house had descended into decline it would be due to be replaced, in accordance with the will or Mandate of Heaven (*Tian ming*). As such the concept became a basic principle in Confucian political thought. In so doing it lent invaluable support to pretenders to imperial power and the statesmen, officials and historians who were required to defend the elimination of a dynasty by its newly arisen successor. Alternatively, the concept could be used to strengthen a link between an existing house and its three illustrious predecessors.

References: Sivin, 1969a: 12; Tjan, 1949: 99.
MICHAEL LOEWE

San xian 三獻
(Three offerings)

San xian refers to the three times a cup of libation is offered to a spirit during sacrifice as described in the *Book of Rites* (*Li ji*). Each offering of the cup marks the presentation of gifts to the gods and spirits, including the libation, a prayer, incense, silk, jade (in great sacrifices), and a feast comprising meat (see *tai lao*) and other viands of unsalted broth, mixed soups, uncooked grains, sauces, dried meats, nuts, edible grasses and cakes. Preparation of food for the gods and spirits, the *Book of Rites* tells us, emphasises simplicity of the fare not pleasing flavours.

The first offering (*chu xian* 初獻) in the sacrifice to Confucius begins with the reading of the prayer and presentation of incense, silk and libation. The silk, libation and prayer are placed on the altar. Only the libation is offered up in the second (*ya xian* 亞獻) and last (*zhong xian* 終獻) offering. For each of these offerings, the consecration officer bows, then prostrates himself, and stands facing north toward the spirit tablet or image. He receives the goblet from an usher on his right, offers it up to the spirit, then hands it to a ceremonial master to his left who replaces the goblet on the altar. Just as the principal consecration officer completes his offering to Confucius, secondary officers (*fen xian* 分獻) perform the same rites to the Correlates and Savants, whose tablets are on altars on the East and west walls inside the main hall, followed by the same rites to the worthies and scholars, whose tablets are in corridors that stretch along the full length of the East and west sides of the temple grounds.

THOMAS A. WILSON

Sancong side 三從四德
(Threefold obedience and four virtues)

This idea neatly sums up the behaviour that Confucians expected from women. The concepts of *sancong* (threefold obedience) and *side* (four virtues) began as separate notions and first appeared in the ritual classics. In fact, it probably was not until late imperial times that these two concepts were combined to create this idealised formula for female conduct. Modern critics have assailed this concept because it posits the inferiority of women and promotes their subordination.

Sancong has been translated as threefold obedience or the three dependencies. The concept indicates that a woman is under the authority of, or dependant upon, a male relative during all three stages of her life. The *Yi li* states, 'Before marrying, she follows (*cong* 從) her father; after marrying she follows (*cong*) her husband; when her husband dies, she follows (*cong*) her son' (*Yi li*, 11: 66). The **Baihu tong** explains the rationale for the threefold obedience by noting that, '[women] partake in the *yin* nature and are lowly, and they do not participate in outside matters. Hence they are obliged to submit to the Three Obediences' (*Baihu tong*, 1: 3). In other words, women have to follow their male relatives due to their lack of voice in public affairs and their natural inferiority.

Nevertheless, whether *cong* here means to slavishly obey one's father, husband, or son's every command, or merely to allow him ultimate say in weighty decisions is not clear. In short, ultimately submitting to a male's authority did not mean that a woman agreed with or went along with all of his decisions. For example, in the **Lienü zhuan**, **Mengzi**'s mother cites the doctrine of the threefold obedience, but she only does so to ease Mengzi's conscience about moving her to another state. In the same biography, she reprimands her son and reverses his decision to divorce his wife (*Lienü zhuan*, 1: 9). Lisa Raphals has shown that, in pre-Tang literature, the motif of a woman either admonishing or providing political advice to her husband or son was a popular one.

The four virtues are traits that every woman should develop. These characteristics are 'wifely virtue' (*fu de* 婦德), 'wifely speech' (*fu yan* 婦言), 'wifely demeanour' (*fu rong* 婦容) and 'wifely work' (*fu gong* 婦功). These names make it immediately evident that every woman is expected to marry; her most important attributes are those that will help her fulfil the role of wife. Ban Zhao's 班昭 (48–?116 CE) *Lessons for Women* (**Nü jie**) provides the earliest description of these virtues. Rather than outstanding talent, wifely virtue means a woman should maintain her integrity and be steadfast in her loyalties. Rather than being a clever conversationalist, wifely speech means a woman should speak words that are proper, carefully selected and timely. Rather than being comely, wifely demeanour means a woman should be clean and tidy. Rather than being extraordinarily skilled in handicrafts, wifely work means a woman should concentrate on weaving, preparing food and welcoming guests (**Hou Han shu**, 84: 2789). Nevertheless, since the Classics do not explicitly spell out what the four virtues are, they were open to interpretation. Dorothy Ko has noted that, during late Ming and Qing times, a number of women reinterpreted wifely virtue to mean literary talent.

References: Ko, 1992: 28–30; Raphals, 1998.

KEITH KNAPP

Sang li 喪禮
(Rites of mourning and burial)

The most elaborate of the Confucian rites of passage consists in the long series of ceremonies associated with death, mourning and burial. The *Book of Rites* is the canonical source for these rituals, discussing aspects of them in several chapters, and treating them as a matter of utmost seriousness, central to the fulfillment of filial piety (*xiao*).

This complex series of rites extended over more than two years. Immediately after the death, the survivors were expected to call back the soul, wash and dress the body, and set out a representation of the dead that could receive offerings. Within a few days they had to perform two laying-out ceremonies in which the body is placed in the coffin and the coffin is packed with clothes and shrouds. At this point the mourners put on mourning garments appropriate to their degree of kinship and began ritualised wailing. They were also expected to send out announcements of the death and receive condolence visits. After preparing the grave they would arrange a procession to the grave. After the burial, they would bring back the spirit tablet and perform the first of a long series of post burial funerary sacrifices. Not until the last was completed would the ancestral tablet be incorporated into the regular ancestral rites.

The concept of the five grades of mourning governed how each individual performed his obligations to the dead. The grade varied by the coarseness of the required garments and how long they were worn (three years, one year, nine months, five months, or three months). Within a family, when a man died, his sons owed him three years of mourning wearing 'untrimmed' hemp garments; his brothers and unmarried sisters, his sons' wives, and his daughters owed him one year of trimmed hemp garments; his father's sisters, his married sisters, his first cousins and his grandchildren owed him nine months; his brothers' grandchildren and his second cousins owed him five months; third cousins and his daughter's husband and children and his mother's brother's sons were supposed to wear relatively fine clothes for three months. In practice, people who owed lower degrees of mourning usually only wore the mourning garments during the funeral procession and burial ceremonies.

Most of the Confucian literature on mourning is above all concerned with the behaviour expected of those in mourning for their parents. Those wearing mourning garments were expected to abstain from comforts, including tasty food and soft beds, and withdraw from many activities, including political office and making offerings at the ancestral altar. They could not marry or officiate at a marriage, and were expected to abstain from sexual relations and from drinking wine. Although the three-year mourning was the standard, officials and Confucian scholars were probably the only ones widely expected to conform closely to its requirements.

Over time, as funerary practices not documented in the Classics gained hold, Confucian scholars debated at length which ones could be considered minor variations of canonical practices, which were harmless

elaborations and which were pernicious violations of the spirit of the Classics that had to be opposed. In Song times, scholars wrote against such practices as cremation instead of burial, playing music at funerals, calling in monks to perform Buddhist services and leaving bodies unburied for long periods of time, often because the descendants were not yet able to secure a grave that would be favourable according to geomancy (*feng shui* 風水). Although cremation seems to have declined significantly after the Song period, the other practices continued through Ming and Qing times, as did Confucian criticism of them.

In late imperial times and into the twentieth century, Chinese continued to treat the funeral and burial of their parents as a major obligation and would devote large shares of family resources to it. Although common practice involved many customs not of classical origin, including not merely the participation of Buddhist monks, but also various acts designed to propitiate the dead or ward off evil forces, the overall shape of funeral rituals remained remarkably faithful to the pattern described in the Classics.

References: De Groot, 1892–1910; Ebrey, 1990b, 1991b and 1991a: 65–152; Kutcher, 1999; McDermott, 1999; Watson & Rawski, 1988.

PATRICIA EBREY

Sannian sang 三年喪
(Three-year mourning)

Wearing mourning garments for parents and husband into the third year (generally to the twenty-fifth or twenty-seventh month) became a Confucian doctrine by mid to late Zhou times. Those wearing mourning garments were expected to observe such austerities as eating simple food and refraining from sexual relations. Their contact with death made them inauspicious, requiring them to avoid ancestral rites, weddings and court audiences and other auspicious events.

The length of the mourning period had to be defended from the time of Confucius on. In *Analects* 17: 21, after a disciple said he thought one year of mourning ought to be enough, Confucius remarked that a gentleman would feel grief for three years. When the Duke of Teng sent an inquiry to Mengzi asking how he should mourn his father, Mengzi replied that three years of mourning wearing coarse clothes and eating gruel had been the practice of the three ancient dynasties (**San dai**) for everyone from the Son of Heaven to commoners. Yet when the duke told his officials that he had decided to follow the three-year mourning, they objected that none of the former rulers of Lu had practised it, nor any of their own state, and in matters of funerals and sacrifices one should follow one's ancestors (*Mengzi* 3A: 2). Mozi ridiculed having to extend the austerities of mourning to three years ('*Jie sang*'). Perhaps because of criticism of this sort, the *Book of Rites* (**Li ji**) includes a short chapter '*Sannian wen*' on the rationale of mourning for three years. It argues that the stipulated lengths do not prolong natural tendencies to grieve, but let people know when it is time to stop grieving. This text attributes to Confucius what came to be the proverbial explanation of the three-year rule: babies are carried by their parents for three years.

In later centuries imperial and private ritual manuals upheld the principle of mourning parents into the third year. Officials normally had to retire from service so that they could return home for the mourning period. Entertaining guests with wine, begetting a child, or otherwise demonstrating failure to adhere to mourning austerities would attract criticism.

Exceptions to the rule of three-year mourning were made for emperors who had to conduct auspicious rites. To keep the symbolism, however, months were converted to days, so that the mourning period lasted twenty-seven days instead of twenty-seven months. Generals leading campaigns and officials whose services were essential were also regularly exempted from the requirement to retire for the full mourning period.

Reference: de Groot, 1892–1910: vol. II: 500–3.

PATRICIA EBREY

Sanzi jing 三字經
(*Three-Character Classic*)

The *Three-Character Classic*, attributed to the great classical scholar **Wang Yinglin**, served as a first primer for children in late imperial China. Its 356 alternately rhyming lines of three characters contained some 500 different characters that encapsulated the basic cosmological and ethical principles associated with Neo-Confucianism. Memorisation of the text, therefore, schooled children not only in basic literacy but also in the rudiments of the state-sponsored worldview. The opening lines of the Classic proclaim 'Men at their birth/ Are at root good,/ Their natures are much the same./ Though by habit they grow distant./ If foolishly not taught,/ The nature then will change./ The way of moral teaching/ Is to value using single-mindedness.' The text then likens the untaught child to unpolished jade; the substance of both may be fine, but the application of sufficient care increases the worth of the substance. The sanctity of family relations and the orderliness of the universe are stressed in succeeding lines. The student is advised to master the Four Books (**Si shu**) before learning the *Book of Filial Piety* (**Xiao jing**), the Five Classics (**Wu jing**), and the orthodox succession of dynasties. Youthful prodigies of diligent learning are then celebrated before the final warning is given to 'Be on your guard/ Suitably exert effort.'

Countless editions of the *Sanzi jing* were published before the Republican era. So influential was the text considered that the Chinese Communist Party in 1994 decided to publish its own *New* (*Xin*) *Three-Character Classic*, designed to glorify the leadership of the party and the greatness of the Han majority culture.

References: Giles, Herbert, 1910; Rawski, 1979; *Xin Sanzijing*, 1995.

MICHAEL NYLAN

Satô Issai 佐藤一齋
1772–1859
(*azana* 字: 大道)

Satô Issai was born in Edo as the eldest surviving son in a family which had served the lord of Iwamura 岩村 domain, in Mino 美農 province, as Confucian advisers for three generations. His father had studied for a period under Hattori Nankaku, a disciple of **Ogyû Sorai**, and had played an important part in the government of his domain for over thirty years. In his childhood Issai became close friends with the third son of the Iwamura daimyo Matsudaira Norimori 松平乘蘊, a boy named Taira 衡 who was four years his senior. In 1790, Issai officially entered Norimori's personal retinue. In 1792, he went to Osaka, where he was able to study for a while under the great Kaitokudô scholar Nakai Chikuzan. In 1793 both he and Taira began studying under Hayashi Kanjun 林簡順, head of the Hayashi college (Shôheikô 昌平黌), but before long Kanjun died without an heir, prompting Sadanobu to order that Taira be adopted into the Hayashi family as heir to Kanjun's position. Taira, henceforth known as Hayashi Jussai 林述齋, then formally took Satô Issai as a disciple. In 1800, Issai was invited by the lord of Hirado 平戸 to Nagasaki, where he was able to meet with visiting scholars from Qing China. In 1805 he became professorial head (*jukuchô* 塾長) of the Shôheikô, which had been converted into the official school for training bakufu officials in 1790. Under his and Hayashi Jussai's leadership, the college came to flourish as never before, attracting superior students from various domains

all over Japan. Although the Shôheikô was supposed to be the bastion of Zhu Xi Learning (**Shushigaku**), especially after the Kansei Prohibition of Heterodoxy (1790), Issai had early on developed a strong personal attraction to Wang Yangming Learning (**Yômeigaku**). Thus it was commonly said that Issai followed 'Shushigaku on the surface, but Yômeigaku underneath' (*yôshu in'ô* 陽朱陰王), though in Issai's case this was not a matter of insincerity but more a matter of a distinction between his public functions and his private beliefs. Issai began to attract major disciples from the age of fifty (1821), and those who became his students between 1830 and 1836 include many of the major scholars of the bakumatsu period: Yoshimura Shûyô 吉村秋陽 (Yômeigaku), **Sakuma Shôzan** (principally Shushigaku), Ôhashi Totsuan 大橋訥庵 (Shushigaku after a period of Yômeigaku), Yamada Hôkoku 山田方谷, Takemura Kaisai 竹村悔齋, Ikeda Sôan 池田草庵 (all Yômeigaku followers), and **Yokoi Shônan**. At the age of seventy, Issai built a retreat near his daimyo's residence and thought of retiring from active service. Later in the same year, he was deeply grieved by the death of Hayashi Jussai and the prison suicide of his disciple, the artist Watanabe Kazan 渡邊華山. Nevertheless, toward the end of the year he was formally appointed a professor of the Shôheikô, which required him to move into an official residence at the college. Here he continued to guide students, give lectures, meet dignitaries, write diplomatic documents and give policy advice to the government until his death.

The most famous of Issai's many works are his four collections of guidelines for life, called the four *Genshiroku* 言志錄, or 'Articulating One's Resolve'. A sampling of these maxims follows.

From *Genshiroku* (age 42): 2. The highest thing is to take Heaven as your teacher. The next is to take a person as your teacher. The next is to take the Classics as your teacher; 6. In learning there is nothing more important than establishing one's resolution (*kokorozashi* 志). However, establishing the resolution is not a matter of forcing oneself. It is just a matter of following what the original mind likes; 18. Whenever things go really well for you, it is only because you have grasped the natural flow of things. There is nothing wonderful beyond that; 20. If one's spirit is all in the face, one cannot avoid chasing after things and acting indiscriminately. Only when one draws in the spirit and makes it dwell in the back is it possible to forget the body. And only then is one really the possessor of one's body (see *Book of Changes*, hexagram 52); 22. Miscellaneous idle thoughts arise helter skelter in the mind because of the disturbances caused by external things. If you constantly use your resolution like a sword to drive out all outside distractions, not allowing them to get inside of you, then your mind will naturally feel clean and clear; 27. A person who truly has a great aspiration is able to be diligent in little things. A person who is truly farsighted does not neglect the little matters; 43. There are many people who regret yesterday's wrongs, but not many who correct today's mistakes; 44. The times when things go as one wishes are the times it is most important to work on stepping back. At all times and in all affairs, there is always the danger that the dragon has climbed too high [See hexagram 1, nine at the top].

From *Genshikôroku* 言志後録 (age sixty): 1. This learning is our lifetime burden. We cannot stop until the day we die. As a matter of course the Way has no ending. 'There is unlimited goodness even beyond Yao and Shun' (**Chuanxi lu**, A22). From the time he set his mind on learning until he was seventy, every ten years Confucius felt that he had made some progress. So he kept up his effort untiringly, unaware that old age was creeping up on him (*Analects* 7: 18). If he had continued past eighty and ninety and reached a hundred, then just imagine how spiritually illuminated and unfathomable he would have been! All those who study Confucius should take Confucius' resolution as their own; 5. All

teachings enter from the outside. Moral effort comes from within. What comes from within must be tested on the outside. What enters from the outside must be reconnected to its roots within. 6. We must know how to value ourselves. Our nature is something exalted received from Heaven, and it should be regarded as the most precious thing. Our body is the continuation of our mother and father, and it must not be treated with disrespect. Our external bearing is what people look up to, and our words are what people place their trust upon. Can we afford not to take them seriously? 16. Some people say that external things are a burden. I say that all things are of one body with myself. There is no need for them to be a burden. It is me who makes them into a burden.

From *Genshi tetsuroku* 言志耄録 (age eighty): 21. The word 'repentance' lies at the crossroads of good and evil. The superior person (*kunshi* 君子) repents and thereby moves himself toward the good, but the petty person repents and thereby completes his evil. Therefore one should take charge of one's repentance by establishing a resolution. Only then can one overcome the vice of vascillation; 27. Though the student needs a great resolution, his efforts should all be small. In affairs, what is small is the beginning. In things, what is small is the subtle sign of what is coming. This is what the *Book of Changes* means by the statement, '"Return" means to discriminate things when they are small.' (See hexagram 24, *Xici* commentary B.)

BARRY D. STEBEN

Satô Nobuhiro 佐藤信淵
1769–1850
(*azana*: Genkai 元海, 椿園, 融齋, 松庵, *tsûshô*: Hyakuyû 百佑)

Satô Nobuhiro was born in Ugo 羽後 province (in modern Akita prefecture) as the son of a scholar of agricultural administration.

At the age of thirteen he travelled around Japan with his father. When his father died some three years later, Nobuhiro followed the instructions in his will and went to Edo to further his education. Here he studied Dutch learning, herbology, Confucianism, astronomy and geography under different teachers, later taking up Shinto studies in the Yoshikawa lineage and *Kokugaku* studies under Hirata Atsutane 平田篤胤. In time he became a prolific writer with his own original ideas of political economy that drew on all of these schools as well as the writings of Dazai Shundai, Hayashi Shihei (an explorer of Hokkaidô who was imprisoned for his strong advocacy of strengthening coastal defence), and Honda Toshiaki (a scholar of astronomy and navigation who advocated foreign trade, colonisation, and the development of Hokkaidô). Nobuhiro's thought reached maturity in the Bunsei period (1818–1830), when he published *Keizai yôryaku* 經濟要略 (An Outline of Economics), *Keizai yôroku* 經濟要錄 (The Essentials of Economics), and *Nôsei honron* 農政本論 (The Fundamental Theory of Agricultural Administration). After becoming Atsutane's disciple, he wrote two works articulating a theory of productive economic power based in agriculture and good agricultural administration and rooted in 'the will of the local fertility gods (*ubusuna no shin'i* 産土の神意),' culminating in the idea of increasing the national wealth in order to bestow an economically and militarily strong state (*fukoku kyôhei* 富國強兵) on succeeding generations. In 1838 he published *Bukka yoron* (A supplementary theory of prices), and in 1845 *Fukkohô gaigen* (An overview of the method of restoring antiquity). In these works, under the influence of ancient Chinese Classics of political economy like *Guanzi* 管子, he developed a thoroughgoing theory of the regulation of commerce aimed at showing a way out of the country's political and economic predicament, emphasising the necessity of trade and its management by the government.

However, because of the downfall of his patron, Mizuno Tadakuni 水野忠邦 (initiator of the Tenpô 天保 reforms in 1841), his programme was not put into practice. He had been banished from Edo from 1832 until 1843, when his works began to draw much attention among bakufu officials because as a result of the Opium War (1841–42). In his later years he advocated the occupation of Sakhalin and the naturalisation of its Tartar inhabitants as a base for invading Chinese territory. In a work of 1857, *Suitô hiroku* 垂統秘錄 (A secret document on bestowing an enhanced patrimony to posterity), he put forth a kind of state socialist vision of a unified, absolutist Japanese state with three executive advisory offices (*dai* 台) and six ministries (*fu* 府), with the population divided into eight professions. However, he did not state specifically whether the shogun or the emperor was to be the centre of the exercise of political power, merely mentioning a ruler whose sovereignty is based on 'the will of the gods.' Because of the way Satô's thought anticipates the image of the Meiji state and its preoccupation with *fukoku kyôhei*, he has received a great deal of attention in modern Japan.

Further reading: Masuda Wataru. *Japan and China: Mutual Representations in the Modern Era.* Trans. Joshua Fogel. Richmond, Surrey: Curzon Press, 2000, pp. 60–7.

BARRY D. STEBEN

School regulations (Xue gui 學規)

Written school regulations perhaps began to appear in the Tang times, if not earlier. The first set of government-issued school regulations that is still extant is that of the Prefectural Elementary School of Jingzhao that was engraved on stone in 1054. Reformers in the late Song issued many school regulations, and this caused strong reaction. When **Zhu Xi** wrote his famous 'Open

Exhortation to the White Deer Hollow Academy' he openly criticised the government-issued school regulations and pointedly called his regulations 'exhortations'. The work is a quintessential Neo-Confucian document on the ideal and behavioural norms of a moral life. Citing famous dicta from the Confucian tradition, and supplemented with Zhu Xi's brief comments, it became the archetype of Chinese schools regulations. Some of the other famous school regulations are such as **Lü Zuqian**'s 'Regulations and Agreements', the 'Norms for Learning' by **Cheng Duanmeng**. All of them take a positive approach by citing classical and Neo-Confucian axioms of behaviour to encourage moral commitment for learning.

By the late Song and Yuan times, practically all academies (**shu yuan**) adopted Zhu Xi's 'Open Exhortation' or had their own school regulations. Zhu Yuanzhang (r. 1368–1398), the founder of the Ming, made some important additions to the movement by personally composing school regulations for the nation's highest educational institution, the **Guozi jian** (also known as **Tai xue**). The regulations he issued in different times were very detailed, and prohibitive and punitive in nature, in drastic contrast to those found in the academies which were characteristically normative. The core prohibition was against student criticism of government politics. This set of authoritarian regulations were throughout Ming and Qing times prominently displayed in all government schools and are famously known as the 'horizontal tablets' (**wo bei** 臥碑). They became an unfortunate caricature to the Neo-Confucian ideal of school regulations.

Most academies continued to issue their own school regulations, and in them one could find the different emphases of various strands of Confucian thought throughout the Ming and Qing times. Practically all the great Neo-Confucian thinkers, ranging from **Chen Xianzhang** to **Wang Shouren** to

Gu Xiancheng all composed one or two school regulations.

The movement of school regulations was closely related to the development of academies. As academies became widespread and important in education, the need for a different set of detailed regulations governing school management emerged. These regulations were often called 'chapters and procedures' (*zhang cheng* 章程) and existed side by side with Neo-Confucian school regulations. The end of the academies in the early twentieth century marked also the end of composing school regulations. Western school mottoes replaced school regulations, although the new mottoes often continued to reflect traditional Confucian concerns. In Republican China, the first four words of Zhu Yuanzhang's famous 'decorum, rightness, incorruptibility, shamefulness, filial piety, brotherly love, loyalty and faithfulness' were adopted as the universal school motto for all schools in China. The *locus classicus* of the four words is *Guanzi* 管子.

Reference: Lee, Thomas, 2000: 594–607, 623–35.

THOMAS H.C. LEE

School rites

Rite (**li**) is central to Confucius' educational thinking and remained throughout Chinese history an essential component of daily life, including that in the schools. It is in the correct and sincere enactment of rites that humaneness (**ren**), the ultimate goal of Confucian education, is completed. Confucius considered the acquisition of the six aristocratic arts as fundamental to the education of a gentleman, and in giving moral and ethical significance to the Six Arts (**liu yi**), Confucius interprets the idea of rite as accomplishing harmonious resonance and interaction between the human and his/her environment, as well as nature.

It is therefore in the punctilious performance that one understands the truth of
perfect society and knows how to accomplish
it. It is believed that the rites canons had
included a chapter devoted to 'school rites'.

The schools as the primary vehicle for
education should naturally be a centre for
rites education and performance, even
though early Han thinkers who were
among the earliest to articulate on the various types of rites did not treat school rites
as an independent category. Most school rites
came into maturity really only in the Later
Han (25–220 CE). The building of a shrine
for Confucius and the awarding of an
honorific posthumous name went back relatively early, perhaps even before the Han
was founded, but the earliest record showing that the Imperial Academy (*Tai xue*) held
the sacrificial rite to Confucius, as a part of
xiang yinjiu (village libation) and archery contest rite is that of 59 CE. Still, the fact that
the Imperial Academy was placed under
the Chamberlain of Ceremonials (*taichang*
太常) reflects the Han thinking that rites
were central to higher education. Han
works include detailed records of rites
marking the occasions of imperial visits to
the Academy, venerating the elders (often
associated with *xiang yinjiu*), presentation
of vegetables (*shi cai*), and venerating sages
(*shi dian*). It was **Wang Mang**, a usurper of
the Han, who paid the greatest attention
to schol rites; he built the Illustrious Hall
(*Ming tang*) and Spiritual Platform (*Ling
tai* 靈臺) for ritual purposes in the premise
of the Imperial Academy.

On the local level, building shrines for
sages (Duke of Zhou (**Zhou Gong**) in this
time), and giving the performance of venerating the sages had been in existence
from the early Han. By the end of the Han,
most of the rites that were performed in
or for schools had largely taken shape:
imperial visits, *shi dian*, *shi cai*, and *xiang
yinjiu*.

The building of a Confucian shrine in the
Imperial Academy dates only to 385 (and as
late as 630 for local schools), and the inclusion of other sages into the Confucian pantheon seems to have started even later, in
the late sixth century. The timely sacrifice
to them was the occasion for performance
of school rites, or vice versa.

The famous *Kaiyuan Rites of the Great
Tang* (*Da Tang Kaiyuan li*) recognises three
school rites: veneration of sages, veneration
of elders and the village libation ceremony.
In actuality, the veneration of elders' ceremonies often were held together with
village libation rites, while the veneration
of vegetable ceremony was regularly, but
independently, performed. Emperors or
crown princes often visited the Imperial
Academy (or Directorate of Education) on
the occasion of the venerating sage ceremonies. Theoretically speaking, these rites
were also held in local schools.

It is useful to refer to the ceremonies in
relation to the civil service examinations
which had risen in importance since the
Tang times. Clearly, candidates were often
expected to perform rites related to
education. Thus, the banquet given by the
emperor in honour of the new recruits
often was also the occasion for holding
village libation rites. The latter was to become standard after 1113, when Emperor
Huizung (r. 1100–1125) of the Song ordered
the discontinuation of congratulatory banquets in its favour.

Emperor Huizong's decision was in
line with the Confucian revival at the time.
The sacrifices paid to Confucius were
greatly elevated and the semi-annual *shi
dian* and the less frequent *shi cai* rites (only
revived in the early twelfth century) were
held with greater attention: there were
clerks in charge of such ceremonies in
local schools. On the other hand, imperial
visits to the Academy became less frequent. One record shows that the most
respected of the Song emperors by the
Confucian scholars, Lizong (r. 1225–1264),
made only three visits. Finally, whether
Wang Anshi (1021–1086) and his son,
Wang Pang 王雱 (1042–1076), should
enter the Confucian pantheon became a

controversial issue through the Southern Song, reflecting the increasingly politicised nature of school rites.

Zhu Yuanzhang 朱元璋 (r. 1368–1398), the founder of the Ming, sought to use school rites for the purpose of political control. He reaffirmed the local significance of the *xiangyinjiu* ceremony; he apparently also saw a greater significance in the *shi cai* than *shi dian* ceremony, because the former was less elaborate, and ordered its performance in all localities. This was in violation of *shi cai*'s school rite nature. But the decision reflected his concern for local control. Nonetheless, it was the *shi dian* rite that was eventually observed on regular basis, though void of true seriousness, throughout the Ming and the subsequent Qing, whereas the *shi cai* rite fell into oblivion and was actually discontinued after 1595.

The school rites had all but demised after the eighteenth century. The great Confucian tradition in ritual performance had outlived its usefulness by this time, and rites became not more than rituals. Catholic missionaries of the seventeenth and eighteenth centuries were evidently not impressed by school rites then staged in local schools.

References: Li Zhizao, 1970; Pang Zhonglu, 1988.

THOMAS H.C. LEE

Schwartz, Benjamin
1916–

Schwartz is one of the most authoritative western scholars of Chinese intellectual history in the second half of the twentieth century. His early scholarship focused on the Communist thought of Mao Zedong (1893–1976) as well as the translations of western ideas offered by **Yan Fu**. In his later monumental study, *The World of Thought in Ancient China*, Schwartz developed one of the most rigorously historical, yet philosophically sensitive, accounts of the life, thought and significance of Confucius and **Mengzi**, casting them as private teachers active in an age of exceptional intellectual activity, one characterised by concern over sociopolitical and religious decay.

JOHN A. TUCKER

Se 色
(Countenance, sensual beauty)

For Confucian writers, *se* has two distinct meanings. Firstly, *se* means one's facial countenance. It is of tremendous importance because if one acts sincerely, one's facial expression will reflect his or her innermost feelings and put them on public display. According to the *Analects*, when Confucius 'passed by [his lord's] place, his countenance (*se*) became serious, his steps became timid, and his words appeared to be insufficient' (10: 3). Nowhere is one's countenance (*se*) more important than in the performance of filial rituals. When asked about filial piety (**xiao**), Confucius replied, 'One's countenance (*se*) is what is difficult' (2: 8). That is because in serving parents one must always have a pleasing countenance, which means one must be inwardly happy, even if one is anxious about their health or disagrees with their orders.

Se also means sensual beauty, which arouses lust. Although Confucius and Mengzi did not view this craving as bad in itself, it could lead men astray from pursuing self-cultivation. Confucius twice opined that, 'I have never seen anyone whose fondness of virtue matched his fondness for sensual beauty' (*Analects*, 9: 18, 15: 13). Although **Xunzi** viewed a liking for beauty as natural, he believed that it led man to his ruin. He said, 'When one is born, his eyes and ears then have desires. One thus has a fondness for music and sensual beauty. If one follows these [desires], licentious and disorderly conduct will appear, and ritual duties and cultural principles will be lost' (*Xunzi*, 23: 1).

References: Hung, ed., 1972a; Lau and Chen Fong Ching, eds., 1996a.

KEITH KNAPP

Setchûgakuha 折衷學派
(The Eclectics)

The term 'Setchûgakuha' is used to group together a number of scholars of the mid Edo period who put forth various different doctrines based on a mixture of the teachings of the various schools of Confucianism, drawing from Han and Tang period commentaries as well as from Song and Ming Neo-Confucianism. Of the ten most prominent Confucian scholars of the second half of the eighteenth century, as many as eight or nine are classified as Eclectics. **Inoue Kinga** and **Katayama Kenzan** are regarded as the principal founders of the 'school'. Other major scholars normally classified as Eclectics include Hosoi Heishû (1728–1801), Nakai Riken (1732–1817), Tsukada Taihô (1745–1832), Yamamoto Hokuzan (1752–1812), Kameda Hosai (1752–1826), Inukai Keisho (1761–1845), and Hirose Tansô (1782–1856). While the Eclectics inherited the philological methodology of the Ancient Learning scholars, particularly **Ogyû Sorai**, they criticised Sorai's theories, redefining the 'Way of the Sages' from Sorai's objective and political emphasis on national administration and popular relief (*keisei saimin*) to the ethical learning and moral edification that formed the original core of Confucianism. They also rejected Sorai's theory that the Way had been invented by the sages, reviving the continuity between nature and morality that had been the hallmark of Zhu Xi Learning. In spite of their similarities with Zhu Xi learning, however, it was apparently their emphasis on freedom and inner realisation that led the teachings of the Eclectics to be prohibited at the bakufu college in the Kansei Prohibition of Heterodoxy of 1790, along with the Sorai school, the teachings of **Itô Jinsai**, Wang Yangming Learning (see **Wang Shouren**), and the 'poeticists and novelists' (much influenced by Sorai). Yet there were quite a few Eclectic scholars who, like Hosoi Heishû 細井平洲 (1728–1801), were very active in establishing new schools as part of their domain's reform programmes. While Eclectic learning declined after the prohibition, it philological methodology was inherited by the school of positivist learning (*kôshô gakuha* 考證學派), and their high regard for Han and Tang commentaries had much influence on nineteenth-century Confucian scholarship.

Source: Kinugasa Yasuki, 'Setchûgakuha', in *Heibonsha daihyakka jiten* (Tokyo: Heibonsha, 1985), vol. VIII, p. 600.

BARRY D. STEBEN

Shan 善
(Good, goodness, to be good at something)

Much attention has been given to the concept of *shan* as 'good' in juxtaposition to *e*, or 'evil', particularly regarding **Mengzi**'s and **Xunzi**'s discussions of human nature. In early texts, however, 'good' is more commonly contrasted simply with what is 'not good' (*bu shan* 不善), and its usages are not at all limited to discussions of human nature. In the **Shang shu**, for example, good is contrasted with what is wanton or transgressive (*yin* 淫) or faulty or excessive (*zui* 罪); good is what is well ordered (*zhi* 治) as opposed to what is disordered (*luan* 亂). In the *Shang shu*, 'good' usually refers to what one does rather than what one is. Doing good (*zuo shan* 作善) invokes the attentions of Heaven, which sends down blessings while visiting calamities upon those who are wanton, such as kings who take leave of virtue (*de*). Virtue and doing good are closely associated: virtue lies in focusing on what is good, and a good government is one in which virtue obtains. Moreover, 'good' can mean 'to be good at something', such as a skill – even one of dubious merits, such as crafty speech – and it can mean to keep something, such as armour, in good condition.

In the *Analects*, the term also means to be good at something, such as singing or a trade, but it more frequently refers to the crafting of human relationships or of the Way (*Dao*). People are described as being good at relationships with others, at teaching others, at reforming their own conduct, or as being good at the Way itself; good people could rule without resorting to harsh punishments. Confucius doubted, however, that he would ever meet either a sage or a truly good person, which indicates just how complex an endeavour doing good had become. The association of good with human action is continued in the *Doctrine of the Mean* (*Zhongyong*), which describes filiality as the continuation of one's ancestor's intentions and affairs (chapter 19).

Mengzi, however, focused instead on 'good' as a quality or tendency deeply imbedded within the latent potentialities of the human being. Contemporary thinkers debated whether the nature (*xing*) was good or not good, and to this discussion Mengzi contributed the notion that humans can be or do good because they have four 'minds' of compassion and commiseration, shame and disgrace, respect and reverence and right and wrong, asserting that the fluid tendency of human nature to do good was like water's natural inclination to flow downward.

Mengzi's notion of good was not juxtaposed to evil, but simply to what was not good, and it was only in the 'Human nature as Evil' (*Xing e pian* 性惡篇) chapter of the *Xunzi* that this concept of negativity entered the discussion. This chapter, constructed as a diatribe against Mengzi, posits that the less negative aspects of the human condition are the result of conscious activity rather than any inherent tendency. Some later interpretations of the writings of Mengzi and Xunzi reduced these thinkers' views of human nature to a polarity between good and evil, giving less attention to the many subtleties of their arguments or to other chapters of the *Xunzi* that develop

markedly different notions of the inherent qualities of the human being.

References: Ames & Rosemont, 1998: 5: 17, 7: 3, 7: 26, 7: 32, 8: 13, 9: 11, 11: 20, 13: 11, 15: 10, and pp. 57–8; Knoblock, 1988–94: vol. III: 139–62; Lau, 1984: 6A: 2, 6A: 6; Legge, 1985c: 55, 186, 198, 217, 622, 628, 634; Shun, 1997a: 210–31.

DEBORAH SOMMER

Shan ren 善人
(Truly good person)

The *Shan ren* is a person of virtuous behaviour who through his or her actions exemplifies humaneness (*ren*) and righteousness (*yi*). One can also associate the political position held by the men of quality (*junzi*) with the ethical character of the *shan ren* – the latter being essential for the former. In *Lunyu* 13: 11 the following is asserted: 'How true is the saying that after a state has been ruled for a hundred years by good men (*shan ren*) it is possible to get the better of cruelty and to do away with killing.' Clearly this is not an ordinary definition of goodness; it is an immensely rigorous philosophical and ethical category, one which cannot readily be found even in the most earnest of scholars. Thus Confucius says in the *Analects* 7: 26: 'I have no hopes of meeting a truly good person. I would be content if I met someone who has constancy (*heng* 恆) . . .'

Reference: Lau, 1979.

TODD CAMERON THACKER

Shang Di 上帝
(Lord on High)

In early received texts such as the *Book of Poetry* (*Shi jing*) and the *Book of Documents* (*Shang shu*), the Lord (Di) on High (Shang) was one of the supreme (if not the supreme) numinous powers within a large pantheon of divine forces that pervaded the celestial, human and terrestrial realms. Although not a creator god, Shang Di was a mythic progenitor who impregnated mortal women who then gave birth to culture heroes. A volatile celestial authority who held dominion over meteorological and political realms, he took a keen interest in human warfare. He bestowed on all human beings a constant nature but maintained covenanted relationships with chosen high-ranking people, particularly those of strong inner power or virtue (*de*) and other efficacious moral qualities, and bestowed a mandate or charge (*ming*) upon these select few. Only the ruler could perform the sacrificial offerings that sustained communications with August Heaven and the Lord on High; the culture hero King Wen, for example, was noted for serving the Lord on High assiduously and was rewarded accordingly.

The Lord on High was often conflated, in early received texts, with Heaven (*tian*); in the writings of Warring States' scholars, the Lord on High appears in quotations from earlier works but is otherwise replaced in importance by Heaven. In the Han, the Lord on High was sometimes associated with the Great One (*Tai yi*). Scholars of the Song dynasty understood the Lord on High as a valence of substance and function (*ti yong*) or as principle (*li*), in effect stripping the Lord of his former martial vigor. Early Christian missionaries used *Shang Di* to translate the Christian God, which has now become a standard name for God in Chinese Christianity.

References: *Book of Poetry*, nos. 224, 236, 245, 258; Chan, Wing-tsit, 1989; Legge, 1985b: 185–6, 189, 286.

DEBORAH SOMMER

Shang shu 尚書
(*Book of Documents*)

The *Shang shu*, *Venerated Documents*, also known as the *Shu jing* or *Classic of Documents* or *Book of History*, is generally regarded as the second of the five Chinese Classics (*Wu jing*), a status that parts of it had already attained by no later than the beginning of the Warring States period (475–221 BCE) and which was officially recognised with the establishment of the Imperial Academy in 135 BCE during the reign of **Han Wudi** (r. 141–87 BCE). Despite this exalted status, the text has been the locus of perhaps the most important controversy in the history of Chinese textual criticism, between so-called 'New Text' (*jinwen* 今文) and 'Old Text' (*guwen* 古文) versions of the text. The text is supposed to have included originally one hundred chapters, selected by Confucius from among all government documents available at his time; titles of these chapters are preserved in the 'Preface to the *Documents*' (*Shu xu* 書序), which however is itself part of the 'Old Text' tradition. Many of these chapters have long been lost. The 'New Text' edition of the text, the establishment of which is credited to one **Fu Sheng** during the reign of Han Wendi (r. 179–157 BCE), includes only twenty-eight or twenty-nine documents (the '*Tai shi*' 泰誓 is a 'New Text' document, but has a different provenance from that of the other twenty-eight documents, and is therefore usually differentiated from them). The 'Old Text' edition is supposed to have been discovered during the renovation of Confucius' ancestral home in Qufu 曲阜 (Shandong) and is said to have been presented at the court of Han Wudi by a descendant of Confucius named **Kong Anguo**; this edition consists of forty-five documents divided into fifty-eight chapters. A scholarly consensus of the last two centuries or so holds that the Old Text tradition, and especially those chapters unique to it, was spuriously created early in the fourth century of the common era. While new evidence may require some revision of this consensus, it seems unlikely that the Old Text tradition *in toto* represents an authentic, independent tradition.

The *Shang shu* is divided into four major sections: the *Yu shu* 虞書 or *Documents of Yu*, five chapters in the Old Text tradition and two chapters in the New Text tradition that purport to derive from the time of Yao and Shun (see **Yao Shun**), now generally regarded as a legendary period; the *Xia shu* 夏書 or *Documents of the Xia* (dynasty), four Old Text chapters and two New Text chapters; the *Shang shu* 商書 or *Documents of the Shang* (dynasty), seventeen Old Text chapters and five New Text chapters; and the *Zhou shu* 周書 or *Documents of the Zhou* (dynasty), thirty-two Old Text chapters and nineteen or twenty New Text chapters. The documents are also generically divided into five different types: Consultations (*mo* 謨), dialogues between kings and their ministers; Instructions (*xun* 訓), advice given by ministers to kings; Announcements (*gao* 誥), pronouncements made by kings to the people at large; Declarations (*shi* 誓), battlefield speeches made by kings; and Commands (*ming*), statements of investiture made by a king to a single individual.

It is important to note that even those chapters accepted by both the 'New Text' and 'Old Text' traditions may have been composed well after the events that they purport to record, so that it is often necessary to pay even greater attention than usual to the language in which the document is written. In general, the texts of the *Yu shu, Xia shu* and *Shang shu* were probably composed for the most part during the fifth and fourth centuries BCE, though the '*Pan Geng*' 盤庚 chapter of the *Shang shu* is often accepted as actually dating to the reign of the Shang king Pan Geng (r. *c.* 1250 BCE) and probably was written earlier than the other chapters of the *Shang shu*, even if not so early as the Shang dynasty itself. It is the chapters of the *Zhou shu*, however, that have usually been regarded as the most important texts of the *Shang shu*, and it is with them that one finds the greatest disagreement regarding date of composition. Most historians regard the five *gao* (Announcement) chapters of the *Zhou shu* (i.e., 'Da gao' 大誥 Great announcement, '*Kang gao*' 康誥 Announcement to Kang (Hou), '*Jiu gao* 酒誥 Announcement regarding wine, '*Shao gao*' 召誥 Announcement of Shao (Gong) and '*Luo gao*' 洛誥 Announcement at Luo) as being authentic documents of the early Western Zhou dynasty, with their authorship attributed variously to King Wu (r. *c.* 1049–1043 BCE), King Cheng (r. *c.* 1042–1006 BCE) or Zhou Gong (d. *c.* 1032 BCE). Opinions regarding the other chapters traditionally assumed to have been composed at the beginning of the Western Zhou are mixed, though there is some consensus, at least in the West, that two of the most important of these in later historiography, the '*Hong fan*' 洪範 (Expansive plan) and '*Jin teng*' 金滕 (Metal coffer), actually date to the late Spring and Autumn or early Warring States period. The last chapters of the *Zhou shu*, the '*Wen Hou zhi ming*' 文候之命 (Command to Wen Hou), '*Fei shi*' 費誓 (Declaration at Fei [also read *Bi*]) and '*Qin shi*' 秦誓 (Declaration of Qin [Gong]), doubtless are authentic documents from the early Eastern Zhou period, as they purport to be.

As might be expected for a work of such importance and disputed authenticity, the *Shang shu* has a rich commentarial tradition. Two commentaries in particular warrant mention in any discussion of the *Shang shu*. The earliest commentary is the **Shang shu da zhuan** attributed to **Fu Sheng** of the second century BCE, though it now exists only in fragments. The *Shang shu zhuan* 尚書傳 or *Kong zhuan* 孔傳 (*Kong's tradition*) is still extant; though it was traditionally attributed to **Kong Anguo**, also of the second century BCE, and was subsequently selected by the **Wu jing zhengyi** project of the Tang dynasty as the standard commentary of the *Shang shu*, many scholars now regard it as a forgery of the fourth century CE.

References: Karlgren, 1950; Legge, 1985c: vol. III; Liu, 1989; Loewe, 1993: 376–89.

EDWARD L. SHAUGHNESSY

Shang shu dazhuan 尚書大傳

(Great Tradition of the Venerated Documents)

The *Shang shu dazhuan* is attributed to **Fu Sheng**, the figure who is also credited with preserving the 'new text' (*jinwen* 今文) version of the *Shang shu* at the time of the Qin dynasty (221–206 BCE) proscription of ancient texts. The work, which survives today only in fragments reconstituted from quotations in medieval sources, contains important information about the twenty-eight *Shang shu* chapters that Fu Sheng transmitted and also about early Han views of ancient history. Whether actually written by Fu Sheng himself, or by his students, the book was certainly in existence in the second century BCE since it seems to have been consulted by **Sima Qian**. The work is cited in the bibliographic monographs of the dynastic histories through the Tang dynasty (618–907), including the mention that **Zheng Xuan** wrote a commentary on it, but by the Song dynasty (960–1279) it seems no longer to have been extant. Reconstituted in the Qing dynasty (1644–1911), the best text is still *Shang shu da zhuan jijiao* 尚書大傳輯教 edited by Chen Shouqi 陳壽祺 (1771–1834).

EDWARD L. SHAUGHNESSY

Shao Bowen 邵伯溫
1057–1134
(*zi* Ziwen 子文)

Shao Bowen was the elder son of famous philosopher **Shao Yong** and he is customarily regarded as a faithful guardian of his father's thought. Shao Bowen was awarded the *jinshi* degree in 1087 but received it on the increasingly rare basis of recommendation rather than by passing the civil service examinations. He thereupon began service as an assistant instructor (*zhu jiao* 助教) in Confucianism and thereafter, over the course of a long bureaucratic career, held a succession of largely provincial posts. At the daily feasts held by the emperor Huizong (r. 1100–1125) to solicit opinion upon his accession, Shao Bowen incurred the resentment of many officials less idealistic than he himself was. He persistently called

for a recommitment to the principles by which the dynastic founder Taizu (r. 960–976) had ruled, the cessation of the vendettas spawned by factionalism and certain social reforms – such as a moratorium on the military conscription of indigent peasants. For his efforts, Shao was transferred to a remote provincial assignment in which he oversaw drainage canals and the construction of other public work projects. During the incursions made into North China by the Jurchen 女真 tribes of the Jin dynasty (1115–1234) in 1126–1127, Shao Bowen lived in the western provinces in relative safety. Upon his death, Shao's own disciple Zhao Ding 趙鼎 (1085–1147; *zi* Yuanzhen 元鎮 *shi* Zhongjian 忠簡), acting as Grand Counsellor (*cheng xiang* 丞相), ordered the conferral of posthumous honours upon his master.

Shao Bowen authored numerous works, several of which are now lost. Of those that survive, we can basically divide them into three types – those specifically and directly bearing on and amplifying the teachings of his famous father Shao Yong, those bearing no overt connection to his father's thought, and those that constitute a mixture of the first two classifications. This last category – although it essentially consists of only two extant works – is really the most revealing in terms of the information conveyed about Shao Bowen's intellectual relationship and indebtedness to his father. The *Yixue Bianhuo* 易學辨惑 (*Clarifying Confusing Elements in the Learning of the Book of Changes*) purports to correct the errors and distortions in Shao Yong's thought perpetrated by Zheng Shi 鄭史 (*fl.* 1060; *zi* Yangting 揚庭), a self-professed disciple. This defence of Shao Yong's approach to the *Yi jing* by his son helps to illuminate an otherwise imperfectly understood dimension of the older man's philosophy. Shao Bowen's *Henan Shaoshi Wenjian Qianlu* 河南邵氏聞見前錄 (*Former Record of Things Heard and Seen by Mr Shao of Henan*) is an informal history of the Song dynasty (960–1279) up until his time. However, more than a fifth of the book – including the last four of its twenty *juan* or chapters – consists almost exclusively of detailed recollections and anecdotes concerning the life and social interactions of Shao Yong. Shao Bowen's intellectual importance is finally underscored by the fact that his own circle grew to include so many of his father's original close associates, including **Sima Guang** and the brothers **Cheng Hao** and **Cheng Yi**.

References: Ching, 1976: 846–9; Jiang, 1994: 109; Wyatt, 1996: 15–7, 21, 26, 60–1, 71, 72, 82–3, 94, 119–20, 132–33, 134, 136, 143–4, 155, 159, 165, 167–8, 170–1, 173–4, 175, 176, 229–32, 233, 252n. 12, 293n. 51, 303n. 10, 307n. 58, n. 61; Wyatt, 1999.

DON J. WYATT

Shao Yichen 邵懿辰
1810–1861
(*zi* Wei Xi 位西)

Born in Hangzhou, Shao Yichen was a successful candidate of Zhejiang provincial-level examination (1831), and served for a long time at various positions of the central government of the Qing dynasty (1644–1911). He was an upright man and was at odds with some of his superiors, so he resigned from the government and returned home. He died in a battle of the Taiping uprising in 1861. His philosophical ideas stemmed from **Zhu Xi**, while his study of the Confucian Classics followed **Li Guangdi**, and his literary studies followed **Fang Bao**, although he did not subscribe to the Han Learning (*Han xue* 漢學). He believed that the aim of classical study was to clarify the great meaning of the world, but he also paid very close attention to textual research. He admired the Confucian studies presented by the masters of the Song dynasty (960–1279) because they engaged in much more textual research and understood Confucius and **Mengzi** better than the scholars of the Han (206 BCE–220 CE), which he criticised as superficial. Shao

insisted in his book on *Music* (*yue* 樂) that there was no original classic work on music such as the **Yue jing**. Actually, music came from poetry (*shi*), and was used as a rite (*li*). He argued in his *A General Discourse on the Classics of Rites* (*Li jing tonglun* 禮經通論) that the **Yi li** totalling seventeen volumes was complete, with no omissions. He expressed his ideas about national administration in his *You xing lu* 憂行錄. His other books include *Shang shu tongyi* 尚書通義, *Xiao jing tonglun* 孝經通論, and *Wei Xi yigao* 位西遺稿.

Reference: Wu & Song, 1992.

OUYANG KANG

Shao Yong 邵雍
1011–1077
(*zi* Yaofu 堯夫, *hao* Baiyuan Xiansheng 百源先生, Anle Xiansheng 安樂先生)

Shao Yong was born into a family of humble scholars that had resided in Fanyang 范陽 (southwest of modern Beijing) for many generations. However, the northern upheaval caused by the incursions of the Qidan 契丹 Liao dynasty (947–1125) forced the Shaos into numerous peregrinations until Shao Yong's father Shao Gu 邵古 (986–1064; *zi* Tiansou 天叟, *hao* Yichuan Zhangren 伊川丈人) eventually settled the family in Gongcheng 共城 in Weizhou 衛州 (in modern Hui 輝 county, Henan 河南). Shao Yong followed in the footsteps of his father Shao Gu and grandfather Shao Dexin 邵德新 (d. 996), both of whom had led learned but reclusive lives. Thus, like **Zhou Dunyi** – with whom he is often linked intellectually but not acquainted – Shao Yong never sat for the **civil service examinations**. But unlike Zhou, who, by availing himself of the hereditary 'shadow' or *yin* 蔭 privilege, went on to a successful bureaucratic career, Shao Yong refused to even once serve in office, despite receiving at least two imperial summonses (in 1061 and in 1069) to do so.

Shao Yong moved permanently to Luoyang in 1049. As a result of his blossoming friendship with Cheng Xiang 程珦 (1006–1090; *zi* Bowen 伯溫) by the mid-1050s, Shao Yong briefly served as instructor to the elder man's sons **Cheng Hao** and **Cheng Yi**. Nevertheless, despite this and other eminent connections, Shao Yong lived in relative obscurity for twenty years – from the time of his arrival in Luoyang until 1069. In that pivotal year, **Wang Anshi** began to install his programme of New Policies (*xinfa* 新法) and the programme's detractors were increasingly impelled to resign from their offices. Luoyang became the most-favoured refuge for many of these disaffected bureaucrats and, as that city's most venerable savant, Shao Yong emerged with increasing prominence as a sagely counsel to the growing corps of conservative anti-Wang resistance that amassed there. In this way, Shao Yong's personal history intersected with that of the Song dynasty (960–1279).

In late life, Shao Yong's closest associates included **Sima Guang**, Cheng Hao, and Lü Gongzhu 呂公著 (1018–89; *zi* Huishu 晦叔). For nearly a decade, Shao, who – apart from teaching – remained unemployed to the end, was the beneficiary of their largess. This influential coterie had for years provided him not only with social engagement but also with many material necessities – including even his home, which he referred to as his 'nest of peace and happiness' (*anle wo* 安樂窩). Shao Yong, for his part, had purportedly imparted much of his wisdom to its members. Thus, understandably, at the time of his death in the summer of 1077, Shao Yong was attended not only by his son **Shao Bowen** but also by such cultural luminaries as Sima Guang, Cheng Yi and **Zhang Zai**.

Thought and works

Although he occupies an unassailable and indispensable position in the evolution of the **Dao xue** (Learning of the Way) lineage, Shao Yong is equally notable for the ways in which he stood apart from his peers. His contrasting lifestyle has already been noted and his open adulation for such latter-day

Daoist iconoclasts as Chen Tuan 陳搏 (895–989; *zi* Tunan 圖南, *hao* Xiyi, Xiansheng 希夷先生, Fulu Zi 扶挌子) was thought to be partly the blame for it. While doubtless inspired intellectually by the **Yi jing** (*Book of Changes*) and possibly representing the foremost practitioner of **Xiang shu xue** (the Learning of Images and Numbers) in his time, Shao Yong neither wrote a commentary on that Classic nor formally articulated his ideas on how it should be interpreted. While his philosophical peers are all noteworthy for their employment of a lexicon of virtue concepts, Shao Yong is notorious for his failure to embrace such a lexicon as fully. Particularly glaring was his failure to emphasise the classic Confucian virtues of *ren* and *yi* – a disposition on his part that ostensibly led **Zhu Xi** to exclude him from the orthodox *ru* version the *dao tong* (transmission of the Way). Nevertheless, in hindsight, by far the most conspicuous of Shao Yong's departures from the newly emerging mainstream of *ru* thought consisted of his failure to adopt *li* or principle as his most exalted concept.

Shao Yong selected an entirely different tool for the purpose of procuring knowledge and that tool was number (*shu* 數). To the degree that we can assume that he also subscribed to Zhou Dunyi's scenario of cosmogonic generation emanating from the *Tai ji* or Supreme Ultimate, then, in Shao's view, number afforded at least three distinct advantages over principle as an operational concept. First, in Shao Yong's system, number was a tangible entity – the first generated of corporeal things. In the unfolding of the universal evolution, Shao recognised other concepts as preceding number – most notably the ethereal and capricious faculty of *shen* or spirit. But number was the first of these emanations that could be used and applied for advancing knowledge. Shao recognised several forms of knowledge but the most subtle and elevated category that becomes accessible through the application of number is a kind of predictive knowledge known as the 'teaching or learning of Before Heaven' (*Xiantian Xue* 先天學). Secondly,

Shao regarded number itself as the perfect mode for describing this generative process because of its inherent regulative functions and these were perhaps best demonstrated by the simple act of enumeration. Still a third and final advantage of number over principle is unrelated to these first two and this is Shao Yong's belief that thoroughly understanding number was necessary for the most efficient and maximal utilisation of the human *xin* (heart/mind). In this way, number not only functioned as a mode but also a medium for Shao Yong, for – like any other object – it served as a field of inquiry for the full application of the mind that leads to sagehood.

Shao Yong's faith in the efficacy of number led him to the formulation of two signature methodological devices that were themselves number-dependent in their operation – *jing shi* (經世 world ordering) and **guan wu**. Although there are areas of considerable functional overlap between the two, Shao Yong applied the former method primarily as a means of temporal, historical and political inquiry and the latter method mainly as a means of natural and human observation. Shao Yong articulated these methods at different stages in his intellectual career. Nevertheless, he employed them jointly and both evinced an irreducible moral component. The former method is especially in full display in Shao Yong's seminal philosophical work – **Huangji jingshi shu** (*Book of Supreme World-Ordering Principles*). Indicative of its political emphasis and goals, it is therein stated: 'If individuals who are destined to order the world (*jing shi*) can flourish across generations . . . within three transformations, the Way of the emperor can be raised' (*Huangji jingshi shu*, 6: 16).

Influence

Although the role of teacher was his only vocational calling throughout his entire life, Shao Yong produced painfully few (and no major) successors to his teachings. The reasons for his dearth of followers, however, are not difficult to discern. His son **Shao Bowen**, though loyal to his father in other respects, discounted himself as a direct exponent of his philosophy; his half-brother Shao Mu 邵睦 (1036–68), though perhaps willing, died before the crystallisation of a complete system. Even those who knew Shao Yong intimately and studied under him for some duration considered his philosophy too abstruse. Moreover, especially upon his death, a tendency to regard Shao's teachings as novel and ungrounded in precedent emerged and hence this caused successive generations of scholars to have even less incentive for perpetuating his philosophy.

Shao Yong instead exerted his influence profoundly in another way. Contrasting starkly with the lack of receptiveness to his teachings was his overwhelming charismatic allure as an individual. Thus, Shao Yong influenced his contemporaries as well as successive generations more through the lofty quality of his bearing as a wise and sagely man than through his scholarship or ascribed philosophical ideas.

Shao Yong received the posthumous title (*shi* 諡) of Kangjie 康節 sometime between the years 1086 and 1094. In 1267, Shao was honoured as an earl (*bo* 伯) and the regularised conduction of sacrifices on his behalf was commenced within the **Kong miao** (Temple of Confucius).

References: Balazs & Hervouet, 1978: 4, 11, 75, 103, 104, 222, 223, 262, 289–90; Birdwhistell, 1989; Bol, 1992: 30, 235, 279, 300, 338, 430n. 142, 445n. 100; Cai, 1973; Collins, 1998: 5, 75, 301, 304, 307, 308, 312; He Zhaowu, 1991: 249, 297; Huang Siu-chi, 1999: 37–56; Jiang Guanghui, 1994: 109, 110; Smith, *et al.*, 1990: 100–35; Wyatt, 1996; Zhao Lingling, 1973.

DON J. WYATT

Shen 神
(Spirit)

Classical texts describe *shen* as the spirit or transformative numinous power of forces of nature, living creatures and human beings. Human beings can communicate with the spiritual forces external to themselves through ritualised votive offerings, and they can also develop this aspect of themselves through various methods of self-cultivation. Later, the term *shen* also became used as an adjective to refer to the spiritlike, supranormal, or 'divine' talents of human beings and other phenomena.

In early texts, celestial and meteorological phenomena such as the sun, moon, stars and the forces of cold and heat were considered spirits and were given thanksgiving offerings, which might consist of such commodities as livestock or jades. Terrestrial formations such as mountains, which were believed to have the powers to provide material resources and produce clouds that sustained human agriculture, were also considered spirits. Even living creatures such as small carnivores that consumed crop-damaging vermin made contributions to humanity, and their spirits, or efficacious powers, were likewise honored with votive offerings.

If even such animals had efficacious powers, how much more was this true of human beings, who were endowed with various souls, energies and transformative processes, one of which also was spirit (see *gui shen*). As people interacted with the external world, their spirits became luminous and eventually ascended from their mortal remains at death. This spirit aspect – soundless, formless, and imperceptible to the senses under most circumstances – continued nonetheless to exist in a post death state of indeterminate nature and could be invoked to be present during sacrificial offerings, where it was 'fed' with food offerings that were eventually consumed by the community of living participants. Spirits inhabited a hidden, invisible realm (*you* 幽) but were nonetheless embodied, traceless, within things and could be invoked to be present in the visible (*ming* 明) realm of ritual performance. Pious sacrificers could invoke the spirits of their own kin, with

whom they had a relationship of blood and vital energy, or *qi*. In addition to performing rites for their own ancestral spirits, people of suitably high rank could also invoke nonkin spirits of natural powers or of deceased famous personages. Such spirits had powers that benefited a community larger than a single clan. As early as the **Zhou li**, for example, regularised offerings were presented to the spirits of deceased scholars and teachers.

In later times, Song scholars such as **Zhu Xi** understood spirits in terms of the contraction and expansion of yin and yang and the coalescence of *qi* – without, however, reducing them to such criteria or depersonalising them, for he maintained a close relationship with the spirit of Confucius, for example, reporting to him the important events of his life. Since Han times, the spirit of Confucius had been the recipient of sacrificial offerings, and by the Song the ever-changing list of Confucian luminaries who were worthy of such rites had expanded into the hundreds, and Zhu Xi's spirit itself eventually joined their ranks.

References: Adler, 2002; Chan, Wing-tsit, 1986b: 142–68, 1987; Gardner, 1995, 1996; Graham, 1992: 108–18; Legge, 1985b; Sommer, 2003.

DEBORAH SOMMER

Shen dao shejiao 神道設教
(To use the divine way to give instruction)

This expression is found first in the ancient commentaries of the *Book of Changes* (*Yi jing*) (*Zhouyi dazhuan* 周易大傳). In the Commentary on the Decision (*tuan zhuan* 彖傳) of the 'Contemplation (view, *guan* 觀)' hexagram, it is said: 'Those below look toward him and are transformed. He affords them a view of the divine way of Heaven, and the four seasons do not deviate from their rule. Thus the sage uses the divine way to give instruction, and the whole world submits to him.' Three meaning-loaded words are used here, each carrying a wide spectrum of connotations. *Shen* could mean divine or spirit. *Dao* unquestionably is the most often invoked idea and here it may mean natural order or law. *Jiao* means a set of teachings or ideologies that sometimes have religious implications. Thus, the expression could suggest that the sage gave instructions on divine teachings, which could be found in the orderly change of the four seasons. There is some natural law or order suggestion here. The secularising tendency in Confucius' thinking reduced the religious connotation in this expression, which in later usage often was to mean only that the sage took lessons from observing the orderly change of nature and used them to teach the common people. In the mind of **Liu Xiang**, '*Shen* could not defeat *dao*'. Here, *shen* was to mean ghosts and carried bad connotations. Its power was no match of that of *dao*. However, it is clear that in Confucian education, sages were expected to play a central role in the discovery of the *dao* and in assuming the responsibility of teaching and transforming the moral life of the common people.

THOMAS H.C. LEE

Shen du 慎獨
(Taking care [to develop] what is singular to oneself, or taking care when alone)

The phrase *shen du* was understood in diametrically different ways in Han classicism and in Cheng–Zhu school of learning (see **Cheng–Zhu xuepai**). The *locus classicus* in the *Li ji*, a compilation dating to the middle of the Former Han (206 BCE–8 CE) but drawing upon earlier ritual statements associated with **Xunzi**, uses the term to refer to the duty of each person to 'take care [to develop] what is singular' to himself or herself in the course of self-cultivation. At its inception, therefore, the term acknowledged variations in human dispositions,

talents and circumstances that can be expressed through rituals, so long as the rituals do not become mechanical and routinised. However, by the Later Han (25–220 CE), Confucian writings often emphasise the necessity to take care when alone, lest one become gradually accustomed to coarse thoughts and behaviours. This is the major theme, for example, of chapter 2 in **Xu Gan**'s *Balanced Discourses* (**Zhong lun**), which enjoins true gentlefolk to constantly maintain the same model behaviour, whether they are alone or with others. In the Cheng–Zhu interpretations of the Classics, 'taking care when alone' became the dominant reading for *shen du*. Such care was seen to be the main sign of internal 'reverence' (*jing*), the attitude that was the very precondition for moral behaviour.

MICHAEL NYLAN

Shen Huan 沈煥
1139–1191
(*zi* Shuhui 叔晦, *hao* Dingchuan xiansheng 定川先生)

Shen Zhu 沈銖, the father of Shen Huan, had studied with Jiao Yuan 焦援, one of the students of **Cheng Yi** who had fled to the Ningbo region after the invasion of the Jurchen. Thus Shen Huan, who later was called one of the Four Masters from Ming Prefecture (**Mingzhou si xiansheng**), became influenced by the teachings of Cheng Yi at an early stage of his life. Later, when he was studying at the Imperial Academy, Shen Huan became a classmate of **Lu Jiuyuan**'s brother Lu Jiuling who gained his *jinshi* degree in 1169, three years earlier than Shen Huan. Accordingly, Shen Huan regarded Lu Jiuling as his teacher. After the examinations Shen Huan served as a teacher in several places. He irritated his superiors because contrary to established custom he sought close contact with his students claiming that men should not be selected because of the results achieved on a single examination day but on the reputation gained over a long time under the observation of their teachers. Minor favours granted to Shen Huan at court and his outspokenness aroused anger and envy among fellow-officials who eventually succeeded in impeding his carreer. The former chancellor Shi Hao 史浩 (1106–1194), one of the leading figures during the reign of Emperors Xiaozong (r. 1163–1190) and Guangzong (r. 1190–1194) and also a native from Ningbo, donated Shen Huan a piece of his own land where Shen taught his students when he was out of office.

Although Shen Huan was mainly influenced by Lu Jiuyuan's Learning of the Mind (*Xin xue*) transmitted to him by **Lu Jiuling**, he also discussed scholarly matters with **Lü Zuqian** and despite some doubts concerning the *Tai ji* diagram of **Zhou Dunyi** did not altogether reject the ideas of **Zhu Xi**.

Unfortunately, Shen Huan's collected works were lost already at the time of **Quan Zuwang**. Besides some works scattered over several sources only his remarks contained in the *Dingchuan yanxing bian* 定川言行編 (*Compendium of Words and Deeds of the Master from Dingchuan*) compiled by **Yuan Xie** can tell us something about his thought. Like **Shu Lin** he was famous for his 'even and practical' teachings. This traditional characterisation implies that Shen Huan did not like abstract speculations about the human 'mind', the central term of Lu Jiuyuan, but instead established a concrete moral doctrine. According to him, the mind could, when cultivated, penetrate even the highness of heaven and the thickness of earth. He considered historical writings to be a burden. They should be read only very selectively because he was convinced that it was possible to read ten thousand books without understanding anything if one did not realise the really important things. He said: 'The most urgent task of us Confucians is nothing more than to establish the basic root and to clarify the basic meaning. If the root does not stand and if the meaning is

not clear then what is the use of discussing a programme for current duties?' And: 'If at daytime looking for it in one's wife and children, and at night being interested in it in one's dreams, and one does not have to be ashamed in both, then we can call this learning.'

HANS VAN ESS

Shen Kuo 沈括
1031–1095
(*zi* Cunzhong 存中, *hao* Mengqi Weng 夢溪翁)

Shen Kuo earned his *jinshi* degree through participation in the civil service examinations held between 1056 and 1063. Shen thereafter had a checkered bureaucratic career – one that was distinguished by service in such varied capacities as a companion to the heir apparent (*taizi zhongyun* 太子中允), a director of astronomy (*sitian jian* 司天監), and a frontier defender against the Qidan 契丹 Liao dynasty (947–1125) while holding an appointment as an investigation commissioner (*chafang shi* 察訪使). Near the end of his career, after being found culpable for a defeat of Chinese forces by the Tangut 唐古忒 western Xia dynasty (1038–1227) that resulted in 60,000 deaths, he was demoted and banished. Shen's legacy has also suffered in traditional accounts because of his reputedly servile involvement as an eager participant in the reforms of **Wang Anshi**. Nevertheless, these detractions notwithstanding, Shen Kuo is far better remembered as a polymath who excelled especially at nature observation and scientific writing. In fact, for the Song dynasty (960–1279), his *Mengqi bitan* 夢溪筆談 (*Notes Taken at Dream Brook*) is the definitive work of its kind. This book consists of a collection of 507 notes – divided into seventeen categories – on an astounding array of subjects, including all aspects of eleventh-century elite cultural life. However, significantly more than half of the book is devoted to the thoughtful recording of information on the natural sciences, engineering and technology as they were practised during Shen's time. Thus, we must regard Shen Kuo's collection as an indispensable primary source attesting to the unmatched level of attainment achieved by Chinese science prior to the twelfth century.

References: Bodde, 1991: 86–7, 259n. 47; He Zhaowu 1991: 341–8; Kasoff, 1984: 8–9, 23–4, 31; Needham, 1959: 4, 36, 38–9, 42, 48, 72, 79, 97, 102, 109, 110, 139, 142, 143, 145, 153, 191, 192, 208, 228, 262, 278, 281, 310, 325, 332, 415, 421, 433, 473, 479, 482, 492, 493, 541, 549, 574–7, 580, 603, 604, 605, 607, 609, 611, 612, 614, 618; Wyatt 1996: 284n. 80.

Don J. Wyatt

Sheng ren 聖人
(Sage)

Sheng means sage, sagacious or wise; *ren*, human being. As an expression, *sheng ren* means 'a sage', as does the shorter *sheng* and also *sheng zhe* 聖者, 'one who is sage'.

In earlier texts such as the **Shi jing** or **Shang shu**, *sheng* was often used in a general, adjectival sense to describe the behaviour or counsels of a person of any rank who exhibited wisdom, intelligence or perspicacity in the governance of the state. Rulers might be sages, but so also might their ministers or even the ministers' staff; an ode from the *Shi jing* (no. 32) lauds a mother who is 'sage and good' (*sheng shan*). Being sage was not a permanent state; the stupid might become sage, but the sage, if careless, might also become stupid. Sagacity was associated with the qualities of reverence (*jing*), knowing (*zhi*), the good (*shan* or *liang* 良), the real (*shi* 實), virtue (*de*), martial valour, circumspection, magnanimity and the ability to pattern oneself on heaven's paradigms.

From at least the time of Confucius, however, being a sage meant having attained a rare and unique kind of moral stature. The relative merits of sages *vis-à-vis* other kinds of people such as worthies (*xian ren*), noble people (*junzi*), or petty people (*xiao ren* 小人) were much discussed, but it was generally agreed that sages represented the epitome of what it meant to be a human being. Scholars debated the various qualities of sages, the processes by which one might, if possible, become one, and the position of the sage within human society and within the larger cosmos.

Confucius despaired of ever meeting a sage and did not think of himself as one, although his pupils did. So did **Mengzi**, who was one of the first to single out Confucius as being unique even among sages. In both the *Mengzi* and the **Xunzi**, several paradoxical views on sages emerge: one is marked by discontinuity and 'otherness'; the other, by consubstantiality and similitude. According to the first view, sages were mythic rulers or specially gifted persons who lived in the irretrievable past; according to the second, sages and one's own self are of the same kind, and one can become a sage through education.

By the Han, many people viewed sages as even more radically other. Thus **Wang Chong** felt obliged to explain that sages did not have superhuman powers, could not foretell the future, and did not have preternaturally gifted sense faculties. Even child prodigies, like everyone else, had to study to develop their exceptional capabilities. Wang Bi (王弼 226–249 CE) likewise dismissed claims that sages did not have human emotions.

Song thinkers offered differing visions of sagehood. Wang Bi's views notwithstanding, **Zhou Dunyi** lauded sages for having no desires and praised them for their sincerity or authenticity (*cheng* 誠). **Shao Yong** believed sages had special powers of perception that were processed through the mind rather than the sense faculties. **Zhang Zai**'s cosmic vision of the *Xi ming* identified sages with the totality of Heaven and Earth, as did his nephews the Cheng brothers (**Cheng Hao** and **Cheng Yi**), who moreover saw the sage as someone who could completely fathom principle (*li*). **Zhu Xi** described a path to sagehood that allowed one access to the sages of the past through book learning and that concomitantly required acting within the world.

References: Ames & Rosemont, 1998: 6:30, 7:26, 7:34, 9:6; Chan, Wing-tsit, 1963d, 1967: 289–308; de Bary & Bloom, 1999: 385–6, 669–84; Forke, 1962; Gardner, 1990; Graham, 1992; Huang Hui, 1990; Knoblock, 1988–94; Legge, 1985b: 50, 198, 257, 332, 499, 640; Legge, 1985c: 54, 194–6, 198, 253, 255, 262, 327, 378, 500, 539, 629; Wang Xianqian, 1988.

DEBORAH SOMMER

Sheng sheng 生生
(Vitality, production and reproduction)

Sheng sheng is defined as the cycles of eternal change (*yi* 易) and endless creation in the universe. This constant production, where change is a successive movement of *yin* and *yang*, is precisely the vitality and reproduction found so centrally in the cyclical cosmological standpoint of the *Book of Changes* (*Yi jing*), in the first part of the chapter of Appended Remarks (*Xici* 系辭上). Chinese cosmology held that from the Supreme Ultimate (*tai ji*), come yin and yang cosmic powers, then the four phenomena (*si xiang* 四象), eight trigrams (*ba gua* 八卦) and sixty-four hexagrams, and ultimately everything in the universe (*wan wu*). This process of change and its function in the principle of the vitality of living systems is deemed the greatest virtue of heaven (*tian*) and earth (*di*). The term also figures in the *Book of Documents* (*Shang shu*), though in a practical rather than cosmological mode, whereby life and all things are combined in a single image.

Reference: *Yugyo Sajon Pyonchan Wiwonhoe*, ed., 1990.

TODD CAMERON THACKER

Shengxue Hui 聖學會
1897–1898
(Association for the Study of Sage-Learning)

The *Shengxue Hui* was a political organisation established in May of 1897 in Guilin, Guangxi province, by the reformist Confucians during the Constitutional Reform Movement at the end of 1890s. The founders of the Association were **Kang Youwei**, Tang Jingsong 唐景崧, Cen Chunxuan 岑春煊, Cai Xibin 蔡希邠, among others. Since the organisation enshrined and worshipped Confucius in a rented *Guangren Shantang* 廣仁善堂, it was also called *Liangyue Guangren Shantang Shengxue Hui* 兩粵廣仁善堂圣學會. There were about two hundred members of the association including young intellectuals and enlightened persons of the time. In the announcement of the founding of the association written by Kang Youwei, the given aims of the association were to respect Confucianism as a religion (*kong jiao* 孔教), to propagate the doctrines of the ancient sages, to train and foster talented persons and to save China. According to the regulations of the association, there were five main tasks: firstly, to meet and study Confucian Classics on every *Gengzi* day 庚子日 (that is, once every sixty days) in order to keep its guiding position in the society; secondly, to collect books that were useful to China including ancient Chinese books and those from the West, and to purchase new equipment for modern natural sciences such as telescopes, microscopes, etc.; thirdly, to publish newspapers in order to propagandise Confucianism and exchange information; fourthly, to establish volunteer schools in order to train highly skilled individuals; and fifthly, to establish schools for developing agriculture, industry and commerce. The *Guangren bao* 廣仁報 was the association's newspaper and a place to publish these new ideas, to oppose the civil service examination system consisting of the *Eight-Legged Essay* (*ba gu wen* 八股文), to encourage the New Text Learning of the

Classics (*Jinwen jingxue*), to propagate the ideas of constitutional reform and create a new society. The association ceased its activities after the collapse of the political reform of 1898.

References: Wang & Yang, 1989; Wu & Song, 1992.

OUYANG KANG

Shi 師
(Teacher)

Like the relationships of ruler and subject (*jun chen*), parent and child (*fu zi*), where the senior to junior relationship is one of the superior receiving the respect (*gong*) of the junior, a teacher traditionally holds a very important position in society. The *Guo yu* (*Conversations of the State*) in fact equate the above three (the ruler, the father and the teacher) as meriting equal devotion, since one's parents give one life, one's teacher demonstrates how life is to be properly lived, and one's ruler is in a position to provide the necessary conditions for a peaceful life by maintaining social order. Though the teacher–student relationship is not included in the five human relationships (*wu lun*), it is often considered an ideal form of friendship, since, as mentioned above, the teacher begets one intellectually, where the parent (one of the five human relationships) begets one physically.

References: Johnston, 1935: 47–8; Morohashi, 1960.

TODD CAMERON THACKER

Shi cai 釋菜
(Presentation of Vegetable Ceremony)

According to the *Book of Rites* (*Li ji*), the school performed the 'Presentation of Vegetable Ceremony' when new pupils were admitted. The vegetable included celery and sea weeds, etc. There is very little information about its performance, although Han sources indicate that this ceremony sometimes was held in conjunction with the rite of 'sacrifice to the sages' (*shi dian*). Obviously, this is a minor and much neglected ceremony. In the Tang times (618–907), however, the ceremony was apparently held monthly, during which seminar sessions were held for open discussion.

The *shi cai* ceremony must have been largely abandoned since the late Tang and therefore when it was revived in the early twelfth century during Cai Jing's (1046–1126) educational reform movement, many people thought that this was the revival of a ceremony discontinued since the Han. The antiquarian restructuring of the Imperial Academy at the time included the reintroduction of the ceremony. It was to be performed in the fall (while *shi dian* was for the spring). It is said that the Academy held this ceremony when admitting Korean students in 1116.

The *shi cai* ceremony appears to have been continued up until late Song, but then fell into oblivion again. The rite was only occasionally performed throughout the later imperial times.

References: Lee, Thomas, 2000: 569; Pang Zhonglu, 1988: 3/8b, 10b, 13a; Zhu Bin, 1996: 318–19.

THOMAS H.C. LEE

Shi dian 釋奠
(Sacrifice to Sages)

According to the *Book of Rites* (*Li ji*), schools performed the *shi dian* sacrifice of the beginning of the four seasons to Confucius and other sages (notably, the Duke of Zhou (**Zhou Gong**)). The content of the sacrificial objects was wine and meat. This classical prescription was adopted and performed fairly regularly through Chinese history, going back probably to the beginning of the Later Han times (25–220 CE), although reliable information exists only for a slightly later period and especially the Wei of the Three Kingdoms Period (220–256).

During the Period of Disunity (220–589), the ritual was held in the compound of the Imperial Academy. The emperor or the crown prince was often in charge of its performance. It was also the occasion for them to meet with students for discussion on the Classics.

By the Tang times (618–907), the sacrifice was held mainly for Confucius and his disciple Yan Hui. The frequency of the rite was apparently reduced to only the spring and the fall. At the same time, however, successful candidates from local examinations were required to participate in the rite when they came to the capital to take the Departmental Examination. During the ceremony, the Imperial Academy also held lectures and discussions. The performance of *shi dian* rites continued in the Song (960–1279) and became fairly routine, in which attention was directed primarily to who could be inducted into Confucian temples so that they could also receive the sacrifice.

The rite increasingly lost its importance under the conquest dynasties, and by the Ming times had become largely an anachronistic ceremony, dutifully but ritualistically performed in the Confucian temple of the Imperial Academy.

References: Gao Mingshi, 1980: 218–36, 1984: 106–22, 144–59; Pang Zhonglu, 1988; Zhu Bin, 1996: 317, 327–8.

THOMAS H.C. LEE

Shi–fei 是非
(This–not this)

The *shi–fei* pair is central to ancient Chinese ethical discussions. *Shi* was a demonstrative 'this'. The translation as 'right' works because saying of 'this one' in context implies it is the right choice. *Fei* preceeds predicate nouns like 'is not a . . .' It similarly denies that the thing is the right choice so *shi* (this) and *fei* (not) represent positive and negative judgements. *Shi* and *fei* are not principles, but situational choices of things, actions or ways of acting.

They also served as the key terms in discussing meaning or semantics. Since discussion of what a term 'picked out' relevant for deciding how *correctly* to follow a *dao* (way, see **Dao qi**), picking the thing to which a term correctly referred was picking the right thing in the context of acting. Knowing how to use a word was knowing how to *shi–fei* (this–not this) or to 辯 *bian* (distinguish) with that word. Questions of knowledge, judgement and belief tended to be formulated as questions about what to *shi* and what to *fei*.

Mozi, Confucius' utilitarian rival, first cast ethical issues in *shi–fei* terms. Later, the idealist Confucian, **Mengzi**, and after him Zhuangzi and **Xunzi** all followed Mozi in making *shi–fei* central to their ethical theorising. Mozi cast his utilitarianism as a system that used the distinction of *li–hai* 利害 (benefit–harm) to guide the application of the terms *shi–fei*. These core distinctions thus governed both normative choice and interpretation. To follow guidance *correctly*, one must get the reference right.

Classical Chinese thinkers intimately link ethical issues to the question of distinction making. Essentially making the right *shi–fei* distinctions is carving the world at its *normative* joints. Technically, *fei* is the key indication of a distinction and, in Daoism, becomes the focus of its sceptical theory of language. We count as knowing a word in the language when we know that something does not count as 'the thing in question' (*fei*). To know a word is to know a contrasting pair of words. To get rid of language is to get rid of *fei*-ing or distinction-making.

Mengzi, seeking to evade the utilitarian conclusion, developed a theory of intuitively right *shi–fei* choices. Mengzi listed the heart of *shi–fei* as the last of his four hearts – the one that leads to moral wisdom.

The innate heart's 'seed' of moral knowledge is our ability to *shi–fei*. Our moral intuition should blossom naturally until it is in tune with the cosmic moral structure. A sage's intuition guiding his choices, thus, perfectly accords with nature.

The other major classical figure who discussed *shi–fei* was Zhuangzi. His analysis also exploited the grammatical features of *shi*. Zhuangzi contrasts *shi* first with its indexical opposite *bi* (彼, the other) then moves to discuss *shi–fei* with the implication that all judgements is perspectival. *Shi–fei* judgements are correct in the way that calling this thing 'this' is correct. Moral judgements reflect our perspectives, not normative joints in reality. This argument also applies to semantic convention. There is no *naturally right* word for a thing. Linguistic traditions are arbitrary (see *wu wei*).

Zhuangzi exploits the bitter dispute between Confucians and Moists to drive this point home. Each has a different discourse *dao*. Accordingly, for key terms of moral discourse, they disagree on 'what counts as 'this' and 'not-this' (*shi*-ing themselves and *fei*-ing their opponents). They disagree about the terms *yi* (righteousness) and *de* (virtue). Zhuangzi also ridiculed Mengzi's intuitive *shi–fei*. Any *shi–fei*, Zhuangzi argued, presupposes something. We cannot get *shi–fei* out of heart/mind without instilling it there. Mengzi reached outside the heart/mind to justify relying on it and again to distinguish between sage and ordinary *heart/mind*.

The last great Confucian of the period countered that on Zhuangzi's own grounds, the only viable standard for what was the correct way to *shi–fei* with a term was the tradition. The standard way to accord with tradition was to study it as a Confucian scholar would. Thus the Confucian, cultivated gentleman or sage's reactions was the standard that society should follow in *shi–fei*-ing. Xunzi argued that the political authority should step in when philosophers and semanticists began to deviate from these traditional patterns of *shi–fei* to preserve the harmony and moral orientation of the community.

Shi–fei (this–not this) 是非 lost its technical use after the classical period as *shi* (this, right) evolved into a connective verb (approximately *to be*). The pair continued to be used as a general reference to issues of right–wrong in Confucian–Buddhist discourse but without drawing on the technical pre-Han meaning.

References: Graham, 1990: 322–59; Hansen, 1992.

CHAD HANSEN

Shi ji 史記
(*The Records of the Historian*)

Judged by any criteria, the *Shi ji* stands out as the work which more than any other moulded the Chinese view and treatment of the past, set the form for official historical writing for some two thousand years and focused the minds of imperial officials on the ideal concepts ascribed to earlier rulers and masters. As perhaps the longest piece of writing as yet to be planned as a unity, and running to 130 chapters, the work sets out to trace the history of mankind from the earliest known beginnings until the time of the principal writer, *c.* 90 BCE. While drawing on existing writings of types exemplified in the received versions of the *Book of Documents* (**Shang shu**), **Chunqiu Zuo zhuan**, **Guo yu** or *Zhanguo ce* 戰國策, the authors were also able to call on records that had been compiled in the course of administering the Han empire and were preserved in the offices of the government. Some of these, such as emperors' decrees or officials' memorials, are presented in summary; other documents, such as the tables of the nobilities, may well have been reproduced directly from official archives, without major change.

As compared with the dynastic histories compiled from Tang times onwards, the *Shi ji* was conceived and completed by two officials as a private venture, with some imperial support, rather than as the sponsored work of an established organ of government. Both **Sima Tan** and his son **Sima Qian** held the office of Director of Astrology (*Taishi ling* 太史令) whose duties included the maintenance of records of astronomical events and certain other activities. How much of the received text derived from Sima Tan and how much from Sima Qian may not be known for certain; but the specific discrimination between and identification of the six categories of thought named as **Yin–Yang** 陰陽, *Ru* 儒, *Mo* 墨, *Fa* 法, *Ming* 名 and *Dao* 道 was the work of the father rather than the son.

The 130 chapters of the work were conceived in five groups. The twelve chapters of Basic Annals (*Ben ji* 本紀) record in chronological sequence the reigns of the preimperial monarchs and lesser rulers, and the emperors of the Qin and the Han, together with the actions in which they were principally concerned. Ten chapters of tables (*biao* 表) set out the dates of their accession and death, year by year details of the succession of the kings (*Zhuhou wang* 諸侯王) and nobles (*Liehou* 列侯) of the Han period and the tenure of office by senior imperial officials. Eight chapters are devoted to select topics such as religious matters, codes of conduct (*Li* 禮), music or economic matters. The book includes thirty chapters (*Shi jia* 世家) which record the succession and family history of leaders mainly of the preimperial states and some notable men of Han times. The remaining seventy chapters of biographies (*Lie zhuan* 列傳) relate the careers, contributions to public life and destinies of individuals who played major parts in the unfolding of preimperial and mainly imperial history. The division between the last two categories is not always clear cut, Confucius appearing in the eight chapters of family records, while **Mengzi** and **Xunzi** are treated in the seventy biographies.

Apart from the disappearance of ten chapters at a very early stage, in general the text of the *Shi ji* appears to have been transmitted without suffering major loss or corruption. Those ten chapters included the Basic Annals for Han Jingdi (r. 157–141 BCE) and **Han Wudi** (r. 141–87 BCE) and the treatises on codes of conduct and music. The received text now includes replacements for all ten chapters and some additional material that was written by **Chu Shaosun**, and possibly as many as fifteen others.

Between them Sima Tan and Sima Qian provided the first systematic account of China's history. The form that they evolved differed from that of earlier records such as the *Spring and Autumn Annals* (*Chunqiu*) which takes events in strictly chronological sequence and which was readopted by **Sima Guang** (1019–86). All the subsequent dynastic histories followed the form initiated in the *Shi ji*.

While drawing on existing sources, Sima Qian at least was by no means unaware of the problem of distinguishing between authentic record and unconfirmed hearsay. He set out to avoid the assignment of praise and blame as was attributed to the *Spring and Autumn Annals*; in the course of his travels he endeavoured to collect information to supplement his sources. But despite his avowed intentions, as in all the dynastic histories so in the *Shi ji* signs of bias are seen in the choice of subjects or the style and extent of their treatment. Thus the account of Ni Kuan 兒寬 varies considerably from that of the *Han shu* which is far more informative; the choice of *li* (codes of conduct) and music as subjects for treatises reveals some of the authors' values that might not have appealed to all of his contemporaries.

Sima Qian had lived through the years of the expansionist policies of Han Wudi's reign (141–87 BCE) and he had seen their effect on government. Although he was a contemporary of **Dong Zhongshu** the ideas of Han Confucianism that the latter was formulating had yet to gain the full acceptance that they received later, and they can hardly have affected the composition of the *Shi ji*. Similarly as yet the kings of the Zhou and their governments were not being regarded as the paragons that deserved emulation. But although neither Sima Tan nor Sima Qian should strictly be described as 'Confucian', the work that they left behind them included many of the ideas that were later included in that mode of thought. Sima Qian's own views, which are revealed in the *Shi ji*'s criticism of Han Wudi's governemt, may well have been accentuated by the punishment to which he was personally subjected. The pertinent comments or appraisals that he appended to each chapter are based on some of his own judgements or prejudices.

The *Shi ji* remained as a model for China's historians throughout the imperial age. It included its own selection and version of mythological accounts of the earliest rulers of mankind. It set the dynastic schemes that formed the basis of imperial Confucian ideology and it provided a means for asserting dynastic legitimacy or, alternatively, denying such claims to an interloper. Some of the chapters laid down principles that became cardinal ideals in a Confucian empire. These included the perennial importance of *Li*; the need to maintain social hierarchies; the individual's duty to serve his superiors; the importance of training scholar officials; and the emperor's obligation to respect the cults of state, as yet addressed to the Five Powers (*Wu di* 五帝), the Lord of Earth (Hou tu 后土) and the Supreme One (Tai yi 太一) rather than to Heaven and Earth. Other chapters trace the start of Confucian scholarship and the transmission of learning by the various schools of the Five Canonical Texts (*Wu jing*).

References: Chavannes, 1969; Hulsewé, in Beasley & Pulleyblank, 1961: 31–43, and in Loewe, 1993: 405–14; Nienhauser, ed., 1994; Watson, 1958.

MICHAEL LOEWE

Shi Jie 石介
1005–1045
(*zi* Shoudao 守道, *hao* Culai xiansheng 徂徠先生)

A leader of the early Northern Song Confucianism, Shi Jie won the *jinshi* title in 1030 and served in various official posts. He surprised many of his contemporaries by ignoring the relatively low social status of Sun Fu (who failed to pass the civil service examinations) and paying Sun Fu great respect for his moral teaching. At his own expense, he built an academy for Sun Fu at Mount Tai in Shandong. In his essay *Tai shan shuyuan ji* 泰山書院記 (*An Account of the Mount Tai Academy*), Shi justified what he did by evoking, among others, **Han Yu**'s essay **Yuan dao** 原道 (*On the Origins of the Way*). He argued that there were two equally important Confucian genealogies for passing on the Way. One was a genealogy of accomplished officials who manifested the Way in governing. The other was a genealogy of teachers who expressed the Way in teaching and writing. For Shi, Sun Fu was a great teacher because he revived the Confucian moral learning after its three hundred year of eclipse since the death of Han Yu.

Han Yu was important to Shi Jie in other respects as well. Influenced by Han Yu's call for expressing the True Way of Confucianism in clear and simple writing, Shi was a fervent critic of the popular ornate style of writing, the *xikun* (西崑) style. In his essay 'Guai shuo' 怪說 (*On Anomalies*), he accused Yang Yi 楊億 (974–1020), the leader of the *xikun* style, of undermining the Confucian moral principles by stressing literary embellishment over moral content.

Throughout his life, Shi was a relentless opponent of Buddhism and Daoism. Considering both religions as 'foreign' (although religious Daoism clearly developed in China), he used them as the straw man to present what he believed to be the indigenous Chinese culture. In his essay 'Zhongguo lun' 中國論 (*A Discussion of the Central Kingdom*), he argued that there was a categorical distinction between the Chinese and the non-Chinese. For him, what characterised the Chinese was their socio-political order built on the Confucian Five Human Relations (**Wu lun**). Since Buddhism and Daoism were 'imported' religions with drastically different social and political agendas, he called on the Chinese to reject them in order to preserve their true Chinese characteristics.

In 1043, shortly before the *Qingli* reform was launched, Shi Jie composed the highly polemic *Qingli shengde song* 慶歷聖德頌 (*An Ode to the Sagely Virtues of Emperor Renzong*). In this, he depicted the launching of the reform as a victory of the virtuous officials in the imperial court over their enemies. Injecting his own moral vision into the reform, he described the reform as an attempt to apply Confucian moral principles to governing. Because of its hyperpole, Shi's writing did not help to publicise the cause of the *Qingli* reform; on the contrary, it made enemies for the reform.

References: Bol, 1992; Song–Yuan xuean, 1996; Qian, 1977; Shi Jie, 1984.

TZE-KI HON

Shi jing 詩經
(*Book of Poetry*)

The *Shi jing*, also known simply as *Shi* 詩, *Poetry* or, since the Han, as **Mao shi** (*Poetry of Mao*) (i.e., the *Poetry* transmitted by **Mao Heng** or Mao Chang 毛萇 [*fl.* second century BCE]), is a collection of 305 poems dating for the most part between about 1000 BCE and 600 BCE. Already by the Spring and Autumn period (771–476 BCE), poems from the collection were routinely quoted in support of political arguments and, slightly later, philosophical arguments, and by the end of the fourth century BCE it was already accorded the status of a *jing* 經, or 'classic'. When the Imperial Academy was established during the reign of **Han Wudi** (r. 141–87 BCE), this status was made official, with chairs assigned to each of three different traditions of transmission of the text: those of Lu 魯 (the transmission of which is credited to one Shen Pei 申培 [*fl. c.* 200 BCE]), Qi 齊 (credited to Yuan Gu 轅固 [*fl. c.* 150 BCE]), and Han 韓 (of Han Ying 韓嬰 [*fl. c.* 175 BCE], whose *Han Shi wai zhuan* 韓詩外傳 is the only work associated with these transmissions still extant). A fourth tradition, associated with Mao Heng and Mao Chang, was not recognised by the Imperial Academy, but gained in popularity throughout the Han dynasty (206 BCE–220 CE), and had become dominant by the second century CE when it was the text used by **Zheng Xuan** for his commentary, *Mao shi Zheng jian* 毛詩鄭箋. By the Tang (618–907), the traditions of Lu, Qi and Han had essentially ceased to be transmitted, leaving the *Mao shi* as the only exemplar of this Classic.

The 305 poems of the *Shi* (titles only are given for six other poems) are divided into three major sections: the *feng* 風 or 'airs'; the *ya* 雅, often translated 'elegentiae' though 'encomia' may be a more appropriate functional translation; and the *song* 頌 or 'liturgies'. Each of these major sections is in turn divided into subsections. In the case of the *feng*, of which there are a total of 160 poems, the divisions are geographical: after two subsections entitled *Zhou Nan* 周南 and *Shao Nan* 召南, referring to the lands given to **Zhou Gong** 周公 (Duke of Zhou) and Shao Gong 召公 at the beginning of the Western Zhou (it seems likely that *nan* 南 refers to the type of music that accompanied these poems), there are *feng* attributed to thirteen different states or regions: Bei 邶, Yong 鄘, Wei 衛 (all three of these pertain to areas around the former Shang capital at Anyang (Henan)), Wang 王 (the capital region at present-day Luoyang 洛陽 (Henan)), Zheng 鄭 (Henan), Qi 齊 (Shandong), Wei 魏 (Shanxi), Tang 唐 (Shanxi), Qin 秦 (Shaanxi), Chen 陳 (Henan), Kuai 檜 (perhaps in Henan), Cao

曹 (Shandong) and Bin 豳 (Shaanxi). The second major section, of 105 poems, is the *ya*, divided simply into the *Xiao Ya* 小雅 or Lesser Encomia and *Da Ya* 大雅 or Greater Encomia. The third major section is the *Song*, also divided quasi-geographically (the division can also be described as cultural): the *Zhou Song* 周頌 or Liturgies of the Zhou, comprising thirty-one of the forty poems in this section; and the *Lu Song* 魯頌 (four poems) and *Shang Song* 商頌 (five poems).

The collection seems to have come together in more or less reverse order of its canonical sequence; that is, the earliest poems are those of the *Zhou Song*, some of which probably go back to the first half of the Western Zhou dynasty (*c.* 1000 BCE) and the rest of which date to just after the major ritual reforms that took place in the middle of that dynasty. The next group of poems, most of which are found in the *Da Ya*, date to the last generation or two of the Western Zhou (*c.* 800 BCE). Most of the *Feng* of various states show signs, both linguistic and contextual, of having been composed during the first century of the Spring and Autumn period (i.e., seventh century BCE). The date of composition of the nine poems in the *Lu Song* and *Shang Song* is, however, also quite late, the poem 'Bi gong' 閟宮 of the *Lu Song* containing an internal reference to the reigning Xi Gong 僖公 of Lu (r. 659–627). While there would seem to be no reason to follow tradition in crediting Confucius with the editing of the collection, there is some reason to suppose that it was actually edited in the state of Lu, thus accounting for the elevation of the Lu poems (which are generically similar to *Feng* and *Ya* poems) to the same status as the liturgies (*song*) of the dynastic powers Zhou and Shang.

The three major sections of the *Shi* also represent three different functions to which the poems were put. The poems of the *song* or 'liturgies', and especially the *Zhou Song*, were, for the most part, sung during the performance of sacrifices in the ancestral temples. The following poem, entitled 'We Lead' (*Wo jiang* 我將, No. 272), is a good example of one such temple liturgy:

> We lead our offerings:
> They are sheep; they are cows;
> May it be that Heaven accepts them.
> The rites properly take as model King
>   Wen's statutes,
> Daily making tranquil the four quarters.
> And so blessed King Wen
> Has accepted and enjoyed them.
> May we morning and night
> Revere Heaven's awe
> And protect it here.

It can be seen that this poem accompanied the sacrifice of sheep and cows to the deceased founder of the Zhou dynasty, King Wen (r. *c.* 1099–1050 BCE), and ends with the prayer that 'we' (i.e., the participants in the sacrifice) should benefit from the sacrifice. These liturgies tend to be very short, and of all the poems in the *Shi* are the only ones marked by irregular line length and absence of end rhyme.

The *ya* or encomia probably originated as entertainment after the banquets that followed major sacrifices, especially as the ritual system evolved from the middle of the tenth century BCE. These encomia were sung by individual singers, who may also have composed the poems (five of the *ya* poems are explicitly 'signed' by their makers, and at least two others also indicate that the singer 'made' [*zuo* 作] the poem). 'Thick the Bramble' (*Chu ci* 楚茨; No. 209) is a particularly good example of this function; it is an extended description of one such sacrifice, the preparations for it, the banquet afterwards, and then also the entertainment itself. While the poem is too long to quote in its entirety, its last two stanzas illustrate this context:

> The rites and ceremonies being finished,
> The bells and drums being set up,
> The filial descendant goes to his place,
> The skilled priest brings forth the
>   announcement:

'The spirits are all drunk.'
The august impersonator then arises.
The drums and bells send off the
   impersonator,
And so the spiritual protectors go back.
The many stewards and noble ladies
Clear away without delay.
The many uncles and cousins
Have finished the private banquet.

The musicians enter to play
In order to bring the comfort of
   after-blessings.
Your meats being presented
None is resentful and all celebrate.
Being drunk, being sated,
Young and old touch their heads to the
   ground.
The spirits partook of the drink and food,
Making the lord be long-lived.
Most kind, most correct,
May he see it to the end,
And have sons' sons and grandsons'
   grandsons
Without interruption to prolong it.

Most of the *ya* poems have a regular style,
being composed of lengthy stanzas of four-
character lines all of which share a common
end-rhyme (the change of stanza usually
being marked by a change of rhyme). Their
content is also similar, being for the most
part songs of praise for both dynastic legends
and contemporary heroes. However, songs
of praise could also be turned to songs of
censure when times turned bad, and some
of the most powerful *ya* poems are indeed
clearly political protests.

The *feng* or 'airs' have also traditionally
be read in a political context, but many
modern interpreters, beginning with Marcel
Granet (1884–1940) in the West and Wen
Yiduo 聞一多 (1899–1946) in China, have
interpreted them as 'folksongs', or at least
as songs representative of personal or
private emotions. The first song in the collection, '*Join, the Osprey*' (*Guan ju* 關雎;
No. 1), has served as the paradigm for all
readers of the *Shi*. Its first stanza already

serves to introduce perhaps the major
poetic development that comes to fruition
in these poems:

   '*Join, join*', the osprey,
   On the river's isle:
   The luscious good girl,
   A fine match for the lord's son.

Stanzas of the *feng* poems are generally
short, often – as here – composed of just two
couplets, the first describing some image
in the natural world and the second a
corresponding image in the human world.
Beginning with the 'Preface to the *Poetry*'
(*Shi xu* 詩序) of the *Mao shi*, this poetic style
has been referred to as *xing* 興, which
can perhaps best be translated as 'arousal';
it indicates a very close correspondence
between the two images, that the nature
image evokes or causes the human image
to 'arise'. It is not always possible today to
understand the correspondence between
the images, but it seems clear that when
Confucius urged his students to study the
Poetry, 'the better to recognize the names
of birds and animals, plants and trees'
(*Analects* 17: 9), he was not interested primarily in botanical taxonomy; rather, like
the poets who created these poems, he too
subscribed to a worldview in which man
and nature were very closely correlated.

The history of *Shi jing* exegesis begins with
Confucius and goes on to include virtually
every major literary figure in the Chinese tradition, and thus is well beyond the scope of
an encyclopedia entry such as this. Readers
today generally divide between 'traditional'
readings, informed by the Mao tradition's
political contextualisation of the poems,
and 'folksong' readings in which individual
poems, and especially those of the *Guo feng*,
are seen as timeless and universal expressions
of human emotions. By tracing the development of poetic types through the three
major sections of the *Shi*, and by noting the
social context of their creation, it may be
possible to reconcile both of these apparently
contradictory interpretations. In any event,

the *Shi jing* is a large and complex enough literary creation to support them both.

References: Granet, 1919; Karlgren, 1950, 1964; Legge, 1985b; Waley, 1937; Wen Yiduo, 1984.

EDWARD L. SHAUGHNESSY

Shi jing 石經
(*Stone Classics*)

By the middle of the second century CE a number of versions of the classical texts and their interpretations were in circulation, some being subject to error, and some of the interpetations being out of official favour. As part of a move to establish an approved version with an orthodox interpretation under official sponsorship, in 175 CE **Cai Yong** and others proposed the preparation of a copy that was to be regarded as the standard for scholars to follow. The works whose texts were engraved on tablets of stone for this purpose included *The Book of Changes* (*Yi jing* 易經), as taught by **Jing Fang the Younger**; *The Book of History* (*Shang shu*), as taught by Ouyang Gao 歐陽高 (a pupil of **Fu Sheng**); *The Book of Poetry* (*Shi jing*), Lu 魯 version; **Dai De**'s work on *Li* 禮; *The Spring and Autumn Annals* (*Chunqiu*); the *Chunqiu Gongyang zhuan*; and the *Analects* (*Lunyu*), Lu version. In this way scholars and students would be able not only to consult the approved version but also to make copies for their own use in the form of rubbings. Following this example of the Later Han, similar projects were undertaken in 240, 833, 950, 1041, 1153 and 1791.

Reference: Tsien, 1962: 73–9.

MICHAEL LOEWE

Shi pin 詩品
(*Ranks of Poetry*)

Zhong Rong 鐘嶸 (466?–518?) probably published his only remaining work, the *Shi*

pin, after 513. Called by **Zhang Xuesheng** 'the source of poetry criticism', the *Shi pin* gives an unsystematic but all-inclusive theory of poetry in its prefaces and it ranks 122 poets who lived from the end of the Later Han (220 CE) to the beginning of the sixth century. Zhong Rong follows the *Da xu* 大序, *Great Preface*, of the *Shi jing* (*Book of Poetry*), in his theory of poetry as originating in emotion and describes the poets and their work in a clearly Confucian framework: Cao Zhi 曹植 (192–232), for example, his greatest poet, is compared with the Duke of Zhou (**see Zhou Gong**) and Confucius, and **Ji Kang** is criticised in terms borrowed from the *Lunyu*.

Reference: Führer, 1995.

DONALD HOLZMAN

Shi pipan shu 十批判書
(*A Book of Ten Critiques*)

A Marxist reassessment of ancient Chinese history published in 1945 by Guo Moruo 郭沫若 (1892–1978), it countered previous studies by Hu Shi 胡適 (1891–1962, *zi* Shizhi 適之) and **Qian Mu**. Guo applied dialectical materialism to ancient texts, revealing their interactive contexts. Specific chapters discussed Confucius, his subsequent disciples, and **Xunzi**. After demythologising Confucius' image through Moist criticisms, Guo criticised 'slavish attitudes' inherent in 'cultivated humaneness' (*ren*) and 'ritual propriety' (*li*), emphasising his 'progressive' metaphysical scepticism and political concerns. In eight other chapters similar criticisms and affirmations are made.

LAUREN PFISTER

Shi tian 事天
(Serving Heaven)

One can serve (*shi*) human beings of higher status such as parents, older siblings, elders, superiors or rulers; political entities such as states; or numinous phenomena such as spirits (**shen**), the Lord on High (**Shang Di**), or, as in this expression, Heaven (**tian**). In the **Shi jing** (ode 236), for example, King Wen was lauded for manifesting his inner power (**de**) and assiduously serving the Lord on High (with which heaven was often associated) and securing blessings for his people. The **Mengzi** more closely associates service to heaven with inner cultivation (see **zhi tian shi tian**) rather than material blessings.

References: Lau, 1984: 1A: 5, 1A: 7, 1B: 3, 7A: 1; Legge, 1985b: 433.

DEBORAH SOMMER

Shibusawa Eiichi 澁澤榮一
1840–1931

Shibusawa Eiichi, the great Confucian financier and entrepreneur, was born in Musashi 武藏 province (modern Saitama prefecture) in a farming family that had grown wealthy through the indigo business. He worked in the family business from a young age, while also developing a voracious appetite for reading and outstanding skill in fencing, the latter of which led to friendships with men of the **Mito School**. Through such friends he came under the influence of *sonnô jôi* ideas, dedicating himself at age seventeen to the destruction of the shogunate. In 1863 he was relieved by his father of his responsibilities as his heir, enabling him to join an anti-Tokugawa plot that was to begin with attacks on foreigners' residences in Yokohama. This brought him to Edo, where he was introduced to a vassal of Tokugawa Yoshinobu 慶喜, later to become the fifteenth and last shogun. Persuaded to give up the plot in view of the increasing strength of the *kôbu gattai* 公武合體 movement, for his own safety he ended up himself becoming a retainer of Yoshinobu's Hitotsubashi branch of

the Tokugawa. In this capacity he worked vigorously to build up the strength of Yoshinobu's Imperial Guard by encouraging enlistment, finding new sources of finance through the rationalisation of trade, and training the new troops using French methods. Realising that the shogunate's survival was in great danger, he tried to dissuade Yoshinobu from accepting the shogunal succession, but without success.

His resulting melancholy regarding his and his lord's fate was relieved when the new shogun ordered him to go to France as a retainer of Yoshinobu's younger brother, Prince Mimbu, to attend the great Paris Exposition of 1867. Early in his voyage he was converted by conversations with a bakufu expert in foreign affairs into a great admirer of Townsend Harris, the first American Consul-General to Japan, and he remained a stauch friend of the United States for the rest of his life. The two years he spent in Europe visiting the most advanced sites of European technology, manufacturing, military power and high culture fundamentally changed his thinking about foreigners, and he returned with an immovable conviction that the source of a country's wealth and power lay in commerce and industry. After inspecting the mammoth Suez Canal construction project (completed in 1869), he wrote in his diary that 'Generally speaking, the western man does not undertake to do a thing for his own sake alone. He aims at the public welfare of his country or community. The magnitude of his schemes and the audacity of his purposes deserve high admiration'. His observation of this great project was one of the sources his later insistence on the importance of the collective or cooperative system for business enterprise, involving the cooperation between private capital and the government. He was also deeply impressed by the fact that in Europe bankers and military leaders treated each other as equals, and that kings made it a priority to promote the interests of their nation's business community, things that were inconceivable within the strict status system of Japan, in which merchants had the lowest official status.

Shibusawa and the prince left France for their return voyage in October 1868, though since 2 January they had been hearing about the momentous changes that were going on in Japan. Shibusawa was determined to avoid official service and devote himself to promoting commerce and industry, but the new Meiji government insisted on appointing him as Head of the Bureau of Taxation. Marquis Ôkuma Shigenobu persuaded him to accept by appealing both to the Confucian exaltation of public service and to the need to help convince doubters that the ex-shogun was supporting the new government. A 'Bureau of Reorganisation' was set up with Shibusawa as head to preside over the revision of the tax system and the nationwide survey that was necessary to implement it. After Ôkuma was replaced by Inoue Kowashi as head of the Treasury Department, the two carried through the unification of national finances following the abolition of the domains. Shibusawa proceeded, as vice-minister from February 1872, to preside over the organisation of the National Bank, the adoption of its regulations and rules, the issuance of paper money and postal and revenue stamps, and the establishment of a stock exchange, all of which were institutions he had learned about in France. He finally tendered his resignation in May 1873, after his patron Inoue had resigned due to opposition to the financial programme he and Shibusawa had been promoting. This was followed in the same year by what Shibusawa's English secretary and biographer Kyugoro Obata calls 'the summit of his life', the founding of Japan's First National Bank. In Obata's words, this 'was the headquarters where the Viscount, the generalissimo of the huge industrial army, commanded the creative and constructive forces for building up the industrial civilisation of modern Japan' (p. 85). The bank was followed by the paper mill, the Tokyo Gas company, and the Osaka Spinning

Company, eventually reaching a total of 250 companies directed and guided by Shibusawa. Yamamoto Shichihei goes as far as to give Shibusawa the chief credit for making possible Japan's rapid modernisation.

Shibusawa, however, is remembered not just for his great contributions to Japanese commerce and industry, but for his synthesis of Confucian ethics with the practice of business. As Obata notes, he made untiring efforts to destroy the traditional notion that morality and the pursuit of profit are incompatible. 'The point he wanted to emphasise was that the correct relationship between morality and economy came from the harmonising of economy with morality, and not morality with economy' (p. 266). In an essay called 'The Theory of the Unity of Morality and Economy' (*Dôtoku keizai gôitsu setsu*), he wrote that the later (mis)interpreters of Confucius 'forgot that productiveness is a way of practicing virtue. They little thought that all sorts of industrial work and the existence of cooperative systems are conducted according to certain regulations based on moral reason and mutual confidence. The result is that they came to believe that poverty is clean and wealth unclean. This misunderstanding tended to separate learning [which became erroneously restricted to the non-productive classes] from practical living'. Confucius' remarks that he could *still* have joy in the midst of poverty and that when the superior man sees an opportunity for gain he thinks of righteousness, meant not that the life of poverty was ideal, but that the ethical man could *if necessary* do without material comforts if they could only be gained through unethical actions. Moreover, Confucius said that a man who 'extensively confers benefits on the people' is not only virtuous, but might well have the qualities of a sage. 'If we hope for the genuine prosperity of the country', Shibusawa insisted, 'we must endeavour to enrich it' through 'industry and commerce conducted according to modern scientific methods'. To do this requires 'the organisation of the cooperative system, which in turn must be controlled by sound and solid moral reason'. Moroever, 'there is but one standard for moral reason, which is the *Analects*, the teaching of Confucius the sage' (pp. 267–9).

For a man in the business world to live a truly moral life, Obata notes, is much more difficult than for, say, a scholar in a university, because of the constant temptations to compromise one's principles for profit or expediency. Thus it was necessary for Shibusawa to nourish and renew his commitment to ethical principles every morning and keep up a constant vigilance in his daily life. In spite of the vast gulf between the life of the businessman and the life of the samurai, in this matter of constant vigilance and daily renewal of moral resolution, the moral teachings developed for the samurai could be directly applied to the character-building called for in a capitalist economy. Thus in the midst of his busy life as a man of affairs, Shibusawa found the time to write poetry in both Chinese and Japanese and to associate himself with literary organisations composed of scholars of Chinese Classics known for their exemplary moral conduct. He himself founded an *Analects* society (Rongo Kai), which arranged lectures by scholars on the *Lunyu* for his family and relatives, and a Wang Yangming (see **Wang Shouren**) society (Yômei Kai), which in his later years held meetings in one of the rooms of his office. He was fond of repeating and writing in his inimitable calligraphy the famous maxim from the *Doctrine of the Mean* (*Zhongyong*) (ch. 20), 'Sincerity is the Way of Heaven. The attainment of sincerity is the Way of men . . . One attains sincerity by choosing the good and holding firmly to it.' Obata notes that 'The older he grew, the more intensely he came to yearn after a high and blameless life'. In the Taishô period he retired from business and devoted himself to philanthropic activities, public welfare projects and the promotion of international goodwill through frequent visits to China, the United States, and a host of other countries. He believed strongly that peace could be preserved if only a friendly relationship could be maintained between Britain, Japan, and the United States.

BARRY D. STEBEN

Shili yuyao 十力語要
(*The Essential Teachings of Xiong Shili*)

Essentially a creative compilation of nearly 200 recorded discussions, pieces of correspondence, speeches and published articles by **Xiong Shili** 熊十力, this book reflects Xiong's lively engagement with colleagues, friends, and students. The majority being correspondence and lectures written between 1924 and 1946, they reveal personal dimensions of the scholar, the contemporary intellectual milieu and his views on Chinese culture, Chinese philosophies, and their comparison to western culture and philosophies. Some involve insightful interpretations and debates over various Chinese scriptures and issues in his **Xin weishi lun** 新唯識論. Published as one volume in 1947, a sequel appeared in 1949.

References: Fang & Zheng, 1995: 71–3; Xiong Shili 1989.

LAUREN PFISTER

Shinju funi 神儒不二
(Shinto and Confucianism are not separate traditions)

During most of the Tokugawa period (1600–1868) in Japan, proponents of Shinto and Confucianism sought ways to reconcile their respective creeds and teachings with one another. These efforts were supplanted during the period's last decades and continuing into the subsequent Meiji era (1868–1912) by the more radical argument that Shinto and Confucianism (*Shinju*) not only shared common assumptions but literally were to be understood as singularly convergent (*gôichi*, 合一) and *not* separate (*funi* 不二) traditions. These efforts in the intellectual and spiritual arenas were congruent with efforts in the political sphere to buttress imperial rule and thereby promote national unity of purpose by collapsing certain traditional binaries, as evidenced in such popular slogans as those asserting that or calling for the 'union of civil and military authority' (*kôbu gattai*), 'the singularity of the literary and martial traditions' (*bunbu fugi*), 'loyalty to the throne and to parents are one' (*chûkô ippon* 忠孝一本), and perhaps the best known slogan of the day 'revere the emperor and expel the barbarian' (*sonnô jôi*, 尊王襄夷). This fusion of Shinto spirituality with Confucian morality formed an important component in the nationalistic ethics taught in Japanese schools during much of the Meiji period and in the ultra-nationalist ideology prominent in Japan through the end of World War II. In more recent times, a popular fusion of Shinto and Confucianism has likewise contributed to various efforts in Japan to articulate a 'national identity'.

PETER ERLING NOSCO

Shiqu ge huiyi 石渠閣會議
(The Conference in the Stone Canal Pavilion)

The court conference of 51 BCE, conducted in the Stone Canal Pavilion (*shiqu ge* 石渠閣) within the western Han imperial palace at Chang'an, was devoted to the interpretation of the officially recognised canon, that is, the Five Classics (**Wu jing**). The debate was apparently triggered by controversies among court scholars over the Gongyang and the Guliang traditions of the **Chunqiu** and from there extended to issues concerning the whole corpus of the Five Classics. The ultimate purpose of the conference was to reinterpret the canon according to the changing political and intellectual circumstances. In concrete terms, the debate is said to have addressed more than thirty individual issues which afterwards were put into writing in the form of extensive 'discussion memorials' (*yizou* 議奏) for each of the Classics. While the memorials, listed in the **Han shu**'s 'Monograph on Arts and Letters' (*Yiwen zhi*, ch. 30), are lost, fragments mostly concerned with questions of ritual and propriety have survived from a summary of the debate. Probably lasting for several months and involving twenty-three scholars, the conference was presided over by **Han Xuandi** and headed by Xiao Wangzhi 蕭望之 (*c.* 110–47 BCE), the Grand Tutor of the heir-apparent. The procedure was highly formalised: one scholar was assigned to raise the questions for debate, another scholar took records of the ensuing discussion, and the emperor himself, according to historical sources, pronounced the final decisions, assuming the highest authority in the interpretation of the Classics. The conference resulted in giving official preference to the *Guliang* tradition over the previously authoritative *Gongyang* tradition of the **Chunqiu**, and in raising the number of chairs for the different traditions of the Classics to twelve.

Reference: Tjan, 1949: 89–93, 128–37.

MARTIN KERN

Shiren pian 識仁篇
(*On Recognising Ren*)

Shiren pian is **Cheng Hao**'s most important discussion of **ren** (humaneness, benevolence), and is thus a foundational text of the Neo-Confucian movement. This short discourse was recorded by **Lü Dalin** and is found in *Ercheng Yishu* 2a (see **Ercheng quanshu**). Cheng Hao discusses Lü's questions concerning personal cultivation, particularly about self-searching and making efforts; he responds that there is no need for special efforts so long as *ren* is 'preserved with authenticity (**cheng** 誠) and reverence (*jing*)'.

Cheng Hao puts understanding or recognising *ren* as first priority for those engaged in learning. The text expresses, in a condensed way, Cheng Hao's characteristic approach to *ren* as the sensitivity that forms one body with all things (see *wanwu yiti*). He cites *Mengzi* 7A: 4 that 'all things are complete in me' to emphasise that in *ren* there is no opposition between oneself and others, and points to **Zhang Zai**'s *Xi ming* as a fuller expression of this idea. Our innately good knowledge and good ability (*liangzhi liangneng* 良知良能), later explored by **Wang Shouren** (see *zhi liangzhi*), is not lost, says Cheng; all that is necessary is to exercise it and enjoy it.

The most accessible English translation of *Shiren pian* is found in Wing-tsit **Chan**'s *A Source Book in Chinese Philosophy*, wherein Chan remarks that the text has been 'a *vade mecum* for many a Chinese scholar'. Among recent Confucian thinkers, *Shiren pian* has received particular attention from **Mou Zongsan** and his followers, and is indeed worthy of reflection for all interested in Confucian philosophy or spirituality.

References: Chan, Wing-tsit, 1963d: 523–5; Fung, 1952: 521–2; Mou, 1963: vol. II: 218–33.

THOMAS SELOVER

Shisan jing 十三經
(The Thirteen Classics)

The *Shisan jing* consists of the *Yi jing*, *Shu jing* or *Shang shu*, *Shi jing*, *Zhou li*, *Yi li*, *Li ji*, *Chunqiu Zuo zhuan*, (*Chunqiu*) *Guliang zhuan*, (*Chunqiu*) *Gongyang zhuan*, *Lunyu*, *Xiao jing*, *Er ya* 爾雅 and *Mengzi*. The collection of the Thirteen Classics was finally established during the period of Shaoxi 紹熙 of Guangzong (r. 1189–94) in the Song dynasty, during which the *Mengzi* was added to the Twelve Classics (*Shier jing*), while the *Erya* had been included as a Classic during the Tang. The title *Shisan jing* appeared in *Yuhai* 玉海 compiled by **Wang Yinglin**. *Shisan jing* was republished in

the twelfth year of Qianlong 乾隆 (1747), under the name '*Qianlong-Chiben* 乾隆敕本 (The Version *by Qianlong Imperial Edict*)'.

During the Jiaqing 嘉慶 (1796–1820) period, **Ruan Yuan** published the *Shisan jing zhushu jiaokan ji* 十三經注疏校勘記, based on previous editions. This has been regarded as the most authoritative text.

Reference: Fung Yu-lan, 1952.

M.H. KIM

Shisan jing zhushu 十三經注疏
(*Commentaries and Sub-Commentaries to the Thirteen Classics*)

When the Confucian canon, after the inclusion of the *Mengzi* in Song times, finally comprised the 'Thirteen Classics' (*Shisan jing*), the thirteen texts first circulated separately from their Han, Wei and Jin commentaries (*zhu*) and Tang and Song subcommentaries (*shu*). In the twelfth century, editions of the Thirteen Classics including the commentaries were printed under the title *Shisan jing zhushu* (*The Thirteen Classics, with Commentaries and Sub-Commentaries*); these were reprinted during Yuan and Ming times. The authoritative version of the *Shisan jing zhushu*, including the standard *zhu* and *shu* commentaries, Lu Deming's 陸德明 (556–627, personal name Yuanlang 元郎, *zi* Deming 德明) phonetic glosses from the *Jingdian shiwen* 經典釋文, as well as additional text critical notes, was published in 1815 by the eminent classicist and philologist **Ruan Yuan** (1764–1849) under the title *Shisan jing zhushu jiaokan ji* 十三經注疏校勘記 (*The Thirteen Classics, with Commentaries, Sub-Commentaries, and Collation Notes*).

MARTIN KERN

Shishuo xinyu 世說新語
(*New Account of Tales of the World*)

The *Shishuo xinyu* is a collection of anecdotes, originally in eight fascicles, concerning the cultural life of the Later Han and Wei-Jin dynasties (220–420), put together about 430 under the name of Liu Yiqing 劉義慶 (403–444), an imperial relative and general of the succeeding Liu–Song dynasty (420–479), though given the compiler's obvious sympathy for witty repartee it has generally been assumed that some staff officer of a less conventional outlook actually carried out the task. Commentary from the next century by Liu Jun 劉峻 (458–521?) of a primarily background documentary nature survives in part, expanding the text to ten fascicles, and illustrates the difficulties felt even soon after the accumulation of its thousand or so anecdotes in reading them against their original historical context; in later times and places (for example, Tokugawa Japan) the problem of retrieving the nuances of long-forgotten Chinese colloquial turns of phrase also occupied – and indeed still occupies – many scholars.

Even so, this collection remains, with its commentary, an important source of information on Chinese thought, especially of the fourth century. Issues such as spontaneity versus conformity (see **Ming jiao**) emerge as topics of vigorous, somewhat formalised debates during this era, all the more remarkably because the political consequences of these arguments, which for parties viewed with disfavour could lead to punishments ranging from demotion to death, are often to the forefront. Amongst the participants, too, we catch glimpses of the first Buddhist monks to have had an intellectual impact in China.

References: Mather, 1976; Xu, 1984.

TIM H. BARRETT

Shiyi jing 十一經
(The Eleven Classics)

The Eleven Classics were published in 953 during the reign of Emperor Taizu (r. 951–954) of the Later Zhou dynasty (951–60). However the edition of the Eleven Classics is not extant and only the titles that are included in the collection are kown. There are two sets of texts that are called 'the Eleven Classics'. The first consists of the *Yi jing*, *Shi jing*, *Shu jing*, the three texts of rites, the three commentaries on the *Chunqiu*, *Lunyu* and *Xiao jing*; the second, as edited and rearranged by He Yisun 何異孫 of the Yuan dynasty (1260–1368) in his *Questions and Answers on the Eleven Classics* (*Shiyi jing Wendui* 十一經問對), includes the *Lunyu*, *Xiao jing*, **Mengzi**, *Da xue*, **Zhongyong**, *Shi jing*, *Shu jing*, *Chunqiu* and the three texts of rites.

M.H. KIM

Shôheizaka Gakumonjo
昌平坂學問所
(Shôheikô 昌平黌)

In 1630, the third Tokugawa shogun, Iemitsu 家光, granted **Hayashi Razan** a four-acre plot of land at Ueno Shinobigaoka 上野忍ケ岡, near the shogunal palace, on which to build an academy (*shoin* 書院), a school building (*jukusha* 塾舍), and a library. Two years later Tokugawa Yoshinao 德川義直 had a Confucian temple built on the site, enshrining images of Confucius and four of his disciples and providing a full set of ritual implements for performing the semiannual *sekiten* 釋奠 rites to Confucius. Yoshinao was founder of Owari 尾張 domain, one of the *go-sanke* 御三家 (three collateral Tokugawa domains of high status with special responsibilities for protecting the shogunate). In 1663, the shogun Ietsuna 家鋼 named the school building the Kôbunkan 弘文館, and Razan's son, Gahô 鵞峰, later adopted this name for the Hayashi family school as a whole. Three years later a charter for the school was adopted, and the curriculum was divided into five departments – classical studies, history, poetry and composition, broad reading, and Japanese classical studies – and ten grades or levels were established in each department.

In 1690 (Genroku 3), the fifth shogun, Tsunayoshi 鋼吉, a strong promoter of

Confucian Learning, granted a somewhat larger plot of land at Yushima-zaka, near the thriving town that had grown up around the Yushima Tenjin 湯島天神 Shrine where the god of learning, Sugawara Michizane 菅原道真 (845–903), was worshipped. The Kôbunkan, with its Confucian temple, was now moved to this site, and expanded in scale and architectural grandeur. The academy was renamed the Shôheizaka Gakumonjo, or simply Shôheikô, and Tsunayoshi himself wrote the calligraphy for the main hall (*taiseiden* 大成殿) of the Confucian temple. The temple – now known as the Yushima Seidô 湯島聖堂 – was augmented by a complex of over twenty structures for use at the time of the *sekiten* ritual, to be presided over henceforth by Razan's descendants. A great *sekiten* was held in the shogun's presence to celebrate the completion of the new buildings in 1691. Tsunayoshi granted a junior imperial rank as well as the ancient title of *Daigaku no kami* 大學頭 ('head of the college for training government officials', a title from the Tang-based *ritsuryô* 律令 government system adopted in the seventh century) to Razan's grandson Hôkô 鳳岡 (Nobuatsu 信篤), and his descendants retained the title through the Tokugawa period. In 1718 specific lecture days were instituted independently of the *sekiten*, and five lecturers were appointed. Under Yoshimune's new educational programme, lectures at the Seidô were held two hours every day, and attendance was opened to commoners as well as *bushi*. A list of attendees was submitted to the bakufu at the end of each month.

While under Yoshimune's educational programme the school acquired some functions characteristic of an official bakufu academy, it retained its basic character as a private academy until it was brought under direct bakufu control by the Kansei educational reforms of 1790–1793 (see **Shushigaku** and **Setchûgaku**). The academy had undergone serious decline during the corrupt Tanuma administration of 1767–1786, crowned by its destruction by fire in 1784. It was rebuilt, but on a smaller scale,

and even the performance of the *sekiten* ritual was suspended. The abuses of the Tanuma era led directly to the Kansei reforms of Matsudaira Sadanobu 松平定信 (1758–1829), a strong believer in Zhu Xi Learning and traditional Confucian prescriptions for socio-political reform based on sumptuary laws, financial retrenchment, ethical self-discipline, and the spread of Confucian moral education throughout society, beginning with the education of government officials from the ranks of direct bakufu vassals of *hatamoto* 旗本 status. In 1792 a system of examinations was introduced, and in 1794, after Hayashi Jussai (1768–1841) had become headmaster, 237 candidates underwent examinations. Gradually, under the direction of able leaders like Koga Seiri 古賀精里 and **Satô Issai**, the academy developed into a flourishing centre of Confucian Learning that turned out a long line of astute political leaders and intellectuals through the challenging final eight decades of the Tokugawa period. Teaching was given at government expense to both commuting and resident students, and the criteria for enrolment were gradually expanded to include domainal samurai and independent scholars, provided they were disciples of Shôheikô teachers and paid their food expenses. In 1841 a programme of daily lectures open to commoners was introduced. After the Restoration the Meiji government took over the school, renaming it the university at the end of 1869, but in July 1870, with the establishment of a modern western-style education system, its 240 years of history came to an end.

Reference: Ooms 1985, pp. 74–80.

BARRY D. STEBEN

Shu 恕
(Consideration)

Confucius once cryptically remarked that his way, or **dao**, was pervaded by a single thread; one of his disciples explained this thread as *zhong* (loyalty or conscientiousness) and *shu*, or consideration (also frequently translated as 'altruism' or 'empathy'). Confucius once explained *shu* as follows: do not impose on others anything you yourself dislike (*Lunyu* 15: 24 and *Zhongyong* 13.3). Some translate *shu* as reciprocity, but *shu* is based on commonality rather than reciprocity. *Shu* transcends expectations about the reciprocal response of others to one's own actions, and it does not imply that one's actions are secondary responses to the behaviour of others (*Daxue* 9: 4). Consideration stems from within the self and moves outward regardless of how one is perceived – or misperceived – by others. Noble people, as Confucius remarked in the opening passage of the *Analects*, act morally but are unconcerned that others do not understand them. Consideration is a moral attentiveness generated by a self that is at once autonomous and yet is empathetically aware of its commonalities with others.

One finds consideration embedded even more deeply in the self in the *Mengzi* (7A: 4), which asserts that the myriad things, not just *shu*, are already replete in one's own person. Acting with consideration is the quickest way of drawing nigh to humaneness (*ren*). In the Song period, the Cheng brothers also associated consideration with humaneness. *Shu* was interpreted by Song thinkers in terms of the development of the mind, substance and function, and applied ethics. Its importance for the Chengs, Zhu Xi, and others is summarised in a small treatise by **Chen Chun** in his *Beixi ziyi*.

References: Ames & Rosemont, 1998; Chan, Wing-tsit, 1963d: 27–8, 785–6 and 1986a, 1986b: 88–96, 1989; Lau, 1984: 7A: 4; Zhu Xi, 1996: 15.

DEBORAH SOMMER

Shu 疏
(Subcommentary)

Shu, literally meaning 'to penetrate', denotes the genre of subcommentary that

was intended to clarify, and to extensively elaborate upon, a chosen primary commentary. In Southern Song times (1127–1279), the collection of the Thirteen Classics with the title *Shisan jing zhushu*, *zhu* refers to the earlier layer of Han through to Jin times (206 BCE–420 CE) commentaries, and *shu* to their later explanations dating from Tang and Song times (618–1279), including the imperially commissioned subcommentaries of the *Wu jing zhengyi*. Together with the *zhu* commentaries that they were expanding upon, the far longer *shu* commentaries were as interlinear readings integrated into the primary text, making the commentaries a physical part of the Classics. In this arrangement, the selected and thereby endorsed primary commentary was canonised through its subcommentary; in addition, the Tang and Song subcommentaries drew extensively on dozens and sometimes hundreds of Six Dynasties' and Sui commentaries in order to discuss, and often to reject, alternative interpretations. One major motive of this strategy to decide among competing readings of the Classics was the need for authoritative and standardised interpretations of the Classics on which prospective office holders could be tested in the civil service examinations. The secondary layer of subcommentaries, especially those compiled under imperial auspices, thus marked a decisive step in canonising the Confucian Classics together with a particular selection of early exegetical texts.

References: McMullen, 1988: 67–112; Pi Xirui 1959: 193–273.

MARTIN KERN

Shu Lin 舒璘
1136–1199
(*zi* Yuanzhi 元質 and Yuanbin 元賓, *hao* Guangping xiansheng 廣平先生, posthumous name Wenjing 文靖)

Shu Lin was the oldest of the Four Masters from Ming Prefecture (Ningbo) (*Mingzhou si xiansheng*). He first heard of the teachings of the Cheng brothers (**Cheng Hao** and **Cheng Yi**) through his father-in-law, who had once been a student of **Yang Shi**. When he later studied at the Imperial Academy in Hangzhou, Shu Lin met with **Hu Hong**'s student **Zhang Shi**. He also learned from **Zhu Xi** and **Lü Zuqian** and in the end became a student of **Lu Jiuyuan**. Although he obtained the *jinshi* degree in 1172 he did not rise as high as **Yang Jian** and **Yuan Xie**, his colleagues from Mingzhou, did. Instead he remained a teacher throughout his life, sometimes giving advice to the provincial authorities concerning such practical matters as the state-monopolies on tea, salt and iron or on labour-services. However, he was interested enough in matters of state-policy to criticise Zhu Xi and others who retired during the middle of 1190s, leaving the power to the ruthless regent Han Tuozhou 韓侂冑 (1152–1207).

Not many writings of Shu Lin have come down to us. **Huang Zongxi**, who wrote as early as during the seventeenth century, declared that the collected writings by Shu Lin had not been transmitted for a very long time. Lost forever are his commentary on the *Mao shi* (*Shi xue fawei* 詩學發微) – a text on which Yang Jian and Yuan Xie commented as well – and his explanations on the *Book of Poetry* and the *Book of Rites* (*Shi Li jiangjie* 詩禮講解). Thanks to Huang Zongxi who collected fragments of Shu's works from his descendants, we have a collection of his philosophical sayings. These are mostly culled from letters which Shu Lin wrote to his friends and students. Under the title of *Shu wenjing ji* 舒文靖集 there survive two chapters (*juan*) of *Collected Works of Shu Lin*. As Huang Zongxi remarked, there are many texts on practical matters but extremely few concerning Shu Lin's more abstract teachings. Of the latter all the *Collected Works* tell us that concerning the term *ben xin* 本心, which was so important for his teacher Lu Jiuyuan, Shu Lin did not believe in a sudden enlightenment through meditation. He thought it could

be reached only through constant moral effort. This is the reason why Shu Lin is credited to have established an 'even and practical' variant of the philosophy of Lu Jiuyuan.

As Quan Zuwang frankly said, there was not much more material on the philosophy of Shu Lin to be obtained than what Huang Zongxi had found. Quan used this material in order to expand the space accorded to Shu Lin in a short biography in the *History of the Song* (*Song shi* 宋史), hoping that his additions might be used in a future revised edition of this work. Together with his fellow-townsman **Shen Huan**, Shu Lin is thus one of the cases which best show that Quan Zuwang in the *Song–Yuan xuean* tried to promote scholars from his own home town (Ningbo) although it may be that they were not very famous outside of this place.

HANS VAN ESS

Shu sheng 述聖
(The Following or Compliant Sage)

Shu sheng is **Kong Ji**'s 孔伋 (*zi* Zisi 子思) title in temple sacrifices to Confucius. Kong Ji's 'compliance' arises from his relationship with his grandfather, Confucius. Kong Ji's father died at an early age and Kong Ji was therefore put in Confucius' care. A passage in the *Doctrine of the Mean* (18), which is attributed to Kong Ji, also speaks of King Wen and King Wu in their respective contributions: 'father establishing' (*fu zuo zhi* 父作之) insititutions of the Zhou, and the 'son following or continuing' this legacy (*zi shu zhi* 子述之). Kong Ji was ennobled as Marquis of Yishui 沂水侯 in 1102 and enshrined in the Temple of Confucius in 1108. He was promoted to a Correlate and ennobled as Duke of Yi 沂國公 in 1267 and given the title of the Compliant Sage Duke of Yi 沂國述聖公 in 1330.

THOMAS A. WILSON

Shu yuan 書院
(Confucian Academies)

Shu yuan were independent or semi-independent educational institutions, primarily within the Confucian tradition. Their main function was to train students in classical studies and philosophical interpretations of Confucian doctrines, in addition to collecting, collating and publishing books. They thrived from the eleventh to the early twentieth century.

Origin of the term
The origin of the private Confucian educational institution can be traced back to the Later Han dynasty (25–220 CE) when some Confucian scholars set up private schools, called *jing she* 精舍 (also called *jing lu* 精盧, 'house of essence', originally meant 'house of heart'), to give oral instruction on classical texts. The term *jing she* was also used to denote Buddhist and Daoist monks' living or preaching quarters since the Three Kingdoms period (220–280).

Along with the establishment of woodblock printing in the Tang dynasty (618–907), a number of book repositories, also used as places for study, had emerged. They were called *shu lou* 書樓, *shu she* 書舍, *shu wu* 書屋, *shu tang* 書堂, or *shu yuan* 書院. The term *shu yuan* first occurred in the Tang dynasty as the name of an imperial library called *Lizheng Shu yuan* 麗正書院 (founded in 717, renamed *Jingxiandian Shu yuan* 集賢殿書院 in 725) and soon used for more than one purpose (*Xin tangshu: Bai guan zhi* 新唐書: 百官志). During the late Tang and Five Dynasties (907–960) the term *shu yuan* was applied to a wide variety of institutions such as studies, libraries, ritual places as well as private schools.

From the Northern Song dynasty (960–1127), the term *shu yuan* mainly denoted institutions which gave instruction at advanced levels, but also establishments differing in size and range of activity. It is worth noting that the ancient term *jing she* continued to be used in the sense of *shu yuan*, referring in particular to high level academies.

The translation of the Chinese term *Shu yuan* by the term 'Academies' is credited to the Jesuit missionary Matteo **Ricci**. In 1595, Ricci visited *Bailudong Shu yuan* 白鹿洞書院 (White Deer Grotto Academy) and described it as 'an Academy of literati', comparing it to the academies that were flourishing in Italy.

Historical development
Academies during the late Tang and Five Dynasties period were basically of a small scale, formalised versions of the Han dynasty scholars' private schools. It was in the Song dynasty that academies developed into a complete system which performed teaching and research, preserving books and paying tribute to Confucius and other sages.

Northern Song rulers expanded civil service examinations and therefore increased the demand both for education and participation in them. While state schools could not meet this growing demand, academies founded by local efforts provided a solution and were highly encouraged by the government. It was estimated that some 140 academies were established in the Northern Song. It was at this time that big academies such as the *Bailudong Shu yuan* 白鹿洞書院, *Yuelu Shu yuan* 岳鹿書院, *Songyang Shu yuan* 嵩陽書院, and *Shigu Shu yuan* 石鼓書院 emerged. Academies reached their peak during Southern Song period (1127–1279) due to the popularisation of the Neo-Confucianism movement.

One of the first Confucian scholars who used the academies as a means to propagate **Neo-Confucianism** was **Zhou Dunyi**. He founded his *Lianxi Shu tang* 濂溪書堂 in 1061, which heralded the link between Neo-Confucianism and academies. Afterwards **Cheng Hao** and **Cheng Yi** spread their teachings in various academies. Cheng Yi also founded the *Yichuan Shu yuan* 伊川書院 (1082).

In the Southern Song, more Confucian scholars recognised that social order and personal fulfillment depended on education and that academies could meet their educational goals and spread their social-philosophical ideas. The great advocate who intensively moulded academies into the educational basis for Neo-Confucianism was **Zhu Xi**. Besides involving himself in the activities of academies, he restored the White Deer Grotto Academy and Yuelu Academy, founded the *Hanquan Jing she* 寒泉精舍, *Zhulin Jing she* 竹林精舍 (also named *Cangzhou Jing she* 蒼州精舍) and *Wuyi Jing she* 武夷精舍.

The academy movement received an enthusiastic response among Zhu Xi's contemporary Confucians and their followers. **Lu Jiuyuan**, **Zhang Shi**, and **Lü Zuqian** all took an active part in the promotion of academies. Neo-Confucian promotion of the academy movement ultimately helped their ideas to be understood and accepted. By the middle of the thirteenth century, *Li xue* (the Learning of the Principle) had achieved approval by the state and the academies were in full swing.

The Mongolian rulers intended to preserve Confucian tradition to stabilise Chinese society. Traditional educational institutions were maintained, particularly those private academies established by Song Confucians. With more academies established along the Yellow River area, Confucian teachings in the South spread or were transmitted to Northern China. By the time of Emperor Shundi (r. 1333–1370) in the late Yuan, the number of existing academies approached approximately one thousand at its height.

After being ignored for more than a century at the beginning of the Ming dynasty (1368–1644), academies were revived with the rise of the *Xin xue* (the Learning of the Heart/Mind) which launched a campaign through academies to challenge *Li xue* as represented by Zhu Xi. Thinkers like **Chen Xianzhang**, **Wang Shouren**, and **Zhan Ruoshui** made special efforts to promote academies. During the reign of Emperor Jiajing (r. 1520–1566) academies were

highly renowned. The number of existing academies in the Ming approximated 1,500, which were distributed throughout distant areas like the lower Zhujiang River. Famous academies formed in the late Ming were *Donglin Shu yuan* 東林書院, *Ziyang Shu yuan* 紫陽書院 and *Jiangyou Shu yuan* 江油書院.

Since mid and late Ming, academies played an important role in guiding public opinion and were sometimes suppressed as centres of unorthodoxy or even subversive thought. Due to political crisis, academies were persecuted on four occasions. The most severe setback was in 1625 when the *Donglin Shu yuan* was destroyed by the eunuch Wei Zhongxian 魏忠賢 (1568–1627).

At first, Qing conquerors prohibited the establishment of academies, fearing that they might produce anti-orthodox thoughts and criticise government as they did during the Ming period. The prohibition was gradually relaxed during the reigns of Emperors Kangxi (r. 1662–1722) and Yongzheng (r. 1723–1735). Soon academies again obtained full support from the government. They were established in administrative divisions at all levels from provinces down to the prefectures, counties and even villages. By the time of Emperor Qianlong (r. 1736–1795), academies had replaced the almost paralytic state schools and became the main educational institutions all over the country. The number of existing academies in the Qing shifted between 1,800 and 3,600.

Reform in Qing academies

In the face of the worsening mid-Qing crisis and impact of western thought, many Confucians began to reevaluate their cultural traditions and forms of education. **Yan Yuan** founded the *Zhangnan Shu yuan* 彰南書院 in 1694 to teach military training, strategy, archery, boxing, mechanics, mathematics, astronomy and history along with the Confucian Classics. A few Han Learning scholars had based their study on academies. **Ruan Yuan** founded two academies the *Gujing Jing she* 詁經精舍, and *Xuehai tang* 學海堂 which concentrated on the phonological analysis of the Classics and produced remarkable works of philology. After the Opium War (1840–1841), western Christian missionaries established church academies in trade ports to teach the Bible, western languages and science. More academies were founded by merchants and taught mainly practical subjects. In 1876, the *Gezhi Shu yuan* 格致書院 was founded in Shanghai. It was the first academy which did not teach Confucian Classics but modern science and technology. After it, more academies were founded to introduce social sciences, sciences and technology in the manner of the western school, for instance, **Zhang Zhidong** founded the *Guangya Shu yuan* 廣雅書院 in 1889, and **Kang Youwei** founded in 1891 the *Wanmu Caotang* 萬木草堂. By 1901 Emperor Guangxu (r. 1875–1908) issued an order to convert academies into modern schools and colleges, which happened four years before the **civil service examinations** were abolished in China.

Sponsorship

Before the thirteenth century, academies were mostly founded by individuals, local communities and clan families, supplemented with donations from local officials. The maintenance of academies largely depended on land income. Courts bequeathed imperial calligraphy, tablets, books and land property to selected academies. This kind of endowment thereafter became a standard practice of the government's official recognition in late centuries.

After the Song dynasty, the growth of the academies can be attributed to a combination of government and local efforts. The tendency to put academies under official sponsorship had been strengthened on a large scale from the Yuan through Qing dynasties. Academies usually received generous funding; in turn, the government took control of the administration as well as the finance of academies. As time went on,

local academies consisted largely of substandard recruits which eventually turned the academies into a place to earn a living.

Texts and methodology

After Neo-Confucianism prevailed in Song society, different schools and groups of Neo-Confucianism, especially Zhu Xi's doctrine, dominated in academies; however, other schools of thought, to varying degrees and intensities, played a supplementary role. The scholarship in academies could be independent of the state school curricula. The headmaster could decide the way his academy developed. Academies therefore frequently were employed as institutional bases by scholars whose ideas were viewed unfavourably by the orthodoxy.

In most Song Neo-Confucian academies training students for the *ke ju* (**civil service examinations**) was rejected. However, in the Yuan period many academies concentrated on training essay-writing for examinations since Zhu Xi's vision of Confucian Classics was the only approved criterion. By the late Qing, preparation for civil service examinations in most academies became the main, if not the entire, task.

The main method of learning emphasised individual self-cultivation under the guidance of a master. Students received instruction individually or in groups. Discussion, debating and exchanges from lectures were encouraged. Philosophical discussions became a fashion in the Southern Song and developed into regularly held large conferences, which usually involved the attendance of several academies during the Ming.

Publishing

The development of academies followed the spread and improvement of printing technology and the subsequent large increase in literacy. In particular, the popularity of woodcut prints in the Southern Song made the publishing work of the academies possible.

Besides its teaching role, a big academy also functioned as a local library and publishing centre. Academies kept records consisting largely of prescriptions, regulations and hortatory essays. The headmaster was in charge of the collation, which ensured textual quality. Instead of local government, the academies financed publication and kept printing plates. Therefore reprinting and distribution became much easier tasks than those of official publications. 'Academic versions' were regarded as high quality and were the most popular.

Besides those common books printed by other publishers, academies specialised in textbooks and related reference books, research works by scholars and study records in academies. The big academies which had extensive activities in publication merging in the Qing dynasty were the *Nanjing Shuju* 南菁書局; *Qixiu Shanfang* 啟秀山房; *Guangya Shuju* 廣雅書局, *Zhengyi Shuju* 正誼書局; *Zunjing Shuju* 尊經書局.

Academies in Korea

Academies (Kr. *So~won*) were introduced into Korea probably around the tenth century. Zealous scholars set up their private academies in the countryside to pursue serious Confucian scholarship, but did not attach public importance to them for the first few hundred years. In 1419 King Sejong (r. 1418–1450) issued an order of commendation for the establishment of academies. In 1543 the court for the first time awarded a royal charter to *Paegundong* Academy 白雲洞書院 (renamed *Sosu,*) founded by Chu Se-bung 周世鵬 (1495–1554) while he served as the magistrate of P'unggi county in Kyongsang province. *Paegundong* Academy, also translated as the White Cloud Grotto Academy, shaped after the renowned White Deer Grotto Academy 白鹿洞書院, itself became the model for hundreds of academies that subsequently sprang up throughout the country. Thereafter until the mid-eighteenth century academies were fully developed under the patronage of the court and overtook county schools (Kr. **hyanggyo**) as centres of local education and scholarship. They were usually affluently endowed through private donations, in addition to royal awards in the form of a name plaque and a generous grant of finances, books, land and servants from the government. Later, however, the academies became involved in the factional politics of the seventeenth and eighteenth centuries, and then fell into disgrace with the government as a result of financial crisis and political conflict. In 1871 the Court issued an order to dismantle academies throughout the country.

Academies in Korea played a dual role not only as educational but also as ritual institutions. Ceremonies commemorating favoured Confucian sages took place in academies and were organised by the local community. It is estimated that there were about 1,300 sages, both Korean and Chinese, who were enshrined in academies. Zhu Xi's Neo-Confucianism dominated in the academies; his works were the orthodox textbooks used extensively in Korean academies, along with Neo-Confucian works of the Korean scholars. It is recorded that Zhu Xi was enshrined in twenty-five academies, even more than Confucius who was enshrined only in eight academies. All other beliefs, customs and traditions that did not comply with Confucian teachings were ejected from the curriculum.

References: De Bary & Chaffee, 1989; Lee, Peter H., 1993; Meskill, 1982; *Zhonghua ruxue tongdian*, 1992.

REBEKAH X. ZHAO

Shuixin School 水心學派

Shuixin School refers to the teachings of **Ye Shi** and his students in the Southern Song. Ye Shi, whose given name was Zhengze 正則, was born in Yongjia 永嘉 county (today's Wenzhou city of Zhejiang province). Ye Shi and his group people were called by his friends as the *Shuixin* School because Ye Shi had been living in his hometown Shuixin village of Yongjia

County in the last sixteen years after he retired from government service. It was during this period that Ye Shi developed the profound criticism of the **dao xue** movement, synthesized *Yongjia* traditions into a more structured form with more convincing arguments and solid historical documentation, and therefore, brought *Yongjia* teachings to the highest level that this School ever reached.

The basic arguments of Shuixin School included different aspects. The most important philosophical argument was that material embodiments had priority over **dao**. The different understanding on the polarity of *dao* and material embodiments became the watershed of Ye Shi and **Zhu Xi**'s theories. Both Ye Shi and Zhu Xi agreed that, *dao* and material embodiments were inseparable; *dao* existed in material embodiments and material embodiments were the manifestations of *dao*. However, Ye Shi believed that material embodiments were formed before the *dao* was present, therefore, material embodiments had priority over *dao*. After establishing such argument as philosophic foundation, Ye Shi further challenged Zhu Xi's view on the Non-Ultimate (**wu ji**) and Supreme Ultimate (**tai ji**). Ye Shi pointed out that the Ultimate was not something mysterious that produced and regulated the myriad things in the world, instead, it was the general attribute of all material things and the perfect state that all material things could achieve when they fully developed or displayed their functions.

As the extension of his philosophical arguments, Ye Shi also offered his views on 'investigating things' (*gewu* 格物) and 'extending knowledge' (*zhizhi* 致知). He pointed out that investigating things was neither investigating principle (**li**) nor investigating mind (**xin**), as Zhu Xi and **Lu Jiuyuan** claimed. To Ye Shi, investigating things was to realise or reflect outside actual entities by using the human mind. Such realisation or reflection started from actual things, and the function of the mind

was to conform itself to such reflection of actual things. Because the process was built on the interactions between the outside actual things and the inside mind, and such interactions could not be accomplished with one move for people to obtain the principle, Ye Shi said, investigating things became a gradual process, not a sudden and momentary enlightenment, as Lu Jiuyuan claimed. In Ye Shi's eyes, Lu Jiuyuan's approach toward cultivation omitted the process of investigating things and therefore created the gap between investigating things and obtaining principle, which would eventually lead people into mystery and agnosticism.

One of the important arguments that the *Shuixin* School advocated was the active involvement of practical governance. He served in different positions at both local and central level of government administrations. He left us lengthy articles with extensive discussions about a restoration plan against Jurchen Jin in North China, military strategies, land system, financial reform, tax collection and bureaucratic operations. In these articles, he advocated institutional changes and applications of historical experiences. By doing so, he set up a good example of how to implement the teachings of the *Yongjia* School.

There is no doubt that the *Shuixin* School provided an alternative approach toward statecraft issues Southern Song government was facing. It was the response to the fundamental changes and increasing pressures which had happened in the Song intellectual community and a substantial challenge to the theory of Zhu Xi who tried to establish *Dao xue*'s authority by narrowing down the scope of *Dao xue* fellowship and by excluding those whom he regarded as contaminated by heterodox ideas.

References: *Song–Yuan xuean*, 1966; Lo, 1974; Niu, Pu, 1998; Tian Hao, 1996; Tillman, 1982, 1992a; Ye Shi, 1959, 1977; Zhou Mengjiang, 1992; Zhou Xuewu, 1988.

Pu Niu

Shushigaku 朱子學
(Zhu Xi Learning)

'Shushigaku' is the standard name in Japanese for Cheng–Zhu School Learning, which was long considered to have constituted the orthodox learning or official ideology (*kangaku* 官學) of the Tokugawa bakufu. This Meiji-rooted view was still assumed in Maruyama Masao's classic *Studies in the Intellectual History of Tokugawa Japan* (written 1940–1944), which descries the rise of 'modern' thought in Edo Japan in the critiques of Shushigaku (which the author viewed as a static medieval thought system) propounded by the Ancient Learning scholars, particularly **Ogyû Sorai**. Studies since the 1960s have dismantled this view of Zhu Xi learning as a bakufu-supported orthodoxy initiated by **Tokugawa Ieyasu** and **Hayashi Razan**, revealing it as largely an *ex post facto* view of history promoted by the Hayashi family and other Shushigaku scholars after the Kansei Prohibition of Heterodoxy of 1790. The prohibition, associated with the restructuring of the Hayashi family's Confucian academy (Shôheikô) into a training college for bakufu officials of *hatamoto* 旗本 status, did make a genuine attempt to establish Shushigaku as the official learning at the bakufu college, a move which required legitimation by association with Ieyasu. Even this prohibition, however, did not aim at establishing a *nationwide* orthodoxy, though the introduction of Shushigaku-based examinations for official posts and the hiring of Shôheikô-trained scholars by domainal schools gradually spread the influence of the bakufu's new educational system through most of the country. The post 1960s view of the development of Tokugawa thought emphasises that Neo-Confucian Learning had considerable difficulty getting established in Japan in the seventeenth century and was incompatible in many ways with Japanese society (see Bitô 1961 and Watanabe 1985), and that the authority of the bakufu was established without any explicit connection with Confucian or Neo-Confucian thought. It also emphasises that the bakufu did not really have a clearly defined official ideology, that whatever legitimating ideology it had in its early stages was drawn more from *sengoku*-period Buddhist and Shinto religious concepts than Confucian rationalism, and that while there were individual daimyô who strongly promoted Confucianism as in Okayama, Mito and Aizu domains, the actual conduct of bakufu government was almost totally divorced from the pursuit of Confucian Learning (see, for instance, Hori 1964 and Ooms 1985). Nevertheless, by the Genroku period (1688–1704), Confucian Learning was truly flourishing, though Shushigaku was already being seriously challenged by the rising popularity of **Itô Jinsai**'s *kogigaku* 古義學, and soon by **Ogyû Sorai**'s *kobunjigaku* 古文辭學. Interestingly, as Araki Kengo has pointed out, their criticisms of Shushigaku were of an opposite nature to the criticisms preferred in China, at least through the end of the Ming dynasty: to put it simply, while Chinese critics attacked the fixed and *a priori* nature of the Cheng–Zhu conception of principle (*ri* 理) as an unnatural restriction on the dynamic nature of the mind, the Japanese critics attacked the *instability* and unreliability of the concept of principle because its standard of practice was rooted in the mind rather than in an objective external reality. As Jinsai said, 'they all look at the mind, but they do not look at the Way' (*Dôjimon*). Some scholars have observed that such Japanese criticisms seem to have been directed most specifically to the teachings of **Yamazaki Ansai**, which were rigorously moralistic and introspective and strongly emphasised the distinction between *ri* (ethical principles) and *ki* (the physical body and material reality). Even among Ansai's disciples, there was a great controversy between Satô Naokata and Asami Keisai over whether moral principles were embodied primarily in the objective political and legal order, anchored in a

Sinocentric universality, or in generally accepted principles of honourable behaviour (*giri* 義理), anchored in the particularity of the Japanese tradition, that might at times require action contrary to the law. Disagreements and differences of approach among different schools of Shushigaku were even more pronounced, with some, like Razan, emphasising the unity of *ri* and *ki*, and some, like **Kaibara Ekiken**, showing as much interest in the empirical study of the natural world as in the promulgation of ethical principles. Other influential teachers and schools of Shushigaku in Edo Japan include **Fujiwara Seika**, the **Mito School**, Zhu Shunshui, **Nakamura Tekisai**, **Arai Hakuseki**, **Muro Kyûsô**, **Asaka Tanpaku**, the **Later Mito school**, and **Sakuma Shôzan**. We should also mention the promoters of the Prohibition of Heterodoxy and the educational philosophy on which it was based – **Rai Sanyô**'s father Rai Shunsui 賴春水, Bitô Nishû 尾藤二洲, Shibano Ritsuzan 柴野栗山, Koga Seiri 古賀精里, Okada Kansen 岡田寒泉 and Nishiyama Sessai 西山拙齋. Moreover, since virtually all Confucian scholars obtained their basic educational grounding in Zhu Xi learning, its teachings exerted deep influence on all the other schools of Japanese Confucianism as well.

BARRY D. STEBEN

Shusun Tong 叔孫通
(Died probably before 188 BCE)

Shusun Tong had been an academician (*boshi*) in the time of the Qin empire (221–206 BCE). At the uprising of Chen Sheng 陳勝 (209 BCE), he fled from Xianyang 咸陽 to his place of origin and joined the cause of Xiang Liang 項梁 and then Xiang Yu 項羽 (233–202 BCE) in their bid to gain control of the whole of China. In 205 BCE he made over to Liu Bang 劉邦 (256–195), then king of Han, accompanying him on his journey to the southwest. Eventually gaining

Liu Bang's confidence, he became an academician when the latter had become first of the Han emperors (Gaozu, r. 202–195 BCE).

It was largely due to Shusun Tong that the concept of codes of conduct or rites (*li*) came to form an integral part in Confucian ideals and imperial institutions. Before the foundation of the Han empire he had formulated procedures for state occasions and he was one of the officials or supporters who chose an auspicious day for the inauguration of the new regime. With the help of thirty colleagues he succeeded in persuading the Han emperor to pay due attention to *li* and to respect the proper hierarchies of the rank and seniority of officials. He served as superintendent of ceremonial (*feng chang* 奉常), and as senior tutor of the heir apparent (*Taizi Taifu* 太子太傅) from 198 BCE. At one point he felt obliged to remind Han Gaozu of the importance of ensuring that the succession to the throne would follow correct lines. He established the approved procedures for setting up the tombs and memorial shrines for deceased emperors, fixing the type of music to be performed there. He once insisted on the need to preserve the authority of the emperor, to the point of avoiding any public acknowledgement that some of his decisions had been mistaken.

A written record that Shusun Tong made of institutional practice was lodged in the imperial depositories of the Later Han (25–220 CE). No more than fragments survive.

MICHAEL LOEWE

Si 私
(Private, personal or selfish)

In the *Book of Documents* (**Shang shu**), *Zhou Guan* 周官 chapter, we find the assertion of 'abandoning self interest in favour of the public good' (*yi gong mie si* 以公滅私). *Si* implies here the self, subjective, particular and individual, or one's private affairs and property, and is contrary to what is 'public' (*gong* 公). Examples of how the concept of *si* as formed in the Confucian Classics include the *Analects* 2: 9 when Confucius assesses his students by taking a closer look at what they do in private and finding them worthy; this implies the subjectiveness of a student's implementation of Confucius' teachings. Moreover, Confucianism takes as fundamental the practical ethical goal of fostering a harmonious community and thereby emphasises the public way (*gong dao* 公道) and public profit (*gong li* 公利) over the private, not only for the general public (*min*), but for the ruler (*junzi*) as well. In this way the philosophical implications of *si* appear. Confucians have since early on consistently rejected self-interests over the political, social and ethical ideal of the public good. In particular, in the Song-dynasty School of Nature and Principle (*Xingli xue*) held *si* to be the foundation of selfishness and desire, and warned against this in statements such as 'preserving the principle of Heaven and prevent human desire'.

References: Lau, 1970, 1979; Morohashi, 1960; *Yugyo Sajon Pyonchan Wiwonhoe*, ed., 1990.

TODD CAMERON THACKER

Si duan 四端
(Four Beginnings)

Si duan, sometimes translated as 'four sprouts' or 'four germs', refers to the innate moral tendencies of human nature. In **Mengzi** 2A: 6 and 6A: 6, the *si duan* are given as: *ceyin zhi xin* 惻隱之心 (the heart/mind of compassion or pity), *xiuwu zhi xin* 羞惡之心 (the heart/mind of shame at evil), *cirang zhi xin* 辭讓之心 (the heart/mind of respect or deference), and *shifei zhi xin* 是非之心 (the heart/mind of [discerning] right and wrong). These are the spontaneous 'sprouts' of **ren**, **yi**, **li**, and **zhi** respectively. **Mengzi** elaborates this spontaneity through the Ox Mountain 'parable' (6A: 8). *Si duan* as moral feelings are thor-

oughly explored in the **Four–Seven Debate** among Korean Neo-Confucians.

References: Chan, Wing-tsit, 1963d: 56, 65; Kalton, 1994; Lau, 1970: 16–27.

THOMAS SELOVER

Si–Meng xuepai 思孟學派
(The Zisi–Mengzi School)

Xunzi probably originated the notion of a Zisi–Mengzi School, i.e. of a spiritual and intellectual filiation between Zisi (**Kong Ji**), Confucius' grandson, and the fourth-century philosopher **Mengzi**, by presenting the relationship between them in a critical light (see *Xunzi*, ch. 6 *Fei shi er zi* 非十二子, Contra twelve philosophers). Just as the **Tian xia** (The whole world) chapter of the *Zhuangzi* 莊子 (ch. 33), and the '*Xian xue* 顯學' (Eminence in learning) chapter of the *Han Fei zi* 韓非子 (ch. 50), this chapter of the *Xunzi* provides a useful survey of currents of contemporary thought and an important insight into the intellectual life of late Warring States China.

But paradoxically enough, Xunzi's condemnation of rival currents within the Confucian heritage itself is even more virulently critical than that of the *Zhuangzi* and the *Han Fei zi* chapters which could reasonably be expected to be so. In fact, Xunzi's particularly violent (and sometimes unfounded) attack against Zisi and Mengzi was to reject him towards the margins of the Confucian mainstream, especially from the Tang dynasty (618–907) onwards, when the process of canonisation of Mengzi started. Thus the question arises whether Xunzi is indeed in good faith, and whether he is to be believed when he bundles Zisi and Mengzi together:

'Some men follow the model of the Ancient Kings in a fragmentary way, but they do not understand its guiding principles. Still their abilities are manifold, their memory great, and their experiences and knowledge both varied and broad.

They have initiated a theory for which they claim great antiquity, calling it the Five Processes theory. Peculiar and unreasonable in the extreme, it lacks proper logical categories. Mysterious and enigmatic, it lacks a satisfactory theoretical basis. Esoteric and laconic in its statements, it lacks adequate explanations. To give their propositions a cloak of respectability and to win respect and veneration for them, they claim: "These doctrines represent the genuine words of the gentleman of former times. Zisi provided the tune for them, and Mengzi harmonised it" (*Zisi chang zhi, Meng Ke he zhi* 子思唱之, 孟軻和之).

The stupid, indecisive, deluded Ru (Confucians) of today enthusiastically welcome these notions, unaware that they are false. They pass on what they have received, believing that, on account of these theories, Confucius and Zigong 子弓 (the text should read Ziyou 子游 but it contradicts the condemnation of Ziyou as a 'base Ru' later on in the chapter) would be highly esteemed by later generations. It is in just this that they offend against Zisi and Mengzi' (*Xunzi* 6, in Knoblock, 1994).

Later tradition, especially from the Han onwards, takes for granted the direct filiation between Zisi and Mengzi. According to the latter's biography in *Shi ji* (chapter 74, pp. 2343 and following), 'Mengzi received instruction from a follower of Zisi'. In the twelfth century, **Zhu Xi** squarely declared that 'Zisi composed the '*Zhongyong*' in order to transmit it to Mengzi.' In other words, talking about a 'Zisi–Mengzi School' is tantamount to establishing a textual filiation between the *Mengzi* and the *Zhong yong*, now a chapter of the *Li ji*. But, as is shown in the article on Zisi, the recent Guodian archaeological finds might shed new light on this traditional view.

Reference: Knoblock, 1988, vol. I: 224.

ANNE CHENG

Si shu 四書
(The Four Books)

If we are to believe the testimonies of the *Song shi* (chapters *Daoxue zhuan* and *Cheng Yi zhuan*), the Cheng brothers (see **Cheng Hao** and **Cheng Yi**) originated the habit of grouping the *Daxue* (*Great Learning*) and *Zhongyong* (*Doctrine of the Mean*) chapters of the *Li ji* (*Book of Rites*) together with the *Lunyu* (*Analects*) and the *Mengzi* into a corpus of 'Four Books' placed on a par with the Six Classics (*Liu jing*). The *Zhongyong* (often coupled with the *Zhou Yi*, the *Book of Changes*) was supposed to provide a source of inspiration for an overarching anthropocosmic conception while the *Daxue* was regarded as the 'entrance gate on the path of virtue' (*ru de zhi men* 入德之門), the *Lunyu* and the *Mengzi* being the basis for a sound reading of the Classics.

ANNE CHENG

Si shu zhangju jizhu
四書章句集注
(*The Collected Annotations on the Four Books*)

This compilation by **Zhu Xi** probably constitutes the core of his exegetical work (altogether, he devoted some forty years of his life to it). In his selection of a new canon extolling the *Da xue* (*Great Learning*) and the *Zhongyong* (*Doctrine of the Mean*) chapters of the *Li ji* (*Book of Rites*), coupled with the *Mengzi* and *Lunyu* (*Analects*), Zhu Xi followed in the footsteps of the Cheng brothers. Zhu Xi's interpretive compendium is composed of the *Daxue zhangju* in one *juan* (section), the *Zhongyong zhangju* in one *juan*, the *Lunyu jizhu* in ten *juan*, and the *Mengzi jizhu* in fourteen *juan*. This succession indicates a didactical order, whereby the student of the Confucian way is supposed to start with the easiest (the *Daxue*) and finish with the more complex (the *Mengzi*).

Claiming to 'take Master Cheng's meaning' (*qu Chengzi zhi yi* 取程子之意), Zhu Xi rearranged the text of the *Great Learning* into one chapter of 'classic' (where Zhu imagined the mutual identity of the text's messages – providing a clear definition and prescription of the goals, principles and procedures for moral self-cultivation and socio-political activism (and Confucius' teachings) and ten chapters of 'commentary' (attributed to Confucius' disciple, Zengzi); he even made an interpolation to fill in what he regarded as a lacuna in the text and excised some characters that he judged to be superfluous. Zhu Xi further added a commentary on the classical passage of **gewu zhizhi** (investigation of things and extension of knowledge to the utmost).

After Zhu Xi's death, this compilation gradually came to be regarded as the 'ladder leading to the Six Classics (**Liu jing**)', in fact it turned out to be a 'ladder to success' since it was to become the basis of the curriculum for civil service examinations starting from 1313 in the Yuan dynasty down to 1905 when the examination system disappeared altogether, followed shortly by the end of the Qing dynasty and the establishment of the Republic.

References: Gardner, 1986; Zhu Xi, 1983.

ANNE CHENG

Siku quanshu zongmu tiyao 四庫全書總目提要

This book includes scholarly notes to the large number of literary works collected at imperial orders from 1773 to 1782 and classified in the four categories of Classics (**Jing**), histories (*Shi* 史), masters of thought (*Zi* 子) and belles-lettres (*Ji* 集). The descriptive accounts and shrewd assessments form the most valuable bibliographical guide to traditional Chinese literature that is available.

References: Hummel, 1943: 120–2; Teng & Biggerstaff, 1971: 18–20.

MICHAEL LOEWE

Sima Guang 司馬光
1019–1086
(*zi* Junshi 君實, *hao* Qiwu Zi 齊物子, Sushui Xiansheng 涑水先生)

As a son already possessing official rank by virtue of the state service of his eminent father Sima Chi 司馬池 (980–1041; *zi* Hezhong 和中), Sima Guang might well have entered the civil service solely on the basis hereditary 'shadow' or *yin* 蔭 privilege. However, being also a child prodigy especially versed in the **Chunqiu Zuo zhuan** (*Spring and Autumn Annals with Zuo's Commentary*), Sima Guang elected to take the examinations anyway and he obtained the coveted *jinshi* degree in 1038. Sima Guang thereafter embarked on an official career almost entirely circumscribed by service at the early Song capital of Kaifeng 開封, and he served there with distinction under four successive emperors. However, after thirty years of continuous service, the distinguished tenure of Sima Guang was disrupted by his great confrontations with Wang Anshi over the latter's New Policies (*xin fa* 新法), which arose while Sima served as vice censor-in-chief (*yushi zhongcheng* 御史中丞). The imperial favour bestowed upon Wang Anshi's views at the expense of all others very shortly drove Sima Guang to resignation from office and into self-imposed exile. Nevertheless, even while residing in Luoyang for the next fifteen years, Sima persevered in his role as the arch adversary of Wang and his policies. Sima Guang was restored to office – as vice director of the Chancellery (*menxia shilang* 門下侍郎) – in the last year of his life, upon the accession of the Zhezong emperor (r. 1086–1100). Dying a mere five months after Wang, Sima made the abolition of the New Policies his final act. He received the posthumous title (*shi* 謚) of Wenzheng 文正 and, in 1267, was canonised as a duke (*gong* 公) in the **Kong miao** (Temple of Confucius).

Thought and works

Perhaps the most common misconception about the thought of Sima Guang is that it was averse to all changes and, consequently, categorically anti-reformist. In truth, much like Wang Anshi, Sima Guang acknowledged that the prevailing bureaucratic structure of his time was fraught with defects and that it demanded change. As evidence, we can note that the two men began their petitions for reform independently but at essentially the same time – approximately the pivotal year 1060. Nevertheless, they differed profoundly over the nature of reform and their differences stemmed mostly from their incompatible conceptions of what the real deficiencies in government were and what was required to remedy them.

Wang Anshi saw the flaws immanent in existing institutions as the great impediment to change and he, accordingly, concentrated his energies on eradicating them collectively. Sima Guang instead saw the various problems besetting the empire primarily as a function of its flawed system of management. For Sima, the real deficiencies resided in the processes whereby those who staffed the complex of institutions that constituted the government were appointed, employed and promoted. Sima advocated a schema that made the personnel pool – rather than the institutions themselves – the targets of reform. In his view, for the sake of the empire, all the functionaries of the state – from high to low – should feel morally compelled to subordinate their selfish interests for the purpose of securing the goal of a grander political good. Thus, Sima Guang's thought was less pointedly directed toward ensuring the well-being of the masses of society than it was committed to safeguarding the political order, the hierarchy, and, at all costs, the territorial sanctity of the state. Maintaining these latter constructs intact would necessarily ensure the welfare of the people. Consequently, we can regard Sima Guang's idea of polity as a kind of 'preservationist' model.

Nonetheless, despite its emphasis on the proper selection and indoctrination of its supporting cast, the most weighty and conspicuous responsibilities in Sima Guang's model of preservation rested with the emperor and his progeny. Ultimately, the success or failure of the entire structure depended entirely upon them. Employing standard analogical reasoning, Sima Guang once compared the emperor's relationship to the government as being like that of an owner's relationship to a great house. In erecting a government, as when building the house, one must lay its foundation (i.e. its people) firmly, prop up its pillars (i.e. its rites and laws) securely, reinforce its beams (i.e. its high officials) amply, etc. Thereafter, in the care of an able descendant, there is no reason why the structure should not last forever. We can discern not only a conservative but an antiquarian dimension in Sima Guang's analogy that stems from the fact that its model of government requires that the emperor himself render it direct and constant attention. It, therefore, contrasts strongly with the images evoked by Wang Anshi's model – images of corps of aggressively activist ministers enlisted into the service of a powerful but relatively passive sovereign.

Despite his prominence as a political actor and theorist, Sima Guang achieved even greater renown as a writer. Most of Sima's surviving writings have been assembled in the conventional scholar's literary collection, which, in his case, bears the title *Wenguo Wenzheng Sima Gong wenji* 溫國文正司馬公文集 (*Literary Collection of Duke Sima Wenguo Wenzheng*). But Sima Guang is best known as a historian and as the author of a singular work of history – the **Zizhi tongjian** (*Comprehensive Mirror for the Aid of Government*).

Influence

The influence of Sima Guang continues to be exerted primarily through his major work *Comprehensive Mirror for the Aid of Government*. While it is ostensibly a dispassionate work of history, the book nevertheless stands as an enduring testament of its author's signature political ideals. Its grounding theme is that history should, at all times, be held before the monarch's face like a cautionary mirror. To be sure, this remains a salient and inescapable message – one that continues to inform the thinking of China's bureaucratic elite just as much today as it did in the years immediately following Sima Guang's death.

References: Balazs & Hervouet, 1978: 69–72, 100–1, 183–4, 232–3, 392–3; Bol, 1992: 30, 70–1, 73, 151, 176, 189–91, 212–53, 329–41; Hartwell, 1971: 690–727; Jiang, 1994: 42, 100, 111; Liu James, 1959: 7, 9, 35, 55, 65, 91, 95, 103, 105–8; Sariti, 1972: 53–76; Wyatt, 1996: 8, 62, 135–6, 141, 144–8, 151–4, 162–5, 165–75, 217–18.

DON J. WYATT

Sima Qian 司馬遷
145?–86? BCE

A member of a family which had produced specialists in astronomy and calendar from Zhou times, in his youth Sima Qian travelled widely in different parts of the Han empire and succeeded his father **Sima Tan** as Director of Astrology (*Taishi ling* 太史令) after his death in 110 BCE. Sima Tan had for some time been compiling his historical account of mankind and he enjoined his son to complete the task that he himself had been unable to finish. Sima Qian started by collecting written material and consulting some of his own contemporay scholars such as **Kong Anguo** on the problems of works such as the *Book of Documents* (*Shang shu*); he then embarked on his task. He took his subject right up to his own time (*c.* 90 BCE) and it is to Sima Qian that is due the credit for compiling and leaving the *Shi ji* very much in the condition in which it exists today.

As Director of Astrology himself, Sima Qian was intimately involved in the changes which were introduced 105–104 BCE, inaugurating a new regnal title (Taichu 太初) and a newly adjusted calendar, and adopting Earth in place of Water as the patron element of the dynasty. His career was severely marred owing to the defence that he expressed on behalf of Li Ling 李陵, who had been obliged to surrender to the Xiongnu 匈奴 in 99 BCE. Such an opinion ran counter to that of **Han Wudi** or his advisers and Sima Qian was punished by castration. Acutely aware of the disgrace that he had suffered and brought upon his family, Sima Qian nonetheless determined to complete the task that his father had left him, dying *c.* 86 BCE.

References: Chavannes, 1969, vol. I: vii–lxi; Watson, 1958; Nienhauser, 1986: 720–3.

MICHAEL LOEWE

Sima Tan 司馬談
d. 110 BCE

For several generations Sima Tan's ancestors had been trained in astro-calendrical skills and in his own turn Sima Tan, also trained in Daoist thought, held the post of Director of Astrology (*Taishi ling* 太史令), perhaps from 140 BCE. Classifying the more important modes of thought that were current in his time in the six groups of **Yin–Yang** 陰陽, *Ru* 儒, *Mo* 墨, *Fa* 法, *Ming* 名 and *Dao* 道, he advised **Han Wudi** (r. 141–87 BCE) to initiate the state worship of Hou tu 后土 (113 BCE) and Tai yi 太一 (112 BCE) and to perform certain rites on Mount Tai 泰. Too old to accompany his emperor on that journey, Sima Tan died in 110 BCE.

At an unknown date Sima Tan had started the work of writing his history, which was in time to be known as the *Shi ji*. He left his son **Sima Qian** earnest instructions for its completion.

Reference: Chavannes, 1969, vol. I: vii–lxi.

MICHAEL LOEWE

Sima Xiangru 司馬相如
c. 179–117 BCE

Suffering from poor health, and a stammerer, Sima Xiangru was not anxious to serve in high office and never did so. Nevertheless, as a native of the southwest he played an important part in promoting the advance of Chinese authority in those distant regions. In his second, and perhaps greater, contribution he brought a long-lasting influence to bear on the development of Chinese literature.

For a short time during Han Jingdi's reign (157–141 BCE) Sima Xiangru served as a Gentleman (*Lang* 郎) and as a Cavalryman in Permanent Attendance (*Wuji Changshi* 武騎常侍). He subsequently became a guest at the court of the King of Liang, returning to his native home in 143 BCE. After a famous romantic attachment and an elopement, he was summoned to the Capital Chang'an and in *c.* 135 BCE he was sent to convey a message of encouragement and reassurance to the peoples of the two commanderies of Ba 巴 and Shu 蜀, thereby reinforcing their loyalty to the Han imperial court. It was largely due to his advice that **Han Wudi**'s government maintained its firm control in the southwest and was able to rely on the support of some of the non-assimilated peoples of those parts. Such policies did not pass without question and Sima Xiangru became subject to criticism and perhaps unfair treatment.

Throughout his life Sima Xiangru took the opportunity to write rhapsodies (*fu* 賦) in which he would call attention to certain public events or issues, commenting on the contemporary way of life and remonstrating with the throne or officials as he saw fit. In an essay that became available after his death (117 BCE) he had recommended that the *Feng* 封 and *Shan* 禪 rites should be performed on Mount Tai 泰; there followed the institution of the state cults to Hou tu 后土 in 114 BCE and to Tai yi 太一 in 113 BCE, and Wudi's ascent of Mount Tai in 110 BCE. His rhapsodies gained considerable admiration, leading the way to the growing popularity of this genre of writing and exciting imitation by poets such as **Yang Xiong**.

References: Hervouet, 1964; Nienhauser, 1986: 723–5.

MICHAEL LOEWE

Simen boshi 四門博士
(Erudite/Academician of the School of the Four Gates)

The erudites in charge of education in the School of the Four Gates (*Simen xue*). The school was first founded as an elementary school in the Northern Wei (386–535) and continued by the Sui (581–618), to admit aristocratic boys under fourteen. As such, it was a preparatory school of the Imperial Academy (***Tai xue***). The School continued to operate throughout the Tang, but the admission age was raised to nineteen and above. Its difference from the Imperial Academy was thus in the family background of the students, a distinction no longer tenable after the ninth century. The School was left to die in the Northern Sung. The *locus classicus* of 'the four gates' is *Book of History* (***Shang shu***), meaning the gates at the four corners of the national territory. Tang government appointed seven erudites to the School.

Reference: Lee, T.H.C., 2000.

THOMAS H.C. LEE

Sirhak 實學
(Practical Learning)

Practical Learning is the scholastic trend that emerged in China and Korea focusing on practical application and actual evidence as opposed to what many saw as the empty theorising and debates of Song and Ming scholarship. The Cheng–Zhu School of the Learning of Nature and Principle (*Sŏngnihak* 性理學) was adopted in early Chosŏn and later flourished. On the one hand, Neo-Confucian theories continued to diversify but also became more finely developed and, on the other hand, any objective unity between various factions was lost as scholars devoted themselves to 'empty' dogmatic theories. Moreover, given the social and economic devastation caused by the Japanese invasions in the 1590s, the Qing invasion in 1636 and the immediate problems they caused, as well as the introduction of Practical Learning and western thought from China, a new practical focus developed in Korea by scholars who pursued policies to resolve the problems facing society. In other words, a more modern consciousness started to take root after the Japanese invasions and flourished during the reigns of Kings Yŏngjo (1724–1776) and Chŏngjo (1776–1800). Practical Learning scholars pointed out the social, economic and political backwardness resulting from traditional Neo-Confucian political ideas, and presented proposals to remedy the situation. To the moralistic Neo-Confucian scholars they accused of empty theorising, they insisted that only after a practical, economically stable livelihood had been established among the people could there be any moral development. They had wide ranging interests and applied this practical approach not only to politics, economics, the military, education and farming, but also to astronomy, medicine, mathematics, geography, language, culture and history. Of course, Practical Learning was also based on the Neo-Confucianism it criticised and it likewise looked on morality as fundamental and held manifesting the **Dao** within human nature (*xing*) as the goal along with a prosperous and stable society.

One of the forerunners in Practical Learning thought, Yi Su-gwang 李睟光 (1563–1628), gave many of his contemporaries an appreciation of the new trend through his introduction, albeit fragmentary, of not only Chinese thought and culture but also western scientific culture, Christian thought and South East Asian geography. Although **Yi I** (Yulgok) gave birth to an age of reform, **Yu Hyŏng-wŏn** 柳馨遠 (1622–1673) called for full-scale reforms of the entire national order. **Yi Ik** continued to develop Yu's ideas. Yi Ik said, 'Before we pursue an ideal government according to the *Dao*, we must first lay the foundation of the land system; if we do not do that we will only become destitute; development will be uneven, and there will be no peace within the kingdom.' In short, for Yi Ik, economic

problems had to be solved first before ideal forms of government could be realised. Moreover, he also held that gentlemen–scholars had to be able to maintain a livelihood; even if they were engaged in industry or even commerce, which until then was scorned by the literati, they could do so without abandoning morality.

Hong Tae-yong developed Practical Learning another step after his return from Beijing, where he deepened his knowledge of natural science. He wrote a famous work, *Euisan Mundap* (*Dialogue on Mount Ui* (the name of a mountain in Manchuria)) which criticises the empty theorising of traditional Neo-Confucianism, rejects speculation and subjective evaluations of things seen from a personal point of view, and asserts an objective view of things as seen from the point of view of Heaven. **Chŏng Yag-yong** was a great synthesiser of Practical Learning thought in the early nineteenth century. He stated that the true value of Confucianism is scholarship that teaches people to be capable of handling whatever comes up, this includes both military skills and culture, as well as how to rule the country and pacify the people. He also criticised traditional Neo-Confucianism for its empty talk and useless theories. Chŏng Yag-yong supported practical scholarship that enriched the nation and strengthened the military. He also introduced western science and techniques. Supported by **Mengzi**'s idea that bad rulers could be deposed, Chŏng Yag-yong rejected the idea that kings ruled by the divine mandate, and instead insisted that rulers existed for the people, not people for the rulers. In short, rulers who failed to look after the livelihood of the people could be deposed. The last major Practical Learning scholar in the Chosŏn dynasty was **Ch'oe Han-gi**. He developed a philosophy based on material force (*qi*). Ch'oe tried to revive the basis of Confucianism by relating Confucian ideas to scientific modernisation. He also gave precedence to experience over theory. In addition, unlike previous Practical Larning scholars, Ch'oe supported the opening up of the country and establishing diplomatic relations with other countries.

In sum, there are a few things common to these Practical Learning scholars. Firstly, a common concern for practical application, something that can be seen in their interest in utility and welfare. Secondly, a concern with evidence and the objective over the subjective and the application of this to various fields of inquiry, i.e., a more modern, scientific attitude. Thirdly, a more critical attitude that pointed out the contradictions in society and the need for reform. Lastly, a more open academic attitude that drew not only on the thought of **Wang Yang-ming**, Evidential Learning (*Kaozhengxue* 考證學), and western thought (*xi xue*), but also on Buddhism and Daoism.

References: Keum Jang-t'ae, 1987; *Sirhakŭi Ch'ŏlhak*, 1996.

NAM-JIN HUH

Sŏ Kyŏng-dŏk 徐敬德
1489–1546
(*zi* Kaku 可久, *hao* Hwadam 花潭)

Sŏ was an early Chosŏn philosopher. His mother was said to have dreamt of Confucius on the night she conceived him. Sŏ was an especially bright child who was very respectful to his elders. At the age of eighteen, upon reading the line 'extension of knowledge lays in the investigation of things' (*zhizhizai gewu* 致知在格物) from the Great Learning (*Da xue*), Sŏ lamented, 'When one pursues one's studies and yet does not first investigate things, though one reads the words, where will one write?' and attached the characters 'heaven, earth, ten thousand things' (Kr. *ch'ŏnjimanmul* 天地萬物) to his wall and every day put great effort into his investigations. Sŏ married at the age of nineteen and by his thirty-first year, was selected by **Cho Kwŏng-cho** to be recommended for a government post without having to take an examination; Sŏ however declined this recommendation, changed his name to Hwadam, and built a study where with ever greater resolution he set about to dedicate himself exclusively to his research and education. Later, at the request of his mother, he sat for the civil service examination and took first place, but ultimately he resigned the post and absorbed himself in researching Neo-Confucian metaphysics (*Sŏngnihak* 性理學), with all later nominations to government office continually meeting his refusal.

Sŏ was particularly clear in his studies of ritual and propriety (*li*), and upon the deaths of Kings Chung Chong (r. 1506–1544) and In Chong (r. 1544), he wore his mourning clothes and grieved for three months.

Sŏ did not introduce to Korea the pure **Zhu Xi** school of thought which was present during the Song dynasty, but he established a unique harmonisation of the philosophical thought of **Zhou Dunyi**, **Shao Yong** and **Zhang Zai**, in which the material force (*qi*) is the single source of the universe (Kr. *kiirwollon* 氣一元論). Within his Neo-Confucian philosophical theory, found in his thesis on the Supreme Void (*tai xu* Kr. *t'aehŏ*), space is replete with primal vital energy (*yuan qi*) which comprises metaphysical objects; the essence of material force is the Great Void. Sŏ explains this in the following way: the essence of material force which is the Great Void is pure, formless and innate (*a priori*). There are no limits to its size and it has no beginning; its origins cannot possibly be investigated. The pure emptiness is completely quiescent (*jing*, see *dong jing*) and this lack of movement (*dong*) is none other than the source of material force. The boundaries of the Great Void are far and yet it is not in any way empty. Thus its existence cannot be referred to as emptiness (Kr. *mu* 無). The rhythm of creation and annhilation of everything is infinite in its transformation; this is none other than the rhythm of material force, like the ebb and flow of wind and waves.

Accordingly, Sŏ ascribes all things in the universe to material force, the infinite, completely full, without beginning nor end, eternal existence, whose sole creative power is depended upon by all. Material force collects and disperses much like water freezes and thaws, but whose original state is ever preserved, but in itself is never subject to annihilation. This theory, akin to the scientific law of the conservation of energy, is called Sŏ's *Ilgijangjonsŏl* (一氣 長存說).

On the relationship of principle to material force, Sŏ said that there can be no principle outside material force, and principle gains its existence from material force, and can never precede material force. Material force has no beginning, and also principle is without a beginning. If principle were first, the material force would have a beginning. This is Sŏ's theory of 'material force as the single source' mentioned above. From this he also asserted the similarity of life and death (Kr. *sasaeng-yŏil* 死生如一), from which he criticised Buddhism, for since material force is not subject to annihilation, but transformation, and all things are but temporary accumulations or deposits of material force, human life is also not part of annihilation but only transformation of material force.

The originality of Sŏ's material force philosophy (Kr. *Kich'ŏlhak* 氣哲學) and its resulting school were highly appraised by scholars like **Yi Hwang** and **Yi I**.

References: Yi Jong-ho, 1998; Yi Nam-yŏng, 1987.

NAM-JIN HUH

Sŏng Hon 成渾
1535–1598
(*zi* Howŏn 浩原, *hao* Ugye 牛溪)

Sŏng Hon was a Neo-Confucian (*Sŏngnihak* 性理學) scholar during the mid-Chosŏn period. As a youth his interest leaned more towards concentrating on scholarship than on getting a government position, but in 1575 he entered government service, even-

tually holding a number of high offices, including fourth state councillor. In 1592 he held a position advising the Crown Prince (Kwanghae-gun). He admired the scholarship of both **Yi Hwang** (T'oegye) and **Yi I** (Yulgok) as two great masters of Neo-Confucianism.

After reviewing some of **Zhu Xi**'s works, Sŏng Hon thought T'oegye's theory of mutual issuance of principle and material force (Kr. *igihobalsŏl* 理氣互發說) agreed with Zhu Xi's theory and wrote to Yulgok for his thoughts on the matter. This exchange started what became the second part of the **Four–Seven Debate**, a debate initiated by **Ki Tae-sŭng** and Yi Hwang. Sŏng asserted that at the original, conceptual level, the Four Beginnings (*si duan*), Seven Emotions (*qi qing*), the heart/mind of the Way (*dao xin*), and the human heart/mind (*ren xin*) were not alike, but when it came to their applications in a person's character and emotion they were similar. Hence he supported Yi Hwang's 'mutual issuance' theory. He also held that the heart/mind of the Way and the human heart/mind could not be reduced to emotion alone and that they should not be spoken of in terms of just principle (*li*) or material force (*qi*), respectively.

Sŏng Hon had a large number of students, and one of them, Cho Hŏn 趙憲 (1544–1592), became the leader of one of the 'Righteous Armies' that was raised to help combat the Japanese invasions in the late sixteenth century. Sŏng's works include the *Ugyejip* 牛溪集, and *Jumun Jikyŏl* 朱門旨訣.

References: Kim Ch'ung-yŏl, 1988; Sŏng Hon, 1976.

NAM-JIN HUH

Song Si-yŏl 宋時烈
1607–1689
(*zi* Yŏngpo 永補, *hao* Uam 尤庵)

Song is one of the representative Confucian scholars of the second half of the

Chosŏn dynasty; he is known as 'the **Zhu Xi** of Korea' and played an important role in determining the spirit of the age in Confucian theories of righteousness (*yi*, Kr. *ŭi*) and propriety (*li*, Kr. *ye*). This trend is related to the humiliation suffered by Koreans at the hands of invading Qing Manchu forces in 1636, and the desire to expel these forces and to even restore the former Chinese Ming dynasty to what he deemed their rightful rule. Song was head of the Noron School, and at the same time was a great scholar of the Learning of Nature and Principle (*Sŏngnihak* 性理學). The scholarly lineage of the **Kiho School** is traditionally held to be **Yi I**, then Kim Chang-saeng 金長生 (1548–1631, *zi* Hee Won 希元, *hao* Sakye 沙溪) (see *Karye Chimnam*), Kim Chip 金集 (1574–1656, *zi* Sakang 士剛, *hao* Sin Tok-chae 慎獨齋) and followed by Song.

Song asserted that the Supreme Ultimate (*tai ji*, Kr. *t'aegŭk*) is 'The Essence' that by moving (*dong*, Kr. *tong*) creates **yang**, and by resting, **yin**. He was supportive of **Yi I**'s theory of the single path of the issuance of material force (Kr. *gibal ildosŏl* 氣發一途說) in the **Four–Seven Debate**, and proposed that both principle (*li*, Kr. *i*) and material force (*qi*, Kr. *gi*) are one, and at the same time two entities. Moreover, in establishing the strict orthodoxy of *Sŏngni*, he took Zhu Xi's thought as the standard and reassessed other schools with conflicting views, to ultimately bring them into line with Zhu's standard, by means of Song's unique perspective on Zhu Xi.

References: Keum   Jang-t'ae,   1998b; *Kihohakp'aŭi Ch'ŏlhak Sasang*, 1995.

JANG-TAE KEUM

Song–Yuan xuean 宋元學案

(*Records of Song–Yuan Scholars*)

Song–Yuan xuean is an important account of Confucian thought in the Song and Yuan periods. It was first compiled by **Huang Zongxi**, who had completed a similar work for the Ming period entitled *Mingru xuean*. Unlike the latter, *Song Yuan xuean* was hardly finished at the hands of Huang Zongxi. His son Huang Bai jia 黃百家 and later **Quan Zuwang** contributed to its compilation in succession. When it was first printed in 1838, it became clearly a work of multiple authors, including editorial contribution from the final editors and compilers He Shaoji 何紹基 (1800–74), Feng Yunhao 馮雲濠 (?–?) and Wang Zicai 王梓材 (?–?). Of the 100 *juans* of the 1838 edition, Huang Zongxi authored only 25 *juans* and Quan Zuwang contributed 45 *juans*. In addition, Quan heavily edited and expanded 17 *juans* by Huang.

Quan's involvement in the completion of the work was significant. From 1745 through 1754, he devoted himself to collection of materials and writing of the work. The presentation of information in the *Song–Yuan xuean* was much improved over that of the *Mingru xuean*. At the beginning of each 'case', Quan provided a table showing the relationship among the scholars within a 'case', followed by a short introduction to the thought of the main thinker of the case or the latter's relationship with other thinkers.

In contrast with the *Mingru xuean*, the approach to the merits of various thinkers was much more inclusive. Quan was critical of Huang's partisan perspective in selection. The large number of Confucians added by Quan indicates much more than the incomplete condition of the project resulting from Huang's death. It signals a different approach to the history of Confucian thought. Quan included important figures like **Ouyang Xiu**, **Fan Zhongyan**, **Sima Guang**, figures who were not interested in the philosophical discussion of human nature and its relationship with the general order of existence. Therefore, unlike the *Mingru xuean*, which was devoted to an account of Confucian scholars who were interested in issues of human nature, the heart/mind, as well as their metaphysical relationship with the general order of existence, the *Sung–Yuan xuean* defined the term *ru* in a much broader sense by virtue of its inclusion of Confucians who made no contribution to the understanding of those issues.

The inclusion of a greater number of Confucians does not mean the lack of an ideological stance in the work as a whole. Quan included anecdotes of, and comments on, the scholar by his contemporaries and scholars of later generations as supplementary notes. Furthermore, he did not shy away from registering his disagreement with Huang Zongxi's view (*Song–Yuan xuean*, 34.3a–b). Quan was able to include biographical information on many Song Confucians, thanks to his involvement in copying the *Yongle dadian* 永樂大典, which preserved many Song texts that had been lost.

KAI-WING CHOW

Sŏnggyun'gwan 成均館
(National Confucian College)

Sŏnggyun'gwan was the National Confucian College, an educational institution, established in Seoul during the Chosŏn dynasty (1392–1910). The term 'Sŏnggyun' was originally the name of the Confucian College in the Chinese Han Dynasty (206 BCE–220 CE). The term itself is taken from a passage in the *The Rites of the Zhou* (*Zhou li*), where 'sŏng' (*cheng* 成) is seen as completing a person's innate potential and 'gyun' (*jun* 均), which literally means 'level', is here taken as evening out or correcting a person's bad habits.

Besides the link to the Zhou dynasty there were institutional predecessors in Korea: there was the National Confucian Academy in Koguryŏ dynasty (tr. 37 BCE–668 CE), the National Confucian College in the Silla dynasty (tr. 57 BCE–935 CE) and the National Academy in Koryŏ dynasty

(918–1392). In 1298, King Ch'ingyŏl (r. 1274–1308) called the institution 'Sŏnggyungam', but King Ch'ungsŏn (r. 1308–1313) changed the name to 'Sŏnggyun'gwan' after he ascended the throne in 1308. In 1356, the name reverted back to 'Sŏnggyungam' as part of King Kongmin's (r. 1351–1374) anti-Yuan policy, but the name once again was changed to 'Sŏnggyun'gwan' in 1362, a name it has since kept. It was moved to the new capital, Seoul (then called Hanyang), at the beginning of the Chosŏn dynasty. In the early part of the new dynasty, Sŏnggyun'gwan continued to use the system it had operated under during the Koryŏ dynasty, but a new system was instituted in 1466.

The traditional curriculum started with the Four Books (*Si shu*), the *Analects*, *Mengzi*, the *Great Learning* the *Doctrine of the Mean* and the Five Classics (*Wu jing*). Building on this foundation, a number of other Confucian texts were read, such as *Reflections on Things at Hand* (*Jinsi lu*), the *Great Compendium of Neo-Confucianism* (*Xingli daquan* 性理大全), as well as historical and legal works. However, the emphasis of the curriculum shifted according to changes in emphasis on the civil service examinations. Lastly, non-Confucian texts, i.e., Daoist and Buddhist texts, were barred from the curriculum.

At the beginning of the dynasty Sŏnggyun'gwan had about 150 students, but by 1429 this number grew to around 200. Almost all the students were sons of literati families. The amount of support it received also increased over time. During the reign of King Sŏngjong (r. 1469–1494) Sŏnggyun'gwan had about 2,400 tracts of land assigned to it for support; by the reign of King Hyojong (r. 1649–1659) this had increased by another 358 tracts. The increase in the number of slaves was even more dramatic. While there were only about 400 slaves in the beginning, this number had increased to several thousand by the eighteenth century, though by the late eighteenth century all slaves in Korea were freed.

By the mid-eighteenth century the situation at Sŏnggyun'gwan had declined. The academic environment started to decline late in the Chosŏn period due to the rise of factionalism and private academies that focused on preparing students for the civil service examinations. Adding to the problem was the number of students at the Sŏnggyun'gwan who ignored their studies because they were caught up in political disputes between various factions. Moreover, this situation continued into the nineteenth century when there was an effort to reform the institution in 1887. This attempt failed. Reforms were implemented after 1894 including the abolition of the Confucian based civil service examinations. In 1895 a new system was initiated. This included a three-year curriculum divided into two parts. Students were selected from a pool of applicants between twenty and forty years of age who had passed the entrance examination. As part of the reforms, new courses were added to the curriculum. Korean history was now a compulsory course and general history, mathematics and topography were optional. But these three courses also became compulsory just a year later, in 1896. Those who passed the graduation exam at the end of the three-year programme received a diploma. In short, these were modifications that respected the tradition of the institution, but, at the same time, helped modernise it. Confucian studies remained a required subject.

There was wholesale change during the Japanese colonial era as a result of colonial policies that undercut educational opportunities. One of these policies was to downgrade the status of Sŏnggyun'gwan by renaming it a 'Classical Studies Institute'. Confucians across the country called for the restoration of Sŏnggyun'gwan but this did not happen until after the Japanese defeat in World War II. In 1946, the National Confucian Society met in order to reestablish the University to continue the traditions of Sŏnggyun'gwan. As a result Sŏnggyun'gwan University was established in September 1946. It is now a University with sixty-four departments spread across six different colleges.

References: Keum Jang-t'ae, 1999; Yi Sŏng-mu, 1967.

JANG-TAE KEUM

Sŏnghak chibyo 聖學輯要
(*Tenets of Sagely Learning*)

When **Yi I** was a scholar–official in government and adviser for the king's education, he presented this book to King Sŏnjo (r. 1567–1608) in 1575, 'stressing the importance of studies of the Classics (Kr. *Kyŏnghak* 經學) and Histories (Kr. *Shisŏ* 史書) for cultivation of scholarship and political administration'. According to the preface, it is a simple arrangement and sample outline of the Way as found in the Four Books (**Si shu**) and Six Classics (**Liu jing**). Its objective is to ellucidate the easily lost way of these voluminous texts, by compiling an abstract of the important core. Yi achieved this by using the *Great Learning* (**Da xue**) as the guiding principle for the *Sŏnghak chibyo*, for he deemed the fundamental principles of the *Great Learning* indispensible to the sages' plans for proper rule, etc. Yi stressed that the *Great Learning* 'is the entrance to virtue (**de**, Kr. *tŏk*)', and accordingly composed his work from its standpoint. In the first chapter it explains the common view of self-cultivation and attaining to the virtue of **ren**. It then divides up the contents under discussion into cultivating one's character (*xiuji* 修己), stabilising the family (*qi jia*), ordering the state (*zhi guo*), and bringing world peace (**ping tianxia**). Finally, Yi I explores the practicality of the *Great Learning* under the title *Sŏnghyŏn Dot'ong* 聖賢道通. He hoped to present to the King the practical applications of these cardinal points of governance; however not only does he succeed in explaining the Way of the ruler, but he also presents an essential philosophical description of the Four Books and Six Classics. The special character of Yi I's scholarship offers people a means of realising themselves. In short, the work can enlighten the intellect and the heart of both ruler and the ruled.

References: Hwang Jun-yŏn, 1995; Yi I, 1985.

NAM-JIN HUH

Sŏnghak Sibto 聖學十圖
(*Ten Diagrams of Confucianism*)

This work by **Yi Hwang** comprises ten concise diagrams of the core principles of *Sŏnghak* scholarship and methods of self-cultivation, which he presented to the king in 1568. Later kings often had folding screens and small manuals of these diagrams at hand at all times to aid in their contemplative introspection; it was also published by royal decree as part of the corpus of ethical teaching materials. Yi's foremost place in Korean Confucianism is evident in his mature scholarly insights into the diagrams and comments by Song–Yuan Cheng–Zhu scholars which he recorded in this work.

Sŏnghak implies the learning of the sages (**sheng ren**, Kr. *sŏngin*) or the learning of the sage–king (*sheng wang*, Kr. *sŏngwang* 聖王). Yi Hwang showed that in the structure of *Sŏnghak* (as it relates to the human mind), principle (**li**, Kr. *i*) and human affairs (Kr. *sa* 事) are matched, the former being the fundamental, universal order and the latter being the everyday world, with reverence (*jing*, Kr. *kyŏng*) controlling this process. This is the core principle of *Sŏnghak*.

Yi's diagrams are composed of two structures of interpretation. The first five diagrams take Heaven's Way (**tian dao**, Kr. *ch'ŏndo*) as fundamental while dealing with practical matters like human ethics and virtuous deeds and affairs (*deye*, Kr. *tŏkkyo* 德業). The latter five diagrams deal with mind and nature (**xin xing**, Kr. *simsŏng*).

There are two types of commentary in the *Sŏnghak Sibto*: one for each diagram and the other for the overall ten. In the history of Korean Confucianism, the *Sŏnghak Sibto* is a classic which has inspired the most abundant research and commentaries upon it. Outside of Korea, the Japanese scholar Takahashi Susumu 高橋進 has written the *Li Taikei Shisa no Taikeiteki Kosei – Seigaku Juzu* 李退溪思想の體系的構成 – 聖學十圖; and Michael C. Kalton has written *To Become a Sage* (1988).

JANG-TAE KEUM

Sŏngho sasŏl 星湖僿說
(*Collected Works of Sŏngho*)

This work by **Yi Ik** records his thoughts and feelings, interests and readings, as well as his answers to his students' questions which he compiled from age forty to eighty. After his death his nephews put these notes in order. Later, Yi's student An Chŏng-bok 安鼎福 (1712–1791, *zi* Paeksun 百順, *hao* Sunam 順庵) reordered the notes by subject, publishing under the title *Sŏngho sasŏl Ryusun* 星湖僿說類選. This edition covers the five main subjects of Heaven and earth (**tian di**, Kr. *ch'ŏnji*), everything in the universe (*wan wu*, Kr. *manmul*), human affairs (Kr. *insa* 人事), Classics and Histories (Kr. *kyŏngsa* 經史), poetry and prose (Kr. *simun* 詩文) with a total of 3,007 items. This book is particularly positive in the reception of western science occuring at the time, with an open attitude towards the prevailing state of society and scholarship. From the Practical Learning (**Sirhak**) standpoint, Yi Ik opposed the traditional adherence of **Zhu Xi**'s system of thought, developing instead his own critical manner.

Reference: Han U-gŭn, 1980.

JANG-TAE KEUM

Soothill, William Edward
1861–1935

Soothill was the third Professor of Chinese at Oxford University, a post first held by James **Legge**. Like Legge, Soothill had extensive experience in China, some twenty-eight years residence there as a Protestant missionary–educator, before returning to Britain as a scholar. Also like Legge, Soothill readily recognised the religious and ceremonial elements in Confucius' thought and in Confucianism generally. However, Soothill saw Confucius more as a theorist emphasising the transcendence of the state over the individual, in matters political and religious. After Legge's translation, Soothill's was the second major scholarly rendering of the *Analects* (**Lunyu**) into English, appearing in 1910.

JOHN A. TUCKER

Su Che 蘇轍
1039–1112
(*zi* Ziyou 子由, *hao* Yingbin yilao 潁濱遺老, the Old Man of Yingbin)

Despite being the younger brother of the famous Northern Song literatus **Su Shi**, Su Che achieved fame in his own right. Both brothers received the coveted *jinshi* degree under **Ouyang Xiu** in 1057. Su Che then passed an imperial decree examination in 1061. His strong criticism of contemporary policies, however, almost cost him his post (Shiba & Franke 1976: 882). Initially associated with **Wang Anshi**'s attempt to reform Song government institutions, he nevertheless fell out with Wang after arguing against various New Policies (especially the Green Sprouts Loan programme, the *qing miao fa* 青苗法). He therefore suffered demotion to provincial posts. Although he enjoyed political rehabilitation in 1086 during the administration of **Sima Guang**, he was subsequently blacklisted as a member of the Yuanyou faction (*Yuanyou dang* 元祐黨), demoted and forced into retirement.

Su Che was a key figure in the movement called 'Sichuan Learning' (*Shu xue* 蜀學) led by his more famous brother. Although, as indicated by his inclusion among the 'eight literary masters of the Tang and Song', Su Che had a great reputation as a literary figure, he also produced classical commentaries (on the **Shi jing** and the **Chunqiu**) and explications of the **Lunyu**, the **Mengzi**, and the *Daode jing* 道德經, including *Laozi jie* 老子解 (Explanations of the Laozi), *Lunyu shiyi* 論語拾遺 (Supplement to the *Analects* of Confucius), and *Mengzi jie* 孟子解 (Explanations of the Mencius). Su also wrote on ancient history (*Gu shi* 古史) and left a sizeable corpus of writings on government policy.

Reference: Shiba and Franke, 1976: 882–5.

ANTHONY DEBLASI

Su ru 俗儒
('Vulgar' or 'crass' classicists)

Even before the Han, a sharp distinction articulated by the Confucian master **Xunzi** had developed between 'vulgar' or 'crass' classicists (*su ru*) and the 'refined Confucians' (**ya ru**). The 'vulgar classicists' regarded the Classics only as a repository of political precedents and literary allusions of some utility in forging a career path – to the consternation of those who saw the Five Classics (**Wu jing**) as the *summa* of moral teachings. Ironically, evidence suggests that the gap between the two types of *ru* widened after the institution of the Imperial Academy (traditionally dated to 124 BCE), if only because a candidate for public office could become a nominal *ru* after attending the Academy for one year and passing an examination in one of the Five Classics.

MICHAEL NYLAN

Su Shi 蘇軾

1036–1101
(*zi* Zizhan 子瞻, *hao* Dongpo jushi 東坡居士)

Su Shi is the most famous member of the Su family of Sichuan. He came to the capital Kaifeng in 1056 and the next year passed the famous *jinshi* examination in which **Ouyang Xiu** changed the standards to emphasise *guwen* 古文 (ancient writing) style. After mourning his mother and passing an imperial decree examination, Su took up government office (Hatch 1976: 907–10). His political career was something of a roller coaster. His outstanding success in the examinations made him a celebrity, and he therefore held important offices. Nevertheless his independence of mind led him to criticise government faults directly. He therefore served much of his career in provincial posts, the result of political exile.

Su was sympathetic to the effort to reform Song government, but he rejected the rigid approach embodied in **Wang Anshi**'s New Policies. Since Su's work stressed the importance of spontaneous response to a changing world, he was particularly opposed to Wang's effort to dictate absolute uniformity among the elite (*shi*) through mandatory classical commentaries and the creation of a national school system (Bol 1992: 272–3). Despite his opposition to Wang, Su was able to recognise good elements in his programme. Thus, he incurred **Sima Guang**'s anger when he defended Wang's reform of the labour service law (*mianyi fa* 免役法), which sought to reduce the burden of such service on the peasantry by levying a cash tax that could be used to hire substitutes (Hatch 1976: 955–7).

Su was known above all for his defence of literary activities as an essential activity of the politically and morally responsible literatus. He thus continued a long tradition that stretched back through Ouyang Xiu into the Tang period. His fame and persuasiveness attracted a number of important disciples, the most famous of whom were **Huang Tingjian**, **Qin Guan**, Zhang Lei 張耒, and Chao Buzhi 晁補之. The breadth of his interests is indicated by the variety of his surviving writings. Not only does his *œuvre* contain a collection of his literary and political writings, it also boasts commentaries on the **Shang shu** (*Dongpo Shuzhuan* 東坡書傳 [Su Dongpo's Commentary on the Shujing]) and the **Yi jing** (*Dongpo Yizhuan* 東坡易傳 [Su Dongpo's Commentary on the Yi jing]), as well as a miscellany (the *Dongpo zhilin* 東坡志林, or East Slope's Forest of Jottings).

References: Bol, Peter K., 1992, 'Su Shih's Tao: Unity with Individuality,': 254–99; Hatch, George, 1976: v.2, 900–68.

ANTHONY DEBLASI

Su wang 素王
(Uncrowned king)

Su wang refers to the title for a man who has the virtues of a king but does not hold the position. The term first appears in the *Zhuangzi* 莊子 where together with *Xuan sheng* 玄聖 (Mysterious Sages) it refers to those who are perfect in the Daoist way of life, namely, emptiness, quietude, limpidity, silence and non-action: 'To hold them in high station is the Virtue of emperors and kings, of the Son of Heaven; to hold them in lowly position is the way of the dark sage, the uncrowned king' (Watson, 1968: 143). **Dong Zhongshu** used this term as the exclusive title for Confucius who, being a plain scholar himself, established the new way for the people and manifested the virtue and culture of the Uncrowned King (**Han shu**, 1962: 2509). Dong argued that in responding to the will of Heaven, Confucius produced (*zuo* 作) the *Spring and Autumn Annals*, which was the business of a new King (Su Yu, 1992: 199). By conferring the title of *su wang* upon Confucius, Dong elaborated on one of the key tenets of the New

Text School (**Jinwen jing xue**), namely, that Confucius purposely 'created' a new doctrine, to lay down the foundation for the new world order. This is echoed in the *Shi ji* when **Sima Qian** remarks that 'being a commoner clad in a cotton gown (布衣) Confucius became the acknowledged Master of scholars for over ten generations. All people in China who study the six arts, from the emperors, kings and princes down, subject them to the authority of the Master. He was indeed the Perfect Sage!' (*Shi ji*, 1962: 1947) It was accepted among later Confucians that the Uncrowned King was the true meaning of the Sage. The uncrowned kingship of Confucius provided a doctrinal justification for the worship of Confucius to be in the highest rank of the state sacrifice, using the same rituals and offerings as those for Heaven, Earth, the Gods of Soil and Grains and the royal ancestors.

XINZHONG YAO

Sun Fu 孫復
992–1057
(*zi* Mingfu 明復, *hao* Fuchun 富春)

Along with **Hu Yuan** and **Shi Jie**, Sun Fu revived Confucian studies in the early Northern Song. He reinterpreted the *Spring and Autumn Annals* (**Chunqiu**) to condemn the usurpation of power by military generals during the Five Dynasties period (506–560). In his *Chunqiu zunwang fawei* 春秋尊王發微 (*Explicating the Subtle Meaning of Honouring the Emperor in the Annals*), he affirmed the authority of a moral and centralised government over feudal lords. He argued that only a strong centralised government could maintain law and order and defend the country from foreign invasion.

References: Qian Mu, 1977; *Song–Yuan xuean*; Wood, 1995.

TZE-KI HON

Sun Yirang 孫詒讓
1848–1908
(*zi* Zhong Rong 仲容)

Sun Yirang, born in Ruian of Zhejiang, was a successful candidate in the civil service examination at the provincial level in 1867 and was appointed as a director in the Ministry of Punishments (*xing bu zhu shi* 刑部主事). He was interested not in fame and wealth but in classical studies. He disregarded various opportunities to serve as a government officer and instead returned to his hometown and concentrated on the study of Classics for about forty years, which resulted in a number of influential books. He paid close attention to the people's education and served as the president of Wenzhou Teachers' College and the director of the Educational Association of Zhejiang province. His father set up a library for him and helped him to collect books and reading materials. When finding that there were many mistakes and misunderstandings in historical doctrines, he endeavoured to compile various materials into his *Za yi lu* 札移錄 to verify the truth and falsity of these records. He insisted that since the time of the Qin and Han dynasties (221 BCE–220 CE), there had not been enough works to explain the **Zhou li**, so he studied it for nearly twenty years and wrote the *Zhou li zheng yi* 周禮正義 (the *Correct Meanings of the Rites of the Zhou*) which became highly praised as an important work on the classic. He compared the political system noted in the *Zhou li* with western political systems, drawing his conclusions in the book entitled the *Zhou li zheng yao* 周禮政要 (*The Essentials of Government Recorded in the Rites of the Zhou*) that China should learn from the West. He admired Mozi's doctrine of universal love, condemning wars, utilitarianism, strengthening the country and extolled them as useful means to develop the society. He engaged in careful textual studies of the *Mozi* 墨子 which enabled him to produce an influential book entitled *Mozi* *jiangu* 墨子閒詁. His book *Qiwen juyao* 契文舉要 was the first book to study the inscriptions on oracle bones of the Shang dynasty in Chinese history. He also wrote many other books that contributed to the textual study of ancient books and languages.

OUYANG KANG

T

Tai he 太和
(Supreme harmony)

Tai he is that manifestation of *qi* (material force) in its pristine undifferentiated state and, hence, the state from which the blending or harmonisation of yin and yang ensues (see **yin–yang**). It therefore bears a close relationship to the *tai ji* because many consider it also to be the primordial *qi* that gives birth to the myriad things or *wu* in the world. The first historical reference to the *tai he* in this sense appears in **Hou Han shu** by Fan Ye 范曄 (398–445), in the biography of **Ma Rong**, wherein it is stated 'to receive the Supreme Harmony aids us in securing myriad blessings' (*Hou Han shu*, 7.1955). However, as a fully articulated philosophical concept, the Supreme Harmony is most closely identified with the Song-period thinker **Zhang Zai**.

The Supreme Harmony is a direct product of Zhang Zai's belief that *qi* constitutes the most elementary substance in the composition of the universe. Moreover, the pre-eminence of the Supreme Harmony in his thinking is borne out by the fact that it is the first of the major concepts to which we are exposed in the most important of his cosmological writings – the **Zheng meng**. In the very first sentence of that treatise, Zhang states that the Supreme Harmony is also called the Way or **Dao**. He then immediately further describes it as enveloping the mutually respondent **xing** or natures of 'floating and sinking, ascent and descent, activity and quiescence'. Moreover, he contends that 'the beclouded, roiling processes of victory and defeat, expansion and contraction all have their beginning in [the Supreme Harmony]' (*Zhangzi quanshu*, 2.1b).

References: Chan, Wing-tsit, 1963d: 495, 500; Fung, 1952: 479, 480; Kasoff, 1984: 36–7, 43, 68, 120, 125–6, 168n. 6.

DON J. WYATT

Tai ji 太極
(Supreme Ultimate)

Tai ji is by far the oldest and most widely accepted term used to denote the generative construct through which the great primordial *qi* (material force) produces the universe and all the diverse *wu* – things both animate and inanimate – contained in it. Regarded as the foundation upon which the two primordial dyads of *qi* that are called yin and yang interact to constitute the universe, the Supreme Ultimate is known by many other names. Among these names are *da dao* 大道 (Great Way), *da ji* 大極 (Great Ultimate), *tai yi* 太易 (Supreme Change), *tai yi* 太儀 (Supreme Regulator), and **tai xu** (Supreme Void). The first mention of *tai ji* and description of its functioning appears in the *Xici zhuan* 繫辭傳 (*Appended Statements Commentary*) or *Da zhuan* 大傳 (*Great Commentary*), the fifth and sixth of the so-called traditional 'ten wings' (*shiyi* 十翼) of the **Yi jing**. Therein, in words destined to be quoted and paraphrased with the utmost frequency by later thinkers, it is tersely stated: 'The *Book of Changes* has a Supreme Ultimate, and this produces the two modes [of *yin* and *yang*]' (*Zhou Yi* 周易, 7.9b).

To be sure, the appropriation of the Supreme Ultimate – together with the commandeering of its associated and probably Daoist cosmographical representation, the *taijitu* 太極圖 (*Diagram of the Supreme Ultimate*) – by **Zhou Dunyi** in the mid-eleventh century certainly represents the most important milestone in the history of the concept. Through his imaginativeness and persistence, Zhou Dunyi parlayed the Supreme Ultimate into a stock fixture within the Confucian tradition. He thereby ensconced it metaphysically – making it a construct that nearly all subscribers eventually came to regard as the first cause of perceived reality. Zhou and his followers thus ensured a sacrosanct place for the Supreme Ultimate within future Confucian discourse and, in doing so, they enshrined it as an ontological necessity. In this way, in subsequent centuries, the once-obscure notion of a Supreme Ultimate became a normative and consistent feature within the individual system of virtually every philosopher – regardless of whether he adhered to the **dao xue** (Learning of the Way), the **xin xue** (Learning of the Mind), or some other persuasion. Indeed, as **Zhu Xi** was to expound conclusively, 'What Master Zhou called the Supreme Ultimate is a name for all that is good – both within Heaven and Earth and among men and things' (*Zhuzi yulei*, 94.7).

References: Birdwhistell, 1989: 56–9, 75, 78, 83–4, 100, 104, 169, 175, 189, 214, 268; Chan, Wing-tsit, 1963d: 14, 263, 271, 463–5, 471, 484, 535, 585, 593, 752, 758; Fung, 1952: 101–2, 182–3, 435, 453, 458–9, 478, 534, 546, 549–50, 552, 559, 589–90, 640; Smith *et al.*, 1990: 105, 112; Wyatt, 1996: 97, 99–103, 121, 200, 241, 280n. 29.

DON J. WYATT

Tai lao 太牢
(Large Beast Sacrifice)

Tai lao refers to the largest animals of the domesticated herd – an ox, pig, and goat – offered as sacrifice to the imperial ancestors, gods of soils and grains, sun and moon, which are ranked as great sacrifices (*da si* 大祀), and to middle level (*zhong si* 中祀) gods and spirits. One of the earliest records of an offering of three victims (*san sheng* 三牲) as sacrifice is found in the *Book of Documents* ('Duke of Shao's Admonition'), where the Duke of Zhou offers it to the God of Soil upon completing the foundations for the royal city. The Large Beast Sacrifice ranks after the 'Single Victim' Sacrifice (*te sheng* 特牲) offered to Heaven and Earth. According to the **Shi ji**, Han Gaozu (r. 206–195 BCE) offered a Large Beast Sacrifice to Confucius in 195 BCE, which established a precedent for subsequent imperial sacrifices to Confucius in Qufu and eventually in the capital. Only the sovereign may slaughter an ox for sacrificial purposes, thus smaller beast (*shao lao* 少牢) sacrifices are offered to gods and spirits when performed at local temples. On occasion smaller beast offerings were used at rites in the capital to signify lower status in the spirit hierarchy (e.g., in the years of 931 and 1753). The victims were separated from the rest of the herd one month before the sacrifice to Confucius (three months before single-victim sacrifices to Heaven and Earth) and kept in a special clean pen (*di* 滌). The victims are slaughtered in the temple kitchen on the morning of the sacrifice and a portion of their blood and fur is buried outside the main gate to inform the spirit that the whole animal is offered in sacrifice. Portions of the meat, now blessed (*fu zuo* 福胙) by its use in the ceremony, are distributed to the celebrants after the ceremony and taken home to be eaten by the family.

THOMAS A. WILSON

Tai shan 泰山
(Mount Tai)

This highest peak in present-day central Shandong province in eastern China rises 4,992 feet (1,522m) above sea-level. During the Han times both *fang shi* wizards and early Confucian scholars designated it as a sacred peak and competed with each other to influence the throne. Mount Tai, known as 'The First Peak' or 'East Peak' among the **Wu yue** (the Five Peaks), was linked to the absolute monarch, also known in his imperial ritual role as 'The One Man'. As it became the site of the famous and mysterious *feng shan* sacrifices to Heaven (*tian*) and Earth (*di*), 'Going to Mount Tai' came to signify gaining possession of the empire. As metaphor, 'Tai shan' signifies something huge, valuable, stable and solid.

References: Chavannes, 1910; Wechsler, 1985.

ANGELA ZITO

Tai xu 太虛
(Supreme Void)

Tai xu – also called the *tian kong* 天空 (Heavenly Emptiness) or the *da kong* 大空 (Great Emptiness) – is the great primordial **qi** (material force) of the universe. It is the *qi* of flux and chaos and, consequently, the starting point for the genesis and maturation of the universe. Viewed in this light, it is unsurprising that we should find the Supreme Void to be quite comparable to **tai ji**, which we may also view as the generative principle that stocks and continually replenishes the universe. There are, however, some crucial differences between the two concepts.

Tai xu – to at least the same degree as its companion concept, **tai he** – is intimately associated with the philosopher **Zhang Zai**. In his **Zheng meng**, he attempted to distinguish the two concepts from each other thus: 'The Supreme Void is formless but, regarding the original state of its *qi*, whether it appears condensed or dispersed, these states are nothing more than the transitory forms of change' (*Zhangzi quanshu*, 2.2). He further stated that the Supreme Void is 'vacuous' to the point of being 'devoid of all obstructions' (*Zhangzi quanshu*, 2.3b). Consequently, while he seems to have used the Supreme Harmony as a generic reference for *qi* in all its potential states, Zhang Zai employed the Supreme Void for the highly specific purpose of describing *qi* only in its most rarefied and imperceptible state. *Qi*, within the context of the Supreme Void, is a vacuous and essentially invisible substance but it is never insubstantial or absent. This conception of *qi* would prove of indispensable importance to Zhang and his successors in formulating their collective rebuttal of the Buddhist doctrine of emptiness.

References: Chan, Wing-tsit, 1963d: 495, 500; Fung, 1952: 479; Kasoff, 1984: 37–43, 46, 48, 50–1, 59, 62–3, 66, 68, 88, 108–9, 125–6, 139–42, 164n. 30, 164n. 33, 169n. 36.

DON J. WYATT

Tai xue 太學
(Imperial Academy)

The *Book of Rites* (*Li ji*) says that in ancient times, the sagely government set up a higher educational institution to admit boys of fifteen years and above. The institution was also the place where the ruler could seek for knowledge and wisdom with regard to government. This classical ideal influenced the Han government's decision to establish the *Tai xue* (in 136 BCE) that was to take charge of teaching Confucian Classics to students recruited primarily from aristocratic families. The admission age was eighteen, and its graduates were guaranteed of office.

The Imperial Academy was the centre of Classical Learning at least until the end of the Period of Disunity (220–589). It is the best documented educational institution in Chinese history. At the height of the development, the Han Imperial Academy had as many as 30,000 students (around 125–144 CE). The congregation of such a large number of students led to two major student movements.

During the Period of Disunity, sons of aristocrats were admitted into either the Imperial Academy or the School of National Youth (*Guozi xue* 國子學), which admitted those of highly ranked aristocrats. Both shared largely the same curriculum and instructional staff, and the educational content continued to be Confucian Classics. The various states took pride in founding the Imperial Academy and their ancillary institutions, as part of the programme of good government. This was a great era of Chinese higher education, and the number of students often was in the hundreds or even thousands. However, the education was eminently aristocratic; it is possible that all sons of aristocrats were expected to attend the two schools.

The Imperial Academy, now often used interchangeably with the School of National Youth, continued in the Tang times (618–907), but its importance declined, and the number of students was also much smaller than before; at no time did the number exceed 1,000. By the end of the ninth century, the Academy was no more.

The Imperial Academy and the School of National Youth were significant during the Song (960–1279) because of the political power students held in their hands, whereas their educational contribution was negligible. Student meddling in Court affairs was a legacy in the Song. At the most critical time of alien invasions of the Song, around 1125–1127, tens of thousands of people, led by the students of the Imperial Academy and other schools in the capital, joined

in demonstrating against the Court's lack of determination to fight the nomadic invaders. The demonstration tradition continued during the next two centuries when students' frivolous life was often permitted because of their ability to intimidate Court officials. Scholarship-wise, the liberal and even sceptic atmosphere that characterised Song Classical Learning had little to do with the academic activities of the Imperial Academy which had largely become a part of the civil service examination system, certifying students' qualifications by graduating them so that they could be exempted from taking the local examinations which had a smaller quota for successful candidates than for students from the Academy (see **civil service examinations**).

Yuan and other conquest dynasties continued to found *Taixue*, which had Chinese and non-Chinese components, using different languages for instruction. Graduates of different schools were afforded different avenues of government service. The vitality of the school as a centre for Classical Learning had completely ended, although **Zhu Xi**'s Neo-Confucian thinking and his Four Books (*Si shu*) were now the orthodox teaching used in the examinations to recruit candidates.

The Ming Imperial Academy, now more often referred to as the Directorate of National Youth (*Guozi jian*), admitted a large number of students. (The state maintained two campuses, one in Beijing and one in Nanjing.) The government often appointed students to internship or clerkship in government offices. The founder of the Ming was wary of the potentials of student unrest, and repeatedly issued injunctions against student meddling in politics. The draconian approach to the potential officials made a mockery of Confucian educational ideals. This was a sad chapter in the history of the Chinese higher education.

The Qing Imperial Academy was not much more than an office to register a special category of students eligible for government's civil service examinations.

Like its counterpart in the Ming, the institution offered little actual instruction, and was educationally insignificant.

The Imperial Academy met with its demise in 1905 when the Qing government reorganised its Directorate of Education into The Ministry of Education. The Imperial Academy, as the educational name of the Directorate, became the Grand School of the Capital (*jingshi da xuetang* 京師大學堂), the predecesor of today's Beijing University.

THOMAS H.C. LEE

Taijitu shuo 太極圖說
(*Diagram of the Supreme Ultimate Explained*)

The *Taijitu shuo* is one of the two seminal writings of **Zhou Dunyi**, the other being the **Tong shu** (*Penetrating the Book of Change*). By means of the *Diagram Explained*, Zhou sought to justify and thereby legitimate the inclusion of an obscure diagram that he had already interposed within the inherited Confucian tradition of his time. This was a diagram that he had most likely either derived indirectly from a Daoist text of the eighth century or acquired directly from a Daoist master contemporary. The fact that Zhou Dunyi succeeded in this effort at appropriation produced the dual effect of establishing his theories as the starting point for all future articulations of **li xue** (Learning of Principle) metaphysics and establishing Zhou himself as the inspired initiator of a new movement.

The extremely short length of the *Taijitu shuo* belies its dramatic philosophical importance. The entire work consists of a mere 228 Chinese characters. Nevertheless, the *Diagram Explained* became subsequently extolled by **Zhu Xi** as the textual wellspring of what scholars of future dynasties would term *Song xue* 宋學 (Learning of the Song Dynasty) – a designation that, even while implying a uniformity of thought that never actually existed, is at least chronologically accurate. Moreover, Zhu Xi regarded the

work as the prime example of the profundity achievable by contemporary writing in the Confucian tradition, and he therefore valued the text on a par with such works as the **Yi jing** and the **Zhongyong**. Of these latter two texts, however, the *Diagram Explained* clearly shares a far greater number of both formal and conceptual attributes in common with the *Yi jing* than with the *Zhong yong*.

The *Diagram Explained* begins with the brief but revealing statement, 'The Non-Ultimate (**wu ji**) and yet also the Supreme Ultimate (**tai ji**)! With movement (**dong**), the Supreme Ultimate produces yang and, with this movement having reached its extreme, there is then quiescence (**jing**), which produces yin' (see **yin–yang**). There can be little doubt about how thoroughly and completely the imagery of this salient opening passage adumbrates the primordial generative functioning of the Supreme Ultimate as it is described in the *Yi jing*. Through an identical process in both works, the Supreme Ultimate undergoes a fluctuating but unceasing pattern of division and subdivision, from which all of the myriad things in the universe arise (*Zhou Yi* 周易, 7.9b).

It thus becomes apparent that Zhou Dunyi had more than a single motivation and purpose in mind in writing the *Diagram Explained*. Zhou did not merely intend for the work to rationalise his insertion of an alien construct into the newly revitalising Confucian tradition of his time. He meant for it to serve as a textual gloss on a diagrammatic depiction of the universe in its ever-evolving state. In this way, the *Taijitu shuo* became a compelling textual instrument to be applied in the service of all those who wished to counter the then-current, highly persuasive theories of cosmogony propounded by both Daoism and Buddhism with a specifically Confucian alternative.

References: Balazs, 1978: 216, 218; Chan, Wing-tsit, 1963a: 463–5; Fung, 1952: 435–51; Liu Wu-chi, 1955: 153–5.

DON J. WYATT

Taixuan jing 太玄經
(*Canon of Supreme Mystery*)

The *Taixuan jing*, completed by **Yang Xiong** in his mature years after he had essentially abandoned *fu* (rhyme-prose) writing as frivolous, is perhaps the most famous of the companions to the *Book of Changes* (*Yi jing*). Han *ru* (Confucians and classicists) had been frustrated in their attempts to find underlying principles of order either in the sequence of the *Yi jing* hexagrams or in the verbal emblems that accompany them. As the single author of the monumental *Canon of Supreme Mystery*, Yang could integrate the structure and content of his masterwork in a fully systematic way, so as to confirm for the sceptics the existence of a comprehensive moral order informing the astronomical, mathematical, musical and social harmonies, while reflecting the most advanced philosophic concepts of his time.

The structure of the *Supreme Mystery* is best understood by comparing it with that of the *Yi jing*. By Yang's time, the *Yi jing* consisted of sixty-four six-line hexagrams, each line of which was either broken (indicating yin) or unbroken (indicating yang). Accompanying each hexagram were six verbal emblems keyed to the six graphic lines of the hexagram (hence the name, the 'Line Texts'). Appended to the entire text of the *Yi jing* were at least six separate commentaries called the 'Wings' (i.e., appendices), though it seems that Yang either had not seen or did not find the *Duan* or Judgement section included in the present 'Ten Wings' to be authoritative.

The core text of the *Supreme Mystery*, like that of its prototype, presents a series of linear complexes, but in contrast to the *Book of Changes*, manipulation of the yarrow stalks according to Yang's explicit directions yields three possibilities for each line of the graph: (1) an unbroken line correlated with Heaven; (2) a line broken once representing Earth; and (3) a line broken twice, symbolising humans living between Heaven and Earth. For the six-line complex of the *Book of Changes*, the *Supreme Mystery* substitutes a four-line graph (the 'tetragram'), whose component parts are read from top to bottom (i.e., in the opposite order from the *Book of Changes*). The four graphic lines of the tetragrams are associated with a hierarchical nest of divisons that is at once geographic and social. From the top there are 3 Regions, 9 Provinces, 27 Departments, and 81 Families. The cosmogonic Mystery, like the emperor in the human realm, is said to occupy the centre, where all phenomena converge.

Turning to the verbal, rather than graphic elements in the *Supreme Mystery*, the 'Head' text (analogous to the *Book of Changes*' summarising Hexagram Statement) names one aspect of the comprehensive Mystery, which it then relates to the progressive waxing and waning of yin and yang *qi* through the calendar year (which, in turn, determines the growth and decline of the myriad things). Loosely patterned after the Line Texts of the *Yi jing* are the nine Appraisals assigned to each tetragram, each of which represents half a day. (Two additional Appraisals are not assigned to a specific tetragram; they exist solely to make up the deficiency of three-quarters of a day between the 364 half days of Yang's basic structure [81 tetragrams $\times$ $4\frac{1}{2}$ days] and the $365\frac{1}{4}$ days in the solar year.) In contrast to the Line Texts of the *Yi jing*, each of which refers to a single specific line of the hexagram, the Appraisals do not purport to reveal the significance of the individual lines in the four-line graphic symbol. The correlation of the Appraisals to time rather than to graphic line accomplishes at least two goals: as a unit the Appraisals reflect the perfect cyclical nature of graduate change in Heaven and Earth through the course of the calendar year, while separately each block of nine Appraisals provides a series of subtly shifting images that work like different refractions of the single theme presented in the tetragram. Together the Appraisals, positioned between the Head Texts and the later autocommentaries of the

Supreme Mystery, serve as metaphoric bridge between the cyclic dominion of fate and the field of human choice and achievement, the latter being the main theme of the extensive autocommentaries which Yang composed for the *Supreme Mystery* on the model of the *Book of Changes*' Ten Wings.

These autocommentaries are also ten in number: The 'Fathomings' (*Xuan ce* 玄測), like the 'Commentary of the Images' (*Xiang zhuan* 象傳), summarise the main significance of each Appraisal. The 'Elaboration' (*Xuan wen* 玄文) discussed only the first tetragram as a microcosm for the entire book, just as the 'Elaborated Teachings' (*Wen yan* 文言) commentary treats only the first pair of hexagrams. The remaining autocommentaries do not interpret individual texts; instead they assess or illuminate the *Mystery* as a whole: The 'Polar Oppositions' (*Xuan chong* 玄衝) corresponds to the 'Sequence of Hexagrams' (*Xu gua* 序卦) of the *Book of Changes*; the 'Interplay of Opposites' (Xuan cuo 玄錯) corresponds to the 'Interplay' (*Za gua* 雜卦). Two commentaries, the 'Numbers' (*Xuan shu* 玄數) and the 'Revelation (*Xuan gao* 玄告) correspond to the 'Discussion of the Trigrams' (*Shuo gua* 說卦) in the *Yi jing*. No fewer than four autocommentaries correspond to the 'Great Commentary': the 'Evolution' (*Xuan li* 玄攡); 'Illumination' (*Xuan ying* 玄瑩); 'Diagram' (*Xuan tu* 玄圖); and 'Representations' (*Xuan yi* 玄捃).

The content of Yang's ten autocommentaries is nearly unparalleled in both the richness of its vocabulary and the breadth of its philosophic import. In those autocommentaries, Yang manages to portray the *Mystery* itself as it relates to **yin–yang** and the **Wu xing** (Five Phases), thereby attaining in his own *Mystery* the standard he ascribed to all 'true' canons, including the *Yi jing*: that it be concise yet pertinent to all situations. Yang prescribes the exact conditions under which one may apply to the gods for illumination through divination. He also defines fate and the role it (as opposed to luck) plays in human fortune.

Most intriguing of all, perhaps, are several passages through which Yang makes the case that adherence to Confucian social norms (especially ritual) is not only the highest duty of humankind, but also its chief source of sustainable pleasure. In moving the reader beyond grim notions of constraint and duty to the connoisseur's 'delight in the Way', Yang (like his classical Greek counterparts) goes a long way towards explaining the best method by which the consuming pleasures (among them, eating, drinking, having sex and politicking) can be turned into pleasures that will sustain the soul, the body and the body politic.

References: Nylan & Sivin, 1987; Nylan, 1993; Zheng Wangeng, 1989.

MICHAEL NYLAN

Taizhou xuepai 泰州學派
(The Taizhou School)

The *Taizhou* School, or *Taizhou* branch, of the Wang Yangming (**Wang Shouren**) school of thought, was named after the native place of the branch's founder, **Wang Gen**. In the twentieth century, the *Taizhou* branch has been referred to as the 'leftist' branch of the Wang Yangming School, due to its appeal to commoners and emphasis upon the idea that any man or woman can become a sage. The *Taizhou* branch counted among its members a large number of commoners, including a woodcutter and a potter, even representatives of the notorious government clerks. Nevertheless, most important figures of the *Taizhou* branch were gentry and officials.

The *Taizhou* branch gained fame for producing a number of individualistic and idiosyncratic thinkers who reflected the increasing ambiguity of social roles in late-Ming society. Adherents of the school were derogatorily referred to by their critics as Wild Chan Buddhists (*kuang chan* 狂禪), alluding to the fact that several members of the branch consciously drew from Buddhist ideas. Several *Taizhou* advocates of syncretism were openly critical of Neo Confucian (see **Neo-Confucianism**) state orthodoxy.

The *Taizhou* branch exerted a great amount of influence during the late sixteenth century, especially in the Yangtze River delta. Important members of the *Taizhou* branch include Yan Jun 顏鈞 (?–?) and his students **Luo Rufang** and **He Xinyin**. Other noteworthy figures are the brothers Geng Dingxiang 耿定向 (1524–1596) and Geng Dingli 耿定理 (1534–1584), as well as **Jiao Hong** and Zhou Rudeng 周汝登 (1547–1629). The most radical figure of this group was **Li Zhi**.

Reference: Huang Tsung-hsi, 1987: 165–201.

STEVEN MILES

Tan Sitong 譚嗣同
1865–1898

Political thinker, scholar and martyr of the Hundred Days of Reform (1898), Tan Sitong was born in Hunan province but grew up in Beijing. As a young boy, he moved from place to place following his father's official posts. Despite his literary talents and wide-ranging curiosity, he had trouble passing the civil service examinations. In 1895, after failing to pass the examinations for the fifth time and having learnt that China was defeated in the Sino-Japanese War, he suffered from a spiritual crisis. He scorned the examination system and the orthodox curriculum. He condemned the 'eight-legged' essay that all examination candidates had to learn to write. For the first time in his life, he realised that China needed drastic changes in order to survive in the global competition for wealth and power.

Having recovered from his personal crisis, Tan stopped taking the examinations and turned his attention to promoting political reform. He befriended other reform advocates like **Kang Youwei**, **Liang Qichao** and Xia Zengyou 夏曾祐 (1863–1924). He read widely and developed an interest in Mahayana Buddhism, western science and the New Text School of Former Han Confucianism. Between 1896 and 1897, he wrote the *ren xue* (Learning of Ren), a work that later made him a leading radical thinker of the late Qing. Although the *Ren xue* was never published before Tan's death, copies of it were circulated among his close friends after its completion.

In the *ren xue*, Tan devoted half of the book to discussing the concept of *ren* (commonly translated as humaneness, benevolence). Combining Song–Ming **Neo-Confucianism** with western science, he used *ren* to refer to the common bond that brought creatures and physical objects together in this universe. For him, *ren* could be understood as the basic material substance, similar to the nineteenth-century concept of ether (transliterated by Tan as *yitai*). On the other hand, *ren* could also be understood as a cosmic force that permeated throughout the universe. From Tan's perspective, the purpose of learning to be *ren* was to build a perfect society based on equality and the innate rights of the individual. To build the perfect society, he criticised any social or political barrier that separated one group of people from another. In particular, he condemned the Three Cardinal Guides (*san gang*) and Five Human Relations (*Wu lun*) for privileging the ruler over the ruled, father over son and husband over wife. He scorned the Chinese system of monarchy because it allowed the rulers to advance their private interests at the expense of the public good. Although not necessarily driven by anti-Manchuism, he blamed the Manchus for using the monarchical system to victimise the Han Chinese.

Tan's radical views on reform earned him a friendship with Hunan province governor Chen Baozhen 陳寶箴 (1831–1900), who was interested in transforming the once backward province into a centre of national rejuvenation. Along with **Pi Xirui**, Tan was invited to organise the *Nanxue hui* (Society of Southern Learning) in

Changsha. As a first step to establish the provincial parliament in Hunan, *Nanxue hui* provided a forum for the elite to discuss public affairs. To press for more changes in the political institution, Tan published articles in the *Xiangbao* 湘報 (Hunan News). Like Kang Youwei, he argued in the articles that Confucius was a *Su wang* (uncrowned king) who defined for posterity the basic principles of a perfect government. As Tan and other reformers were pressing for change, tension began to build up as the Hunanese conservatives pressured Governor Chen to give up his sponsorship to *Nanxue hui*.

In the early months of 1898, Tan was invited to go to Beijing for an imperial audience with the young and ambitious Emperor Guangxu (r. 1875–1908). Following the imperial audience, he was appointed a secretary of Grand Council. In the summer of that year, along with Kang Youwei and Liang Qichao, he helped to launch the Hundred Days of Reform, in which the emperor issued 103 reform decrees to change the political, economic and educational systems. Conservatives opposed the reform, and in September a *coup d'état* led by Empress Dowager Cixi (1835–1908) ended the Hundred Days of Reform. In a deliberate act of martyrdom, Tan refused to flee during the *coup d'état*. Along with five other young reformers, he was caught and executed. Through death, he became a symbol of self-sacrifice and was remembered for his selfless dedication to the cause of the nation. Published posthumously, the *ren xue* became a popular text among the reformers and the revolutionaries for its critique of Confucian social customs and the monarchical system.

References: Chang Hao, 1997; Fung, 1952; Kwong, 1996.

TZE-KI HON

Tang Boyuan 唐伯元
1540?–1598?
(*zi* Renqing 仁卿, *hao* Shutai 曙臺)

A scholar and official, Tang is best known as an ardent critic of **Wang Shouren**. Tang was a native of Chenghai in Guangdong who received the *jinshi* degree in 1574. He went on to serve as a magistrate in Jiangxi Province before being promoted to posts in the Boards of Personnel and Works in Nanjing. In 1585 Tang submitted to the throne a copy of the 'stone classic ancient text' (*shijing guben* 石經古本) of the *Da xue* (*Great Learning*), suggesting that it be made the standard text of the Classic in the civil service examinations. This 'stone classic' version had been fabricated by Feng Fang 豐坊 (receiving his *jinshi* degree in 1523). At the same time, Tang in his memorial fervently objected to a commemorative tablet in honour of Wang Yangming being placed in the *Kong miao* (The Temple of Confucius). The Wanli emperor (r. 1573–1620) rejected both of Tang's suggestions and punished him with demotion.

In his *Mingru xuean*, **Huang Zongxi** identifies Tang with the school of **Zhan Ruoshui**. Tang vehemently opposed Wang Yangming's *xin xue* (Learning of the Heart/Mind) and instead advocated the theory that human nature is good (*xing shan* 性善) but that the heart/mind contained both good and evil. Hence, Tang emphasised the role of *li* (rites) in overcoming or controlling oneself (*ke ji* 克己), as well as the importance of studying the Classics. Tang thus anticipated the critique of Wang Yangming proffered by many Confucians of the Qing dynasty (1644–1911), as well as their emphasis upon ritual learning.

Reference: *Mingru xuean*, 1985.

STEVEN MILES

Tang Jian 唐鑑
1778–1861
(*zi* Jinghai 鏡海)

A native of Shanhua 善化 of Hunan province, Tang was a Classicist and philosopher. He gained his *jinshi* degree in 1809 and was assigned a bachelor (Shujishi 庶吉

士) of the Hanlin Academy. He then was appointed as a Hanlin corrector 檢討, later a provincial administrative officer in Zhejiang, Guangxi, Anhui, Shanxi areas. After retiring from head of the royal ritual department (Taichang shiqing 太常寺卿) he became the master of the Jinling Academy 金陵書院. He later was called to the court to answer Emperor Xianfeng 咸豐 (r. 1851–1861) on state affairs fifteen times. He returned to his hometown in 1852 and led a plain life until he died at the age of eighty-four.

Tang held a special interest in the study of human nature and principle, and was influenced by Neo-Confucian schools of **Cheng Hao**, **Cheng Yi** and **Zhu Xi**. He wrote a work on the development of Neo-Confucian schools entitled *Xuean xiaozhi* 學案小識 in which he especially adored **Lu Longqi**, an early Qing Neo-Confucian as the leading exponent of the Cheng–Zhu teaching. He also compiled *The Complete Works of Zhuzi* (*Zhuzi Quanji* 朱子全集) with commentaries and notes. His other works included *Zhuzi nianpu kaoyi* 朱子年譜考異, an investigation into the chronological life of Zhu Xi, and *Xingshen rike* 省身日課, Daily lessons of examining oneself on moral points. His other works on the Classics include those on the *Book of Changes* (*Yi jing*) and the *Book of Rites* (*Li ji*) entitled *Du yi xiaozhi* 讀易小識, *Yi fansheng lu* 易反身錄 and *Du li xiaoshi Ji* 讀禮小事記.

REBEKAH X. ZHAO

Tang Junyi 唐君毅
1909–1978

Perhaps the most prolific and internationally recognised philosopher among Modern New Confucians who expatriated to Hong Kong in 1949, Tang Junyi grew up in western China and later studied philosophy in Nanjing 南京 under **Fang Dongmei** and **Xiong Shili** before his leaving the mainland. Resisting the anti-traditional trends of the post May Fourth era, Tang remained interested in Chinese intellectual traditions. During the 1930s he developed an informed appreciation of modern German aesthetics and studied the philosophical systems of Kant and Hegel. He wrote a lyrical allegory on human life in the early 1940s, full of literary vigour and existential insights, portraying basic features of a dialectically extended and multi-levelled view of reality later systematically elaborated in his more formal philosophical works. Joining **Qian Mu** in starting a new school in Guangzhou in 1947, Tang moved with the school to Hong Kong in 1949 as its academic dean. This institution afterwards became New Asia College (Xinya shuyuan 新亞書院), Tang remaining there also when it became part of a larger modern university (The Chinese University of Hong Kong). In 1958 he helped in writing a lengthy 'Confucian Manifesto' in Chinese and English versions, signing it along with **Mou Zongsan**, **Xu Fuguan**, and **Zhang Junmai**. During his years in Hong Kong, Tang published many works arguing for the modern relevance of Confucianism within a broadly systematised and more comparatively oriented philosophy of intellectual-and-spiritual culture (*jingshen wenhua* 精神文化). In addition he wrote multi-volume works on the history of Confucian philosophical traditions.

Confucianism, Confucian philosophy and modernity

As in the 1958 Confucian Manifesto, Tang asserted that the core philosophical concern of Confucian-informed culture is the relationship between the heart/mind (*xin*) and the nature (*xing*). He demonstrated this through his interpretations of a broad selection of ancient Chinese texts and studies of the basic values they advocated. Willing to adopt a modern and even critical attitude toward Confucian traditions at times, Tang identified the key contributions of 'Confucian philosophy' to the modern age in its promotion of a moral self (*daode ziwo* 道德自我) and its nurture of cultivated humaneness (**ren** 仁). This freed him to some degree from identifying Chinese culture with its ancient ritual traditions, and provided justifications for reconsidering the distinctive ways a modern humane culture would develop.

An articulate apologist for a modern form of Confucian culture, Tang was well informed about the cultural and philosophical crises felt in Europe during the post-World War II period. He opposed taking existential despair or philosophical scepticism as the basis for life, and consistently rejected Soviet and Chinese forms of Communism as unjust and immoral. Nevertheless, he saw inherent positive values in developing scientific and technological systems as well as democratic institutions within modern China, but insisted that they must be grounded upon a self-conscious moral awareness. Consequently, like all modern Confucian scholars, he was motivated by an intense concern about the fate of Chinese culture in general and Confucianism in particular – which he took to be the main expression of this culture – within the postwar era.

Confucianism from a historical perspective
Among Tang's later contributions was his extensive exploration in the history of Confucian philosophy. In various essays he focused on a selective set of Confucian philosophical categories, while his more lengthy works presented the history of Confucianism as a sequence of developments following the three initial categores of the **Zhongyong**, that is, dealing with the nature, the Way (*dao*), and teaching (*jiao*).

Following the lead of modern Confucian scholars such as **Fung Yu-lan**, Tang identified the origins of Confucianism with the teachings of **Confucius**. He argued that seminal commitments for a moral self engaged with everyday life appeared already in the teachings of Confucius and **Mengzi**. This focus Tang describes through later Confucian commentaries as 'engaging oneself with what is immediately before one' (*dang xia zhi nian* 當下之念). A fuller philo-

sophical development of these commitments appeared in the writings of Song–Ming Confucians, their summit appearing in the works of **Liu Zongzhou**. Liu's teaching of a creatively dynamic and metaphysical moral-mindedness overcame the dilemmas caused by **Zhu Xi**'s explicit metaphysical dualism and **Wang Shouren**'s implicit moral quietism. Though Tang also gives credit to **Wang Fuzhi**'s writings as a Chinese source for his own version of 'culture', paralleling Tang's Hegelian-informed reflections on cultural developments and their institutions, he nevertheless stands against Wang Fuzhi's departure from the Wang Yangming School's insights into the moral self and its idealistic identification with all beings. Liu Zongzhou's achievement is for Tang the more philosophically enriched and synthetically comprehensive Confucian vision, developing the original ideas set out first in teachings of Confucius and Mengzi. This vision, Tang insists, parallels the moral heights articulated also in the teachings of Buddha and Jesus.

Confucian philosophy in a comparative cultural perspective
Arguments for the philosophical importance of the metaphysically justified Confucian moral self, which transcends the empirically grounded 'actual self', were articulated by Tang within his own distinctive philosophy of culture. His final systematic expression of this philosophy, a two-volume work completed just before his death, developed into a complicated Hegelian-like phenomenology of the Way, uniting Confucian moral consciousness and a Whiteheadian-like vision of unending humane creativity. Human experience can reach and transist into nine distinct realms (*jing jie* 境界), all divided into three different levels. At the highest level, where subjective and objective dimensions are transcended, Tang identified realms of Christian salvation, Buddhist enlightenment and Heavenly-decreed Confucian sageliness. While Tang expressed general appreciation for all three expressions at

this level, he advocated the specific contributions and superlative achievement of the Confucian vision.

While Confucius' influences have been intensely challenged in twentieth-century settings in China, Tang argued that the sources of these influences run deep, deeper than the sources of sceptical modernity and modern revolutionary movements. Expecting always that these modern expressions would ultimately prove to be effete, Tang was disappointed at the end of his life that a more full Confucian renewal had not already taking place.

References: Fang & Li, 1995: vol. III, 5–72; Huang Chün-chieh, 1995; Pfister, 1995.

LAUREN PFISTER

Tang lü shuyi 唐律疏議
(*Tang Penal Code and Commentary*)

The *Tang Penal Code and Commentary* contained the penalties prescribed by the state for a range of 502 specific offences. Drafted by a commission and first presented to the emperor in 653, it was deliberately less severe than its precursor codes. Its provisions embody what has been called the 'Confucianisation of Chinese law', a process whereby the concepts of Confucian teaching influenced the definition of offences. The most serious crimes, against the dynastic house or against the head of family, were thus concerned with relationships central to Confucian teaching. Many offences were 'status specific', described in terms of the Confucian kinship system. The memorial of submission, by Zhangsun Wuji 長孫無忌 expressed the traditional Confucian ideological position that penal law was inferior to ritual as a means of bringing about social order, that force was less effective than persuasion and that the code would be 'little used if times were pure'. Nonetheless the code and the penal agencies of the government greatly influenced later dynastic criminal codes throughout East Asia.

The code was given a voluminous subcommentary by its compilers and this greatly elucidates their thinking on the punishments they prescribed. The version that is extant, based on that presented in 653, dates from 737 and incorporates revisions made in the intervening decades.

References: Ch'u, 1961; Johnson, 1979 & 1997.

DAVID MCMULLEN

Tao Yuanming 陶淵明
365–427
(*zi* Yuanliang 元亮)

Tao Yuanming, also known as Tao Qian, came from a prominent southern family, probably of non-Han origin, known for its support of the Jin dynasty (265–420). Tao lived most of his life, however, supported by farming, with only occasional forays into public office, which he found most uncongenial. This we know from several pieces of prose and more poetry, which is accounted amongst the very best in China before the Tang (618–907), and which offers a remarkably direct account of the feelings and problems of a modest, principled and highly sympathetic individual with a distinct fondness for alcohol. Creating a satisfactory biography from these apparently self-revealing sources has, however, proved an elusive task. His distaste for bureaucratic service puzzles many later Chinese commentators, who assume that some underlying point of principle was at stake, though scholars in western universities have found his stated lack of enthusiasm for paperwork rather non-problematic. As for the ideas underlying such works as his '*Xing* 形, *ying* 影, *shen* 神' (body, shadow, spirit), though obviously they reflect in some sense both the debates of the age and (most prominently) his own emotions concerning mortality, the actual relationship between poetic creativity and intellectual environment has proved hard to pin down. The stated conclusions to his meditations do not go beyond accepted Confucian norms, though the influence of the *Liezi* 列子, a work which had become known in his lifetime, is also perhaps detectable. How to regard the thought of the *Liezi* remains, of course, a problem in itself.

References: Lü Qinli, 1979; Davis, 1983.

TIM H. BARRETT

Taylor, Rodney
1944–

Taylor is one of the leading western scholars of the late twentieth century who emphasise the profoundly religious character of Confucianism as one of its quintessential features. Taylor's early work on the Ming Neo-Confucian scholar, **Gao Panlong**, focused on Gao's advocacy of quiet-sitting (*jing zuo*) as a practice conducive to attaining sagehood. Taylor understands religion as involving an ultimate self-transformation towards the absolute, one realised fully in the achievement of sagehood. In Taylor's later scholarship, while quiet-sitting continues to figure prominently in his analyses, religious aspects of ancient Confucianism, especially those related to the notion of Heaven (*tian*), are emphasised.

JOHN A. TUCKER

Ten Savants (*Shi zhe* 十哲)

In 712 the Ten Savants (or ten wise men) were formally distinguished from Confucius' other personal disciples and given special status in the Temple of Confucius (see *Kong miao*). Images of these ten disciples had been painted on the walls of the temple in the capital before then, although they were not formally enshrined. Images of Confucius' seventy-two disciples were used in the Temple of Confucius in Qufu as early as 178 CE and received sacrifices there as early as 72 CE. Evidence from Qufu also suggests ten

disciples were separated from the others in cult sacrifice no later than 540, when a stele reports the repairs of images of Confucius and 'ten worthies' (*shi xian* 十賢) standing in attendance. These ten men were elevated in the imperial temple in 712 on the grounds that Confucius singled them out as excelling in one of four disciplines (*si ke* 四科): virtue and conduct, oratory and discourse, governance and serving and literary scholarship (*Analects* 11: 2). Commentaries on this passage and ritual specialists maintain that this remark was not intended to be an exhaustive inventory, but applied to those disciples with Confucius during his troubles in the states of Chen and Cai (*c.* 492–489 BCE). The formation of this group in the temple at this time is significant for it follows the contentious years of the seventh century when the court debated whether Confucius or the Duke of Zhou was the principal sage of this cult. The latter was finally removed from the temple in 657 and sacrifices to Confucius' disciples Yan Hui and the twenty-two masters of the Confucian canon resumed. The distinction between a Correlate and a Savant at this time was liturgical rather than structural in that, between 712 and 1267 Yan Hui held both statuses simultaneously. Eventually this distinction was made explicit, particularly after Yan Hui was separated from the Savants (see **Twelve Savants**).

The following discusses the Ten Savants within the groups of the four disciplines, which were explicitly invoked in 712, then draws from the *Analects* and other early sources to situate each man in the discipline to which he was assigned.

Virtue and conduct 德行
That Confucius probably regarded this as the broadest and perhaps most basic of the four disciplines is marked by his inclusion of Yan Hui. Of the four disciplines, virtue and conduct nonetheless most aptly characterises the man (see *Four Correlates* and *Fu Sheng*). It was said that Yan 'loved learning and was not constrained to any one part of

the sage'. **Min Sun**'s actions were guided by filiality toward his kin and he never accepted appointment from unvirtuous rulers, thus he never lived off tainted emolument. **Ran Geng** was one of Confucius' earliest disciples. His activities are not well documented, although it is known that when Ran fell ill, Confucius was deeply concerned. In the *Mengzi* (2A: 2) it is said that, with Yan Hui and Min Sun, Ran Geng embodied sagehood, though it was not fully developed. **Ran Yong**, according to Confucius, could be 'given charge to [rule as sovereign] facing south' (6: 1). He once pressed Confucius over a vague position on the value of ruling with simplicity. Sceptically, Ran Yong said simplicity in practical governance is acceptable so long as one personally abides in reverence, whereas ruling with simplicity while also personally abiding in it would be excessively simplistic (6: 2). **Xunzi** spoke of Ran Yong and Confucius together as embodying this school.

Oratory and discourse 言語
Occupying an ethically somewhat more ambiguous status, the men who excelled in oratory and discourse nonetheless played a crucial role in negotiating Confucius' relations with the rulers of his day. Both men in this group – **Zai Wo** and **Duanmu Si** (Zigong) also spent considerable time advising dukes. This required not only eloquence but also keen insight into the Master's teachings. Several manuals on the Confucius temple cult record an unverified anecdote from the *Kong congzi* in which Zai Wo cited several concrete examples to explain to the King of Chu why Confucius will never accept a finely appointed luxurious carriage. Duanmu Si later argued that by using only concrete examples of how Confucius lived his life, Zai Wo's explanation 'failed to exhaust the beauty of the Master's Way', which is 'as lofty as Heaven and deep as the ocean'. The Master, however, favoured Zai Wo's concrete reasoning to Duanmu Si's flowery rhetoric. The

image of Zai Wo in the *Analects* is not flattering, which suggests that the text's later compilers were not disposed toward praising Zai Wo rather than that Confucius praised an unworthy man in the *Analects* (11: 2). Zai Wo's rhetorical virtuosity nonetheless occasionally got the better of him, such as when he suggested by clever wordplay that the Zhou sovereigns sought to instil fear in their subjects (*Analects* 3: 21). Confucius was less ambivalent over Zai Wo's moral calibre; he said, 'One cannot carve rotten wood' (*Analects* 5: 10). Duanmu Si also achieved considerable notoriety for his dealings with kings and statesmen, which are recorded in the *Zuo zhuan* (see **Chunqiu Zuo zhuan**) as well as the *Analects*. Confucius once called him a vessel. What kind of vessel? Duanmu Si inquired. 'A *hu* and *lian*', the Master replied. That is, the vessels used for the main grain offering in sacrifices to the royal ancestors during the Xia and Zhou (*Analects* 5: 4). Such rites were among the most important a sovereign performed, thus Confucius regarded this disciple as a man of great worth, even if he had not attained the calibre of the *junzi* (2: 12). Confucius also praised Duanmu Si's grasp of the *Poetry* (1: 15). Duanmu Si mourned Confucius' death longer than the other disciples by building a hut by Confucius' grave (*Mengzi* 3A: 4).

Government and serving 政事
Ran Qiu and **Zhong You** – the two men included in this group – were both known for their administrative talents rather than careful attention to Confucius' teachings. Ran Qiu recognised his own talents in *Analects* 11: 26 when he said that he could nurture the peoples' material livelihood if given the task of governing a medium-size state, while he would defer to the lord (*junzi*) the matters of rites and music. Commentators note that Ran Qiu recognised his abilities and limitations in this passage and was not dismissing the importance of rites. Elsewhere, Confucius expressed confidence in Ran's abilities to

govern a large city (5: 8) and lamented Ran's employment in the Ji household (11: 17), which usurped royal prerogatives by performing rites restricted to the Son of Heaven (e.g., 3: 1). A man from the wilderness outside of the state of Lu, Zhong You, was believed capable of managing the military administration of a large state. Impetuous and excessively courageous by nature, Zhong You was warned by Confucius against acting prematurely (5: 14) and to be mindful that the practice of virtues was not merely intuitive but required learning (17: 8). Han sources further record two early encounters between Zhong You and Confucius in which the former expresses his fondness for using the long sword as a means of moral suasion and Confucius admonishing him by explaining the importance of virtue.

Literary scholarship 文學
Literary scholarship refers here to the *Poetry, Documents, Rites,* and *Music.* One may construe these traditions as either textual or oral for it is unclear whether they had actually been inscribed at this point or whether they were still principally oral traditions. The *Analects* provides little insight into why Confucius thought of **Yan Yan** as learned. According to other sources dating to the Han, however, Yan Yan purportedly inquired about the Rites and Confucius informed him of sacrifices to Heaven, Earth, the God of Soils and the royal ancestors. Yan withdrew to study the *Rites* and was sometimes called 'He who practised the Rites' by the disciples. The *Analects* provides more ample evidence for **Bu Shang** as a careful thinker about the value of learning. 'Broad learning', he said, 'and sincere resolve in one's purpose; thorough inquiry and reflection upon what is near: humaneness lies in this' (19: 6). Following a conversation about the meaning of a piece in the *Book of Poetry*, Confucius proclaims, 'Shang has enlightened me. Only with the likes of you can one discuss the *Poetry*' (3: 8).

THOMAS A. WILSON

Tennôsei 天皇制
(The Emperor System)

The term *tennôsei* appeared in the early Shôwa period (1926–1989) in Marxist discourse, and it came to be accepted as a social science term for Japan's distinctive monarchical system. In the narrow sense, it refers only to that system as it was constituted from the **Meiji Restoration** to the end of the Second World War, but in the broad sense it includes the imperial institution in its premodern and postwar forms. The word is sometimes used not only to refer to the system of state authority, but also to the ideology, social order and ultranationalist value system that centred on the imperial institution. While this ideology, centring on the concept of *kokutai* 国体, was identified most closely with state Shinto and supported by the ancient creation mythology recorded in the *Kojiki* and *Nihon shoki*, it incorporated important elements derived from Japanese Confucian thought, particularly from the **Yamazaki Ansai** school, the **Later Mito School**, and the teachings of Meiji thinkers such as **Motoda Nagazane**, **Nishimura Shigeki**, and **Inoue Tetsujirô**. The semi-legendary connections of the origins of the imperial institution with ancient Korea and Confucianism are discussed in the article on Emperor Ôjin. Historically, it was Prince Shôtoku (d. 622) who first brought Confucianism explicitly into the ideology of the Japanese state, though it was overshadowed by Buddhism. Emperor Kanmu (r. 781–806), the founder of the capital at Heian, was among the early emperors who, while supporting Buddhism, followed Confucian principles in attempting to build a strong centralised government independent of interference by religious institutions. From the Heian period onward, however, the rituals of state presided over by the emperor were derived mainly from Shinto and Esoteric Buddhism, rather than from Confucianism.

BARRY D. STEBEN

Ti 悌
(Fraternal)

Ti is usually translated as 'brotherly' or 'fraternal' and is used interchangeably with the word *di* 弟, which literally means 'younger brother'. The **Baihu tong** explicitly links these two words: 'A younger brother (*di*) is *ti* (brotherly). His heart is obedient (*shun* 順) and his conduct generous' (*Baihutong*, 29: 55). What *ti* specifically designates is the respect and deference that a younger brother owes his elder brother. The **Xunzi** says, 'Those who are able to employ [propriety (*li*) and righteousness (*yi*)] to serve their elder brothers are called brotherly (*di*)' (*Xunzi*, 9: 16a).

As for the specific actions that embody this virtue, traditional illustrative stories posit three types. They are (1) yielding wealth or food to one's brother, (2) taking his place when he is in danger, and (3) after his death, supporting his widow and orphans. For example, cannibalistic rebels caught Zhao Xiao's 趙孝 (first century CE; *zi* Changping 長平) younger brother. Zhao bound himself and told the rebels that he would be much tastier than his skinny sibling (**Hou Han shu**, 39: 1299). When Xu Miao's 徐苗 (d.302; *zi* Shuzhou 叔冑) brothers died, for over forty years, he lived with and supported their children and widows. At the end of that time, he yielded all of his wealth to his nephews (*Chuxue ji* 初學記, 17: 426).

Nevertheless, brotherly conduct (*ti*) should not merely be confined to siblings; one should extend it to all of one's seniors and superiors. This is because one's seniors are similar to one's elder brothers. The *Xunzi* states, 'What do the rites (*li*) consist of? Respecting the noble, being filial (**xiao**) to the elderly, being brotherly (*di*) to one's seniors, and kind (**ci**) to the young' (*Xunzi*, 27: 16). Confucius thus said, 'at home a young man should be filial (*xiao*); outside the home, he should be brotherly (*ti*)' (*Analects*, 1: 6). The *Li ji* provides us with a sense of brotherly (*ti*) behaviour outside the home: 'Upon the appearance of some-one elderly, then carts and pedestrians avoid his or her path. Along the road, one who has white streaks in his or her hair is not allowed to shoulder his or her burden. Thus, brotherly conduct (*di*) reaches the roads and paths' (*Li ji*, 25: 39). When men in authority are brotherly, it transforms the behaviour of the people at large. The **Da xue** states, 'When those above treat the elderly as elderly, then among the people filial piety (*xiao*) will flourish; when those above treat seniors as seniors, then among the people brotherly conduct (*di*) will flourish' (*Li ji*, 43: 2).

Confucian writers oftentimes pair *ti* together with its complement, *xiao* (filial piety). These two values address the two most important relationships within the Chinese family: the ties between father and son and brothers. Hence, the advocacy of these two values was always an important priority. Confucius said, 'Being filial (*xiao*) and brotherly (*ti*) are the basis of benevolence (**ren**)' (*Analects*, 1: 2). Mengzi went even a step further and asserted that: 'The Way of Yao and Shun (see **Yao Shun**) is nothing more than being filial (*xiao*) and brotherly (*di*)' (*Mengzi*, 6B: 1).

References: *Chuxue ji*, 1962; *Hou Han shu*, 1965; Hung, ed., 1972a, 1972b; Lau & Chen, 1992a, 1994, 1995, 1996a.

KEITH KNAPP

Ti yong 體用
(Substance and function)

The basic meanings of *ti* as an independent term are 'body', 'corpus', 'substance' or 'form'; *yong* means use, usage, activity or implementation. As a paired combination, the two terms are usually translated as substance and function. In that sense, *ti* usually refers to the essential, unmanifested, inner qualities of a thing, event or phenomena and generally speaking indicates its ontological dimensions. *Yong* refers to its external, applied, manifested, active or processual dimensions. *Ti* can also be used to refer to one thing and *yong*, something else entirely with which the first entity is compared or contrasted. *Ti* can also refer to a thing and *yong*, to actions performed on or with that thing. The terms are often used abstractly and very loosely, however, and not necessarily systematically, and in parallel phrases *yong* sometimes takes precedence over *ti. Ti yong* is a hermeneutic lens through which literati have interpreted and constructed numerous dyadic concepts and parallel expressions.

One of the first parallel occurrences of the terms *ti* and *yong* appears not in pre-Han classics but in Wang Bi's 王弼 (226–249) commentary on the *Laozi*, where Wang commented on the nature of nonbeing (chapter 38). *Ti yong* was also frequently used in Tang dynasty Hua-yan, Tiantai and Three-Treatise Schools of Buddhism and became firmly established there; Ji-zang 吉藏 (549–623), for example, employed the terms to explicate the polysemous nature of all dharmas, and Tiantai Buddhists used them to evoke the contemporaneity of multiple layers of truth, the collapsing of all time into an instant, and the totality of suchness contained within a discrete entity.

The expression eventually came into the common vocabulary of Song literati thinkers such as **Zhang Zai** (in his **Zheng Meng**), **Shao Yong**, and particularly **Cheng Yi** and **Zhu Xi**. Shao Yong, for example, incorporated the pair of terms into his complex cosmological vision and applied them not only to contemporary phenomena but to the content of the ancient classics and to the character of the culture heroes and sages of antiquity and their various states and dynasties. He perceived the sage–kings, for example, as the substance of the **Yi jing**, and he saw images and numbers as the function of that text. Thus he, too, collapsed time and multiple realms into a contiguous seam, but the content, textual sources and historical dimensions of his vision were quite different than those of the Buddhists.

Shao Yong developed this elaborate web of correlations in his understanding of *ti* and

yong, but Cheng Yi focused instead on comprehensive unity. Cheng Yi was noted for his statement in the preface to his commentary on the *Yi jing* that substance and function are of one source (體用一源) and that there was no difference between what was manifest and what was hidden. Similar expressions were also employed by contemporary Buddhists, and some claim this notion is derived from the *Avatamsaka Sutra*. For Cheng Yi, nonetheless, substance abided in the Way and in moral principles.

Zhu Xi was largely indebted to Cheng Yi in his understanding of substance and function and used them to explicate cosmological, ethical and ontological principles and to craft the principles shaping the human condition. He employed the terms more profusely than perhaps any other thinker and used them to interpret a diverse array of phenomena that ranged from objects of daily use to the operations of the human mind. He at once attempted to establish the discrete nature of both *ti* and *yong* while emphasising their perfect contiguity and simultaneous instantiation. Substance referred to principle (*li*), for example, and function was usage, but there was substance within function and function within substance. Substance referred to a thing (such as a fan, the eye, the human body or water) and function referred to how that thing moved or was used (fanning, seeing, walking or flowing, respectively). Substance and function were at once different and yet never apart from one another. At the level of the human being, their conjoinedness was reflected in the masterful synthesising powers of the human mind, whose substance was nature and whose function was feelings and emotions. For Zhu Xi, substance and function were also flexible, relative terms, in the sense that when different phenomena were compared with one another, the relationship of substance and function might shift: when discussing yang, for example, yang was substance and yin was function, but in discussing yin, yin was substance and yang was function.

References: Birdwhistell, 1989; Chan, Wing-tsit, 1963d: 323, 368–9, 403–5, 570 and 1967, 1989: 222–34, 1996: 175–8; Teng Ai-min 1986.

DEBORAH SOMMER

Tian 天
(Heaven/Nature)

Tian is the sky, the heavens or heaven; particularly in later texts, it is the operational principles of the cosmos. In early works such as the **Shi jing**, heaven is understood as a place, a creative life-source, and a sovereign divinity or power. As a place, heaven is the atmospheric and celestial realm above the earth that on the one hand is a constant source of life-giving light and rain and on the other is a changeable, destructive power that sends down famine, death and chaos. Heaven is also the abode of ancestral spirits who in the afterlife can descend and ascend to intervene in human affairs. As a creative life-source, heaven gives birth to the human race, and as it bestows life and forms human nature (*xing*) it also establishes social norms. Heaven often responds to human supplication and moral ardour, but its responses are dangerously unpredictable and its ways are difficult to fathom. As a sovereign divinity or power, Heaven is endowed with intelligence and emotions, particularly anger, and takes a very active and watchful role in human affairs. Its identity is sometimes vaguely merged with that of the Lord on High (**Shang Di**), but as Heaven's actual appearance is not described, one can only conjecture as to whether it was understood as an anthropomorphic divinity. Human rulers, who bear the title of child or Son of Heaven, are enjoined to follow a mandate (*ming*) based on virtue (*de*) or risk heaven's fatal punishments. The **Shang shu** asserts that Heaven sees as the people hear and see, so Heaven's attentions are with the people as much as with the ruler.

Vestiges of Heaven's complex and ambiguous nature are still seen in the **Lunyu**. Although Confucius' disciples once complained that they rarely heard their master's views on the way of heaven (**tian dao**), it is nonetheless clear that Confucius saw Heaven as an awe-inspiring source of life, as the font of his own virtue, and as an ultimately just power who set him on the path to sagehood. Heaven's sometimes cruel unfathomability is reflected in his lament at the death of his favourite pupil, Yan Hui, that Heaven has bereft him. Yet Confucius elsewhere asserts that he bears no ill will against Heaven and feels assured that Heaven would not destroy him or his culture. He moreover claims that he understands Heaven and that Heaven understands him – a sentiment rarely, if ever, voiced in the **Shi jing**. Confucius, however, claimed to not understand the mandate of Heaven until he had reached the age of fifty.

Heaven is even less dangerous and less unknowable in the **Mengzi**, where it plays a largely benevolent role in human affairs. Here heaven is associated with the ordered, moral principles that operate within the universe and infuse the human frame. Heaven bestows life itself and gives human beings minds (*xin*) that can guide their senses and allow them to understand their heaven-bestowed natures (*xing*). It is through self-development, not supplication, that humans can serve heaven (**shi tian**). Heaven charges human beings with a moral imperative, but this mandate also has a personal, individualised aspect that has been expanded from the state-level mandate once largely the preserve of rulers.

In the *Zhongyong* of the **Li ji**, heaven has also lost most of its fearsome aspect and is partnered with the earth; together, they are the living totality of the observed natural world and are a treasure-house of cosmic proportions. Through self-perfection, humans can form a trinity with Heaven and Earth and participate in their completeness. Not only can humans understand Heaven (something even Confucius found problematic), but they can actively engage in its transformations through personal development.

The *Xunzi* similarly asserts that humans may form a triad with Heaven and Earth, but in this ternion Xunzi emphasises the role of human beings in determining their own fates. He dispels the notion that heaven interferes arbitrarily in human affairs or can inspire fear and dread. On the contrary, Heaven's operations are predictable, impartial, observable and constant; calamitous or felicitous events in the human realm are due to human folly or accomplishment, respectively, not to Heaven's wilful wrath or pleasure. Heaven is not morally neutral, however, for it is associated with the way (*dao*). It endows humans with physical bodies, faculties and emotions; provides for human sustenance; and endows people with minds (*xin*) that are capable of understanding the way. Through the performance of ritual, which Xunzi understands not simply as scripted offerings but as the entire complex of human culture conceived of at its most abstract and aesthetic levels, humans realise their own potential and create harmonious relationships with heaven and earth.

For the Song scholar **Zhang Zai**, Heaven is not only a fearsome entity but is a nurturing parent who is espoused to the earth. In his *Xi ming*, he describes Heaven as his father and earth as his mother and describes himself as a minute creature who is yet afforded a significant place in their presence. Other Song scholars understood heaven in less personalised, familial terms and envisioned it more abstractly as the fundamentally moral operational principles of the universe. The Cheng brothers identified Heaven with the way; the human mind was one with the mind of Heaven. They spoke more often of Heaven's principle (*tian li* 天理, a notion that had appeared in the *Li ji* but came to play a much larger role in Song thought), which in their writings was associated with moral values and informed all things. The complete apprehension of heaven's principle might be clouded by excess human desires (*ren yu* 人欲), but innate to the human condition was the ability of the self to overcome such negativities. **Zhu Xi**'s notions of heaven were indebted to the Chengs, and he associated Heaven with Mengzi's four cardinal virtues of humaneness, wisdom, rightness and ritual. But in his cosmology the notion of the Great Ultimate (*tai ji*) takes on greater significance than Heaven. And Chen Chun does not include the notion of Heaven in his *Beixi ziyi*, his study of significant philosophical concepts of the age.

References: Ames & Rosemont, 1998: 2: 4, 5: 13, 7: 23, 9: 5, 9: 6, 11: 9, 14: 35, 16: 8, 17: 19; Chan, Wing-tsit 1963b and 1986, 1989: 184–96; de Bary & Bloom, 1999; Hall & Ames, 1987: 195–215; Lau, 1984: 3A: 5, 5A: 5, 5A: 6, 6A: 15, 6B :15, 7A: 1; Legge, 1985b, odes 194, 198, 207, 210, 229, 235, 254, 255, 257, 260, 288; Legge, 1985c, pp. 271, 292; Watson, 1963: 79–88; Yu Yamanoi, 1986.

DEBORAH SOMMER

Tian dao 天道
(The way of Heaven)

The way of heaven is the way (*dao*), path or set of norms heaven (*tian*) follows in its interactions with the natural and human realms. Human beings are morally obligated to follow these norms, which are the operational principles of the cosmos. By complying with the way of Heaven, which actively participates in human society and prevails over mortal folly, human beings can succeed in their own endeavours; they transgress the way of Heaven at their own peril. The *Shang shu* claims that it is the way of Heaven to make the good prosper and to punish the wicked. Its mandate favours those who are humble, respectful, follow the path of rightness, maintain their virtue and adhere to ritual.

The *Chunqiu Zuo zhuan* similarly associates the way of Heaven with ideals of human behaviour, particularly regarding the proper relationships between sovereigns and ministers. Such relationships should be guided by loyalty, trustworthiness, magnanimity and reverence. The way of heaven also guides the relationship between the human and numinous realms, which is conducted through the performance of ritual. Ritual itself accords with the way of Heaven but is here understood ideally as virtuous conduct rather than the mere outward performance of oblations and sacrifices. The way of Heaven is constant and cannot be swayed by mechanical supplications.

But for all its constancy, the content of the way of Heaven was, however, elusive to some, as is evidenced by the complaint of Confucius' disciples that they seldom heard their master expound on the subject. The constancy of the way of Heaven was nonetheless asserted in the **Zhongyong** (ch. 26), where heaven is partnered with the earth, with whom it gives birth to all things. Here, the way of heaven is noted for its depth, breadth, generosity and enduringness. The world is ontologically grounded, then, on principles tending toward human prosperity.

The *Xunzi*, however, takes pains to distinguish the way of Heaven and the way of Earth from the way of human beings, which is instead epitomised by the conduct of the noble person (*junzi*). **Mengzi**, however, conjoins the ways of Heaven and human beings through the moral quality of integrity or sincerity (*cheng*), which he equates with the way of Heaven. By internalising this integrity and enacting it in one's conduct (conduct that is then not far from that of Xunzi's noble person), one is able to nurture one's family, earn the trust of friends and superiors, and govern well. The way of Heaven, then, is firmly implanted in the human realm.

References: Ames & Rosemont, 1998: 5: 13; Chan, Wing-tsit, 1963a; de Bary and Bloom, 1999; Knoblock, 1988–94, vol. II: 71; Lau, 1984: 4A: 12; Legge, 1985a: 495, 626, 671, 718, 823; Legge, 1985c: 65, 183, 186; Shun, Kwong-loi, 1997a: 16.

DEBORAH SOMMER

Tian di 天地
(Heaven and Earth)

Tian di signifies not only the natural world or universe, but also is a frequently used metaphor for what is above and below, the yang and yin which when united become the origin or basis of life. The *Book of Documents* (**Shang shu**) says of this unity: 'Heaven and Earth is the parent of all things'; an idea echoed in the *Doctrine of the Mean* (**Zhongyong**) 1(5): 'A happy order will prevail throughout Heaven and Earth, and all things will be nourished and flourish.' This unity also plays a triadic role with humans (**ren** 人), the **san cai**. From a Confucian perspective this interrelationship of heaven, earth and humans share a similar nature and are harmoniously, rather than antagonistically, interacting. The single Way (*dao*) of this interaction is characterised by three modes: the Way of Heaven (*tian dao*), the Way of earth (*di dao*) and the Way of humans (**ren dao**). In chapter 3 of the first part of the Appended Remarks, the *Book of Changes* (**Yi jing**), it is stated that '. . . change is a paradigm of heaven and earth, and it shows how one can fill in and pull together the Way of Heaven and Earth. Looking up, the sage uses [the change] to observe the configuration of heaven, and, looking down, he uses it to examine the patterns of earth . . .' and later in chapter 7 it continues, '. . . exhalted, [the Sage] emulate heaven, and, humble, they model themselves on earth'.

References: Legge, 1861, 1966; Morohashi, 1960; Yao, 2000.

TODD CAMERON THACKER

Tian di zhi xing 天地之性
(The nature of Heaven and Earth)

As explained by the Cheng–Zhu School (**Cheng–Zhu xuepai**), the 'nature of Heaven and Earth' is equivalent to the **benran zhi xing** (original nature), and it is superior to and to be distinguished from the *qizhi zhi xing* (physically endowed nature). The nature of Heaven and Earth is that primordial and ethereal nature that is dispensed to each person upon birth and it is always invariably good. This nature of Heaven and Earth, which is immanent in all of us, generates entirely from *li* (principle) and demonstrates no dependency whatsoever upon *qi* (material force), which can differ markedly in its grade and allocation from person to person.

A reference in the Classic *Xiao jing* – 'man is most prized because of his nature of Heaven and Earth' – actually became the basis for stressing the cultivation of this particular nature at the expense of the physically endowed nature (*Xiao jing*, 'Shengzhi Zhang' 聖治章, 9: 1.7b). Or, as Zhu Xi once explained, 'Whenever we discuss the nature of Heaven and Earth, then we must speak by concentrating on principle. Whenever we discuss the physically endowed nature, then we must speak in terms of the commingling of principle and *qi*. If not for the prior existence of this principle, we never would have this *qi*. It is possible for *qi* to exist for a time and then dissipate and yet, as for the nature [of Heaven and Earth] – it is always forever intact' (*Zhuzi yulei*, 4.10).

Reference: Chu, 1922.

DON J. WYATT

Tian ming 天命
(Mandate of Heaven)

The doctrine of the *Tian ming* proclaimed the essential place in the cosmic system for a king or later an emperor to rule over mankind with the support of a superhuman authority. It allowed for the correct removal of a ruler if he showed himself unfit to bear the charge that he carried; and a leader of a movement to remove such a ruler would do so with the full support of Heaven, whose purpose he would be

implementing, and in the expectation that he would himself succeed to rule with Heaven's blessing. This was a highly valuable doctrine for those who sought to explain and legitimise their own seizure of power by conquering a predecessor. As an inbuilt principle of Chinese official historiography it brought an inevitable bias into the dynastic records. But while the origins of the doctrine can be traced to some of the earliest of China's writings, it did not yet command uninterrupted acceptance. It was not incorporated in the concept of imperial government until nearly two centuries after the foundation of the first empire. In time the doctrine included the view that Heaven would choose to warn a ruler of offences that had prejudiced his right to rule, such warnings being manifested in strange happenings in the skies or in disasters that struck the earth.

According to the Mandate of Heaven, once an enthroned recipient of the charge had shown himself as unworthy he forfeited Heaven's blessing and the charge was transferred elsewhere. This principle was applied anachronistically to legitimise the means whereby the Shang 商 house had displaced that of the Xia 夏, and the kings of the Zhou 周 those of the Shang; for Jie 桀 and Zhou 紂, the last rulers of Xia and Shang, had shown themselves to be oppressive tyrants who had flouted Heaven's will.

In place of *Di* 帝, or *Shang Di* 上帝 the god worshipped by the kings of the Shang, *Tian*, Heaven, was seen by the kings of the Zhou as a universal god to whom worship was due from all peoples who lived on earth, as represented by their king. As Heaven's nominated monarch, those kings styled themselves as the 'Sons of Heaven' (*Tian zi*). The conjuction of five planets of 1059 BCE was at one time interpreted as a visible and material sign that Heaven's gift of earthly majesty was about to descend on the kings of the Zhou, whose reign started *c.* 1045 BCE. An inscription on a bronze vessel (Da Yu ding 大盂鼎) of 981 BCE states the principles of the doctrine, and there are at least seven references to it in the *Book of Poetry* (**Shi jing**) and six in the *Book of Documents* (**Shang shu**). Crucially some of these concern the transfer of rule from Shang to Zhou, explained in one instance as being due to the failure of the kings of the Shang to render due worship to *Tian*. Two passages even enjoin the founders of first the Shang and then the Zhou houses to eliminate their predecessors in preparation for their own receipt of the Mandate. One passage of the *Poetry*, which is cited in the **Mengzi**, is at pains to point out that the Mandate is in no way fixed permanently in one ruling house.

Of necessity the claim to be blessed by Heaven's Mandate implied the existence of one and only one legitimate ruler of mankind. But new political conditions prevailed following the flight east of the last of the kings of western Zhou in 771 BCE. A large number of leaders came to exercise authority over limited areas simultaneously and it was not feasible for any one of them to claim to be the choice of Heaven; and in the later conditions, of the seven major kingdoms of the Warring States period, any such claim would be contested fiercely. Some of the writers of these centuries, notably Confucius and Mengzi, harked back nostalgically to the days of the kings of the Zhou, now seen to have ruled with the greatest beneficence to the advantage of all mankind. References to the Mandate in the **Chunqiu Zuo zhuan** or *Analects* (**Lunyu**) reflect such thoughts but cannot claim the application of the doctrine at the time when those texts were being written.

A further, and radical, change in dynastic and political terms followed the foundation of the Qin empire in 221 BCE. For the establishment of a single monarch on this occasion brought with it a rejection of the ideals that had been ascribed to the kings of the Zhou and their institutions. With their own views of the basis and purpose of imperial authority, the new masters of China did not regard the worship of

Heaven as part of their duties. Rather did the theories of **Wu xing** 五行 militate against the concept of a single deity who commanded universal power; the state cults of the Qin, and then those of the Han, were addressed at first not to Heaven but first to the four and then to the five *Di* whose powers operated in successive stages and of whom one was singled out as patron of the ruling house.

A return to a faith in Heaven's gift of authority was comparatively slow. In a memorial of 202 BCE Lou Jing 婁敬 contrasted the rule of the Zhou with that of the first of the Han emperors, but he did not question the manner in which Liu Bang 劉邦, the Founder of the Han dynasty, had acquired power; nor did he support it by appealing to the blessing of Heaven. There are no references to the *Tian ming* in the **Xin yu** of **Lu Jia**, nor does the term itself appear in the three basic memorials of **Dong Zhongshu** to whom, however, some of the elements of the doctrine may be traced. In his concept of the universe Dong Zhongshu identified the three constituent and interdependent estates of Heaven, Earth and Man, the last comprehending all living creatures; and he saw the exercise of sovereignty as an essential element in the comos, resting on the authority conveyed by Heaven. He does not specify Heaven as the power that could encourage or validate the transfer of sovereignty from one house to another; but in explaining strange phenomena and natural disasters as the means whereby Heaven expresses its warnings to a ruler he emphasises what was to be cited as an integral principle of the doctrine.

There is little to show that Dong Zhongshu's views received general approval during his lifetime, but they were much in agreement with the new ideas of government and its purpose that were coming into currency from perhaps 80 BCE. Apart from certain anachronistic references, specific mention of a ruler who has received the Mandate (*Shou ming zhi wang* 受命之王) together with evocation of the kings of the

Zhou and citation from the *Book of Poetry*, is seen perhaps for the first time in Han history in one of the memorials put forward by **Kuang Heng** (*c.* 44 BCE). At the time Kuang Heng was still a junior official, and his memorial predated the transfer of the cults of state from the Five Powers (*Wu di* 五帝) to Heaven. Introduced *c.* 30 BCE, this change was far from permanent, being revoked and reintroduced on several occasions until 5 CE, when, under the influence of Wang Mang 王莽, the cult to Heaven was finally installed at Chang'an.

In the meantime **Liu Xiang**, who had been writing at a somewhat critical moment in dynastic fortunes (16 BCE), invoked the concept of the *San tong* 三統, noting that the Mandate was not vested in one single family. He cited from Confucius' interpretation of the *Poetry*, with respect to the transfer of the Mandate from the Shang to the Zhou. At an even more critical time, **Xia Heliang** called for the Han dynasty to bring about a restoration of its authority, and the ensuing decree of 5 BCE accepted the duty of seeking a renewal of the Mandate.

But it was in the reign of **Wang Mang** (9–23 CE) that the Mandate of Heaven first enters into dynastic discussions in full force. It is cited in the requests made by officials that he should accede to the imperial throne; it is quoted in a document entitled *Fu ming* 符命 that he circulated on an empire-wide basis immediately after doing so. In the troubled circumstances of Wang Mang's last years a bold official tried to turn the tables by suggesting to Wang Mang that, in accordance with the Mandate, imperial authority should revert to the house of Liu. After Wang Mang's death supporters of a number of contenders to power argued that Wang Mang himself had acted against Heaven and had forfeited the Mandate, which they were thereby themselves due to receive. Whereas the concept had not been mentioned when Han Gaozu (r. 202–195 BCE) and Han Wendi (r. 180–157 BCE) were

being urged to ascend the throne, it featured in the calls addressed to Liu Xiu, the future Guangwudi, first of the Later Han emperors (r. 25–57 CE). Wang Mang had bequeathed to his successors the means of strengthening their claims to rule the world under the protection of Heaven.

MICHAEL LOEWE

Tian ren 天人
(Heaven and human beings)

Tian is Heaven; *ren*, human beings. Since earliest times the relationship between them was of central concern for every matter from personal self-cultivation to the governance of the state. Also significant in this relationship is the role of the Earth (*di* 地), and together, the realms of Heaven, Earth and Human Beings encompassed all known phenomena.

In many early texts, the relationship between Heaven and human beings was one fraught with considerable danger for mortals, and heaven's power and authority elicited at once both fear and reverence. On the one hand, Heaven was a capricious and unassuageable power capable of destroying human life by causing famine; on the other, it was also viewed as a source of life and as a righteous authority that charged human rulers with a mandate (*ming* 命) to rule morally. Sovereigns who did not maintain an ethical form of governance were forcibly punished by Heaven – or at least by rival claimants to sovereignty who claimed to be acting in Heaven's name. Communicating with Heaven and interpreting its signs was primarily the prerogative of rulers and high-ranking officials, and the common people were afforded little direct access to Heaven's powers.

Heaven, earth and humans were organised into an ordered cosmos in mythic cosmogonic accounts in the *Shang shu*, which relate how the sage rulers Yao, Shun and Yu surveyed the Heavens and the earth, perceived the regularities and periodicities intrinsic to the natural world, and created a hierarchically structured social order. To accomplish this, they relied not on revelation or superhuman abilities but upon ordinary powers of human observation and upon principles of organisation, division and calculation; thus they transformed an amorphous and floodlike primordiality into a predictable and measured environment suitable for human habitation. They moreover instantiated a system of ritual votive offerings or sacrifices (*ji si* 祭祀) that facilitated communications between the heavenly, human and earthly realms and the numinous powers that inhabited them.

The principles of this ritual system were later described in greater detail in such texts as the *Li ji* and *Zhou li*, which describe cosmological systems comprised of a heavenly realm inhabited by spirits (*shen* 神), a human realm inhabited not only by mortals but also by ghosts (*gui* 鬼), and an earthly realm of terrestrial powers (*zhi*). Living human beings were the beneficiaries of all the numinous powers of the universe – the sun, moon, cold and heat, rain, soil and so on – and were obligated to recompense (*bao* 報) them with votive offerings of foodstuffs and other commodities. Offerings were presented by a tiered hierarchy of sacrificers who performed rites only to their counterparts in rank in the numinous realm: only the ruler might sacrifice to Heaven, only the enfeoffed lords might sacrifice to the mountains and rivers of their own realms, and so on. Performing offerings was crucial to the stability of the state. This ritual system persisted until the early twentieth century.

By the late Zhou, however, heaven becomes less associated with unstable meteorological powers or with celestial imagery and was understood more abstractly – and beneficently – as a source of life and moral values. The relationship between Heaven and human beings is alluded to in the *Lunyu*, although Confucius' disciples complained of rarely hearing their master discuss the topic. It is nonetheless clear that Confucius saw Heaven as a great and just power whose silent operations humans could ultimately comprehend.

Heaven moreover moved beyond the purview of the ruler or the performance of the state cult and became instantiated within each person and accessible to all through self-cultivation. Texts such as the *Zhong yong* posit that humans can participate in a tripartite relationship with Heaven and Earth not only through the outward manifestations of ritual but through the inward refashioning of the self: the perfection of the quality of integrity or sincerity (*cheng* 誠) has a transformational power that resonates with Heaven and Earth. In both the *Mengzi* and the *Xunzi*, Heaven is embedded in the human mind or heart (*xin*), which guides the physical frame and the senses and allows humans to participate in the generative powers of Heaven (*shitian zhitian* 事天知天). **Xunzi** emphasised, however, that humans should accept their unique responsibilities in this ternion and not mistakenly attribute their own fates to the powers of Heaven or Earth (see *tianren xiangfen*).

Han scholars such as **Dong Zhongshu** articulated this relationship in greater detail and understood it in terms of a mutual resonance between Heaven and human beings (*tianren ganying*). In his systematised vision of the relatedness of all phenomena, he proposed that not only the mind but also every bone and joint in the human body responds sympathetically to fluctuations in the heavens and on earth.

The Song thinker **Zhang Zai**, however, perceived his own relationship to Heaven and Earth in personal, familial terms and conceived of it as that between a child and its parents. And instead of correlating the human body with analogous phenomena, his *Xi ming* erases the boundaries between the human body and the larger universe altogether: that which suffuses the universe, he claims, is in fact his own body (*ti* 體). Much later, **Wang Shouren** expanded upon a similar notion of the body and claimed that the ideal person considered Heaven, Earth and the myriad things to be one body. Human beings enacted this unity by following the eight steps of **Da xue** (the *Great Learning*) and by implementing it in their daily actions.

Zhang Zai's nephews **Cheng Hao** and **Cheng Yi** lauded those who identified themselves with Heaven and Earth, and, unlike Dong Zhongshu, they understood this relationship in terms of unity rather than correlation: the human mind is one with the 'minds' of Heaven and Earth. They conceived of Heaven abstractly as a principle imbued with moral values, and even asserted that all phenomena are in fact just this *tian li* 天理, or heavenly principle. Human desires can becloud it, but through effort these negativities can be overcome and the self realised.

Zhu Xi's complex philosophical system attempted to explain how ontological principles are enmeshed with ethical values and how a human being comprehends them through the mind and enacts them in practice. He understood the principles of Heaven and Earth as the Great Ultimate (*tai ji* 太極), which he moreover associated with the principle of the mind.

References: Ames & Rosemont, 1998; Chan, Wing-tsit, 1963a and 1963b, 1986b, 1989; de Bary & Bloom, 1999; Knoblock, 1988–94; Lau, 1984; Legge, 1985b and 1985c; Sun Yirang, 1987; Yu Yamanoi, 1986.

DEBORAH SOMMER

Tian ren ganying 天人感應

(Resonance between Heaven and human beings)

Tian is Heaven; *ren*, human beings. *Gan* means to invoke, evoke, or bestir and *ying* means to respond or resonate. *Ganying* is a mutual resonance or mutual sympathy between two or more phenomena. *Tian ren ganying*, the mutual resonance between heaven and human beings, was developed most prominently by **Dong Zhongshu** in his **Chunqiu fanlu**, although notions of mutual response are found in earlier sources such as the *Yi jing* (Book of Changes), the *Xunzi*, and the *Lüshi Chunqiu*.

The idea of mutual resonance is hinted at in the *Yi jing*, although the relationships between the heavenly and the human realm are not systematically articulated there. In the explanations (*tuan* 彖) to the hexagram *xian* 咸, which is associated with the visually similar *gan* 感, mutual resonance occurs between dyads such as hard and soft or between two *qi*. Heaven and Earth bestirs all things and gives birth to them, an activity that in the human realm is paralleled by the sage, who bestirs the human mind.

Moving from the mind of the sage to the nature of human beings in general, the *Xunzi* goes so far as to state that human nature (*xing*) itself is harmonious and mutually responsive (*ganying*) from birth (*Zheng ming pian* 正名篇, the Chapter on Rectification of Names). Xunzi, however, emphasises what is unique to both the heavenly and the human realm and does not underscore their convergences (see *tianren xiangfen*).

Resonances between human and heavenly realms are described at greater length, however, in the *Lüshi Chunqiu*. Here, phenomena that are of the same *qi* or that are of the same kind (*lei* 類) resonate with or attract (*zhao* 召) one another. To be of the same kind is to be of the same class or category of phenomena and to share a fundamental, ontological similitude. In the *Lüshi Chunqiu*, for example, musical notes are phenomena of the same kind and hence resonate with one another, or water is attracted to damp places. Similarly, the actions of the ruler elicit certain responses from Heaven, which are manifested through omens. In this system of resonances, the depth of the sovereign's moral cultivation is directly proportional to the prosperity of the realm.

Dong Zhongshu incorporates these notions of mutual resonance, kind and also of visual similitude (xiang 象) into a much more elaborate system of relationships that encompasses the entire universe. Human beings participate in a triadic relationship with heaven and earth, and correspondences between these three realms are marked by observable or calculable phenomena: the human body's 360 joints correspond to the number of days in a year, human breath is like the wind, the head is rounded like the domed heavens, the feet are flat like the earth, and so on. The human body is a simulacrum of the cosmos.

This visual multiplicity of observable phenomena, however, rests upon fundamental principles not readily apparent to the senses. Principles of yin and yang (see **yin–yang**) suffuse the human body and fluctuate with the forces of yin and yang in the larger universe. Yin is associated with sadness, death and the season of autumn, for example; yang, with joy, life and the season of spring. Humans are enjoined to adjust their ritual calendars accordingly, scheduling funerary rites for autumn and celebratory rites for the spring. Thus, human behaviour resonates appropriately with the natural world.

Not only these calendars but all circadian rhythms, emotional fluctuations, agrarian timetables, political schedules and historical cycles of the human realm resonate deeply with heavenly cycles, for both realms are fundamentally of the same kind (*yi lei he zhi, tian ren yi ye* 以類合之, 天人一也). In Dong's vision of the cosmos, phenomena of the same kind activate and respond to one another in a complex universe perpetually in motion but pervaded by constant principles. The mandate of the ruler and the sage is to facilitate the orderly and timely progression of human and natural events, and this is accomplished through enacting humaneness (*ren*) and rightness (*yi*).

References: Chan, 1963d: 271–88; Knoblock, 1988–94; Knoblock & Riegel,

2000: 282–6, 439–43, 522–30; Su Yu, 1992; Wang Xianqian, 1988.

DEBORAH SOMMER

Tian ren heyi 天人合一

(Heaven and human beings in harmony as one)

In this expression, **tian** is Heaven; **ren**, human beings; **he**, to be in harmony; and **yi** is one or unity. The phrase is commonly found in modern secondary studies of Confucian thought, where it refers in general to a wide range of premodern notions about the relationships between heaven and human beings. According to these modern interpretations, the idea that Heaven and Earth are in harmony as one dates to Zhou times. The specific expression *tianren heyi*, however, does not occur in texts of that date, although the more general notion that the heavenly and human realms are integrally related is elaborated in many texts of that age, particularly in the **Mengzi** and the **Zhongyong**. The *Mengzi*, for example, posits that cultivating the nature and the mind are tantamount to serving heaven (**shi tian**; *Mengzi* 7A: 1) and claims that all things are complete within the self (7A: 4). This is not, however, the same as saying that heaven and human beings are one. The **Zhongyong** (*Zhongyong* 22) and the **Xunzi** assert that human beings can participate in the operations of Heaven and Earth, but this participation is conceptualised as a triad, not a unity.

The Han scholar **Dong Zhongshu** in his **Chunqiu fanlu** (*juan* 35, *Shencha minghao* 深察名號) used the expression *tianren zhi ji, he er wei yi* 天人之際, 合而為一, that is, 'the junctures of Heaven and human beings are harmonious as one'. The larger context of this statement, however, is not at all a disquisition on the oneness of Heaven and human beings but is primarily a discourse on the principles of correlation between terms and reality. Dong's philosophical system elsewhere is informed by notions of correlations, correspondences, resonances and resemblances between largely discrete or analogous entities (a differentiation suggested in the expression above by the term *ji*, which means 'boundary' or 'juncture') – not on principles of ontological unity.

The Song scholar **Zhang Zai**, however, did in fact specifically use the expression *tianren heyi*, and his philosophical system is characterised by expressions of unity and oneness: the myriad things are one, the way is one, human nature is the single origin of the myriad things, and the universe is grounded in a commonality of **qi**, and so on. In his ***Zheng meng*** (*Qiancheng pian* 乾稱篇 and *Chengming pian* 誠明篇), he asserts that not only Heaven and human beings but also existence (*you* 有) and nonexistence (*wu* 無), inside and outside, activity and tranquility and yin and yang are in harmony as one. In fact, the entire universe is informed by a Great Harmony (*tai he* 太和) that underlies all cosmic fluctuations and transmutations. In his ***Xi ming***, Zhang Zai dissolves distinctions between his own body and the substance of the entire universe and evokes intense filiations with heaven, which he envisions as his own parent.

References: Chan, 1963d: 271–88, 495–517 and 1996: 97–9; Jiang Guozhu, 2001: 87–96; Jiang Guozhu, 1982: 34–53; Su Yu, 1992: 288.

DEBORAH SOMMER

Tian ren xiangfen 天人相分
(The different concerns of Heaven and human beings)

Tian is Heaven; *ren*, human beings; *xiang* signifies a parallel or mutual relationship between phenomena. *Fen* means to divide or to distinguish, or to be a division or portion of something. More abstractly, it can also refer to one's apportioned lot or station in life. Here, *xiang fen* is translated 'different concerns', as the original context of this idea, which is found in the **Xunzi**, refers to the dis-

tinct concerns appropriate to heaven and human beings, respectively.

In the chapter 'On Heaven' (*Tian lun* 天論), one actually finds this notion in the slightly different expression *tianren zhi fen* 天人之分. **Xunzi** is not arguing here that human beings and Heaven are unrelated. He is, on the other hand, arguing that Heaven's ways are constant and that those who believe its operations are based on arbitrary principles are mistaken. Heaven has its concerns, and humans have theirs, and Heaven responds predictably to human conduct: certain kinds of behaviour (such as diligence and frugality) elicit good fortune, but others (negligence and extravagance) beget misfortune. The ups and downs of human systems of governance, agriculture and economy are not attributable to erratic interference from Heaven but are a matter of human concern foremost. Hence, by emphasising 'differentiation' Xunzi seeks to instil in human beings a greater sense of responsibility for their own actions. Sages understand this responsibility, seek to develop human powers to the utmost, and thus truly participate in a triadic partnership with heaven and earth.

References: Knoblock, 1988–94; Wang Xianqian, 1988; Watson, 1963.

DEBORAH SOMMER

Tian xia 天下
(The world)

Tian xia denotes the world, or in context, the Asian world or simply all of China. In contrast to a material or natural world, as for example **tian di** (Heaven and earth), *tian xia* has a subtle spiritual element. Under the rule of the Sage (**sheng ren**), the spiritual fulfillment of the world can be established. Confucian examples of the benevolent and beneficial effects of such reigns include the Three Sovereigns and Five Emperors (**sanhuang wudi**). Moreover, these model political references to the ruler (**junzi**) carrying out his duty to the State are commonplace in Confucian texts. For example, in the *Great Learning* (**Daxue**) 5, 'Their States being rightly governed, the whole world (*tian xia*) was made tranquil and happy'. This ideal state of peace in the *tian xia* had already been lost in Confucius' day and was never again reestablished. Confucius said in the *Analects* (**Lunyu**) 16: 2, 'When the Way prevails in the Empire [*tianxia*], the rites (**li**) and music (**yue**) and punitive expeditions are initiated by the King [*tian zi*].' When this spiritual rule prevails upon the Empire, genuine peace is within reach. Without it, a sustained fall into moral and political collapse is inevitable. This was a view clearly held by **Mengzi**, who says of kingly rule (*wang dao*) as such '... There is one way to win the Empire; win the people ... win their hearts ... amass what they want for them and do not impose what they dislike on them. That is all. The people turn benevolent as water flows downwards ...'

References: Lau, 1970, 1979; Legge, 1966; Morohashi 1960.

TODD CAMERON THACKER

Tian zi 天子
(Son of Heaven)

The Son of Heaven is a representative of the Heavenly Lord (*tian di* 天帝), administering by proxy the latter's true ethical principles with incontrovertable authority and virtue. He is said to have received the Mandate of Heaven (**tian ming**), and as a sage rules the people benevolently. Through this mandate he serves the people, not vice versa. Take, for example, the paradigmatic statement in the **Mengzi**, 7B: 14, 'Mengzi said, 'The people (**min**) are of supreme importance; the altars to the gods of earth and grain come next; last comes the ruler (**jun**). This is why he who gains the confidence of the multitudinous people (**min**) will be the king (**tian zi**); he who gains the confidence

of the king will be a feudal lord (**zhu hou**) ...'

References: Lau, 1970; Morohashi, 1960.

TODD CAMERON THACKER

Tianjue renjue 天爵人爵
(The dignities of Heaven and the dignities of man)

A phrase used by **Mengzi** (6A: 16) when discussing the relationship between worldly nobility, expressed by noble ranks, 'the dignities of man', and moral nobility, characterised by values such as selflessness, a sense of the right, wholeheartedness, trustworthiness and joy in the tireless doing of good, 'the dignities of Heaven'. Mengzi contended that worldly honour derived ultimately from these moral values, and could not stand in their absence. In ancient times men had cultivated the dignities of Heaven, and those of man had followed as a matter of course. In the present, men had come to cultivate the dignities of Heaven as a means to attain the dignities of man, but after their success, they courted ruin by discarding the former while clinging to the latter.

GARY ARBUCKLE

Tianli renyu 天理人欲
(Heavenly pattern (*v.*) human desires)

Tian li, also translated 'Heavenly Principle' or 'Principle of Nature' (see **li**), is the natural pattern of things and of the heart/mind (**xin**). In the Daoist Classic *Zhuangzi*, Cook Ding says that he relies upon 'Heaven's structuring' (*tian li*) in carving up oxen. **Cheng Hao** said that *tian li* was what he had discovered on his own. The reciprocal opposition of *tian li* and *ren yu* (human desires) is found in the 'Yueji' (Record of Music) chapter of the *Book of Rites* (**Li ji**). According to the Neo-Confucians, when *ren yu* (more explicitly *si yu* 私欲,

selfish desire) increases within the heart/mind, *tian li* is diminished and vice versa; the perfectionist goal was complete elimination of selfish desire.

References: Chan, Wing-tsit, 1963d; Graham, 1981: 64; Wang Meng'o, 1984.

THOMAS SELOVER

Tok Sŏki 讀書記

The *Tok Sŏki* was a collection of the Classics by late Chosŏn dynasty Confucian scholar **Yun Hyu**. He departed from **Zhu Xi**'s traditional system, implementing his own original interpretation by organising the Classics starting with the *Doctrine of the Mean* (*Zhong yong*) and *Great Learning* (*Da xue*), then adding the *Book of Filial Piety* (*Xiao jing*), *Book of Poetry* (*Shi jing*), *Book of Documents* (*Shang Shu* see **Shang shu**), *Book of Rites* (*Li ji*) and *Spring and Autumn Annals* (*Chunqiu*). The special nature of his system is apparent by his breaking away from the Four Books (*Si shu*) and Five Classics (*Wu jing*) organisation, and by placing special emphasis on the *Book of Filial Piety* and *Book of Rites* (inner chapter) rather than Zhu's concentration on the *Book of Changes* (*Yi jing*). The object was to conduct an inquiry into an ideal social system and its practical organisation while pursuing realistic and practical goals. With his critical mind, Yun presented new insights from the various Classics, which are recorded in the *Hyokyung Oechŏn* 孝經外傳 and *Neichik Waigyung* 內則外記.

Reference: Keum Jang-t'ae, 1998a.

NAM-JIN HUH

Tokugawa Ieyasu 德川家康
1542–1616

Tokugawa Ieyasu, eldest son of Matsudaira Hirotada 松平廣忠, lord of Okazaki Castle 岡崎城, founded the Tokugawa bakufu after his Eastern army defeated the western army in the Battle of Sekigahara 關原 on 15 September 1600. He was formally appointed Shogun by the emperor on 12 February 1603. Although a devout believer in Pure Land Buddhism, Ieyasu developed a considerable respect for Confucian political ideas during his participation in the national-unification campaigns of Oda Nobunaga (1534–1582) and Toyotomi Hideyoshi (1538–1598). While stationed in Kyushu with Toyotomi Hideyoshi in 1593, he was introduced to **Fujiwara Seika**, a Zen scholar well versed in Neo-Confucianism. He invited Seika to lecture on the *Zhenguan zhengyao* 貞觀政要 (Jn. *Jôgan seiyô*), a guide to government based on historical lectures given to his retainers by the brilliant Tai Zong (r. 618–649), second emperor and consolidator of the Tang dynasty. In 1599, while still nominally a vassal of Hideyoshi's son Hideyori, he ordered the printing of the **Kongzi jiayu**, two classics on military strategy entitled *Liutao* 六韜 and *Sanlue* 三略, and later the *Analects*, the *Doctrine of the Mean* (*Zhongyong*), and the *Great Learning* (*Daxue*). In the spring of 1600, while acting as Hideyori's regent in Osaka, he ordered the printing of copies of the *Zhenguan zhengyao*. Two months after his victory at Sekigahara, he invited Seika to come to Edo, but Seika declined. It was at this time that Ieyasu first heard about Seika's talented disciple, **Hayashi Razan**. After long efforts by a disciple of Seika to arrange a meeting with Razan, in 1605 Ieyasu finally assembled a group of three high-ranking scholars to test Razan's knowledge of Chinese history. Razan performed extremely well, and after several more meetings Ieyasu proceeded to employ him as an adviser, document-writer and negotiator – functions that had traditionally been performed by Sinologically trained Gozan Zen monks. Further books that Ieyasu had printed between 1605 and 1616, using a movable-type printing press newly introduced from Korea after Hideyoshi's invasion of 1592, included a history of the founding of the Kamukura shogunate (*Azuma kagami* 吾妻鏡) as well as writings demonstrating the compatibility of Buddhism and Confucianism and the inseparability of military and civil skills in government. One of two massive works printed in 1614 – the year when Ieyasu eliminated his last rival, Hideyori, in the Osaka campaigns – was the fifty-volume *Qunshu zhiyao* (Jn. *Gunsho chiyô*) 群書治要, a collection of writings on the essentials of government compiled at the behest of Tang Tai Zong. It should be noted, however, that no specifically Neo-Confucian writings were printed in Ieyasu's time. Razan was employed by the bakufu from 1608 as a document writer and adviser for the second shogun, Hidetada 秀忠. He was not successful, however, in injecting Neo-Confucian ideas into shogunate ideology until well into the shogunship of Ieyasu's grandson, Iemitsu (r. 1623–1651). Even then, as elements of a discourse legitimating the authority of the shogunate, the Neo-Confucian ideas Razan introduced were very much intertwined with Shinto concepts. Even during his lifetime Ieyasu was commonly referred to as 'the great divine ruler' (*daijinkun* 大神君), and after his death he was deified as the god 'Great Avatar Shining in the East' (*Tôshô daigongen* 東照大權現) and worshipped at the Tôshôgû 東照宮 shrine in Nikkô 日光

Reference: Ooms, 1985: 50–62.

BARRY D. STEBEN

Tominaga Nakamoto 富永仲基
1715–1746
(*na*: 德基; *azana*: 子仲; *tsûshô*: Saburôbei 三郎兵衛)

Tominaga Nakamoto was born in Osaka as the third son of one of the five founders of the **Kaitokudô** merchant academy, Tominaga Hôshun (also known as Dômyôjiya Kichizaemon), a soy sauce manufacturer who provided the site for the academy. Little is known about Nakamoto's life, but he apparently studied under Miyake Sekian (1665–1730), the head lecturer of the

academy, from 1725. Miyake is known for his pragmatic combination of the ideas of different schools of Confucianism, including **Yômeigaku**, and for his affirmation of the moral equality of high and low, which legitimated the idea that merchant commoners engaged in practical trades should also pursue Confucian Learning. Tominaga was expelled from the Kaitokudô in 1730 for writing an essay pointing out the constructed nature of the Confucian Classical texts, but he continued his studies at a nearby school under Tanaka Tôkô, a former friend of **Ogyû Sorai**. Afflicted with a weak constitution and a chronic pulmonary ailment, he spent a great deal of time in bed reading, developing a vast knowledge and a penetrating intellect. At about nineteen, he was employed by the Ôbaku 黃檗 Zen temple in Kyoto, Manpukuji 萬福寺, to assist in the preparation of a new edition of the Tripitaka. Later he opened his own school and devoted himself to teaching and writing. In 1738, he wrote a work called *Okina no fumi* 翁の文 (Jottings of an Old Man) in which he argued that neither Confucianism, Buddhism, nor Shinto was an appropriate teaching for the Japanese in the present-day. The first two were the Ways of other countries, and religious systems are inevitably distorted and made artificial when transplanted from one culturo-linguistic system into another. As for Shinto, like Confucianism and Buddhism, none of its various teachings are really derived from antiquity, all of them having been formulated for later ages by thinkers competing for supremacy through their mystical formulae and deceiving people under the pretense of teaching them. In the place of all three religions he advocated 'the Way of sincerity' (*makoto no michi* 誠の道), a down-to-earth way of ethical living that accorded with the native Japanese preference for 'direct, unadorned, honest language' and involved simply carrying out wholeheartedly and with precision the ordinary tasks of one's daily life. At the age of thirty, in the year before his death, Nakamoto published *Shutsujô gogo* 出定後語

(Words Uttered Subsequent to Emerging from Samadhi), a difficult work in *kanbun* 漢文 that offered a penetrating historical critique of the various doctrines of Buddhism. In it he demonstrated that the Buddhist texts were not, as they claimed to be, *buddhavaçana* (the word of the Buddha), but products of historical development that grew out of interschool polemics. 'The history of moral ideas, in other words, is not at all the unfolding of insights into what is true, but ambitious struggles over orthodoxy that produce falsifications and that render them utterly unreliable as a stable source of ethical authority for the present' (Najita, 1987: 103). Such an awareness of the polemical nature of doctrinal texts inevitably draws one toward the investigation of the patterns of language use, which Tominaga undertakes in *Shutsujô gogo*. He identifies three distinguishable elements in language that differentiate the doctrinal content of any proposition: the person (人), the era (世), and the rhetorical category (類). The first is the subjective, and thus relative and sectarian perspective inherent in any assertion. The second refers to the fact that language changes over time, so that the meaning of an assertion does not transcend the language of a particular era in which it is embodied. As for the rhetorical categories of religious discourse, Tominaga distinguishes five types: (1) the stretching of the meanings of terms from the concrete to the abstract or spiritual, (2) the use of all-inclusive abstract terms to define the 'spiritual essence' of the particular (*han* 泛), (3) the expression of spiritual essence in terms of concrete virtues (*ki* 磯, see **Mengzi** 6B: 3), (4) the twisting and reversing of the conventional meanings of terms (*han* 反), and (5) the use of language to convey change from one state into another totally different state (*ten* 轉). The result of the use of all these rhetorical devices over time is that 'ordinary human beings are deceived into believing religious and moral assertions that have no grounding in existential human reality'

(p. 111). *Shutsujô gogo*, needless to say, was excoriated by the Buddhists, but in a later period it won high praise from the Nativist scholars **Motoori Norinaga** and Hirata Atsutane 平田篤胤 (1776–1843), contributing significantly to the development of their own critiques of Buddhism and Confucianism. Hirata Atsutane even entitled his own denunciation of Buddhism *Shutsujô shôgo* 出定笑語 'Words of Laughter Uttered after Emerging from Samadhi' (1817). In the twentieth century, Tominaga was again rescued from relative obscurity by the distinguished historian of Chinese historiography, Naitô Konan 內藤湖南 (1866–1934), who wrote that 'Originally, the Japanese are exceedingly crude when it comes to constructing logical methods of research . . . In this area, both Jinsai and Sorai stand out as rather exceptional, but, among Japanese intellectual historians, only Tominaga Nakamoto can truly be said to have constructed his research method on a logical basis' (*Naitô Konan zenshû*, vol. IX, p. 376). The rediscovery of Tominaga played a role in the establishment of the modern field of Japanese intellectual history parallel to the role played by Naitô's discovery of the Qing historian **Zhang Xuecheng** in the establishment of the field of Oriental history (*Tôyô shigaku* 東洋史學).

For the original text of *Okina no fumi*, see Ienaga *et al.*, *Nihon bungaku taikei 97, Kinsei shisôka bunshû*, pp. 539–561; for *Shutsujô gogo*, see Mizuta Norihisa and Arisaka Takamichi, *Tominaga Nakamoto – Yamagata Bantô*, NST, vol. 43, pp. 11–138.

Reference: Najita, 1987: 101–21.

BARRY D. STEBEN

Tong shu 通書
(The *All-Embracing Book*)

Whereas the **Taijitu shuo** mainly constitutes a terse but powerful commentary on its corresponding namesake diagram, the *Tong* *shu* – which originally bore the title *Yi tong 易通* (hence, *All-Embracing Book on the Book of Changes*) – is nothing other than the commentary of the great philosopher **Zhou Dunyi** on the *Yi jing* itself. Moreover, whereas the *Taijitu shuo* is a largely theoretical treatise, the *Tong shu* appears to be more of a work of practical application. Finally, from the standpoint of contrast, although it is significantly longer than its companion work, it is nonetheless also a relatively short work in one volume (*juan*), divided into forty chapters.

At the absolute centre of the *All-Embracing Book* and absolutely vital to our own acquisition of any informed understanding of it is the interpretation of Zhou Dunyi's conception of his cardinal virtue **cheng** (sincerity, authenticity or genuineness). For Zhou Dunyi, *cheng* – in addition to being the fount of sagehood – was the great repository of all virtues, wherein the 'five constants' (**Wu chang**) of **ren, yi, li, zhi**, and **xin** all reside and flourish. Through the perfection of *cheng*, one achieves sagehood because he has thereby succeeded in reclaiming his nature (**xing**) and returning it to its ideal state. Thus, while it was ostensibly written as a technical gloss on the *Yi jing*, the *All-Embracing Book* is actually more properly regarded as the primary vehicle for the espousal of Zhou Dunyi's own personal philosophy.

References: Balazs, 1978: 216, 217; Chan, Wing-tsit, 1963d: 465–80; Fung, 1952: 442–51.

DON J. WYATT

Tongcheng pai 桐城派
(The Tongcheng School)

The Tongcheng School refers to the school of prose that modelled upon the style of 'Tang Song Eight Masters' (*Tang–Song bada jia* 唐宋八大家). There was no Tongcheng School until the eighteenth century when Yao Nai 姚鼐 (1731–1815) began to appropriate a formerly common prose style and its ideological use for writers from his native place Tongcheng. In 1776 he first alluded to the existence of a lineage of prose writers from the Tongcheng county: **Fang Bao**, Liu Dakui 劉大櫆 (1698–1779) and Yao Nai himself. Three years later, in the anthology he compiled, entitled *Guwen cilei zuan* 古文辭類纂 (Classified Anthology of Ancient Proses), which included prose writers from different periods and the only Qing writers included were Fang Bao and Liu Dagkui.

The prose style of Tang–Song writers had been advocated by Ming writers like Tang Shunzi (1507–1560) and Gui Youguang. In the early Qing, there were many scholars and writers who shared a common interest in the Tang–Song style of ancient prose and its didactic function in propagating the Cheng–Zhu Learning as the Confucian orthodoxy. Lü Liuliang, **Lu Longqi**, Li Guangdi were among the most well-known literati who shared these literary and ideological positions. In addition, there were Dai Mingshi 戴名世 (1653–1713) and Fang Fao, both from Tongcheng, who shared these literary and ideological interests. Not all writers of ancient prose were qualified to be included in the Tongcheng School as Yao Nai conceived it. Apparently because of Dai's execution in 1713 as a result of his conviction of disloyalty, he was not included in Yao Nai's lineage of writers from Tongcheng. Yao clearly did not want to be affiliated with a 'rebel'. Fang Bao was included for another obvious reason. He was the editor-in-chief of the *Qinding sishu wen* 欽定四書文 (*Imperial Edition of Essays on the Four Books*), an anthology of examination essays commissioned by the Qianlong emperor (r. 1736–1795).

The major ideas of the method of prose writing Yao Nai appropriated for the Tongcheng writers were formulated by Fang Bao who advocated *yifa* 義法 (moralising method of writing) as the criterion for measuring the quality of ancient prose. By *yifa* Fang meant 'writing with order' (*yan youxu* 言有序) and 'writing with substance' (*yan you wu* 言有物). In terms of style, Fang argued that writing should have the qualities of *qing* 清 (pure), *zheng* 正 (rectifying), *gu* 古 (ancient) and *ya* 雅 (elegance); specifically these requirements referred to avoidance of heterodox expressions and vulgarities as well as promotion of Cheng–Zhu Learning.

Yao Nai himself contributed to the rhetoric of ancient prose of the Tongcheng School by embracing 'evidential studies' (*kaozheng xue* 考證學), which had come to set the standard of literary learning since the mid-eighteenth century. He advocated the need to attend to three aspects of prose writing: 'moral truth' (*yili* 義理), 'evidential scholarship' (*kaozheng* 考證), and 'literary writing' (*cizhang* 辭章).

The subsequent rise of the reputation of the Tongcheng School in the second half of the nineteenth century clearly owed more to **Zeng Guofan** than to Yao Nai as the former became a hero in suppressing the Taiping revolution and a patron of literary and scholarly activities.

References: Chow, 1994; Wei Jichang, 1988.

KAI-WING CHOW

Tonghak 東學
(Eastern Learning)

Late in the Chosŏn dynasty, in 1860, Ch'oe Che-u 崔濟愚 (1824–1864) founded a religion based on the belief of 'serving Heaven' (Kr. *Shich'ŏnju* 侍天主). He also advocated protecting the country and aiding the masses (Kr. *Pogug anmin* 保國安民). This popular religion he called 'Tonghak' (Eastern Learning) in order to emphasise its opposition to western science and religion, then called 'western Learning' (*xi xue*). Tonghak was renamed *Ch'ŏndogyo* 天道教 (Teaching of the Ways of Heaven) by Son Pyŏng-hui 孫秉熙 (1861–1922) in 1905. Whereas Ch'oe Che-u had promoted

becoming a superior person through service to Heaven (**tian** Kr. *Ch'ŏn*) and protecting the country and aiding the masses (**min**), under the stewardship of Ch'oe Si-hyŏng 崔時亨 (1827–1898) the doctrine of 'serve men as you would serve Heaven' (Kr. *Sain Yŏch'ŏn* 事人如天) was developed, and since everything came to be seen as endowed and created by Heaven, a pantheistic 'everything is Heaven' theory developed. Under Son Pyŏng-hui the idea that 'Man is Heaven' (Kr. *Innaech'ŏn* 人乃天) was established and that the theory that Heaven and humanity combined as one (**tianren heyi** Kr. *Ch'ŏnin habil*) was further developed.

These ideas greatly influenced attempts at social reform. Instead of vertical relationships between higher and lower, ruler and follower, Tonghak leaders advocated horizontal relationships where everyone was equal. In short, Tonghak established a social character as a popular religion promoting the destruction of the traditional social order.

Changes in Tonghak thought
Up until his late thirties Ch'oe Che-u was spiritually adrift and engaged in ascetic practices when, in 1860, he awakened to the teachings of what he would call the new religion 'Tonghak'. This realisation was due to a sudden religious experience that shook his entire body and soul, and it is claimed that after hearing, then speaking to, Heaven, its spirit descended on him and he knew the Way of Heaven. From 1861 on, he made a magical charm based on this experience of achieving the Dao, and started to proselytise this new belief of serving Heaven. He gathered many believers who would recite at home the thirteen-character phrase he had made: 'Serve God and you will be in harmony with all creation. Keep God in your thoughts at all times and you will come to understand all there is to know.'

Tonghak combines elements of Confucianism, Buddhism and native folk religion. Socially it sought to protect the country from foreign invasion and internally it sought to relieve the suffering of commoners. Ch'oe Che-u compiled *Scripture of Tonghak Doctrine* (Kr. *Tonggyŏng daejŏn* 東經大全) and *Songs of Yongdam* (Kr. *Yongdam yusa* 龍潭遺詞). These texts deal with the concepts 'Heaven' (Kr. *Ch'ŏn*), 'Ruler of Heaven' (Kr. *Chuch'ŏn*) and 'God' (Kr. *Hanŭnim*), but these were not fixed terms; rather they changed along with the changes in society. For Ch'oe Che-u, all people, literati and commoners alike, regardless of class, could become superior persons as long as they served Heaven with reverential awe.

Ch'oe Si-hyŏng

Ch'oe Che-u was martyred in 1864. His successor Ch'oe Si-hyŏng, proselytised, established religious doctrines and had copies of *Eastern Scripture* printed. He also strengthened the organisational structure of the group. Ideologically, he wanted to free people from social distinctions and concentrated on leading people out of their subordinate social positions. Besides differences based on class, he also wanted to free people from distinctions based on gender or age. Whereas Ch'oe Che-u advocated serving God, Ch'oe Si-hyŏng advocated serving human beings as one would serve Heaven. Moreover, he advocated reverence toward Heaven, toward mankind and toward all things in general. He also taught that anyone could become a sage or a superior person by reverently serving Heaven.

Tonghak spread rapidly, fostered in part by the oppression of commoners by corrupt officials and the constant threat of foreign invasion by Japan and the western powers. This led to peasant movements that fought against foreign imperialists. Ch'oe Si-hyŏng was martyred in 1898.

In the 1894 (Kabo) Reforms, Tonghak leaders helped lead the call for social equality. They also supported the rule of requiring the traditional styled hair, topknots, to be cut. As part of the quest for modernisation, Son Pyŏng-hui changed the name of *Tonghak* (Eastern Learning) to *Ch'ŏndogyo* (Teachings of the Way of Heaven) in 1905. They also began participating in the movement to open the country and contributed to a new education movement by operating many schools. *Ch'ŏndogyo* continued to take root among the people and it played an important role in the March First Independence Movement.

References: Ch'oe Dong-hui, 1980; Kim Sang-gi, 1947.

JANG-TAE KEUM

Tu Wei-ming 杜維明
1940–

Tu is one of the world's leading interpreters of Confucianism. Tu understands Confucianism not as a historical relic but as a rich and profoundly spiritual humanistic tradition offering a vital and relevant philosophy of life for the modern world. The focus of Tu's early scholarship was **Wang Shouren**, the Ming-dynasty Neo-Confucian whose thought was, according to Tu, a more faithful transmission of Confucius and **Mengzi**'s philosophy than had been achieved by **Zhu Xi**, the Song Neo-Confucian master whose commentaries on ancient Confucian writings prevailed during the Ming and Qing dynasties. In elevating Wang's teachings, Tu highlighted the importance of self-cultivation and the quest for sagehood in Confucianism, religious themes which recur regularly in his writings.

While Tu emphasises the religious nature of Confucianism, he does so within the context of a cosmology of 'continuous being' and 'spontaneously self-generating life process', one lacking any ontological claims, positive or negative, regarding a providential, theistic God. Within such a cosmos, Tu sees the Confucian project of self-cultivation in anthropocosmic terms, emphasising a person's ultimate on-going achievement of a sense of identity, as one body, with Heaven and Earth. Through such unceasing achievement, Tu claims, one realises open-ended self-transformation of a profoundly religious and inherently cosmic sort. Tu is careful to warn that notions such as 'self' cannot be understood in terms of categories associated with western individualism, but must be conceived of in relation to the Confucian belief that the self is a Heaven-endowed, divinely all-embracing open centre of our relationships with other people and the cosmos at large. Consequently, Tu emphasises that human-relatedness and communalism are essential dimensions of religiosity.

Some of Tu's more recent works explore the relationship between Confucianism, East Asian modernity, and economic culture, pointing out that development of modernity and the achievements of capitalistic economies need not be based on departures from or rejection of Confucian traditions. Without resorting to the simpleminded claim that a functional equivalent of Max Weber's Protestant ethic resides in Confucianism, Tu has highlighted various aspects of the Confucian faith which provide rich resources for East Asian communities to develop distinctive varieties of capitalism and democracy. At the same time, Tu challenges Confucians by noting that the goals of Confucian self-cultivation can be realised more fully in liberal democratic societies than in traditional authoritarian ones. Tu has also explored the relationship between Confucianism and human rights, noting that while the Confucian tradition lacks the concepts of liberty and human rights, that it is hardly incompatible, and in many significant ways, conducive to, the full realisation of them. Tu further emphasises that Confucian humanism and its core values enhance the universal appeal of human rights.

JOHN A. TUCKER

Twelve Savants
(Shier zhe 十二哲)

The Savants ranked after Confucius and the Correlates in the Confucius temple hierarchy. There were **Ten Savants** in the temple between the eighth century, when they first received sacrifice separately from the other disciples, and the thirteenth century. In 1267, the Southern Song court promoted **Zhuansun Shi** to Correlate status. Yan Hui presumably held separate status as Correlate by this time, so there were still Ten Savants in the temple until the Song master **Zhu Xi** was elevated to savant status by an enthusiastic patron – the Kangxi emperor – in 1712. **You Ruo**, a personal disciple of Confucius, was elevated to savant in 1738, thereby constituting the Twelve Savants, which remained unchanged to the twentieth century.

THOMAS A. WILSON

U

Ŭisan mundap 醫山問答
(*Dialogue on Mount Iwulu*)

This text by Practical Learning (**Sirhak**) scholar Hong Tae-yong (洪大容 1731–1783, *zi* Tokpo 德保, *hao* Damhun 湛軒) presents his view of nature and scientific thought. It is included in the appendix to his *Collected Works*. It is composed of a roughly 12,000-character set of questions and answers by two people, Silong 實翁 and Huhja 虛子. Huhja was a vastly studied and experienced Chosŏn scholar who for sixty days associated with Chinese scholars in Beijing, but who, meeting with disappointment, was on his way back to Korea, when he met up with the reclusive Silong, at Yishan Lüshan 醫山閭山 in Nanmanzhou 南滿州. The work records their debates.

Hong also for the first time in Asia clearly stated how the earth's rotation leads to day and night. In addition, the origins of life, earthquakes, tides, meteorological phenomena, etc. were discussed. Huhja speaks for the traditional Chosŏn scholar while Silong represents the newly received western scholarship.

References: Chang Myŏng-suk, 1994; Hong Tae-yong, 1984.

NAM-JIN HUH

Waley, Arthur David
1889–1966

Waley was the most outstanding translator and interpreter of Confucius' thought in the first half of the twentieth century. Waley's interest in Confucianism and expertise in Chinese, acquired while working at the British Museum between 1913 and 1926, culminated in his *The Analects of Confucius* (1938). Waley's translation differed from earlier ones by not following the commentaries of **Zhu Xi**, which Waley characterised as 'Neo-Confucian'. While acknowledging that Zhu Xi's insights had prevailed throughout the ages, Waley's historically minded interpretations sought to convey what Confucius, as known solely through the *Analects* (**Lunyu**), meant to communicate to his contemporaries.

JOHN A. TUCKER

Wan Sida 萬斯大
1633–1683
(*zi* Congzong 充宗)

Wan Sida, a native of Jin county (Zhejiang), was the elder brother of the celebrated historian **Wan Sitong** and a student of **Huang Zongxi**. The significance of Wan's thought lies in the fact that it is representative of the ritualist reorientation of Confucianism in the early Qing. Since 1673, Wan had fully committed to the investigation of ancient rites and their implications for application in his times.

Strong interest in building lineage in the early Qing had prompted many Confucians to study the *Zhuzi jiali* 朱子家禮 (*Family Rites of Master Zhu*), which provided models for the two types of lineages: one based on an ancestral rite enshrining the ancestors of 'four-generations' (*si shi* 四世) and the other based on an apical ancestor (*shizu* 始祖). For purist Confucians like **Chen Que**, these rites were applicable only to aristocrats and could not be extended to ordinary officials and commoners. The debate over applicability revolved around the understanding of the ancient 'descend-line system' (*Zong fa* 宗法), which many insisted could not be revived. In a treatise entitled 'Descent-line system', Wan marshalled textual evidence from the Classics and ancient history to demonstrate that those who opposed adoption of the *zongfa* operated on a mistaken exposition by the Han classicist **Zheng Xuan** and that the two models of ancestral rite prescribed in the *Zhuzi jiali* could be adopted without reviving aristocracy, lending credit to *Zhuzi jiali* as a reliable source of authentic rites. These important writings were included in his *Xueli zhiyi* 學禮質疑 (*Doubts Regarding the Study of Rites*). His other major works included *Zhouguan bianfei* 周官辨非 (*Correcting the Errors of the Rites of the Zhou*).

Reference: Chow, 1994.

KAI-WING CHOW

Wan Sitong 萬斯同
1638–1702
(*zi* Jiye 季野)

A native of Jin county (Zhejiang), Wan Sitong was renowned for his erudition and his contribution to the drafting of the *Ming Shi* (*History of the Ming Dynasty*). Invited by Xu Yuanwen 徐元文 (1634–1691), director of the Office for the Compilation of the History of the Ming dynasty, and urged by his mentor **Huang Zongxi**, he began to work on the project as a private scholar. Wan was more than a historian; his knowledge of the Classics and rites was unmatched in his times. Under Xu Qianxue's 徐乾學 (1631–1694) patronage, Wan was involved in the compilation of the voluminous study of rites, entitled the *Du li tongkao* 讀禮通考 (*A Comprehensive Study of Rituals*).

Wan's growing interest in classical and ritual studies was in part a result of his discontent with the polemics over the teachings of **Wang Shouren** in particular and *dao xue* Confucianism in general. Wan was the best-known student of Huang Zongxi who regarded himself as a follower of Wang Yangming. But Wan Sitong later was attracted to the teachings of Pan Pingge 潘平格 (1610–1677), who called for a complete repudiation of Song and Ming *dao xue* for its infusion with heterodox ideas. Wan was reprimanded by Huang for his attraction to Pan's view. Reluctant to be enthralled in ideological debate, he turned to concentrate on his commitment to writing a history of the Ming and the study of the Classics and ritual.

Wan Sitong was involved in debates about issues in classical and ritual studies, especially regarding lineage structure and its focal rite – ancestral worship. His 'Treatise on the Grand Worship' (*ti shuo* 禘說) and a series of studies of 'Temple systems' (*miao zhi* 廟制) from the Zhou dynasty through the Ming were crucial to the understanding of the practice of ancestral rite and hence the models of lineage organisation in high antiquity. These treatises and other essays were included in his *Qunshu yibian* 群書疑辯 (*Doubts and Clarification of Various Books*). His other important works include *Lidai shibiao* 歷代史表 (*History in Tables*) in 60 *juan*s.

References: Chow, 1994; Liang Qichao, 1957: 86–90.

KAI-WING CHOW

Wang Anshi 王安石
1021–1086
(*zi* Jiefu 介甫, *hao* Banshan 半山)

Being descended from a family of recently emerged, low-level bureaucrats, Wang Anshi was appointed to local office only on the basis of his obtaining the *jinshi* degree with distinction in the civil service examinations of 1042. For nearly two decades thereafter, Wang's career was uneventful, as he continued to serve in minor posts and even declined to assume the few more elevated posts for which such individuals as **Ouyang Xiu** recommended him. Then, in 1060, Wang Anshi accepted his first capital appointment in the accounts department in the State Finance Commission (*sansi* 三司) and his profile began to rise mercurially. In 1069, at the behest of the emperor Shenzong (r. 1067–1085), Wang assumed the post of participant in determining government matters (*canzhi zhengshi* 參知政事), which made him the chief ministerial authority in the empire. From this vantage point, he unveiled and began to institutionalise his ambitious and sweeping programme of New Policies (*xin fa* 新法).

The New Policies – a series of measures mainly designed to achieve financial solvency for the government while shoring its defences – became the major determinant in the remainder of Wang Anshi's career and life histories. Put into effect by a mobile cadre of mainly youthful and enthusiastic officials with personal ties and allegiances to Wang himself, the New Policies drew opposition from numerous conservative factions whose members construed the government sponsored measures as extreme, invasive and misguided. In 1074 and in 1076, the furor generated by the resistance to his policies even drove Wang Anshi to resign from office. After 1076, despite his final removal from the central political stage and his acceptance of only honorary posts, Wang witnessed his reform programme maintained intact until Shenzong's death in early 1085. Wang himself died in 1086 and, within that year, nearly all of the New Policies were either diluted beyond recognition or entirely rescinded.

The worldview of Wang Anshi was shaped by many of the same factors as that of his contemporary **Li Gou** and, consequently, we should not be surprised that Wang should have held many similar opinions as Li and reacted similarly on the basis of what were essentially the same perceptions. However, we must also see Wang's collective responses to his sociopolitical environment as advancing significantly beyond Li's. Both Li and Wang saw that China confronted perennial problems on the economic, fiscal, and administrative fronts. But whereas Li never moved beyond theorised solutions, Wang – animated by an unflagging activist spirit – ensured that his solutions took tangible form.

The programme of reform that Wang Anshi thrust upon China was a marvel of comprehensiveness. Once he had obtained power, Wang responded to the recurrent problems of land concentration and tax evasion on the part of the wealthy by instituting a new, empire-wide registration of land-ownership, with the aim of imposing a more graduated property-based taxation system. He sought to alleviate the plight of the heretofore disenfranchised peasantry most directly by granting government grain loans at highly favourable, low-interest rates. He sought to bolster the financial standing of the government by establishing state-run granaries and pawnshops. He sought to improve national defence through such tactics as requiring frontier families to engage in horse husbandry. He even strove to improve the civil service examinations by redirecting their content away from literary (and especially poetic) foci and more toward the affairs of practical statecraft, as represented by the new requirements of having to write an essay and three policy proposals.

Throughout all this activity, we can detect in Wang Anshi's thought an unbridled fascination with the potential of what the state can do to remake society. It was precisely the extremes to which he took this viewpoint that most provoked the enmity of his critics. These individuals – led most prominently by **Sima Guang** – eventually ascribed Legalist underpinnings to Wang's entire agenda. The grandiose intrusions of too many of Wang's reform measures only confirmed this view. Not only did the grain loans tend to supplant the government granaries but the interest rate exacted eventually rose prohibitively to 30 per cent or more and the loans themselves became compulsory, with severe punishments in cases of default. The state monopolies Wang established threatened to subsume all commercial enterprise because independent merchants and traders could not compete with them. Although Wang succeeded in replacing the age-old system of corvee with a tax, the tax was imposed on people – such as widows and childless families – who had formerly been exempt from such conscripted labour. In this way, ironically, Wang Anshi's utilisation of government as the primary tool for refashioning society became the victim of its own excesses. The completeness with which his policies impinged on the lives and livelihoods of the people is precisely what doomed them.

Wang Anshi's extant writings comprise the *Linchuan Xiansheng Ji* 臨川先生集 (*Collected Works of Master Linchuan*) and are voluminous, consisting of 100 chapters (*juan*). They are also uncommonly diverse. The '*Wanyan Shu*' 萬言書 (*Myriad-Word Memorial*) or originally '*Shang Renzong Huangdi Yanshi Shu*' 上仁宗皇帝言事書 (*Memorial Discussing Affairs Submitted to the Renzong Emperor*) is by far Wang's most memorable work, for his entire reform agenda is laid out in this 1058 document. Nevertheless, despite his public posture on the subject, Wang Anshi's engagement in literary pursuits is striking. He was, for example, an important poetic stylist and the author of nearly 1,500 poems.

Aside from the arguable possibility of **Wang Mang**, Wang Anshi is the most important reformer in China's history prior to the twentieth century. Moreover, the fact that Wang Anshi shares a legacy of infamy that is similar to Wang Mang's is unsurprising. Almost without exception, later chroniclers have portrayed both men as ministers who overstepped their stations, who manipulated and misused the authority of the Chinese emperorship, and who – by resorting to political discord and showing disrespect for custom – led the respective dynasties that had produced them to the verge of ruin.

References: Balazs & Hervouet, 1978: 393–4; Bol, 1992: 189–91, 212–53, 269–82, 336, 339; Hsieh, 1979: 3–4, 159–203, 210–11; Liu, James, 1959; Lo, 1976: 41–53; Meskill, 1963; Williamson, 1935; Wyatt, 1996: 138, 139, 143, 149, 151, 152–3, 154, 155, 156–7, 158–9, 164.

DON J. WYATT

Wang ba 王霸
(Kings and hegemons)

Wang and *ba* refer to two types of rulers and their corresponding methods of rule – the king and the hegemon. According to Confucians, kings rule by following the *dao* (Way) and cultivating their own moral charisma, or virtue (*de*). In this way, they are able to win the hearts of the people and bring peace and prosperity to their kingdoms. Ultimately, a true king will be granted the Mandate of Heaven (*Tian ming*), unify China and rule over it peacefully. Hegemons rule by wise use of intelligent ministers and resources, enabling them to establish and maintain a state that is militarily and economically strong. Yet, they do not win the hearts of the people and will fall short of the peace and prosperity of a true king's rule. Although able to build and maintain a large state, the hegemon will fail to gain the Mandate of Heaven.

While the ideal form of Confucian rulership was the true king, early in the tradition Confucians began to recognise the abilities, if not the complete legitimacy, of hegemons. Hegemony is most closely associated with the rule of Duke Huan of Qi 齊桓公 (?–643 BCE), who employed Guan Zhong 管仲 (?–645 BCE) as his prime minister. Duke Huan's character was far from cultivated, and he made no attempt to embrace Confucian teachings. Despite this lack of virtue, he was able to build Qi into a powerful and prosperous state. Confucius, **Mengzi**, and **Xunzi** all decry the lack of a true king and the failures of hegemons such as Duke Huan. Yet, at the same time these hegemons are recognised as being preferable to the chaos and disorder of tyrants such as Jie 桀 (the last king of the Xia dynasty) and Zhou 紂 (the last king of the Zhou dynasty). Hegemons bring stability and order to the state, establishing laws and standards for the people to follow and effectively administering the state's resources. Mengzi even admits that 'the people under a hegemon are happy and secure. Under a king, they are expansive and content' (*Mengzi*, 7A: 13).

When discussing forms of rulership, Xunzi also ranks the hegemon between the king and the tyrant. Both king and hegemon are able to use people, opportunities and resources to their advantage. However, the king does so by following the *dao* through practising the rites (*li*) and establishing social norms (*yi*). The hegemon does so by establishing standards (*fa* 法) and promoting trust (*xin*) among ministers and people. 'The mutual trust between ruler and subject was as close as one's upper and lower teeth closing together. No one under Heaven dared claim to be their equal' (Xunzi, *Wang ba* chapter). Moreover, the king and hegemon have in common a commitment to some standard of behaviour other than their innate desires for pleasure and profit (*li* 利). For Xunzi they are preferable to the tyrant who uses force to maintain his rule and seeks only pleasure and profit.

T.C. KLINE III

Wang Bo 王柏
1197–1274
(*zi* Huizhi 會之, *hao* Luzhai 魯齋, *shi* Wenxian 文憲)

Wang Bo was an important teacher of Neo-Confucian ideas at several academies (**Shu yuan**) during the latest years of Southern Song dynasty. His family had been living in Jinhua 金華 (Zhejiang) for generations. His grandfather Wang Shiyu 王師愈 (1122–1190, *zi* Yuzheng 與正 or Qixian 齊賢) was a follower of the Neo-Confucians **Zhu Xi**, **Zhang Shi**, **Lü Zuqian** and especially **Yang Shi**, who taught him the 'right' interpretation of *the Book of Changes* (**Yi jing**) and the *Analects of Confucius* (**Lunyu**). This tradition was continued by Wang Bo's father Wang Han 王瀚 (?–1211, *zi* Bohai 伯海, *hao* Ding'an 定庵) who educated his son in the thoughts of Zhu Xi and Lü Zuqian. After having lost his father at age of fourteen (fifteen *sui* 歲) he first intended to participate in the civil service examinations. But soon he got tired of the preparation and became rather an admirer of the military achievements of Zhuge Liang (181–234). Therefore he styled himself as Changxiao 長嘯 (or 'long howl'), according to a saying by Zhuge Liang.

After turning thirty, he finally went back to his Neo-Confucian roots he had neglected for such a long time. He gave up his style name Changxiao, because he felt that it was contradictory to the Confucian principle of reverence (*jing*). He studied diligently under He Ji 何基 (1188–1268, *zi* Zigong 子恭, *hao* Boshan 北山), a former disciple of **Zhu Xi**'s follower **Huang Gan**, and adopted his new style name: Luzhai. After ten years of study, he was engaged to be a professor at several academies. During his activities there, he attracted many students, and it is said that even the venerable old men (*qide* 耆德) of the district revered him using the same etiquette as his disciples. His education method began with the Four Books (**Si shu**) and culminated in the principle of **Jingshi zhi yong**. In this way he contributed to the development of the Zhu Xi tradition. The major disciple of Wang Bo was **Jin Lüxiang**, who continued the transmission of Zhu Xi's teachings. Wang Bo died in 1274, only two years before the Southern Song capital Lin'an 臨安 was captured by Mongol troops. 450 years later (in the year 1724) his tablet was placed in the Temple of Confucius (**Kong miao**).

Almost all his works are comments on the Classics. The most important are the *Shuyi* 書疑 (*Doubts about The Book of History*) and the *Shiyi* 詩疑 (*Doubts about The Book of Poetry*). Here he only expresses his doubt on the tradition of the **Shang shu** and the **Shi jing**, but not on its origins. Sometimes his views are contradictory to the 'main-stream' of the Song Neo-Confucians, but have always been highly esteemed by his later commentators.

Reference: Zhao Zhiyang, 1984.

CHRISTIAN SOFFEL

Wang Chong 王充
27–96? CE
(*zi* Zhongren 仲任)

The Han scholar Wang Chong is best known as the compiler of the **Lun heng**, a collection of critical essays on thought and folklore. The main sources of the details of his life are a short biography in *juan* 79 of the *History of the Later Han* (**Hou Han shu**) and two of the last sections of the *Lun Heng*: Section 84, 'Responses' (*Dui zuo* 對作) and Section 85, 'Autobiography' (*ziji* 自紀). Whether these latter two chapters are primarily biographical or autobiographical is unclear, however, and their authorship and date are a matter of conjecture.

According to Wang's brief biographical entry in the *History of the Later Han*, he was from Shangyu 上虞 in Kuaiji 會稽 in what is now Zhejiang province. He came from a poor family but was noted for his filial piety (*xiao*) as a child. As he could not afford books, he learned by haunting the bookshops of Luoyang and was acclaimed for his photographic memory. Wang studied at the Grand Academy (**Tai xue**) and was a pupil of the historian and official Ban Biao 班彪 (3–54 CE). On the occasion of an imperial visit to the academy, he composed the now-lost work 'On the Six Scholars' (*Liu ru lun* 六儒論). He eventually returned to his native region, where he lived an unassuming life as a teacher and held several minor regional offices. Wang was noted for an idiosyncratic but ultimately convincing style of rhetoric, although his critiques of commonly held beliefs encountered much resistance. Not known for his social graces, he encountered political obstacles and left office. He became reclusive late in life, and as he neared his seventies he adopted a strict daily regimen developed to eliminate desires. It was at this time that he wrote a book, now lost, in sixteen chapters titled *On the Cultivation of the Nature* (*Yang xing* 養性). Wang died at home of an illness some time during the Yungyuan 永元 era (89–104).

Much of this information is repeated in the two biographical chapters in the *Lun heng*, which are far longer, much more embroidered with detail, and hence probably less reliable. These chapters are largely apologia for Wang's lowly background and unconventional philosophical views. Here

his ancestors are described as homicidally violent and brutal; Wang, by contrast, was a precociously studious and mild-mannered child who developed into a person of great integrity and intellectual independence. He composed two additional works that are no longer extant: *Censures on Social Mores* (*Ji su jieyi* 譏俗節義) in twelve *pian*, which was written in simple language for wide consumption, and *On Governance* (*Zheng wu* 政務), a work on political administration.

His greatest legacy, however, is his *Lun heng* itself, even though it accrued few commentaries until late imperial times.

References: *Ershiwu shi*, 1986: vol. II: *juan* 79, modern p. 946; Forke, 1962; Huang Hui, 1990; Loewe, 1993: 309–12 and 2000: 4–5; Twitchett & Loewe, 1986.

DEBORAH SOMMER

Wang Fu 王符
c. 85–165

Wang was the author of the **Qianfu lun**, who was from Anding 安定, on the northwestern frontier, where Qiang 羌 invasions occured during his lifetime and were recorded in his book. We know little of his parentage except that his mother was a concubine. However, his friends included two scions of consort clans: one was **Ma Rong**, the great exegete and teacher, and the other was Dou Zhang 竇章, who served as Privy Treasurer while his daughter was a favourite of Emperor Shun (r. 125–44), until 131 or 132. In addition, Wang knew the great scientist Zhang Heng 張衡 (78–139), who advised Emperor Huan (r. 146–167); and the great calligrapher Cui Yuan 崔瑗 (78–143). Pearson (1989) argues that these friendships gave him much insight on the political matters he discussed in his *Qianfu lun*.

Wang Fu's work is classified as Confucian (*rujia*) in the *Sui shu* 隋書, but he clearly disagreed with many tenets of the orthodox yin–yang Confucianism of his era. His work is more practical than abstract and theoretical, the quality identified by Hsiao Kung-ch'uan as typical of Chinese political thought, as 'what Xunzi meant by speaking of "learning carried to the point of implementation, there to stop", or, as Wang Yangming said, "Acting is the fulfillment of knowing"' (Hsiao 1979, pp. 7–8, note 13).

Wang argued that imperfections as well as strengths could be useful, even in officialdom. He argued for greater honesty in recommendations, more autonomy for local officials, greater thrift in government and society, and reinforcement of troops defending the frontier. While influenced by **Xunzi**, Wang was extremely outspoken in his criticisms, an exemplar of a worthy (*xian ren*) to **Han Yu** and of the Confucian tradition of dissent according to Pearson.

References: Pearson, Margaret, 1989; Kinney, 1990.

MARGARET PEARSON

Wang Fuzhi 王夫之
1619–1692
(*zi* Er Nong 而農)

Wang Fuzhi, one of the most important and famous thinkers, historians and philosophers in Chinese history, was born into an intellectual family in Hunan and lived during a time of distinct social contradictions and conflicts. When he was twenty years old, he studied at the *Yuelu Academy* 岳麓書院, one of the oldest and most famous academies in ancient China; he later was a successful candidate in the imperial examinations at the Hubei Provincial level (*ju ren* 舉人). He experienced the peasant uprising led by Li Zicheng 李自成 and saw the destruction of the Ming dynasty (1368–1644). When the Manchus oppressed his native province of Hunan, he raised a small army to fight for the protection of the Ming cause. After their inevitable defeat, he had to retire when he was only thirty-three years old and lived at *Stone Boat Mountain* (*Shi*

Chuan Shan 石船山) for about forty years. He wrote most of his works there and was called Mr Chuan Shan 船山先生. Wang Fuzhi had a very wide knowledge of astronomy, geography, calendars, mathematics and was knowledgeable in literature, history, Confucian classics and philosophy in general. He endeavoured to carry on the theory of **Zhang Zai** and is correctly described as Zhang's successor. He paid very close attention to recapitulating the experiences and lessons of the history of the flourishing and decline of Chinese dynasties, to reflecting on traditional Chinese culture (especially Confucianism), to the examination of Buddhism and Daoism, and to formulating his own systematic ideas. His special contributions to Chinese history were his theories of history, politics and philosophy.

Wang Fuzhi was a careful student of history and treated these historical lessons as guides for today's decision making. He thought that the purpose of learning was to probe the laws of movement in human history. His theory of history encompassed the following main ideas. Firstly, he insisted on an evolutionary view of history. By criticising the viewpoints of historical retrogression, he described human history as an evolutionary and developing process. He called for people to respect the here and now more than the past. Secondly, he confirmed that there are some inner laws in the development of history, which he called ways or principles (*dao*, or *li*). He believed that under the effect of social laws, the movement and the development of human history were subject to inner trends, which he called 'material force' (*shi* 勢). Principle and material forces were the two aspects of social movement. The interaction of the laws and the trends makes social progress an objective, necessary process. But this social necessity is realised by the accidental activities of certain historical individuals. In this way, Wang Fuzhi dialectically explained the relationships between necessity and probability as well as functions of the masses and individuals in social development and movement. Thirdly, he maintained that there must be respect towards humanity in the relationship between human beings (**ren**) and Heaven (**tian**) (*ji min yi jian tian* 即民以見天). For Wang Fuzhi, Heaven is complex and difficult to see and to master, so that Heaven, as used by the sages, should be treated as the Heaven of the people. He insisted on respecting human desires, the satisfaction of their needs and the realisation of their nature. He called for the proper treatment of the relationship between humanity and the world by combining the principles of the world and people's desires (*li yu he yi* 理欲合一).

In politics, Wang Fuzhi urged that decisions be made according to actual conditions of the time. Since he lived in a society with distinct contradictions among different nationalities in China, he stressed that one must distinguish between Chinese (*hua xia zu* 華夏族) and barbarians such as *Yidi* (夷狄), and to prevent invasion and the influence of *Yidi* on Chinese culture (夷夏之防). Wang Fuzhi insisted on protecting and satisfying the public and people's benefits (*gong tian xia* 公天下). He divided public benefits into two kinds: national common benefits and people's basic benefits. He thought that the rulers' responsibilities were to protect the benefits of their citizens. If they did not want to or failed to do so, they should be removed from power. He declared that the basic rule of administration was to manage its officers strictly and to treat the people with tolerance. He called for punishing corrupt officials, reducing exploitation, repression and the burden of the people, by encouraging the increase of social production, thus enriching the people. To maintain social stability, he advocated the use of both criminal laws and moral teachings. He thought that each of these had different functions in social administration. Influenced by Confucian ideas which stress moral teaching over punishment, Wang claimed that moral teaching should be implemented prior to punishment. Rulers should first teach people with virtues and honour, and then apply punishment if necessary.

The main characteristic of Wang Fuzhi's philosophy was his idea of the co-construction of *qian* and *kun*. His ontology is a kind of material force (**qi**) monism that takes *qi* as the basic element of the world. According to Wang, material force can be divided into two main kinds: *qian* 乾 is the positive aspect (yang), while *kun* 坤 is the negative aspect (yin; see **yin–yang**). The interrelationship and interaction of *qian* and *kun* (yin and yang) constitutes all things in the world. The world consists only of concrete things, all of which are different entities formed by the movement of yin and yang. Principles (*li*) exist in the movement of force and things but not out of the *qi* and things (*li zai qi zhong* 理在氣中). If there were no material force movement and concrete things, then there could not be *ways* (*wu qi wu dao* 無器無道). The dialectical relationship between yin and yang forms the universal contradiction of the world and is the basic force to prompt the movement, the development and the progress of the world. The movement of the world is a dialectical process of stability and change.

In his epistemology, Wang Fuzhi stressed the importance of studying external things and of adjusting our theoretical understandings according to the facts. As to the relationship between cognition and action, he emphasised their dialectical mutual interaction but insisted on the precedence of action over cognition. For him, people could learn while they were acting and practising but could not act only from learning (*xing ke jian zhi, er zhi bu ke jian xing* 行可兼知，而知不可兼行).

Wang Fuzhi wrote many books that had a wide influence on subsequent Chinese history. On history, there are the *Du Tongjian lun* 讀通鑒論, *Xu Chunqiu Zuoshi zhuan boyi* 續春秋左氏傳博議, *Song lun* 宋論, *Yong Li Shi Lu* 永歷實錄, among others; on politics, the *Huang Shu* 黃書, *E Meng* 噩夢, etc; on philosophy, the *Zhangzi Zhengmeng zhu* 張子正蒙注, *Zhouyi waizhuan* 周易外傳, *Zhouyi neizhuan* 周易內傳, *Shang shu yinyi* 尚書引義, *Du Sishu daquan shuo* 讀四書大全說, *Laozi yan* 老子衍, etc. Contemporary scholars are paying special attention to the ideas and doctrines contained in his works.

References: Chan, Wing-tsit, 1963d; Wu & Song, 1992; *Zhongguo ruxue baike quanshu*, 1997.

OUYANG KANG

Wang Gen 王艮
1483–1541
(*zi* Ruzhi 汝止, *hao* Xinzhai 心齋)

Wang Gen is known as the founder of the **Taizhou xuepai** (Taizhou branch) of the Wang Yangming School (**Wang Shouren**), referring to his native town Taizhou in northern Jiangsu. Originally named Wang Yin 王銀, Wang came from a family of salt-farmers with little scholarly background. He was trained as a tradesman for most of his youth, studying as much as he could on his own. After becoming an independent salt-maker at twenty-one, Wang's business prospered enough to allow him more time for study and meditation. At the age of twenty-five, Wang accompanied his father on business to Shandong and there visited the **Kong miao** (Temple of Confucius) at Qufu. This trip made Wang realise that Confucius was a man just like himself, thus spurring his ambitions toward sagehood. Wang achieved further enlightenment when, in 1511, he dreamt that he saved the masses from a falling Heaven. Awakening soaked in sweat, Wang realised that his heart was where Heaven, Earth and all things coincided. Wang then began to advocate zealously the reform of local customs and the revival of the ancient in his own life, inspired by a passage from **Mengzi** in which the sage asks how one could speak the words and perform the actions of the sage–king Yao (see **Yao Shun**) without wearing the same type of clothing as Yao. Thus Wang designed as best he could a simple cotton gown of the type he imagined to have been worn by the

sage–king, and, wearing it together with an ancient hat, traipsed about town carrying a ceremonial tablet. Above his door he hung a placard announcing that his teaching had been passed down from the ancient sage–kings to Confucius, and that he was willing to impart it to anyone who sought it earnestly, regardless of age, status or ability.

The next turn in Wang's quest for sage-hood came when, on the advice of a friend, he set out to visit Wang Yangming at the latter's post in Jiangxi. Initially reluctant to accept Wang Yangming's superiority, Wang Gen eventually became a disciple, following the scholar–official Wang on his way back to Yuyao. It was Wang Yangming who changed the younger Wang's name from 'Yin' to the more scholarly 'Gen'. Returning home after this initial meeting, Wang Gen built himself a cart modelled on the one he thought Confucius had used in his travels, and proceeded to Beijing, where his odd dress and cart attracted much negative attention from critics of Wang Yangming. Sensing the damage that Wang Gen was causing for the movement, Wang Yangming's followers pressured him into leaving the capital. When Wang returned and next visited Wang Yangming, the latter refused to see him for three days.

When Wang Yangming died in 1529, Wang Gen returned to Taizhou where he opened a school of his own. There he accepted students regardless of their social status, from gentry to commoners. Likewise, perhaps reflecting his own origins as a commoner, Wang promoted the idea of the common man as sage. Wang suggested that study, a spontaneous and joyous activity, was open to every common man and woman (*yufu yufu* 愚夫愚婦). Underlying this effort to popularise the pursuit of sage-hood was Wang's emphasis upon learning gotten for oneself (*zide* 自得). Nevertheless, among his most important students was the official Xu Yue 徐樾 (obtaining his *jinshi* degree in 1532).

Wang's interpretation of *gewu* 格物 (investigation of things) is based upon the concept of reciprocity, proceeding from individual self-cultivation, the root, to the ordering of society, the branches. Like Wang Yangming's *liang zhi* 良知 (innate knowledge of good), *gewu* for Wang Gen meant essentially the 'rectification of affairs'. That is, the first step in self-cultivation is the application of one's own moral sense to all affairs. Wang Gen interpreted *gewu* as finding the root or pattern that lies in oneself. Like a compass for measuring circles, this is a pattern by which the right shape of a thing is regulated. For Wang, the fundamental task in cultivation was to give peace or security to the self (*an shen* 安身) with an emphasis upon natural spontaneity (*zi ran* 自然). Wang's conception of the self is primarily the physical or bodily self (*shen* 身). This fundamentally differs from Wang Yangming's understanding of the self, in that the latter's theory of *liangzhi* places emphasis upon the mental self, the **xin** (heart/mind). In an essay entitled *Mingzhe baoshen lun* 明哲保身論 (*Clear Wisdom and Self Preservation*), Wang Gen expounded upon this theme, stressing that *liangzhi* requires a genuine love of oneself and one's self-preservation.

Wang Gen sought to base the distinction between orthodoxy and heresy upon what he referred to as the daily uses of the people (*baixing riyong* 百姓日用). According to Wang, the **Dao** of the sage was no different from the daily uses of the people. Consequently whatever diverged from the daily uses of the people was heresy. Wang derived this notion of *baixing riyong* from a passage in the **Yi jing** (*The Book of Changes*) that reads, 'The kind (**ren**) man discovers it [the Dao] and calls it kind. The wise (**zhi**) man discovers it and calls it wise. The people use it day by day (*baixing riyong*) and are not aware of it' (*Yi jing, xici*, A).

Despite his popularisation of the ideal of sagehood, Wang Gen did not find around him a large number of sages. He hoped to discover people who would meet his concept of the hero as described in an essay he wrote entitled, 'Qiu Shan fu' 鰍鱔賦 (Rhapsody on the Loach and Eel). In this parable, a loach saves the life of a floundering eel without seeking gratitude or credit, but rather out of a spontaneous act of generosity. An observer asks where such *ren* (humaneness) can be found among men, and recalls Mengzi speaking of the great man or 'hero' (*da zhangfu* 大丈夫) (*Mengzi*, 3B: 2). Wang makes this an ideal for his own time, imagining heroic leaders (*haojie zhi shi* 豪傑之士) rising up to roam about the empire, helping people in need out of spontaneous humaneness.

References: de Bary, 1991: 155–202; Huang Tsung-hsi, 1987: 173–7; Wang Gen, 1912: 2: 10a–b.

STEVEN MILES

Wang Guowei 王國維
1877–1927

Historian, literary critic and Qing loyalist, Wang Guowei was born to a scholar family in Haining, Zhejiang province. Like many other young Chinese, he was shocked by China's defeat in the Sino-Japanese War (1894–1895). Realising that China was behind in the global competition for wealth and power, he stopped taking the civil service examinations and turned his attention to the 'new learning'. In 1898, he moved to Shanghai and joined the staff of *Current Affairs* (*Shiwu bao*). In his free time, he studied Japanese and English at the Eastern Language Institute (*Dongwen xueshe*) set up by Luo Zhengyu 羅振玉 (1866–1940). Impressed by his talents, Luo became his life-long friend.

Inspired by his Japanese teacher Fujita Toyohachi (1869–1929), Wang developed a strong interest in the philosophy of Kant and Schopenhauer. Applying philosophy to literary criticism, he broke new grounds in the study of Chinese literature. In his study of *The Dream of the Red Chamber* (*Honglou meng*), he examined the novel as a piece of literature rather than as an autobiography of the author Cao Xueqin. In examining the development of lyrics in the Song and the Yuan periods, he demonstrated that there was unique literary style in each historical period. In the *Renjian cihua* 人間辭話 (*Remarks on Lyrics in the World of Man*, 1909), he explained the aesthetic principles for evaluating literature based on an analysis of the lyrics of the Tang and the Song periods.

In part to show his loyalty to the Qing, Wang accompanied Luo Zhenyu in a move to Japan after the 1911 Revolution. During his five-year stay in Kyoto, he developed a strong interest in history while assisting Luo in cataloguing the newly discovered archaeological findings in Dunhuang. Having returned to Shanghai in 1916, he established himself as the leading expert of ancient history by verifying the conventional accounts of the Shang dynasty (1766? BCE–1027? BCE) with archaeological evidence. In his critically acclaimed articles on the genealogy of the Shang royal family, he showed that *The Records of the Grand Historian* (*Shi ji*) is a reliable source of ancient history.

Based on his study of the Shang dynasty, Wang played an important role in the historiographic debate of the 1920s. Led by Gu Jiegang 顧頡剛 (1893–1980), the 'historical doubters' questioned the historicity of the 'Three Ages' (the Xia, the Shang and the Zhou) and challenged the authority of the Five Confucian Classics (*Wu jing*) as records of the past. In response, Wang proposed in the *Gushi xinzheng* 古史新証 (*New Evidence Concerning Ancient History*, 1927) a two-pronged approach of comparing the archaeological evidence with textual records. He argued that many received textual records, including the Five Confucian Classics, are reliable sources of ancient history.

Despite being a leading scholar of ancient history, Wang found himself out of place in Republican China. Still wearing a skull cap and a queue, he became a symbol of the defunct Qing. From 1924, he worked for the deposed Manchu emperor Puyi

in the capacity of a 'Companion of the Southern Study' (*Nanshufang xingzou*). At the height of his academic career, he drowned himself in a former imperial park in 1927.

References: Chen Yinke, 1927; Bonner, 1986; Yuan & Liu, 1996.

TZE-KI HON

Wang Ji 王畿
1498–1583
(*zi* Ruzhong 汝中, *hao* Longxi 龍溪)

Wang Ji was among the most innovative immediate disciples of **Wang Shouren** (Yangming). One of the most important and controversial figures of the Wang Yangming School, Wang Ji was at times criticised for what some critics took to be his unorthodox views. A native of Shaoxing near Wang Yangming's hometown of Yuyao in Zhejiang, Wang Ji in fact traced his descent to the same ancestor as Wang Yangming. Wang Ji passed the provincial examination and became a *juren* in 1519. When Wang Yangming returned to Yuyao and started teaching, Wang Ji and **Qian Dehong** were among the first of his students. Both Wang Ji and Qian were given charge of teaching the numerous students who came to Yuyao seeking to learn Wang Yangming's doctrines. In 1526 Qian and the younger Wang went to take the metropolitan examinations in Beijing, but returned before the palace examinations because of veiled attacks on their teacher. Both proceeded to the examinations a second time in 1529 but returned again, this time due to the death of Wang Yangming. Qian and Wang Ji, who became the two primary immediate disciples of Wang Yangming, established the Tianzhen 天真 Academy in Hangzhou in their teacher's honour and both finally received their *jinshi* degrees in 1532. Wang served as an official in Nanjing until he was dismissed in 1542. Thereafter, he travelled widely in southern China, teaching and lecturing.

In his *Tianquan zhengdao ji* 天泉證道紀 (*Account of Proving the Way at the Tianquan Bridge*), a testimony of Wang Yangming's resolution of a debate between Wang Ji and Qian Dehong, Wang Ji offers his interpretation of his teacher's famous Four Dicta. Wang Ji's innovations were largely developed from the notion, found in the first dictum, that the substance of the heart/mind (*xin zhi ti* 心之體) is beyond good and evil. Wang Ji went on to insist that the intentions (*yi* 意), knowledge (*zhi*) and things/acts (*wu*) described in the second through fourth dicta are also beyond good and evil. That is, because substance (*ti* 體) and its functions (*yong* 用) essentially derive from one dynamic source (*ji* 機), therefore the mind, intention, knowledge and things are actually all one thing. Consequently, Wang Ji emphasised the transcendence of ethical categories of good and evil that occurs with the recognition that in oneself the mind is independent of moral judgements while being at the same time the source of such judgements. For Wang, this meant that the mind must be free of all preconceptions that were part of any doctrines, including the classical canon. Therefore, the sage can follow the dictates of his heat/mind without fear of making any moral transgression. This idea came to be known as the Four Negatives (*Si wu* 四無), in contrast to Qian Dehong's Four Positives (*Si you* 四有). When Wang Ji and Qian queried Wang Yangming about their different interpretations of the Four Dicta, the latter suggested that both were correct, but that Wang Ji's Four Negatives were more appropriately employed only by men of superior understanding.

Wang Ji referred to the absoluteness of the mind-in-itself, which was equated with **liang zhi** 良知 (innate knowledge of good), as the springs of life (*sheng ji* 生機). According to Wang, this is already developed in everyone; one simply needs to wake up to its full meaning through *xin* (faithfulness) in the capacity of *liang zhi*. Wang Ji's notion that the absoluteness of *liang zhi* is already developed in everyone is referred to as the doctrine of the ready-made *liang zhi* (*liangzhi xiancheng lun* 良知現成論). In short, Wang Ji developed Wang Yangming's thought by placing a greater weight upon inner enlightenment, in contrast to Qian Dehong's emphasis upon gradual and persistent effort.

Wang Ji is also noted for his efforts to blend Confucianism with Buddhist and Daoist ideas. For Wang, self-understanding takes precedence over Classical Learning. In Wang's view, the only legitimate criterion of the validity of a teaching is the extent to which it satisfies the requirements of *liangzhi* in getting it oneself (*zide* 自得). As a result, the differences among the Three Teachings (**san jiao**) become less important. According to Wang, the shared basis of the Three Teachings is the original nature the understanding of which is arrived at by *liangzhi*. This syncretic impulse in Wang Ji was seen by critics as accentuating Chan Buddhist tendencies in the thought of Wang Yangming.

Finally, Wang Ji was influential in the thought of **Nakae Tôju**, the putative founder of the Wang Yangming School in Japan. Wang's thought also inspired many religious messianic Neo-Confucian activists in the late Tokugawa era.

References: de Bary, ed. (1970): 121–44, 1991; Huang Tsung-hsi, 1987.

STEVEN MILES

Wang Ling 王令
1032–1059
(*zi* Fengyuan 逢源, also Fengyuan 逢原)

While, for much of his short life, there was little in which he would not dabble, Wang Ling suddenly took a serious liking to strenuous study. **Wang Anshi** so marvelled at his emerging talents that he even arranged for Wang Ling to marry his wife's younger sister – Wu Shi 吳氏 (1035–1093). Wang Ling derived his poetics from the Tang masters

Han Yu and Meng Jiao 孟郊 (751–814; *zi* Dongye 東野), such that the level of his knowledge of their works was both lofty and extensive. For one who died so young, Wang Ling was also extremely prolific. In addition to composing his poetic opus *Guangling ji* 廣陵集 (Collection of Guangling), he wrote commentaries on and annotations to both the **Lunyu** and the **Mengzi**. However, Wang Ling's most enduring literary achievement was in the realm of elementary education, for he is also the author of an exquisite primer – the *Wang Xiansheng shiqi shi mengqiu* 王先生十七史蒙求 (*Master Wang's Selection of Excerpts from the Seventeen Histories in Response to the Needs of the Unenlightened*). Being a compendium of the statements and actions of famous figures, the work consists of pairings of analogous historical examples that Wang intended for beginning students to recite aloud and thus memorise.

Reference: Balazs & Hervouet, 1978: 322.

DON J. WYATT

Wang Mang 王莽
46 BCE–23 CE

In view of the historians' need to brand Wang Mang as an illegitimate ruler of China, it could be expected that they would ignore any actions taken in his name or in his reign to promote what were to become the orthodox Confucian doctrines of state. It follows that statements to the effect that Wang Mang took an active part in asserting the values ascribed to the kings of the Zhou or in adopting preimperial practices would be understated rather than overstated, or that such actions would be credited to others. How far Wang Mang took a personal part in determining the terms of his decrees or statements that were backed by just such motives may not be known; but according to our sources he traced the line of imperial sovereignty to Yao and Shun (see **Yao Shun**), laying particular

emphasis on Shun. More than any other personality who is reported for the Former Han, he praised and emulated the Duke of the Zhou (**Zhou Gong** 周公), seeking comparison with him as a regent who was implementing the will of Heaven. As emperor, Wang Mang adopted institutional titles and systems that were ascribed to Zhou times and operated them in the very different circumstances of an empire; and he claimed to be ruling as emperor in accordance with the Mandate of Heaven (**Tian ming**). Vilified as he has been, it has to be acknowledged that in his short reign he was more influential in deliberately fostering Confucian ideas than any of the emperors of Former Han, including **Han Wudi** (r. 141–87). See also *Han Shu, Ming tang, Tian ming*.

References: Bielenstein, in Twitchett & Loewe, eds., 1986, vol. I: 223–40 (for a reassessment of Wang Mang and a rejection of his description as an 'usurper'); Thomsen, 1988.

MICHAEL LOEWE

Wang Maohong 王懋竑
1668–1741
(*zi* Yu Zhong 予中)

Wang Maohong, born in Bao Ying (Jiangsu), was a successful candidate in the Jiangsu provincial level examination in 1718 and took his *jinshi* degree in the following year. He served in the Hanlin Academy 翰林院 for some years after 1723, but soon left that position and returned home to concentrate on classical studies in his later years. While following the theory of idealistic philosophy in the Song dynasty (960–1279), Wang was especially influenced by **Zhu Xi**. He criticised theories dealing only with quietness (**jing**), insisting that quieteness and movement (**dong**) should be treated on equal terms, because for him both quietness and movement are characteristics of human beings and are essentially related and interacting to each other, in a way similar to one's breathing in and out. He was dissatisfied with the available books explaining Zhu Xi's theory, and therefore spent about twenty years on careful textual research of Zhu's original works and ideas. In his four *juan Zhuzi nianpu* 朱子年譜 with two *juan Kao yi* 考异 and two *juan Fu lu* 附錄, he comprehensively identified and corrected many misuses of Zhu Xi's works and misunderstandings of his ideas. The works Wang left were regarded as singularly important achievements in Zhu Xi studies during that period. He advocated textual studies and based his investigations on the original works, in order to explain the scholars' own historical ideas. His book on the **Mengzi** (*Mengzi Xu Shuo kao* 孟子序說考) examined different works of different ages and compared them in an effort to explain the original ideas of Mengzi. Wang's other books include the *Zhuzi Wenji zhu* 朱子文集注, *Zhuzi Yulu zhu* 朱子語錄注, *Du jing jiyi* 讀經記疑, *Du shi jiyi* 讀史記疑, among others.

Reference: Wu & Song, 1992.

OUYANG KANG

Wang Mingsheng 王鳴盛
1722–1798
(*zi* Fengjie 鳳喈, Litang 禮堂; *hao* Xizhuang 西莊, Xizhi 西沚)

A native of Jiading 嘉定 (Shanghai), Wang was a classicist and historian. He had studied the Confucian Classics as a student of Shen Deqian 沈德潛 (1673–1769) and **Hui Dong** at the Ziyang Academy 紫陽書院 in Suzhou 蘇州 before he gained the *jinshi* degree in 1754. He was appointed as a compiler 編修 in the Hanlin Academy. Having served in various positions in the capital and provinces, he retired as the Chief Minister of the Court of Imperial Entertainment (*guang lu si qing* 光祿寺卿) in 1763.

Wang's major contribution to scholarship was his critical studies of the Seventeen Dynastic Histories, entitled *Shiqi shi shangque* 十七史商榷, first printed in 1787 and later incorporated in the Guangya Congshu. In this book he conducted a thorough examination and correction of the materials and facts involved in the Seventeen Dynastic Histories and provided correct details on places, official posts, institutions and affairs mentioned in the histories. Making a critical break with the allegedly forged Old Text version of the *Book of Documents*, he produced a work entitled *Shangshu houan* 尚書後案 (*Later Commentaries on the Book of Documents*), in which he reconstructed in large measure the Han dynasty text of the **Shang shu** by collecting fragmentary commentaries from **Zheng Xuan**, **Ma Rong**, and **Kong Anguo**. He also wrote a work on the Institutes of the Zhou dynasty entitled the *Zhouli junfu shuo* 周禮軍賦說. His miscellaneous notes, classified under ten headings and entitled *Eshu bian* 蛾術編, covered a wide range of ancient political systems, characters, historical figures, tablet inscriptions, utensils and geography. His literary works, composed before 1763, were printed in about 1766, under the title *Xizhuang shi cungao* 西莊始存稿, while the works produced during the latter part of his life were published in an 1823 collection entitled *Xizhi jushi ji* 西沚居士集.

References: Hummel, 1943–4; Loewe, 1993; *Qing shi gao*, 1970.

REBEKAH X. ZHAO

Wang Pin 王蘋
1082–1153
(*zi* Xinbo 信伯, *hao* Zhenze 震澤)

Wang was a late student of the Cheng brothers (see **Cheng Hao** and **Cheng Yi**), who enjoyed only a modest bureaucratic career. His scholarship impressed the Emperor Gaozong (r. 1127–1162) during an audience, and he was rewarded with *jinshi* status and a low-ranking post in the palace library. He later worked on the *Veritable Records of Shenzong's Reign* (*r. 1068–1085*) (*Shenzong shilu* 神宗實錄). He eventually ran afoul of the controversial minister Qin Gui 秦檜 (1090–1155, *zi* Huizhi 會之) and was stripped of his posts. He ended his official career in a temple sinecure.

According to Quan Zuwang, Wang was an important link in the transmission of ***dao xue*** learning in two distinct ways. Firstly, Wang was credited with spreading the teachings of the Chengs into the southeastern region of Wu 吳 (Jiangsu). Secondly, he acted as a bridge between the disciples of the Cheng brothers and the so-called thinkers of the mind (*xin xue*). The source of his inspiration was **Yang Shi**, but his reputation has rested on the similarity between his ideas and those of **Lu Jiuyuan**. Although censured by **Zhu Xi**, he was praised by Wang Yangming (*Song–Yuan xuean*, 29.1a). What survives of his writings certainly reveals a willingness to draw on Daoist and Buddhist sources to explain his ideas.

Wang's writings included an unfinished commentary (now lost) on the ***Lunyu***. His literary collection, the *Wang Zhuzuo ji* 王著作集 (*The Literary Collection of Editorial Director Wang*) is still extant.

References: *Song–Yuan xuean*, 1966; Wang Pin, 1782.

ANTHONY DEBLASI

Wang Shouren 王守仁
1472–1529
(*zi* Boan 伯安, *hao* Yangming 陽明)

Better known as Wang Yangming throughout East Asia, Wang Shouren was born on 31 October 1472 in Yue 越 in the district of Yuyao 餘姚 near Hangzhou, a descendant of the great calligrapher Wang Xizhi (321–379). He evidently combined great powers of concentration with an insatiable curiosity. The story is told that when he was married at the age of seventeen, on his wedding night he became so engrossed in a conversation with a Daoist priest that he forgot to return home. In 1492 he received the *juren* degree, but failed the *jinshi* exam in both 1493 and 1496. In 1499 he passed the *jinshi* exam, ranking second among all the examinees. Within a short time he was appointed to positions of considerable responsibility, first in public works, then in justice, examinations and military affairs. His practical experience in administration had a profound effect on the development of his own philosophy, making him aware of the limits that real life often places in the way of abstract theory.

As his reputation grew, Wang began to attract students drawn by his independent frame of mind. He was already criticising the tendency of teachers to focus on flowery language and empty memorisation, instead encouraging students to concentrate on their own motives and purposes in learning, to start out by purifying themselves before they directed their efforts to learning about the more conventional subjects of history and philosophy.

At this point he experienced such a reversal of his fortunes that it provoked a fundamental reevaluation of his life. When a number of prominent officials were imprisoned by the palace eunuch Liu Jin in 1506, Wang wrote a memorial protesting the action. He was ordered to receive forty lashes in the presence of the emperor, after which he was transferred to a remote post in the southern province of Guizhou. Isolated and confronted with all manner of personal hardship, he underwent a liberating experience of intellectual enlightenment in 1508 that led in the following year to the articulation of his doctrine of the unity of knowledge and action (***zhixing heyi***).

After 1510 he climbed rapidly in the administrative hierarchy. In 1517 he was given the responsibility of suppressing a local rebellion in Fujian province. His immediate and remarkable success in putting down that and other rebellions and then in implementing policies of good government – such as building schools – that would restore confidence in the future greatly enhanced his reputation. In 1519 he was named governor of Jiangsi province, where once again he implemented a series of reforms that won widespread praise.

His success inspired jealousy among some officials of the emperor's court, and his official career fell into decline. From 1521 to 1527, he retired to his home in Yue. It was in these years that he developed his doctrine of the extension of innate knowledge (*liang zhi* 良知), which represented a synthesis of his basic philosophy. His willingness to depart from the orthodox commentaries of **Zhu Xi** provoked intense criticism by those scholars loyal to the Song philosopher. In 1528 he was called back into public service to suppress a rebellion in Guangsi, which he did but at the cost of his health. He died *en route* to his home on 9 January 1529.

Thought

Wang Yangming is generally credited with making three specific contributions to Chinese philosophy: his understanding of the term 'investigating things' (*gewu* 格物), his doctrine of the unity of knowledge and action (*zhixing heyi*), and the extension of innate knowledge of the good (*zhi liang zhi*).

As he pursued the subject of the investigation of things, he was compelled to redefine the context in which the term was defined by the Song Neo-Confucian thinkers. Zhu Xi had defined it as the pursuit of objective knowledge outside of oneself, a pursuit that was a prerequisite to sagehood. The problem for Wang Yangming was that not everyone had the time or resources to devote to such study. This would seem contrary to Mengzi's belief in the essential goodness of human nature and the possibility that everyone can achieve sagehood. As a consequence, Wang Yangming changed the meaning of the term from what had been accepted since Zhu Xi to 'making one's intentions sincere'. The way to purify those intentions was to eliminate selfish desires (*ren yu* 人欲).

The doctrine of the unity of knowledge and action (*zhixing heyi*), which Wang Yangming began preaching in 1509, the year after his experience of enlightenment, also addressed the problem of making sagehood available to the everyday person, not just the scholar. It did so by emphasising the existence of principle, *li*, in the mind, and by defining knowledge primarily as moral knowledge or knowledge of the good, i.e., wisdom. Action, in turn, meant activity that conformed to one's knowledge of the good, and that was not separated by selfish desires. Thus one could learn virtue not just by studying it but equally by putting it into action, which everyone can do. As he said, 'knowledge is the beginning of action, and action is the completion of knowledge' (Chan, 1972: 10).

Through meditation, or quiet-sitting (*jing zuo*) one can recover one's true – and good – self, and eliminate selfish desires. Contemplation, to which Wang Yangming was powerfully attracted throughout his life, and which he frequently engaged in, was therefore seen as a means to an end, but never as an end in itself and never as a means of escaping the cares of the world.

Wang Yangming's crowning achievement was his doctrine of the development, or extension, of the innate knowledge of the good, *zhi liang zhi*, as the true path to sagehood. He defined innate knowledge as the 'original substance of the mind', by which he meant the knowledge of right and wrong. By 'development' or 'extension' (*zhi* 致) he meant the constant effort or exertion necessary to purify one's heart/mind of selfish desires. Mere knowledge in the abstract of what is right and wrong is not sufficient for the attainment of sagehood – one must act in accordance with that knowledge, and through that very action deepen one's understanding of the knowledge. By sagehood Wang Yangming meant becoming a fully authentic person, true to oneself, genuine, at ease with oneself and with the world at large. His doctrine was in part derived from **Mengzi**'s admonition that 'the sense of right and wrong is common to all men' (Mengzi 7A: 15). This quality is the fundamental basis of human dignity, compassion and moral action.

To distill his thought into a short statement, he developed in 1527 his Four Dicta: 'In the original substance of the mind there is no distinction between good and evil; when the will becomes active, however, such distinction exists; the faculty of innate knowledge is to know good and evil; the investigation of things is to do good and remove evil'. He wrote that his insight was 'achieved from a hundred deaths and a thousand sufferings' (Chan, 1972: xxxvi). The heart/mind, *xin*, was the source of all our perfection as well as the instrument of our improvement. It was the ultimate, transcendent truth, and through it we can transcend ourselves. Wang was therefore much less concerned than his counterparts in the Zhi Xi School with issues such as principle, *li*, or material force, *qi*, or the Supreme Ultimate, *tai ji*. For him everything was embodied in heart/mind.

Wang Yangming's views inspired controversy by their independence of spirit and particularly by their differences with the orthodox interpretations of Zhu Xi. Two publications in particular drew the most sustained criticism. The first was Wang Yangming's repudiation of Zhu Xi's edition of the Confucian Classic, the **Daxue** (*Book of Learning*), entitled *Daxue guben pangzhu* 大學古本旁注 (*Old Version of the Great Learning, with Side Commentaries*). Zhu Xi claimed that the text as it had been handed down to the Song dynasty contained errors. He reissued the text, which changed the order of the sections in order to give greater support for his own interpretation of the meaning of the 'investigation of things' as the means of making the intentions sincere. Wang Yangming restored the original order, which appeared to give priority to making the intentions sincere, in accordance with his view that the central issue was what took place in the heart/mind (*xin*) not what one learned by studying the Classics.

His second controversial publication was a study of Zhu Xi's letters, *Zhuzi wannian dinglun* 朱子晚年定論 (*Definitive Ideas of Zhu Xi as Developed Later in Life*), in which Wang Yangming extracted excerpts, out of context, appearing to suggest that Zhu Xi had changed his mind on important subjects later in life. These changes, not surprisingly, appeared to support Wang Yangming's own interpretation. Although these two publications did much to enhance Wang Yangming's own scholarly reputation, they also prompted charges of unfair scholarship, since he appeared to have deliberately misrepresented the ideas of the Song philosopher to justify his own positions.

Significance

Wang Yangming has inspired praise as well as blame. Most observers regard him as the greatest philosopher in China since Zhu Xi in the twelfth century. But many accused him of promoting a destructive form of individualism by later philosophers who justified all manner of bizarre behaviour as expressing their 'innate knowledge'. Some Qing philosophers like **Gu Yanwu** even went so far as to blame Wang's philosophy, in part, for the eventual decline of the Ming dynasty.

The textual exegesis movement was promoted by a follower of Wang Yangming in the late Ming, **Jiao Hong**. This led to one of the principal intellectual currents of the Qing dynasty. His followers included **Qian Dehong**, **Huang Wan**, Nie Bao 聶豹 (1487–1563), **Wang Gen**, **Wang Ji**, and his favourite student, **Xu Ai**.

Wang's independence of mind, together with his focus on the standards of the mind itself, encouraged in those who followed him a tendency to set their own standards. Many became eccentric and opposed to external authority of any kind. Others tended to drift back to the emphasis on cultivating serenity through quiet-sitting of the Zhu Xi School. He was important as well in the movements that arose in reaction to him. The Donglin movement of Confucian revival at the end of the Ming blamed

Wang's followers for the decline of dynastic institutions.

Wang Yangming's influence extended to Japan and Korea as well as China. In Japan his philosophy, known as Yomeigaku, had the effect of strengthening the movement for reform during the late Tokugawa. It inspired some of the most important Meiji reformers such as **Yoshida Shôin** and Saigo Takamori (1827–1877). In Korea the Zhu Xi School dominated the intellectual horizon, as it did in China. But Wang Yangming's philosophy also inspired a dynamic movement under the leadership of **Chóng Chedu** in the Yi dynasty (1393–1910).

References: Chan, Wing-tsit, 1972: 63–92; Ching, 1976; Chu, Hung-lam, 1998: 47–70; Cua, 1982, 1993: 611–47; Nivison, 1953; *Philosophy East and West* 23 (January/April) 1973; Tu, 1976b.

ALAN T. WOOD

Wang Shu 王恕
1416–1508
(*zi* Zongguan 宗貫, *hao* Jiean 介庵, Shiqu 石渠)

Wang Shu was a native of San Yuan 三原 (Shanxi). He obtained his *jinshi* degree in 1448, at which time he received an appointment to the Hanlin Academy, although he soon left this position eventually to become prefect of Yangzhou. He remained in government service for forty-five years, and became well known during his tenure as Minister of Personnel. Although Wang was permitted to take leaves of office on the occasions of both his mother's and father's deaths, he returned to service a short while thereafter (only two months in the case of his mother). His administrative talents ranged from a successful bandit suppression campaign in 1466 to the compilation of a history of the Grand Canal in 1471. Wang's work has been preserved in fellow official Wang Qiong's 王瓊 (1459–1532) 1496 work *Portrait of the Grand Canal* 漕河圖志.

Wang also became famous for his denunciations of the court's use of eunuch advisers and what he determined to be the excessive court patronage of Buddhism. In particular, Wang accused the eunuch Qian Neng 錢能 of colluding with Vietnamese Lê court officials during an imperial mission to purchase gemstones. Surprisingly, the court eunuch had nothing but praise for Wang when the two officials finally met again at court in about 1480. However, Wang had begun to lose allies at court late in his career, and his criticisms of the imperial decisions did not go unnoticed. In 1486, under intense political pressure from the emperor himself, Wang Shu retired from government service. However, he was recalled by imperial decree from the subsequent ruler in 1488. In 1493, Wang was again denounced and removed from office, allegedly for poor judgement in the selection of officials and for an excessive desire to remain in the limelight. He died at the age of ninety-two after spending his last years editing and annotating his collected works. In retirement, Wang also established a school in his home region of Sanyuan called the Hongdao 宏道 Academy.

Wang's works include an autobiography and several collections of his memorials, as well as philosophical writings such as *Thoughts on the Book of Changes* (*Wanyi Yijian* 玩易意見) and a book of various commentaries on other Confucian classics *Thoughts of Master Shiqu* (*Shiqu Yijian* 石渠意見). In these works Wang voiced doubts regarding some of the famous Southern Song scholar **Zhu Xi**'s commentaries on the Confucian Classics. Wang chose to express his independent views of these works, and such opinions have left Wang with the reputation for idiosyncratic thinking. However, Wang focused largely on practical political matters, and his limited commentary on the Classics reflected this point of view. As **Huang Zongxi** commented 'as to what concerns the great roots of learning, (Wang) probably did not achieve them'. Julia **Ching** notes that Wang's scholarship in

Confucian Learning of his time was limited, but he instead distinguished himself in government service, following in the footsteps of fellow northern **Neo-Confucian Xue Xuan**.

References: Giles, H. 1898: 841; Goodrich & Fang, eds., 1976: 1417; Huang Tsung-hsi, 1987: 99–100; Huang, Z., 1985: 9: 158; Wu & Song, eds., 1992: 1096.

JAMES A. ANDERSON

Wang Su 王肅
195?–256
(*zi* Ziyong 子雍)

Son of a famous exegete on classics and Wei statesman, Wang Lang 王郎, Wang Su made commentaries on all the books of the canon that had great authority in the Imperial Academy. His fame was such that his daughter became the wife of the son of the usurper of the Wei dynasty (220–265) and thus his grandson mounted the throne as the first emperor of the Jin. In the traditional Han method of exegesis, Wang Su was counted as the seventeenth successor of the New Text scholar **Fu Sheng** in the study of the *Shang shu* which is perhaps one of the reasons he waged a relentless war against the great Han exegete **Zheng Xuan** whose independent views tended to destroy the old method of canonical study by reference to hereditary schools of interpretation. Not content with attacking Zheng Xuan's views directly, Wang Su either forged or tinkered with a book already in existence purporting to contain quotations from Confucius, the *Kongzi jiayu*. He added his own commentary pointing out how Zheng Xuan's views went against those of Confucius himself given in the *Kongzi jiayu*. Although his commentaries on the canon were used in the Imperial Academy during the Jin dynasty (265–420) and his ideas were followed in court ritual, Wang Su's views were seldom quoted in canonical studies after the Jin and his forgery of the *Kongzi jiayu* has been

almost unanimously acknowledged since the eighteenth century.

Reference: Kramers, 1950.

DONALD HOLZMAN

Wang Tanzhi 王坦之
330–375

One of the most famous of the adepts of 'Pure Talk', *Qingtan* 清談, fashionable conversation on philosophical or literary themes, Wang Tanzhi is above all known for his opposition to the philosophy of Zhuangzi 莊子. He wrote an essay called 'On Rejecting Zhuangzi', *Fei Zhuang lun* 廢莊論, in which he criticised Zhuangzi for producing a philosophical system cut off from the needs of ordinary humanity. When paragons of virtue and men of high, single-minded morality were unable to 'enter into the *dao* (Way)', how much more was it difficult for ordinary men to achieve the mystical experience and the kind of self-realisation taught by Zhuangzi. By aiming too high at absolute absorption into the All, Zhuangzi lost sight of the real world and led men to let themselves go in dissipation. What is interesting in this very short essay is not so much the criticism of Zhuangzi, which is fairly well taken, but the fact that Wang Tanzhi preaches a syncretic philosophy in which Zhuangzi is presented as a muddleheaded thinker who failed to understand the basic mystical truths that Confucius and Laozi both espoused centuries earlier.

DONALD HOLZMAN

Wang Tao 王韜
1828–97
(*zi* Ziquan 紫詮, *hao* Zhongtao 仲弢)

Reformist thinker and statecraft scholar, Wang Tao was born to a village tutor family in Suzhou, Jiangsu province. He abandoned his examination candidate's career after passing the first level of the civil service examinations. From 1849 to 1862, he became an editor/translator for a British publishing house in Shanghai. During those thirteen years, he taught himself western history, science and technology. Based on his knowledge about the West and his statecraft learning, he offered advice to provincial officials on naval defence and foreign relations. In his letters to the provincial officials, he was among the first to point out that China was no longer the 'Middle Kingdom', but a member of the community of nations.

In 1862, Wang left Shanghai for Hong Kong because of his link with the Taiping Rebellion. In Hong Kong, he assisted **James Legge** in translating the *Shang shu* into English. In 1867, he went to Scotland to help Legge translate the rest of the Five Confucian Classics (*Wu jing*). For three years, he travelled widely in England, France and Russia. Having returned to Hong Kong, he published his reflection on the trip in the newly founded newspaper, *Xunhuan ribao* 循環日報. In these short essays as well as in his translated work on the Franco-Prussian War, Wang applied the *Yi jing* concept of change to current affairs. He argued that the Chinese had to respond to the challenge of the West by drastically reforming their political, economic and educational systems. Some of Wang's ideas were adopted in the Self-Strengthening Movement led by Li Hongzhang 李鴻章 (1823–1901).

References: Cohen, Paul, 1974; McAleavy, 1953.

TZE-KI HON

Wang Tingxiang 王廷相
1474–1544
(*zi* Ziheng 子衡, *hao* Junchuan 濬川)

Wang Tingxiang stands out as one of the most independent thinkers of the Ming Dynasty, and is particularly known for his explicit promotion of **Zhang Zai**'s philosophy of *qi* (material force).

Wang's father had been banished from Shanxi to Yifeng in Henan for military service. Somehow, the elder Wang managed to become a local landowner. As a result, his son Wang Tingxiang became a registered Yifeng native. He passed the provincial examinations in 1495 and earned the *jinshi* degree in 1502, receiving appointment in the Hanlin Academy. During these years in the capital, Wang became friends with the poets Li Mengyang 李夢陽 (1475–1529) and He Jingming 何景明 (1483–1521), both leading figures in the archaist movement in poetry. Together with Li, He and others, Wang became known as one of the Earlier Seven Masters of Ming poetry.

Soon, however, Wang was censored by the powerful eunuch Liao Tang 廖堂 (?–?) for abusing his authority while serving as a regional inspector in Shaanxi in 1511. Wang was demoted and removed from office before gradually climbing back up the bureaucratic ladder through various provincial posts, such as director of education in Sichuan (1517–1521) and Shandong (1521–1523). After a period of mourning, Wang rose to the position of Sichuan governor in 1527.

At this time, Wang became embroiled in the partisan politics of the great rites controversy (*Dali yi* 大禮議) surrounding the new Jiajing emperor (r. 1522–1566) in the 1520s. The controversy resulted from the fact that the previous emperor had died without a son and without naming an heir to the throne. The Jiajing emperor was the grandson of the Chenghua emperor (r. 1465–1487) and an imperial concubine, a fact that should have made him an illegitimate heir. Nevertheless, highly placed officials encouraged his accession to the throne in the interest of dynastic stability. Fictionally adopted by the deceased emperor, the new Jiajing emperor was expected to treat him, an uncle, as his father in court rituals. Despite the objections of his highest officials, most of whom were ardent followers of **Zhu Xi**, the new Jiajing emperor insisted on honouring his true father as the imperial father in court ceremonies. Wang

Tingxiang, as well as officials enamoured with the philosophy of **Wang Shouren**, supported the emperor in his decision to honour his parents in court rituals rather than the deceased emperor. Consequently, Wang Tingxiang became part of the pro-emperor group led by Zhang Fujing 張孚敬 (1475–1539), and his career profited from this. Beginning in 1528, Wang spent over a decade at various posts in the southern and northern capitals culminating in his appointment as grand guardian of the heir apparent in 1539. Finally, in 1541, Wang was dismissed from office.

Wang's most important philosophical position was his refutation of the Song Neo-Confucian theory that *li* (principle) originates *qi* (material force) Instead, Wang developed the notion, first articulated by Zhang Zai, that all principle comes from material force (*wanli jie sheng yu qi* 萬理皆 生於氣). As Wang described it, 'Inside and outside of Heaven, all is *qi*. All on Earth, as well, is *qi*. The vacuous and concrete aspects of things are all *qi*. Connecting the extremes above and below, it is the actual substance of creation and transformation' (*Wang Tingxiang ji*, 753). In other words, *qi* according to Wang creates all things.

Wang Tingxiang developed his own theory of the relationship between *li* and *qi* in his critique of **Cheng Yi** and Zhu Xi. According to Wang, *qi* can be classified into *yuanqi* (primordial material force) and *shengqi* 生氣 (produced matter); the latter has form whereas the former lacks it. According to Wang, *li* is contained in both types of *qi*. In Wang's understanding, *li* refers to the order or pattern of *qi*, but does not exist prior to *qi* and consequently cannot be said to produce it. Because *qi* is the only actual or concrete substance in the universe, while *li* is only its order or pattern, and moreover because *qi* is constantly transforming, therefore *li* and by extension the *Dao* are also unceasingly being altered. In particular, the principles of human society are constantly changing with the times. This directly refutes the notion promoted

by Zhu Xi that principle ultimately is an absolute, unchanging phenomenon.

Moreover, Wang was highly critical of the notion of *xing* (nature). While Neo-Confucians after Zhu Xi typically interpreted nature as independent from *qi*, Wang suggests that nature is in fact constituted from *qi*. What accounts for contrasting natures among individuals, in Wang's view, is the purity or turbidness of one's *qi*. Wang argued that the notion drawn from **Mengzi** and popularised by the Neo-Confucians that human nature is good therefore cannot be held as true. Because one's nature is unceasingly transformed along with *qi*, Wang believes that a person's nature can thereby be transformed through practice. Therefore, in a tone somewhat reminiscent of **Xunzi**, Wang believed that human nature was subject to modification by learning.

During the latter half of the Ming dynasty, Wang Tingxiang's emphasis upon *qi* was widely influential. In addition, the thought of Wang, **Luo Qinshun** and **Wu Tinghan**, with its shared emphasis upon physical reality and the affirmation of the desires, had a deep impact among Japanese Neo-Confucians as well. Wang, Luo and Wu greatly influenced **Kaibara Ekiken**, and provided the starting point in the development of *kogaku* (Ancient Learning) School thought represented by **Itô Jinsai**, **Ogyû Sorai** and others. More recently, beginning in the 1950s, Wang, along **Huang Wan**, Lü Kun 呂坤 (1536–1618) and **Wang Fuzhi**, has been celebrated by Marxist materialist philosophers in the People's Republic of China for his advocacy of 'materialistic monism'. Wang's two most important philosophical works are *Shenyan* 慎言 (*Cautious Words*) and *Yashu* 雅述 (*Recounting Refinement*). Both of these works are recollections of Wang's philosophical and ethical essays compiled and published by his disciples, the first in 1533 and the second in 1539.

References: Chen, 1994; Nosco, 1984: 138–65; Wang Tingxiang, 1989.

STEVEN MILES

Wang Tong 王通
584–617
(*zi* Zhongyan 仲淹)

Wang Tong was a great Confucian scholar of the Sui dynasty (581–618). He presented to the throne the 'Twelve Schemes for Grand Peace' (*taiping shier ce* 太平十二策) in 603, though it is apparent that they were not adopted by Emperor Wen (r. 581–604). According to **Zizhi tongjian** (ch. 179), the emperor subsequently called upon him several times to serve in the court but he declined the invitations, and took an early retirement when Emperor Yang (r. 604–618) ascended to the throne.

During the early seventh century when Buddhism was reaching its height, according to his disciples it was with him that the great principles of the Confucian sages were brought to completion, and when he died, his students claimed that he was the only one who had known what Confucius would want them to know and to learn; they therefore conferred on him the private posthumous title of Wenzhong zi 文中子. However, the *Sui shu* does not include Wang among its bibliographies, and the *Jiu Tang shu* 舊唐書 (the *Old History of the Tang Dynasty*) and the *Xin Tang shu* 新唐書 (The *New History of the Tang Dynasty*) mention him only incidentally in their chapters 163 and 196 respectively. It seems that although Wang might have enjoyed a considerable scholarly reputation during his lifetime, the information we have today may not be sufficient for us to give any credibility to the accounts of his disciples.

Wang was said to have written a number of books including his commentaries on the Six Classics, which however have long since been lost. His thoughts on Confucianism are primarily preserved in a short text modelled on the *Analects of Confucius* (**Lunyu**), entitled '*Zhong shuo* 中說' (The Middle Sayings), also known as *Wenzhong zi*. In this work, Wang demonstrated a firm belief in traditional Con-fucian doctrines, and claimed that he was the proper successor to the Duke of Zhou (**Zhou Gong**) and Confucius. He believed that **li** (ritual/rites, propriety) had been completely lost and it was his mission to recover it. Benevolence and righteousness were the basic sources for educating the people, which provided the foundation for peace and harmony in society. At the same time Wang also demonstrated a clear tendency to syncretism based on Con-fucian ideas, intending to unite the three doctrines of Confucianism, Daoism and Buddhism into a single tradition, and to make use of some of the Buddhist and Daoist doctrines to further Confucian polit-ical and moral ideals. His understanding of the relationship between the human heart/mind (**ren xin** 人心) and the heart/mind of the Way (**dao xin** 道心) informed one of the essential Neo-Confucian doctrines in the Song dynasty (960–1126). He also pointed at the contradiction of **xing** (nature) and *qing* (情, emotion or sentiment), emphasising the effectiveness of *jing* (quiescence 靜) and **cheng** (sincerity). In this sense it may be said that Wang was one of the early Confucian scholars who made a contribution to the later revival of Neo-Confucianism in the Song, especially in the area of the the-oretical and philosophical reconstruction of Confucian doctrines.

M.H. KIM

Wang Xinjing 王心敬
1656–1738
(*zi* Er Ji 爾緝)

Wang Xinjing, born in E Xian 鄂縣 (Shanxi), was a preeminent student of **Li Yong**, a famous scholar in the Qing dynasty. He was recommended as a '*Good and Upright Man*' (*Xian Liang Fang Zheng* 賢良方正) in 1736 by imperial decree but he failed to reach the capital due to old age. He had a wide range of knowledge and especially excelled in the study of the *Book of Changes* (*Yi jing*). His work entitled *Discourse on the Book of Changes* (*Yi shuo* 易說) carefully explained the concepts and principles of the book. For him, the contents of *Yi* were not only related to nature, but also centrally related to human affairs; thus a good knowledge of the *Yi* would help people to avoid serious mistakes and to live a better life. He believed that Confucius and other sages got their true spirit from the *Yi jing*. He criticised the Diagram of the River (*He Tu* 河圖) and the Scripts of the Luo (*Luo Shu* 洛書) for misunderstanding the original idea of *Yi*, pointing out that all later Confucians who stressed aspects of the contents of the *Yi* like Images (*Xiang* 象), Numbers (*Shu* 數), Principle (*Li* 理) and Divination (*Bu wu* 卜巫), were actually departing from the true spirit of the *Yi*. He viewed the interaction of yin and yang as actually indicating social movement (see **yin–yang**). He greatly respected the *Doctrine of the Mean* (**Zhongyong**) and treated it as Zi Si's (**Kong Ji**) most important work on *Yi* and *Dao*. His other works include the *Shang shu zhiyi* 尚書質疑, *Shi jing shuo* 詩經說, *Li ji zhuan* 禮記撰, *Chun Qiu yuanjing* 春秋原經, *Fengchuan ji* 丰川集. He was hailed as the person who perpetuated and enriched *Zhou Yi* studies in the Shanxi area of his time.

Reference: Wu & Song, 1992.

OUYANG KANG

Wang Yansou 王岩叟
1044–1094
(*zi* Yanlin 彥霖)

Wang Yansou was particularly learned in the Classics as he demonstrated in 1061 when he came first in the provincial, metropolitan and palace examinations in the Classics (*ming jing* 明經) (*Song shi*, 1977: 342: 10891). After initially serving in low-ranking positions, he was recommended to Emperor Zhezong's (r. 1086–1100) court

and appointed an Investigating Censor (*jiancha yushi* 監察御史). There followed a series of promotions that saw him achieve an important role in the court. He eventually became one of the leaders of the so-called Hebei faction (*Shuo dang* 朔黨) during the *Yuanyou* 元祐 reign period (1086–1093). Ultimately accused of forming a faction, he was sent to a provincial post where he died.

Wang had an enduring reputation as an official who offered forthright criticism on a broad array of government policies. This included opposition to some of **Wang Anshi**'s New Policies (e.g., the law commuting labour service to cash). Classical scholarship, however, was his most important intellectual activity. He produced, for example, commentaries on the *Yi jing*, the *Shi jing*, and the *Spring and Autumn Annals*. According to **Zhu Xi**, Wang did have some contact with **Cheng Hao** but was certainly not among the latter's disciples (*Yi Luo yuanyuan lu* 14.1b).

References: *Song shi*, 1977; Zhu Xi, *Yi Luo yuanyuan lu*.

ANTHONY DEBLASI

Wang Yingchen 汪應辰
?–1176
(*zi* Shengxi 聖錫)

Wang's original name had been Wang Yang 汪洋. He was a native of the region of Yushan 玉山 in Xinzhou 信州 County (in modern-day Jiangxi), hence his title Master Yushan. Wang's followers would have a strong influence later on the trends in Confucian thought beginning in the Southern Song period, namely **Zhu Xi**'s *Dao xue* Learning and **Lu Jiuyuan**'s *Xinxue* Learning. Wang was born into a farming family, and his earliest Confucian training came from Yu Tuanshi 喻湍石 (?–?), who had entered the region as the newly appointed District Defender 尉 and had seen great potential in young Wang. Yu's programme of instruction closely followed the Yi Luo 伊洛 School teachings of **Cheng Hao** and **Cheng Yi**. After he had finished a short period of study, Yu suggested that Wang pursue a career in government service. At the age of eighteen in 1135 Wang Yingchen received his *jinshi* degree. The Song emperor Gaozong (r. 1127–1163) is said to have read Wang's exam papers, and to have thought that Wang was an established scholar from his mature style of writing. Therefore, Wang was given the highest official rank for that session of the examinations. When Wang was called before the emperor, Gaozong presented the young candidate with a specially prepared copy of the Confucian classic *Doctrine of the Mean* to mark his academic achievement. Wang's first official appointment was as Proofreader in the Palace Library (*mishu sheng zhengzi* 秘書省正字).

Wang was actively involved in court debate over Song–Jin tensions along the northern frontier. When the Jurchen Jin forces threatened the border region of Henan in 1141–1142, Wang prepared a military defence. However, Qin Gui 秦檜 (1090–1155) and his pacifist faction presided over the court in this period, and court policy soon dictated that no military response should be arranged. Wang eventually memorialised the court to argue that he opposed the order not to coordinate a strong defence to face the horrible threat from the impending Jurchen invasion. His public opposition was said to have irritated Qin Gui, and Wang was soon demoted to the position of Controller-General (*tongpan* 通判) to Jianzhou 建州 prefecture. Wang eventually took up residence at Mt Chang's 長山 Xiao Buddhist Temple 蕭寺 where he took work as a lecturer.

After Qin had died and his faction had fallen out of imperial favour, Wang Yingchen attempted to return to court. Eventually he worked his way up the official hierarchy to the position of Head of the Ministry of Personnel (*shangshuli*

bulang 尚書吏部郎). Later he took the position of Vice Minister of the Ministry of Revenue (*hubu shilang* 戶部侍郎) and Hanlin scholar, among other high positions. Wang Yingchen was honest but unyielding in his official service. When he was not afraid to speak his mind, lesserminded officials would cast aspersions on his character. Wang became embroiled in further court debate, and he was subsequently demoted in rank. Wang soon retired from official life and lived in solitude until he died at the age of fifty-nine.

Wang drew on a wide range of sources in developing his brand of Confucianism. During his earliest period of exile Wang developed his eclectic philosophical thought. When in his youth Wang married the daughter of Yu Tuanshi, the dowry he received was in the form of books. It was with this gift that Wang learned of the teachings of the Cheng brothers. Through the Cheng brothers Wang took an interest in 'ritual, music, legal codes and government' (*li yue xing zheng* 禮樂刑政), whereby the centrality and harmony within both ritual and music would lead one to the principle of the *Dao*. When he was young, Wang Yingchen often associated with loyalist literary figures **Lü Benzhong** and **Hu Anguo**, and adopted their teachings as well. Wang Yingchen also studied with **Zhang Jiucheng**'s Heng Pu 橫浦 School soon after Wang had received his first official appointment. However, Wang eventually distanced himself from the Heng Pu School and associated himself more closely with Lü Benzhong's Zi Wei 紫微 School, because Zhang was known to be unduly partial to Buddhist practices. Wang was also a student of Yang Shi for a period.

Huang Zongxi quoted Zhu Xi as saying that Wang had mastered many different schools, but that he never became content with one system of learning. Such a statement from Zhu Xi was probably based on Zhu's criticism of Wang's foremost student Lü Zuqian that Lü was overly analytical in his thought and never spent enough time to determine right from wrong in personal conduct. Wang's writings were later compiled as *Wending Ji* 文定集 (*The Collected Works of Wang Wending*).

References: *Song–Yuan xuean*, 1966: 1451–5; Tillman 1992b: 86.

JAMES A. ANDERSON

Wang Yinglin 王應麟
1223–1296
(*zi* Bohou 伯厚 or Houzhai 厚齋, *hao* Shenning 深寧)

Wang Yinglin is an important representative of the so-called 'polymaths' of the Southern Song dynasty (1127–1279). His ancestors fled to South China after the end of the Northern Song dynasty and settled eventually in the prefecture Yin 鄞 (today Ningbo 寧波, Zhejiang), where Wang Yinglin was born. Under the strict supervision of his father Wang Hui 王撝 (1184–1253, *zi* Qianfu 謙父) he began his diligent studies of the canonical Confucian works in his early youth. At the age of nineteen *sui* 歲 (eighteen years) he already obtained his *jinshi* degree and in 1256 even passed the hardest of the examinations in Song dynasty – the 'polymath examination' (*boxue hongci* 博學宏詞 or 博學宏辭). Afterwards he had an unsteady career at the court of the Southern Song emperor until he finally retreated from the post of Minister of Rites (*libu shangshu* 禮部尚書) in late 1275, only a few months before Mongol troops stormed the capital Lin'an 臨安 (today Hangzhou 杭州). He spent the last twenty years of his life at his family residence working on his compilations and teaching his students.

While preparing for the 'polymath examination', Wang Yinglin wrote the '*Sea of Jades*' (*Yuhai* 玉海), one of the most important encyclopedias of that time. During seclusion of his later years he compiled many commentaries on the Classics and other traditional historical works. The most abundant of these is the collection *Recordings of Observances from Arduous Studies* (*Kunxue jiwen* 困學紀聞), which also gives some information about his thoughts during his late years, since it was finished only after 1280. His educational efforts can be felt in his elementary book *Purple Pearls of Elementary Learning* (*Xiao xue ganzhu* 小學紺珠) and his commentaries on the Han-dynasty primer – the *Hastening to Achievement* (*Jijiu pian* 急就篇). The *Sanzi jing* however is most likely not written by Wang Yinglin, although it is often so stated.

Wang Yinglin had studied under several teachers belonging to different schools of Confucianism. Qing dynasty scholars like **Quan Zuwang** make him a successor of **Lü Zuqian**, while in recent times **Qian Mu** tried to prove that he continued the tradition of **Zhu Xi**. Others even write that his thought is based on the school of **Lu Jiuyuan**. As connections to all these schools of thought can be found in Wang's writings, it seems that we must give up this kind of schematic classification when dealing with scholars like Wang Yinglin. He emphasises broad learning as well as a high moral standard to be observed by any serious scholar. Qing dynasty scholars – like **Yan Ruoju**, **Quan Zuwang** and He Zhuo 何焯 (1661–1722, *zi* Qizhan 屺瞻, *hao* Chaxian 茶仙 or Yimen 義門) – were mostly impressed by his philological techniques and especially appreciated the collection of notes *Kunxue jiwen*, as well as Wang Yinglin's attempts to reconstruct lost works, e.g. the *Zhou Yi Zheng Kangcheng zhu* 周易鄭康成注 (*Commentaries of Zheng Xuan on the Yi jing*). However, it can be shown that Wang Yinglin's painful feelings concerning the brutal end of the Song dynasty (1276) also had a great impact on his philological work of the latest years.

References: He Zeheng, 1981; Langley, 1986; Qian Mu, 1974.

CHRISTIAN SOFFEL

Wang Yuan 王源
1648–1710
(*zi* Kunsheng 昆繩)

Wang Yuan, born in Da Xin, Beijing, was a successful candidate in the provincial level imperial examinations in 1693, studied under **Yan Yuan** in his later years and finally became a member of the School of Yan Yuan and **Li Gong**. He was disgusted with Song Neo-Confucianism, considering it to be merely empty talk that would bring calamity to the country and the people. His most important work was the *Ping Shu* 平書, which contains his main ideas about the reform of the state and social institutions. His main contribution was in economics, stressing the need for an improvement in the social position of commerce. He redivided the traditional social order of professions, calling for protection and encouragement of farming and commerce, and for lifting the position of commerce and business in society. Firstly, reflecting upon the requirement of the new and rising classes of industry and commerce, he insisted that businessmen should share the same social position as the literati and officialdom. He highlighted a proposal to collect taxes according to the amount of one's capital, to abolish unnecessary taxes, and to ensure that businessmen do not lose money in their businesses. This was the first tax system proposal that would benefit the development of commerce. Secondly, with regard to land policy, he insisted that land owners should plough the land themselves (*You tian zhe bi zi geng* 有田者必自耕) and suggested that the state should buy land and then divide it for the peasants. Thirdly, as for financial administration, one of his suggestions was to set up a tax system similar to today's income tax system in the area of commerce. Fourthly, in order to enhance the abilities of financial administration, he suggested that students should study the subject of financial administration. He also suggested setting up a financial department in the official system of government.

Besides the *Ping Shu*, Wang Yuan also wrote *On Soldiers* (*Bing lun* 兵論), *General Words on the Study of the Book of Changes* (*Yi xue tongyan* 易學通言), and *Juyie Tang wenji* 居業堂文集, of which only the last is extant.

Reference: Wu & Song, 1992.

OUYANG KANG

Wang Zhi 王植
1681–?
(*zi* Huaisan 槐三, *hao* Hansi 憨思)

A native of Shenze 深澤 (Hebei), Wang was a Classicist and philosopher. He gained his *jinshi* degree in 1721 and served as county magistrate in Guangdong and Shandong. He retired in 1749 and dedicated the rest of his life to scholarly writing.

Wang proposed a synthetic perception between the Learning of the Heart/Mind (*xin xue*) and the Learning of Principle (**li xue**). He believed that moral principles as well as social criteria were innate in human nature (*xing*) rather than separate from the latter. He advocated that political and social practice were essential processes in maintaining one's heart/mind. From this point of view, he praised **Zhou Dunyi**, **Zhang Zai** and **Shao Yong** and proclaimed **Lu Jiuyuan**'s and **Wang Shouren**'s teachings as 'empty learning'.

Wang also made an intensive study of phonology. He supported **Gu Yanwu** and **Jiang Yong** in dividing ancient vowel sounds into certain groups. He pointed out that this division was fundamental to the analysis of ancient and modern sounds. He therefore criticised **Mao Qiling**'s phonological studies.

Wang's works include the *Records of the Origin and Sources of the Learning of the Way* (*Dao xue yuanyuan lu* 道學淵源錄); the *Primary Meaning of the Correcting the Unenlightened* (*Zhengmeng chuyi* 正蒙初義), and the *Explanations of the Book of Supreme World-Ordering Principles* (*Huangji jingshi shu jie* 皇極經世書解).

REBEKAH X. ZHAO

Wangming lun 王命論
(*On the King's Mandate*)

In the disunited state of China that followed the end of **Wang Mang**'s 王莽 reign in 23 CE, Ban Biao 班彪 (3–54 CE) advised Wei Ao 隗囂 (?–?), one of the contenders for power, on the nature of sovereignty. In his essay, which is entitled *Wangming lun*, Ban Biao emphasised the essential need for a monarch to enjoy the full support of Heaven and to possess the qualities that make him fit for the charge. In supporting the legitimacy of the Han house of Liu 劉, he added that true sovereignty does not depend on force alone; and he traced the ancestry of the Liu family to the legendary ruler Yao (see **Yao Shun**).

Reference: de Bary, Chan & Watson, 1960, vol. I: 176–80.

MICHAEL LOEWE

Wanwu yiti 萬物一體
(Unity with all things)

Wanwu yiti, literally '10,000 things, one body', is a summary statement of the relationality of **ren** with the myriad things (see **wu**, things). The idea is traceable to **Mengzi** 7A: 4, where we find a statement '*wanwu jie bei yu wo*' 萬物皆備於我, generally translated as that 'all things are complete in me'. It is not simply a microcosmic image of self-sufficiency but a macrocosmic vision of unity with the cosmos, similar to **Zhang Zai**'s belief that 'All people are my brothers and sisters, and all things are my companions' (see **Xi ming**).

The classic statement of *wanwu yiti* comes from **Cheng Hao**: 'the person of *ren* forms one body with heaven, earth and the myriad things; none is not oneself' 仁者以天地萬物為一體, 莫非己也 (*Ercheng ji*, p. 15, see also his *Shiren pian*). The passage uses visceral imagery of pain and itch to describe bodily unity. For Cheng Hao, it is humane sensitivity that forms one

body. One's unity with all things is not a result of deliberate intention but naturally so according to heavenly pattern; however, the awareness of somatic unity is usually blocked by selfish desires (see **tianli renyu**).

Wanwu yiti is not an oceanic experience of being one with the world, but rather one with all things, each in its own integrity. A well-developed statement of sympathetic resonance forming one body is found in **Wang Shouren**'s *Da xue wen*, where Wang points out that the person of *ren* forms one body even with inanimate objects like tiles and stones. *Wanwu yiti* also informs **Tu Wei-ming**'s notion of the 'continuity of being'. It may be called the Confucian creed of commonality.

References: Chan, Wing-tsit, 1963d: 497, 523, 530 and 1963c: 56, 272–4; Cheng & Cheng, 1981: 15–17; Tu, 1985: 35–50.

THOMAS SELOVER

Wei guwen Shang shu
偽古文尚書
(*Spurious Old Text of the Venerated Documents*)

The *Wei guwen Shang shu* refers to the text entitled *Kong Anguo Shang shu* 孔安國尚書 that Mei Ze 梅賾 (*fl.* 317–322) presented to the Eastern Jin court in 317. This text was supposed to have been identical to the 'Old Text' (*guwen* 古文) version of the **Shang shu** that **Kong Anguo** was supposed to have discovered in the wall of Confucius' mansion and to have presented to the court of **Han Wudi** (r. 141–87 BCE), but which had been lost when the Western Jin capital at Luoyang 洛陽 (Henan) was sacked in 311. The text, which included also a commentary attributed to Kong Anguo, was quickly recognised as the orthodox version of the *Shang shu*, being adopted for both the *Shang shu Zheng yi* 尚書正義 (*Correct Meaning of the Venerated Documents*) and the Kaicheng Stone Classics (*Kaicheng shi jing* 開成石經) projects of the Tang dynasty (618–907). However, beginning already in the early

Southern Song dynasty (1127–1279), scholars, including **Zhu Xi**, recognised that the seventeen documents exclusive to the 'Old Text' version of the *Shang shu* were qualitatively different from the twenty-eight documents said to have been also in its 'New Text' version. By the Qing dynasty (1644–1911), great efforts were made to demonstrate that these seventeen documents and especially the commentary attributed to Kong Anguo must have been written after the time that Kong Anguo lived, presumably early in the fourth century. The spurious nature of these texts was demonstrated most fully in *Guwen Shang shu shu zheng* 古文尚書疏證 (*Proofs of the Old Text of the Venerated Documents*) by **Yan Ruoju**.

References: Legge, 1985c: vol. III; Loewe, 1993: 376–89.

EDWARD L. SHAUGHNESSY

Wei Liaoweng 魏了翁
1178–1237
(*zi* Huafu 華父)

Wei Liaoweng was from Sichuan where he received instruction from followers of **Zhang Shi**. He was awarded the *jinshi* degree in 1199. At age twenty-six or twenty-seven he met two senior disciples of **Zhu Xi** with whom he continued his studies and became a great admirer of Zhu's learning. In his preface to *Zhuzi nianpu* 年譜 (*Chronological Biography of Master Zhu*) by Li Fangzi 李方子 (?–?, *zi* Gonghui 公晦) he praised Zhu's achievements as not inferior to those of **Mengzi**. In his political career, Wei was successful in local administration but repeatedly frustrated at court where his proposals for reform were unwelcome. In this he resembled **Zhen Dexiu**, a fellow 1199 *jinshi*, with whom Wei is often coupled. Both men stood out as eminent and politically engaged *daoxue* scholars of the generation after Zhu Xi.

Wei devoted much of his energies to textual studies. His *Jiujing yaoyi* 九經要義 (*Essential Meanings of the Nine Classics*) are highly valued for their careful scholarship and the clarity of his presentation of the findings of earlier commentators. Especially highly prized are his *Yaoyi* of the three ritual texts, foremost the **Yi li** (*Book of Ritual*) which he praised as the root while relegating the **Zhou li** (*Rites of Zhou*) to the branches. In addition to his *Zhou yi yaoyi* 周易要義 he compiled a *Zhou yi jiyi* 周易集義 consisting of commentaries by Song scholars. Another work of interest is Wei's *Gujin kao*, 古今考 (*Examination into Past and Present*) greatly expanded by Fang Hui (方回 1227–1307). His *Reading Notes* (*Dushu* 讀書) and *Collected Writings* (*Wenji* 文記) further confirm Wei's erudition.

In his preface to Li Boyong's 李伯勇 collection of commentaries (*Wenji* 53) Wei included a statement later quoted by the *Siku Quanshu* editors discussing Wei's own *Essential Meaning of the Zuozhuan and Chunqiu* (*Zuozhuan Chunqiu Yaoyi* 左傳春秋要義). He wrote that only in his own dynasty was it realised that the *Annals* are the great model for ordering the world and the 'essential documents of the transmission of the heart/mind' (*chuanxin zhi yaodian* 傳心之要典) (a phrase also found in **Hu Anguo**'s introduction to his commentary to *The Annals*).

Elsewhere, particularly in writings addressed to the emperor, Wei again emphasised the centrality and sublimity of the heart/mind, raising it even above Heaven and Earth: 'Heaven comprehends and controls (*tong* 統) the original life-force (**yuanqi**) to cover all things, and Earth comprehends and controls (*tong*) the original form to support all things. Heaven and Earth are so vast that nothing can be added. But man with his single heart/mind combines the abilities of Heaven and Earth, provides the substance (**ti** 體) of all things, to establish its place among them, to rule (*zhu* 主) Heaven and Earth, to command (*ming*) all things, to open and close *yin* and *yang*, and to encompass creation, advance and retreat through past and present' (*wenji* 15). In his most famous memorial Wei wrote that the heart/mind is the **tai ji**, that the human heart/mind is also the *taiji* of Heaven and Earth and thus orders *yin* and *yang* and commands all things'. While the emphasis on the emperor's heart/ mind is similar to that found in Zhu Xi or Zhen Dexiu, Wei goes beyond them in assigning it a cosmic role.

Wei does not share Zhen Dexiu's moral rigorism. He emphasised that the sage (i.e. Mengzi) taught that the desires should be made few but did not teach that people should be without desires and cited such benevolent desires as that for **ren** (humanness). He then quoted **Hu Hong** that Heavenly principle and human desires are the same in their operation but different in their feelings (*tongxing yiqing* 同性異情), a doctrine Zhu Xi had found objectionable.

Wei Liaoweng's extensive writings await study in depth. While he does not appear to have worked out a full fledged philosophical system, he was a remarkably productive scholar and a *daoxue* thinker who admired but did not always follow Zhu Xi.

References: Balazs & Hervouet, 1978; Franke, 1976: vol. III: 1180–3; Ito Shigehiko, 1976: 8–11, 115–37, 445–52; Liu, James, 1993: 336–48; *Song yuan xuean*, 1966.

CONRAD SCHIROKAUER

Wei Yuan 魏源
1794–1857
(*zi* Mo Shen 默深)

In 1815, at the age of twenty-two, Wei Yuan underwent a drastic transformation in his life. A native of Hunan, he had been since a child an ardent student of both the evidential 'Han Learning' and the moralistic 'Song Learning'. Like thousands of aspiring candidates of the civil service examinations, he faithfully followed the two schools of teaching in order to win a post in the government. In 1815, he paid a visit to the capital Beijing, in the hope of broadening his social circle to increase his chance of passing the examinations. By a stroke of luck, he met first with the New Text scholar Liu Fenglu 劉逢祿 (1776–1829), and then with a recent convert to the New Text School **Gong Zizhen**. For the

first time in his life, he saw the close link between studying the Confucian classics and ordering the world. Immediately following the meeting, he studied the foundational text of the New Text School with Liu Fenglu – Gongyang's commentary of the *Spring and Autumn Annals* (**Chunqiu Gongyang zhuan**). He spent day and night discussing textual matters with Gong Zizhen and became a devout follower of the New Text School.

Wei was attracted to the New Text School because of its emphasis on linking classical scholarship with governing. Summarised in the phrase 'applying the Classics to the practical use of administration' (**Jingshi zhi yong** 經世致用), the New Text School of the Qing dynasty stressed the importance of locating the subtle political messages hidden in the archaic texts. Behind and beyond the 'subtle words' (*weiyan* 微言) of Confucian texts, the New Text scholars argued that there was a 'profound metaphoric meaning' (*dayi* 大義) accessible only through oral transmission. Hence, what appeared to be a neutral description of the past could turn out to be a blueprint of political renewal for the present. A case in point was Confucius' account of history in the *Spring and Autumn Annals*. On the surface, Confucius' account was an impartial report of what had happened from 722 to 481 BCE. But on closer inspection, it implied a political vision based on the gradual progress of the 'Three Ages' – Age of Disorder (*juluan shi* 據亂世), Age of Approaching Peace (*shengping shi* 升平世) and Age of Great Peace (*taiping shi* 太平世). Reading the *Spring and Autumn Annals* in this light, the New Text scholars asserted that the Confucian text was a call to political reform in response to the needs of the times.

Living in a time when the Qing suffered from both internal disintegration and foreign defeats, Wei had good reason to find the New Text School appealing. As a junior officer in Jiangsu in the 1820s and 1830s, he was exposed to the mismanagement of the salt trade and the government's failure to maintain the grand canal. In 1842, he was shocked by the news that the Qing had signed the Nanjing Treaty with Britain.

The Qing's defeat in the Opium War made him realise how rapidly the empire had declined from its zenith in the eighteenth century. Immediately he wrote the *Shengwu ji* 聖武記 (*Record of the Imperial Military Achievements*, 1842) to remind his readers how militarily powerful the Qing once was a century and half before. He advised his readers to pay special attention to national defence because the foreign powers appeared to have the upper hand in military technology. In the final years of his life, he was troubled by the loss of law and order in the Taiping Rebellion (1850–1864). Having spent a tremendous effort in organising local forces to defend against Taiping rebels, he witnessed at first hand the destruction of the once prosperous lower Yangzi area. On his deathbed, he knew that the Qing of the *Shengwu ji* was gone forever.

Following the teaching of the New Text School, Wei became a leading statecraft scholar of the late Qing. Under He Changling 賀長齡 (1785–1848), he edited the multi-volume *Huangchao jingshi wenbian* 皇朝經世文編 (*Collected Writings on Statecraft of the Reigning Dynasty*, 1825) to call attention to the need for institutional reform. Divided into eight sections, the collection brought together writings since 1644 that dealt with education, administration, recruitment, rituals, defense, punishment and public work. In 1844, appalled by the lack of knowledge of the Qing officials in dealing with the British during the Opium War, he compiled the *Haiguo tuzhi* 海國圖志 (*An Illustrated Account of Maritime Countries*). Expanding on Lin Zexiu's *Sizhou zhi* 四州志 (*A Survey of the Four Continents*), the *Haiguo tuzhi* provided the first comprehensive account of the globe to Chinese readers. Consisting of fifty chapters, it offered general information on different countries in the world, including their religions, cultures and calendars. In the preface to the book, Wei made it clear that China would not be able to defend herself unless she undertook drastic reform immediately. His famous line *shi yi zhi changji yi zhi yi* ('learning the best skills of the barbarians in order to control the barbarians') later became the catchphrase during the Self-Strengthening Movement (1860–1894).

As a classical scholar, Wei made two contributions to the New Text School. Firstly, he underscored the importance of **Dong Zhongshu**'s commentary on the *Spring and Autumn Annals*. Before him, the New Text scholars focused mainly on **He Xiu**'s commentary rather than on Dong's. In his *Dongzi Chunqiu fawei* 董子春秋發微 (*Explaining the Esoteric Meaning of Dong Zhongshu's Commentary on the Spring and Autumn Annals*), he redressed this imbalance by elaborating on Dong's contribution to the study of the *Annals*. Secondly, he reinterpreted Confucian Classics from the perspective of the New Text School. Among his many writings, he wrote commentaries on the *Shi jing* (*Book of Poetry*) and the *Shu jing* (*Book of Documents*) – the *Shi gu wei* 詩古微 (*The Ancient Esoteric Meaning of the Book of Poetry*, 1836) and the *Shu gu wei* 書古微 (*The Ancient Esoteric Meaning of the Book of Documents*, 1855). These two commentaries were the authoritative New Text readings of the two Confucian Classics.

References: Mitchell, 1972; Zhou & Yang, 1981: 171–93; Leonard, 1984.

TZE-KI HON

Wei Zheng 魏徵
580–643
(*zi* Zixuan 子玄)

Wei Zheng was a fearless adviser to the second Tang emperor, Taizong 太宗 (r. 626–649), and one of the prime movers in the early Tang attempt to impose order of the whole scholarly tradition, principally by directing major compilatory works. Among his high posts were the directorship of the imperial library, during his tenure of which he collected and attempted to reassemble early stone engravings of the text of the Confucian canon; he was a codirector of the first state ritual code of the dynasty; he also compiled a guide to good administration that drew from a wide range of sources, the

Qunshu zhiyao 群書治要, and directed the project for writing histories of five of the pre-Tang dynasties. He was the only high minister of Taizong's reign to write a commentary, to a reordered version of the **Li ji** that may have been intended to prescribe for state rituals.

Even more than **Fang Xuanling**, Wei Zheng was committed to urging Confucian policies on the emperor. He earned a reputation for directness in criticising any feature of Taizong's conduct that he considered did not conform to his ideals. Such was his integrity that Taizong generally accepted his remonstrations, with the result that he was idealised as exemplifying the prestigious minister–emperor relationship. He used historical precedent to urge Taizong to exemplify austerity, openness, restraint over grandiose projects, lenient punishments and willingness to accept remonstration.

Like Fang Xuanling, Wei Zheng has left little indication of his views on religious belief at the personal level. His Confucianism is, like Fang's, characteristically medieval in its focus on policies, institutions and compilatory scholarship.

Reference: Wechsler, 1974.

DAVID McMULLEN

Wen 文

The word *wen* defies any specific translation. A central concept of Chinese civilisation since Western Zhou times (1045?–771 BCE), it has continuously changed along with the development of cultural paradigms, meaning different things in different contexts and periods. Defined in the dictionary *Shuowen jiezi* 說文解字 (100 CE) as 'crossing lines that represent interlacing patterns' (*cuohua* 錯畫也, 象交文), *wen* in Zhou times referred to aesthetic patterns like those in textiles, tattoos, on bronze vessels, or, acoustically, of melodies. By extension, it denoted 'refinement' or 'cultural accomplishment' and the appearance of ritual form and demeanour; as such, it was used in posthumous titles already in Western Zhou

times. The dichotomies of *wen* (civility) versus *wu* 武 (martiality), and *wen* (refinement) versus *zhi* 質 (substance) point at the broader implications of 'civil culture' or 'civilisation' that were understood to distinguish the Zhou both historically from their predecessors and culturally from non-Chinese peoples. From very early on, *wen* also meant 'writing', 'written character', 'writing(s)' and 'culture' in general. In the **Lunyu** (*Analects*), Confucius says he has embodied in himself 'this culture [of the Ancients]' *siwen* 斯文 (9: 5).

Only after a long, gradual process from Eastern Zhou through Late Han times (771 BCE–220 CE), when writing finally became the most prestigious emblem of cultural expression, did *wen*, together with compounds like *wenzhang* 文章, *wencai* 文彩, or *wenxue* 文學, come to be primarily understood in terms of refined writing and the learning of canonical texts. In the late period of the Former Han dynasty (206 BCE–8 CE), at a time when the first major imperial dynasty had long passed its political, military, and cultural zenith, influential scholars and statesmen like the chancellor **Kuang Heng** drew on the old discussion of refinement vs. substance (see **Lunyu** 6: 18, 12: 8) in order to propose a new classicism be adopted at court. Accusing contemporary Han ritual practice as being excessively 'ornate' (*wen*) and not in accord with the ancient ideas of substantial simplicity, as they were allegedly espoused in the classical canon, scholars now made the written canon the ultimate standard of ritual practice, further contributing to the shift in importance from ritual to textual *wen*. According to Kuang Heng and other conservative ritualists of his times, the return to the authentic and sincere ritual forms of antiquity was both a cultural and political necessity.

This cultural shift towards the primacy of the written text was accompanied by a reinterpretation of the *wen* of the pre-Confucian culture-heroes who now became credited with texts. In Han times, Confucius himself was finally related to all the Five Classics (**Wu jing**) either as author, compiler or commentator. The postface to the *Shuowen jiezi* significantly expanded earlier ideas about the origin of writing that had been formulated in the 'Appended Remarks' (*Xici*) commentary to the *Yi jing*: according to the *Shuowen jiezi* postface, Chinese graphs derived from the *Yi jing* trigrams and, with them, ultimately from natural patterns. In Six Dynasties times, e.g., in the first chapter of the **Wenxin diaolong**, the cosmological explanation of the script was extended to the nature of refined literature (*wen*). Cosmic patterns (*wen*) were associated with the human patterns (*wen*) of the written literary text (*wen*); these patterns of literary form, like syntactic and semantic parallelism, were now celebrated as directly resonating with cosmological principles, such as the complementary pair of yin and yang (see **yin–yang**). The formal variety of refined literature became the primary representation of *wen*, as such both echoing and replacing the multifold appearances of ritual aesthetics in Zhou and early imperial times. In a technical sense, as reflected in the genre theory of the *Wenxin diaolong, wen* now specifically denoted rhymed forms of literature (as opposed to unrhymed forms, *bi* 筆). Along with the discovery of the tonal nature of the Chinese language in the sixth century, new forms of parallelistic prose and poetry were developed, and elaborate formal rules for the composition of highly intricate verse were designed at the southern courts of the Qi (479–502) and Liang (502–557) dynasties, finally resulting in the form of Tang regulated verse (*lüshi* 律詩).

Already in the early decades of the Tang dynasty (618–907), voices like those of **Wei Zheng** and Chen Zi'ang 陳子昂 (661–702 *zi* Boyu 伯玉) condemned the formal ornateness (*wen*) and lack of moral instruction in the literary style that the Tang had inherited from the southern dynasties. Both Wei and Chen evoked the rhetoric of Warring States and Han discussions on music and the old topos of the decline of **Shi jing** (*Book of Poetry*) style poetry to bemoan that 'the Way

(*dao*) of literature (*wenzhang*) has been in decline for five hundred years' (Chen Zi'ang). Such views continued to be proposed by prominent scholars like Li Hua 李華 (d. *c.* 769; *zi* Xiashu 遐叔), Dugu Ji 獨孤及 (725–777; *zi* Zhizhi 至之), or Liang Su 梁肅 (753–793; *zi* Jingzhi 敬之 and Kuanzhong 寬中), all of whom insisted on the importance of literature (*wen*) for the government and moral instruction of the people. But it was not until the late eighth or early ninth century, when under the leadership of **Han Yu** a new powerful ideology of 'ancient style literature' (*guwen* 古文; not to be confused with the notion of *guwen* as 'old text' versions of the Classics), favouring discursive prose genres over poetic forms, gained prominence. Perceiving of the virtual collapse of the Tang empire after the An Lushan (d. 757) Rebellion as a deep civilisational crisis, Han Yu argued that the decline of Chinese culture had resulted from the strength of foreign cultural influences and the religious ideologies of Daoism and Buddhism. Condemning – like others before him – Six Dynasties and Tang excesses of literary form on the expense of moral substance, he requested a return to the sincerity, clarity and moral didacticism of the writings from the 'Three Dynasties' Xia, Shang and Zhou as well as from the Han in order to revive the Confucian Way (*dao*) through its main cultural expression in the form of the literary text (*wen*). Han's friend **Liu Zongyuan** maintained that one should 'illuminate the Way by means of literature (*wen*)' (*wen yi ming dao* 文以明道); two centuries later, the **dao xue** philosopher **Zhou Dunyi** coined the famous formula that 'literature is the means to convey the Way' (*wen yi zai dao* 文以載道). Such views about the centrality of literary expression for the promotion of the Confucian Way were not uncontested among Song thinkers; the influential **Cheng Yi** is known for his opinion that literary expression is 'harmful' (*hai* 害) to the Way.

Despite the Neo-Confucian ambivalence about literary *wen* (and about the position

Han Yu had been granted in the transmission of the Way), Han's *guwen* ideal was embraced by many of the best writers, scholars and statesmen since Song times (960–1279). Already during the Song, ancient style literature anthologies began to appear, in Ming times culminating in the canonisation of the 'eight great masters of Tang and Song [literature]' with Tang Shunzhi's 唐順之 (1507–1560; *zi* Yingde 應德) *Jingchuan wenbian* 荊川文編. Collections of *guwen* prose, enshrining a conservative and orthodox notion of *wen vis-à-vis* both more formalistic literary trends on the one side, and the rise of vernacular genres on the other, enjoyed broad circulation as textbooks, celebrating the Tang and Song revival of ancient literary and moral culture. The most influential of all these anthologies, reprinted in many editions and continued through follow-up compilations still in Republican times, was Yao Nai's 姚鼐 (1732–1815; *zi* Jichuan 姬傳) *Guwenci leizuan* 古文辭類纂 of 1779. This anthology for the first time arranged *guwen* texts not chronologically but on the basis of a pragmatic genre theory of literary prose in which literary forms were defined according to their didactic or situational use, thereby emphasising the social and political significance of literary *wen* for traditional Chinese culture (*wen*) as a whole.

References: Bol, 1992; Kern, 2001; von Falkenhausen, 1996; de Weerdt, 1999.

MARTIN KERN

Wen Tianxiang 文天祥

1236–1283

(*zi* Lüshan 履善 or Songrui 宋瑞, *hao* Wenshan 文山 or Xinguo gong 信國公)

Wen Tianxiang was a native of Jishui 吉水 (Jiangxi). His ancestors belonged to the middle-class gentry and were quite wealthy but never held higher official posts. His original name was Yunsun 雲孫, but he participated in the local district exam-

ination (*xiangju* 鄉舉) under his style (*zi*) Tianxiang which became his name thereafter. In 1256 he obtained the *jinshi* degree. Impressed by the strong patriotism of Wen's examination essay, Emperor Lizong (r. 1225–64) personally chose him to win the top honours.

Later, his entire life was devoted to the resistance against the Mongols, who at that time were about to conquer all of South China. During 1275–1279 he led many unsuccessful military campaigns against the Mongol troops. In 1279 he was captured near the last bastion of the Song at Yashan 崖山 (Guangdong) and was – in spite of his attempt to starve himself to death on the way – deported to Yanjing 燕京 (today Beijing). After being kept in prison there for several years, he was put to death to prevent the possibility of a Chinese uprising.

During the following centuries he was commonly worshipped as a patriotic hero. But only in 1844 was his tablet placed in the western wing of the Temple of Confucius (***Kong miao***). Sacrificial services have continued to take place until today.

Wen Tianxiang's complete writings are collected in the *Wen Wenshan quanji* 文文山全集 (*Complete works of Wen Tianxiang*).

Reference: Brown, 1986.

CHRISTIAN SOFFEL

Wenhua yishi yu daode lixing
文化意識與道德理性
(*Cultural Consciousness and Moral Rationality*)

In this two-volume work **Tang Junyi** 唐君毅 (1909–78) presented in 1957 his own systematic philosophy of culture based on Confucian understandings of 'moral rationality' (*daode lixing* 道德理性) and a revised account of 'cultural consciousness' (*wenhua yishi* 文化意識) informed by German idealist traditions and modern cultural histories. While Tang recognised that cultural activities are concretely objectified in many expressions, it is cultured human consciousness that is their source. Arguing that moral rationality is the ground for all forms of cultured human consciousness and their related cultural activities, Tang developed detailed accounts of three realms of cultural activities – social (family, economy, government), pure (religion, sciences, arts) and conserving (physical, military, legal and educational) activities – to demonstrate his claim. Most of these activities only involve moral consciousness as an unselfconscious (*fei zijue* 非自覺) and therefore latent (*qianfu* 潛伏) stimulus and value orientation, while religious consciousness approaches moral rationality from a 'trans-selfconscious' (*chao zijue* 超自覺) metaphysical perspective. Only moral activity motivated by moral consciousness is a fully selfconscious cultural activity.

Tang argues that when moral consciousness is expressed in moral behaviour, it becomes a cultural resource for creativity and renewal in all cultural spheres, here following themes found in the teachings of **Mengzi**, **Zhu Xi**, **Wang Shouren**, and **Wang Fuzhi**. Ultimately, cultures rise up because moral consciousness is creatively realised in cultural activitities fully justified by moral rationality, but they begin to decline because the creative impulse in moral consciousness is lost or de-emphasised due to preferences for cultural enjoyments.

References: Fang & Li, 1995: vol. III, 50–72; Fang & Zheng, 1995: 242–6.

LAUREN PFISTER

Wenwu zhi dao 文武之道
(The Way of King Wen and King Wu)

In the *Analects* (**Lunyu**) 19: 22, Zigong (**Duanmu Si**), a disciple of Confucius, responds to a question concerning the identity of Confucius' own teacher. Zigong replied that Confucius studied with no particular teacher but learned from everyone, since all people in some measure embodied the Way of Wen and Wu.

This way is understood here to mean the Way of sage rulership and learning that was perceived to have been modelled by King Wen (r. 1099?–1050? BCE) and his eldest son and successor King Wu (r. 1049/45?–1043? BCE), the two founding rulers of the Zhou dynasty. 'Wen' means 'culture' or 'learning', and by Confucius' time the very name of King Wen was synonymous with a repository of idealised Zhou cultural ideals that included the securing of the Mandate of Heaven (**Tian ming**), the establishment of benevolent rule, and the triumph of virtue over wantonness (the latter a quality the Zhou attributed to the Shang culture they had just conquered). King Wen's skills as a military strategist may have been more noteworthy than his learning, but he is nonetheless accredited with shaping an early version of the *Book of Changes* (**Yi jing**). His prowess as a sire of the Zhou culture who sits posthumously at the right hand of the Lord (**di**) is lauded in the elegiac hymn 'King Wen' (ode 235) of the **Shi jing**. His son, King Wu, is praised in the following ode (ode 236). 'Wu' means 'martial', and the military victories King Wu won at the famous battle of Muye, which strategically established the success of the Zhou claim to sovereignty, are described there.

References: Ames & Rosemont, 1998: 19: 22; Legge, 1985c, odes 235 and 236; Lewis, 1999; Loewe & Shaughnessy, 1999.

DEBORAH SOMMER

Wenxin diaolong 文心雕龍
(*How Writers Compose and the Elegant Rhetoric they Employ*)

Liu Xie 劉勰 (466?–536?) was a fervent Buddhist who spent much of his creative life in monasteries and finally became a monk. The rigorous organisation of his masterpiece, the *Wenxin diaolong* (*How Writers Compose and the Elegant Rhetoric they*

Employ), is unique in China and is probably the result of his long acquaintance with Buddhist logic, but there is no other Buddhist influence in this work. On the contrary, Liu Xie insists in the first four sections that the greatest literature be thoroughly founded in the Confucian Canon. For him Confucianism is the 'essential point, the key' (*shuniu* 樞杻) that allows a true understanding of all literature.

Reference: Kôzen Hiroshi, 1970.

DONALD HOLZMAN

Wenxuan wang 文宣王
(Exalted King of Culture)

Confucius, who had held the title of duke since 1 BCE, was elevated to 'Exalted King of Culture' in 739 CE. The liturgy was altered in 723 when royal four racks of hanging bells and chimes were used in the sacrifices to him rather than three used in sacrifices to dukes, thereby implying Confucius' higher ritual status. His title of king in 739 made this higher status explicit and his ritual statue was turned facing south in the two imperial Directorates of Education, the direction faced by the Son of Heaven. Yan Hui, who was already called the second sage (**Ya sheng** 亞聖) since 720, was ennobled as Duke of Yan 兗公, the savants as marquises, and Zeng Shen as earl. The descendants of Confucius were given the title of 'Exalted Duke of Culture' (*Wenxuan Gong* 文宣公).

THOMAS A. WILSON

Wenyi zaidao 文以載道
(The aim of literature is to transmit the Way)

'The aim of literature is to transmit the Way [of the Ancients]', a near-quotation from the twenty-eighth paragraph of the '*Wenci*' 文辭, 'Elegant Words', of the **Tong shu** 通書, *All-Embracing Book* (also known as the *Yi* 易 *Tong shu*, All-Embracing Book on

the *Yi jing*), by **Zhou Dunyi**. This phrase has entered the language and has come to be used as a general description of didactic and moralistic literature, and has been applied both to traditional Confucian thinkers as well as to more recent socialist realists.

DONALD HOLZMAN

Wu 物
(Things)

Wu is a common Chinese word with a range of meanings similar to the English word 'thing/s'. Its modern compounds include *ren wu* 人物 (personage), *wen wu* 文物 (cultural artifacts), *dongwu* 動物 (animals) and especially the inclusive *wan wu* 萬物 (the 10,000 or myriad things in the world). In Confucian thought, the focus of interpretive reflection on *wu* has been a passage from the *Great Learning* (**Da xue**) about investigation of things (*gewu* 格物, see **gewu zhizhi**). In this phrase as elsewhere, *wu* is often glossed as 'affairs' (*shi* 事) or 'the external situation' (*waijing* 外境), showing that there is no hard demarcation between concrete objects and their matrices.

The basic Confucian approach to *wu* is realistic; there are few worries about the limits of sense perception that would correspond to Immanuel Kant's mysterious and inaccessible 'thing-in-itself'. However, in Confucian writings as also in Buddhist or Daoist sources, *wu* sometimes stands for problematic attitudes or desires that are stimulated by contact with things. In **Mengzi** 6A:15, **Mengzi** remarks that people become petty because '*wu jiao wu*' 物交物 ('material things act on the material senses' or 'the physical senses interact with physical things'). To avoid prejudice, **Shao Yong** advocated viewing things on their own terms (*yiwu guanwu* 以物觀物). **Zhang Zai** said in the *Western Inscription* (**Xi ming**), 'The people and I are close kin, the *wu* and I are companions'. The fullest realisation of this companionship was expressed by the

Neo-Confucian ideal of 'forming one body with all things' (***wanwu yiti*** 萬物一體).

References: Chan, Wing-tsit, 1963d: 59; Chen Lai, 1993: 103–5; Wu Yi, 1986: 52; Zhang Zai, 1985: 62.

THOMAS SELOVER

Wu chang 五常
(Five constant virtues)

The five fundamental Confucian virtues are ***ren*** (humaneness, benevolence), ***yi*** (rightness, righteousness), ***li*** (ritual, propriety), ***zhi*** (intelligence, wisdom), and ***xin*** (trust, faithfulness). Confucius took *ren* to be the most central in his overall philosophy. In the *Analects* 9: 29 and 14: 28, Confucius also mentions humaneness and wisdom as two of the three ways of the men of quality (*junzi*). **Mengzi** grouped the first four together in the *Mengzi* 6A: 6. In the *Book of Rites*, it is stated that 'The ancient Kings (in framing their music) laid its foundations in the feelings and nature of men; they examined (the notes) by the measures (for the length and quality of each); and adapted it to express the meaning of the ceremonies (in which it was to be used.) They (thus) brought it into harmony with the energy that produces life (***sheng***), and to give expression to the performance of the 'five regular constituents of virtues' (*wu chang*).

It was **Dong Zhongshu** who explicitly added the fifth element, *xin*, and related the *wu chang* to the Five Phases (*wu xing*) in his philosophy. Referred to as 'five virtues' by Dong in his *Duice* 對策, the five constant virtues are said to be the Way (*dao*) to proper self-cultivation and moderation of one's behaviour. Later, Dong's theories were taken up by the later Han dynasty scholar Ban Gu 班固 (32–92) in his ***Baihu Tong***, where the five are termed *wu xing* 五性, the five dimensions of human nature. The Five Constant Virtues are often paired together with the Three Cardinal Guides (***san gang***) and termed *gang chang* 綱常.

References: Chan, Wing-tsit, 1963d: 279; Legge, 1966: 108; Morohashi, 1960.

TODD CAMERON THACKER

Wu Cheng 吳澄
1249–1333
(*zi* Youqing 幼清, *hao* Caolu 草廬)

Wu received his education during the Southern Song (1127–1279) and was barely thirty when the Mongols extinguished that regime. Born into a poor family with a scholarly tradition in Fuzhou 撫州 prefecture in Jiangxi, his precocity was matched only by his diligence: at an early age he memorised substantial portions of ***Lunyu***, ***Mengzi***, and the Five Classics (***Wu jing***). His early training was in the **Zhu Xi** lineage *via* Rao Lu 饒魯 (*fl.* 1256), the teacher of Wu's mentor **Cheng Ruoyong**. But Wu also studied with Cheng Shaokai 程邵開 (1212–1280), who attempted to harmonise the teachings of Zhu Xi and **Lu Jiuyuan** at the Academy of the Unity of *Dao* (*Daoyi shuyuan* 道一書院) he established in Jiangxi. In these early years, Wu wrote on the transmission of the Way, the *dao tong*, feeling that he had a responsibility to perpetuate Confucian principles and criticised classical study that overemphasised exegesis; these themes were central to Wu's intellectual development.

Wu failed to pass the *jinshi* examination in 1271, and after the Mongols invaded Jiangxi, Wu's sympathies with the resistance forces under **Wen Tianxiang** led to seclusion with his friend Zheng Song 鄭松 (d. 1307). Wu worked on the ritual classics, and he and Zheng discussed ideas of dynastic legitimacy, *zheng tong* 正統. In 1286, his boyhood friend Cheng Jufu 程鉅夫 (1249–1318) searched out scholars to serve in Dadu 大都 (Beijing) on behalf of Khubilai. Wu declined, but Cheng had the commentaries Wu wrote while in retreat transcribed and disseminated through the Directorate of Education, which made Wu famous in scholarly circles.

Refusing local appointments in favour of private teaching, at the age of sixty Wu became Proctor of the Directorate of Education 國子監丞 in Beijing in 1309 and Director of Studies in 1311. He devised a four-part curriculum there emphasising Classical Learning (*jing xue*), concrete practice (*xing shi* 行實), literary arts (*wenyi* 文藝), and administration (*zhi shi* 治事) and was part of the debate over the restoration of the examination system under Emperor Ayurbarwada (Renzong, r. 1311–1320). As a fourth generation disciple of Zhu Xi, Wu supported a curriculum that included Zhu's commentaries on the Four Books (*Si shu*), but he felt that a programme confined solely to this, or one based on *belles-lettres*, was too narrow and the competitive ambience too stifling. As a southerner, and especially one with ties to southern Daoists such as Wu Quanjie 吳全節 (1269–1346), who supported him while he was in Beijing, Wu was outside of the Northern intellectual establishment that owed its allegiance to **Xu Heng**. Moreover, Wu supported the ideas of **Lu Jiuyuan** and criticised the exegetical emphasis of Xu's disciples. Wu left precipitately in 1312, issuing a statement that stressed a Zhu–Lu balance between textual study and moral intro-spection that endeared him even less to scholars in the north.

For the next twenty years or more, Wu worked on commentaries ('observations', *zuanyan* 攢言) on the *Book of Changes* and the *Book of Documents*. Between 1323 and 1325 he served as Chancellor of the Hanlin Academy in Beijing, undertaking the compilation of the *Yingzong shilu* 英宗實錄 (*Veritable Record of the Yingzong emperor* (Shidebala, r. 1320–1323)). In his last five years, he completed commentaries on the *Spring and Autumn Annals* and the *Book of Rites*.

Wu's classical work was original and rivalled Zhu Xi's. He amplified Zhu's doubts about the Old Text (*guwen* 古文) portions of the *Book of Documents*, gave equal status to the the *Guliang* 穀梁, *Gongyang* 公羊 and *Zuo* 佐 commentaries on the *Spring and Autumn Annals*, established coherent editions of the riutal classics and wrote commentaries on the Daoist classics. But it is in his own philosophical writings that Wu was most original. Wu pursued metaphysical inquiry to its limits in investigating the Supreme Ultimate, **tai ji**, concluding that there are limits to understanding the universal process. One should explore the moral universe experientially, transforming the nature through the mind in moral act. The **dao** must be crystallised within oneself (*ning dao* 凝道), and Wu criticises his intellectual forbears, **Chen Chun** and Rao Lu, who became bogged down in exegesis, claiming that it took him four decades to achieve a breakthrough, a moral enlightenment.

He envisaged a synthesis of Zhu and Lu and accorded Lu as prominent a place in the Neo-Confucian pantheon as he did Zhu. His appropriation of Lu's ideas, which blended well with his introspective tendencies and Daoist interests, kept the emphasis on interiority alive in Yuan and into the Ming and Qing, and he anticipated the development of the Learning of the Heart/Mind (*Xin xue*) in Ming thinkers such as **Zhan Roshui**, **Chen Xianzhang**, and **Wang Shouren**, who had a special affintiy for Wu's ideas; in the Qing, Li Fu 李紱 (1675–1750) also championed Wu, especially when he was attacked by orthodox thinkers who felt that he should not have served the Yuan. The attention paid in the Ming and Qing eras to Wu's classical studies, his philosophy and his career indicates that he was one of the most influential scholar–thinkers in the Neo-Confucian tradition.

References: Chan Hok-lam, 1981: 68; Chang, Carsun, 1957: I, 342–6; Chen Gaohua, 1983: 282–5; Chen Yuan, 1966: 32–4, 219, 228–9; Forke, 1938: 290–7; Gedalecia, 1981, 186–213; 1982: 279–326, 1999 and 2000; Lao Yan-shuan, 1981: 114, 118; Liu Ts'un-yan, 1986: 521, 524–5, 533–5, 540–2; *Song Yuan xuean*, 1966: 92: 1a–58a (1440–

70); Sun K'o-k'uan, 'Yu Chi', in Langlois, 1981: 233, 240; Yu Ying-shih, 1986: 228; *Yuan shi* 1976: 171.

DAVID GEDALECIA

Wu ji 無極
(Non-Ultimate)

Wu ji is an ancient philosophical concept, originally Daoist, but spanning various schools and applications in Chinese thought. Non-Ultimate is by definition beyond description and transcends human limits of understanding, but it has been characterised as the original, formless source of the universe, or in Laozi's words, 'a shape that has no shape, an image that is without substance' (*Daode jing* 14). For Laozi it is the simple state of the universe, while for Zhuangzi, it is its infinite state. *Wu ji* was introduced into Confucian philosophy through the intermingling of Daoist theory. In **Zhou Dunyi**'s *Taijitu shuo*, the Great Ultimate (*tai ji*) is said to come from the Non-Ultimate, but this is contradictory to the predominence of 'Being' (*you* 有) in Confucian thought, as opposed to the non-being (*wu* 無) foundation of Daoism, sparking various debates on the matter by **Zhu Xi**, among others.

References: Chan, Wing-tsit, 1967; Morohashi, 1960.

TODD CAMERON THACKER

Wu jing 五經
(The Five Classics)

Wu jing are the Five Classics of *Yi* (*Changes*), **Shi** (*Poetry*), **Shu** (*Documents*), **Li** (*Rites*), and **Chunqiu** (*Spring and Autumn Annals*). The concept developed in Former Han times, apparently derived from the **Liu jing** (Six Classics) or **Liu yi** (Six Arts) but leaving out the (presumably lost) Classic of *Music*. According to the **Han shu**, **Han Wudi** restricted imperially sponsored scholarship to the Five Classics and established academic chairs (**Wu jing boshi**) for their instruction in 136 BCE, making their study 'official learning' (*guan xue* 官學). While the term *Wu jing* is not attested beyond doubt before 51 BCE, the Five Classics remained the core of the later expanding Confucian canon.

Reference: Nylan, 2001.

MARTIN KERN

Wu jing boshi 五經博士
(Academicians of the Five Classics)

Han Wudi (r. 141–87 BCE) accepted **Dong Zhongshu**'s recommendation to make Confucianism the state ideology. Confucian Classics therefore became the core content of Imperial Academy (*Tai xue*) education. In 136 BCE, Five Confucian Classics (**Wu jing**) were chosen for teaching: they were the *Book of Poetry*, the *Book of Documents*, the *Book of Changes*, the *Book of Rites* and the *Spring and Autumn Annals*. Each Classic was represented by one dominant school of interpretation (commentary), taught by one academician (*boshi*). Subsequent development saw the addition of more schools, so that in the beginning of the Later Han (25–220 CE), a total of fourteen (some sources suggest fifteen) schools were inducted and the number of academicians reached as many as seventy at some point.

During the Later Han, the *Classic of Music* was also established as a course and had its *boshi*, but this Classic never succeeded to win universal acceptance as a genuine ancient text. The term, academicians of Six Classics (**Liu jing**), was thus used only briefly.

After the Han, the name, *boshi* 博士, was no longer used exclusively for teachers of Classical Learning in the Imperial Academy. The words of *Wu jing* (Five Classics) were less frequently used when referring to the academcians who continued to teach various versions of commentaries in the Academy until they ultimately lost their status as the sanctioned authority of the Classics. In late Imperial times in China, the title became honorific, usually given to the descendants of respected Confucian worthies.

The Han *boshi* were limited to those of fifty and above. There were also methods for evaluating their qualification, of which, however, we know next to nothing.

References: Pi Xirui, 1959; Wang Guowei, 1956; Yang Hongnian, 1982.

THOMAS H.C. LEE

Wu jing yiyi 五經異義
(*Different Interpretations of the Five Classics*)

Xu Shen is usually known for having written the *Shuowen jiezi*. Yet he did produce another work, namely the *Wu jing yiyi* in which he listed different opinions concerning institutional and intellectual problems of his time brought forward by competing schools of scholarship during the Han (206 BCE–220 CE). The *Wu jing yiyi* was lost sometime after the Tang, but about 150 passages of it were recovered by Qing scholars mainly from the subcommentaries to the Thirteen Classics dating from the Tang and the Song. Fortunately, these commentaries and some encyclopedias quoted extensively from the *Wu jing yiyi*.

A full entry in the *Wu jing yiyi* usually consisted of three items. Firstly, it is an opinion associated with a so-called '*jin*' (new) tradition which was officially recognised during the Han; which secondly is followed by a '*gu*' (old) opinion, in most cases related to the *Zuo zhuan*, the **Zhou li**, **Guwen Shang shu** or the **Mao shi**, and thirdly is then Xu Shen's own estimation which usually, but not always, was in accordance with the 'old' opinions. According to authorities writing in the nineteenth and the twentieth century, 'old' and 'new' refer to scriptures which were in the former case written down before the reform of the writing system

under the Qin (221–206 BCE) and after it in the latter case.

At the end of the Han **Zheng Xuan** refuted many of Xu Shen's opinions, and as early as during the Tang the text of the *Wu jing yiyi* was transmitted together with Zheng's refutations under the title of *Bo* 駁 (*Refutations to*) *Wu jing yiyi*. Although we cannot know whether *Zuo zhuan*, *Zhou li* and *Mao shi* were, as supposed by Chinese scholars at the turn of the twentieth century, transmitted in the old characters abolished under the Qin, it is clear from frequent references in the **Hou Han shu** (*History of the Later Han*) that these texts together with the *Guwen Shang shu* were considered as a group containing materials which differed sharply from those contained in the '*jinwen*' texts. At least as far as the representation of Xu Shen is concerned, it seems that the 'old' texts were used as a basis for arguing in favour of the political system inherited from the Qin, as opposed to a return to the older system of the Zhou. The arguments of this reformist faction are brandished as 'new' in the *Wu jing yiyi*. This recompiled text is our most important source for the so-called Old Text/New Text Controversy of the Han.

References: Liao Ping, 1886; Miller, 1977–8: 1–21; van Ess, 1993.

HANS VAN ESS

Wu jing zhengyi 五經正義
(*The Correct Meanings of the Five Classics*)

In the early part of the Tang dynasty, Taizong (r. 626–649) was compelled to order the compilation of orthodox standard commentaries on the canonical books, because there existed so many different versions of commentary upon the Confucian Classics (*jing* 經). Taizong, eventually, commissioned the great scholar **Yan Shigu** to establish definitive texts of the canonical books, and in 638 ordered **Kong Yingda** and other scholars such as Yan Shigu,

Sima Caizhang 司馬才章, Wang Gong 王恭 and Wang Tan 王談 to write detailed sub-commentaries upon them. A first draft of these was completed in 642, but further work was necessary, and revision continued until well into the 650s. These texts and subcommentaries known as the *Correct Meanings of the Five Classics* (*Wu jing zhengyi*) have remained authoritative, and provided the foundation for classical Confucian education throughout the Tang. However, they were mainly used for the official school text and people tended to memorise them only for the official examinations. It was an effective way of unifying scholarly thought, but owing to this, during the Tang dynasty, new and progressive scholarly tendencies were not fostered. At the same time it was not a good method to recover the spirit of ancient Confucianism. In Tang Gaozong's reign (649–683) the final revision of the standard subcommentaries on the *Wu jing zhengyi* came into being. It consists of 180 *juan* (volumes).

Reference: Fung Yu-Lan, 1952.

M.H. KIM

Wu lun 五倫
(Five Human Relations)

The exposition of the five human relations can be found in the **Mengzi** (3A: 4): love (*qin*) between father and son (*fuzi*), duty (*yi*) between ruler and subject (*jun chen*), distinction (*bie* 別) between husband and wife (*fu fu*), precedence (*xu* 序) of the old over the young (*zhang you*), and faithfulness (*xin*) between friends (*peng you* 朋友). The three relations of ruler and the ruled, father and son and husband and wife known as the Three Cardinal Guides (*san gang*). Though naturally there are other relations of great social importance, for example, truth between teacher (*shi*) and student, and authority between officer and soldier, they can be derived from the existence of these fundamental five. Later in the *Mengzi* 4A: 12

the foundation on which the five human relations rests is said to be faithfulness/trust (*xin*), an essential element for one's moral cultivation since if one is truly faithful and sincere, then one can transform oneself and others. Without it, however, one cannot please one's parents, nor win the trust of friends, and ultimately one then cannot understand what is good.

The ten duties (*shi yi* 十義) which follow from these five relations are a practical derivation of how the mutual relations will be manifest in society. They are as follows. The father cherishes (*ci* 慈) his son, while the son in turn is filial (*xiao*). The ruler favours (*en* 恩) the subject, while the subject is loyal (*zhong*); the husband is dutiful (*yi*) to his wife, while the wife obeys or listens (*ting* 听); the elder is gracious (*hui* 惠) to the junior, and the junior is obedient (*shun* 順); and lastly, the friend (*peng* 朋) gives (*shi* 施) to the friend (*you* 友), while the latter repays (*bao* 報) this debt. In the Ming dynasty, Shen Yi 沈易 (?–?) edited an education manual for children entitled the *Book of Five Human Relations* (*Wulunshu* 五倫書).

References: Lau, 1970; Morohashi, 1960.

TODD CAMERON THACKER

Wu Shidao 吳師道
1283–1344
(*zi* Zhengchuan 正傳)

Wu hailed from Jinhua prefecture in Zhejiang. In his youth, he wrote poetry and studied the writings of the late Song Confucian **Zhen Dexiu**, which motivated him to become a scholar. He was awarded a *jinshi* degree in 1321 and served in the Directorate of Education 國子監 and the Board of Rites.

Wu's mentors were the late Song Jinhua Neo-Confucians **Jin Lüxiang** and Xu Qian 許謙 (1270–1337), who declined to serve the Yuan but who became influential teachers. They were both critical of the Lu Jiuyuan school and of Buddhism, and they transmitted the teachings of **Zhu Xi** to their students (including Wu), shifting the emphasis from metaphysics (*li* 理) to concrete political issues. For Xu, this emphasis implied the Confucianisation of the law, and Wu was deeply influenced by this Jinhua brand of Neo-Confucian thought.

Wu wrote studies of the *Book of Changes* (*Yi jing*), *Book of History* (*Shang shu*), *Book of Poetry* (*Shi jing*), and the *Intrigues of the Warring States* (*Zhanguoce* 戰國策). But he is best known for his study of the commentary on the *Spring and Autumn Annals* by **Hu Anguo**, the Northern Song Confucian, who had viewed the *Annals* as a kind of penal code. Wu's interpretation of Hu's commentary, which was influenced by the ideas he inherited from Jin and Xu, became the standard for the civil service examinations that were reinstituted in 1315.

Wu's son, Wu Chen 吳沈 (d. 1386) followed in his father's scholarly footsteps. He became one of the four Jinhua masters in the early Ming period, along with Zhan Tong 詹同 (*fl.* 1350–1374), Song Lian 宋濂 (1310–1381), and Yue Shaofeng 樂韶鳳 (*fl.* 1355–1380), and served in the Hanlin Academy and the Directorate of Education.

References: Liu Ts'un-yan, 1986: 536; *Song–Yuan xuean*, 1966: 82; Sun Kekuan, 1976; *Yuan shi*, 1976: 190.

DAVID GEDALECIA

Wu Tinghan 吳廷翰
1489–1559
(*zi* Chongbo 崇伯, *hao* Suyuan 蘇原)

One of several materialists of the Ming dynasty (1368–1644), Wu Tinghan was actually more influential in Tokugawa Japan than in his native China. In recent years he has received attention in Mainland China as an early advocate of materialist monism. Wu was a native of Wuwei 無為 in Nan Zhili (modern-day Anhui) who attained the *jinshi* degree in 1521. After serving at several posts in the Board of Personnel, Wu incurred the displeasure of his superiors and was sent to provincial posts in remote Guangdong.

At first a follower of **Zhu Xi**, Wu later became inspired by **Wang Tingxiang**'s theories, sharply criticising both Cheng–Zhu Learning of Principle and **Wang Shouren**'s *xin xue* (Learning of the Heart/Mind). Wu did not completely reject Zhu Xi's views, but he did emphasise the central importance and priority of *qi* (material force), equating it with *li* (principle). Wu's critique of Zhu Xi, entitled *Jizhai manlu* 吉齋漫錄 (*Jottings from the Auspicious Studio*), was written in 1543.

Along with Wang Tingxiang and **Luo Qinshun**, Wu Tinghan greatly influenced such Japanese Neo-Confucians as **Kaibara Ekiken**, whose thought most closely resembled that of Wu. Moreover, **Itô Jinsai**, **Ogyû Sorai** and other scholars associated with the *kogaku* (Ancient Learning) School developed their ideas by addressing the monism and naturalism of Wu, Wang Tingxian and Luo Qinshun. Itô Jinsai, for example, was at first inspired by Zhu Xi but eventually became discontented with him and in turn drew from Wu Tinghan.

References: de Bary & Bloom, 1979: 231–305; Nosco, 1984: 138–65.

STEVEN MILES

Wu-wei 無為
(Non-action)

Wu-wei is normally viewed as a Daoist concept, but scholars note echoes of the doctrine in Confucius' account of the ruler who 'governs' with the force of example, simply 'being in place'. Laozi's famous paradoxical *wu-wei* slogan exhibits a puzzle in the concept. To obey an instruction to *wu-wei* is to *wei* 為. We can illuminate the puzzle if we focus on what *wei* (do:deem) means. The sound *wei* is used for several semantically linked characters. One *wei* (is only) is an ancient is-verb and another translates well as 'to call' or 'to mean'. It is the most common way to fix reference. The *wei* in the phrase *wu-wei* is the key verb used in constructing ancient Chinese belief contexts. English 'X believes that S(ubject) is P(redicate)' becomes X *yi* (with) S(ubject) *wei* (deems it) P(redicate). English X knows that S(ubject) is P(redicate) (when P is nominal) becomes X *zhi* (knows) S(ubject's) *wei* (deems it) P(redicate noun). These facts suggest an implicit confluence of the notions of *deeming, being called,* and *being* of a type/category. Laozi's wider purpose is thus to call social norms of language into question. They interfere with natural spontaneity. Thus we should avoid governing our action by those category distinctions – by *wei*-ing. If we stop *wei*-ing then our actions will be spontaneous and free from social constraint and control. We will be *wei* (doing) without *wei* deeming.

Wei (deem:do) has still another semantic role (usually marked in modern dialects with a tonal change). Translators commonly render this role as 'for the purpose of'. This suggests that social deeming, classifying are guided by some purpose. And finally, that same *wei* (do:deem) with a *ren* (human) radical added, forms a character also pronounced *wei* 偽 which translators typically render as 'artificial' or 'false'. This suggests the distinctions, categories etc. we employ are not 'in nature' but are products of social conventions.

Xunzi exploits these aspects of *wei* as he argues (against **Mengzi**) that moral goodness is *wei* (artificial), not natural (**tian**) and that the sages' moral purposes lay behind the conventions of language when combined with the rituals of Confucianism. Xunzi was, accordingly, quite in favour of *wei*-ing.

Later Neo-Confucians, more in a Mengzi mould, viewed morality as continuous with nature and thus again associated perfect virtue with *wu-wei*, though they disapproved of Laozi's 'quietism'. The rejection of passivity and quietism is even more markedly signalled by the choice of names by the early Modern Confucian reformer, **Kang**

Youwei (Kang 'have deliberate moral action').

References: Hansen, 1983: 24–55, 1992; Lau, tr., 1963.

CHAD HANSEN

Wu xing 五行
(Five Phases or Five Agents)

Though *xing* is often translated 'element', this translation is misleading if by 'element' it is meant an entity of quiescence rather than the dynamic. In Chinese philosophy there are five basic components of the formation of everything in the universe (*wan wu*): wood (*mu* 木), fire (*huo* 火), earth (*tu* 土), metal (*jin* 金) and water (*shui* 水). Each symbolises an indispensable factor for human life, and is utilised as a means of explaining, through its own unique characteristic of material force (**qi**), the source and function of everything which exists in the universe. The character *xing* 行 implies in this case 'mixture', of which each agent 'moves' cyclically and differently from the constant principles of the others, and this can be found in general in nature and specifically in the seasons, and again in general in history and specifically in human affairs.

Later in the Warring States period (475–221 BCE), the school of **Zou Yan** (305–240?) applied the theory of cyclical changes based on the five agents to explain the cyclical aspects of history and the change of the dynasties. Each of the five agents demonstrates a dominant virtue which when rising dominates all natural and human affairs, while in due time it would decline and give way to the virtue of another agent. This 'principle of history' was known as the *wude zhongshi shuo* 五德終始說. The theory of the five agents was later modified in the Han dynasty, when the arrangement of the agents was known as the *wuxing xiangke shuo* 五行相克說. Each of the historical periods was assigned an agent and therefore a particular virtue, for example the rule of Yellow Emperor (Huangdi 黃帝) was dominated by the virtue of earth, which gave way to the virtue of wood in the Xia dynasty, which in turn was replaced by the virtue of metal in the Shang dynasty, which in turn by the virtue of fire of the Zhou, and therefore the changes of dynastic rule were said to be a cyclical sequence in the same way that wood overcomes earth, earth overcomes water, water overcomes fire, fire overcomes metal, metal overcomes wood, and so on.

Dong Zhongshu introduced the theory of the five agents into the Confucian system, by which a theory of Heaven–human correlation was established. The five agents start with wood and end with water, while earth stands at the centre becoming the dominant agent. The five agents not only replace each other (*xiang ke* 相克) but also give rise to each other (*xiang sheng* 相生). The former is used to illustrate the relationship between governmental offices, while the latter is compared to the relationship of father and son. The cyclical relationship of the five agents is not only used to explain the historical changes of dynasties, but also for a new regime to justify its overthrow of the previous one, such as **Wang Mang**'s replacement of the Former Han dynasty, and the Yellow Turbans (a reactionary movement whose adopted colour yellow represented earth) which almost overthrew the Later Han. Throughout the Han, *wu xing* theory was combined with **yin–yang** theory, and the creation of everything in the universe was said to be due to the power of the *wuxing*.

References: Morohashi, 1960; *Yugyo Sajon Pyonchan Wiwonhoe*, 1990.

TODD CAMERON THACKER

Wu Yubi 吳與弼
1391–1469
(*zi* Zipu 子溥, *hao* Kangzhai 康齋)

Wu Yubi was a native of Congren 崇仁 in Mingfu 明撫 Prefecture (modern-day Jiangxi). Wu was born into a scholar family. His father had served as dean of the Directorate of Education (*guozi jian siye* 國子監司業). When he was young, Wu practised composing *shi* and *ci* poetry, as well as historical essays. In 1409 when he was fourteen years old, Wu went with his father to Nanjing, where Wu became a student of the tutor to the imperial family, Yang Pu 楊溥 (1371–1446) of the 'Three Yangs' fame. At this time, Wu, following his father's instructions, engaged in a close reading of **Zhu Xi**'s 1173 text *Records of the Origins of the Yi Luo School of the Cheng Brothers* (*Yi-Luo yuanyuan lu* 伊洛淵源錄).

Through his studies, Wu became deeply engrossed with the teachings of the Cheng Brothers, particularly **Cheng Hao**. As **Huang Zongxi** noted, '(Wu) observed that if the elder Cheng could take pleasure in watching hunting, by inference sages and worthies were also human; who could then say that sagehood could not be acquired by learning?' He also concluded that government service would not hinder his efforts to become a sage. Therefore, Wu publicly abandoned preparation to take the civil service examinations, and instead withdrew to his room for two years of obsessive study. In 1411 his father finally forced Wu to return to his hometown, with the hope that married life would temper his son's fanatical behaviour.

Wu never sought public office nor did he change his eccentric behaviour. Moreover, his approach to self-cultivation was not rooted in textual study, and so his own literary output was limited, aside from his well-known work *Ri Lu* 日錄 (*Daily Record*). Yet Wu's reputation for scholarship spread, and Wu eventually had a number of students who wised to study with the reclusive master. At this point Wu's teachings entered the stream of Neo-Confucian development that would lead to the teachings of Wang Yangming. Wu's students included Lou Liang 婁諒 (1422–1491), the one very likely to teach Wu's teachings to a young Wang, and **Chen Xianzhang**, whose own inward-looking teachings closely resembled Wang and whose best student **Zhan Ruoshui** became a close friend of Wang's.

The late Ming scholar **Liu Zongzhou** would have nothing but praise for Wu Yubi, seeing in the teachings of this reclusive scholar the origins of the Ming period's most important currents of thought. As Liu wrote, 'he did not give himself to writing and publishing but understood the truth of the Way. His words and actions were all peaceful and serene. In what concerns his action in later life, he set a sublime example to the world while remaining content, without any undue display for publicity's sake. Unless he had acquired the Way, how could he have acted so?'

References: Huang Tsung-hsi, 1987: 22, 71, 53–4; Wu & Song, 1992: 1095–6.

JAMES A. ANDERSON

Wu yue 五岳
(The Five Peaks)

The Five Peaks or five sacred mountains, included the eastern **Tai shan** in Shandong; the southern, Hengshan in Hunan; the western Huashan in Shanxi; the northern Hengshan in Hebei, and the central peak of Songshan in Henan. In Han correlative cosmology of *Wu xing* (Five Phases), earthly topography linked to heavenly virtues, and mountains were thought to stabilise the surrounding landscape as a good monarch would do the social world. They also connected Earth (*di*) to Heaven (*tian*), providing a gathering place for the rain-clouds so necessary to good harvests and prosperity in an agricultural civilisation. Buddhist and Daoist temples dot each of these ranges, testifying that they shared a respect for mountains with the state Confucian tradition.

Reference: Chavannes, 1910.

ANGELA ZITO

Wude zhongshi 五德終始
(Cyclical succession of the Five Powers)

In this expression from Qin and Han cosmological discourse, *wu* is the number five; *de*, the inner power of something or someone. The Five Powers are more commonly known as the Five Phases (*wu xing*) – earth, metal, fire, water, and wood – which are understood as processes rather than substances. *Zhong* means 'end'; *shi*, 'begin'. Hence, the expression refers to the cessation and reemergence in the cosmos of each of the Five Powers in turn. Moreover, the ontological structure of the cosmos is deeply enmeshed with events in the human realm: the alternation of the powers is integrally tied to the demise of old regimes and to the generation of their successors. **Sima Qian**'s *Shi ji* (*juan* 6), for example, records that the First Emperor of the Qin subscribed to this belief. The conquered Zhou dynasty was dominated by the power of fire, he believed, and just as water overcomes fire, so must his succeeding Qin dynasty have the power of water. He formulated the insignia of his court regalia to display that perceived association with water.

Sima Qian names **Zou Yan** (*fl. c.* 250 BCE) as an important developer of the Five Powers concept (*Shi ji* 74), although Zou's works are now lost. The concept is also developed in such texts as the *Lüshi Chunqiu* (239 BCE), **Dong Zhongshu**'s *Chunqiu fanlu* (as the Five Phases), and in the 'Monthly Ordinances' (*Yue ling* 月令) chapter of the *Li ji*, where the permutations of the Five Powers are cadenced by the seasons of the year rather than shifts in political power.

References: Graham, 1989; Li Zehou, 1986; Watson, 1993a: 43.

DEBORAH SOMMER

Wufeng xuepai 五峰學派
(School of Mount Five Peaks)

Wufeng School is the name for the group of scholars associated with **Hu Hong**. Its most important representative is **Zhang Shi** who, however, was later considered the founder of the Nanxian 南軒 School. Among the names of the followers of Hu Hong we find all junior members of the Hu family, namely his son **Hu Dashi** and his nephews Hu Dayuan 胡大原 (?–?) and Hu Daben 胡大本 (?–?). Among those deserving further mention is Biao Juzheng 彪居正 (?–?), probably Hu Hong's oldest student, some members of the Xiang 向 family, who had been one of the first clans at Kaifeng during the Northern Song and who, like the Hu, were refugees in Hunan.

The basic texts to which all these scholars adhered were the Commentary to the *Spring and Autumn Annals* (*Chunqiu zhuan* 春秋傳) of **Hu Anguo** and *Knowing Words* (*Zhi yan* 知言) of Hu Hong. Although they belonged to the few groups who resisted Zhu Xi's grip to power, they were soon overshadowed by the latter's superior intellectual capacities. **Zhu Xi** as well as **Lu Jiuyuan** made remarks concerning a lack of original ideas among the Wufeng group after the death of Hu Hong and Zhang Shi. There are hardly any important members of this school after the turn of the thirteenth century.

HANS VAN ESS

Wuyi xuepai 武夷學派
(The School of Hu Anguo)

Wuyi xuepai is the term for a loosely defined and intellectually heterogeneous group of scholars named after the place of birth of its founder **Hu Anguo** in Fujian. After the death of **Yang Shi** in 1135, Hu Anguo became the single most important person transmitting the teachings of the Cheng brothers (**Cheng Hao** and **Cheng Yi**) for a number of years. Besides his famous adoptive son **Hu Yin** and his even more renowned son **Hu Hong**, both of whom were strongly anti-Buddhist, we find among the persons listed as adherents of the Wuyi School the names of Hu Ning 胡寧 (?–? *zi* Hezhong 和仲), another son of Hu Anguo known to posterity only because he wrote the first subcommentary to his father's commentary to the *Chunqiu*, Hu Anguo's son-in-law Fan Rugui 范如圭 (1102–1160, *zi* Boda 伯達 or Bokui 伯逵) and the Buddho-Confucian Hu Xian 胡憲 (1086–1162, *zi* Yuanzhong 原仲, *hao* Jiqi xiansheng 藉溪 Master of Ji creek), a nephew of Hu Anguo belonging to a branch of the Hu family which had stayed in Fujian when Hu Anguo himself had moved to Hubei. Hu Xian was one of the first teachers of **Zhu Xi**. The editors of *Song–Yuan xuean* add several more persons as followers of the Wuyi School because it is known that they were in contact with Hu Anguo or because they spent some time near his place at Mount Heng. The most important names in this category are those of Zeng Ji 曾幾 (1084–1166, *zi* Jifu 吉甫, *hao* Tushan xiansheng 茶山 先生, Master of Tushan) whom Hu Anguo criticised because of his Buddhist inclinations and who was the teacher of the most prolific Southern Song poet Lu You 陸游 (1125–1209, *zi* Wuguan 務觀), and of Hu Quan 胡銓 (1102–1180, *zi* Bangheng 邦衡, *hao* Danan xiansheng 澹庵先生, Master of Danan) who in turn was the teacher of **Yang Wanli**.

HANS VAN ESS

X

Xi ming 西銘
(*Western Inscription*)

The *Xi ming* enjoys the reputation of being the most brilliant gem amidst the already brilliant philosophical corpus of **Zhang Zai**. Originally this extremely brief essay was but a portion of the seventeenth and last section of the author's **Zheng meng**. However, over time, because of the power and poignancy of its message, the *Western Inscription* (so called because Zhang had its text inscribed on the window of the western wall of his studio) became thought of as singular and thus published as a distinct document. Aside from the **Taijitu shuo** of **Zhou Dunyi**, no other work in the evolving tradition of **Dao xue** (Learning of the Way) has exercised influence in such stark disproportion to its length.

The paramount theme of the *Western Inscription* is that of the mutual interrelationship between **tian di** (Heaven and Earth) and all humankind. 'Heaven is my father and Earth is my mother', writes Zhang Zai, 'and even such a small being as I finds an intimate niche in their midst' (*Zhangzi quanshu*, 1.1). Zhang Zai then advances beyond this opening statement to posit a claim that is even more radical. 'All people are my kin', he further contends, 'and all things are my companions' (*Zhangzi quanshu*, 1.3). There can be no doubt that the all-encompassing language of the *Western Inscription* – precisely because it became so earnestly regarded by all those subscribing to it – had the effect of expanding the boundaries of Confucian ethics to heretofore unimagined parameters.

References: Balazs & Hervouet, 1978: 218, 326; Chan, Wing-tsit, 1963d: 497–500; Fung, 1952: 493–6.

DON J. WYATT

Xi xue 西學
(Western Learning)

Western Learning was the term for the influx of pure and applied science, political doctrines, military theory and technology, which was introduced from Europe and America, particularly during the second half of the nineteenth century and at the beginning of the twentieth century. Its sudden and overwhelming influence rendered Confucianism in China and Korea completely helpless to criticisms levelled at it as 'backward' or old fashioned, inherently unable to progress with the necessary and groundbreaking speed of reform. Only in Japan was Confucianism swiftly and successfully adapted by scholars to provide ethical guidelines in the time of modernisation and industrialisation of the Meiji era (1868–1912). In Korea in the nineteenth century, Western Learning was a name synonymous with Christian teachings of God, salvation and sin, especially the dogma of the Catholic church.

Reference: Yao, 2000.

TODD CAMERON THACKER

Xia Heliang 夏賀良
?–5 BCE

Relying on the teachings of Gan Zhongke 甘忠可 (?–?), during Han Aidi's reign (7 BCE–1 BCE), Xia Heliang expressed the view that the Han dynasty (206 BCE–8 CE) stood in need of rededication, and a decree of 5 BCE accepted that it was necessary to seek a renewal of Heaven's Mandate (*Tian ming*). Steps that were intended to symbolise such a search failed to improve the state of the dynasty and at the rejection of Xia Heliang's message he was condemned to death. When **Wang Mang** wished for recognition as a 'Temporary Emperor' (9 CE), he referred to the way in which Gan Zhongke and Xia Heliang had called for a response to the Mandate of Heaven.

MICHAEL LOEWE

Xiahou Sheng 夏侯勝
152?–61? BCE

A nephew of **Xiahou Shichang**, Xiahou Sheng, who was known as Xiahou the Elder, was a specialist in the *Book of Documents* (*Shang shu*), texts on *Li* 禮 and the Lu 魯 tradition of the *Analects* (*Lunyu*). A pupil himself of Jian Qing 蕑卿 (?–?) and Ni Kuan 兒寬 (?–?), after the accession of **Han Xuandi** (74 BCE) he was ordered to give instruction in the *Book of Documents* to the young Empress Dowager. As an outspoken critic of the policies of **Han Wudi**'s reign (141–87 BCE), Xiahou Sheng was imprisoned for two years, later to be exonerated and to reach high office.

Xiahou Sheng also gave instruction to his cousin Xiahou Jian 夏侯建 (?–?, *zi*

Changqing 長卿), who was known as Xiahou the Younger. Both men produced their commentaries on the *Book of Documents*. Xiahou Jian criticised that of Xiahou Sheng as being diffuse, and his own took the form of an exegetical commentary (*Zhang ju* 章句). He was appointed an academician. Following the conference of 51 BCE, posts were established for academicians to specialise in the teachings that both men had provided for the *Book of Documents*.

Reference: Tjan, 1949, vol. I, table II.

MICHAEL LOEWE

Xiahou Shichang 夏侯始昌
?–?

An uncle of **Xiahou Sheng**, Xiahou Shichang had been trained in the *Book of Documents* (*Shang shu*) and himself gave teaching in the Qi 齊 version of the *Book of Poetry* (*Shi jing*) to Xiahou Sheng and others. Appointed senior tutor (*Tai fu* 太傅) of Liu He 劉賀 (reigned for twenty-seven days in 74 BCE) he died of old age.

MICHAEL LOEWE

Xian ren 賢人
(Worthy)

Xian means 'worthy' or 'to be worthy'; *ren* means 'human being' or 'person'. The precise nature of worthiness is described only faintly in early texts, but it was believed that one could readily perceive it visually in others. One of its opposites was *bu xiao* 不肖, literally, 'to not resemble', or to fail that visual examination and thus to be suspect of moral dissembling. Worthiness was a quality not so much of rulers themselves as of the candidates they selected to implement government operations. Appointing, retaining, revering, and promoting worthy individuals and distinguishing them from the unworthy was the task of rulers who sought thereby to secure their reigns from chaos (*luan*). Rulers ignored the advice of worthies at their own peril. Yao and Shun were lauded for abdicating in favour of worthies.

Worthiness was a quality that transcended the prerogatives of both birth and rank, and rulers were advised to promote worthies regardless of their seniority. To be worthy was associated particularly with capability (*neng* 能) – not in the sense of task- or trade-specific skills, which are specialised and limited – but with broader-based talent. To be unworthy was to be incapable. Worthiness was also associated with the good (*liang*), the righteous (*yi*), and the virtuous (*de*). Worthies were averse to profligacy and extravagance. Confucius, for example, praised Yan Hui as a worthy because he was extremely poor and yet happy. Bo Yi and Shu Qi, worthies of ancient times, died of starvation in the wilderness, yet found the meaning of humaneness (*ren*) and avoided disgrace.

References: Ames & Rosemont, 1998: 1:7, 4:17, 6:11, 7:15, 13:2, 15:10; Knoblock, 1988–94: vol. I: 103–4, vol. II: 60, 71, 94, 95, 162, 168–88; Lau, 1984, 1B: 7, 1B: 16, 2A: 4, 2A: 5; Legge, 1861, *Confucian Analects*: 387, 405–11; Legge, 1985b: 360–1 and 1985c: 53, 181, 295, 316.

DEBORAH SOMMER

Xian ru 先儒
(the Former scholars)

'Former Scholars' referred to exegetes and court academicians (*boshi*) of the Confucian canon who, as early as the Tang dynasty, received sacrifice in the imperial Temple of Confucius (see **Kong miao**). Before the Song dynasty they were called either 'Former Teachers' (*xian shi* 先師) or 'Former Worthies (*xian xian*). Long before 'Former Scholars' were formalised in the temple nomenclature, the term was routinely used to invoke the most prominent authorities on the canon in discussions on the Classics,

court debates, and in appointments of court academicians. The Chamberlain for Ceremonials at the Eastern Jin court (317–420) already singled out most of the exegetes whom the Tang court would later enshrine in the temple. From Ming times on, the Former Scholars – represented by images before 1530 and tablets thereafter – were located at the southernmost end of the eastern and western corridors of the temple, and were ranked last, after the Sage, Correlates, Savants and Former Worthies in the hierarchy of the temple, and thus received a reduced offering during imperial sacrifice to Confucius.

In 647 twenty-two persons were enshrined in the temple as Former Teachers (*xian shi*). Prior to this moment the temple cult was largely limited to the propitiation of the Sage and his personal disciples. The enshrinement of the canonical masters in 647 invoked a passage in the *Record of Rites* that states that 'school officers offered libation sacrifice to their former teachers' ('Wengwang shi zi', *Li ji*) and effectively established exegesis as a new criterion of admission into the temple. These included Confucius' disciple **Bu Shang** (*zi* Zixia 子夏), known for his study of the *Poetry* (he was included among the Savants in 720), and the three principal commentators on the *Spring and Autumn Annals*: Zuo Qiuming 左丘明, Gongyang Gao 公羊高, and Guliang Chi 穀梁赤. Also enshrined were eighteen scholars of one or several canonical books: **Fu Sheng**, Gao Tangsheng 高堂生 (a Han academcian of the **Yi li**), **Dai Sheng**, Mao Chang 毛萇 (a scholar on **Shi jing**), **Kong Anguo**, **Liu Xiang**, Zheng Zhong 鄭眾 (?–83, a specialist of the **Zuo zhuang**, **Zhou li**), **Jia Kui**, Du Zichun 杜子春 (30?–58?, an exegete of the **Zhou li**), **Ma Rong**, Lu Zhi 魯植 (?–192, Ma Rong's disciple), **Zheng Xuan**, Fu Qian 服虔 (an exegete on *Zuo zhuan*), **He Xiu**, **Wang Su**, **Wang Bi** (the author of a major commentary on *Yi jing*), **Du You**, and **Fan Ning**.

When, in 739, noble titles were conferred upon Confucius and his disciples in the temple, the canonical masters did not receive any noble rank. In 1009, twenty-one masters, now referred to as 'Former Scholars', first received noble titles of earl (*bo* 伯), when the **Ten Savants** were promoted to dukes and Confucius' disciples were promoted to marquises (*hou* 侯). Some of Confucius' disciples retained their titles of earl and were elevated over the Former Scholars in the temple as Former Worthies. The blurred distinction between personal disciples and canonical exegetes was further complicated in 1084. When **Mengzi** was enshrined as duke and placed among the Correlates in the temple, **Xunzi**, **Yang Xiong** of the Han, and **Han Yu** of the Tang were enshrined as earls and placed among the Former Scholars. While the enshrinements of 647 established canonical exegesis as a new criterion of canonisation in the Temple of Confucius, the additions of 1084 established other criteria for canonisation. Mengzi and Xunzi were not Confucius' personal disciples, nor did they write commentaries on the canon; rather they authored their own books – later classed among the 'various masters' (*zhuzi* 諸子) of late antiquity. While Yang Xiong wrote an important commentary on the *Book of Changes*, he was primarily known for his own book which was also included among the various masters. Han Yu wrote on the canon and expounded upon his own teachings in the form of the essay written in the ancient style of the Classics.

The next major additions to the ranks of Former Scholar, which came at the end of the Song dynasty (960–1279), established a pattern for enshrinement that would be the dominant mode until the eighteenth century. In 1241, the five principal masters of the **dao xue** School of Confucianism – **Zhou Dunyi**, **Zhang Zai**, **Cheng Hao**, **Cheng Yi**, and **Zhu Xi** – were enshrined as Former Scholars. The enshrinement of these men was extraordinary not because they lived during the same dynasty that canonised them. In his proclamation announcing the first imperial canonisation of **dao xue**

Confucianism, Emperor Lizong (r. 1224–1264) enunciated a new criterion for enshrinement: 'No one received Confucius' *Dao* after Mengzi died. Only in our own dynasty', he continued, did 'the learning that ended long ago, finally converge' in the writings of these five masters. The new criterion for canonisation was a genealogical principle based on the Song doctrine called the genealogy or transmission of the Way (**dao tong**), which held that only Mengzi received the Way of Confucius and that after his death the Way was not transmitted in the world until the *dao xue* masters received the Way through direct apprehension of the truth in such books as **Lunyu** and **Mengzi**. In the remaining years of the Song and in successive dynasties other recent masters were enshrined as Former Scholars on the basis of the genealogical principles of transmission of the *dao*.

During the Ming dynasty the court debated many aspects of the temple cult, including the status of several Confucians enshrined in the temple. In 1530, several Former Scholars were removed from the temple for a variety of reasons. Xunzi was removed because his doctrine that human nature is evil conflicted with Mengzi's teachings. Seven canonical exegetes who received sacrifice in the temple since the seventh century were removed: Dai Sheng because he was a treacherous official; Liu Xiang because of involvement in shamanism; Jia Kui abused prophesies; Ma Rong used factional contacts to enrich his family; He Xiu practised improper divination; Wang Su conspired with Sima Shi to seize the throne at the end of the Wei dynasty (220–265); Wang Bi's learning was based on Laozi and Zhuangzi; and Du Yu instituted abbreviated mourning rites. Five other exegetes were demoted to local cults because of obscurantism in their learning: Lu Zhi, Zheng Zhong, Zheng Xuan, Fu Qian and Fan Ning. This left eight exegetes among the Former Scholars in the temple: Zuoqiu Ming, Gongyang Gao, Guliang Chi, Fu Sheng, Gao Tangsheng, Mao Chang, Kong Anguo and Du Zichun. Much of the rationale for removing these exegetes from the temple was that their views were inconsistent with Cheng–Zhu orthodoxy of the Ming court, although not all of the figures enshrined in Ming times were proponents of Cheng–Zhu thinking, perhaps **Lu Jiuyuan**, enshrined in 1530, was the most prominent among them. Yet, to the bitter end, the Ming court was the Cheng–Zhu School's most resolute advocate: in 1642, just before its final demise, the Ming court promoted six *Daoxue* masters from Former Scholars to Former Worthies, and placed them after Confucius' personal disciples.

The Kangxi emperor (r. 1662–1922) largely continued the Ming tendency of promoting Cheng–Zhu orthodoxy in temple enshrinements, but this trend was partly reversed under the Yongzheng emperor (r. 1723–1736). Beginning in the second year of his reign, for example, the court returned Zheng Xuan and Fan Ning, who were removed in 1530, to the ranks of Former Scholars. Twenty other scholars were enshrined for the first time, including **Yin Chun**, **Wei Liaoweng**, **Huang Gan**, **Chen Chun**, He Ji 何基 (1188–1268), **Wang Bo**, and **Zhao Fu** of the Song, **Jin Lüxiang**, Xu Qian 許謙 (1270–1337), and Chen Hao 陳澔 (1261–1341) of the Yuan, **Luo Qinshun** and Cai Qing 蔡清 (1453–1508) of the Ming, and **Lu Longqi** of the Qing. During the nineteenth century, other prominent Confucian thinkers were added to the ranks of the Former Scholars: **Liu Zongzhou** was admitted in 1822; Tang Bin 湯斌 (1627–1687) in 1823; Huang Daozhou 黃道周 (1585–1646) in 1825; Lü Kun 呂坤 (1536–1618) in 1826; and Sun Qifeng 孫奇逢 (1584–1675) in 1828. While many, perhaps most, of these thinkers tended to favour *dao xue* School thinking, clearly many were not. The temple was also opened to scholar–statesmen who were primarily known for the defence of their dynasty, such as Zhuge Liang 諸葛亮 (181–234), statesman of the Han, who was enshrined in 1724 and Lu Zhi 陸贄 (754–805), statesman

of the Tang, who was admitted in 1826. In 1908 **Wang Fuzhi**, **Huang Zongxi**, **Gu Yanwu**, who had opposed and even openly fought against the Manchus in the mid-seventeenth century, were admitted to the temple.

THOMAS A. WILSON

Xian sheng 先聖
(the First Sage)

Confucius was given the title 'First Sage' in 628 CE. For several years in the 620s and 650s the Duke of Zhou (**Zhou Gong**) received primary sacrifices in the temple as First Sage, when Confucius was demoted to the secondary status of First Teacher (*xian shi* 先師) and Yan Hui 顏回 (see **Fu Sheng**) was removed. After considerable debate during the first half of the seventh century it was determined that though both men were sages, as chief minister during the founding kings of the Zhou dynasty, the Duke of Zhou should receive secondary sacrifices in the temple devoted to the Zhou sovereigns and that Confucius should receive primary sacrifices in the temple devoted to the canonical traditions of the Confucian Classics. Confucius was restored to First Sage in 657 and Yan Hui was given the title of First Teacher.

THOMAS A. WILSON

Xian wang zhi dao 先王之道
(The Way of the Former Kings)

The 'Former Kings', to Warring States period and later thinkers, were the sage rulers of the Xia, Shang and Zhou dynasties who had formulated or personally embodied, it was believed, exemplary social mores, model standards of governance, righteous martial valour, remarkable filial piety, pious regard for spiritual beings, and so on. Although literati did not necessarily have any particular king in mind when using the phrase in a general sense, they were most often referring to such semilegendary figures as Yao, Shun (see *Yao Shun*), Yu and Kings Wen and Wu (see *Wenwu zhi dao*).

The Former Kings were sometimes contrasted with the 'later kings', that is, more 'modern' or 'contemporary' rulers whose methods of governance might fundamentally differ from principles outlined in classical texts. Such contrasts often pitted the values of antiquity against their contemporary applications and questioned the viability of applying ancient mores to modern issues.

But for those who advocated the Way, or *Dao*, of the Former Kings, this Way was not a mere object of historical inquiry but was to be implemented in contemporary life. **Mengzi** believed not only that the humane Way of Yao and Shun could be enacted in contemporary governance, but that everyone could themselves become a Yao or Shun. **Xunzi**, for example, equated the Way of the Former Kings with humaneness, ritual/ propriety, rightness and acting according to the principle of centrality. Contemporary *ru* or scholars, he asserted, modelled themselves after such figures.

References: Knoblock, 1988–94: vol. II: 63– 84; Lau, 1984; Wang Xianqian, 1988: 114–47.
DEBORAH SOMMER

Xian xian 先賢
(The Former Worthies)

The *xian* 賢 (Worthies) followed the *zhe* 哲 (the Savants, see **Ten Savants**) and preceded *xian ru* (the Former Scholars) in the temple hierarchy of late imperial times. Their tablets were located in the side corridors of the temple complex with the Former Scholars and were thus physically separated in the temple complex from the Sage (**Confucius**), the **Four Correlates**, and the Savants (the persons in the latter two groups were often called 'worthies' as well), whose tablets were located in the main hall at the centre of the complex. The Worthies enshrined in the temple of Confucius can be divided into three groups: (1) personal disciples of Confucius, most of whom received sacrifice in the temple from the earliest years of the imperial cult; (2) disciples of **Mengzi** who were enshrined in 1724; and (3) masters of the *dao xue* School, who were promoted from Scholars to Worthies in the Ming dynasty as part of a process of institutionalising this school's teachings as imperial orthodoxy.

In the early centuries of the imperial cult, the term 'Former Worthy' was an informal temple designation first for the masters of the canon – who were eventually called the Former Scholars – then for personal disciples of Confucius. The *Jiu Tangshu* (7.159) records imperial sacrifice at the Imperial Academy (see **Tai xue**) to twenty-two worthies (i.e., canonical masters) in 712. Before the Song dynasty (960–1279) the canonical scholars received irregular sacrifice as masters (*zi* 子) and were ranked after Confucius' disciples. From the early Song on, Confucius' personal disciples (numbering seventy, seventy-two or seventy-seven depending upon sources used) were usually referred to as worthies and held higher noble rank than the scholars. Until the mid-Ming, the designations worthy and scholar were used both as formal temple rank and as an informal name for one group or another. In 1530 the posthumous noble titles of everyone enshrined in the temple were removed, thereby formalising the hierarchy of sage, correlate, savant, worthy and scholar.

Confucius' disciples
Before the establishment of an imperial cult in the capital, emperors and imperial entourages honoured Confucius' disciples in Qufu. As early as 72 CE, Emperor Ming (r. 58–75) offered sacrifice (*ci* 祠) to Confucius and seventy-two of his disciples, a precedent that was followed by a number of later emperors. The earliest sacrifices to Confucius' disciples in the capital were probably in 720, when their images were painted on the temple walls to receive

secondary offerings with the twenty-two worthies. Imperial propitiation of most of Confucius' disciples was rarely justified on substantive grounds of individual achievement, but rather on grounds that they had heard the Master personally. The early sources used by court authorities to identify these disciples, particularly **Sima Qian**'s *Shi ji* and the *Kongzi jiayu*, list only the names, courtesy names (*zi* 字), and/or ages (as determined in relation to Confucius' age) of forty-eight of them. Sima Qian supplemented this information with passages from the *Analects* for twenty-nine of Confucius' better-known followers. The Tang court elevated ten of the Master's known disciples as Correlate (*pei* 配) or Savant (zhe 哲). Of the remaining sixty-seven, three were later promoted: Zeng Shen 曾參 (see **Zong sheng**) was promoted to Correlate and **Zhuansun Shi** 顓孫師 to savant in 1267, and **You Ruo** 有若 (*zi* Ziyou 子有) was promoted to Savant in 1738. Summaries of these entries in *Shi ji* (Chapter 67) are included for several men below, followed by a list of the remaining disciples.

Tantai Mieming 澹臺滅明 (*zi* Ziyu 子羽). Tantai was said to be exceedingly ugly and Confucius initially suspected that his talent was limited. But Tantai cultivated his conduct without taking shortcuts (*Lunyu* 6.14) and eventually established a significant following in the South. Confucius realised his error, and said, 'I favoured men who were skilled orators and erred with Zai Wo [whom Confucius later described as a piece of "rotten wood"]. I selected men on the basis of appearance and erred with Ziyu.'

Fu Buqi 宓(虙)不齊 (*zi* Zijian 子賤). Confucius regarded Fu Buqi as a gentleman (*junzi*) (*Lunyu* 5.3) and once lamented that he never had the chance to govern anything but a small domain.

Yuan Xian 原憲 (*zi* Zisi 子思). Yuan once asked Confucius about shame. Confucius replied that 'One can accept payment in a state that possesses the Way, but to accept payment from a state that does not possess the Way is shameful' (*Lunyu* 14.1).

After Confucius died, Yuan Xian fled to the marshes. Later, Zigong (see **Duanmu si**) became the Prime Minister of a state and found Yuan Xian in poverty. Zigong asked if he was ill, to which Yuan Xian replied, 'He who has no wealth is called poor. He who studies the Way but is unable to practice it is called ill. I may be poor, but I am not ill!' For the rest of his life, Zigong was ashamed of his words.

Gongye Chang 公冶長 (*zi* Zichang 子長). Confucius said that 'one could offer one's daughter in marriage to the likes of Gongye Zhang. Even if he found himself in prison he would be without fault' (*Lunyu* 5.1). Later, Confucius did indeed marry his daughter to Gongye Chang.

Nangong Kuo 南宮适 (*zi* Zirong 子容) who married the son of Confucius' older brother.

Zeng Dian 曾蒧 (also written as 點, *zi* Xi 晳), Zeng Shen's father. The Master quizzed four disciples about their wishes. Zilu 子路 (see **Zhong You**) quickly proclaimed that in three years he could lead the people of a medium size state under siege to gain courage and know the proper course. **Ran Qiu** said that in three years he could lead the people of a small area to self-sufficiency, but that he would leave matters of rites and music to someone more worthy. Gongxi Chi 公西赤 said that he would like to assist in the sacrifices at the royal temple and meetings of the feudal lords. When asked of his wishes, Zeng Dian waited for the sound of his zither to fade away, then said, 'My choice differs from the other three . . . In late spring, when the spring clothing is put away, to go swimming in the Yi River with several young men and other youths, to sit in the breeze on the platform of the Rain Altar, then sing all the way home.' The Master sighed and said, 'I'm with Dian' (*Lunyu* 11.25).

Yan Wuyou 顏無繇 (*zi* Lu 路), Yan Hui's father, who also served Confucius. The Yan family was poor. When Yan Hui died, Yan Wuyou asked if he could sell Confucius' carriage to pay for the funeral. Confucius replied that he didn't sell his carriage to pay for his own son's funeral (*Lunyu* 11.8).

Shang Qu 商瞿 (*zi* Zimu 子木) received the tradition of the *Book of Changes* (see **Yi jing**) from Confucius and passed it on to others to establish a textual tradition that existed in Sima Qian's day.

Gao Chai 高柴 (*zi* Zigao 子羔). Confucius instructed Zigao, but considered him slow. Confucius objected when Zilu employed Zigao in the service of the Ji family – known for its usurpation of royal privileges (e.g., *Lunyu* 3.1, 3.6) – because he was not ready to serve in government. 'You will make a thief of him', he said, to which Zilu quipped, 'There are people there. There are altars to soils and grains there. Why practice learning only after study?' Confucius replied, 'This is why I detest sycophants' (*Lunyu* 11.25). The figure of the innocent Gao Chai is used here to illustrate the potential for insulting the spirits and tyrannising the people when one is called to serve before undergoing proper training.

Qidiao Kai 漆雕開 (*zi* Zikai 子開). Confucius wanted to send Qidiao Kai to serve in office. When Qidiao demurred that he had not yet gained the confidence to do so, Confucius was greatly pleased (*Lunyu* 5.6).

Sima Geng 司馬耕 (*zi* Ziniu 子牛). When his talkative and fidgety disciple asked about humane men, Confucius replied that they speak haltingly, with difficulty. Sima Geng queried, 'He who speaks with difficulty can be called humane?' Confucius answered, 'Acting humanely is already difficult, why shouldn't we speak about the humane with difficulty too?' (*Lunyu* 12.3).

Other disciples who are listed as Worthies include Fan Xu 樊須 (*zi* Chi 遲), Gongxi Chi 公西赤 (*zi* Zihua 子華), Wuma Shi 巫馬施 (*zi* Qi 期), Gongxi Ai 公晳哀 (*zi* Jici 季次), Gongbo Liao 公伯寮 ('Liao' also written 繚, *zi* Zizhou 子周) who was removed from the temple in 1530 because he sued Zilu (Zhong You), Liang Zhan 梁鱣 (*zi* Ziyu 子魚), Yan Xing 顏幸 (*zi* Liu 柳), Ran Ru 冉孺 (*zi* Zilu 子魯), Cao Xu 曹卹 (*zi* Zixun 子循), Bo Qian 伯虔 (*zi* Zixi

子析), Gongsun Long 公孫龍 (*zi* Zishi 子石), Ran Ji 冉季 (*zi* Chan 產), Qin Zu 秦祖 (*zi* Zinan 子南), Qidiao Chi 漆雕哆 (*zi* Lian 斂), Yan Gao 顏高 (*zi* Ziqiao 子驕), Qidiao Xifu 漆雕徒父, Rangsi Chi 壤駟赤 (*zi* Zixi 子徒), Shang Ze 商澤, Shizuo Shu 石作蜀 (*zi* Ziming 子明), Ren Buqi 任不齊 (*zi* Xuan 選), Gongxia Shou 公夏首 (*zi* Cheng 乘), Gongliang Ru 公良孺 (*zi* Zizheng 子正), Hou Chu 后處 (*zi* Zili 子里), Qin Ran 秦冉 (*zi* Kai 開) who was removed from the temple in 1530 because the *Kongzi jiayu* did not list him as a disciple and it was suspected that the *Shi ji* mistakenly recorded him as a disciple but he was restored to the temple in 1724, Xirong Zhen 奚容蒧 (*zi* Zixi 子皙), Gongjian Ding 公肩定 (*zi* Zizhong 子中), Yan Zu 顏祖 (*zi* Rang 襄), Tiao (or Qiao) Shan 鄡單 (*zi* Zijia 子家), Gou Jingjiang 句井彊, Hanfu Hei 罕父黑 (*zi* Zisuo 子索), Qin Shang 秦商 (*zi* Zipi 子丕), Shen Dang 申黨 (*zi* Zhou 周), Gongzu Gouzi 公祖句玆 (*zi* Zizhi 子之), Rong Qi 榮旂 (*zi* Ziqi 子祈), Xian Cheng 縣成 (*zi* Ziqi 子祺), Zuoren Ying 左人郢 (*zi* Xing 行), Yan Ji 燕伋 (*zi* Si 思), Zheng Guo 鄭國 (*zi* Zixi 子徒), Qin Fei 秦非 (*zi* Zizhi 子之), Shi Zhichang 施之常 (*zi* Ziheng 子恆), Yan Kuai 顏噲 (*zi* Zisheng 子聲), Bushu Cheng 步叔乘 (*zi* Ziche 子車), Yan Zhipu 顏之僕 (*zi* Shu 叔), Yuan Kangji 原亢籍, Yue Kai 樂欬 (*zi* Zisheng 子聲), Lian Xie 廉絜 (*zi* Yong 庸), Yan He 顏何 (*zi* Ran 冉) who was removed from the temple in 1530 because the *Kongzi jiayu* did not list him as a disciple and it was suspected that the *Shi ji* mistakenly recorded him as one but he was restored to the temple in 1724, Shu Zhonghui 叔仲會 (*zi* Ziqi 子期), Di Hei 狄黑 (*zi* Xi 皙), Pang Xun 邦巽 (*zi* Zilian 子斂), Kong Zhong 孔忠, Gongxi Yuru 公西與如 (*zi* Zishang 子上), Gongxi Zhen 公西蒧 (*zi* Zishang 子上), Lin Fang 林放 (*zi* Ziqiu 子丘) who was enshrined for the first time in 739 and removed in 1530 on the grounds that he was not listed as a disciple in either the *Shi ji* or *Kongzi jiayu* but was restored to the temple in 1724, Qu Yuan 蘧瑗 (*zi* Boyu 伯玉) who was enshrined for the first time in 739 and removed in 1530 because Confucius did not treat him as a disciple and was indirectly critical of him in a conversation with his servant (*Lunyu* 14.25), and was restored in 1724.

Mengzi's disciples
In 1113, eighteen of Mengzi's disciples were enshrined in the Temple of Mengzi located in his home county of Zou 鄒 (modern-day Yanzhou, Shandong province). Four of Mengzi's followers were enshrined as Former Worthies in 1724. Yuezheng Ke 樂正克 (*zi* Zhengzi 正子) was ranked as Correlate in the Temple of Mengzi in Yanzhou in 1113. Mengzi said of Yuezheng Ke, that he 'loved the good', a quality that could draw all the good within the four seas to his side (the *Mengzi* 6B: 13, see also 7B: 25). Gongdu Zi 公都子 was involved in the well-known debate in the *Mengzi* on the internal nature of righteousness (6A: 5). Wan Zhang 萬章 was the central disciple in the fifth book of the *Mengzi*, which is named after him, and features an extended discussion on the ancient sage–kings, Yao, Shun, and Yu. Gongsun Chou's 公孫丑 queries on the circumstances under which one should serve a lord are recorded in several chapters of the *Mengzi* (e.g., 2B.2, 6, 14).

Dao xue masters
In the first departure from the principle that the 'Worthies' should be composed of personal disciples of the ancient sages, six Song masters of the *Dao xue* School received sacrifice in the temple as Former Worthies in 1642. The Chongzhen emperor (r. 1628–1644) recognised that the Ming court's imperial anthology of Confucian writings called the *Great Collections on the Five Classics and the Four Books* (*Wu jing Si shu daquan* 五經四書大全) was dominated by the writings and commentaries of **Zhou Dunyi**, **Cheng Hao**, **Cheng Yi**, **Zhu Xi**, **Zhang Zai**, and **Shao Yong**. 'It is evident', he proclaimed, 'that the learning of Principle was greatly illuminated in the Song' by these men. This reorganisation of the Worthies and Scholars in the temple hierarchy effectively enshrined the separation of scholars of Cheng–Zhu orthodoxy from all other Confucians after the death of the ancient sages Confucius and Mengzi. Zuo Qiuming, the supposed author of the *Zuo zhuan* (see **Chunqiu Zuo zhuan**) was also promoted to Former Worthy in 1642 on the grounds that he directly received the *Spring and Autumn Annals* from Confucius.

Thomas A. Wilson

Xiang shu xue 象數學
(Learning of image and number)

Traditionally, the 'Learning of Image and Number' forms one of the two distinct methodological approaches for understanding the *Yi jing* (*The Book of Changes*). In contrast to the more text-bound and hermeneutical approach represented by **Yili zhixue** (Learning of Meaning and Principle), *Xiang shu xue* affords the inquirer a mode of access that relies almost exclusively on the manipulation and interpretation of the *Yi jing*'s own visual constructs and components. The oldest text in which *Xiang shu xue* is discussed is the **Chunqiu Zuo zhuan** (*Spring and Autumn Annals with Zuo's Commentary*); it affords us the following description: 'Divination by means of the tortoise [plastron] involves image, and divination by means of the plant stalks incorporates number. In being produced, things (*wu*) give rise to images; images then lead to fecundity (*zi* Zi 滋); fecundity results in numbers' (*Zuo zhuan*, Duke Xi 15th year). Of the prevailing approaches to understanding the *Yi*, *Xiang shu xue* appears to have been the most ancient. The Southern Qi-dynasty scholar Lu Deng 陸澄 (423–494; *zi* Yanyuan 彥淵) remarked that 'although different schools for the study of the *Book of Changes* have existed since [the time of Confucius' disciple] Shang Qu 商瞿 (*fl.* 500 BCE; *zi* Zimu 子木), they all converge in taking image and number to be their progenitor' (Wang Yinglin 王應麟, *Hanyi wenzhi kaozheng* 漢藝文志考證, 1.10). But despite its great antiquity and its early acceptance as the favoured approach for interpreting the *Yi jing*, from about the end of the eleventh century CE onward and largely owing to the efforts of **Cheng Yi** and his successors, *Xiang shu xue* became increasingly displaced by *Yili zhixue*.

References: Birdwhistell, 1989: 4, 55, 59, 62, 74, 203, 210, 225, 258; Smith, *et al.*, 1990: 18, 19, 175, 179, 217–18, 225; Wyatt, 1996: 4, 91–2, 93, 226, 249, 277.

DON J. WYATT

Xiang yinjiu 鄉飲酒
(Village Libation Ceremony)

The tri-yearly performance of this rite was for local officials to remind the ruled subjects of the importance of moral rectification and to elect the righteous as role models. The core of the rite was to serve wine to the elected. The canonical authority came from the *Rites of Zhou* (**Zhou li**) and the *Rites of Literati* (**Yi li**), and therefore the rite included remnants of ancient rituals (notably the rites of archery contest, *she li* 射禮).

Starting with the Han, it was celebrated mainly in the schools. By the period of Disunity (220–589), during the Northern Wei (386–535), this became an annual affair, held in winter, with mass participation. The Sui (581–618) then established it as a school rite, even though throughout the Sui and Tang it continued to be considered also as a local ritual for moral rectification purposes and administered by local officials. Further, paying homage to the elders became its centre-piece by the mid-Tang when it reached its height in importance.

The rise of the **civil service examinations** in the Tang added to the educational significance of the rite. The party for new recruits was now also the occasion to cel-ebrate the *xiang yinjiu* rite. By the early twelfth century, the ceremony to mark the nomination of local examination candidates was simply named *xiang yinjiu*. It was thus held once every three years by local government offices, often also accompanied by archery contests. In the Ming and Qing times (1368–1911), this ritual continued to be organised *pro forma* by local officials, often on school compounds and on a semi-yearly basis. However, it had all but lost its original meaning of respecting the elderly and symbolising good government.

References: Hsiao Kung-chuan, 1960: 208–19, 625, 628; Pang Zhonglu, 1988.

THOMAS H.C. LEE

Xiangshan ji 象山集
(*Collection of Works by Lu Jiuyuan*)

This collection – in 36 chapters (*juan*) – comprises the complete philosophical and literary production of the philosopher **Lu Jiuyuan**. It is sometimes also titled *Xiangshan Quanji* 象山全集 (*Complete Works of Lu Jiuyuan*) or *Lu Xiangshan Xiansheng quanji* 陸象山先生全集 (*Complete Works of Master Lu Jiuyuan*). Featured foremost in the collection is Lu Jiuyuan's correspondence, in chapters 1 through 17, and his dialogues with peers and students, in chapters 34 and 35. The importance of these chapters cannot be overstressed because it was primarily through these letters and conversations that Lu articulated his philosophical agenda, ideas and programme. Brief essays on the Classics and other sundry topics are contained in chapters 21 through 24 and 29 through 31. Of these essays, the most celebrated is one on the nobility of man over and above all other creatures in chapter 30. It is included among the essays that Lu had successfully exploited in the civil service examinations. Chapter 36 consists of a chronological biography (*nianpu* 年譜) compiled by Lu's disciple **Yuan Xie**. The remaining chapters – 18–20; 25–28; 32–35 – contain miscellaneous materials – ranging from biographies to poetry to funeral inscriptions – that scholars have deemed minor.

In contrast to similar works dating from earlier eras of the Song dynasty (960–1279), we know much about the textual history of the *Xiangshan ji*. Lu Jiuyuan's son Lu Chizhi 陸持之 (*fl.* 1187–1226) initiated its compilation. But, afterward, successive generations of Lu Jiuyuan's disciples – including ultimately such notables as **Wang Shouren** – expanded the collection, until it finally assumed its present form in the early sixteenth century.

References: Balazs & Hervouet, 1978: 423; Chan, Wing-tsit, 1963d: 574–87; Fung, 1952: 572–9.

DON J. WYATT

Xiao 孝
(Filial piety)

Filial piety, a basic Chinese virtue celebrated in many Confucian texts, is the dutiful submission of children to their parents. The use of the term *xiao* dates back to the early Zhou, when it referred primarily to ritual service to deceased parents. Many western Zhou bronzes are inscribed with references to the owners making an offering of their filial piety to their deceased father or ancestors, and the *Book of Poetry* uses the term mostly in this sense as well. By the time of Confucius, however, the meaning of filial piety had been broadened to include relations with living parents. In the *Analects*, Confucius urges viewing filial piety as a virtue that goes much further than merely feeding parents. It should involve showing respect to them, knowing how to tactfully offer advice to them, and keeping in mind their needs and concerns. At the same time, it still involved service after death, and Confucius explicitly mentioned giving parents a proper funeral and offering sacrifices to them as essential elements in filial piety.

From early times those who carried filial devotion to extremes were seen as moral heroes. The **Chunqiu Zuo zhuan** includes two anecdotes of sons who preferred death to refusing to obey their fathers' completely unjustified commands. It also includes the story of Duke Zhuang of Zheng 鄭莊公 (r. 743–701 BCE) who swore never to see his mother again until they met in the Yellow Springs because he had discovered she was plotting against him. Later he repented and dug an underground passage to allow a reconciliation that would not violate his oath.

Even though filial piety was strongly associated with the followers of Confucius, it never became a particularly controversial virtue. Both Mozi 墨子 and Laozi 老子 took for granted that the world is in better order when the people are filial. Although Han Feizi 韓非子 (280?–233 BCE) pointed out to rulers how the Confucian notion of filial piety could lead to divided loyalty on the part of subjects, in chapter 51 on filial piety and loyalty, he presented absolute obedience to the father as supporting absolute loyalty to the ruler. In later periods of Chinese history, few questioned that filial devotion was a virtue. Buddhists, in adapting to China, did not challenge the weight placed on filial piety; rather they argued that their teachings allowed a child to fulfill his filial duties to the utmost, for instance by aiding the salvation of deceased ancestors. Daoists of the Song and later regularly promoted filial piety in their moral tracts.

The exaltation of filial piety was carried to extreme heights in the Han period (206 BCE–220 CE). In the *Book of Rites* (*Li ji*), Zengzi 曾子 (see **Fu Sheng**) asserts that true goodness, propriety, righteousness and sincerity all lay in reverent, persistent service to parents and cautious behaviour that avoids bringing shame on them. The *Book of Filial Piety* (*Xiao jing*) attributed to Confucius the statement that 'Filial piety is the root of all virtue and the source of all teachings.' The Han government made filial piety a criterion for selecting men to office and rewarded extreme acts of filial piety. Depictions of paragons of filial piety were a common theme in Han art. Some of the passion for extreme forms of filial piety seems more like religious passion than calculating acts. Truly devoted children, for instance, would cut off a piece of their flesh to feed an ill parent, confident that it would cure them. Stories of such self-sacrificing filial exemplars were eventually collected into the widely circulated *Twenty-Four Filial Exemplars* (**Ershisi xiao**).

Confucian tracts for children invariably stressed the virtue of filial piety. Besides the *Book of Filial Piety*, and the Tang imitation of it for girls, *The Classic of Filial Piety for Girls* (*Nü Xiao jing* 女孝經), works like **Zhu Xi**'s *Elementary Learning* (**Xiao xue**) devoted considerable space to giving examples of filial devotion.

The moral weight assigned to filial piety had pervasive effects on Chinese culture and social organisation. Proverbs and popular literature show the contempt people had for those who flouted or ignored the demands of filial piety. Law codes treated violations of filial piety, such as cursing parents or accidentally causing them bodily harm, as major crimes. The opinion of Mengzi that the worst of unfilial acts was to fail to have (male) descendants, often quoted in later ages, not only shaped Chinese family dynamics but also Chinese population growth.

References: de Bary & Bloom, 1999: 529–31; Ebrey, ed., 1993: 64–8, 238–44; Kelleher, 1989; Kutcher, 1999; Liu Kwang-ching, ed., 1990.

PATRICIA EBREY

Xiao jing 孝經
(*The Book of Filial Piety*)

The *Xiao jing* is made up of a concatenation of dialogues where Confucius is seen to lecture his disciple Zengzi 曾子 (Zeng Can or Zeng Shen 曾參, see **Fu Sheng**) – no other one of Confucius' disciples appears in the text – who is shown waiting in attendance on his master and content with interjecting a few respectful comments or questions. William Boltz (1993: 141) aptly describes the *Xiao jing* as 'a comparatively small work, of not more than two thousand characters, dealing with the virtue of *xiao* (filial piety) in its predictable contexts, i.e., with respect to one's behaviour towards parents and other seniors, and also in connection with the comparable attitude of fealty and duty one is traditionally called upon to show towards one's lord (*jun* 君)'.

The current text is in nine chapters (*juan* 卷), divided into eighteen sections (*zhang* 章), most of which end with a quotation from the **Shi jing** (in one case from the **Shang shu**), which contributes further to present the *Xiao jing* as an unmistakably Confucian book. Because it appears in large part to be a record of questions and answers between Confucius and Zengzi, it was early on assumed that Confucius or perhaps Zengzi was the author. The **Shi ji** chapter 67 (p. 2205) records that Confucius 'composed' (*zuo* 作) the *Xiao jing*, which is interpreted conventionally to mean that Confucius recited it to Zengzi who in turn wrote it down. Such was the view that prevailed between the Han and the Tang periods, whereas Song scholars considered it to have been written down by later followers.

The bibliographical chapters of **Han shu** (chapter 30, pp. 1718–1719) and of *Sui shu* (chapter 32, pp. 933–5) both record the *Xiao jing* as having been extant at the start of the Han period (206 BCE–220 CE). According to William Boltz (1993: 143), the sizeable citations from the *Xiao jing* that are to be found in the **Lüshi Chunqiu**, known to have been compiled around 239 BCE, are enough evidence that this date 'can safely be taken as a *terminus ante quem* for the composition of the *Xiao jing*'. Furthermore, the *Han shu*, followed by the *Sui shu*, claims that the *Xiao jing* was transmitted in the Former Han by **Zhang Yu** who is also known to have prepared an edition of the **Lunyu** (*Analects*) while acting about 48 BCE as teacher to the heir apparent, the future Emperor Cheng (r. 33–7 BCE).

It is to be noted in this respect that the *Xiao jing* and the *Lunyu* share in common the form of dialogues between Confucius and his disciples, and that Zengzi also features in the latter work where he is extolled as a paragon of filial piety. There is in the first part of Book 8 of the *Lunyu* a cluster of sections which exclusively record sayings by Zengzi, starting from the well-known scene where he is seen on his death-bed showing to his disciples that, as a supreme sign of filial piety, he has managed to keep his body intact, just as his parents had given it to him at birth. The relationship between Zengzi and the theme of filial piety is corroborated by the general similarity in style and context of the *Xiao jing* to the 'Zengzi wen' 曾子問 (Zengzi's questions) sections of the *Li ji*. It may be that both pieces were originally part of the same text which was then split up with the former dealing more specifically with filial piety, leaving the remaining aspects of ceremony and ritual to the latter.

Whether the composition of the *Xiao jing* predates the Han or not (according to Michael Nylan, the startling 'discovery' of this text in the early Han smells of downright forgery), the book clearly takes on a canonical value in its association with Confucius, and as such, it becomes involved in the textual struggles of the period, there being a *jinwen* (New Text) version known as the *Zhengzhu Xiao jing* 鄭注孝經 ('The Classic of Filial Piety with a Commentary by Zheng', who was dubiously identified as the great Later Han exegete **Zheng Xuan**) and a *guwen* (Old Text) version known as the *Kong Anguo zhuan Xiao jing* 孔安國傳孝經 ('The Classic of Filial Piety in the Tradition of Kong Anguo'), although its case seems to be strengthened by the citations from the *Zuo zhuan* and the *Guoyu* present in the text, this transmission by **Kong Anguo**, just as his alleged transmission of the *Lunyu* and the *Shang shu*, is probably spurious.

Whatever the case may be, the political import of the debate appears blatantly with the analogy set up by the book between *xiao* which concerns mainly the father–son relationship (*fu zi*), and *zhong* (loyalty, devotion) which is more specific to the ruler–minister (or subject) relationship (*jun chen*). The latter can be said to be conceived of on the model of the former, the structure of the state (*guo* 國) being modelled on that of the family (*jia* 家), as is recalled by the modern compound *guojia* 國家 meaning the state. As Michael Nylan remarks, 'quite specifically, the *Hsiao ching* [*Xiao jing*] argued that habits of respect and obedience taught within the family circle develop the crucial attitudes of reverence and loyalty needed for political loyalty ... Filial piety begins in service to one's parents, centres in service to one's lord, and ends in establishing (a name for) oneself' (*Xiao jing*, chs. 1, 7).

The neatly drawn parallel between filial piety and political loyalty is effectively established in a range of texts by the middle of the Former Han, while finding a form of political instrumentation in that *xiao* becomes the posthumous designation for the Han emperors and the decisive criterion for recommendation of candidates to official positions. In the cosmological vision of **Dong Zhongshu**, loyalty to the ruler is, just like filial piety of the son to the father, as 'natural' as the submission of Earth to Heaven. The Han cult of filial piety as the basis of loyalty to the state set the model for later dynasties.

References: Boltz, 1993; Chen, Ivan, 1908; Hsiao, Harry Hsin-i, 1978; Nylan, 1996.

ANNE CHENG

Xiao kang 小康
(Lesser prosperity)

In the *Evolution of Ritual* (*Li yun*) chapter in the *Book of Rites* (*Li ji*), Confucius contrasts a mythic former age of Great Harmony (**Da tong**) with a succeeding protohistorical age of Lesser Prosperity. People in his utopian Great Harmony were well-off but not greedy and were compassionate toward all;

the great Way (**Dao**) prevailed, and a public-spiritedness pervaded all under Heaven. The moral exemplars Yu, Tang, Wen, Wu and the Duke of Zhou ruled during the following age of Lesser Prosperity, when people were acquisitive and enmeshed with family concerns rather than the public commonality.

References: Legge, 1986: reprint, vol. XXVII: 364–7.

DEBORAH SOMMER

Xiao xue 小學
(Primary education, elementary school, elementary learning)

Xiao xue originally meant elementary schools. According to *Book of Rites* (**Li ji**), aristocratic children aged eight should attend elementary schools, though the details of the schools are not clear. There is no evidence that the Han government established elementary schools, although it is entirely possible that elementary education was available to noble children.

By the Period of Disunity (220–589), government-sponsored elementary schools, such as the School of the Four Gates (*Simen xue* 四門學) in the capital, had become commonplace. During the Tang (618–907), most local government schools had elementary schools affiliated with them. This was to continue in the Song and after. In the Ming times (1368–1644), community schools (*she xue* 社學) rose in importance; most of them were basically elementary educational gatherings. Elementary schools usually taught such famous primers as *Jijiu* 急就, *Thousand Characters Essay* (*Qianzi wen* 千字文), *Hundred Surnames* (*Baijia xing* 百家姓) and *Three Character Classic* (**Sanzi jing**), etc. Pupils also learned writing and basic calculating skills. The more advanced took on the *Analects* (**Lunyu**) and *Classic of Filial Piety* (*Xiao jing*).

The mass appearance of primers led Ban Gu 班固 (32–92), the author of *History of the Former Han* (**Han shu**), to use *xiao xue* to mean primers and elementary texts.

This usage came back in force in the eighteenth century when Evidential Learning (*kao zheng* 考證) scholars used *xiao xue* to mean the philological study of ancient texts.

In the twelfth century, when **Zhu Xi** published his elementary text and named it *xiao xue*, he gave the expression its third meaning: proper learning for children. After him *xiao xue* became widely accepted as meaning elementary learning.

References: Ci Xiaofang, 1998; Lee, Thomas, 2000.

THOMAS H.C. LEE

Xiao zong 小宗
(Minor lineage)

In the idealised kinship structures of the received ritual texts of the late Warring States and early Han periods, a minor lineage is described as a branch or lateral line of a *da zong* 大宗, a major lineage. Both lineages descended ultimately from the same ancestor. A child from a minor lineage could be adopted into a major lineage to serve as its head, requiring him to shift ritual obligations due to his natural father to his adopted ancestor. Distinctions between lineages were significant for maintaining mourning rituals, whose strictures were more severe the closer the relationship to the deceased.

References: Hsu & Linduff, 1988: 163–71; Legge, 1986: vol. XXVIII: 40–67; *Li ji*, 'Sang fu xiao ji', 'Ta zhuan'; Steele, 1966: vol. II: 18–19; *Yi li*, 'Sang fu'; Zheng Xuan, 1990: *juan* 11.8a, modern p. 148.

DEBORAH SOMMER

Xiaozi zhuan 孝子傳
(*Accounts of Dutiful Offspring*)

Xiaozi zhuan are collections of stories in which sons and daughters go to extraordinary lengths to serve their parents. That is, the narratives show how, through their concrete actions, historical figures embodied the virtue of filial piety (*xiao*). One of the most famous of these stories concerns Guo Ju 郭巨 who decided to bury alive his infant son so that he would have enough food for his mother. Happily, upon breaking the ground with his shovel, he found that Heaven rewarded his virtue with a pot of gold. Stories like this were meant to both inspire elite adults and provide them with models of ideal behaviour.

From the Later Han (25–220) through the Tang (618–907), *Accounts of Filial Offspring* circulated in China's elite circles. An indication of their popularity is the fact that emperors authored several of them. Wu Zetian 武則天 (r. 684–705), China's only female emperor, compiled a *Xiaonü zhuan* 孝女傳 (*Accounts of Filial Women*). These works became source materials for primers, such as **Zhu Xi**'s *Xiaoxue* and Li Han's 李瀚 *Mengqiu* 蒙求 (*The Quest of the Unschooled*), and the later collections of filial offspring tales known as '*The Twenty-four Filial Exemplars*' (**Ershisi xiao**). *Accounts of Filial Offspring* also made their way to Japan and Korea, where they introduced Chinese-style filial piety. With the exception of two manuscripts in Japan (which seem to be two recensions of the same text), none of the *Accounts of Filial Offspring* survives, except as fragments in encyclopedias and in manuscripts from Dunhuang 敦煌.

References: Knapp, 1996; Kono, 1954; Tokuda, 1963: vol. I.

KEITH KNAPP

Xie Liangzuo 謝良佐

c. 1050–*c.* 1120
(*zi* Xiandao 顯道, master Shangcai 上蔡先生)

Xie Liangzuo was one of the leading disciples of **Cheng Hao** and his brother **Cheng Yi**; he and **Yang Shi** were called heroes of the Cheng School 程門龍象. Xie's main contribution to the creative development of ***Dao xue*** was his interpretation of *ren* 仁 as

jue 覺 (sensitivity, awareness) and as having a generative seed-like quality.

Life and career

Born in Shangcai 上蔡 in present-day Henan, Xie attained the *jinshi* degree in 1085 and received an appointment at a prefectural school. He later served in several local government posts, including Yingcheng 應城 in present-day Hubei and Mianchi in present-day Henan. While he was in Yingcheng, **Hu Anguo** came to see him and was so impressed with the alertness of Xie's subordinates that he became Xie's student.

A decisive moment in Xie's political career came when he was granted an imperial audience by Emperor Huizong (r. 1100–1125) in 1101, while he was serving at the Imperial Library. According to reports, after the audience Xie commented that 'the Emperor's intent is not sincere' (*Shangyi bucheng* 上意不誠). Subsequently he was assigned to a minor post as superintendent of bamboo and lumber grounds (*jian zhumu chang* 監竹木場) in Luoyang. Later he was stripped of official status, having been implicated by rumour and linked to the so-called Yuanyou faction. His life ended without further opportunity for service, in the period of strife leading to the loss of north China to the Jurchen Jin dynasty (1115–1234).

Neo-Confucian contributions

In 1078, when Xie was approximately twenty-eight years old, he journeyed to the district of Fugou 扶溝 (in present-day Henan) to see Cheng Hao, who was serving as District Magistrate (*zhixian* 知縣). According to one account of their first meeting, Cheng treated Xie with the courtesy due to a guest, but Xie protested that he wanted to become his student. When he was undeterred after being quartered in a cold dark corner for more than a month, Cheng accepted him as a formal disciple. Cheng Hao at one point criticised his students for only studying his words, urging them to devote themselves to practice. When Xie asked what to practise, Cheng suggested quiet-sitting (*jing zuo*).

The best-known anecdote of interaction between Xie and his teacher was while Xie was showing off his knowledge by reciting a book of history. Cheng Hao chided him as 'trifling with things and losing purpose' (*wanwu sangzhi* 玩物喪志), causing Xie to redden and perspire. This reaction, said Cheng, showed the heart/mind of natural compassion (*ceyin zhi xin* 惻隱之心), the incipience of *ren*. Xie was known as a diligent disciple who took his mistakes very seriously; after a year's effort, he reported to Cheng Yi that he had succeeded in getting rid of 'boasting' (*jin* 矜).

The most significant and controversial of Xie's contributions to Confucian thought was his interpretation of *ren* as *jue* 覺, with the connotations of 'awareness', 'awakening', 'sensitivity' and 'alertness'. **Zhu Xi** later criticised Xie's teaching on *ren*, saying that his approach would lead to confusing desires with *li* (principle/pattern). However, Xie himself was particularly careful about distinguishing heavenly principle and personal desire (*tianli renyu*). The point of Xie's teaching on humane sensitivity was to overcome a false sense of separation between oneself and things that he called '*wuwo zhi xin*' 物我之心. In this, he was closely following Cheng Hao's teaching of *wanwu yiti* (unity with all things).

Xie's thought is known primarily through the *Shangcai yulu* 上蔡語錄 (*Recorded Sayings of the Master from Shangcai*), recorded by Zeng Tian 曾恬 (?–?) and **Hu Anguo**. Zhu Xi edited Xie's *yulu* in 1159 as his first major project. Like several other Cheng disciples, Xie wrote a full-length commentary on the *Analects* that became one of the sources for the *Si shu jizhu*. Xie's commentary, *Explanations of the Analects* (*Lunyu jie* 論語解), exemplifies the Neo-Confucian practice of 'savouring the text' (*wanwei* 玩味), imagining oneself directly addressed by Confucius' advice. Xie's preface to the commentary, his only surviving literary work, illustrates his inten-

tion to lift the study of the Sage's words beyond mundane philology to intellectual and spiritual engagement.

Zhu Zhen, a leading disciple of Xie, wrote of him that '. . . as a worthy, he personally transmitted the *Dao xue* learning; none in the world could match him'. Standard accounts of **dao xue** trace Xie's transmission lineage to Hu Anguo, **Hu Hong**, and **Zhang Shi**, marking his particular role in the development of the Hunan School (see *Yuelu xuepai*). **Huang Zongxi**, first compiler of *Song–Yuan xuean*, held that Xie was the best among all the Cheng brothers' disciples. Xie's insights on *ren* remain fruitful themes for later generations; see recent studies by Bäcker, Chu and Selover.

References: Bäcker, 1982; Chan, Wing-tsit, 1967: 52–3, 171–2, 151; Chen & Zhu, 1992; Dong, 1995: 18–20; Franke, 1976: 413–15; Hervouet, 1978: 221–2; Huang & Quan, 1966: 915–38; Mao, 1986: 504–5; Sato, 1986; Selover, 2002; Tillman, 1992b: 75–80.

THOMAS SELOVER

Xin 信
(Trust, faithfulness)

Xin was added by **Dong Zhongshu** to comprise the five constant virtues (**wu chang**) of humaneness (**ren**), righteousness (**yi**), propriety (**li**) and wisdom (**zhi**). *Xin* not only has a very concrete aspect different from that of the other four constants, it is the foundation on which the others rest. In the *Shuowen jiezi* 說文解字 (*Explanations of Scripts and Elucidation of Characters*), the etymological description of the character is of sincerity; an ideographical combination of 'person' (*ren* 人) and 'speech' (*yan* 言), implying a lack of deception in one's words. In the *Analects* (**Lunyu**) 1: 4, Zengzi says, 'Every day I examine myself on three counts: . . . In my dealings with my friends, have I failed to be trustworthy in what I say? . . .'. In the *Mengzi* 3A: 4, **Mengzi** clearly ascribes *xin* to the relation of friendship (*pengyou youxin* 朋友有信). In the *Doctrine of the Mean* (*Zhongyong*) 20, there is a similar mention of the attainment of the Way (*da dao*) and the need for the trustworthiness of one's friends is emphasised as a universal element in the proper fulfillment of one's overall duties to others. **Zhu Xi** took *xin* further, to imply a unification of one's words with one's actions, and held that the relationship between friends is 'sincere' in this manner, a correct path or right way in one's dealings with friends.

Expanding from the self and others to the self and society, Confucius in the *Analects* 12: 7 gives an example of *xin* and the requisites of government: 'The Master said, 'Give them [the people] enough food, give them enough arms, and the common people will have trust in you.' And when asked about the last of these to give up, Confucius replies, 'Death has always been with us . . . but when there is no trust, the common people will have nothing to stand on.' Similarly in the *Spring and Autumn Annals* (*Chunqiu Zuo zhuan*), the third year of Duke Yin, there is an admonition to a ruler that, '. . . you have bound all the princes to you by your propriety (*li*) and trustworhiness (*xin*); and will it not be improper to end with an opposite policy? . . .' In this way, *xin* extends between individuals or groups.

In the Han dynasty, the five constants each had a corresponding member of the five agents (*wu xing*), the five colours (*wu se* 五色) and five directions (*wu fang wei* 五方位), with *xin* associated with *tu* 土 (earth), *huang* 黃 (yellow), and the *zhongyang* 中央 (centre). The premise was that *xin* related human society and the world, human and human, and human and nature. It is likely that because of Confucius' deepening of the concept of *xin* with his association of devotion to duty (*zhong*) in *zhong xin* (忠信), the *Doctrine of the Mean* was influenced in its own development of the central concept of sincerity (*cheng*), and consequently in Confucianism as a whole.

References: *Chunqiu Zuozhuan*; Lau, 1970, 1979; Morohashi, 1960; *Yugyo Sajon Pyonchan Wiwonhoe*, ed., 1990.

TODD CAMERON THACKER

Xin 心
(Heart, mind, heart/mind)

The character *xin* presents particular problems for the translator. In some usages, the term refers to a component of the physical body that is responsible for what in modern terms might be called mentation, and hence it is somewhat analogous to the brain or the mind. Yet Chinese illustrated medical texts indicate that the *xin* is the organ in the chest cavity known in western medicine as the heart. Moreover, the *xin* is also associated with the powers of feeling and emotion, and hence it is closer to western conceptualisations of the heart as a seat of affect and the emotions. Depending upon the context, then, the term *xin* is often translated as either 'mind' or 'heart', although many translators employ some neologism combining both terms – 'mind-and-heart', 'mind/heart', 'heart-mind', and so on – to indicate the range of meanings implied by the Chinese term. Here the less cumbersome 'mind' will be used to designate *xin* in both its cognitive and affective aspects (although it has many more aspects besides), but without any intention of thus establishing a parallel with the modern western understanding of the mind.

Outside of these understandings of *xin*, the notion has moreover complex metaphoric and conceptual applications, as the mind does not always reside in a human body. In such early compilations as the *Book of Documents* (*Shang shu*), the incorporeal Way itself is possessed of a mind (*dao xin*), whose subtlety is paralleled with the precariousness of the human mind (*ren xin* 人心). According to that text, not only humans but also the Lord on High (*Shang Di*) and Heaven (*tian*) are possessed of 'minds'.

Of pre-Han thinkers who had considerable influence on later understandings of the mind, **Mengzi** and **Xunzi** were two of the most important for formulating its moral dimensions and its salient characteristics, respectively. Mengzi asserted that the mind was bestowed by Heaven, that its function was thinking, and that those who developed it through self-cultivation could attain the epitome of what it meant to be a human being. In another instance, Mengzi posited not one but four 'minds' or 'beginnings' (*si duan*), which he understood as inherent potentialities, attitudes or tendencies possessed in common by all people that were the roots of the virtues of humaneness (*ren*), rightness (*yi*), ritual propriety (*li*), and wisdom (*zhi*). **Xunzi** articulated the dimensions of the inner world of the mind, which for him is the faculty that governs the body and understands things. By virtue of its inherent qualities of emptiness, unity and stillness (*xuyi er jing*), the mind can understand the Way and one can attain a great, clear brightness or clarity (*da qingming*).

The cultivation of the mind was not an end in itself, according to a programme for personal, familial and social development outlined in the *Great Learning* (*Da xue*). There the 'rectification' (*zheng* 正) of the mind was one step in a process that on the level of the individual entailed the enhancement of knowledge through inquiry into the phenomenal world and through establishing the sincerity and integrity of one's thoughts. This personal development was then extended to the members of one's clan, one's state and eventually the entire world. Building upon this text, later writings on statecraft, for example, emphasised the importance of rectifying the mind of the ruler in order to establish the prosperity of the state.

The *Great Learning* much influenced Song scholars such as the Cheng brothers and **Zhu Xi**, who moreover emphasised the moral nature of the mind, its original goodness and the commonality of its attendant

virtues present within all human beings. Song discourses on the mind focused upon its relationship with human nature, the emotions (*qing*), evil (*e*), and material force (*qi*). By the Song, the mind had acquired cosmological valences whereby it was associated (by Zhu Xi, for example, who understood the mind as conscious awareness) with the Supreme Ultimate (*tai ji*) and the movements of yin and yang (see **yin–yang**). The ontological implications of the mind expanded also as it became identified with principle (*li*); for **Lu Jiuyuan**, for example, the mind *was* principle.

For the Ming scholar **Wang Shouren**, who was deeply influenced by Mengzi, the *Great Learning*, and Song scholarship, the development of the mind was a key process in the path of sagehood. This development came from within and extended outward, for the mind already naturally possessed within it the 'highest good' described in the *Great Learning* and was moreover endowed with the quality of innate knowing (see *liangzhi liangneng*). Bestowed by Heaven, innate knowing was a faculty of conscious awareness and moral discernment.

References: Chan, Wing-tsit, 1963c, 1996; de Bary & Bloom, 1999: 708–11, 725–37, 842–51; Graham, 1992; Knoblock, 1988–94; Lau, 1984, 2A: 6, 6A: 1; Legge, 1985c.

DEBORAH SOMMER

Xin ji li 心即理
(The mind is principle)

Song thinkers formulated in various ways the relationship between the mind (*xin*) and principle (*li*), but the notion that the mind is itself principle was developed especially by **Lu Jiuyuan**. Building upon **Mengzi**'s notion of the mind and its innate tendencies, Lu asserted that all human beings have minds replete with principle and that the mind and principle are coextensive with the universe through both space and time. Centuries later, **Wang Shouren** further developed, in his *Chuanxi lu*, this idea that the mind is principle.

References: Chan, Wing-tsit, 1963c, 1996: 15–21; de Bary & Bloom, 1999: 714–17.

DEBORAH SOMMER

Xin lun 新論
(*New Treatises*)

Though only fragments remain of the *Xin lun* by **Huan Tan**, those fragments attest to the versatility and brilliance of their author on matters calendrical, musical, medical, economic, historical and ethical. They also provide valuable evidence on important figures known to Huan Tan personally, for example, **Wang Mang**, founder of the short-lived Xin dynasty (9–23 CE), and the classical masters **Liu Xin** and **Yang Xiong**. So while the founder of the Later Han refused to heed the advice Huan Tan proferred in 26 CE, the original *Xin lun* (in 16 or 29 *pian*, depending on the recension) earned Huan Tan a place in history and guaranteed that due honour would be paid to the man whom Huan served as master, Yang Xiong.

Considered more reliable than those from later sources, fragments preserved in Song and pre-Song collectanea or encyclopedias allow us to reconstruct Huan's main ideas. Huan lambasted the characteristic follies of his contemporaries in the ruling elite: their fascination with prognostication texts, portents and alchemy; their pursuit of wealth and power at all costs; their innate corruption cloaked in bureaucratic niceties; their pettifogging scholasticism; their excessive adoration of the past; and their profound ignorance of ordinary realities. Unorthodox in his defence of the 'new music' condemned by classicists, he urged fellow classicists to employ all sorts of music, literature and science in educating the people.

Reference: Pokora, 1975.

MICHAEL NYLAN

Xin Qingnian 新青年
(*New Youth*)

Xin Qingnian was an influential magazine established in Shanghai in September of 1915 during the period of the New Cultural Movement. Chen Duxiu 陳獨秀 (1879–1942) was one of its founders and the editor-in-chief. Its first issue was entitled *Qingnian zazhi* 青年雜志 (*Youth Magazine*); published monthly by Shanghai Jun Yi Press. From the second issue, it was renamed *Xin Qingnian*. Since Chen Duxiu accepted an invitation to teach at Beijing University, the editorial quarters of the magazine moved to Beijing in 1919. The magazine readership increased from about 1,000 at first to about 15,000 in 1917. After the success of the Russian Revolution in October 1917, it was the first journal to propagandise Marxism in China. When the Chinese Communist Party was created in 1921, *Xin Qingnian* became for a time its official journal. Its publication ceased in July of 1926. Influential scholars like Chen Duxiu, Li Dazhao 李大釗 (1889–1927), Hu Shi 胡適 (1891–1962), Qian Xuantong 錢玄同 (1887–1939), were its editors and contributors, many of whom published their most influential papers there. The main aims and the achievements of the journal were such as follows. Firstly, it was set out to spread the ideas of science and democracy. Chen Duxiu developed 'science' and 'democracy' as two doctrines for new youth and two flags for the new cultural movements. Secondly, it encouraged opposition to the feudal social system and demanded social revolution; the editors and authors of the journal joined the social movement against Yuan Shikai's attempt to restore the imperial system. Thirdly, the magazine harshly criticised Confucianism as the aristocratic ideology of feudalism, thus opposing any efforts to reestablish its social position. Fourthly, it concentrated on criticising feudalistic moral standards and demanded a new moral system. Fifthly, it encouraged and supported cultural revolution including proposing vernacular language instead of ancient Chinese. Finally, it imparted these new ideas to the next generation.

References: Wang Jin, Yang Jianghua, eds., 1989; Wu & Song, 1992.

OUYANG KANG

Xin shu 新書
(*The New Book*)

The fifty-eight chapters of the *Xin shu* (ascribed to **Jia Yi**) may be divided into the three categories of memorials addressed to Han Wendi (r. 180–157 BCE), discussions on ritual, possibly deriving from Jia Yi's talks with his pupils, and historical anecdotes that lend strength to the lessons of political life.

Of the essays included in the collection the best known is the one entitled '*Guo Qin lun*' 過秦論 which should best be taken to mean 'Identifying the mistakes made by Qin'. Included in the **Shi ji** and in part in the **Han shu**, this essay goes further than categorising the activities of the Qin government as wicked; it acts as a warning to the contemporary government of Han Wendi to avoid committing the same errors as Qin emperors, thereby deserving a similar end. In this sense the essay may be read as an attempt to maintain the established system of imperial government which had not been seen in the time of Confucius and which rested on the structure and organisation that the Qin had initiated. In so far as the essay criticises the Qin, and in particular the First Qin Emperor (r. 221–210 BCE), on the grounds of a failure to abide by recognised ethical standards, it has often been taken as an appeal to practise the ideals of humaneness (*ren*) and righteousness or justice (*yi*) that Confucius and his followers advocated.

The doubts that have been raised regarding the authenticity of all or parts of the received text of the *Xin shu* have met with the reaction of some scholars in its defence.

References: de Bary, Chan & Watson, 1960: vol. I: 150–2; Nylan, Michael, in Loewe, ed., 1993: 161–70.

MICHAEL LOEWE

Xin weishi lun 新唯識論
(*New Doctrine of Consciousness Only*)

This is the major work representing **Xiong Shili**'s philosophical system. After learning and teaching the Buddhist doctrine of Consciousness Only (*Weishi lun* 唯識論), Xiong became convinced that these teachings were inadequate. His subsequent transformation of thought involved a reinterpretation of many Buddhist concepts, reworked progressively into a systematic Confucian monistic worldview. *New Doctrine of Consciousness Only* was first published in eight chapters of classical Chinese in 1932; a revised colloquial version, consisting of four parts in nine larger chapters accompanied by charts and further explanatory notes, appeared in 1944.

Basic to Xiong's philosophy is an ontological claim: human life and the universe are 'originally not separate'. Though the external world of 'things' (*wu* 物) does exist, it is not ontologically separate from the human 'heart/mind' (*xin*). There is ultimately no difference between the 'essence' and 'utility' of all things (*tiyong bu er* 體用不二). This monistic ontology (*benti* 本體) embodies a constantly changing reality, as elaborated in **Wang Fuzhi**'s *Commentaries to the Appendix of the Book of Changes* (*Zhouyi waizhuan* 周易外傳, *Zhouyi neizhuan* 周易內傳). Though there are 'openings' of mental awareness (*pi* 闢) and 'closings' (*xi* 翕) of materialisation in the universal process, it remains a mutually intertwining ontological whole.

The 'original heart/mind' (*ben xin* 本心), the metaphysical awareness which grounds the self and things, is the source of all values. Xiong identifies it with Confucian humaneness (*ren* 仁) and **Wang Shouren**'s 'innate knowledge of good' (*liang zhi* 良知).

Xiong's philosophy significantly influenced the philosophical writings of **Tang Junyi**, **Mou Zongsan**, and **Xu Fuguan**.

References: Cheng & Bunnin, 2002; Fang & Li, 1995: vol. I, 470–7; Fang & Zheng, 1995: 67–71; Lin Anwu, ed., 1990; Xiong, 1985.

LAUREN PFISTER

Xin xing 心性
(The mind and the nature)

Xin in this expression is the mind or heart; *xing* is the nature. Although in some usages the expression can be understood as a compound that means 'the nature of the mind', it is more commonly understood as being composed of two paired terms and hence means 'the mind and the nature'. In later imperial times, the expression 'learning of the mind and the nature' (*Xinxing zhi xue*) referred to Song learning.

Song scholars were hardly the first to discuss those terms together, however. **Mengzi** had much earlier asserted that the mind and the nature are developed in tandem. Those who fully develop their minds understand the nature, he claimed; those who understand the nature understand Heaven. Cultivating the mind and the nature were moreover tantamount to serving Heaven. Hence Mengzi established a contiguity between the inner life of a person and the larger world beyond the self, and self-cultivation thus was a process bearing cosmic significance. 'Serving' was a duty commonly owed to a human superior, but here Mengzi established a direct relationship between the individual and Heaven itself.

Xunzi discussed the relationship of the mind and the nature in the context of the satisfaction and control of desire. Emotions (*qing*) were one aspect of the nature bestowed by Heaven, and desires were the responses of those emotions. The reason the desires did not otherwise develop inappropriately was due to the mind, which controlled them.

In the Song, **Zhang Zai** understood the relationship of the mind and the nature in terms of harmony but nonetheless also asserted that the mind is in charge of the emotions. The nature unfolded from the harmony of the Supreme Vacuity (*Tai xu*) and material force (*qi*); the mind was the harmony of the nature and awareness (*zhi jue* 知覺). The mind furthermore brought together the nature and the emotions. By expanding one's mind and fully developing the nature, one could transcend the limits of sense perception, fathom the myriad phenomena of the world, and become merged with all things in the cosmos.

Cheng Yi understood the mind and the nature in terms of principle: the nature, the mind and Heaven itself were all manifestations of the same principle. Principle was one, Cheng asserted, but it manifested itself in diverse ways. The nature, moreover, was identified with *qi*. Cheng Yi believed the mind was originally good, but upon being aroused it might manifest negative aspects. The nature was also fundamentally good, but one's capability (*cai*), which stemmed from *qi*, might become either good or bad, depending upon the clarity or murkiness, respectively, of one's *qi*.

For **Zhu Xi**, who was much influenced by both Zhang Zai and Cheng Yi, the mind and the nature were closely interrelated. All things had their principle, which was ultimately one and was beyond form, but principle was moreover particularised in individual human beings and inhered in *qi*, which was of the realm of form and materiality. The nature of human beings was this principle and was the Way itself. The mind, for Zhu Xi, was associated with the Supreme Ultimate (*Tai ji*) rather than Zhang's Supreme Vacuity. There was a principle of consciousness that, when it was given form, was the mind, which was the supervisor of the physical frame. The mind might become clouded with desires, but by inquiring into things (following the steps of self-cultivation articulated in the *Great*

Learning (*Da xue*) one might develop clarity and understanding.

Lu Jiuyuan placed more emphasis on the mind and principle than the mind and the nature, asserting that they were one and that the mind was the cosmos itself. When asked about the relationships between the mind, the nature, capability and emotions, Lu replied that they were all just one thing manifested differently. In the Ming, **Wang Shouren** drew upon the *Great Learning* and the *Mengzi* in his interpretations of the mind and the nature. He criticised Zhu Xi for purportedly implying that the mind and the nature were two different things; for Wang, the mind was the nature, and the nature was principle and was the highest good. Wang emphasised the mind's inherent ability to know or understand things (see *liangzhi liangneng*) and the importance of seeking moral principles within the mind and enacting them in one's daily life.

Dai Zhen, however, understood the natures of humans, animals and things in terms of differences and particularities rather than unity. The nature was the manifestation of different amalgamations of sanguine humours, *qi*, the Five Phases (*wu xing*), yin and yang (see **yin–yang**) and what he called the 'knowing mind' (*xin zhi* 心知). Following Mengzi, he did not include principle in this formulation.

References: Chan, Wing-tsit, 1963a: 572–87, 1963b, 1996; Chin & Freeman, 1990; de Bary & Bloom, 1999: 684–9, 710–11; Graham, 1992; Knoblock, 1988–94; Lau, 1984, 7A: 1.

DEBORAH SOMMER

Xin xue 心學
(The Learning of the Heart/Mind)

Human heart/mind (*xin*) occupies a central place in the Neo-Confucian understanding of how human beings become human. Idealistic Neo-Confucians believe that and human beings achieve moral action, transform and transcend themselves via their understanding, will and self-cultivation and self-development. The core of the Learning of the Heart/Mind or *Xin xue* in the Song-Ming period is therefore concerned with the investigation of how the human heart/mind grasps principles of reality, reason and value and fulfils itself. It is **Lu Jiuyuan** (Lu Xiangshan) who holds that this heart/mind of ours is the vehicle for principle (*xin ji li*) and embodies the very essence of *li* the principle. He says that 'My heart/mind is the cosmos and the cosmos is my heart/mind.' In this maxim one sees that Lu has treated heart/mind as the ultimate reality and hence not separable from the *li* as understood as an ultimate principle of reality and knowledge. It is clear that to equate heart/mind with the world-reality is not to deny the objective reality of things but to attribute a deeper significance to the reality of things in terms of the unity, dynamism and moral value content of the heart/mind. In this regard one must agree with Lu that his philosophy of the heart/mind originates from **Mengzi**. But on the other hand, in so far as the heart/mind acquires the significance and identity of *li*, it is still part of the *li* tradition as established in the Northern Song period. In this regard we may simply note that Mengzi is the originator of the *Xin xue* as well as the originator of *Li xue* in the sense that he propagates that *li* and *yi* (righteousness) of things and human beings can be found only in our heart/mind.

It is not until **Wang Shouren** that the *Xin xue* becomes the prevailing influence of his time. It was indeed in the hands of Wang that *Xin xue* acquires an independent status. In contrast with, or as an opposite to *Li xue*. Wang enriches and develops the *Xin xue* by way of his deep experience of both the metaphysical function and moral function of the heart/mind under critical and stringent conditions for self-understanding and self-transcendence. He comes to hold that the heart/mind is *li*, which means that it is the heart/mind alone that presents the subtle and important truths of being and life. He further notices that it is in the practice and action of life that knowledge of the heart/mind becomes real and that it is in the knowledge of the heart/mind that one forms a decision and commitment to action and practice. In this sense knowing and action generate each other. The creative interaction between knowledge and action is crucial for the development of the moral character of a person. In his final view on fulfilling the innate knowledge of good, Wang comes to see the utimate reality and value of human life as consisting of realising the inner goodness of reality in terms of understanding, action and reflection. Although Wang formed a large school of the heart/mind in the middle Ming period and his influences have spread far and wide in China and Japan throughout the modern period, there are other distinguished heart/mind philosophers such as **Chen Xianzhang** and **Zhan Ruoshui**. Whether the thesis of *Xin xue* is derived from Chinese Chan Buddhism is also a philosophical and academic issue in the Song–Ming philosophy. But one cannot deny that the *Xin xue* has presented a distinguished position of its own which no doubt has its roots in classical Confucianism and in the *Li xue* of the Song period.

CHUNG-YING CHENG

Xin xue 新學
(New Learning)

The term has been used to mean many different things in the history of Confucianism. First, *Xin xue* is used to refer to the learning of the Xin dynasty (9–23 CE) when **Liu Xin** promoted the Old Text versions of the Classics, which differed from the current learning of the New Text School. In the 1890s, in order to advance his theory of reform, **Kang Youwei** in his *Xinxue weijing kao* attacked the *Xin xue* as based on the

forged Classics, and asserted that the learning of the New Text School was the only true Confucian Learning. Secondly, it is used to describe the approach to classical studies developed by the Northern Song scholar **Wang Anshi**, who composed commentaries on the *Book of Poetry* (*Shi jing*), *Book of History* (*Shang shu*), and *Rites of Zhou* (*Zhou li*) with a view toward actualising, in Song times, his own idealised vision of what he held to be the fundamental principles of Zhou governance. Whereas he is best known for his controversial practical applications of ancient learning to contemporary issues, his cosmological system (based on the theory of the Five Phases (*Wu xing*) and described in his *Hong fan zhuan* 洪範傳 and conceptualisations of the human body (which emphasise the significance of the physical frame) remain lesser known. Thirdly, *xin xue* is a term used by scholars of the nineteenth and twentieth centuries to refer to the learning of the West (**xi xue**), in contrast to *jiu xue* (the Old Learning) of the Chinese, who called for the replacement of the traditional Confucian doctrines by the western ideology. According to these scholars, the contrasts between these two kinds of learning are, for example, that the Old Learning emphasises the three guidelines (**san gang**), while the New Learning promotes equality, that the Chinese governed the state by means of filial piety, while the West by means of a public spirit, and that the Chinese promoted the love of one's own kin (**qinqin**), while the West gave prominence to the worthy.

References: Bol, 1989: 151–85, 1992: 212–53; Liu, James, 1959; Lo, 1976.

DEBORAH SOMMER

Xin xue weijing kao 新學偽經考
(*Inquiry into the Forged Classics of the Xin Dynasty*)

Having recovered from a spiritual crisis in 1878, **Kang Youwei** left his teacher Zhu Ciqi

朱次琦 (1807–1881) and studied the Confucian Classics on his own. After years of intensive study, he abandoned the eclectic approach of learning that Zhu preached, and adopted the New Text School of Former Han Confucianism. In 1889–1890, he met with the Hunanese scholar **Liao Ping**, who showed him the fundamental differences between the New Text School and its rival, the Old Text School. A year later, in 1891, he wrote the *Xinxue weijing kao* in which he offered a comprehensive critique of the Old Text School.

In the late Qing, the New Text and the Old Text scholars concentrated on different Confucian Classics. The Old Text scholars favoured the Classics collected by Liu Xin and **Zheng Xuan**. The Classics were considered to be more authentic because they were purportedly saved from the burning of books in the Qin dynasty (221–206 BCE). In contrast, the New Text scholars focused on another group of Classics, including Gongyang's commentary on the *Spring and Autumn Annals* (*Chunqiu Gongyang zhuan*). Written in *li* (隷) style of calligraphy, the New Text Classics were honoured by the Former Han Emperors, who created special official posts to study the Classics. To further separate themselves from the Old Text scholars, the New Text scholars stressed the need for going beyond the 'literal meanings' of Confucian texts in order to comprehend their 'profound metaphoric messages'. They were more interested in applying Confucian teachings directly to institutional reform than in pure academic philological studies.

In the *Xinxue weijing kao*, Kang's goal was to discredit the Old Text School as a valid school of Confucian Learning. Ironically, to achieve his goal, he employed the philological method that the Old Text Scholars perfected to disprove their claims. Firstly, with ample examples, Kang demonstrated that the Qin's burning of books was not as comprehensive as many historians had suggested. Some of the key Confucian Classics – including those that were adopted by the New Text scholars – were passed on to the Former Han scholars without damage. Hence, the Old Text scholars were wrong in claiming that their classics were more genuine than the New Text Classics.

Secondly, based on meticulous textual studies, Kang showed that the Old Text Classics were spurious. They were forged by Liu Xin to support **Wang Meng**'s usurpation of the Former Han (202 BCE–8 CE). Kang asserted that it was wrong to call the Old Text School the 'Han learning', although it was known that way among the Qing scholars. Because Liu's forgery was to serve Wang Meng's Xin dynasty (9–23), Kang suggested that the Old Text School should be called the **Xin xue** (New Learning). In calling the Old Text School the 'Xin Learning', Kang's intention was to make the New Text School the genuine Han learning. For him, the New Text School was the genuine Han learning not only because it was untamed by forgery, but also because it was a Former Han learning that predated Wang Meng's usurpation.

Immediately following its publication, the *Xinxue weijing kao* became the centre of controversy. On the one hand, **Liao Ping** accused Kang of plagiarism. He claimed that Kang stole ideas from his writings such as the *Jingu xue kao* 今古學考 (*Studies in Old and New Text Learning*, 1886), '*Pi Liu pian*' 闢劉篇 (*Refuting Liu Xin*, 1888), '*Zhisheng pian*' 至聖篇 (*Essay on Comprehending the Sage*, 1888) and the *Guxue kao* 古學考 (*Studies in the Old Text Learning*, 1894). On the other hand, the Old Text scholars condemned Kang for misrepresenting their thoughts and undermining Confucian orthodoxy. In 1894, the government stepped in and burned copies of the *Xinxue weijing kao*. During the Hundred Days of Reform in 1898, Kang was able to reprint the *Xinxue weijing kao* with the support from Emperor Guangxu (r. 1875–1908). But the failure of the reform resulted in yet another suppression of the *Xinxue weijing kao*.

Compared Kang's other work the **Kongzi gaizhi kao**, the *Xinxue weijing kao* did not offer any specific plan to change the political institution. But it was political in the sense of challenging the dominant ideological paradigm of the time, i.e., the Old Text School. As **Liang Qichao** pointed out many years later, the *Xinxue weijing kao* was an important milestone in the development of Qing thought. It was another step that the Qing scholars made in 'liberating themselves from dogma by restoring the ancient teaching' (*yi fugu wei jiefang* 以復古為解放).

References: Fung, 1952; Hsiao Kung-chuan, 1979; Liang Qichao, 1920; Qian, 1937.

TZE-KI HON

Xin yu 新語
(*The New Words*)

Following the warnings that he had given to Han Gaozu (r. 202–195 BCE) on the need to improve his style of government, and the emperor's invitation to express his views in writing, **Lu Jia** submitted a set of essays on the subject in a book of twelve chapters, which was entitled *Xin yu*. Doubts that have been cast on the authenticity of all or parts of the received text of that work have in general been allayed, with some obvious cases of interpolation, and the work was described by the editors of the *Siku quanshu zongmu tiyao* 四庫全書總目提要 as the most mature expression of Confucian opinion for the Han period apart from the writings of **Dong Zhongshu**.

The book recognises the relationship between Heaven (*tian*) and Earth (*di*) and sees human affairs within that context. While strange phenomena are to be regarded as an expression of Heaven's warnings, the book is concerned with human values and relationships rather than with superhuman forces. Full credit is given to the culture heroes and monarchs of mythology in their work of improving the lot of human beings and raising their moral standards. For his own time, the author refers to the ideal of the man of quality (*junzi*) whose successful leadership is based on moderation, the pursuit of ethical aims and the attraction of loyal support by means of tacit example rather than forceful action. The true ruler of humankind must frame his actions so as to follow the sequences of Heaven and he must practise clemency rather than resort to legal prescriptions. He should be ready to recognise good qualities and abilities in any man, however mean his background; but the way of the hermit is to be deprecated as it runs counter to the fulfilment of social duties and of service to one's fellow men. While the imposition of excessively severe punishments leads to the fall of evil rulers, good rule is based on trustworthiness; the decline of a ruler's authority is due not to the decisions of Heaven but to the faults of man. The *Xin yu* cites the reported actions and sayings of Confucius and invokes the *Book of Poetry* (**Shi jing**) and *Book of History* (**Shang shu**). It stresses the value of moral virtues as exemplified in humaneness (**ren**) and righteousness (**yi**).

MICHAEL LOEWE

Xing 刑
(Punishments, recision)

Principles for the application of *xing*, or punishments, were described as early as the 'Punishments of Lü' (*Lü xing*) chapter of the **Shang shu**, which outlined the careful due process observed in the ministration of the 'five punishments' of branding, cutting off the nose, amputation of the feet, castration and death. Officials who administered punishments were considered 'shepherds of Heaven' and were themselves subject to the punishments of Heaven if their decisions were biased, harsh or careless. In doubtful cases, punishments were to be remediated with fines. The 'Punishments of Lü' asserted that unduly severe punishments actually created instead of ameliorated crime and disorder; punishments should ideally be implemented by an administration guided by virtue (*de*) who was moreover moved to teach virtue to the people.

Punishments were one means for governing the people, but a number of early thinkers held that, although they were necessary in extreme cases, punishments were far from an ideal method of statecraft. As a means of maintaining the authority of the rulers, such strictures had severe drawbacks, for they had the potential of inciting chaos. Punishments, it was believed, should first be clearly promulgated and then sparingly and consistently applied. Confucius, for example, asserted that if punishments were not appropriate, then the people would become confused. He emphasised governing the people instead with virtue (*de*), for otherwise the people would simply try to avoid punishments without developing a sense of shame (*Analects* 13: 3 and 2: 3). **Mengzi** encouraged rulers to soften harsh punishments and to provide first for the welfare of the people, implying that crimes were committed largely by persons acting out of desperation, people who would then become further entrapped by the penal system. For **Xunzi**, excessive punishments were a sign of a clumsy, desperate ruler who had little understanding of subtler, more charismatic forms of maintaining order and establishing moral authority.

Although in early texts *xing* often means punishment, in other contexts it often appeared as a pair with de 得, 'to obtain' or also *de* 德, virtue, inner power or rewards. As a compound, *de xing* are rewards and punishments (or, following Major, accretion and recision), the ruler's two 'handles' for ordering the state. The worthy accrued rewards and miscreants were diminished (sometimes literally, in the case of corporal excisions) by punishments. *De xing*, as accretion and recision, described not only this administrative augmentation and reduction but also the waxing and waning of cosmological forces through the permutations of the seasons. Forces of growth increased during the summer months and declined

in the winter, and rulers correlated their own measures of reward and punishment with the seasons, granting emoluments and even amnesties in the warmer months and executing punishments in the winter.

Over the succeeding centuries, these basic attitudes and principles shaped the practice of statecraft of the many literati who served in official positions in the state bureaucracy and were responsible both for the formulation of legal codes and the practical application of their statutes.

References: Bodde & Morris, 1967; Creel, 1980; Hulsewe, 1985; Major, 1987; Wilkinson, 1998.

DEBORAH SOMMER

Xing 性
(The nature, human nature)

The fundamental characteristics of the nature, or human nature, have been endlessly debated by literati thinkers, who have postulated various theories concerning its perceived inherent ethical tendencies; its relationship to other phenomena such as Heaven, the material or vital fore (*qi*), the mind (*xin*) and emotions (*qing*); and the potentialities and processes for developing it throughout life.

In early texts such as the *Book of Poetry* (**Shi jing**), the *Book of History* (**Shang shu**), and the *Spring and Autumn Annals* (**Chunqiu Zuo zhuan**), the term *xing* encompassed more than just human nature and in some usages meant life itself. The radical on the right-hand side of the character as it is commonly written in received texts is *sheng*, which means life. *Xing* also referred to the autochthonous or inherent characteristics of the earth or land of a particular place; the nature of a certain locale was reflected even in the livestock raised there. The nature of human beings was related to the nature of the earth and of other phenomena. The *Chunqiu Zuo zhuan* (Duke Zhao 25th year) describes the interrelationship between the nature of humans, the nature of Heaven and Earth, the six *qi*, and the Five Phases. When these latter phenomena become imbalanced, human beings lose their natures.

One passage from the *Shang shu* names something called the heavenly nature but does not describe it other than to lament that it was not properly attended to in times of famine and distress. Other passages claim that the nature is constant and was bestowed even on ordinary people by **Shang Di**. It was associated also with habituation and repetition; the nature could be developed through daily adjustments, but even negative behaviours could become one's nature if allowed to progress. Overall, however, in these early texts the nature is mentioned almost incidentally and relatively little attention is given to describing its characteristics or direction.

Even Confucius' disciples lamented that they rarely heard Confucius talk about the nature. Their voiced concern, nonetheless, reflects an increasing interest in the subject at the end of the Spring and Autumn period (770–476 BCE). When Confucius did mention the nature, it was in the context of human beings rather than of the earth or animals, and he was more specifically concerned about what people shared in common and how they differed. He distinguished between habituation and the nature, implying that the nature was something beyond habituation in his assertion that in terms of the nature humans are similar but in terms of habit or practice they become very different.

Warring States thinkers, however, developed more systematic analyses of the nature and of its perceived inherent tendencies toward the good, toward what was not good, or toward some direction in between. **Mengzi**, for example, asserted that the nature was possessed of inherent tendencies and that all people shared this nature in common. The nature had the potentiality to become good (*shan*), provided it was not crushed by external circumstances beyond

its control; it tended toward the good just as water was naturally inclined to flow downhill. Humans were moreover innately endowed with the virtues of humaneness, rightness, ritual/propriety and wisdom.

The **Xunzi** describes several different perspectives on the nature. The best known of these is elaborated in the chapter 'Human Nature is Evil or Abhorrent' (see **Xing e lun**), which asserts that human nature is evil and that goodness is the result of conscious effort guided by the ritual formulations and other teachings of the sages. In the 'Rectification of Names' chapter, however, the *Xunzi* claims simply that the nature is what is natural and spontaneous from birth, and the 'Dispelling Obfuscation' chapter asserts that the inborn nature is associated with knowing or wisdom.

The nature was more closely conjoined with Heaven in the **Zhongyong**, which opens with the statement that the nature is endowed by Heaven and that following the nature is the Way. This short text was extremely influential in Song and later discussions of human nature.

Han thinkers combined elements of Warring States thought on the nature and added new political implications. **Dong Zhongshu**, for example, associated the nature with Heaven and humaneness, and stated that goodness develops from the nature with education, but averred that not all of the nature is necessarily good but inclines toward selfish gain. Heaven, fortunately, set up kings to provide the guidance necessary for developing the nature appropriately.

In the Song, **Zhou Dunyi** was inspired by the transformations and processes elaborated in the *Yi jing* regarding his notions of human nature. For him, the nature was the completion of the Way, a phenomenon he understood as good and as the fluctuation of the forces of yin and yang (see **yin-yang**). **Zhang Zai** expanded the notion of the nature to include a cosmological vision that encompassed Heaven and Earth: the nature, for him, was the operational process of the universe itself, which, embodying the original *qi*, became the nature of Heaven and Earth (*Tiandi zhi xing*) and the source of goodness in human nature, while manifesting in material formation, became the physically endowed nature (*Qizhi zhi xing*) and the source of evil in human activities. The original nature, which was fundamentally tranquil, needed development in terms of transforming the latter in order to make the physically endowed nature accord with heavenly principle. The path to this began with the investigation of things, one of the elements of the *Great Learning*, **Da xue**.

The Cheng brothers, much influenced by the *Zhong yong* and Mengzi, asserted that the nature is from Heaven and is essentially good. Following Zhang Zai, they closely associated the nature with principle (*li*) and with *qi*. One's nature stemmed from Heaven, but problems potentially might develop from one's capability or endowment (*cai*), which might be either good or evil. Capability stemmed from *qi*, which might be either murky or clear. Mengzi had earlier claimed that the nature tended toward the good just as water flowed downhill, but the Chengs cautioned that water might become either clear or muddied as it flowed to the sea, and that one was thus enjoined to maintain its clarity. Zhu Xi similarly associated the nature with Heaven and principle, and claimed that the nature and the Way are fundamentally the same; the virtues of humaneness, rightness, ritual/propriety and wisdom were grounded there. Difficulties arose when people drifted away from this nature, which might be obscured by muddied *qi* but nevertheless required *qi* and materiality as a place to inhere. Human desires might obscure the nature, but they could be cleared with effort. The development of the nature was manifested in the proper maintenance of the relationships between human beings.

Wang Shouren, following the *Great Learning*'s assertion that the Way of the great learning lay in abiding in the highest good, claimed that the nature was in fact already the highest good, and that the nature and *qi* were consubstantial. Wang believed that Zhu Xi's programme of the development of the self and the nature was in some respects too belaboured, and Wang emphasised the innate powers that human beings inherently possess for self-realisation and understanding.

The Qing scholar **Dai Zhen** crafted a thorough historical and philosophical analysis of previous theories of human nature – and even of the nature of animals and plants – critiquing Song scholarship in the light of his understanding of pre-Han texts and his distaste for perceived Buddhist and Daoist influences on Song thought. Dai understood human nature in terms of yin and yang, the permutations of *qi* and the Five Phases, the sanguinous humours and the mind.

References: Ames & Rosemont, 1998: 5:13, 17:2; Chan, Wing-tsit, 1963c, 1996: 7–14; Chin & Freeman, 1990: 113–36; de Bary & Bloom, 1999: 302–5, 667–713; Knoblock, 1988–94: vol. III: 110, 127, 139–62; Lau, 1984, 6A: 1–6; Legge, 1985a: 704, 708; 1985c, ode 252; 1985d: 185, 203, 271, 349, 429.

DEBORAH SOMMER

Xing Bing 邢昺
932–1010
(*zi* Shuming 叔明)

Born during the Tang–Song interregnum, Xing Bing was at the centre of classical scholarship during the early years of the Song dynasty (960–1279). Having passed the examination on the Nine Classics (*Jiu jing*) early in Song Taizong's reign (r. 976–997), he was subsequently appointed lecturer and academician in the Hanlin Academy by the Emperor Zhenzong (r. 998–1022), in which capacity he lectured on the *Spring and Autumn Annals* (*Chunqiu*) in the palace. During his career, Xing enjoyed the favour of these two emperors. His service was frequently rewarded with imperial gifts and gold. This service was not limited to simply academic matters. He was apparently able to discuss contemporary policy issues as well (*Song shi*, 1977: 431.12799–800). When he died of illness in 1010, he had reached the post of Minister of Rites (*Libu shangshu* 禮部尚書).

Xing's scholarly reputation led to a series of appointments to commissions preparing standard commentaries on the Classics. These included the three ritual texts (the *Li ji*, the *Zhou li*, and the *Yi li*), the three commentaries to the *Chunqiu* (the *Zuo zhuan*, the *Gongyang zhuan*, and the *Guliang zhuan*), the *Xiao jing*, the *Er ya* 爾雅 dictionary and the *Analects* of Confucius. Xing's commentaries on the *Analects*, *Er ya* and *Xiao jing* were eventually included as the standard subcommentaries in **Ruan Yuan**'s 1815 *Shisan jing zhushu*.

Xing's work stressed explaining the language of the Classics. Thus, he can be seen as continuing the tradition begun in the Han and developed in the Tang that stressed textual exegesis.

References: Ruan Yuan, *et al.*, 1980; *Song shi*, 1977.

ANTHONY DEBLASI

Xing e lun 性惡論
(Human nature is abhorrent)

The slogan 'Human Nature is Abhorrent' was the rhetorical riposte devised by **Xunzi** to counter **Mengzi**'s theory that 'Human Nature is [Innately] Good' (*xing shan lun*). Attempting to explain both variations in human behaviour and the origin of social morality, Mengzi argued that each human being is endowed at birth with the Four Beginnings (*Si duan*) of social morality: the heart of compassion, the heart of shame, the heart of deference, and the heart that discriminates right from wrong. These Four Beginnings have only to be fostered (positively, by suasive example and economic sufficiently; more negatively, by a lack of interference in the development process) for each human being to attain moral maturity. Xunzi strenuously objected to such a view, lest it lead to relativism, to anti-conventional behaviour, or to a misunderstanding of the all-important roles of ritual and hierarchy. 'The inborn nature does not understand ritual and righteousness. It is conscious deliberation that causes a person to seek to know them. It is the search itself that produces them. Thus people have no [innate] sense of ritual and righteousness [at birth] nor do they understand them' (chapter *Xing e*).

Learning to model oneself on the ancient sage–kings so as to continue their social and political institutions, Xunzi stressed, is an artificial act absolutely reliant upon a sophisticated understanding of ritual's crucial role in productive social interactions. Neither the slow study and emulation of moral exemplars nor the painstaking acquisition of conscious powers of moral and practical discrimination is in any way 'natural' to human beings (unlike greed, covetousness and the desire to dominate). Thanks to the 'god-like' prescience of the sages, ritual has been devised in such a way as to completely 'satisfy' human desires (e.g., those for community and symbols) while dramatically 'constraining' them. Ritual can be used, then, to school persons in righteousness.

Outside his chapter 'Human Nature is Abhorrent', it is clear that Xunzi, like Mengzi, believes that each person is endowed with sufficient basic tendencies toward the good, which must be developed if they are to grow into full humanity. But Xunzi departs from Mengzi in stressing the inherent frailty of such tendencies; hence the need for careful guidance by teachers, parents and rulers throughout the maturation process, to insure that humans are guided to morality. The goal of human morality at its best, according to Xunzi, is to maintain a harmonious balance of the emotions and desires in the face of changing external circumstances. The attainment of such an admirable balance in a single human being represents the culmination of the concerted efforts of a great many individuals, including the ancient sage–kings, who devised the social and political institutions that foster goodness in the individual; teachers, parents, friends and rulers, all encouraging the person to desire goodness above all else; and the person concerned, who must continually struggle to overcome the contrary impulses to break community and ignore useful social conventions.

MICHAEL NYLAN

Xing ji li 性即理
(Nature is principle)

Xing ji li is the term, usually translated as 'nature is principle', used by **Cheng Yi** to express his basic belief that the essence of human nature is principle (*li*). According to **Chen Chun**'s understanding of the term, 'from birth man possesses principle complete in his mind. The chief items of principle are simply humanity, righteousness, propriety, and wisdom' (Chan, 1986: 47). Principle cannot exist by itself but requires the body as its vehicle. The body is formed by material force, *qi*, and the nature that infuses the body by principle, *li*. Because *li* is good, man's nature is fundamentally good. Evil derives from the effect of impurities contained within *qi*.

Reference: Chan, Wing-tsit, 1986b.

ALAN T. WOOD

Xing li 性理
(The nature and principle)

The term *xing* is the nature, or human nature; *li* is principle. The two terms appear independently, not as a pair, in pre-Han texts but do appear together some time after the Han in such contexts as **Kong Yingda**'s commentary to Ode 263 of the *Book of Poetry*, where the expression is used as a compound and refers to the essential nature of a thing. The expression *xingli* became important philosophically, however, only around the Song, where the terms *xing* and *li* were used as a pair but not as a compound.

Cheng Yi and **Cheng Hao**, for example, elevated the notion of principle to a significant place in their system of thought, and they moreover equated the nature and principle. The nature, for the Chengs, was bestowed by Heaven. It was inborn, yet no distinction was made regarding whether the nature was internal or external, for one formed one body with all things (following **Mengzi**'s assertion to that effect). The nature was good; one's capability (*cai*), however, might be either good or evil, depending on the clarity of one's material force (*qi*). Principle, for the Chengs, was also good and was deeply associated with moral values. It was inexhaustible and was the Mandate of Heaven; principle was one but manifested itself in many different ways and in all things. Fathoming principle and developing one's nature were one and the same process. By conjoining human nature and principle, the Chengs intimately connected human beings with the fundamental grounding of the universe. The universe, then, was fundamentally good, other than when one moved away from one's inborn nature, and it was real. Such a vision of the world stood in contrast to the cosmology of Buddhist thinkers, whom some literati understood (or misunderstood) to presuppose that the world was vacuous, unreal or empty in a negative sense.

Zhu Xi followed the Chengs regarding this equation between the nature and principle. He stated that the virtues of humaneness, rightness, ritual/propriety and wisdom were themselves human nature, which he moreover equated with the Way. Zhu also asserted the importance of *qi* as a kind of matrix in which principle inhered. Principle was above form, but *qi* was of the realm of form and might be either clear or murky (see *li qi*).

To Ming and later literati, notions of the nature and principle were considered such important hallmarks of Song thought that they often referred to Song learning as the learning of nature and principle (see *xingli zhi xue*). This is reflected in the titles of such Ming compilations of Song learning as the *Xingli daquan* 性理大全 (Great Compendia of Nature and Principle) or the much later *Xingli jingyi*, which included works even by thinkers such as **Zhou Dunyi**, for whom the concepts of nature or principle were not central. Some Qing scholars such as **Dai Zhen**, however, perceived the Cheng brothers' and Zhu Xi's notion of principle as the Buddhist notion of emptiness in disguise and criticised Song learning as slipping away from the teachings of the Classics.

References: Chan, Wing-tsit, 1975, 1996: 7–14, 133–46; Chin & Freeman, 1990: 69–102; de Bary & Bloom, 1999: 689–737; *Shisan jing zhushu*, 1979: modern p. 576.

DEBORAH SOMMER

Xing ming 性命
(Nature and fate)

If 'Heaven' (*tian*) refers to whatever is not under human control, then four basic sorts of 'decrees or mandates' (*ming*) shape numerous aspects of human existence: the king's Mandate to rule over subjects by Heaven's grace (**Tian ming** 天命), man's very life (*ming*), personal destiny (also *ming*, referring to what cannot be altered by human agency) and the basic nature (*xing*). Each of these four represents a gift or mission from on high.

The degree to which humans are autonomous beings capable of making significant choices is a question that underlies nearly all the writings in the Five Classic corpus including the *Book of Poetry* (*Shi jing*) and

Book of History (*Shu jing* or **Shang shu**). The earliest canons presuppose the operations of an anthropomorphic Heaven dispensing good and ill fortune to the ruling family, in the process facilitating the natural course of events by which the elite's chosen actions generally determine their ends. (From such early premises there evolve later theories, such as that of Wang Chong's **Lun heng**, which describes all good and ill fortune as the spontaneous result of the multiple interlocking cycles of cosmic *qi* mandating the fates of the person, the family, the region, and the state). But even those canons register complaints from 'the people below' who feel that they have been unjustly punished by a Heaven for the wrongs committed by their political superiors (e.g., *Ode* no. 131).

At no time in early China do we find an emerging consensus on the relative weight that a human being's actions have in determining his condition, nor on the degree of Heaven's intervention in human operations (for instance, in presenting humans with timely opportunities to do good or ill), whether Heaven is viewed as deity or as the combined process of the regular cosmic cycles. The debates grow more explicit in texts beginning with the *Analects* (*Lunyu*). Usually attributed to Confucius' circle of disciples, the *Analects* cites a popular saying that makes 'death and life . . . wealth and rank' depend upon the will of Heaven (12: 5). The Confucius of the *Analects*, however, in numerous passages (e.g., 7: 14–15, 7: 36, 12: 5) regards the idea of fate or predestination as a sorry pretext that humans employ when they wish to avoid undertaking serious moral commitments. According to Confucius, the human will, if properly committed, can secure many of the benefits most avidly sought by humans, including happiness, steady associations with like-minded friends and allies, and psychic ease, except in exceptional cases where a person's *xing* is unaccountably damaged. Fate, then, has little to do with the all-important question of moral choice, let alone psychic equanimity. (Mozi, too, argues that fatalism prevents most humans from doing their utmost to excel, which suggests that Wang Chong was not the first to insist that nearly everything in life, from one's looks to worldly success, is predetermined before birth.)

Confucius' brief statement in the *Analects* that 'he who does not understand *ming* has no way to become a noble man' (20: 3) virtually required all his followers to give serious consideration to *xing* ('man's basic nature'), its needs and its functions – despite the fact that the Master reportedly never offered his opinions on *xing* (5: 13). Nearly all the Warring States, Qin, and Han period thinkers were preoccupied with describing the effect of *xing* on the human disposition toward morality (phrasing the 'nature *v.* nurture' issues most often in terms of what was 'internal' or 'external' to the inborn nature). One of the most systematic of these discussions appears in the **Mengzi**, where that thinker challenges the commonsense notions of his opponent, Gaozi 告子 (?–?), who thinks the 'basic nature' consists of the inherently amoral desires for food and sex, while 'morality' represents no more than an overlay of culture laid upon the basic nature. (Gaozi's position was later elaborated and refined by **Xunzi**, who insisted, however, that the overlay of good could become a virtual 'second nature' to the noble man single-minded enough in his pursuit of the Way.) Mengzi, by contrast, insists that all humans at birth have an innate moral potential, though he concedes that prevailing societal conditions (especially material insecurity and the bad examples of superiors) can prevent the full development of that potential for the good.

After Han, thinkers offered only a few revisions to these basic positions. **Zhang Zai**, for example, tried – not altogether successfully – to disentangle fate from chance, by restricting the term 'fate' to 'what is identical with the basic nature . . . which Heaven itself is not able to change' and reserving 'chance' for the purely accidental. The Tang politician Li Mi 李泌 (722–789), the Ming teacher **Wang Gen**, and **Wang Fuzhi** were among those who preferred to argue that a person could 'make [his or her own] fate' by overcoming difficulties to achieve success.

References: Fu Sinian, 1952; Lau, 1970; Mori, 1971.

MICHAEL NYLAN

Xing qing 性情
(The nature and feelings)

Xing is the nature, or human nature; *qing* refers to the affective faculties, emotions or feelings. In later literature, *qing* also meant exalted passion or intense emotional ardour, but in literati contexts the term referred to more quotidian feelings. Over the centuries, scholars debated such topics as the fundamental qualities of the nature, the number and characteristics of the emotions and their relationship to the nature, the mind and vital force (**qi**).

The nature and feelings were sometimes considered at odds with one another, but in one of the earliest appearances of the terms as a pair they were not so juxtaposed. The *Wen yen* 文言 section of the *Book of Changes* (*Yi jing*) for the hexagram *qian* 乾 associates them with the qualities of advantage and firmness, respectively, two of the four qualities of *qian* (along with origination and flourishing).

In the ***Xunzi***, both the nature (which some sections of the text describe as evil, or *e*) and feelings require the external guidance of a teacher and must be honed through accumulated effort and study and inquiry. Laxity makes one a petty person, but with effort one can develop the nature and the feelings and form a triad with heaven and earth. Excessive strictness, on the other hand, renders one ineffective as a leader.

The ***Li ji*** offers several visions of the nature and feelings. The opening section of the *Doctrine of the Mean* (*Zhongyong*), originally a chapter of the *Li ji*, describes the nature and the emotions, but in separate passages and not, strictly speaking, as a pair. The nature is bestowed by Heaven. Four emotions of joy, anger, sorrow and joy are outlined in the context of states both before and after they are aroused or manifested. The state before they are aroused is called equilibrium; the state when they are aroused and are fully developed is called harmony. The 'Evolution of Ritual' (*Li yun* 禮運) chapter of the *Li ji*, however, lists seven rather than four emotions: joy, anger, sorrow, fear, love, dislike and desire. These emotions did not have to be learned but were naturally within one.

In the Tang, **Han Yu** postulated various grades of human nature (superior, middling and inferior) and attempted to correlate them systematically with the different feelings. The nature, for Han Yu, was present at birth and had five virtues (**Mengzi**'s 'Four Beginnings' (*si duan*) of humaneness, rightness, ritual/propriety and wisdom plus the virtue of trustworthiness). The feelings, of which there were seven, were produced only by contact with things. The superior grade of person always abided by the Mean in the expression of the feelings.

In the Song, **Zhu Xi** understood the feelings as Mengzi's Four Beginnings and saw the nature as principle; on a more theoretical level, he perceived the nature as substance and the feelings as function (see *ti yong*). Following **Zhang Zai**, he asserted that both the nature and feelings are connected by the mind. His statement that the Four Beginnings are manifestations of principle (*li*) and the Seven Emotions are manifestations of material force (*qi*) were very influential in the 'Four–Seven' Debates in Korea, where scholars discussed the integration and dichotomisation of principle and vital force.

References: Chan, Wing-tsit, 1963d: 450–4, 630–2, 1989: 174–5, 249–51; Chung, 1995; Kalton, 1994; Knoblock, 1988–94: vol. I: 223, vol. II: 81–2.

DEBORAH SOMMER

Xing sanpin shuo 性三品說
(Theory of the three types of human nature)

A remark attributed to Confucius in the *Analects* is the ultimate inspiration of the 'three types of human nature' theory, which dominated in intellectual circles during the Han through Tang periods. Confucius said, 'Human natures do not vary much; it is custom that makes for divergence . . . Only those who are the very wisest and the very most stupid do not change' (17: 2), effectively dividing human natures into three separate categories. Most Han thinkers, including **Dong Zhongshu**, **Yang Xiong**, and Wang Chong, repeated this statement as rationale for instituting broad educational reforms. According to the Han Confucians, humans at birth have in their original endowment a host of contradictory impulses and desires, including those for food, sex and community. Just as the artisan works jade to release its true beauty from rough-hewn pieces, any moral deficiency in the person can be polished and carved away until an 'elegant and accomplished' person emerges.

Xun Yue, author of the *Shen jian* 申鑒 (*Extended Reflections*), repeated the sentiment, arguing that human nature came in three types (*sanpin*), of which neither the highest (the sage) nor the lowest (the incorrigibly evil) were liable to change, but the vast majority in the middle could be maintained as sociable beings through concerted efforts, presumably those of their moral exemplars, their parents, teachers, and rulers, no less than their own. Xun Yue continued, 'Even where the human nature is good, it relies on moral training for its perfection, and where it is evil, it relies on penal law for its suppression. Only those who are the very wisest and the very most stupid do not change.'

Han Yu of the Tang (618–907) was a major proponent of the *sanpin* theory. Following **Mengzi**, Han believed that human nature contained within it the seeds of humaneness (*ren*), righteousness (*yi*), ritual/propriety (*li*), wisdom (*zhi*), and trustworthiness (*xin*). In reaction to external phenomena, human beings expressed their internal states through seven characteristic forms: joy, anger, sorrow, fear, love, hate and desire. But because human beings at birth received differing relative strengths, both in their capacities for the good and in their emotional responses, the person could be made more moral or immoral, when internal imbalances met external experiences. Han Yu's *sanpin* model sought to resolve the obvious contradictions between **Mengzi**'s famous slogan, 'human nature is good', and **Xunzi**'s proposition, 'human nature is not a pretty sight to see'. But by the time of the Song Neo-Confucians, another paradigm for human nature had been put forward (that human nature reflected *tian li* 天理, Heaven's principles), so the *sanpin* theory fell from favour.

MICHAEL NYLAN

Xing shan lun 性善論
(Human nature is good)

The slogan that 'Human Nature is [Innately] Good' is ascribed to **Mengzi**. In Confucius' view, the process of individual self-cultivation is what moves a person from the immoral to moral state. The vast majority of people, at least, are perfectible, it is human effort that makes the difference. Confucius remarked that too many of his disciples mistook the inherent difficulty of self-cultivation to mean that they were fundamentally unsuited to or indeed, incapable of the process, when the path to goodness required greater effort (*Analects*, 6: 10). The ardent desire to develop humaneness (*ren*) would guarantee its achievement.

Mengzi, by contrast, argued quite another view of human nature: that the Four Beginnings (*si duan*) of morality (the heart of compassion, the heart of shame, the heart of deference and the heart of knowing right from wrong) form parts of the basic human endowment, along with desires for food and sex. To critics who believed that humans would not act so badly, if they began life with innate tendencies towards the good, Mengzi replied with two parables: that of the baby crawling towards the well and that of Ox Mountain. Any person's first impulse will be to rush to rescue a baby crawling towards a well, though that noble impulse may ultimately be overcome by baser impulses reflecting greed, indifference or revenge. And Ox Mountain had been so denuded of its original forest cover by earlier woodsmen and domestic animals that the local inhabitants assumed that it had never been forested at all. From such examples, Mengzi demonstrates that the evident lack of goodness in human lives does not mean that some humans never received an original endowment of goodness. It means rather that each person's original endowment needs to be nourished daily, if it is to flourish. The way to nourish the original endowment of goodness is to build up one's moral muscles by continual exercise of the good (defined as actions that are benevolent, dutiful, ritually correct and wise). Then the original endowment, weak as a young seedling or an infant, will grow stronger.

Those who rule 'with their hearts and minds' must be capable of leading those of less moral discrimination to exercise the good. By instituting the basic provisions of benevolent government, good rulers and administrators provide both the economic security and the suasive example that are prerequisites if ordinary people are to be led to engage in the process of self-cultivation on their own. But if the preconditions for human flourishing are met by the state, society will certainly flourish, for human beings will only be developing as is natural, rather than being forced by external circumstances (e.g., economic deprivation or lack of a strong moral environment) into unnatural behaviour that is immoral.

Mengzi's view of human nature, which was extremely influential, especially in

Neo-Confucian theories, nonetheless was attacked by moralists who feared that speaking of the natural goodness of human beings would open the door to relativism and anti-conventional behaviour.

MICHAEL NYLAN

Xing shan qing e 性善情惡
(Good nature and evil dispositions)

Dong Zhongshu formulated a persuasive synthesis of the Warring States thinkers' opposing views of human nature, which accounted for its 'mixed' character (i.e., its good and evil tendencies) while confirming its ultimate origins in Heaven (which most thinkers presumed to be good): Human nature, according to Dong, derived from *yang qi*, which accounted for its innate tendencies towards the good. The emotions, by contrast, derived from *yin qi*, and so were liable to imbalance and excess, qualities abhorrent to the gentleman (*e* 惡). In their totality, however, human beings were by definition good, as their lives were the gift of Heaven, the same presence that had given birth to *yang qi* and *yin qi*.

MICHAEL NYLAN

Xing shen 形神
(Form and spirit)

Xing means visible form or shape and in its widest sense can refer to the form or shape of any thing. Often, however, it refers specifically to the physical frame of the human body. In such usages it is often contrasted with a less tangible aspect of the human being such as the *shen*, or spirit, an ineffable numinous aspect that can be developed and transformed through self-cultivation.

For **Xunzi**, form and spirit were intimately connected with heaven. In the cosmology of his 'Discourse on Heaven' (*Tian lun* 天論), the emotions, sense faculties, mind (*xin*), and physiological processes of the individual person were understood as participating in heaven's operations. Form and spirit were the very completion of the work of heaven; when they were manifest, they gave rise to the heavenly emotions (*tian qing* 天情). Xunzi also understood *xing* as the physical form or body, which was one of the five heavenly sense faculties (*tian guan* 天官), along with the ear, eye, nose and mouth.

In the Song, **Zhou Dunyi** incorporated *xing* and *shen* into the cosmological vision of his *The Diagram of The Supreme Ultimate Explained* (*Taijitu shuo*). For Zhou, the Great Ultimate (*tai ji*) was more signficant than the heaven of Xunzi, but like Xunzi Zhou saw the development of the human being in terms of the appearance of form and the manifestation of spirit, which in turn gave rise to understanding and the emotions. Somewhat later, **Zhang Zai** saw the cosmos as a Supreme Harmony (*tai he*) of paired fluctuating processes. Here, form and spirit were understood in terms of vital force (*qi*) and the formless, respectively.

References: de Bary & Bloom, 1999: 670–6, 682–7; Knoblock, 1988–94: vol. III: 15–16; Wang Xianqian, 1988: 308–10.

DEBORAH SOMMER

Xingli zhi xue 性理之學
(The learning of nature and principle)

Used in a general sense, this expression refers to the learning or teachings (*xue*) on nature (*xing*) and principle (*li*) of any scholars who emphasise such subjects. More particularly, however, the expression usually refers to the teachings on those concepts by such Song scholars as **Cheng Yi**, **Cheng Hao**, **Zhu Xi** and their followers. The Cheng brothers and Zhu Xi did associate human nature with principle; nonetheless, the label 'learning of nature and principle' or the shorter 'learning of principle' (*li xue* 理學) was favoured by later followers rather than by the Cheng brothers or by Zhu Xi himself. The latter, for example, more commonly thought of his work as the 'learning of the Way' (*dao xue* 道學) or 'learning of the sages' (*sheng xue* 聖學).

The expression 'learning of principle' can be traced only to the early thirteenth century, when it referred to **Zhou Dunyi**'s perceived revival of an ancient learning of principle from a period of desuetude that had purportedly persisted since the late Warring States period. The exact provenance of the label 'learning of nature and principle' is less certain. But by at least the early Ming, the titles of such compendia as the *Xingli daquan* 性理大全 (Great Compendia of Nature and Principle), a collection of writings of over one hundred Song scholars, attests to the term's popularity. In this usage, 'learning and principle' evokes a range of Song Learning much broader than that of the Cheng and Zhu traditions. In modern studies in English, the term is often translated as 'Neo-Confucianism'.

References: Chan, Wing-tsit, 1996: 285–8; de Bary, 1989.

DEBORAH SOMMER

Xingshang xingxia 形上形下
(Above form and below form, or formless and form)

This expression is derived from an enigmatic passage in the *Appended Remarks* to the *Yi jing*: 'above (*shang*) form (*xing*) there is the Way; below (*xia*) form there are objects' (*Xici* 1.12). The relationship between the valences of 'above' and 'below', however, was not articulated in the *Book of Changes*. From Han commentaries on down, nonetheless, 'above form' has been variously understood as that which is intangible, formless, without form or beyond form; in modern usages, it is sometimes used as a translation for the English 'metaphysics'. 'Below form', on the other hand, has been associated with the realm of physical forms and tangible phenomena. The objects (*qi* 器, see

Dao qi) of the passage above were often understood in antiquity as bronze vessels – dense forms intended for highly visible ritual display. Above and below were also understood temporally, instead of spatially, as being 'anterior' and 'posterior', respectively, to forms that appeared and vanished in the cycles of transformation whose meaning could be divined through examining the trigrams of the *Book of Changes*.

The concepts 'above form' and 'below form' were of relatively little importance until the Song. At that time, thinkers such as **Zhang Zai**, the Cheng brothers, and **Zhu Xi**, all of whom commented on the *Book of Changes*, incorporated them into their debates on the relationships between cosmological principles and ethical values. **Lu Jiuyuan**, **Luo Qinshun**, **Wang Fuzhi**, and **Dai Zhen** developed their own configurations of form and the formless.

References: Chan, Wing-tsit, 1996: 129–31, 179–81; Graham, 1992: 122–4; Lokuang, 1986.

DEBORAH SOMMER

Xinti yu xingti 心體與性體
(*Essence of Heart/Mind and Essence of Human Nature*)

In this three-volume work published sequentially between 1968 and 1969 **Mou Zongsan** presents revisionary arguments about the nature of Song dynasty Confucianism, which are very influential in contemporary New Confucianism. The core of these arguments rest on how Song scholars explained the essence of heart/mind (*xinti* 心體) and its relationship to the essence of (human) nature (*xingti* 性體). Mou contends that the proper understanding presents heart/mind and nature as essentially one but phenomenally distinguishable, particularly as discerned in appropriate moral effort (*gongfu* 工夫).

After making a lengthy summary statement about the character of Song Confucianism, describing its moral metaphysics and arguing against its contemporary opponent, **Ye Shi**, Mou devotes four-fifths of the work to studying six major Song figures, their teachings, and their controversies. Detailed descriptions of their approach to moral cultivation, their explanations of the key concepts, and their textual studies are presented. Mou concludes, contrary to long-standing scholarly traditions, that because **Zhu Xi** and his predecessor, **Cheng Yi**, destroy the metaphysical union of heart/mind and nature they are not the true inheritors of orthodox Confucian teachings from the pre-Qin period. The authentic transmitters are **Cheng Hao**, his successor **Hu Hong**, and others, who explained the essence of nature from the *Zhongyong* and the commentories on the *Yi jing*, and elaborated the essence of heart/mind from the *Lunyu* and *Mengzi* texts. A third party of scholars including **Lu Jiuyuan** work out less adequate arguments which incline in the right interpretive direction.

References: Fang & Li, 1995: vol. III, 417–20; Fang & Zheng, 1995: 278–82; Mou, 1991.

LAUREN PFISTER

Xinwai wu wu 心外無物
(Outside of the mind there are no things)

The Ming scholar **Wang Shouren** asserted that outside of the mind, there are no things or principles. By 'thing' Wang did not mean material objects but the objects or foci of the intentionality, or will, of the mind: when one's intentionality was directed toward exercising humaneness (**ren**) or filiality to others, for example, then humaneness or filiality were 'things', the foci of that intentionality. Humaneness or benevolence hence were not external to one but were already present within the mind. The investigation of things and making the will sincere were items enumerated in the *Great Learning* (**Daxue**), which deeply influenced Wang.

References: Chan, Wing-tsit, 1963c; Ching, 1976b; Wang Shouren, 1992.

DEBORAH SOMMER

Xinya xueyuan 新亞學院
(New Asia College)

Xinya shuyuan, or New Asia College, was established in Hong Kong by refugee Chinese intellectuals in October 1949. Promoting a broad humanistic education rooted in Chinese traditions, its 'New Asia' ideal included a vision of a new and modern China. The school had special links with Confucian traditions through its principal, the traditional Chinese historian, **Qian Mu**, the New Confucian philosopher, **Tang Junyi**, and the German-trained economist, Zhang Pijie 張丕介 (1905–1970). While the meagerly supported faculty and minuscule student body met in Kowloon 九龍, the principal raised the school's status through Taiwanese and American academic and financial support. In 1963 New Asia College was institutionally linked with two local colleges, forming an alternative Chinese-style university within the British colony. In 1973 New Asia College moved to its modern mountain-top facilities in Shatin 沙田, providing education for over 2,000 students. By 1976 it was fully integrated into the larger and more centralised Chinese University of Hong Kong (*Xianggang Zhongwen daxue* 香港中文大學) system.

In 1955 the two character school motto, *cheng ming* 誠明, exemplifying the 'New Asia spirit', was adopted from the *Zhongyong* 中庸: 'authentic living' and 'intellectual enlightenment'. In consonance with the New Asia spirit Tang Junyi, **Mou Zongsan, Xu Fuguan** 徐復觀 and **Zhang Junmai** drafted a lengthy 'Confucian Manifesto' in 1958, promoting Song–Ming Confucian moral cultivation, humane democracy and controlled scientific development. The College still nurtures this intellectual spirit through the Qian Mu lecture series established by Ambrose King, including among its initial lecturers Qian Mu himself and Joseph Needham.

References: Fang & Li, 1995: 22–4; Pfister, 1995; Qian Mu, 1989; *Xinya yanjiusuo*, 1981.

LAUREN PFISTER

Xiong Shili 熊十力
1885–1968

Perhaps the most creative philosopher within **Modern New Confucianism**, Xiong Shili's gradual approach to Confucianism reflected China's epochal changes. Born as Jizhi 繼智, one of six sons in a poor family from Hubei 湖北 province, he was trained at home in classical Confucian texts, but was orphaned as a teenager. Influenced by revolutionary teachings of **Wang Fuzhi**, Xiong studied military arts and later joined in the 1911 revolution. Disappointed by the ineffectiveness of military means in resolving human problems, especially after a failed military coup in 1917, he decisively turned toward studying, publishing his first book in 1918. In Nanjing 南京 he studied the teachings and logic of Chinese Buddhism for two years under the Buddhist reformer, Ouyang Jian 歐陽漸 (1871–1944; *zi* Jingwu 竟無, Jianwu 漸吾), and in 1922 was hired to help **Liang Shuming** teach Buddhist philosophy at Beijing University. During the subsequent decade Xiong's own philosophical commitments were shaped and strengthened, resulting in the publication of his life-long major work, the *New Mere Consciousness Doctrine* (*Xin weishi lun*).

From Yogacara Buddhism to Modern New Confucianism

Though the book's title refers to the 'consciousness-only' (*weishi* 唯識) school of Mahayana Buddhism, Xiong advocated within it a new interpretation of Confucian philosophy resembling teachings of Heart/Mind Learning (*Xin xue*). This philosophical system was conceived and refined

through years of reflection, teaching and debates, being gradually written down in several versions: the first version in classical style appeared in 1932; a revision in demotic language, in 1944; and a final revision, in 1953. These versions developed from a recognisable reliance on *Weishi* Buddhism in interpreting seminal Confucian concepts toward an exclusive commitment to cosmological and metaphysical ideas Xiong found in the *Book of Changes* (*Yi jing*). Written in lively engagement with different schools of Buddhism, Daoism and the modern scientific approach, Xiong's argumentation illustrated his creative independence as well as an intense concern for a revival of an original and creative Confucianism.

As in the doctrines of Yogacara or Consciousness-only Buddhism, Xiong argued that the enlightened human consciousness or 'original mind' (*benxin* 本心) is metaphysically inseparable from all things, even though the 'customary mind' (*xixin* 習心) of uncultured persons habituates itself to the independence of human consciousness from external things. As in Yogacara, human consciousness and the universe are presented as being a continuous flow of ephemerally connected and always changing manifestations. There is consequently a non-duality in their essence and function (*tiyong bu er* 體用不二). Relying on images from the *Book of Changes*, the subtle interaction of 'openings' (*Pi* 闢) and 'closings' (*Xi* 翕) indicates how the original mind and material things flow together in their momentous connections. On the basis of this unusual account of a dynamic monistic realism Xiong established his own interpretation of the inwardly sagely and outwardly regal Way (**Neisheng waiwang**). Sagely insight revealed the particular kind of monistic metaphysics that Xiong counted as the true contribution of Confucianism to philosophy at large, and the regal traditions of special Confucian texts promoted a progressive and revolutionary political philosophy which Xiong saw as highly relevant to the development of Confucianism in the post traditional era. On the basis of these philosophical commitments and especially his metaphysics, Xiong criticised Buddhist teachings as 'passive' and metaphysically wrong in distinguishing between a higher consciousness and the external world. The unitary set of transforming phenomena in the universe constitute reality for Xiong, and is not to be transcended by an other-worldly Nirvana (*niepan* 涅槃). He also vigor-ously opposed scientific attitudes which assume that the self and the world exist independently or 'objectively', but did not expand on or elaborate his justifications. More significantly, he argued in writings of the 1950s, especially in *On the Ru* (*Yuan Ru* 原儒), that his metaphysical vision was in fact the underlying worldview of Confucius' mature teachings.

A new Confucian fundamentalism

Xiong was convinced that dynamic monism constituted a proper account of Confucius' original worldview, the true Way of the 'inner sage' (*nei sheng* 內聖). Confucius was not only involved in the transmission of the Five Classics (*Wu jing*), according to Xiong, but more significantly was the creator of the metaphysically redolent divinatory work, the *Book of Changes*. Only after Confucius was fifty years old did he study the *Book of Changes* and its 'Great Way' (*Da Dao* 大道), his previous teachings having dealt only with a 'minor peace' (*xiao kang* 小康). Besides the *Book of Changes*, Xiong con-sidered Confucius' seminal works to be the *Spring and Autumn Annals* (*Chunqiu*), the *Rites of Zhou* (*Zhou li*), and the 'Evolution of the Rites' chapter (*Li yun*) in the *Book of Rites* (*Li ji*). From them Xiong envisioned the 'externally regal' way (*wai wang* 外王) as politically 'revolutionary', leading through democratic institutions to socialism where 'all under the heavens is shared in common' (*Tianxia wei gong* 天下為公). Xiong criti-cised almost all previous Confucian writings as inadequate. **Mengzi** and **Xunzi** had departed from the 'Great Way' and settled

for a 'minor peace'. Subsequently Han scholasticism initiated a 'dark age' of falsified Confucianism lasting two millen-nia. Xiong strongly criticised the dualistic teachings of **Zhu Xi**, but maintained a critical admiration for the monistic meta-physics taught by **Zhang Zai** and Wang Fuzhi. Only the Heart/Mind Learning of the Liu–Wang tradition, and especially the teachings of **Wang Shouren**, appeared to match up to his own metaphysical and epi-stemological commitments.

Xiong's interpretation of Confucian political philosophy was highly controversial, receiving pointed criticisms from **Liang Shuming** and Xiong's notable student, **Xu Fuguan**. Nevertheless, his philosophy stands as a watershed in the initial creative develop-ment of Modern New Confucianism. Its influence is formidable, especially as it is re-considered and extended by **Mou Zongsan**. Standard accounts of twentieth-century Chinese philosophy identify him as one of the first generation Modern New Confucians.

References: Bresciani, 1992; Cheng & Bunnin, 2002; Ding Weixiang, 1999; Fang & Li, 1995: vol. I, 429–69; Fu Weixun, 1996; Guo & Zhang, 2001; Guo Qiyong, 1990, 1993; Xiong Shili 1985, 1988a/b, 1989.

LAUREN PFISTER

Xishan xuepai 西山學派
(School of Cai Yuanding)

This term designating the school of **Cai Yuanding** should not be confused with the school of **Zhen Dexiu** which carries the same name in the *Song–Yuan xuean*.

The main stem of the *Xishan xuepai* is the learning of the Cai family. It is said that Cai Yuanding taught his learning on the Confucian canons to his three sons leading each of them to specialise in one part of it. Thus, his eldest son Cai Yuan 蔡淵 (1156–1236) published an elementary book on the oracle of the *Yi jing* and another one explaining his father's teaching on the Great Ultimate (*Tai ji*). His second son Cai

Hang 蔡沆 – also called Yu Zhifang 虞知方 since he was adopted by Cai Yuanding's cousin – wrote explanations on the hidden meaning of the **Chunqiu**. His third son **Cai Chen** elaborated his father's theory on the numbers of the Great Plan (*Hongfan* 洪範), the famous chapter of the **Shang shu** which led to his own school, **Jiufeng xuepai**.

Cai Yuanding's grandsons continued the development of the learning of the Cai family. In the Ming dynasty the works of the Cai family were collected in the *Caishi jiuru shu* 蔡氏九儒書 (*The Works of the Nine Scholars of the Cai family*).

Cai Yuanding himself as a leading follower of **Zhu Xi** was befriended with many other followers of Zhu Xi. Several of Zhu Xi's pupils were his pupils, too. He also was a friend of the brothers Liu Yue 劉爚 (1144–1216) and Liu Bing 劉炳 (*fl.* 1178). Liu Yue later wrote the epitaph for Cai Yuanding. Other friends of him were the ministers Zhan Tiren 詹體仁 (1143–1206) and Lou Yue 樓鑰 (1137–1213). Lou Yue, leaving a voluminous work collected as *Gonggui wenji* 攻瑰文集, became well known for his chronicle of the famous minister **Fan Zhongyan**.

References: Bohn, Hermann G., 1998; *Song–Yuan xuean*, 1966; Wang & Feng, 1962.
DENNIS SCHILLING

Xiu shen 修身
(Personal cultivation, self-cultivation)

Both Confucius and **Mengzi** believed that the acquisition of moral training and the proper acting out of personal virtue was tentative to the construction of a good social and political order. The *Book of Rites* (**Li ji**) systematically details the process (the so-called 'eight steps' (**ba tiaomu**), in which the perfect world could be realised. Personal cultivation is the first step.

Discussions on personal cultivation intensified after **Zhu Xi** made this *Book of Rites* chapter (the 'Great Learning' **Da xue** chapter) one of the Four Books (**Si shu**). Although

Neo-Confucian thinkers were aware of the Buddhist and Daoist approaches to moral life, most of them were satisfied with what Zhu laid out in his *Elementary Learning* (*Xiao xue*) and *Reflections on Things at Hand* (*Jinsi lu*). Zhu Xi believed that the individual's sincere intention and rectification of the heart/mind were the foundation of his personal moral perfection. Indeed, the idea of *shen* 身 could properly be understood as personhood, the accomplishment of which was the goal of human existence. In practical terms, Zhu Xi's idea was simple, it all began with the near and immediate: to learn how to behave oneself correctly, in such things as sprinkling water and sweeping the floor, one could learn about correct behaviour, tentative to genuine moral cultivation.

The concern about the rectitude of personal heart/mind grew in force in the Ming times, and became the central teaching of **Wang Shouren**. Wang and his disciples believed that because humans were born with a natural capability of doing good, the programme for personal cultivation was therefore not more than maintaining that original goodness, preventing it from the disruptive external influences. In a paradoxical way, Wang's philosophy really did not require systematic personal cultivation. However, many Ming thinkers practised meditation and quiet-sitting. They adopted such rigorous disciplinary approaches as a way to personal moral cultivation. Wang's approach was more down to earth. He emphasised an educated person's social responsibility, and actually considered the proper management of social interaction as complementary to an individual's reflections on moral issues. His method of learning demonstrated his belief that personal unity with moral truth was not more than a unity between the person and nature. Thus, he and his followers often talked about natural and relaxed reflection, assisted by chanting or singing, interspersed amid teaching and learning sessions. Other thinkers were more serious in their *xiu shen* programmes. In their works one sees suggestive influences of Buddhist monastic rules and even Daoist inner (physiological) alchemy.

For a commoner, personal moral cultivation meant only living a remorseless life by heeding the teachings of scholars. In popular morality books and other writings intended for the general readership, personal cultivation became the acting out of the moral precepts, often simplistic, distilled from all 'three teachings' (*san jiao* 三教). They taught a kind of utilitarian calculus as justification for virtuous life. Such a pragmatic approach remained a powerful force informing Ming and Qing scholars and commoners alike about personal cultivation.

Personal cultivation continued to remain the educators' concern in early twentieth-century China and was made a subject required of all students.

The influence of Wang Shouren (Wang Yangming) in Japan made *xiushen* an important component of **Bushidô** and the idea that action and personal moral cultivation, especially in terms of self-discipline, are one has remained a widely accepted notion in Japanese life.

References: de Bary, 1975, 1989; Lee, Thomas, 2000.

THOMAS H.C. LEE

Xu Ai 徐愛
1487–1517
(*zi* Riren 日仁, *hao* Hengshan 橫山)

Xu Ai was known as the most promising disciple of **Wang Shouren** (Wang Yangming), before dying at a young age. Hailing from Wang Shouren's native county of Yuyao in Zhejiang, Xu was also Wang's brother-in-law. Xu received the *jinshi* degree in 1508 and served briefly as a prefect in Shanxi before being assigned to various posts in the southern capital of Nanjing. In the early 1510s, Wang was also serving in Nanjing, where he discussed with Xu his interpreta-

tions of *gewu* 格物 (investigation of things) and his ideas on the unity of knowledge and action, as well as emphasising the importance of gathering oneself together (*shoulian* 收斂). Thus Xu became, from 1510, the first disciple of Wang.

In 1516 Xu Ai returned to Yuyao to visit his family and died in the following year at the young age of thirty. Wang Yangming remembered Xu as his greatest disciple and referred to him as his Yan Hui, the favourite disciple of Confucius who also died at an early age. This comparison also implies that it was Xu, as opposed to subsequent disciples, who really got the true teaching of Wang Yangming. **Huang Zongxi** concurs with this view in his **Mingru xuean** (*Records of Ming Scholars*). Xu Ai and **Qian Dehong** recorded Wang Yangming's lectures in the **Chuanxi lu** (*Instructions for Practical Living*), Xu having been responsible for the first part of the work based on his discussions with Wang in Nanjing.

Reference: Huang Tsung-hsi, 1987: 109–10.

STEVEN MILES

Xu Fuguan 徐復觀
1903–1982

Placed with **Tang Junyi** and **Mou Zongsan** as one of the most significant scholars-in-exile in **Modern New Confucianism**, Xu Fuguan distinguished himself as an editor, Chinese intellectual historian and critically informed advocate of modernisation of Confucianism. Unlike his colleagues, he pursued a distinguished military career before turning decisively toward academic study of Chinese culture. Born as Xu Bingchang 徐秉常 into a poor teacher's family living in Xishui 浠水 county of Hubei 湖北 province, he became involved in political affairs in the early 1920s. Travelling to Japan to study economics and military science in 1928 in Meiji University 明治大學 and other institutions, he returned to China in 1931 to serve for fifteen years in military organisations, reaching the rank of major general. Retiring honourably in 1947, partly motivated by disenchantment with contemporary politics but also convinced of the need for cultural revival by **Xiong Shili**, Xu changed his name to Fuguan under Xiong's inspiration and started a small monthly jounal in Nanjing to initiate his intellectual career. A disciplined textual interpreter and broad-ranging writer, Xu published materials related to Chinese culture in political history and theory, intellectual history, philosophical studies, aesthetics and literature. The following major themes were advocated during his prolific career as an elderly New Confucian intellectual.

In political theory Xu advocated the Confucian humane government (**ren zheng**) over authoritarian forms, arguing against past and modern abuses of Confucian teachings to support authoritarianism. In the **Mengzi** he found proto-democratic values, particularly in its *minben* 民本 or 'demophilic' teachings, and so argued for the establishment of a Chinese moral democracy combining Confucian humanist virtues and modern democratic institutions. These and other themes of cultural revival were discussed by Xu and other New Confucians in the *Democratic Review* (*Minzhu Pinglun* 民主評論), which he founded in Hong Kong in 1949 and edited for seventeen years.

Philosophically speaking, Xu argued for the centrality of the Confucian teachings related to the heart/mind (**xin**) and (human) nature (**xing**), presenting a complicated and influential justification of this claim in his *History of the Theory of Human Nature in China* (**Zhongguo renxinglun shi**). Xu claimed that the source for these theoretical debates came in an early turn away from religious transcendence toward a humane and literary cultivated spirit (*renwen jingshen* 人文精神) stimulated by a consciousness of moral anxiety (*youhuan yishi* 憂患意識). Only by personal discipline in moral effort (*gong fu* 工夫) could anyone grasp these moral concerns and put them into practice. These themes were re-addressed in detail in the 1958 'Confucian Manifesto', which Xu signed with Tang, Mou, and **Zhang Junmai**. They insisted there that authentic Confucianism and the possibilities for its modernisation through scientific and democratic developments could not be understood without comprehending the Song–Ming doctrines about the relationship of the heart/mind and (human) nature.

In the aesthetic realm Xu took the freedom or 'wandering' (*you* 游) advocated by Zhuangzi 莊子 as the ground for all Chinese aesthetics, pointing out that Confucius also spoke of one dimension of moral effort as 'wandering in the arts' (*Lunyu* 7: 6).

References: Cheng & Bunnin, 2002; Fang & Li, 1995: vol. III, 579–866; Fang & Zheng, 1995: 294–323; Huang Chün-chieh, 1995.

LAUREN PFISTER

Xu Gan 徐幹
170–217
(*zi* Weichang 偉長)

Xu Gan was a native of Ju 據 Prefecture, Beihai 北海 Kingdom. He was a philosopher–literatus whose representative writing is the collection of essays, **Zhong lun** (*Balanced Discourses*). Although he is not a major figure in Chinese intellectual history, traditionally he has been accorded a place as a representative philosopher of the Later Han (25–220 CE) period. Despite having been accorded a lasting reputation in Chinese literary culture as one of the 'Seven Masters of the *Jian an* 建安 period (196–220)', we know little about Xu Gan's life. What little is known derives largely from the unsigned 'Preface to Xu Gan's *Balanced Discourses*' and brief notes in *San guo zhi* 三國志 and its commentary. He held positions on the staff of the Minister of Works (*si kong* 司空) some time between 197–208, and as Instructor (*wen xue* 文學) to the Leader of Court Gentlemen for Miscellaneous Purposes (*wu guan zhong lang jiang* 五官中郎將) after

Cao Pi's 曹丕 (187–226) appointment to that position in 211. He also served as Instructor of Linzi 臨菑 District some time during or after 214, when Cao Zhi 曹植 (192–232) was made Marquis of Linzi. Xu Gan was also offered two other positions. *Xian xian xing zhuang* 先賢行狀, records that Cao Cao 曹操 (155–220, *zi* Mengde 孟德) offered him an unspecified special appointment, and that later he was also offered the post of Magistrate (*zhang* 長) of Shang'ai 上艾 District. In both cases, he declined on the grounds of ill health. The unsigned preface to *Zhong lun* describes the period of his last years as one of self-imposed isolation and impoverishment.

References: Makeham, 1994; Makeham, tr., 2002.

JOHN MAKEHAM

Xu Guangqi 徐光啟
1562–1633, baptised as Paul in 1603

Xu Guangqi is considered in both western and Chinese sources as the most prominent Chinese Christian at the beginning of the seventeenth century. This is largely due to the position of Grand Secretary he occupied at the end of his life. He thus became an example of the success of the Jesuits' missionary policy towards the elite. His conversion (1603) and his passing the Metropolitan Examination (1604) were closely linked in time. While preparing the examinations, Xu, like his contemporaries, wrote several commentaries on the Classics: *Maoshi liutie jiangyi* 毛詩六帖講意 (*c.* 1617), *Shi jing zhuangao* 詩經傳稿 and *Kaogong ji jie* 考工記解. Characteristic of these texts is Xu's preoccupation with practical studies such as the rhyme-structure of the odes or the 'names and things' of the artisan offices of the Zhou dynasty (1045?–256 BCE). Both his contact with Christianity and his appointment in official duties further developed this practical concern, and this consequently evolved into preoccupation

with mathematics, military defence or agriculture. Together with Matteo **Ricci**, he translated a book on Eucledian geometry *Jihe yuanben* 幾何原本 (*Elements of Geometry*, 1607). In 1629, his proposal to put Jesuits to work on the calendar reform was accepted. Xu Guangqi was of the opinion that Christianity could complement the Confucian tradition and correct Buddhism. This idea appears most clearly in his memorial defending Christianity *Bianxue zhangshu* 辨學章疏 (1616), in which he depicts western countries as having realised the ideal of the *Li yun* 禮運 utopia. Therefore western Learning (**Xi xue**) was advantageous for the whole nation. Because of Xu's fame, after his death, several Christian religious writings have been (wrongly) attributed to him.

References: Ubelhor, 1968: 191–257, 1969: 41–74; *Xu Guangqi ji*, 1984; Xi & Wu, 1986.

NICOLAS STANDAERT

Xu Heng 許衡
1209–1281
(*zi* Zhongping 仲平, *hao* Luzhai 魯齋)

Xu was the most important promoter of the Neo-Confucian revival in North China during the Mongol period. He was born in Henan into a peasant family that suffered during the Mongol conquest of North China, and Xu was taken captive in 1232. By the 1240s, Xu had become an authority on the *Book of Changes* (**Yi jing**) and studied Confucian thought with Dou Mo 竇默 (1196–1280), a northern scholar who had been captured by the Mongols. The two soon came to the attention of **Yao Shu**, who had retired in 1241 to Sumen 蘇門 mountain to study the Neo-Confucian thought he had learned from **Zhao Fu**, shortly before in Beijing. Xu was deeply impressed by Zhao's teaching when he met him at Sumen and soon obtained the Song commentaries on the Classics from Yao. In this way, Xu became acquainted with Neo-Confucian cosmology, metaphysics and political thought, especially as taught by **Zhu Xi** in his interpretations of the Four Books (*Si shu*), which he copied while at Sumen, and later on he would write his own commentaries on the Four Books and the *Book of Changes*. His acquaintance with Zhu's commentaries was an exhilarating and transforming experience that forever influenced the way he approached education, and Xu became the prime moving force in transmitting Zhu's thought in early Yuan times.

Despite his respect for Zhu's commentaries, Xu downplayed the value of exegesis in his pedagogy. Instead, he emphasised Zhu's compilation the *Elementary Learning* (*xiao xue*) in teaching his students the value of performing everyday chores as a first step in ethical self-cultivation. In 1255, he wrote a commentary on the work in vernacular Chinese based on his lectures called *The Essential Meaning of the Elementary Learning* (*Xiaoxue dayi* 小學大義). The *Elementary Learning* was the primary teaching text when Xu served in the Directorate of Education. He said that 'even if one studied nothing else, there would be no cause for regret', and believed that its down-to-earth expression of Confucian principles was ideal in the teaching of Mongols and Central Asians. Xu's emphasis on Zhu Xi's commentaries on the Four Books set the pattern for the dissemination of Confucian ideas in Yuan times, ultimately leading in 1315 to the revival of the civil service examination system on a Four Books basis, which became the standard over the following six hundred years.

After Khubilai's enthronement in the spring of 1260, Xu was recommended to the emperor by Dou Mo, and joined the court at Kaiping 開平 (later Shangdu 上都) in Inner Mongolia. In 1266 he wrote a five-point memorial exhorting Khubilai to use the *Great Learning* (**Daxue**) and the **Mengzi** as models for administering the state, stressing that the ruler had to win the hearts and minds of the people through love and impartiality, following Mengzi's

admonition that the sovereign should always seek to serve the people. In recommending that Chinese methods of government should prevail, Xu stressed the importance of enriching the people, selecting good officials, promoting universal education for Mongols and Chinese alike and enacting judicious legislation. Xu cited the example of Emperor Wen 文 of the Han dynasty (r. 179–157 BCE), who took on the concerns of the people as if they were his own. In using ideas from the *Great Learning* to underscore the Confucian basis for the relationship between ruler and minister and the necessity for the ruler constantly to scrutinise his own conduct and policies, Xu was trying to persuade Khubilai of the value of becoming a Chinese-style emperor, and many of the emperor's subsequent decrees reflect Xu's influence. As Xu said: 'If those above do not treat those below with proper respect and deference, those below will not exert themselves to the utmost'.

In 1267, Xu was appointed as Proctor of the nascent National College (*Guozi xue* 國子學) and taught members of the royal family at the Classics Mat, using such texts as the *Comprehensive Mirror for Aid in Government* (*Zizhi tongjian* 資治通鑑) by the Song scholar **Sima Guang** and the Tang dynasty work *Essence of Government in the Zhenguan Period* (*Zhenguan zhengyao* 貞觀政要). Xu also drew up plans to reform governmental structure, reform court ceremonies, establish community schools and restore the civil service examinations over the next few years. In 1270 he was appointed to the Secretarial Council, where he sought to curb the influence of the powerful minister Ahmad, and the following year took up his appointment as head of the Directorate of Education (Guozi jian 國子監), which was charged with educating the children of Mongol, Central Asian and Chinese officials.

The curriculum instituted by Xu in the Directorate of Education emphasised the *Elementary Learning* (and especially Xu's own commentary on it), the *Classic of Filial Piety* (**Xiao jing**), and the Four Books, especially the *Great Learning*, which were conceived of as gateways to the Five Classics (***Wu jing***). Xu also wrote his own primers on history and ritual. He stressed reading and recitation of the Classics, calligraphy and arithmetic, but also personalised instruction and moral development, and some of his dialogues with students have been preserved. Many of Xu's students had highly successful careers. In the debates over the nature of a restored examination system, Xu Heng favoured a system stressing exegesis steeped in Song Neo-Confucian ideals, over and against a more *belles-lettristic* approach, which had been in vogue for some time among Jin 金 dynasty (1115–1234) literati.

Xu was critical of Buddhism and Daoism, religious and philosophical, though he felt that the ideas of Laozi had relevance for the ruler and for one's outlook on fate. Confucianism was the superior philosophy, and Xu's thought is clearly in the Zhu Xi mould, though much of his ethics is derived from the ideas of the late Song thinker **Zhen Dexiu**, who, using ideas from the *Doctrine of the Mean* (*Zhongyong*), stressed the purification of one's nature as the key to moral enlightenment. Above all, however, Xu's emphasis on the rectification of one's mind, *zhengxin* 正心, had to be translated ultimately into practical action that would improve society, and in this respect Xu was drawing on ideas from the *Great Learning*.

References: Abe Takeo, 1972: 30–6; Chan Hok-lam, 1982: 52; Chan, Wing-tsit, 1982: 211–14, 216–18; Chen Yuan, 1966: 22–3, 26, 34, 289; de Bary, 1982: 20–7, 36–49, 131–45; Forke, 1938: 286–90; Gedalecia, 1981: 202–3; Langlois, 1981: 10 'Introduction'; Liu Ts'un-yan, 1986: 523–4, 530, 542; Liu, Ts'un-yan and Berling, 1982: 497–9; Rossabi, 1981: 280–1; *Song Yuan xuean*, 1966: 90: 2a–10b; Sun Qifeng, *Lixue zongchuan*, 1880: ch. 19; Tu, 1982: 242–3; Yuan Ji, 1972; *Yuan shi*, 1976: 158.

DAVID GEDALECIA

Xu Shen 許慎
c. 55–149 CE

At the restoration of scholarly pursuits to imperial favour under Han Andi (r. 106–125 CE), Xu Shen presented to the court his *Shuowen jiezi* 說文解字 (*Explanations of Scripts and Elucidation of Characters*), which he had compiled with the intention of clarifying the classical writings. The work sets out the meanings of some 10,000 characters which were classified in six types, and arranged under 540 elements, together with variant forms as seen in different types of inscription. The work includes citations of classical writings that were drawn from the Old Text versions, of which Xu Shen was a known protagonist. He was also the author of one of the earliest annotations to the *Huainan zi* 淮南子.

Reference: Boltz, 1993: 429–42.

MICHAEL LOEWE

Xuansheng Wenxuan Wang
玄聖文宣王
(Dark Sage, Exalted King of Culture)

Confucius held the title of ***Wenxuan Wang*** (Exalted King of Culture) from 739. The emperor gave him the title of 'Dark Sage, Exalted King of Culture' in 1008 during a visit to Qufu, Confucius' home town. At the same time, the emperor also posthumously ennobled Confucius' father as Duke of Qi 齊國公 and his mother as Grand Mistress of Lu 魯國太夫人. The title Dark Sage alludes to non-canonical stories about Confucius as the son of a black water god that impregnated Confucius' mother at Mt Ni when she prayed for a son. This is one of the few official acknowledgments of this lore, although the word 'dark' was replaced by the word 'supreme' 至 in 1013.

THOMAS A. WILSON

Xue 學
(Learning)

Confucius' *Analects* is the most widely learned and memorised books in Chinese history. It begins with this word, *xue*, which could best be rendered as 'learning'. Confucius indeed uses 'love of learning' as his self-definition: 'The Master said, In a hamlet of ten houses you may be sure of finding someone quite as loyal and true to his word as I. But I doubt if you would find anyone with such a love of learning' (the *Analects*, 5: 27).

Xue is also often used for a physical school. For example, the school for sons of ranking officials or aristocrats was called a *xue* for 'national sons or youth (*Guozi* 國子)', and the school for astronomy a *xue* for '[knowledge of] heavenly patterns (*Tianwen* 天文)'.

Most importantly, *xue* means systematic knowledge that contains an inner logic and consistency and that is of moral significance, capable of withstanding challenges. It is thus learning in broad sense, and is like a school of thought. It was Zhuangzi 莊子 (fourth century BCE) who first used *xue* in this sense. Subsequent uses of it in the Han times suggest that an intellectual lineage of a certain version of learning or interpreting the Classics was a *xue*. In later times, the scholarship identified with founder-teacher was commonly called *xue* of the founder-teacher.

In daily use, *xue* was no more than learning to take and pass the civil service examinations. In this sense, it was a far cry to what Confucius said of it as the ultimate purpose of learning, to achieve the joy of moral perfection: learning for one's own self in moral sense. Authentic *xue* thus consisted of personal moral cultivation and the comprehension of one's standing within the process and parameter of his learning as a moral human being.

THOMAS H.C. LEE

Xue Jixuan 薛季瑄
1134–1173
(*zi* Tulong 土龍, *hao* Genzhai 艮齋)

Xue Jixuan was one of the leading scholars of *Yongjia* School (**Yongjia xuepai**). Xue was born into an official family in Yongjia area and was involved in different military actions against Jurchen Jin in his life. Xue's contribution to the *Yongjia* School was his definitions and clarifications on the fundamental arguments of *Yongjia* teaching and therefore, set the basic tone for the school's future development. Xue emphasised the priority of understanding concrete things over obtaining abstract **dao**, and he was famous for his practical and broad knowledge ranging from history, astrology, geography, to justice, agriculture and literature. He was the first person in the *Yongjia* School to use Confucian Classics as historical records, and questioned the succession and transmission of the Way (**dao tong**). He clearly indicated that integrity and utility could not be separated from each other and the balance in between should be well maintained. Xue also set up the good example for practising *Yongjia* teachings in public services at both central and local level, in which he provided unique perspectives on restoration strategies, defense systems, financial budgeting and reforms on government institutions. Xue's ideas were further developed by later *Yongjia* scholars, particularly his close student **Chen Fuliang**, and Chen's student **Ye Shi**.

References: *Song–Yuan xuean*, 1966; Niu, Pu, 1998; Qian Mu, 1953.

PU NIU

Xue Xuan 薛瑄
1389–1464
(*zi* Dewen 德溫, *hao* Jingxuan 敬軒)

Xue Xuan was a native of Xi He Jin 西河津 near Mt Mingshan 明山. In 1421 he received his *jinshi* degree. Around 1426 Xue was appointed to the position of Investigating Censor (*Jiancha yushi* 監察御史). In 1436 Xue was dispatched to Shandong as an Educational Intendant to certify students readying themselves for the provincial civil service examinations. Due to a personal conflict with the dictatorial eunuch Wang Zhen 王振, Xue Xuan was falsely accused, arrested and sentenced to death, although he was later released and instead exiled to his home region. Around 1450, Xue again took a position in Nanjing as Chief Minister of the Court of Judicial Review (*Dalishi qing* 大理寺卿). After Emperor Yingzong was restored to the throne (1457), Xue moved to the central court position of Right Vice-Minister of Rites (*Libu you shilang* 禮部右侍郎), serving concurrently as Chancellor of the Hanlin Academy. While at these positions, Xue once again ran into controversy, when he again faced false charges. At this time the powerful official Shi Heng 石亨 was at court, and his opposition proved to be too much for Xue. Xue Xuan subsequently pleaded illness as a cause for his early retirement from government service. He spent the next eight years until his death teaching a growing number of students. When he was young, Xue had studied the *Four Books* and the *Five Classics* with his father. Xue's main works include *Dushu lu* 讀書錄 (*A Record of Book Readings*).

While Xue Xuan can be considered a disciple of the Cheng–Zhu School of Neo-Confucianism, he believed that his own work continued to develop and refine **Zhu Xi**'s teachings. Specifically Xue Xuan denied that *li* (principle) inevitably appears before *qi* (material force), but instead that *Li* is found within *qi* and therefore cannot be said to manifest itself either before or after *qi*. As Xue points out in *A Record of Book Readings*, 'there is a seamless connection between *li* and *qi*, and therefore the instrument is the *dao*, just as the *Dao* may be called the instrument'. Xue maintained that because *li* provided the connections and proper arrangement between the myriad phenomena, *qi* could not be considered an element separate from this arrangement. Regarding the Supreme Ultimate (***tai ji***), Xue argued that its *li* could be found only in *qi* as well. He did not agree with Zhu Xi's contention that the *li* of the Supreme Ultimate preceded the emergence of *yin* and *yang*, and in fact produced these forces. However, he accepted Zhu Xi's notion that while *qi* may be reconstituted continually, *li* remains absolute. As Xue writes '*Li* is like the sun, while *qi* resembles a flock of flying birds. *Li* takes advantage of *qi* to multiply and to move, just as the sun rests upon the back of a bird and flies.'

Xue Xuan presented several critiques of Buddhist practices in this work. For example, he pointedly criticised **Lu Jiuyuan**'s style of 'quiet-sitting' (***jing zuo***), suggesting that Lu's practice did not differ enough from the similar Chan Buddhist technique. He also developed Zhu's method concerning 'the investigation of things' (*gewu*), emphasising the collective utility of one's sensory perception.

References: *Song–Yuan xuan*, 1966: *juan* 7; Wu & Song, 1992: 1094–5; *Zhongguo zhexueshi tonglan*, 1994: 299.

JAMES A. ANDERSON

Xun Shuang 荀爽
128–190 CE
(*zi* Ciming 慈明)

Xun Shuang, also named Xu 諝, was a twelfth-generation descendant of **Xunzi**. He is known for classical scholarship with an overt political agenda. In 166, he was appointed a palace gentleman (*Lang zhong* 郎中) after recommendation for 'Supreme Filial Piety' (*zhi xiao* 至孝). He then wrote a memorial promoting ***xiao*** (filial piety) and the supremacy of family ties over political obligations. In 189, the court named him Superintendent of the Palace (*Guangluxun* 光祿勳) and quickly elevated him to Minister of Works (*Sikong* 司空). *Yi zhuan*

易傳, one of his commentaries on the Five Classics (**Wu jing**), interpreted symbolism in *The Book of Changes* (**Yi jing**) as representing a violent but ultimately triumphant struggle by the good forces of the *shi* 士 (scholar) against the ill forces of the consort clans, eunuchs and even the person of the emperor. In the *Han yu* 漢語(*Conversations on the Han*), Xun Shuang represented certain disastrous Former Han events as warnings about contemporary affairs. He produced *Gongyang wen* 公羊問 (*Questions on the Gongyang Commentary*), a collection of essays titled *Xin shu* 新書 (*New Documents*), and *Bian chen* 辯讖 (*Critiquing the Prognostication Texts*), wherein he rejected the view that the prognostication texts and apocrypha (**chen wei**) recorded esoteric teachings of Confucius. His larger works are lost but for parts of *Yi zhuan* preserved in later commentaries; sections of the *Han yu* may have been incorporated into his nephew **Xun Yue**'s *Han ji* 漢紀 (*A Record of the Han*).

References: Chen Chiryun, 1968, 1975, 1980, 1986; Hulsewé, 1993.

MARK L. ASSELIN

Xun Yue 荀悅
148–209 CE
(*zi* 仲豫 Zhongyu)

Xun Yue was one of three leading Confucian scholars of the Later Han period (25–220 BCE), along with **Wang Fu** and **Zhongchang Tong**, concerned with the art of governing. He was a thirteenth-generation descendant of **Xunzi** and the nephew of **Xun Shuang**. For much of his early adult life, with the eunuchs dominating the court, Xun Yue, under the pretext of illness, lived in retirement. In 196, the emerging 'protector' Cao Cao 曹操 (155–220, *zi* Mengde 孟德) summoned him to office. He was appointed a gentleman of the Yellow Gates (*Huangmen shilang* 黃門侍郎), promoted to Inspector of the Imperial Library (*Mishu jian* 祕書監) and finally named a palace attendant (*Shizhong* 侍中). He, his cousin Xun Yu 荀彧 (163–212, *zi* Wenruo 文若), and **Kong Rong** would conduct lectures and long discussions in the palace. Xun Yue is credited with writing *Chong de* 崇德 (*Esteeming Virtue*), *Zheng lun* 正論 (*Discourse on Rectification*), *Shen jian* 申鑒 (*Extended Reflections*), and *Han ji* 漢紀 (*A Record of the Han*); only the latter two survive, and in the case of *Shen jian*, in a considerably corrupt form. *Shen jian*, in five chapters (*pian*), is a compilation of essays, treatises, dialogues and notes covering a wide variety of topics of practical concern to governance (e.g., education, military matters, ritual). *Han ji*, also known as the *Qian Han ji* 前漢紀 (*A Record of the Former Han*) and *Xiao Xunzi* 小荀子 (*The Lesser Xunzi*), in thirty *pian*, is an abridged version of the **Han shu**. It was presented to the throne in 200 CE. On the emperor's request, the work was organised chronologically, in imitation of *The Spring and Autumn Annals* (**Chunqiu**). In *Han ji*, Xun Yue shrewdly invested the *symbol* of the emperor with enormous cosmic and moral significance, which demonstrated his allegiance to the Han dynasty; this freed him to criticise *actual* emperors for failing to aspire to intellectual and moral excellence. He was generally supportive of the *shi* 士 (scholar), who, by taking up the messy business of governing, kept the emperor untainted by the conflicting interests and compromises inherent in governing. Yet he criticised those scholar–officials who had deviated from the Way and had become corrupt and oppressive. He reserved top censure for those who had formed partisan ties with non-family members. His high regard for the centrality of the family resembles that of Xun Shuang, but being a loyalist, he did not promote the interests of the family to the exclusion of the needs of the state. He advocated de-centralisation through refeudalisation which he maintained provided the proper checks and balances: the people, who had the option to revolt, the feudal lords, who provided the ruler support and correction and the ruler, who established order through clearly delineated and justly administered rewards and punishments. Xun Yue was not as pessimistic as Zhongchang Tong, but believed that strict imposition of punishments could yet restore the Way.

References: Chen Chi-yun, 1975, 1980, 1986, 1993; Hsiao, 1979; Hulsewé 1993.

MARK L. ASSELIN

Xunzhai xuepai 巽齊學派
(The School of Ouyang Shoudao)

The *Xunzhai xuepai* is one of the schools of thought (*xuepai*) mentioned in the **Song-Yuan xuean**; it is named according to the alternative name (*hao* 號) of its founder, **Ouyang Shoudao**. **Quan Zuwang** says it is uncertain through which persons a connection to the school of **Zhu Xi** can be established; the strong influence of the Zhu Xi school, however, is undoubted.

The members of this school are scholars of the late Song or early Yuan period. The most important of them is surely **Wen Tianxiang**, the great hero in the last years of the demise of the Song dynasty (960–1279). The fact that Ouyang Shoudao's pupil Wen Tianxiang is part of this school might be an important reason that most of the other members are Song patriots as well, e.g. Deng Guangjian 鄧光薦 (?–1297?, *zi* Zhongfu 中父 or 中甫, *hao* Zhongzhai 中齋), Luo Kaili 羅開禮 (?–1278?, *zi* Zhengfu 正甫, *hao* Shuixin 水心), and Zhang Qianzai 張千載 (?–?, *zi* Yifu 毅父 or 毅甫). These people followed Wen Tianxiang during his military campaign to save the Song dynasty, and some of them also accompanied him during his stay in prison in Yanjing 燕京 (today Beijing).

But, nevertheless, not all members of this school were involved in politics: we find also the Xing Tianrong 邢天榮 (?–?) and Dong Jingshu 董景舒 (?–?), who were poets devoted to *ci* 詞 and *fu* 賦 poetry.

CHRISTIAN SOFFEL

Xunzi 荀子
313?–238? BCE

Traditionally, Xunzi is recognised as the third scholar in the Confucian lineage, following Confucius and **Mengzi**. Xunzi was born in the state of Zhao. His name was Xun Kuang 荀況, but he came to be known as Xun Qing 荀卿, Xun the Minister. Despite the amount of historical information we have concerning his life, there is no general agreement on the dates of his birth and death. Scholars place his dates as early as 340 BCE–245 BCE and as late as 310 BCE–219 BCE. The difference in dates is due partly to a passage in the **Shi ji** that states that Xunzi left his home for the state of Qi 齊 at the age of fifty. However, there are good reasons for believing that this number should be read as fifteen and not fifty and that the later dates for Xunzi's life are correct. As a consequence, Xunzi probably lived to see the unification of China under King Zheng of Qin 秦政王, who became known as the First Emperor of the Qin dynasty (r. 221–210 BCE).

We know little about Xunzi's family or childhood, but through his writings, he reveals a thorough training in the arts of the aristocracy – including hunting, archery, warfare, reading and writing, ritual activity – as well as an education in classical literature. Since only wealthy families could afford an education of this sort, we can safely surmise that he was born into a relatively affluent family. Compared to our limited knowledge of most other early Chinese figures, we know a great deal about Xunzi's life. Besides his biography in the *Shi ji*, we also have a longer biography written by **Liu Xiang**, who edited and compiled the first version of the extant text of Xunzi's writings. When the biographies are coupled with evidence from Xunzi's writings, we can create a rather detailed picture of his life. Several elements of his biography deserve particular mention: the breadth of his education, his political career and his importance as a Confucian teacher. As mentioned above, Xunzi left home at the age of fifteen to continue his studies in Qi at the Jixia 稷下 Academy. As a thriving centre of intellectual activity, the Jixia Academy offered Xunzi the opportunity to study and learn from the best scholars of the Warring States period (475–221 BCE). This education was not restricted to only Confucian teachings. From his writings it is clear that he was exposed to the teachings of most, if not all, of the major schools of philosophy of his time. In addition to giving Xunzi a background in these schools of thought, the breadth of his education helped him to adopt and adapt arguments and methods from rival schools in the defence of the Confucian Way. Often when Xunzi most vehemently criticises another school of thought, he simultaneously adopts and modifies some of his opponents' arguments, turning them to the defence of Confucianism. This practice can be seen most clearly in relation to the philosophies of Mozi and Zhuangzi. Xunzi soundly criticises both thinkers for failing to understand properly the Way (*dao*), yet his own position owes a great debt to each.

Like most of the scholars of his day, Xunzi spent much of his career travelling to various states advising rulers, teaching students and sometimes being employed as an official. Unlike either Confucius or Mengzi, Xunzi did in fact hold office, although eventually he was dismissed from office for political reasons. What is most significant about his travels and official service is that he observed firsthand the treachery and intrigue of Warring States politics and warfare. Xunzi lived through the end of the Warring States period when conflict and struggle among states was the rule rather than the exception. During this time, the Qin state gradually consolidated its power and captured more and more territory, leading to the eventual unification of China into an empire. Xunzi's experience of the political events of his time left a lasting impression. On the one hand, he came to recognise the ability and power of the Qin form of

political organisation, based on the teachings of Shang Yang 商鞅 (390?–338 BCE). On the other hand, he also witnessed the failure of the Qin to win the hearts of the people and build lasting peace and prosperity in its territories. Xunzi's proposed solution was to organise the state in such a way that it took advantage of the organisational skills of the Legalists, yet remained committed to promoting the Confucian ritual order, an order based on the benevolent treatment of the people. Xunzi argues well for this position in his writings on military affairs and rulership.

Having started as a student at the Jixia Academy, Xunzi came to be one of its most respected and senior scholars. His distinguished place among the intellectuals of his time is attested to by his being appointed head libationer (Jijiu) of the Jixia Academy – the highest-ranking, honorary participant in an official state ritual – an unprecedented three times. Xunzi's connection to the Academy reveals his active participation and leadership within the philosophical community at a time when philosophical discussion and the work of governing the state were thought to require and complement one another. This intellectual environment afforded him opportunities to study under the most distinguished philosophers of his day, to influence many contemporary teachers through discussion and debate, and to instruct a number of exceptionally talented students. Aside from his own writings, his role as teacher ensured him an important place in the Confucian tradition. Xunzi's students played a significant role in the transmission and shaping of later Confucianism. Many of the extant Confucian texts read by later generations were transmitted to Han Confucians by Xunzi's students. For example, among his students, Fouqiu Bo 浮邱伯 conveyed the text of the *Guliang Commentary to The Spring and Autumn Annals* to Shen Pei 申培 (*fl. c.* 200 BCE); Zhang Cang 張蒼 transmitted the (*Chunqiu*) *Zuo Zhuan*, commentary to *The Spring and*

Autumn Annals; and **Mao Heng** learned the interpretations of poems of *The Book of Poetry* (**Shi jing**) from Xunzi and then taught them to his son Mao Chang 毛萇. Together the Maos wrote what became the orthodox commentary on *The Book of Poetry*. Without the work of Xunzi's students in preserving, interpreting and transmitting these texts, they might have been lost.

Xunzi's best known and politically successful students were Han Fei 韓非 (280?–233 BCE) and Li Si 李斯 (?–208 BCE). Han Fei became a well-known philosopher in his own right, writing essays and memorials explaining and defending the Legalist school of thought. Han Fei believed that the means of effective governing lay in developing bureaucratic methods for the control of political power. Like Xunzi, he wrote numerous essays explaining the techniques of governing and providing philosophical justifications for them. But, unlike his teacher, Han Fei focused not on the power of ritual, moral cultivation, or the virtue of the ruler, but exclusively on the techniques for exercising and maintaining political power. After reading Han Fei's essays, King Zheng of Qin implemented many of his policies during Qin's campaign of conquest and in the administration of the subsequent Qin dynasty. Li Si was more actively engaged in the Qin conquest as a member of the Qin court, directly advising King Zheng and helping to create the policies that enabled Qin to unify China and found the first dynasty. The political skills of Li Si and the writings of Han Fei provided central components for the foundation of the Chinese imperial state. Yet, in spite of the remarkable contribution these two students made in orchestrating the unification of China and the creation of the imperial bureaucracy, their success had a negative impact on Xunzi's standing within the Confucian tradition because the Qin dynasty was widely regarded as a brutal and repressive regime. Since, from the Chinese point of view, teachers are responsible for the actions of their students, Xunzi was held accountable for the repressive measures advocated by his two students.

In addition to the work of his students, Xunzi's own writings had a profound influence upon later Confucianism. At the end of the Warring States period, Confucius' teachings were receiving serious criticism from several different schools of thought. Mengzi's earlier defence of the master's teachings was no longer proving to be persuasive. A new, and more sophisticated defence of the Confucian Way was needed and Xunzi provided just such a defence. He directly addressed the criticisms of rival philosophers and developed an interpretation of the Confucian Way that took them into account. Xunzi's writings, collected in a work entitled **Xunzi**, constitute the most coherent, sophisticated and complete explanation and defence of the Confucian Way in the early period. Many of the themes that he directly addressed and elaborated continued to influence and stimulate debate throughout the later tradition.

Xunzi was the first Confucian to designate a textual canon to be used in moral cultivation. He included five works in the canon – *Li* (*Rites*), *Yue* (*Music*), *Shi* (*Poetry*), *Shu* (*Documents*), and **Chunqiu** (*The Spring and Autumn Annals*). Over the course of time the Confucian canon would change, yet the set of texts established by Xunzi endured as its central core. More importantly, the notion of a canon and its contribution to moral cultivation remained a mainstay of the tradition.

Along with the canon, Xunzi emphasised the fundamental role of the teacher in classical Confucian education. Although the importance of the teacher is implicit in the writings of Confucius and Mengzi, Xunzi provided explicit justification for the role teachers must play in moral cultivation. Moreover, he more thoroughly described the role of teachers and their significance in the process of guiding others through moral cultivation. Both his emphasis on the importance of teachers and his explicit justification of their role in moral education remained characteristic features of the later tradition.

In addition, Xunzi expanded the understanding of tradition and argued for the necessity of both hierarchy and a unified set of standards with which to guide cultivation. All of these ideas became integrated into and came to be defining features of the Chinese imperial orthodoxy. While Xunzi was not the only philosopher in the early tradition to discuss these issues, he offered some of the most sophisticated analyses of these topics and was the only thinker to bring them together in a systematic fashion. For these reasons he may be identified as the most influential proponent of these ideas in the early Confucian tradition.

Xunzi also emphasised the importance of *xue* (learning or study) as opposed to *si* 思 (reflection or introspection) in the process of moral cultivation. He accused Mengzi of putting too much emphasis on *si* and not enough on *xue*. This emphasis on study guided by a teacher would remain central to Confucian education until the writings of Mengzi gained greater prominence in the Tang dynasty (618–907). Given that Xunzi claimed that human nature is bad (*xing e*), it made sense to stress the importance of learning guided by a teacher who had already undergone the process of cultivation himself. Before being shaped in moral education, reflection or introspection on one's own inclinations and tendencies would not provide any guidance for cultivation. Xunzi's opposition to both Mengzi's position on the character of human nature and Mengzi's emphasis on introspection, coupled with his connection to Han Fei and Li Si, caused later Confucians largely to ignore or deemphasise Xunzi's contributions to the Confucian tradition. Until very recently most scholarly effort was focused on the writings of Confucius and Mengzi to the relative neglect of Xunzi.

References: Gu Jiegang, 1987, 94–140; Kline & Ivanhoe, 2000: ix–xvii; Knoblock, 1988.

T.C. KLINE III

Xunzi 荀子
(*The Book of Xunzi*)

The *Xunzi* consists of the collected writings of **Xunzi**, a third-century BCE Confucian and the third, great scholar in the Confucian lineage following Confucius and **Mengzi**. The text contains thirty-two chapters, the majority of which are essays on a single topic or theme. Unlike many other early texts, such as the **Lunyu** or **Mengzi**, written primarily by disciples and later followers, almost the entire text was written by Xunzi himself. Given that the text is organised into essays on particular topics, and that it is primarily the work of a single author, the *Xunzi* is generally coherent, clear and consistently well written. These essays cover a broad range of topics from military affairs and governance to music and ritual to moral psychology and the character of human nature. The text has a somewhat complex history of compilation, which creates further problems when we try to determine the authenticity of various sections. Yet, in general the text can be accepted as an authentic collection of the writings of Xunzi from the third century BCE.

For most early Chinese thinkers, the extant versions of the texts containing their writings did not take form until sometime in the Han dynasty (206 BCE–220 CE). The same is true of the *Xunzi*. **Liu Xiang** compiled the *Xunzi* in the first century BCE. In his preface to the work, he claims that he began with a collection of 322 different essays or sections of essays from a work entitled the *Sun Qing shu* 孫卿書. He then rejected 290 of these essays because they were duplicates. Finally, he properly collated and ordered the remaining 32 sections into a work that he entitled the *Sun Qing xinshu* 孫卿新書. (The use of 'sun' 孫 rather than 'xun' 荀 for Xunzi's family name is explained by scholars in various ways, but all agree that properly it should have been written 'xun'.) Although Liu Xiang did append a preface to the work, he did not provide any commentary or annotation.

Nevertheless, the significance of Liu Xiang's work should not be underestimated. If he accurately reports on his own work, then only 10 per cent of the original material was collected into the final version presented to the emperor. In addition to his organisation of the chapters in the work as a whole, it is likely that Liu Xiang also arranged and edited the versions of each chapter, eliminating interpolations and rearranging passages that he believed were misplaced. He presumably created the titles for each chapter as well. Overall, Liu Xiang probably provided a great service in cleaning up a text that was in need of restoration. Yet, although we can learn a great deal about Xunzi's philosophy from the content of the text, we cannot learn anything from the structure or organisation of the work, as it is Liu Xiang and not Xunzi who is responsible for its organisation.

Although the *Xunzi* was originally compiled in the first century BCE, it was not until 818 CE that the first commentary on the text was written by a man named Yang Liang 楊倞. This date is surprisingly late. By the ninth century several commentaries had been written on both the *Lunyu* and *Mengzi*. Nevertheless, Yang Liang's comments are particularly insightful and still used by modern scholars. In addition to writing a commentary on Liu Xiang's edition of the text, Yang Liang also rearranged the order of the chapters. He left the first twenty-three chapters mostly intact, but rearranged the final chapters, moving those more suspect further to the end of the work. In fact, the present version of the *Xunzi* is based on Yang Liang's rearrangement and not Liu Xiang's earlier ordering of the text. More specifically, modern versions are based on the Shide Tang 世德堂 edition from the Ming dynasty, first published in 1530 and still readily available in the Qing dynasty.

From the Song dynasty to the modern period the *Xunzi* was not regarded as a significant text of the Confucian tradition and very little scholarly attention was paid to the text, yet in the modern period sev-

eral very thorough and influential commentaries and studies on the text have been published. Earliest among these studies is Wang Niansun's 王念孫 (1744–1832) annotations to the *Xunzi* included in his larger work, *Dushu zazhi* 讀書雜誌, published in 8 *juan* from 1812–1831. Wang Niansun makes use of and considers most of the earlier scholarship on the text. His notes are carefully researched explanations and conclusions about textual variants and emendations. Yet, he pays relatively little attention to the text's philosophical content. At the end of the nineteenth century, various significant commentaries and studies of the text were combined with a new commentary and text of the *Xunzi* in the *Xunzi jijie* 荀子集解 by Wang Xianqian 王先謙 (1842–1917). This edition with collected commentaries has become an indispensable edition for much scholarship. Early modern Japanese scholarship produced an edition of the text published in 1820 with commentary by Kubo Ai 久保愛 and additional notes by several other Japanese scholars entitled *Junshi zôchû* 荀子增注. Similar to Wang Niansun's edition, several sets of annotations and commentary are included alongside the text.

Despite this somewhat complicated history of compilation, scholars agree that the majority of the *Xunzi* is a collection of the writings of Xunzi. This means that the *Xunzi* is the first Confucian work that can be positively identified as being written by its purported author, and the large majority of the *Xunzi* is thought to consist of authentic writings, even if some of these are not in their original form. However, questions have been raised concerning the authenticity of several parts of the text, especially the last six chapters, 27–32. Scholars have raised questions about both the content and nature of these chapters. This portion of the text tends to be more heterogeneous and less tightly connected to the central themes of the rest of the work. In addition, it is believed that in rearranging the text, Yang Liang placed these chapters at the end because he questioned their authenticity and concluded that they were probably compositions or compilations of later students or followers of Xunzi. There is some merit to these suspicions. Nevertheless, when viewed as a whole, the work is surprisingly coherent and consistent, more so than most early texts. Even these later chapters fit well within the scope and systematic philosophy of the rest of the text. Given the difficulties introduced by Liu Xiang's and Yang Liang's rearrangements of the text, the overall coherence of the work is strong *prima facie* evidence for treating the entire work as authentic. At the very least, we may regard judgements of inauthenticity based on the content or style of exposition with considerable scepticism.

In addition, extensive parallels between the *Xunzi* and three other early texts further suggest the authenticity of the *Xunzi*. The *Hanshi waizhuan* (see **Han Ying**), *Dadai li ji* 大戴禮記 (see **Dai De**), and *Li ji* (The Book of Rites) all contain extended passages that parallel sections of the *Xunzi*. In most cases, these passages are not instances of citation of traditional material by two different authors, nor is it the case that Xunzi is quoting these works. Instead, there is good evidence that the authors or compilers of these works are citing the writings of Xunzi. These quotations, or references, also lend support to the conclusion that the extant text of the *Xunzi* contains authentic writings. Such evidence not withstanding, scholars still disagree about which chapters should be considered as definitely authentic writings of Xunzi and which should be treated with caution.

As is the case with Chinese scholarship on the *Xunzi*, western study of the text began relatively late. James **Legge**, who made the first serious translations of the Confucian classics into English, translated only one chapter of the *Xunzi*, chapter 23, *Xing e* (Human Nature is Bad). He did so as a portion of the preface to his translation of the *Mengzi*. Homer Dubs, in 1927, published *The Works of Hsüntze*, the first selected trans-

lation of the *Xunzi* in English. This work included nineteen chapters of the text: chapters 1–2, 4–11, and 15–23. Since that time, two more selected translations have been published, one by Burton Watson, and one by Eric Hutton, who for the most part follows Watson's selection of passages. The first complete translation of the text into English was completed in 1994 by John Knoblock and consists of three volumes entitled *Xunzi: A Translation and Study of the Complete Works*. Complete translations of the *Xunzi* have also been published in German, by Herman Köster, and in Japanese, by Kanaya Osamu 金谷治. Concordances based on Wang Xianqian's edition of the text have also been published, first in the Harvard–Yenching series, which is now out of print, and recently in the ICS series of concordances published by The Chinese University of Hong Kong. Both of these concordances include a complete copy of the text itself.

In arranging the text, Liu Xiang and Yang Liang appear to have grouped chapters loosely on the basis of their content. John Knoblock has proposed that we recognise four basic divisions to the text based on content. The first six chapters address the topic of moral cultivation and the various methods of Confucian education. This division of the text begins with a chapter discussing Xunzi's understanding of the importance and methods of learning (*xue*). Each of the following five chapters engages and elaborates topics introduced in the first chapter. The second division of the text covers chapters 7–16. Most broadly, these chapters concern the relationship of the individual to his social and political environment. Several of the chapters discuss political theory and ethics, as well as conceptions of the ideal ruler. Traditionally, it is believed that chapters 17–24, the third division of the work, contain the philosophical substance of the *Xunzi*. In these chapters, Xunzi addresses questions concerning the nature and relationship of humans to *tian* (Heaven), *yue* (music), and *li* (ritual). Additionally, he explains and defends his views on moral psychology, moral failure and the character of human nature. These chapters are particularly philosophically rich, yet they cannot be understood properly unless they are placed into the context of the discussions found in the rest of the text. The fourth and final division of the text, chapters 25–32, consists of Xunzi's poetry, historical anecdotes and collected proverbs and fragments of conversation. Yang Liang and other scholars have suggested that many of these chapters were compiled by students or later followers. However, as noted earlier in terms of content, these chapters fit consistently with the rest of the work.

Within Chinese and western scholarship on the Confucian tradition, the *Xunzi* has enjoyed a resurgence of interest in the late nineteenth and twentieth centuries. The *Xunzi* was popular with late nineteenth-century reformers, since Xunzi could be identified as an early representative of a proto-scientific viewpoint, one that was based on empirical observation rather than grand metaphysical theories or superstitious belief. More recently, the *Xunzi* has been recognised by western scholars as containing the most philosophically sophisticated defence of the Confucian worldview in the early period. Part of this interest in the *Xunzi* has been due to the fact that modern scholars often agree with Xunzi's rejection of any innate, moral direction to human nature. Consistent with their rejection of intuitionist theories of morality, such as those developed by Shaftesbury, Hutcheson and Butler, modern western scholars often find Xunzi's position more congenial to their own viewpoint than that of Mengzi. In addition, Xunzi directly addresses questions concerning ritual, moral cultivation and the relationship of human beings to their social and natural environment in sophisticated and insightful ways, many of which not only provide ways to explain and defend the Confucian worldview, but are of interest to contemporary western philosophers as well.

References: Dubs, 1928; Hutton, 2000; Kanaya 1962; Knoblock, 1988; Köster, 1967; Lau, 1996a; Loewe, 1993: 178–88; Watson, 1963.

T.C. KLINE III

Xuyi er jing 虛一而靜
(more commonly 虛壹而靜, Emptiness, unity, and stillness)

This expression from the *Jie bi* 解蔽 ('Dispelling Obfuscation') chapter of the *Xunzi* describes three fundamental qualities of the heart/mind (*xin*) that allow it to understand the Way (*Dao*). The mind is always storing information, but the content of this information does not impede the understanding of new material; hence, the mind is called 'empty'. (Xunzi's notion of emptiness owes nothing to the Buddhist concept of *sunyata*, as the *Xunzi* predates the entry of Buddhist texts to China by several centuries.) The mind is confronted with a multiplicity of diverse phenomena, but it is nonetheless capable of understanding different things at the same time; herein lies its unity. The mind is always moving, even in dreams, yet it nevertheless is possessed of stillness, for it does not allow phantasmagoria to impinge upon its acuity.

Someone who develops these three qualities fully may be said to embody the Way. Xunzi calls the state of emptiness, unity and stillness a 'great, clear brightness' (*da qingming*), a sublimated sense of perspicacity and depth in both space and time. Xunzi admonishes the reader to develop these qualities of the mind – although he does not provide any techniques for their development – as they will hone the acumen of persons responsible for staffing the government and fending off the forces of disorder.

References: Knoblock, 1988–94; Wang Xianqian, 1988; Watson, 1963.

DEBORAH SOMMER

Ya ru 雅儒
(Refined *ru*)

From at least the time of **Xunzi**, the term *Ya ru* was employed by self-identified followers of Confucius' ethical Way to distinguish themselves from the *Su ru* ('vulgar classicists'), regarded as mere *wenli* 文吏 ('literate clerks'). While the clerks prided themselves on being well versed in legal affairs, in record-keeping, or in turning out fine literary phrases to mask harsh administrative measures, they did not maintain the practices and values associated with the moral exemplars associated with the Five Classics' (*Wu jing*) heroes and with Confucius. By contrast, the 'refined *ru*' by definition took moral practice as their chief preoccupation, even at the risk of losing their careers.

MICHAEL NYLAN

Ya sheng 亞聖
(Second Sage)

Mengzi was ennobled as the Duke of Zou in 1083 and received secondary sacrifices (see *Pei xiang*) as a correlate in the temple of Confucius (*Kong miao*) the next year. The *Mengzi* was widely influential among Confucian thinkers during the Song dynasty (960–1279) and was formally canonised as one of the Four Books (*Si shu*) in the civil-service-examination curriculum during the Yuan dynasty (1260–1368). The title Ya sheng 亞聖, the second sage, was originally applied to Yan Hui (see *Fu sheng*) in the Tang dynasty (720), but was formally conferred upon Mengzi in the Yuan dynasty (1333), when the latter was ennobled as Duke of Zou, the Second Sage 鄒國亞聖公, although Mengzi had been referred to as the second sage as early as in the second-century CE commentary on the book by **Zhao Qi**.

THOMAS A. WILSON

Yamaga Sokô 山鹿素行
1622–1685
(*na* 名: Kôkô 高興, 高祐; *azana* 字: Shikei 子敬; *gô* 號: Inzan 因山; *tsûhô* 通稱: Satarô 左太郎, Bunsaburô 文三朗, Jingozaemon 甚五左衛門)

In western scholarship Yamaga Sokô is often described as one of the pioneers of the so-called 'ancient learning movement' (*kogaku*) in Tokugawa Confucian thought. However, Sokô's inclusion in this movement is largely due to the continued acceptance among western scholars of **Inoue Tetsujirô**'s tripartite division of Japanese Confucian philosophy into (1) a **Zhu Xi** school, (2) a Wang Yangming (**Wang Shouren**) School, and (3) an Ancient Learning school. By positing the latter, Inoue provided for a distinctively Japanese development within the history of Tokugawa Confucian thought when otherwise it seemed that Japanese scholars were, as he stated, 'spiritual slaves' of Zhu Xi. Also, Inoue's writings on Tokugawa thought appeared in the early twentieth century, following the Sino-Japanese War (1894–1895), and Japan's ascent as the new power in Asia. Swayed by imperial Japan's military victories, Inoue cast the Ancient Learning School as the harbinger of Meiji military power by suggesting that Ancient Learning scholars, beginning with Sokô, attacked and prevailed over the Song philosophy of Zhu Xi by pioneering distinctive expressions of Japan's 'national morality' (*kokumin dôtoku*) and 'national essence' (*kokutai*).

While Sokô did criticise Zhu Xi and much of Song thought, he never claimed to have been part of an Ancient Learning movement. Instead he referred to his brand of Confucianism as 'Sagely Learning' 聖學 (Jn. *seigaku*), borrowing a rubric earlier used by Song Neo-Confucians to describe their learning. Though Sokô did assert that his ideas sought to revive the philosophy of Confucius and the Duke of Zhou while forsaking that of Song Confucians, scrutiny of Sokô's writings reveals that his ideas, in genre, method and content, owed more to **Neo-Confucianism**, the movement which he purportedly rejected, than to the original ideas of Confucius or the Duke of Zhou. As a former student of **Hayashi Razan**, Sokô was influenced decisively by **Chen Chun**'s (1159–1223) *Beixi ziyi* and Razan's colloquial explication of the same work, the *Seiri jigi genkai*. Sokô's considerable debt to Neo-Confucianism is most evident in his brief treatise, the *Seikyô yôroku* (Essential Lexicography of the Sagely Confucian Teachings). Though the latter is clearly modelled after Chen Chun's *Ziyi*, and can easily be viewed as a revisionist response to it, the *Seikyô yôroku* earned Sokô exile from

Edo for nearly a decade, following its publication in 1665. The Tokugawa bakufu viewed the *Seikyô yôroku* as intolerable not so much due to its doctrines as its hyperbolic, anti-Song rhetoric. Despite Sokô's intemperate polemic, his views are not radically different from those of some Chinese and Korean Neo-Confucians who, despite their disagreements with Zhu Xi and other Song thinkers, have been characterised nevertheless as Neo-Confucians.

Sokô was also a prolific author of texts related to samurai interests. Perhaps his most famous work was the *Bukyô shôgaku* 武教小學 (*Elementary Learning for Samurai*). Sokô's martial teachings enjoyed considerable popularity among samurai and *rônin* in Edo prior to his exile in 1666 to Akô, a tozama domain. While he was allowed to lecture in Edo following his pardon in 1675, Sokô never attracted the kind of following that he had enjoyed as a younger scholar. While his school remained in Edo for another generation, it eventually disappeared from the shogun's capital in favour of distant tozama domains where Sokô's status as an intellectual offender against the bakufu was not considered especially damning. One of these domains, Chôshû, produced the most remarkable successor to Sokô in the promotion of the Yamaga teachings in Tokugawa Japan, **Yoshida Shôin**. Due to Shôin's instruction of Chôshû samurai who later became leaders of the Meiji regime, Sokô's ideas eventually enjoyed far more respect and even reverence in Meiji times than in the Tokugawa. In large part, Sokô's Meiji popularity resulted from the extremely positive appraisals offered by Inoue Tetsujirô.

Inoue's views were highly nationalistic and imperialistic, even though they crystallized decades before the very worst developments along these lines. Inoue admired Sokô in part because Sokô had authored the *Chûchô jijitsu* 中朝事實 (*True Reality of the Central Empire*), a work of mytho-history arguing that Japan, not China, was the true 'Central Empire' because it most fully embodied the values of loyalty and fidelity. Sokô emphasised that Chinese dynastic lines had been repeatedly overthrown, while in Japan the imperial line remained unbroken. The *Chûchô jijitsu* was not a particularly influential work in Tokugawa Japan; however, in the late Meiji period, as Japan defeated China and then Russia (1904–1905), it seemed prophetic. Inoue lauded it as one of the most significant expressions of Japan's *kokutai* 國體 (national polity) ever. With great exaggeration and little more than coincidental evidence, Inoue also praised Sokô as the teacher of the then famous forty-seven *rônin* and as the founder of *bushidô*, a notion that had only attained popularity following publication of Nitobe Inazô's work by the same title. While Nitobe suggested that '*bushidô*' or Japan's ethic of chivalry, was an unwritten code, Inoue insisted that there was a distinctively Japanese literary tradition behind *bushidô*, and that in many respects it began with Sokô, the so-called constitutional theorist of *bushidô*. Postwar scholarship on Sokô rarely repeats these claims because they lack significant corroboration, and seem more an inversion of Sokô's own samurai teachings, meant to provide a responsible role for samurai as civil leaders of the nation rather than promote a willingness to die for a national–imperial cause.

References: Hirose, 1940–2; Hori, 1959; Inoue, 1902; Tahara & Morimoto, 1970.

JOHN A. TUCKER

Yamazaki Ansai 山崎闇齋
1618–1682
(*azana*: Keigi 敬義)
and the Kimon School 崎門學派

The school of learning founded by Yamazaki Ansai is important not only for its wide influence in the Edo period – it was reported even in the latter half of the seventeenth century to have some six thousand disciples – but also because it was drawn

upon as a major source of Japan's national ideology or theory of *kokutai* 國體 (national polity) in the modern period. In terms of philosophical meaning, the Japanese reading marks (*kunten* 訓點) that Ansai provided for the Four Books and Zhu Xi's commentaries totally followed Zhu Xi, rejecting later glosses and commentaries as 'muddled and obstructed in the highest degree'. Ansai's faithfulness to Zhu Xi was proverbial, to the point that he laid a particular claim to the title of **dao xue** 道學 (Jn. *Dôgaku*) that the Cheng–Zhu School was identified with in China, as well as to its concept of **dao tong** 道統 (Jn. *dôtô*), or 'the orthodox transmission of the Way'. That is, Ansai viewed himself as the true inheritor in Japan of the 'orthodox transmission' of Confucian Learning, and his school developed a clear consciousness of itself as distinguished from all other schools of Confucianism – even other schools of Zhu Xi learning – and as specially charged with the mission of defending the orthodox transmission from heterodox ideas. This consciousness of separateness was reproduced in the eyes of other scholars as well, often combining with a rather negative view of the Kimon school as excessively narrow, exclusive, imitative and serious in their single-minded dedication to the study *and practice* of the Confucian Way. Indeed, Ansai put great emphasis on 'realising for oneself' (*tainin jitoku* 體認自得) the 'method of mind' (*shinpô* 心法) that had been passed down from the ancient sages through the Cheng–Zhu School, which required training the mind through quiet-sitting (*seiza* 靜坐) in order to eliminate desires and learn to rest in the unmoving, deepest level of the mind. Thus he was against broad learning for its own sake, which would distract the student from the core task of awakening the mind. His method of practice, however, was not exclusively focused on the mind, but on the unification of mind and body in religious worship, ritual practice, and attention to every movement of the body in daily life. This is what is called 'reverence to straighten the inner life (敬以直內)', a level of practice that for Ansai included both mind and body. The outer side of practice, however, what is called 'rightness to square the external world (義以方外)', was also very important. Thus it was essential to understand correctly what rightness in various different situations is, an understanding that can be cultivated through the study of history. Ansai planned to write a national history, but he reportedly burned his manuscript when he heard that **Hayashi Razan** was engaged in the same task.

His disciple Asami Keisai 淺見絅齋 (1652–1711), however, inherited Ansai's strong concern for understanding 'the supreme righteousness in accord with name and status (*taigi meibun* 大義名分)' in history. Keisai's most famous work was *Seiken igen* 靖獻遺言 (Immortal Words of Acquiescent Self-dedication), a compilation of the writings and records of famous loyal ministers in China who were not favoured by their times, such as Qu Yuan 屈原, Tao Yuanming 陶源明, and **Wen Tianxiang**, with references to the deeds of other loyal ministers in Chinese and Japanese history. Keisai also shared Ansai's reverence for the unbroken Japanese imperial line as the ultimate embodiment of unchanging ethical principle (*ri* 理) and the ultimate object of loyalty, and like Ansai he argued that, for the Japanese, Japan and not China should be regarded as the centre of the world. Thus he has generally been regarded as the chief inheritor of Ansai's 'orthodox line' (*seitô* 正統) of teaching, even though he was actually excommunicated (*hamon* 破門) by Ansai in his later years because of disagreements regarding Ansai's attempts to synthesise Confucianism and Shinto. Also excommunicated around the same time was Ansai's other favourite disciple and Keisai's chief opponent in the debate over the meaning of samurai loyalty, Satô Naokata 佐藤直方 (1650–1719). It is this debate about loyalty that first compelled Kimon thinkers, and

then thinkers in other schools, to investigate the full implications of Zhu Xi's teachings regarding loyalty and legitimacy in the Japanese institutional context, wherein political legitimacy was peculiarly divided between the imperial court and a shogunate or military government.

A crucial dimension of this debate is the debate whether the words *chûgoku* 中國 and *chûka* 中華, which in Confucian texts signify not only the state we know as 'China' but also a superior culture and civilisation that constitutes the centre of a world order, should be used in Japan to refer to China or Japan. The concept of *chûka* was inseparable from its opposite concept, *iteki* 夷狄 (Ch. *yidi*), or 'barbarian lands,' which, if the Sinocentric concept of world order were taken seriously, is a category that would include Japan. In discussing the loyalty of the samurai in Confucian terms, an insistence on the universal validity of the Sinocentric world order would, if pushed to its logical extreme, lead to the idea that the samurai owed their ultimate loyalty to the Chinese emperor, which of course was absurd and offensive. But an insistence on the peculiarity or difference of Japan would tend to undermine the concept of the universality and absolute binding power of Confucian moral norms, which Confucian teachers were determined to establish. This dilemma became unusually intense within the Kimon School, because of its particular insistence on the concept that 'there is only one truth.' Thus the situation of Ansai excommunicating his most gifted disciples is actually reproduced again and again in the history of the school in an unusual tendency for teachers to break off relations with one another because of disagreements perceived to be irreconcilable. In spite of his great reverence for Ansai, Naokata wrote that, 'Within the universe, there is only one principle. Therefore there is no place for the existence of two Ways. If Confucianism is correct, then Shinto is heterodox. If Shinto is correct, then Confucianism is heterodox (*ja* 邪) . . . How could there be a principle by which one could follow both of them? I do not comprehend the meaning of the mixed faith of our master.' He also thought that his teacher had gone too far in declaring that a person who does not follow the 'Way of Japan' based on the 'Age of the Gods' book of the **Nihon shoki** is a 'son of a foreigner' who cannot be said to be the son of his own father and mother. Concordant with these views was his view that the Japanese emperors were ordinary human beings, so they should be subject to the same judgement as a human ruler: if their rule was extremely lacking in virtue, it should be possible to overthrow them. The much-touted continuity of the imperial line, to Naokata, did not reflect its divine origin and sacred nature, but was only a matter of custom. For Keisai, on the other hand, 'To be partial toward a foreign country is a great heresy. Even now, if Confucius and Zhu Xi should attack Japan on the orders of an alien government, we should be the first to march forward and blow off their heads with our cannons . . . This precisely is what is called the great rightness (*taigi* 大義) between lord and vassal . . . Worldly Confucianists read [Confucian] books and in their hearts become aliens . . . People imitate the people of alien countries because they do not know the true Way.' This may seem like an extreme position, but in the context of the various positions taken by Ansai's followers, he was actually trying to work out a middle position between Confucian universalism and Shintoist particularism. In ancient China, he said, 'the way of ancestral spirits, men, and gods was also made correct and clear, so that it did not degenerate into the strange and heterodox, but the Shinto of Japan degenerated into the mystical and mysterious, becoming a shallow and base form of learning.'

Keisai's scenario of a hypothetical invasion from China is a beefed-up version of a famous statement of Ansai that if Confucius and Mencius came and attacked Japan, it is the Way of Confucius and Mencius to take them prisoner. This episode had such appeal as an expression of the independence of the Japanese people in refusing to blindly follow a foreign ideology that it was put into modern Japanese school textbooks. Indeed, in the panegyrics about Ansai in modern Japan, this stance regarding the autonomy (*shutaisei* 主體性) of Japan *vis-à-vis* China was always featured prominently as a major reason for his greatness as a teacher. His school is still commonly described as the first school to really accomplish the 'Japanisation' of Confucianism, and Japanese nationalists (including the promoters of the controversial new history textbooks) still argue in the same vein that the Japanese should take *Japan* and her history, not China or the West, as their basic standard of thought and action. Tani Shinzan 谷秦山 (1663–1718), a follower of Ansai's Suika Shinto 垂加神道 teachings, wrote that 'Those in the service of Edo should take the shogun as fundamental. Those in the service of a domain (*kuni* 國) should take the lord of that domain as fundamental. The people of Japan should take Amaterasu Ômikami 天照大神 as fundamental. The people of China should take Confucius as fundamental. This is the highest point of reasonableness (*dôri* 道理). You are also a Japanese. In spite of that, to advocate discarding Amaterasu and taking Confucius as fundamental – is this not the most grievous error?' The teacher he is attacking here was Miyake Shôsai 三宅尚齋 (1662–1741), the third of the so-called 'three outstanding teachers of the Kimon School (*Kimon sanketsu* 崎門三傑)', whose position was quite close to Naokata's. Yet Shinzan had similar criticisms of Keisai, to whom he wrote: 'First you speak of the Way of Heaven and Earth, and then you speak of the correct lineage (*seitô*) of Heaven and Earth. In always speaking from the position of 'heaven and earth', you are not revering Japan, but are captivated by China. Indeed, since you so adulate the Chinese, before long you ought to be able to get a salary increase from China!' The word 'correct lineage', as seen above, was similar in meaning to the concept of the orthodox transmission of the Way (*dôtô*). However, Shinzan continued, 'The correct lineage of heaven and earth is the same as the correct lineage of ruler and subject (*kunshin* 君臣), and the correct lineage of ruler and subject is the same as the correct lineage of heaven and earth. In this country, if the correct lineage of ruler and subject is correct, the correct lineage of heaven and earth is correct. In the western land [China], because the correct lineage of ruler and subject is not established, even though heaven and earth exist, their correct lineage is not established. Truly, Confucius and Zhu Xi did not lie. This is already made clear in Master Yamazaki's *Kôyûsô* 拘幽操.'

Here the concept of 'orthodoxy' as correct doctrine is conflated with the concept of 'legitimacy' as the correct lineage of rulers, which in Japan was identified with the 'eternally unbroken' imperial line. Since Confucianism is a system of learning the fundamental purpose of which is to bring about a stable social order and good government, there is a natural connection between the realm of doctrine and the concept of political legitimacy. However, because of the historical pattern of regular dynastic change in China, it was impossible for the ideas of 'correct doctrine' and 'moral truth' (**Dao** 道) ever to be identified with one particular blood-line of rulers. This identification developed naturally, however, in the realm of Shinto political concepts because, in the ancient mytho-history surrounding the founding of the imperial line, the myths regarding the beginning of heaven and earth are directly tied to the myths concerning the birth of the 'Middle Country of the Reed Plains (*ashihara no nakatsu kuni* 葦原中國)' and its rulers, so that the gods of Heaven, the imperial ancestress Amaterasu, and the successive generations of emperors (*tennô* 天皇) are all connected together in one lineage. This was the meaning of Ansai's teaching, emphasised by the Suika Shinto

wing of his school, that 'Heaven and man are only one' (*tenjin yuiitsu* 天人唯一). As Maruyama Masao wrote (1980), 'All forms of Japanism that based themselves on these myths had no choice but to universalise the imperial ancestral gods themselves into world gods and either see Japan as the 'parent country of all countries', or else cut Japan off from the world and confine it in a closed uniqueness that had no connection to the logic of universality vs. particularity' (p. 47). The work of Ansai referred to above, *Kôyûsô* (Fidelity in Imprisonment), was one of the basic texts of his school, because it provided an archetypal description of what Ansai and Keisai regarded as the highest form of loyalty, i.e., loyalty that is not conditional on the 'virtue' of one's ruler or lord (*kun* 君). The work was a commentary on **Han Yu**'s essay of the same name (Ch. *Juyoucao*), which extols King Wen's unswerving loyalty to King Zhou 紂, the evil last ruler of the Shang dynasty, even while Wen was unjustly imprisoned by his lord. The idea of obedience as the Way of the vassal was already put forward in Zhu Xi's interpretation of the *Juyoucao*, and it was exalted by Ansai as 'the principle that the vassal or son does not speak of his lord's or father's wrongs'. In a lecture Keisai gave on this work, he finds the essence of the perfect sincerity and loyalty of King Wen in 'the heart of deep attachment and fellow feeling (*kenken sokudatsu* 繾綣惻怛) that he calls 'not having a trace of the mind of resentment (*urami* 怨み) towards one's lord'. When the modern concept of the Japanese *kokutai* was laid down in the Meiji Constitution (1889) and the Imperial Rescript on Education (1890), the two bases of legitimacy that had already been synthesised in the Kimon teachings, 'blood' and 'sagely virtue', were officially unified. From then on, the concept of deep and unconditional loyalty that had been taught to the samurai by Ansai and Keisai was made the basic ethical teaching for all Japanese. It should not be thought, however, that the Naokata-Shôsai branch of the school died out. Actually, it was the first school of Confucianism to recover its footing after the Meiji Restoration, and a book called *The Complete Works of Satô Naokata* – with the offensive passages regarding the imperial line expunged – was published even in 1941.

Source: Maruyama Masao (trans. Barry D. Steben), 'Legitimacy and Orthodoxy in the Kimon School,' translation of 'Ansaigaku to Ansai gakuha' (*Nihon shisô taikei*, vol. 37, 1980), in *Sino-Japanese Studies*, vol. 8, no. 2 (March 1996), pp. 6–49 and vol. 9, no. 1 (October 1996), pp. 4–33. See also Ooms: 194–286; and Bitô, 1961: 40–134.

BARRY D. STEBEN

Yan Fu 嚴復
1854–1921

Native of Houguan 侯官 prefecture in Fujian, Yan Fu was a leading late Qing intellectual. He was a prolific translator and an authority on western political thought. His rendition of writings by Charles Darwin, Herbert Spencer, Adam Smith, John Stuart Mill and C.L. Montesquieu shaped generations of Chinese intellectuals in their quest for modernising their country.

Born to a respectable scholar–gentry family, Yan spent his early life preparing for the civil service examinations. He took lessons in Confucian Classics and learnt to master the elegant *guwen* 古文 prose. With the death of his father in 1866, he gave up his examination candidate's career and gained his admission to the navel school of the Fuzhou shipyard. At the Fuzhou shipyard (which was established as part of the Tongzhi Restoration), he learnt English and western naval technology. Graduating with high honours in 1871, he was sent to England to study. His two-year stay in London (1877–1879) opened his eyes to the wealth and power of Victorian England, and led him to conclude that the Chinese had to take immediate action to catch up with the West. Having returned to China, he worked under Li Hongzhang (1823–1901) and became the superintendent of the Beiyang Naval Academy in Tianjin. Although being respected as an expert in 'new learning', he was frustrated by the limited scope of the Self-Strengthening Movement.

China's defeat in the Sino-Japanese War (1894–1895) was a turning point in Yan's life. Like many Chinese who were shocked by the country's humiliating defeat in the war, Yan sought for a solution by introducing western learning to China. In his first major translation, the *Tianyan lun* 天演論 (*On Evolution*, 1898), he summarised Thomas Huxley's *Evolution and Ethics* and explained Herbert Spencer's critique of Huxley. Written in elegant *guwen* prose and frequently citing passages from such classical texts as the *Book of Changes* (*Yi jing*) and the *Laozi*, he introduced to his audience the Social Darwinist idea of natural selection. Through rendering the unfamiliar in terms of the familiar, he publicised the concept of 'the survival of the fittest'. By warning his readers that China was behind in the current stage of natural selection, he drove home the point that immediate actions had to be taken to save the country.

While Yan explained the natural law of evolution in the *Tianyan lun*, he clarified the goal of China's reform in the *Yuan fu* 原富 (*On Wealth*, 1900). A translation of Adam Smith's *The Wealth of Nations*, he used Victorian England as an example to demonstrate how economic liberalism had contributed to the wealth and power of the state. In the translation, his emphasis was less on Adam's economic liberalism than on how the state should strive for wealth and power. For Yan, the current stage of natural competition was dictated by the fierce competition among nation–states. To survive in this competition for wealth and power, China had to adopt western systems and values.

After a few interruptions during the Boxer Rebellion in 1900, Yan continued his translation of western works. In two works he published in the 1900s – the *Qunji quanjie lun* 群己權界論 (*On the Boundaries of* the *Rights of Society and of the Individual*, 1903) and the *Fa yi* 法意 (*Spirit of the Laws*, 1909) – he introduced his readers to western liberal thoughts. In *Qunji guanjie lun*, he rendered John Stuart Mill's *On Liberty* into a treatise on how to release the energy of the individual to better the interest of the state. He argued that western democratic institutions (including legal code, freedom of assembly and freedom of speech) were effective measures to make the state rich and powerful. Similarly, in the *Fa yi*, he presented Montesquieu's *Spirit of the Laws* as a discussion of the power of the legislators in reforming a society. By contrasting a 'government of law' (*fa zhi*) with a 'government of good men' (*ren zhi*), he introduced the concept of the rule of law that was lacking in the Confucian tradition. Yet, like liberal institutions, Yan never considered the rule of law as an end in itself, but a means for China's search for wealth and power.

Yan was disappointed with the 1911 Revolution. The political and social chaos after the revolution showed him that radical political measures were not necessarily effective in bringing about change. Partly to express his disillusionment with the Republic, he supported Yuan Shikai's revival of the monarchical system in 1915. In his last few years, he was a leading opponent of the New Culture movement.

References: Li Zehou, 1979; Schwartz, 1964.

TZE-KI HON

Yan miao 顏廟
(Temple of Yan (Hui))

Devoted to the cult veneration of Confucius' principal disciple Yan Hui 顏回 (see **Fu sheng**), this temple was also called the 'Temple of the Returning Sage' (*Fu sheng miao* 復聖廟), based on his posthumous title conferred in 1333. Another name of this temple is 'Temple of Humble Alley' (*Louxiang miao* 陋巷廟) – literally the

Temple of a 'narrow alley' – which alludes to Confucius' praise of Yan Hui's perseverance in the face of his family's poverty: 'Venerable, indeed, is Hui! A single bowlful to eat, a ladle-full to drink, living in a poor alley. Others could not endure his hardships, yet Hui's joy does not falter. Venerable, indeed, is Hui!' (*Analects* 6.11).

Yan Hui was correlate (*pei* 配) in sacrifices devoted primarily to Confucius the First Sage at least since 241 CE. Although Yan Hui's status would always be tied to the First Sage, a separate cult – or a cult devoted specifically to the veneration of Yan Hui – did emerge some time during the imperial era. A local Yan Hui cult, either within or distinguishable from the cult of Confucius, probably developed before the construction of a temple devoted to him, particularly among his biological descendants, but there is no evidence to substantiate such claims.

Han sources mention a Yan Temple and Yang Guangxun's (*jinshi* degree in 1586) *Humble Alley Gazetteer* (*Louxiang zhi* 6), completed in 1601, refers to one built in 739. Like the formation of a Yan Hui cult, the early construction of temples is not unlikely, but there is little physical or corroborating evidence to substantiate such claims. The present temple can be traced back to the twelfth century when the Jin 金 controlled north China. A stele dated 1190 (Jin Mingchang 1) refers to the rebuilding of a temple for the 'Duke of Yan 兗, the Second Sage', which is the posthumous title he held from 720 to 1333. Yan Hui was renamed the 'Returning Sage' by the Yuan court when a stele commemorating the event was placed outside the present-day Yan temple. Some evidence suggests that before the Yuan, the Yan Temple was located near the Northeast corner of the wall of the ancient town of Queli 闕里 and that it was moved to its present location on the Humble Alley some time in the Yuan. The senior lineage heir typically assumed responsibility for managing the temple sacrifices.

The structures that constitute the present temple complex and its overall layout are very similar to those of the Temple of Confucius (see **Kong miao**). The main hall houses the spirit image of the recipient of the temple sacrifice, which is flanked by two corridors and faced by a wall with three entries into the complex. There is also a fasting quarters and a storage room for sacrificial vessels and other items. The names of the gates and buildings, however, identify this as a distinctively Yan Hui space. Most of the names allude to passages in the *Analects* that give definition to Yan Hui and his relationship with Confucius. The temple, located northeast of the Kong's Mansion (**Kong fu** 孔府) is situated on the North side of Humble Alley. In references to Confucius' response to Yan Hui's query on the meaning of humaneness (**ren**): 'To return to ritual by mastering the self is humaneness' (*keji fuli*, 克己復禮為仁) (12.1), the main gate is called *Fusheng men* 復聖門 (the 'Returning Sage Gate') and the main hall, *Fusheng dian* 復聖殿 (the 'Returning Sage Hall'). The middle gate inside the temple complex is called Guiren men 歸仁門 (the 'Abiding in Humaneness Gate'); the secondary gate to the East is called *Keji men* 克己門 (the 'Mastering the Self Gate') and the other to west is called Fuli men 復禮門 (the 'Returning to Ritual Gate'). Two other side gates are called *Bowen* 博文 ('Broadening Culture') and *Yueli* 約禮 ('Essentialising Rites'), in references to *Analects* 9.11 in which Yan Hui sighs that whenever he catches a glimpse (*yang zhi* 仰之) of the Master's way it recedes farther away. Yet, he continues, 'The Master is good at leading me at each step. He broadens me with culture and brings me back to the essentials by means of rites'. The last gate that leads into the grounds in front of the main hall is called *Yangsheng men* 仰聖門 (the 'Glimpsing the Sage Gate').

The liturgy of sacrifices to Yan Hui followed those offered to Confucius. Beginning as early as 1317, Yan Hui too had his correlates in sacrifice. His son Xin 歆, thirty-fourth-generation descendant **Yan Zhitui**, the notable author of the *Yan Family Regulations* (**Yanshi jiaxun**), fortieth-generation descendants Zhenqing 真卿 (709–785) and Gaoqing 杲卿 (692–756), both prominent Tang ministers in the eighth century, received sacrifices in the Eastern corridor. Three persons received sacrifices in the western corridor: Yan Hui's grandson Jian 儉; thirty-third-generation descendant Jianyuan 見遠; and thirty-seventh-generation descendant **Yan Shigu**, who wrote the standard critical notes on the *Han shu*.

Thomas A. Wilson

Yan Ruoju 閻若璩
1636–1704
(*zi* Baishi 百詩, *hao* Qianqiu 潛邱)

Born in Huian 淮安 (Jiangsu 江蘇), Yan was a classicist, mathematician and geographer. He worked as personal literary adviser to Xu Qianxue 徐乾學 (1631–1694) and assisted in Xu's compilation of *Daqing yitong zhi* 大清一統志, a major topographical project commissioned by Emperor Kangxi (r. 1662–1722).

Yan's major contribution to classical studies is his proving that the twenty-five chapters of the Old Text version of ***Shang shu*** presented by Mei Ze 梅賾 (317–322) were spurious. Although a few scholars in the Song, Yuan and Ming times had suspected the spurious nature of this text, Yan was the first to thoroughly examine the subject. In the work of *Shang shu guwen shu zheng* 尚書古文疏證 (*Inquiry into the Authenticity of the Old Text Shang Shu*) he cited 128 specific instances and made an intensive textual analysis of the work. This work is also a remarkable example of Han Learning (*Han xue* 漢學) which brought broad historical knowledge, highly refined philological skills and extraordinary textual observations in the analysis of a single work. Yan's attack on the Old Text version of the *Shang shu* promoted a sceptical attitude towards the

Classics among the Qing scholars and gradually brought along a reviving interest in the *Jinwen jingxue* of the Late Han.

Yan also disproved the attribution of the *Daxue* to Zeng Shen 曾參 (505 BCE?–435 BCE?) who was traditionally considered to have been the author of the important treatise. Yan compiled two works on place names in the *Si shu* (Four Books) entitled *Sishu Shidi* 四書釋地 and *Shidi Yulun* 釋地 餘論 which had enduring value both to geographical and classical scholarship. His other works included *Mengzi Shengzu nianyue kao* 孟子生卒年月考 (*An Investigation of the Dates of Mengzi's Birth and Death*), and the *Rizhilu buzheng* 日知錄補正 in which he collected a list of over twenty errors in the well-known work *Rizhi lu* written by **Gu Yanwu**.

References: Hummel, 1943–4; Liang, Qichao, 1959; Loewe, 1993; *Qing shi gao*, 1970.

REBEKAH X. ZHAO

Yan Shigu 顏師古
581–645

Yan Shigu, a member of a family that claimed descent from Yan Hui 顏回 (see **Fusheng**), Confucius' favourite disciple, and that produced outstanding scholars over the medieval period, and the grandson of **Yan Zhitui**, was one of the most important and productive commentators and ritual specialists of the early Tang. He worked in the scholarly agencies and never attained high political office. His fame rests chiefly on his textual work, his commentaries and critical editions of the Confucian Classics. In 631, the emperor commissioned him to determine the authentic texts of the Confucian Classics, the **Zhou yi**, **Shang shu**, **Mao shi**, **Li ji** and **Chunqiu**. He also compiled a list of standard form characters, the *Yanshi ziyang* 顏氏字樣, which circulated widely. Yan's commentary to the **Han shu**, presented to the throne in 641, occupies a place in commentarial scholarship parallel to that of **Kong Yingda**'s subcommentary series to the Five Classics. Like them, it drew together and reviewed earlier commentaries; like them it exemplified the 'moderate scepticism' that was current in official circles in the early seventh century. Yan worked on the *Sui shu* 隋書, the politically sensitive history of the Sui dynasty (581–618). He was also a member of the commission for the first Tang state ritual code and drafted directives for a planned performance of the **Feng shan** 封禪 rites on mount Tai 泰 (see **Tai shan**).

Reference: McMullen, 1988.

DAVID McMULLEN

Yan Yan 言偃
506–? BCE
(*zi* Ziyou 子游)

A native of Changshu 常熟 (forty kilometres north of Suzhou, Jiangsu), Yan Yan was a prominent disciple of Confucius known for his studies of ancient ritual canons. He received sacrifices in the temple as one of the **Ten Savants** in 712, was ennobled as Marquis of Wu 子游吳侯 in 739, promoted to Duke in 1009, given the title of Duke of Danyang 丹陽公 in 1113, and called Master Yan Yan 言子偃 in 1530, when everyone enshrined in the temple was stripped of their noble titles. A shrine 吳公祠 was built for him in Jiangsu in the late twelfth century and another shrine was built in Yanzhou.

THOMAS A. WILSON

Yan Yuan 顏元
1635–1704
(*zi* Yizhi 易直, *hao* Xizhai 習齋)

Yan Yuan, a native of Boye 博野 (Hebei), began as a believer of Cheng–Zhu Learning. He has been hailed as the founder of the Yan–Li School 顏李學派, a school of

Confucianism that stresses practice over bookish learning and vacuous theorising about human nature. Yan championed practical learning that was useful to society. He was inimical to learning with no manifest application to practice. Consequently, modern scholars compare his teachings to those of the American pragmatists. He taught his students various types of learning that were generally classified as statecraft learning. In his 'Treatise on Preserving Government' (*Cunzhi bian* 存治編), which he wrote in his twenties, Yan advocated the restoration of the 'Well-field' (*jing tian*, 井田) and 'feudal' (*feng jian*, 封建) systems of the high antiquity.

Yan first was a faithful follower of Cheng–Zhu learning. However, his adherence to the mourning rites prescribed by the *Family Rites of Master Zhu* (*Zhuzi jiali* 朱子家禮) almost cost him his life. This traumatic experience precipitated a totalistic rejection of the teachings by Song and Ming ***dao xue*** Confucians. He came to the conclusion that their teachings and in fact all the teachings of Song and Ming *daoxue* thinkers were heterodox, having been corrupted by Buddhism and Daoism. While many contemporary exponents of Cheng–Zhu learning condemned the teachings of **Wang Shouren** and his followers as Buddhist in essence, Yan reminded them that the Cheng brothers, **Zhu Xi** and all the Song *dao xue* Confucians were equally guilty of spreading Buddhist ideas under disguise. All of them infused the Confucian texts with heterodox ideas.

His repudiation of all variety of Song and Ming *dao xue* was grounded in his rejection of the ontological dualism underlying their ethical teachings. The positing of a notion of bifurcated human nature – an essential nature and a physical one – justified the dismissal of the physical nature as a source of evil. He saw in this view the Buddhist notion of *liu zei* 六賊 (six destructive elements). But neither Confucius nor **Mengzi** talked about human nature in this manner, Yan argued.

Like many Confucians in the early Qing, Yan endorsed a *qi* concept of human nature. His view of human nature was clearly advanced in his treatise entitled 'Treatise on Preserving Human Nature' (*Cun xing bian* 存性編). The natural endowment of human beings was not inherently evil. It was practice in the form of bad habits that constituted human evils. Accordingly, Yan's ethical theory underscored the importance of developing good habits, and particularly through practising the correct rites. Morality could only be cultivated in practice. Similarly, immorality was practice resulting from bad habit. Yan therefore proposed a programme of moral cultivation foregrounding the need to eradicate bad habits.

Yan considered practice, especially of rites, the fundamental doctrine of the Duke of Zhou (**Zhou Gong**) and Confucius, and repudiated the *dao xue* approach to moral education, which dwelt upon the need to understand principles (*mingli* 明理). What Confucius taught, Yan argued, was 'practice' (*xi* 習). This stress on practice was underscored in his major teachings.

Yan was distrustful of the Four Books (***Si shu***) as the core canon of Confucian teachings and had written comments on what he thought to be mistakes in the *Rectifying the Mistakes of the Four Books* (*Si shu zhengwu* 四書正誤). He was critical of the Song *dao xue* scholars who treated 'quiet-sitting' (***jing zuo***) as a method of moral cultivation. In his 'Treatise on Preserving Learning' (*Cunxue bian* 存學編), he spelled out his interpretation of Confucianism, which he grounded in the *Rites of the Zhou* (**Zhou li**). What captured the core teachings of ancient sages was the Duke of Zhou's method of teaching 'three things of the village' (*xiang sanwu* 鄉三物). They were 'six virtues' (*liude* 六德) and 'six practices' (*liuxing* 六行): humaneness (***ren***), sageliness (***sheng***, see **Sheng ren**), righteousness (***yi***), loyalty/honesty (***zhong***), harmony (***he***), and 'six treasuries of nature' (*liufu* 六府): water, fire, metal, wood, earth, grains. All these should be the objects of study and the concerns of a Confucian. They simply articulate the centrality Yan placed on material and practical aspects of human conditions as opposed to teachings about quiet-sitting and abstract theorising about human nature.

With this stress on practice, Yan offered his unique reading of the phrase **gewu zhizhi**. Knowledge (*zhi*) was object-based. *Wu* 物 (*things*) referred to the 'three things of the village'. '*Ge*' means 'to fight' a tiger, stressing the use of the body in the process of fighting. By such rendering, *gewu* was deprived of its *dao xue* connotation of investigating abstract principles (*li*), instead, it underscored the practice of the 'Three things' as the meaning of *gewu* and the knowledge gained through practice was the process of *zhizhi* (extension of knowledge). Yan's teachings were introduced to scholars in the Lower Yangtze region through his disciple **Li Gong**.

References: Chow, 1994; Liang Qichao, 1957: 104–32; de Bary, 1975.

KAI-WING CHOW

Yan Zhitui 顏之推
531–591?
(*zi* Jie 介)

Yan Zhitui was born into one of the scholarly families of northen (Shandong) origin which had fled south in the early fourth century CE to take up residence under the Eastern Jin and subsequent southern regimes; his own life spanned the stable early years of the Liang Wudi (r. 502–549), through the violent upheavals of the mid-century to the climactic warfare that finally saw the reunification of China in 589; these vicissitudes he survived only by a reputation for scholarship and a fair amount of luck, to produce in his old age works which illuminate much of the language, life and thought of the times.

His troubles began with the rebellion of Hou Jing 候景 in the southern capital in 549, in which he was captured and almost killed, though after the defeat of the rebellion in 552 he was able to serve Emperor Yuan (r. 552–554) until 554 in the new imperial library at Jiangling 江陵, which was in that year largely destroyed by Western Wei (535–551) invaders, who again took him as a captive to their northwestern capital of Changan 長安, whence he escaped in 556 to the northeastern state of the Northern Qi (550–577). Under this unpromising non-Chinese regime he achieved a respite from disaster for two decades, rising to direct the Wenlin guan 文林館 or Literary Academy from 572–574 in their capital at Ye, before the Northern Zhou (557–581), successor state to the Western Wei, invaded and took him as a captive once again to Changan. To the Northern Qi period of his life would appear to belong what is now known as the *Yuanhun zhi* 怨魂志 (*Treatise on Vengeful Ghosts*) and also the compilation during his directorate of the *Xiuwendian yulan* 修文殿御覽 (*Imperial Encyclopedia from the Hall of Literature*) which can be shown to have played an important part in the evolution of Chinese works of reference. Although he was eventually given low government office by the Northern Zhou in 580, this dynasty was in its turn replaced by the Sui in 581, and this dynasty finally gave him the security and support for his scholarship allowing him to involve himself in projects such as the creation of the *Qieyun* 切韻 (Dictionary of Rhymes) and the writing of his **Yanshi jiaxun**. His exact date of death is unknown; he seems to have lived under the Sui for about a decade.

Amongst these writings, the *Yuanhun zhi* survives in a form which relies primarily on the reconstitution of quotations reassembled in the Ming; it has been translated in full by Cohen (1982). Campany (1996) points out that thematically the work falls within a genre, usually also covering the Grateful Dead, which relied on the conception of interaction between Heaven and humanity, rather than Buddhist ideas of karma. Such genre considerations may explain why Yan, a self-declared Buddhist, omits Buddhist themes here, though they occur in the *Yanshi jiaxun*. Campany also considers briefly the very much smaller quantity of material surviving from Yan's *Jiling ji* (Collected Records of Marvels), once apparently a substantial compilation. The massive *Xiuwendian yulan*, now lost except for quotations and adaptations of its material into later works, is not listed under Yan's name; it was based on an even larger encyclopedia compiled by **Liang Wudi**, and was particularly influential in Japan.

The *Qieyun*, too, is not listed as a work compiled by Yan individually, but he was again clearly instrumental in prompting a group of scholars to compile it. It is similarly largely lost as such, though its material was absorbed into later works, and the surviving evidence in this case shows us that in a reunited China Yan's careful concern over pronunciation allowed his group to bring together northern and southern variants of the 'mandarin' speech, which the Chinese elite had been at pains to preserve, into one new standard form of spoken Chinese. Its pattern of rhymes became standard for composing poetry in the Tang, though quite soon his speech standard was supplanted by a new received pronunciation influenced by the dialect of the Changan area. Phonology is one concern which emerges also in Yan's best-known work, the *Yanshi jiaxun*, but we know that his later years were also concerned with studies of music and of the calendar.

Yan Zhitui's family were never powerful, but his great-great uncle Yan Yanzhi 顏延之 (384–456) found fame as a defender of Buddhism, while his grandson **Yan Shigu** (581–645) became an illustrious expert on the history of the Han dynasty. Some later scholars liked to look down on Yan Zhitui as a less than pure Confucian on account of his religious beliefs. But without families such as his, dedicated to the preservation of scholarship under the most adverse circumstances, China would have been a far darker place.

References: Campany, 1996; Cohen, Alvin, 1982; Dien, 1962: 43–64 and 1976; Pulleyblank, 1994.

Tim H. Barrett

Yang Jian 楊簡
1141–1226
(*zi* Jingzhong 敬仲, *hao* Cihu 慈湖, *shi* Wenyuan 文元)

Yang Jian was one of the Four Masters from Mingzhou (Ningbo region) (***Mingzhou si xiansheng***) and probably the most important student of the famous **Lu Jiuyuan**. After passing the palace examination in 1169 he got a position near Hangzhou where he met with his teacher. During this first encounter, Lu Jiuyuan expounded his teachings about the 'original mind' (*ben xin* 本心). **Quan Zuwang** defends Yang Jian against his adversaries who later ridiculed him for making *ben xin*' the centre of his own teachings whereas Lu Jiuyuan in their view pointed at the importance of this concept only so as to provide a first entry into his thought.

The critique has to be seen against the background of rivalries between the first generation of students of **Zhu Xi** and Lu Jiuyuan. Yang Jian consequently developed Lu Jiuyuan's ideas and eliminated in his own texts the concepts of *li* (principle) and *qi* (material force) advanced by Zhu Xi. In his commentary to the *Book of Changes* (***Yi jing***), for example, Yang Jian did not use the word *li* at all. **Chen Chun** complained that as a consequence of their 'original mind' teachings Yang Jian and his students rejected the famous '*Zhangju*' commentaries of Zhu Xi and read only the original texts of the classics and the collected explanations of older commentators. This was probably a reaction to the wide dissemination of *Zhangju* which had almost supplanted the classics themselves.

According to the polemics of Chen Chun, Yang Jian did nothing else than meditating and concentrating on the self, thinking that he thereby had found the correct teachings which had not been transmitted for a thousand years. As a matter of fact, Yang Jian stressed the importance of the words 'heart/mind' (*xin*) and 'self' (*ji* 己) even more than his teacher. For example, in a short treatise called '*Jiyi* 己易' he gave the novel explanation that the word *yi* (*change*) in the title of the *Book of Changes* did not mean 'change' but 'self'. For him the heart/mind (*xin*) was the mental basis for all things. Accordingly, he said that it was wrong to think that the Changes represented transformations of Heaven and Earth and not of one's self. The perfect heart/mind, the famous 'heart/mind of the Way' (*dao xin*) found in the *Book of History's* chapter *Counsels of the Great Yu* (*Da Yumo* 大禹謨), was a heart/mind without intentions and without thinking. But it was also a moral heart/mind with the capacity to perceive things. Besides his commentary on the *Yi jing*, Yang Jian also wrote a commentary to the *Mao shi* claiming that the guiding element of all three hundred poems was the 'heart/mind of the Way', a theme which can also be found in many pages of the twenty chapters of his *Surviving Works of Master Cihu* (*Cihu yishu* 慈湖遺書).

Reference: Zheng Xiaojiang, 1996.

HANS VAN ESS

Yang qi 養氣
(Nourishing the vital force)

A minor theme in early Confucianism, mentioned by both **Mengzi** and **Xunzi**, probably in an attempt to appropriate concepts popular elsewhere. As such, the references are noteworthy as the initial reaction of Confucian thinkers to the challenge of the cosmologies which would come to permeate their thought during the Han.

In the *Mengzi*, the reference occurs in the debate with Gongsun Chou 公孫丑 (2A: 2) where Mengzi claims that his special talents include 'nourishing my superabundant

vital force'. He goes on to argue that mere mechanical nourishment of the material force is futile – it is intimately bound up with moral principles and cannot be nurtured in their absence (see **haoran zhi qi**). In the *Xunzi*, the concept appears in chapter 2, 'On Self-Cultivation', as 'controlling the vital breath and nourishing life' or 'controlling the vital breath and nourishing the mind'. Xunzi's prescription to gain these ends is, unsurprisingly, ritual and the guidance of a good teacher.

References: Knoblock, 1988: 145–8, 153–4; Riegel, 1979: 433–58.

GARY ARBUCKLE

Yang Shi 楊時
1053–1135
(*zi* Zhongli 中立, master Guishan 龜山先生)

Yang Shi was known as one of the heroes of the Cheng brothers' school 程門龍象 along with **Xie Liangzuo**. A native of Jiangle 將樂 in Nanjian 南劍 prefecture (present-day Fujian), Yang's primary place in later Confucian intellectual genealogies is as initiator of the southward transplanting of the Chengs' *dao xue*. With the subsequent warfare and Song dynasty loss of north China, the preservation of the Neo-Confucian initiative among those who fled south was crucial to its survival.

Life and activities
As a young man, Yang Shi was unusually talented and showed literary promise. He attained the *jinshi* in 1076 at the age of twenty-four, but did not take office immediately, due to illness. In 1081, he was posted to Xuzhou 徐州 in present-day Jiangsu. On his way to take up the appointment, Yang stayed for several months with Cheng Hao in Yingchang 潁昌 in present-day Henan and joined his group of disciples. When Yang resumed his journey to Xuzhou, Cheng Hao made his famous

prophetic remark, 'Now my Dao is heading south' (*Wudao nan yi* 吾道南矣).

Among the Cheng disciples, Yang developed a particularly close friendship with **You Zuo**, and continued an intimate correspondence with him throughout his life. His letters to You reveal a person of humour and sensitivity, as well as a strong sense of duty and family ties. In 1093, on the way to another post, Yang went to study with Cheng Yi in Luoyang; there is a famous story of him and You Zuo standing in attendance on a dozing Cheng Yi while a foot of snow fell outside.

Like others in the Cheng school, Yang was strongly opposed to **Wang Anshi**'s 'new policies' regime. He later pressed a proposal to strip Wang Anshi of his posthumous official honours and his place in the Confucian temple. During the Southern Song, Yang attracted considerable fame as the Chengs' leading disciple, such that Emperor Gaozong (r. 1127–1162) summoned him to the court as an intellectual adviser when he was already seventy-five years old.

Yang had a large family of five sons and four daughters. In 1123, Yang's second wife, *née* Chen, died. In his funeral memorial for her, Yang praised her as intelligent and discerning, having studied the Classics, histories, and 'hundred schools' of Chinese thought. In this, she was a kindred spirit to Yang himself.

Neo-Confucian contributions

Yang is distinguished in later Confucian tradition as the 'link' in the orthodox transmission lineage between the Cheng brothers and the great **Zhu Xi**. One of Yang's student followers, **Luo Congyan**, became the teacher of **Li Tong**, who in turn became the first Confucian teacher of Zhu Xi. The idea of one orthodox lineage (**dao tong**) bears a family resemblence to the contemporaneous social development of the *zongzi* 宗子, the primary descent line within families.

In his teaching, Yang placed special emphasis on **cheng** (sincerity, authenticity) as the touchstone of personal cultivation. He brought together the cultivation methods of investigation (*gewu* 格物) and introspection (*fanshen* 反身), holding that the most effective way to '*gewu*' was to discover the principles (*ze* 則) of one's own bodily forms and everyday conduct. Proximity to Buddhist introspective methods led to Yang's approach being criticised as Buddhistic. He insisted, though, that the pattern or principle of all under heaven could be grasped through one's own person because, as Cheng Yi said, **liyi fenshu** 理一分數 ('the principle is one; manifestations are many').

Yang developed an independent line of thinking, as shown by his debate with Cheng Yi over the implications of **Zhang Zai**'s 'western Inscription' (**Xi ming**). Though Cheng disagreed, Yang argued that Zhang's expansive statements about considering all people as one's brothers (and sisters) could be misunderstood in the direction of Mozi's 'universal love' (*jian ai* 兼愛), denying the importance of specific family relationships. From a pedagogical point of view, Yang wanted more emphasis on the 'functions' of **ren**.

Yang Shi edited Cheng Yi's *Yichuan Yizhuan* 伊川易傳 and is associated with the *Ercheng Cuiyan* 二程粹言 (see **Ercheng quanshu**). His own writings include commentaries on **Lunyu** and **Zhongyong** as well as the *Guishan ji* 龜山集 and his *yulu* 語錄; his commentaries on Daoist texts are not extant. Between 1115 and 1125, Yang lectured in Eastern Grove temple in Wuxi 無錫 (present-day Jiangsu), later the site of the famous Donglin Academy (see **Donglin xuepai**), the centre of Confucian Learning and political conscience during the late Ming. Though Yang has been known primarily as a link in the *dao tong* transmission, this reputation ought not to obscure his own wrestling with the content of *Dao xue* and his personal realisations.

References: Chan, Wing-tsit, 1963d: 550–1; Chang, 1988: 163–218; Ching, 1976a; Dong, 1995: 244–5; Hervouet, 1978: 221–2, 406;

Huang & Quan, 1966: 939–61; Jameson, 1990; Yang, 1965.

THOMAS SELOVER

Yang Tingyun 楊庭筠
1562–1627
(baptised as Michael probably in 1611)

Yang Tingyun pursued an average official career, his highest position being Vice Governor of the Metropolitan Prefecture (1624). His wide interests fit well into the syncretic ambiance of Late Ming intellectual life. On the one hand, he was a Confucian scholar writing commentaries on the Classics, especially *Yi jing* (all apparently lost even if *Wanyi weiyan zhaiyao* 玩易微言摘鈔 (*Excerpts of Subtle Words Examining the Yi jing*) was described in *Siku quanshu zongmu tiyao*). On the other hand, he most probably participated as a lay-Buddhist in the movement around the monk Zhuhong 袾宏 (1535–1615). After his conversion to Christianity, he rejected his Buddhist past, but searched for a Confucian–Christian synthesis. Yang Tingyun took up the defence of Christianity against Confucian criticism, and explained its doctrine and organisation in *Daiyi pian* 代疑篇 (1621). His *Daiyi xupian* 代疑續篇 (1635, posthumously published) treats the question of Orthodox Transmission. It is not only a defence of Christianity, but also an indirect apology of the Confucian tradition in reference to Christianity. His works treat a wide variety of theological and philosophical subjects (including the question of God, incarnation, heaven and hell, human nature, etc.) of which he acquired a very substantive knowledge. The case of Yang Tingyun shows that it was possible for a highly educated scholar–official to integrate virtually all basic elements of the Christian doctrine into his own world view, without rejecting the Confucian heritage.

References: Standaert, 1988; Yang Zhen'e, 1944.

NICOLAS STANDAERT

Yang Wanli 楊萬里
1127–1206
(*zi* Tingxiu 廷秀, *hao* Chengzhai 誠齋)

Yang Wanli came from Jishui 吉水 in Jiangxi. He successfully passed the palace examination in 1154 and was subsequently appointed to a post in the southwestern part of Jiangxi, only to become an aide in the prefecture of Yong 永 in Hunan afterwards. This was the place near Mount Heng where Zhang Jun 張浚 father of the philosopher **Zhang Shi**, had been banished because of his opposition to Qin Gui 秦檜 (1090–1155, *zi* Huizhi 會之). Zhang Jun's admonition to study with a sincere (*cheng*) intention became the reason for Yang to call his study the 'Studio of Sincerity' (*Cheng zhai* 誠齋), a name which also became his *hao*. When Zhang Jun again rose to power in 1161 he recommended Yang Wanli. Yang in turn was instrumental in recommending **Zhu Xi** and his followers to Emperor Xiaozong (r. 1162–1189) in 1185. On several occasions he opposed his emperors and the regent Han Tuozhou 韓侂冑 (1152–1207).

Yang Wanli wrote a commentary to the *Book of Changes* (**Yi jing**) in twenty chapters under the title of *Chengzhai yi zhuan* 誠齋易傳. There are also several chapters of short philosophical remarks bearing the title *Yong yan* 庸言 (*Constant Words*), an allusion to the canonical *Zhongyong*. The content of these sayings concerns rules for the superior man in his dealings with the world, notes on historical persons and explanations of philosophical and moral terms. In many of the entries opinions of **Yang Shi** are quoted. As a specialist of the *Book of Changes* Yang Wanli was interested in the theory of *yuanqi* and in speculations concerning the Five Agents/Phases/Elements (**Wu xing**). He put forward the theory that the *Book of Changes* was not the product of the sages of antiquity but the direct emanation of Heaven and Earth. Humaneness (*ren*) was, according to him, a capability (*cai*) of every human being, whereas righteousness (*yi*) was a means to teach the people to order their resources.

However, Yang Wanli did not have many followers as a Confucian philosopher. Similarly to the somewhat older Lü Benzhong, who is also to be considered a Confucian, what made him well known throughout the ages was his contribution in the field of poetry. Together with Lu You 陸游 (1125–1210) and Fan Chengda 范成大 (1126–1191) Yang Wanli belongs to the three great poets of the early Southern Song dynasty. Coming from Jiangxi it seems quite normal that he should have been inspired by masters of the Jiangxi School such as **Huang Tingjian**. Yet, like Lu You he burned all his early poems after he experienced a Chan–Buddhist enlightenment in 1178. He compared the process of becoming a real poet to that of a Chan adept who obtains sudden enlightenment only after having studied under several masters whom he eventually transcends. Like Lü Benzhong to whom Yang Wanli can be compared because he too wrote a *Shi hua* 詩話 (*Chengzhai shihua* 誠齋詩話, *Criticism of Poetry from the Studio of Sincerity*), he used the term of *huofa* 活法 (life method) in order to describe his ideas concerning the superiority of genius over literary craft. Although the term *huofa* was used by Confucians it sounds suspiciously like a Chan ideal. Thus, Yang Wanli's poetic experience once again shows how close Confucianism and Chan could sometimes be during the Southern Song.

References: Schmidt, 1976; Nienhauser, 1986.

HANS VAN ESS

Yang Xiong 楊雄
53 BCE–18 CE

Master Yang Xiong, the first Confucian classicist and the greatest of the pre-Song metaphysicians, is best known for two major philosophical works: the *Canon of Supreme Mystery* (*Taixuan jing*) and the *Model Sayings* (*Fa yan*), both of which explore the interaction between significant cosmic and social patterns by explicit reference to earlier canonical traditions.

A student of Yan Junping 嚴君平 (?–?), Yang Xiong travelled from Chengdu (modern Sichuan) to Chang'an (modern Xi'an), then the capital of the Former Han dynasty (206 BCE–8 CE), in his early thirties, in order to seek preferment at the court. As the foremost poet of his age, Yang Xiong was appointed to a position that was in effect poet laureate to the court in 10 BCE. In his middle age, after the death of a beloved son, Yang experienced a sense of profound revulsion for his earlier poetic efforts. Condemning court poetry as inherently frivolous, if not downright immoral, Yang turned to composing works of philosophy. The first was the *Canon of Supreme Mystery*, which like its prototype, the *Book of Changes* (*Yi jing*), correlates the significant patterns of the universe with different combinations of solid and broken lines accompanied by brief texts and ten autocommentaries. However, the *Mystery* adjusts the structure and imagery of the *Changes* to better address Han preoccupations with correlative thinking, fate and time. As the first grand synthesis of Chinese thought to successfully weave together into one organic whole the elements drawn from early Confucian ethics and ritual, the quietist metaphysics associated with classical Daoism, the proto-scientific **yin–yang** and Five Phases (**Wu xing**) correlative theories, historical studies, alchemy and astrology, the *Mystery* came to occupy a place in Chinese intellectual history roughly comparable to that of the *Summa* of Thomas Aquinas in the West. By his synthesis, Yang meant to direct human effort away from a detailed examination of the shifting phenomenal world and refocus attention upon the preservation of ritual norms and cultural patterns. Undoubtedly, the *Mystery*'s most important philosophical contribution is its account of individual human destiny, which Yang believed to result from the interplay of four major factors: time (meaning the predestined 'present opportunities' resulting from the conjunction of various concurrent cosmological cycles), virtue (or 'character'), tools (including civilised institutions and moral training) and position (social rank and physical location). Of these four factors, only virtue is completely subject to human control, so Yang found adherence to the Good as defined by the Confucian ritual 'Way' to be the single most reliable method of improving personal fate. In the course of outlining this theory of fate, the *Mystery* pinpoints the logical fallacies inherent in various philosophical positions that competed with Confucian classicism for general approval during Yang's time.

Following a draft of the *Taixuan jing* before 2 BCE, there came at least four lengthy philosophical poems whose style parodies the prose-poems of Yang's youth. Two of these *fu* 賦 are dedicated to the defence of his provocative masterwork, the *Mystery*. Around 12 CE, Yang finished the *Model Sayings*, which adopts both the format and style of the Confucian *Analects* (**Lunyu**) to provide a relatively straightforward catechism for the would-be sage. The *Fa yan* evaluates the conflicting goals of immortality, fame, power and scholarship to disentangle prevailing notions that confused conventional notions of the 'good life' with ideas of the Good. As its main theme is the need to immerse oneself in the model of the former sages, the *Model Sayings*, like the *Analects*, devotes considerable attention to the reassessment of historical figures whose conduct or writings were considered worthy of emulation. Like its companion work, the *Mystery*, the *Model Sayings* also at every turn argues the practical benefits of humane interventionist government, while continually countering what Yang considers to be oppressive ideologies (a group that for Yang includes the immensely popular theories associated with the immortality cults, with historical determinism, and with harsh punishments).

When Yang died in 18 CE, he left unfinished a third remarkable work on significant pattern, the *Fang yan* 方言 (*Regional Expressions*). As the first Chinese dialect dictionary, the *Fang yan* is far more than a sourcebook of philological glosses culled from disparate sources. It is a synchronical word list that focuses on rare expressions in an attempt to trace linguistic boundaries and connections. In a surviving letter, Yang justified the enormous task of compiling this text in fairly standard Confucian terms: Since regional cultures evolve from a complex of factors, the wise ruler must have at his disposal texts dealing with such matters so that government policies may be suitably adjusted to varying locales. According to the testimony of his devoted disciple **Huan Tan**, Yang near the time of his death was also busily engaged in the promotion of one astronomical-cosmological theory, the *huntian* 渾天 theory, which viewed the round earth as the centre of the universe, on an analogy with a yolk at the centre of an egg.

Thanks to the volume and quality of his output, Yang's stature as Confucian master remained essentially unchallenged until the Southern Song period (1127–1279). A mere century after his death, Ban Gu 班固 (32–92) hailed Yang as one of the three great classical masters of the Former Han, in company with **Liu Xin** and **Liu Xiang**. The cosmological and ethical principles articulated in Yang Xiong's various writings, as interpreted by Song Zhong 宋衷 (d. 218), became the basis of the '*Mystery Studies*' 玄學 curriculum at the Jingzhou Academy organised under Liu Biao 劉表 (d. 233). And after the Academy was disbanded upon Liu Biao's death, the several hundred Jingzhou masters and their students scattered throughout the Three Kingdoms, setting up private, semi-private, and state-sponsored centres of learning which ultimately shaped the thinking of exegetes as different as Yu Fan 虞翻 (164–232), Wang Bi (226–249), and **Wang Su**. During the unified empires of Sui, Tang and Song, enthusiasm for Yang's writings continued unabated, with a broad spectrum of thinkers (e.g., **Han Yu**, **Sima Guang**, **Shao Yong**, and **Su Shi**) acknowledging their intellectual debts to him. But in the twelfth century, proponents of the Cheng–Zhu's True Way of Learning saw Yang's holistic views as a barrier to the propagation of their own teachings; in their efforts to overturn certain pre-Song moral constructs, they tried to undermine Yang's stature by denouncing his character, moral cosmological vision and eclecticism. Their objections centred on three main areas: first, that Yang, though an ardent champion of **Mengzi** (at a time when Mengzi was far less esteemed in classical circles than **Xunzi**), had proposed an influential theory of human nature that contradicted the one proposed earlier by Mengzi; second, that both Yang and his chief disciples dared to liken Yang's work to two sagely Classics revered by the Song Confucians, specifically the *Analects* and the *Book of Changes*; and third, that Yang had dared to serve both the Han and Xin dynasties, when Song standards strictly forbade service to 'two masters'. Nonetheless, as most Chinese philosophical works dating to the first millennium have been lost, the *Canon of Supreme Mystery* and *Model Sayings,* two undisputed classics, together provide one of the best avenues to understanding early Confucian ideology in its formative stage.

Students interested in Yang's thought would do well to begin with David Knechtges' translation of *The Han Shu Biography of Yang Xiong (53 B.C.–A.D. 18)* (Tempe, Arizona State University, 1981); Timotheus Pokora's *Hsin-lun (New Treatises and Other Writings by Huan T'an (43 B.C.–28 A.D.)* (Ann Arbor: University of Michigan, 1975), passim; and Michael Nylan's translation of *The Canon of Supreme Mystery* (Albany, State University of New York, 1993). But advanced students will wish to study as well Suzuki Yoshijirô's 鈴木由次郎 masterwork, *Taigen no kenkyu* 太玄の研究 (*Research on the Supreme Mystery,* Tokyo: Meitokusha, 1964), which explains the *Mystery*'s debts and contributions to previous Han cosmological theories.

MICHAEL NYLAN

Yangming xuepai 陽明學派
(Schools derived from the teachings of Wang Yangming)

The term *Yangming xuepai* refers to the schools of philosophy based upon the thought of the Ming dynasty philosopher **Wang Shouren**, better known by his alternative name Wang Yangming 王陽明. Often regarded as the greatest philosopher in China since **Zhu Xi**, Wang set Chinese thought in a new direction by focusing his attention on the cultivation of the heart/mind (*xin*) as the most efficacious method of becoming a sage. Wang Yangming made three specific contributions to the body of Confucian philosophy he inherited. The first was his understanding of the term 'the investigation of things' (*gewu*), by which he meant the need to purify the heart/mind of selfish desires. His second contribution was the doctrine of the unity of knowledge and action (*zhixing heyi*), which he interpreted to mean that virtue could not be fully understood intellectually without putting it into practice, nor could it be fully put into practice without understanding it intellectually. For Wang, 'knowledge is the beginning of action, and action is the completion of knowledge'. His third contribution was embodied in the phrase 'the extension of innate knowledge' (*liang zhi*). Representing the culmination of his philosophy, this doctrine held that one's innate knowledge provided the unchanging standard of right and wrong, the guide to action whose main purpose was to do good and eliminate evil.

Wang believed that each person contains within himself the knowledge necessary to achieve sagehood. By placing more emphasis on the cultivation of one's individual heart/mind, and less on the mastery of an objective body of knowledge emphasised by the orthodox Zhu Xi School of **Neo-Confucianism**, Wang manifested a distinctive independence of spirit that became one of the hallmarks of the school associated with his name.

After Wang's death those who followed in his footsteps have been generally divided into two groups. The first remained loyal to his basic doctrines, and might be referred to as a centrist group. Among the most important figures in this line of descent were **Qian Dehong**, who was likely the most loyal of Wang's disciples to the basic tenets of Wang's philosophy. Other prominent figures were Nie Bao 聶豹 (1487–1563), who stressed the role of contemplative solitude in cultivating sagehood, and Luo Hongxian 羅洪先 (1504–1564), who emphasized scholarship as constituting an important method of self-cultivation. The second group descending from Wang Yangming tended to emphasise one aspect of the master's thinking, especially the need for independent thought and individual cultivation. The philosophers most responsible for the latter development were **Wang Ji** and **Wang Gen**, among Wang Yangming's most accomplished students. Wang Ji developed the thought of his teacher by focusing on the process of inducing a state of inner enlightenment to the point that he was accused of adopting the techniques of Chan Buddhism. He was probably the most original of Wang Yangming's students. Wang Gen founded what came to be called the Taizhou 泰州 School (see **Taizhou xuepai**), in the lower Yangtze. This school was known in particular for its focus on independent thinking, which led its critics to accuse it of promoting eccentric behaviour. Some of the most prominent members were **He Xinyin**, **Luo Rufang**, and **Li Zhi**. He Xinyin's life was full of action, not thought. He was distinguished by a propensity to take extreme measures in organising followers to confront what he regarded as social injustice. His independence of spirit clashed with many in authority and he ultimately died of mysterious causes when in prison. Luo was greatly influenced by the disciples of Wang Gen, and chose to follow a career of public administration while simultaneously exerting every effort to purify his own character.

Li Zhi is perhaps the most fascinating of the many intellectual descendants of Wang Yangming. Li developed a strong critique of Zhu Xi's Neo-Confucianism, rejecting the manner in which it stifled creative thinking and fostered a kind of intellectual sterility designed to curry favour with those in power. Li advocated an independence of mind and spirit, and a respect for individual freedom, that automatically set him in opposition to the scholarly conventions of his day and mark him as one of the most original personalities of the Ming dynasty.

The long-term impact on Chinese thought of Wang's followers was profound, turning philosophers away from a preoccupation with metaphysical theorising, mere 'knowledge', in favour of a preoccupation with verifiable, empirical 'action'. Wang's distrust of knowledge alone as the key to achieving sagehood inspired in subsequent thinkers a turn toward consideration of more practical problems and away from the 'empty words' of abstract theory. At the same time, many of Wang's descendants retained Zhu Xi's emphasis on classical scholarship. The outcome was a form of synthesis that took scholarship itself as a realm of investigation and action, producing the school of empirical research that dominated the Qing dynasty. The foundations were laid by the generation of scholars who bridged the end of the Ming and the beginning of the Qing. Scholars like **Huang Zongxi** were admirers of both Wang Yangming and the orthodox line of Neo-Confucianism descending from Zhu Xi. In the Qing the quintessential proponent of the doctrine that knowledge and action are intimately related was **Yan Yuan**, who founded his own school emphasising the importance of pragmatic knowledge and criticising the emphasis of many of his contemporaries on 'book learning'. The notion that scholarly knowledge should be of practical use to society at large permeated the Qing dynasty and may constitute the most important enduring legacy of the school of thought initiated by Wang Yangming.

References: de Bary, 1981: 145–247; Tang Chun-i, 1970: 93–119.

ALAN T. WOOD

Yanshi jiaxun 顏氏家訓
(*The Family Instructions of the Yan Clan*)

The *Yanshi jiaxun* by **Yan Zhitui**, were written towards the end of the author's life, to judge from taboo characters and other indications of a Sui dynasty (581–618) date. It is not the first such compilation of clan rules known to us, but it is by far the most complete early example, having been transmitted more or less in its entirety, and its influence may be seen in many later works. The author lived in both north and south before the Sui reunion, so the determination of unified norms, especially linguistic norms, is inevitably one of his main concerns, and may explain why the work was valued and cited in the decades immediately following its composition. Another obvious theme is how to ensure family survival in uncertain times, in which the degradation and even extinction of once noble families was not uncommon. His advice therefore carries a practical and prudential message which some later found short of Confucian idealism. Admonitions to his family to maintain a faith in Buddhism, and also the vision of a perfect society as one under the sway of the Buddha of the Future, certainly show a complete absence of the purist, revivalist strain of **Neo-Confucianism**, but reflect well the demoralised conditions of the late sixth century. In literary terms the amount of Buddhist material alluded to is actually quite negligible. This in itself, however, may not reflect the author's actual degree of commitment to Buddhism, but rather the conventions of what was already an established genre of writing – conventions and norms are, to repeat, very much at issue in the work.

Even so, the message that the best policy is to devote oneself to study, if need be to only 'several hundred volumes', demonstrates both an irreducible Confucian commitment to the classical tradition, and the constant circulation in private hands – even in violently destructive times – of a much larger body of literature than at the same point in the history of western Europe. Of course as head of a scholarly family, the author's aims were much more than minimal, and he strives to pass on to his children a wealth of arcane and pedantic information – extending even to Daoist religious literature, which for sectarian reasons the author rejects entirely as a religious influence – that shows a China in the middle of a period of climactic warfare preserving an undiminished respect for learning. As a result the *Yanshi jiaxun* has been mined as a resource by social historians and yet more so by philologists, though it also provides important testimony as to what a Buddho-Confucian life might be, and so illustrates a possible alternative to Neo-Confucianism narrowly defined. The historical importance of this alternative, the rhetorical defence of which has tended to be less dramatic than that of a more uncompromising stance, has perhaps been underrated. The *Yanshi jiaxun* has been competently translated into English, and a worthwhile modern typeset variorum edition now exists as well.

References: Teng Ssu-yu, 1968; Wang Liqi, 1980.

TIM H. BARRETT

Yantie huiyi 鹽鐵會議
(The Imperial Conference on the State Monopolies on Salt and Iron)

In 81 BCE, six years after **Han Wudi**'s death, an imperial court conference of scholars and statesmen was convened to discuss the hardships of the population and the administrative measures to deal with them. An account of this debate was later compiled by Huan Kuan (*fl. c.* 50 BCE) under the title ***Yantie lun***. The primary issues were the state monopolies on the production and marketing of salt and iron established in 119 BCE; while the *Yantie lun* shows the critics of Han Wudi's policies (including the monopolies) mostly as winners in the debate, the monopolies were abolished nationwide not before 44 BCE and were reinstated three years later; only the liquor monopoly, set up in 98 BCE, was abolished in 81 BCE. This situation suggests that the *Yantie lun*, while being the only extant source of some detail on the conference, provides an idealised picture of its results. As the state monopolies on salt and iron were directly related to the control of private wealth as well as to the nature and functions of government, the conference addressed a broad range of fundamental issues that had shaped imperial policies under Han Wudi: the government's active role in the economy and in the distribution of material welfare among the population; meritocratic principles in the appointment and control of officials; military expansion of the empire and border defence; extensive foreign trade; large-scale conscript labour and military service; the firm application of law and punishments. While the governmental side in the conference argued that these measures secured peace, economic stability and general welfare, the critics denounced them as a continuation of Qin policies and instead proposed a less controlling and demanding government that should embody traditional principles and lead the population to prosperity through moral instruction.

References: Loewe, 1974, 90–112; Gale, 1931; Gale, Boodberg & Lin, 1934; Twitchett & Loewe, 1986: 187–90.

MARTIN KERN

Yantie lun 鹽鐵論
(*Discourses on Salt and Iron*)

Compiled by Huan Kuan 桓寬 (probably *fl.* 50 BCE), the *Yantie lun*, which is set out in dialogue form, purports to be a record of the discussions ordered in 81 BCE for an investigation of current popular hardships. The title of the work fastens on one particular question of imperial policies, whether to retain or to abolish the monopolies established over the production of salt and iron in 119 BCE. The received account of the debate in fact covers major problems of principle, such as the aims, duties and responsibilities of government, the conflict between ethical ideals and the demands to attain material prosperity and the lessons to be learnt from the policies and mistakes of the past.

Of the two parties to the debate, one criticised and one defended the intensive and expansionist measures of **Han Wudi**'s (r. 141–87) government. The spokesmen for the government saw virtue in enriching the population by controlling and coordinating its working lives and efforts and by expanding imperial interests in distant territories; the critics reacted sharply against the burdens that such policies had imposed on the population and against the principle that the interests of the empire merited priority over those of the individual.

Compiled perhaps some forty years after the debate itself, and after major changes of imperial policies, the sixty sections of the *Yantie lun* show the critics as winning most of the arguments.

References: Translations of parts of the documents are to be found in Gale, 1931; and Gale, Boodberg & Lin, 1934, vol. LXV: 73–110; see also Loewe, 1974, ch. 3.

MICHAEL LOEWE

Yao Shu 姚樞
1203–1280
(*zi* Gongmao 公茂, *hao* Xuezhai 雪齋)

Yao was a scholar known for his administrative service under Khubilai (r. 1260–1294).

After the Mongols overran the North in the 1230s, Yao met the captive Confucian scholar **Zhao Fu**, who introduced Yao to **Zhu Xi**'s commentaries. Zhao taught at Yao's Academy of the Supreme Ultimate (*Taiji shuyuan* 太極書院) in Beijing (founded in 1238), which had an extensive library.

Between 1241 and 1251, Yao, then retired at Sumen 蘇門 mountain in Henan, met **Xu Heng** and introduced him to Song thought. It was through Yao's efforts that Xu first came to the attention of high officials in the employ of Khubilai. At Sumen, Yao printed up Zhu Xi's commentaries on the *Elementary Learning* (**Xiao xue**), the Four Books and the compendium of Neo-Confucian philosophy by Zhu Xi and **Lü Zuqian**, *Reflections on Things at Hand* (**Jinsi lu**), and Khubilai soon hired him as an adviser and tutor. One of Yao's most famous works is an eight-point memorial applying the moral principles of the *Great Learning* (**Da xue**) to government. Yao assisted Khubilai in his conquest of Southern Song, advising him to spare the local population. He also sought to reform the appointment system and to establish centralised judicial procedures. In the 1270s, Yao was part of the debate over the renewal of the civil service examination system on a **Neo-Confucian** curricular basis, and in his last years he served in academic positions, including the Hanlin Academy.

Yao's brand of Confucianism was practical: he compiled sayings from the Classics, stressed morality in government, and championed the role of the scholar in politics. He was an accomplished poet and calligrapher, but his importance lies in his promotion of Neo-Confucian studies in North China in the early years of Mongol rule.

References: Chan, Wing-tsit, 1982: 197–8; Chen Yuan, 1966: 22; de Bary, 1981: 21–2; Langlois, 1981: 219, 271; Liu Ts'un-yan, 1986: 522–3, 531; de Rachewiltz, 1993: 387–405; Rossabi, 1981: 271; *Song–Yuan xuean*, 1966: 90: 10b–11a (p. 1427); Sun K'o-k'uan, 1981: 219; *Yuan shi*, 1976: 158.

DAVID GEDALECIA

Yao Shun 堯舜
(Yao and Shun)

Yao and Shun were mythic rulers of high antiquity whose virtues and whose pronouncements on good governance are recorded in the *Book of History* (**Shang shu**). Yao was noted for his respectful demeanour, intelligence and his ability to create a harmonious society. He organised a system of stable governance wherein skilled ministers were employed to create a calendrical system to calibrate human endeavours with the movements of the heavens and to supervise public works.

At the end of his reign, when Yao sought voluntarily to abdicate his rule to a successor, he selected a nonkin commoner called Shun, whom he chose moreover as a son-in-law for his two daughters. He selected Shun for his singular filial piety and his ability not only to live harmoniously with his loutish parents and brother but also to educate them and transform them. Shun exemplified the personal virtues of his predecessor Yao. As a ruler, he promulgated moral principles; regulated the canons of measurement, sacrificial offerings and criminal law; established strong relationships with the chieftains of the realm; and appointed a bureau of ministers to supervise the departments of government.

In later times, the very mention of the names Yao and Shun evoked nostalgia for the perceived halcyon days of antiquity when rulers were benevolent and self-sacrificing. Yao and Shun became exemplars of a primordial, idealised, sovereignty that few later rulers could hope to equal.

References: Legge, 1985c; Lewis, 1999.

DEBORAH SOMMER

Ye Shi 葉適
1150–1223
(*zi* Zhengze 正則, *hao* Shuixin 水心)

Ye Shi has been regarded as the representative of the **Yongjia** School Yongjia xuepai in the Southern Song because his life, including his political career and intellectual orientation, was the concentrated expression of *Yongjia* teaching.

Ye Shi was born in Yongjia county (today's Wenzhou city of Zhejiang province). He was also called by his friends Mr Shuixin 水心 since he lived in Shuixin Village of Yongjia County after retiring from government service. Ye Shi's life experienced three important periods. In the first period from the time he was born in 1150 to 1178, Ye Shi committed himself to studying Confucian Classics, especially the teachings prevailing in Yongjia areas until he passed the national examination with second place at the age of twenty-nine. The *Yongjia* teachings he received at this stage produced heavy impacts on the formation of his theory against ***dao xue*** and other concurrent Confucian schools in future. The second period from 1178 to 1206 was the most important period for Ye Shi's political career and intellectual development. After serving different positions in local administration for fourteen years, Ye Shi was promoted to the central government in 1192, and became one of the key figures who directed the court *coup* of 1194, which led to Emperor Guangzong's (r. 1189–1194) resignation. Three years later he was dismissed from public service in the Qingyuan Proscription 慶元党禁 against the ***dao xue*** group, however, Ye Shi was reactivated in 1201 when the Southern Song government asked for his support to prepare the war against the Jurchen Jin in the North. Ye Shi assumed civil and military responsibilities during the war to protect the capital city in the Hui River 淮河 area. The failure of military adventure in 1206 led Ye Shi to permanent retirement from government service and closure of his political career. The third period of Ye Shi's life was his last sixteen years spent in the Shuixin village for research and teaching until he died in 1223. It was during this period that Ye Shi developed the profound criticism of the *dao xue* movement, synthesised *Yongjia* traditions into a

more structured form with more convincing arguments and solid historical documentation, and brought Yongjia teachings to the highest level that this school ever reached.

Ye Shi identified himself as one of the practitioners of the *dao xue* movement until the late 1190s. In 1188 his defence of **Zhu Xi** and whole *dao xue* fellowship at court against Lin Li's 林栗 attack highlighted Ye Shi's relationship with the *dao xue* group. Starting in the mid-1190s, Ye Shi's critics on *dao xue* had been intensified after he gradually realised his essential differences from the *dao xue* group, and eventually departed from *dao xue* and became one of its most uncompromising critics.

Ye Shi developed and fulfilled *Yongjia* teachings from different aspects. The most important philosophical arguments for Ye Shi was that material embodiments (*wu*) had priority over ***dao***. The different understanding of the polarity of *dao* and material embodiments became the watershed of Ye Shi and Zhu Xi's theories. Both Ye Shi and Zhu Xi agreed that *dao* and material embodiments were inseparable; *dao* existed in material embodiments and material embodiments were the manifestations of *dao*. However, Ye Shi believed that material embodiments were formed before the *dao* was present, therefore, material embodiments had priority over *dao*. After establishing such an argument as a philosophic foundation, Ye Shi further challenged Zhu Xi's view on the Non-Ultimate (***wu ji***) and the Supreme Ultimate (***tai ji***). Ye Shi pointed out that the Ultimate was not something mysterious that produced and regulated the myriad things in the world, instead, it was the general attribute of all material things and the perfect state that all material things could achieve when they fully developed or displayed their functions. Again, Ye Shi stressed that the Ultimate could not be separated from all material things and had to be manifested in material things, in other words, the establishment of the Ultimate should be based on all material things, therefore, the Ultimate should only be understood through all material things.

As an extension of his philosophical arguments, Ye Shi also offered his views on investigating things (*gewu* 格物) and extending knowledge (*zhizhi*), the widely accepted approach to self-cultivation in the Song Confucian community. He pointed out that investigating things was neither investigating principle (*li*) nor investigating the mind (*xin*), as Zhu Xi and **Lu Jiuyuan** claimed. To Ye Shi, investigating things was to realise or reflect outside actual entities by using the human mind. Such realisation or reflection started from actual things, and the function of the mind was to conform itself to such reflection of actual things. Although Ye Shi's position kept consistent with his basic philosophical arguments, he might overemphasise the role of actual things or material world in the process until he presented his approach toward personal cultivation. Because the process was built on the interactions between the outside actual things and inside mind, and such interactions could not be accomplished with one move for people to obtain the principle, Ye Shi said, investigating things became a gradual process, not a sudden and momentary enlightenment, as Lu Jiuyuan's School claimed. In Ye Shi's eyes, Lu Jiuyuan's approach toward cultivation omitted the process of investigating things and therefore created the gap between investigating things and obtaining principle, which would lead people into mystery and agnosticism. To describe his approach toward obtaining principle, Ye Shi pointed out that investigating things started from seeing and hearing, which generally referred to people's practical experience, completed by thinking, the function of mind. The interaction between the inside and the outside would be the only path toward apprehension of perfect knowledge.

In current studies about Song Confucianism, Ye Shi is always coupled with another major *Zhedong* 浙東 scholar **Chen Liang** because of their shared stance on some national political and economic issues, and their criticism of the *dao xue* movement and fellowship. The view grasped the core of Ye Shi and Chen Liang's relationship, but neglected that Ye Shi and Chen Liang had quite different views on some major issues. Both realised the importance of rich people to the society, but Chen Liang focused more on how to gain the interest for merchants, while Ye Shi appealed for policy changes toward wealthy people on behalf of the government's own interest. The different views on the polarity of integrity and utility became the major issue which divided the two scholars. By synthesising integrity and utility, Chen Liang tried to unify utilitarian orientations and Confucian virtues. However, in the eyes of Ye Shi, Chen Liang had gone to an extreme in pursuing sociopolitical consequences so the unity or balance of integrity and utility was broken.

One of the important contributions Ye Shi made to the *Yongjia* School was his active involvement in practical governance. He served in different positions at both local and central levels of government administrations. He left us lengthy articles with extensive discussions on restoration plans against the Jurchen Jin in North China, military strategies, land systems, financial reform, tax collection, and bureaucratic operations. In these articles, he advocated institutional changes and applications of historical experiences. By doing so, his practice set up a good example of how to implement the teachings of the *Yongjia* School.

There is no doubt that Ye Shi and his teaching provided an alternative approach toward statecraft issues that greatly puzzled the Southern Song government. Ye Shi responsed positively to the fundamental changes that had happened in the Song intellectual community and challenged Zhu Xi's understanding of *Daoxue* which in one way or another expanded the scope of Neo-Confucian theories and practices.

References: Lo, 1974; Niu, Pu, 1998; *Song–Yuan xuean*, 1966; Tian Hao, 1996; Tillman,

1982, 1992a; Ye Shi, 1959, 1977; Zhou Mengjiang, 1992; Zhou Xuewu, 1988.

Pu Niu

Yi 義
(Rightness, righteousness, appropriateness)

The term *yi* has been frequently translated, for lack of a more suitable English counterpart, as 'righteousness'. The less felicitous 'rightness', however, might more accurately invoke the term's sense of 'appropriateness' or 'fittingness' of a path of action or direction of thought to a particular context and moment of time. To reflect the morally imperative nature of such courses of action, the term is also sometimes translated as 'duty', 'dutifulness' or 'morally proper conduct'; especially in later usages, it also means 'meaning' or 'signification'. The concept was developed at some length by Confucius and then greatly elaborated by **Mengzi**, for whom it became one of the cornerstones of the life admirably well lived.

In the *Analects*, the quality of rightness was ideally part of the basic character or disposition of the *junzi*, or noble person, who developed that quality through ritual/propriety and trustworthiness. What was rightly or appropriately to be done in a particular context was something one learned by listening and observation, and such actions often required a measure of courage to execute. Confucius expressed anxiety about not enacting what was appropriate when he observed or heard what was fitting to a particular occasion. Thus, even though rightness might initially be part of one's character, it was also always shaped by what one learned through one's interactions with others in the world. Rightness for the noble person required a significant measure of flexibility, for Confucius remarked that the noble person was neither set on particular paths nor actively contrarian to others but instead sought what was appropriate. For Confucius, rightness was frequently contrasted with *li* 利, which was profit, benefit or personal advantage (see *yi li*). Following the path of rightness was one of the hallmarks of the noble person; petty people concerned themselves instead with the pursuit of personal benefits.

Mengzi more assertively stated that rightness was part of a human being's inherent constitution. Human beings, for him, were possessed of four 'minds' or 'hearts' (*xin*) as surely as they were possessed of their four limbs: the minds or 'beginnings' (*duan* 端, see *si duan*) of commiseration and compassion, shame and disgrace, respect and reverence and right and wrong. These minds were associated with the qualities of humaneness, rightness, ritual and wisdom, respectively. In a famous debate with the philosopher Gaozi 告子 on the goodness (*shan*) of human nature (*xing*), Mengzi asserted that the mind of shame and disgrace and the concomitant quality of rightness were aspects of the human constitution that facilitated the development of goodness.

Merely being possessed of rightness was not enough; it was a path or road one had to follow throughout one's life. Along with the practice of humaneness, it in effect constituted one of the two greatest obligations impingent upon human conduct. (By way of comparison, **Xunzi** paired rightness more commonly with ritual than with humaneness.) Rightness, which was a quality more precious than life itself, began within the family with one's respect for elders and was eventually to be extended to all under heaven, shaping what one should and should not do to others, and also what one should not allow others to do to oneself. Concerns about profit might cloud the pursuit of rightness and were regarded with some circumspection.

Rightness was one of the primary concerns of later literati thinkers. The Han scholar **Dong Zhongshu** looked to the *Zuo's Commentary on the Spring and Autumn Annals* (*Chunqiu Zuo zhuan*), which he believed had been compiled by Confucius, as an important source of teachings about rightness. Dong understood rightness as the principle of perfecting the moral qualities of the self, a necessary prerequisite for then governing others; relationships with other people were sustained by the parallel quality of humaneness. The Tang scholar **Han Yu** also paired humaneness and rightness in his critique of Laozi, Mozi and the Buddhists, whom he perceived as undermining the primal Way and virtue. **Lu Jiuyuan** in the Song contrasted the literati tradition, which he associated with rightness, with the Buddhists, whom he perceived as selfishly concerned instead with personal advantage. Lu's younger contemporary **Chen Chun**, drawing upon Mengzi's notion of the 'Four Beginnings', understood rightness as one of the Five Cardinal Virtues, which for Chen were Mengzi's Four Beginnings plus the additional quality of trustworthiness. He interpreted these five in light of Five Phases (*wu xing*) theory, associating rightness with the phase metal and the razor-sharp discriminating qualities of the mind.

References: Ames & Rosemont, 1998: 1: 3, 2: 24, 4: 10, 4 :16, 7: 3, 15: 18; Chan, Wing-tsit, 1963d: 575–6 and 1986b: 69–85, 134–42; de Bary & Bloom, 1999: 306–9, 569–70; Hall & Ames, 1987; Lau, 1984: 2A: 6, 6A: 6, 6A: 10, 7A: 33; Knoblock, 1988–94; Shun, 1997a.

DEBORAH SOMMER

Yi 一
(One)

The concept of 'one' has taken various forms in Chinese philosophy, but it is generally used to characterise the essence, function and implementation of the Way (*dao*). It is nature's unity, as in the *Book of Changes* (*Yi jing*), where Heaven (*tian*) is given the number one, while Earth (*di*) is two. In the *Xunzi* 'one' is identified with the unity of one's mind, while in Neo-Confucianism it is synonymous variously with the fundamental creative principle of material force (*qi*), nature (*ziran* 自然),

Great Ultimate (*taiji*), human nature (*xing*), unity, desirelessness (**Zhou Dunyi**), clear seeing (**Zhu Xi**), etc.

Reference: Morohashi, 1960.

TODD CAMERON THACKER

Yi Byŏng-do 李丙燾
1896–1989
(*hao* Dukye 斗溪)

A historian who held various senior posts in the National Academy of Sciences, Yi graduated in 1919 from the department of history at Waseda 早稲田 University in Japan, after which he taught in a high school. In 1934 he assumed the office of the first president of the *Jindan* Academy, which was founded by scholars opposed to a materialist historical viewpoint, establishing thus their own objective historical research. The Academy's publication was entitled the *Jindan Bulletin*. Although Yi and many participating Academy scholars did not directly contribute to the independence movement against Japanese occupation, they did make great contributions in setting and maintaining the overall high standards of historical research and Korean cultural research. From 1941 Yi lectured at Ehwa Women's College, and from 1945 was a professor at Seoul National University. In 1954 he was appointed a life fellow of the National Academy of Sciences. Later, in 1962 he became an emeritus professor at Seoul National University and in 1966 became both a professor and head of the Taetong Cultural Institute at **Sŏnggyun'gwan** University. Yi's students became leading professors and scholars after 1945 in Korean academic circles.

In 1980 Yi was appointed to the National Advisory Council on State Affairs, and he received both the Korean Order for Cultural Merit and the National Academy of Sciences Award of Merit. His many works include *An Overview of Korean History, A*

Study of the Koryo Dynasty, Korean History and Guiding Principles, among others.

References: Yi Byŏng-do, 1972, 1987.

NAM-JIN HUH

Yi Gan 李柬
1677–1727
(*zi* Konggŏ 公舉, *hao* Wiam 巍巖)

Yi was a Neo-Confucian (*Sŏngnihak* 性理學) scholar of the mid to late Chosŏn dynasty who held various important government posts. He asserted the limitlessness of principle (Kr. *it'ong* 理通) and the oneness of principle (Kr. *iil* 理一) as a basis for his view on the homogeneity of the nature of human beings and things (Kr. *inmulsŏng sangdongron* 人物性相同論) and also asserted the complete goodness of the 'not yet occuring' (*weifa*, Kr. *mibal* 未發) phase of mind. With this, he came to debate with his classmate **Han Wŏn-jin** for a period of six years concerning the similarities and differences between the nature of humans and that of things (Kr. *inmulsŭng sanginon* 人物性相異論) and on the theories of goodness and evil of the 'not yet occuring phase' of human nature. At this time, Han was studying under **Kwŏn Sang-ha**. Yi debated with Kwón, which led to Yi's system of thought forming the basis for the *Nakron* (洛論) school while Han's formed the *Noron* (湖論) school.

Yi took the view that the Supreme Ultimate (*tai ji*, Kr. *t'aegŭk*), five constant virtues (*wu chang*, Kr. *osang*), Mandate of Heaven (*Tian ming*, Kr. *ch'ŏnmyŏng*) and that which is original (*ben ran*, Kr. *ponyŏn*) were the same, a view based on the assertion that human nature and the nature of things (Kr. *mulsŏng* 物性) are identifiable. The four are simply names designating the same thing, and at first there are no distinctions between that and this (Kr. *p'ich'a* 彼此), cause and effect (Kr. *ponmal* 本末), part and whole (Kr. *p'yŏnjŏn* 偏全), large and small and so on and so forth. Thus when the

Mandate of Heaven and the five constant virtues are looked at from the perspective of a single source (Kr. *irwon* 一原), their characters (Kr. *hyŏnggi* 形器) transcend existence and accordingly humans and things are indistinguishable in terms of part and whole. This is Yi's explanation of 'that which is original is human nature' entitled *Ponyŏnjisŏng* (**benran zhixing**). Yi Gan's works include the *Wiamchip* 巍巖集, and *Mipalpyŏn* 未發辯.

References: Yi Ae-hŭi, 1990; Yi Gan, *Wiamjip.*

NAM-JIN HUH

Yi Hang-no 李恒老
1792–1868
(*zi* Yi-sul 而述, *hao* Hwasŏ 華西)

Yi was a representative scholar of Neo-Confucian Learning (*Sŏngnihak* 性理學) towards the end of the nineteenth century and the initiator of resistance to 'western imperialism' (Kr. *Wichŏng Chuksaron* 衛正斥邪論). His own theory held fundamental differences from that of the **Kiho School**. For example, while the Kiho School held that material force (*qi*, Kr. *gi*) has control over principle (*li*, Kr. *i*) and is superior and active, Yi maintained that the essence of the heart/mind (*xin*, Kr. *sim*) is determined by principle. Yi's theory of principle being preceding material force (Kr. *chuinonch'ŭk* 主理論的) was taken up by his pupils after his death. Kim Pyung-mok 金平默 (1819–1888) advanced a theory of the mind ruling principle (Kr. *simchuisŏl* 心主理說), while another pupil Yu Chóng-gyo 柳重教 (1821–1893) took a view of the mind ruling material force (Kr. *simchugisŏl* 心主氣說), thus through these pupils an intense series of debates was sparked within *Sŏngnihak.*

Yi's discussions of the differences and similarities between the nature of humans and that of things, although not inclining one way or another on the matter, was not simply a compromise, but rather was part of his fundamental theory of principle and material force.

References: *Chosŏn Hugiŭi Hakp'adŭl*, 1996; Keum Jang-t'ae, 1984.

JANG-TAE KEUM

Yi Hwang 李滉
1501–1570
(*zi* Kyungho 景浩, *hao* T'oegye 退溪)

Yi Hwang, better known by his alternative name (*hao*), T'oegye, was one of the most active Confucian scholars during the mid-Chosŏn dynasty and was certainly the most famous, along with **Yi I** (Yulgok). He confirmed **Zhu Xi**'s thought as the standard for Korean Neo-Confucianism (*Sŏngnihak* 性理學), put forward a theory of self-cultivation centring around the practice of 'attentativeness' or 'reverence' (*jing* 敬) and had an enormous influence on the direction and character of Neo-Confucianism in Korea. His everyday life revealed his practice of the Learning of the Way (*dao xue*) in the way he upheld the ideal of the scholar–gentleman. These things made a deep impression on his students. He did not have one particular teacher in his own clan (family) and spent part of his youth studying the *Book of Changes* (**Yi jing**). In fact, he studied so much he became ill. Having passed the civil service examinations at age thirty-four, Yi Hwang took up a government post, but as the political situation was turbulent due to the incursion of foreign powers he volunteered to serve in the countryside. At the age of forty-nine he resigned from his post and returned home and, despite numerous requests from the throne that he accept an official post, he, for the most part, stayed in retirement. In the **Four–Seven Debate** Yi Hwang, in the end, adopted a theory of 'mutual issuance of principle and material force' (Kr. *Igi hobalsŏl* 理氣互發說). Rather than seeing this as a dualistic theory he believed that it was a standardisation and combination of a simplified monistic theory that portrayed both sides of a complicated relationship between material force (*qi*) and principle (*li*).

Self-cultivation
Attaining 'serious attentiveness' was one of Yi Hwang's basic themes, where attentiveness superintends the heart/mind (*xin*); it is a state of internally cultivating one's nature and externally reflecting on and suppressing the possibility of evil in one's acts. Fulfilling one's potential by manifesting Heaven's endowment, i.e., the heart/mind following the original principle of 'attentiveness', is both the goal and the starting point in the Learning of the Way. Yi Hwang unified the methods for realising this by recognising that the practice of attentiveness and understanding the theory of human nature (*xing*) are not two distinct issues, and therefore put forward a theory that knowledge and practice go hand-in-hand, while rejecting various theories either simply combining the two into one or making the relationship between them sequential.

Ten Diagrams on Sage Learning
Yi Hwang wrote the *Ten Diagrams on Sage Learning* (**Sŏnghak Sibto**) when he was sixty-eight years old (1568), as a present for King Sŏn Cho. It is an encapsulation of his mature thought. The book illustrates the fundamental doctrines of Neo-Confucianism through ten diagrams with accompanying comments, all dealing with how to become a sage. There are two basic ways of looking at the *Ten Diagrams on Sage Learning*. The first focuses on the practice of sage learning. Here the standard of practice is seen in the third and fourth diagrams on *Elementary Learning* (**Xiao xue**, Kr. *Sohak*) and the *Great Learning* (**Da xue**, Kr. *Taehak*), respectively. The principles underlying this are in the first two diagrams, based on the Supreme Ultimate (*tai ji*) and the western Inscription (**Xi ming**). Diagrams five through ten present concrete themes of practice. These diagrams show an organic link between theory and

practice. By the second method, the first five diagrams, based on the Heavenly Way, are seen as illustrations of human relations, and the last five, based on human nature, focus on reverential awe (Kr. *Kyŏng-wi* 敬畏). Moreover, both directions, from the Way of Heaven down to human relations and from human nature upward to the Heavenly Mandate (*Tian ming*), correspond to each other, something reflected in the correspondence between Heaven and humanity.

Continuation and influence

Yi Hwang had a large number of followers, many of whom were leading scholars of the time, including Cho Mok 趙穆 (1524–1606), Yu Sŏong-ryong 柳成龍 (1542–1607), Kim Sŏng-il 金成一 (1538–1598), Chŏng Ku 鄭逑 (1543–1620). These scholars were among those leading the school of thought perpetuating Yi Hwang's ideas, which came to be called the Yŏngnam School (**Yŏngnam Hakpa**). Although the scholars continued Yi Hwang's line of thought there were also diverse developments within the Yŏngnam School, particularly the line of thought developed by Chŏng Ku and his followers who formed the basis of those Southerners from the Yŏngnam region residing near Seoul. This line was later continued by **Yi Ik** and his followers who in turn influenced the Practical Learning (*Sirhak*) School in Korea.

There was later a bifurcation of Neo-Confucian thought in Korea as a result of disagreements between Yi Hwang's followers and the followers of Yi I, a famous Neo-Confucian scholar thirty-five years younger than Yi Hwang. Yi I had great respect for Yi Hwang's scholarship despite some major disagreements. Some of T'oegye's followers recorded his words and edited a volume entitled *Words and Deeds of Master T'oegye* (Kr. *T'oegye sŏnsaeng Ŏnhaengnok* 退溪先生言行錄). A later scholar, Yi Sang-chŏng 李相靖 (1710–1781), edited a collection of T'oegye's letters and, even later, Yi Ik arranged T'oegye's sayings and deeds and used his theories to make *Collected Sayings of Yi T'oegye*. **Chong Yag-yong**, on reading

T'oegye's letters was also moved to write a similar book.

Study and teaching

T'oegye's thought was founded on a thorough study of Zhu Xi's writings and commentaries on the Classics. In addition, both *Reflections on Things at Hand* (*Jinsi lu*) written by Zhu Xi and **Lü Zuqian**, and the *Classic of the Heart-Mind* written by **Zhen Dexiu**, a follower of Zhu Xi's thought, played an extremely important role in the development of his thought. T'oegye often used both of these texts for teaching his students. Moreover, the *Grand Compendium of Nature and Principle* (*Xingli daquan* 性理大全) was also important.

'Abiding in serious attentiveness' (Kr. *Kŏgyŏng* 居敬) and 'thoroughly fathoming principle' (Kr. *Kung-i* 窮理) form two poles around which T'oegye's thought developed. Other important themes include the idea that knowledge and action advance hand in hand (Kr. *Chihaeng byŏngjin* 知行並進), and attentiveness and moral senses are likewise mutually supporting (Kr. *Kyŏng-i raeji* 敬義來持). His metaphysics developed the Neo-Confucian themes of human nature and feelings in terms of principle and material force. It is over the relationship of these in relation to the Four Beginnings (*si duan*) and Seven Emotions (*qi qing*) that the **Four–Seven Debate** occurred first between Yi Hwang and **Ki Tae-sŭng**. This debate had a lasting influence on the development of Korean Neo-Confucianism. Yi Hwang's *Ten Diagrams on Sage Learning* also influenced many scholars, and not only in Korea. His thought influenced **Hayashi Razan** and **Yamazaki Ansai**, among others, in Japan, and there was a reprint of his *Ten Diagrams* in China in 1926 with laudatory poems by Chinese scholars appended. Lastly, the T'oegye Society was founded in Korea in 1970 to promote studies of his thought, and a journal was also established to further these ends.

References: Keum Jang-t'ae, 1998a; Yu Yŏng-jong, 1987.

JANG-TAE KEUM

Yi Hyŏn-il 李玄逸
1627–1704
(*zi* Iksŭng 翼升, *hao* Galam 葛庵)

Yi was the second of three brothers who were central figures in the Yŏngnam Neo-Confucian (*Sŏngnihak* 性理學) school of thought. Yi also established the T'oegye (**Yi Hwang**) school tradition. He took his first government post at the age of fifty, though in 1680 on account of the death of his mother and the political struggles of the western and Southern Yŏngnam factions which saw the former in control, Yi retired to concentrate on his writings, including the development of his criticisms of **Yi I**'s *Sŏngni* 性理 theory. In 1689 the Southern school was back in influence in government and Yi was promoted. But in 1694 again the tides turned, and Yi was exiled to Hamgyung Do. At this point, Yi critically investigated various *Sŏngni* theories and supported in his work that of Yi Hwang. In his seventies, his place of exile was moved to Gellado and by the age of seventy-three, he was finally free to return to his hometown and live out his days.

Yi's nineteen-point detailed criticism of Yi I's **Four–Seven Debate** and his extensive inheritence of Yi Hwang's views, led to the theoretical deepening of the T'oegye school of *Sŏngni*. He compared the *Sŏngni* theory of Yi I with Yi Hwang's views, revealing a black and white divide between them with no possibility of reconciliation.

Yi's minute debates on the Four–Seven Debate with Chŏng Si-han 丁時翰 (1625–1709, *zi* Kunik 君翊, *hao* Udam 愚潭), his disciple Sin Ik-hwang 申益愰 and others led to his fundamental *Sŏngni* perspective inheriting Yi Hwang's two source view (Kr. *iwonnon* 二元論), though he differed from Yi Hwang in that he held that principle's (*li*, Kr. *gi*) movement is spontaneous.

This school lineage starts from Yi Hwang to Kim Sŏng-il 金誠一 (1538–1593, *zi* Sasun 士純, *hao* Hakbong 鶴峰), Chang Hong-hyo 張興孝 (1564–1633, *zi* Haengwŏn 行源, *hao* Kyungdang 敬堂), to Yi, and then to his son Yi Chae 李栽 (1657–1730, *zi* Yuchae 幼材, *hao* Mil'am 密庵) and grandson Yi Sang-chŏng 李象靖 (1710–1781, *zi* Kyungmun 景文, *hao* Taesan 大山).

JANG-TAE KEUM

Yi I 李珥
1536–1584
(*hao* Yulgok 栗谷)

Yi I, better known as Yulgok, was a Confucian scholar and politician during the mid-Chosŏn dynasty (1392–1910). His mother was renowned as embodying the traditional Korean ideal of motherhood. She taught her son so well that Yi I was said to have been able to compose poetry by the time he was eight years old. His mother died when he was sixteen and he went into mourning for three years in accordance with ritual requirements. At the age of nineteen he withdrew to a temple on Kumgang Mountain to study Buddhism but returned a year later and again focused on classical studies. Yi I married at the age of twenty-two, met **Yi Hwang** (T'oegye) at twenty-three, and passed the **civil service examinations** later that year, in which he composed a well-known response to the examination questions. But, it was not until he was twenty-nine that he first took a government post. Yi I held several high positions and, not long before his death in 1583, he sent a memorial to the throne expressing his concerns over the security of the country and the need to develop and train a stronger standing army. His request was denied and the country was ill-equipped to repulse the Japanese when they first invaded in 1592. Yi I died at the age of forty-nine but by that time he had become famous and had also established twenty or so academies across the country.

In 1545, when he was only nine, Chosŏn society was wracked by a literati purge that cost some scholars their lives and sent still more into exile. Because of the dangerous political climate many scholars decided to forgo pursuing government posts and instead retired in order to study. However, twenty years later some of those purged earlier regained power and it was soon after this that Yi I took a government position. Yi Hwang (T'oegye) was one of the scholars who took office at that time (1567). In spite of these scholars coming to power, many old customs or corrupt practices remained and basic reforms could not be carried out, resulting in increasing social disorder and a weaker military. It was in this environment that Yi I stressed the importance of working to achieve realistic results corresponding to contemporary needs of society; efforts that failed to do so would create a situation where 'even former sages and worthies would be unable to accomplish anything'. These practical concerns are inextricably linked to the rest of his **Neo-Confucianism**.

Yi I and **Sŏng Hon** exchanged several letters dealing with principle (*li*), material force (*qi*), and human nature (*xing*), over the course of a year. Sŏng Hon, who originally had doubts about Yi Hwang's theory of 'mutual issuance of principle and material force' recognised that it might be sound, and asked Yi I what he thought about it. Yi I replied that Yi Hwang developed an overly dualistic approach partly in response to the situation and times in which he lived, just as **Sŏ Kyŏng-dŏk** (Hwadam) had developed an overly monistic approach in his. Yi I, living in what he thought was an age of newly found confidence, addressed the issue with confidence based on his knowledge of the tradition. He stressed that principle and material force are never separate. Moreover, the heart/mind was also one. The concepts of the heart/mind of the Way (Ch. *dao xin* 道心) and the human heart/mind (Ch. *ren xin* 人心) were rooted in this, so that, even though they were valid concepts, in the end, they referred to the one heart/mind.

Like Sŏ Kyŏng-dŏk before him, Yi I emphasised material force, particularly, its imperishability and dynamism. Yi I praised Sŏ's insight into material force as the activating aspect of the **dao**, but criticised his work for not grasping principle as the source of material force. Yi I stressed the profundity of principle and material force, and although he, again like Sŏ Kyŏng-dŏk, associated principle with the Supreme Ultimate (**tai ji**), he criticised Hwadam's monistic conception of material force because it was not compatible with his belief that 'principle unifies, material force delimits' (Kr. *litong giguk* 理通氣局). On the other hand, Yi I, like Yi Hwang, made a clear distinction between principle and material force and asserted the superiority of principle. He also held principle as the foundation of material force and that the two could not be admixed. Although Yi I and Yi Hwang advocated the theory of principle's issuance, what they meant by the issuance of principle is quite different. Whereas Yi Hwang held a theory of mutual issuance, i.e., principle and material force issuing simultaneously (Kr. *Ho bal* 互發), Yi I insisted on the 'unity of the issuance of material force with principle mounting it' (Kr. *gibal lisung ildo* 氣發理乘一途) and thought Yi Hwang's theory was 'dualistic'. In this sense, Yi I's theory can be seen as an alternative to, and critique of, the monistic theory of Sŏ Kyŏng-dŏk and the dualistic theory of Yi Hwang. Although Sŏ Kyŏng-dŏk and Yi Hwang were contemporaneous their ideas were antithetical. Yi I, recognising the reality of material force and the transcendence of principle, proposed an alternative theory and stressed the profundity of principle and material force. Thus, the relationship between the Supreme Ultimate and **yin–yang**, and between principle and material force was one yet two, and two yet one. According to Yi I, principle permeates everything and original principle is ubiquitous, but there is no movement of principle outside the changes in reality, i.e. material force. In short, universal principle permeates the uniqueness of individual things.

Yi I thought the distinction between morality and profit or benefit was a false one, for him the relationship of these two concepts was clear – they were indivisible. Moreover, they were seen in terms of right and wrong in a way that linked morality and public benefit with being right, and saw personal benefit as harmful and wrong. 'Indeed, implement things that bring peace to the nation and benefit the people and never implement things that harm the people or endanger the nation.' Although this was seen as constant and the institutions developed had to be appropriate for implementing it, Yi I also thought institutions had to respond to things in a way which corresponded to the needs of the times.

References: Ch'oe Yong-sŏng, 1997; Huh Nam-jin, 1981; Hwang Jun-yŏn, 1995; Yi I, 1968, 1985.

NAM-JIN HUH

Yi Ik 李瀷
1682–1764
(*zi* Jasin 自新, *hao* Sŏngho 星湖)

Yi was a late Chosŏn-dynasty (1392–1910) Confucian scholar who had an important influence on the Practical Learning (*Sirhak*) School in Korea. He also trained a large number of students, which enabled a Sŏngho School (*Sŏngho hakp'a* 星湖學派) to develop. He was part of the southern faction (mostly made up of people who were affiliated with the Yŏngnam School but who lived near the capital, Seoul). He gave up seeking a government post and instead concentrated on scholarship after his father and an older brother were killed in a power struggle.

Early on Yi Ik followed **Yi Hwang**'s teachings, e.g., his ritual and metaphysical theories, supported Yi Hwang's ideas on the **Four–Seven Debate**. He also edited a collection of Yi Hwang's sayings as well as a new volume on the Four–Seven Debate. Even though Yi Ik carried on the Neo-

Confucian (*Sŏngnihak* 性理學) tradition he also presented a new practical focus. His scholastic method can be summarised as the pursuit of a sceptical spirit and focusing on present reality. Moreover, although his scholarship depended on an analysis of the Classics, he was not dogmatic and pursued new interpretations.

Yi Ik had a deep interest in western thought and religion, namely science and Catholicism, both of which were being transmitted to Korea in the seventeenth-century. Both also had an enormous impact on eighteenth-century Korea. He was one of the scholars who gained a deeper understanding of western science in the early eighteenth century. Not only did he hold western science in higher regard than Chinese science, he also thought that if the former sages reappeared they would do so too. Yi Ik also discarded the traditional view espousing the superiority of Chinese culture over that of non-Chinese 'barbarians' and the corresponding theory of Sinifying the barbarians. He saw in Catholicism some things he thought reinforced Confucian ethics, but he also critically examined it.

Yi Ik's students, however, split into two main groups over the issue of western science and Catholicism. There was an anti-western group that criticised Catholic teachings. This group included Sin Hu-dam 慎後聃 (1702–1761) and An Chŏng-bok 安鼎福 (1712–1791). The more positive camp included Kwŏn Ch'ul-sin 權哲身 (1736–1801) and Yi Ka-hwan 李家煥 (1742–1801). He also taught **Chŏng Yag-yong**. In this sense Yi Ik was an intermediary in both the introduction of Western Learning (**xi xue**) and its criticism.

Yi Ik formed a political policy moulded on the ideas of **Yi I** (Yulgok) and Yu Sŏng-wŏn, and called for reforming the social system. He also promoted policies to preserve and protect the common people as well as the equal well-field system and the liberation of slaves. In addition, he advocated that scholars should be able to devote themselves to farming and that officials should be chosen based on talent as well as recommendations and the civil service examinations.

References: Han U-gŭn, 1980; Kim Myong-gŏl, 1989.

JANG-TAE KEUM

Yi Jin-sang 李震相
1811–1878
(*zi* Yŏ-roe 汝雷, *hao* Hanju 寒洲)

A late Chosŏn Confucian scholar, Yi learned the Chinese classics and histories (Kr. *kyŏngsa* 經史) from his father. In 1871 Yi started the opposition movement to the edict requiring local Confucian schools (**Shu yuan**, Kr. *Sówón*) to be shut down or destroyed, and in 1876 he made plans to raise a defensive force against possible foreign aggression, although with the quick Japanese attack that year and their victory, his plans became irrelevant. At the same time, Yi often expounded upon the worrisome trends in the importation of Catholicism and western science. The main axis of his thought was precedence of principle (*li*, Kr. *i*) (*zhu li lun*, Kr. *chuinon* 主理論) of **Zhu Xi** and **Yi Hwang**. His own views on the precedence of principle were as follows: though the interval between Heaven and Earth is filled by **yin–yang** and material force (*qi*, Kr. *gi*), the controlling power behind changes in material force is the principle of the Supreme Ultimate (*tai ji*, Kr. *t'aegŭk*). Although the Supreme Ultimate has no form, before the creation of everything in the universe it already exists and is not awaiting the existence of the form of material force. When there is the Supreme Ultimate, there is activity and tranquillity (*dong jing*, Kr. *tongjŏng*), where there is activity and tranquillity there is division of yin and yang. When principle gives rise to material force, because the former is in material force, they move together and are tranquil together, but principle is the leader and material force is the physical form of activity and tranquillity.

Yi's works include the *Yi Jin-sang Munchip* 李震相文集, *Lihak Chongyo* 理學綜要, *Sarae chibyo* 四禮輯要, *Chunchu Jipjun* 春秋集傳, and the *Kujirok* 求志錄.

References: Yi Jin-sang, 1980, 1982.

NAM-JIN HUH

Yi jing 易經
(*Book of Changes*)

The *Yi jing*, also known as *Zhou Yi* 周易 or *Changes of the Zhou*, has been regarded as the first of the Chinese Classics since no later than the Former Han dynasty (206 BCE–8 CE). With canonical commentaries (*Yi zhuan* 易傳) that are supposed to have been written by Confucius himself, virtually all subsequent Confucian scholars have studied and commented on the text. But the place of the text in Chinese intellectual and literary history is by no means limited to Confucian schools. It has also been a fundamental text for Daoists and has been used by many Buddhists as well. Not only this, since its first publication into Latin in 1687, the *Book of Changes* has also become one of the best known Chinese texts in the West. The 'Xici zhuan' 繫辭傳 or *Commentary on the Appended Statements*, the most important of the canonical commentaries, says 'the *Changes* is on a level with Heaven and Earth and therefore is able comprehensively to assay the way of Heaven and Earth' (*yi yu tian di zhun, gu neng mi lun tian di zhi dao* 易与天地准，故能彌綸天地之道). Indeed, the text has often been treated as a microcosm comprehending the way of all the world.

The *Yi jing* is divided into two portions, a *jing* or 'classic' and *zhuan* or 'commentary', which were composed at different times but which since the Han dynasty have been considered together as one integral text. The *jing* portion is comprised of sixty-four units, each based on a diagram (*gua* 卦) composed of six lines that are either solid (–), understood to represent the *yang* principle, or broken (--), representing the *yin* principle. The combination of these six lines gives a shape such as ䷀ or ䷁. In the West, these six-line diagrams are routinely referred to as 'hexagrams'. There is no discernible pattern to the sequence in which the hexagrams appear in the text, except that they invariably come in pairs, the hexagrams either being inversions of each other (e.g., ䷂ and ䷃, the third and fourth hexagrams in the received sequence) or, in the cases where this would produce an identical hexagram, opposites of each other (e.g., ䷜ and ䷝, the twenty-ninth and thirtieth hexagrams). Each of these hexagrams is named, the names being of one, or sometimes two, Chinese characters. The name is followed in the text by a statement, usually short and quite formulaic; this statement is known as the 'hexagram statement' (*gua ci* 卦辭). Following the hexagram statement come six 'line statements' (*yao ci* 爻詞 or often simply *yao* 爻). These line statements are associated with the lines of the hexagrams by introductory tags indicating the position (*wei* 位) and nature (*de* 德) of the line; i.e., whether it is solid or broken. The positions are counted from bottom to top as 'initial' (*chu* 初), 'second' (*er* 二), 'third' (*san* 三), 'fourth' (*si* 四), 'fifth' (*wu* 五) and 'top' (*shang* 上), while the nature of the line is enumerated as either 'six' (*liu* 六) in the case of *yin* or broken lines or 'nine' (*jiu* 九) in the case of *yang* or solid lines; the combination of these two aspects gives tags such as *chu jiu* 初九, 'Initial Nine', *liu er* 六二, 'Six Second' (often translated as Six in the Second), or *shang liu* 上六, 'Top Six'. Then follows the line statement proper. Line statements may be comprised of any combination of three different types of text: an image, often just one clause of two or four characters, describing some aspect of the natural or human world, but sometimes also resumed with a rhyming couplet of four-character clauses that tie the image more explicitly to the human world; an injunction, usually introduced with the word *li* 利, 'beneficial', advising some formulaic course of action (e.g., 'beneficial to

see the great man' [*li jian da ren* 利見大人], 'beneficial to cross the great river' [*li she da chuan* 利涉大川], etc.); and a technical divination prognostication or verification, such as 'auspicious' (*ji* 吉), 'ominous' (*xiong* 凶), 'dangerous' (*li* 厲), 'no trouble' (*wu jiu* 無咎), 'regrets gone' (*hui wang* 悔亡), etc. The images are very often related to the name of the hexagram, and are often interrelated either by rhyme or by changes associated with the position of the line in the hexagram, or both. The text of *Ding* 鼎 (䷱) Caldron hexagram, the fiftieth hexagram in the canonical sequence, illustrates these various components of the *Yi jing*.

Caldron: Prime, auspicious, receipt.
Initial Six: The caldron's upturned feet.
Beneficial to expel the bad and gain a consort and her child.
No trouble.
Nine Second: The caldron is full: my enemy has an illness, it cannot reach me.
Auspicious.
Nine Third: The caldron's ear comes off: Its movement is blocked, the pheasant fat is not eaten, the borderland rains diminish.
Regret; in the end auspicious.
Nine Fourth: The caldron's broken leg: Overturns the duke's stew, his punishment is execution.
Ominous.
Six Fifth: The caldron's yellow ears and metal bar.
Beneficial to divine.
Top Six: The caldron's jade bar.
Greatly auspicious. Nothing not beneficial.

Although tradition ascribes the writing of this *jing* portion of the *Yi jing* to the sagely founders of the Western Zhou dynasty, King Wen (r. 1099?–1050? BCE) and Duke of Zhou (**Zhou Gong**) (d. 1032? BCE), and although it may well contain some material from about this time, it was probably not edited into its received form until toward the end of the Western Zhou (1045?–771 BCE) or even into the Eastern Zhou period (770–256 BCE). The text is quoted several times in the **Chunqiu Zuo zhuan** or *Zuo's commentary* on the *Spring and Autumn Annals,* usually in connection with the performance of milfoil divination. Internal evidence within the text of the *Yi jing* also suggests that this *jing* portion of the text was originally used in the performance of divination, as indeed later traditions concerning its composition and early use also attest. It is not clear just how the text was created in this connection. We do know that divination was routinely performed at the royal courts of ancient China, and the topics of divination could range across all aspects of life. Usually the topic of divination was some hope or wish that the diviner had. Milfoil divination was a special type of divination that involved sorting stalks of the milfoil or yarrow plant (*Achillea millefolium*). This procedure of sortilege produced a result that could be expressed numerically; in the divination tradition associated with the *Yi jing* these results were limited to groups of six. Presumably over time certain particular divinations came to be remembered as paradigmatic in some way, and the topics of these particular divinations – or perhaps more especially the images that the diviners associated with these divinations – were then associated in a generic way with a particular line, and then from that with a particular hexagram. Eventually lines were produced for each of the six lines of all sixty-four hexagrams, the lines within a single hexagram being consciously related to each other. Finally, the injunctions and divination terminology were probably added to the text as it continued to be used, now as a sort of handbook, in still further divinations.

As such a handbook of divination, the *Yi jing* is said to have been not subject to the Qin proscription against ancient texts in 213 BCE (see **Fenshu kengru**), and therefore to have been transmitted without interruption into the Han dynasty. The 'Rulin zhuan' 儒林傳 chapter of the **Han shu** provides a sketch history of the text's trans-

mission beginning with Shang Qu 商瞿 (b. 523 BCE), a first-generation disciple of Confucius, through Tian He 田何 (*c.* 202–143 BCE) at the beginning of the Han. Over the course of these centuries, the text probably began gradually to circulate together with the commentaries that would be recognised as canonical with the establishment of the Imperial Academy during the reign of **Han Wudi** (r. 141–87 BCE). These commentaries transformed the *Yi jing* into a wisdom text, even if its original divinatory nature was never forgotten (indeed, many traditions of *Yi jing* scholarship continued to focus on divination). It was as a wisdom text that it was elevated to the status of first among all of the Classics. The text circulated throughout the Han dynasty among both 'New Text' (*jinwen* 今文) and 'Old Text' (*guwen* 古文) scholars, with the 'New Text' tradition dominant throughout the Han, and it was the basis for the Xiping Stone Classics [*Xiping shi jing* 熹平石經] text of the *Yi jing* of 175 CE, of which about 20 per cent has been recovered (Qu Wanli, 1961). The 'Old Text' tradition became dominant thereafter, due largely to the prestige attached to the commentary written by Wang Bi (226–249), the earliest complete commentary still extant. From that time to the present, the text has never been out of circulation. The history of its exegesis would require something like a history of Chinese thought, too big a topic to be taken up here.

However, one of the great developments of twentieth-century Chinese scholarship, modern archaeology, deserves to be mentioned in connection with the *Yi jing*. In 1973, a silk manuscript of what we have been calling here the *Yi jing,* i.e., the texts of the sixty-four hexagrams, together with various types of commentarial texts (including a version of the '*Xici zhuan*') was found at Mawangdui 馬王堆 in Changsha 長沙 (Hunan). This Mawangdui manuscript, which dates to about 190 BCE, is the earliest text currently extant; with the exception of numerous phonetic loans, it matches the received text quite closely with one very significant difference: the sequence of the sixty-four hexagrams is completely re-arranged, the sequence of the Mawangdui manuscript being based on a mechanical combination of two sequences of the 'eight trigrams' (i.e., the eight possible three-line diagrams that can be formed by combining three solid and broken lines. (Shaughnessy 1996) While it would seem that this sequence owes to Han-dynasty divination traditions, it has caused scholars to reconsider how the *Yi jing* may have originally looked. Archaeology gives scholars reason to expect that they will have new evidence in the future with which to investigate this. Indeed, even as the present encyclopedia goes to press there are rumours that a still earlier text of the *Yi jing*, written on bamboo strips and dating to about 300 BCE, has recently been unearthed at Jingmen 荊門 (Hubei) and is now stored at the Shanghai Museum.

References: Legge, 1882: vol. XVI; Loewe, 1993: 216–28; Qu, Wanli 1961; Rutt, 1996; Shaughnessy, 1996; Wilhelm, 1950.

EDWARD L. SHAUGHNESSY

Yi li 義利
(Rightness and profit)

Yi in this term is rightness, righteousness or appropriateness and is here contrasted to *li*, which is variously understood as profit, benefit, gain or personal advantage. Potential (but not inevitable) conflicts between the pursuit of rightness and acquisition of gain were explored as early as the **Lunyu** and **Mengzi**, and they remained significant points of debate thereafter.

For Confucius, wealth was acceptable, but one had to have acquired it in an acceptable way, and he eschewed either rank or prosperity that was acquired without attention to rightness. Poverty, for him, was not an obstacle to apprehending the Way; gain was one of the topics, along with fate and humaneness, that he rarely discussed.

In the *Analects*, benefiting oneself personally without regard to rightness was unacceptable, whereas benefiting the people or the state at large was a sign of magnanimity.

Gain or benefit was not, then, inherently negative; the problem lay in the pursuit of personal benefit at the expense of benefiting others. Several passages in the *Analects* and the *Great Learning* (**Daxue**) praise officials who belaboured themselves to benefit the masses but condemn those who sought instead to enrich themselves at others' expense. When the pursuit of personal gain became the focus of the energies of people responsible for governance, it was believed, then various ills would befall the state. A state, hence, did not consider benefit itself to be a benefit, but instead considered rightness, which put the benefit of all before the gain of one person, to be true benefit (*Great Learning* 10).

It is this potential conflict of interest between self-enrichment and the enrichment of others that is at the heart of most discussions of rightness and profit. Fears of the seduction of profit and optimism about the strength to overcome it are expressed by Zilu (**Zhong You**) in the *Analects* 4: 12, where he notes that completely developed persons, when they see a chance for gain, think instead of rightness. Confucius asserted that when confronted with the choice between the two, one should always choose the latter. The ability to make this choice made one a noble person, or *junzi*, whereas a predilection for profit made one a petty person.

Some passages in the *Mengzi* seem more chary of gain and question the policy even of benefiting the state at large. For example, when King Hui of Liang asked Mengzi whether he could provide anything to profit the king's state (rather than the king personally), Mengzi responded that sooner or later, most pursuits of profit turn selfish. For the sake of the welfare of all and to preserve the security of the ruler himself, the king should focus instead on rightness and humaneness and avoid speaking of profit altogether. The choice to elect rightness over gain could be a life-and-death decision; given a choice, rightness should not be avoided even if it resulted in one's own demise.

In the Song era, **Zhu Xi**'s concern with rightness over profit was expressed in the rather poor circumstances under which he lived for most of his life and in his refusal to accept gifts he deemed inappropriate. He insisted on clear distinctions between rightness and profit in his debates with **Chen Liang** on those topics. Chen asserted that the two were not in essential conflict. Rightness, associated with heavenly principle, and profit, associated with human desire, could function in tandem and were not essentially in conflict, Chen claimed.

Lu Jiuyuan discussed rightness and personal gain at length, and in one public lecture on the subject he was said to have left his listeners in tears. Building upon the work of Mengzi, Lu asserted that rightness was part of the original mind of human beings. For Lu, rightness was associated with public-mindedness, whereas profit was associated with selfishness. Literati concerned themselves with the former, interacted with the realms of heaven, earth and other human beings, and sought to bring good governance to all under heaven. Lu believed that Buddhists were occupied with 'selfish' goals of seeking *bodhisattvahood* and left the world and their own families to pursue those aims.

Chen Chun also understood the notions of rightness and profit in terms of heavenly principle and human desires, respectively, and he catalogued various manifestations of the desire for gain in his **Beixi ziyi**. He associated rightness with impartiality and sharing; profit, with selfishness and greed. He asserted that material objects, the pursuit of an honest living or even marks of status and rank were not necessarily in and of themselves at issue; it was the motivations toward selfish personal gain they might incite that were problematic.

References: Ames & Rosemont, 1998: 9: 1, 4: 16, 19: 1, 20: 2; Chan, Wing-tsit, 1963d: 572–7 and 1986a: 69–85, 134–42, 1989: 61–89, 197–211; Hall & Ames, 1987; Lau, 1984: 1A: 1, 6A: 10; Shun, 1997a.

DEBORAH SOMMER

Yi li 儀禮
(*The Rites of Literati*)

The *Yi li*, compiled in the Warring States period in seventeen chapters (*pian*), is the first extant text to focus exclusively on ceremonial practices. Originally called either the *Shi li* 士禮 (*Rituals of Knights/Officials*) or *Li jing* 禮經 (*Rites Canon*), the text consists largely of detailed and specific descriptions of rites and liturgies to be employed by *shi*, a group whose composition changed from low-ranking members of the aristocracy in the *Chunqiu* period to 'men of service' in the Warring States and Han periods. Higher-ranking aristocrats (i.e., dukes) are mentioned only in a few passages devoted to court audiences; commoners not at all. The traditional attributions to the Duke of Zhou (**Zhou Gong**) as author and Confucius as editor are untenable, but content, grammar and text history all testify to the relative antiquity of the *Yi li*, as compared with its two companion texts, the *Li ji* and the **Zhou li**, which after **Zheng Xuan** were treated as a single corpus. In the Western Jin (265–317), the *Rites Canon* was rechristened the *Yi li* (*Ceremonials*), to distinguish it from the two other ritual canons in the corpus.

The received text of the *Yi li*, as stated by **Liu Xiang**, prescribes rites in this order of chapters: (1) *shiguan li* 士冠禮, the capping ceremony of common officers, representing the main rite of passage for males of twenty to manhood; (2) *shihun li* 士婚禮, the proper ceremonies of betrothal and marriage; (3) *shixiangjian li* 士相見禮, the exchange of courtesy visits between common officers; (4) *xiangyin li*, 鄉飲禮 the district symposium; (5, 7) *xiangshe li* 鄉射禮 and *dashe li* 大射禮, archery contests at the district and state level; (6) *yan li* 燕禮, banquet etiquette for aristocrats and great officers;

(8) *pin li* 聘禮, diplomatic visits; (9) *gongshi daifu li* 公食大夫禮, feasting a great officer; (10) *jin li* 覲禮, the vassal's audience with the king; and seven chapters (11–17) prescribing mourning attire and rites for every degree of relation among the aristocracy; post burial rites for the common officer; and procedures for sacrifices at the ancestral temple. (The chapter order varies from the orders proposed by the Former Han ritual masters **Dai De** and **Dai Sheng** and from the order found in partial versions of Han *Yi li* text excavated in 1959, in Wuwei [Gansu]). Notably, the *Yi li* omits mention of military rituals and state-sanctioned violence, despite their obvious significance in the early empires. Prescriptions in these chapters are invariably presented as straightforward descriptions of actual practice in an orderly state that is curiously feudal and bureaucratic at the same time. Devoid of literary embellishment, the *Yi li*'s prescriptions include no dialogue or anecdotal material. Instead, most *pian* (chapters) contain 'notes' (*ji* 記) appended to the basic 'description' of action; in *pian* 11, numerous comments labelled as *zhuan* ('interpretive traditions') have also been inserted within the main text.

While some modern readers are put off by lengthy 'reports' of the formal exchange of pleasantries, avid readers of Jane Austen or Miss Manners will find surprisingly little 'translation' required to move from one gentleperson's culture to another. The modern verdict that the *Yi li* is 'dull' – and so, unworthy of scholarly attention – suggests the stupendous achievement of the *Yi li*'s compilers, who successfully projected upon an idealised distant past a perfect aristocratic code (not unlike the European chivalric code, minus its romantic overtones), in hopes of hastening its adoption by all who aspire to true nobility of the spirit. This new code, embodied in an elaborate etiquette, imagines hosts and guests, no less than family members, bound together by their mutual determination to exemplify the charismatic virtue that alone confers true honour. And because it stipulates the exact wording, precise gestures, and suit of clothes to be employed at each stage of major rites, the *Yi li* text represents an important, even revolutionary tool by which to increase social mobility, for aspirants to high culture might just as easily learn admirable social skills by studying its text as by consorting with actual elites.

Etiquette books by and for classicists in imperial China, including that by **Zhu Xi**, took the *Yi li* as their model. Elites and would-be elites closely followed its prescriptions for capping, marriage, mourning and sacrifice. As a genninely older text, the *Yi li* is not that easy to comprehend. Readers still rely upon Zheng Xuan's commentary and Jia Gongyan's 賈公彥 (*fl.* 650) subcommentary. Hu Peihui's 胡培翬 (1782–1849) *Yi li zhengyi* 儀禮正義 (*Correct Meaning of the Yi li*) and Ruan Yuan's 阮元 (1764–1849) *Yi li zhu shu fu jiao kanji* 儀禮注疏附校勘記 (*Collated Notes on the Yi li Commentaries*) to elucidate the text; and Zhang Huiyan's 張惠言 (1761–1802) *Three Rites' Pictures* to illustrate it. Two translations are currently available to western readers: Séraphin Couvreur's 1914 *Cérémonial* (rpt Paris: Cathasia, 1951); and John Steele's 1917 *The I li, or Book of Etiquette and Ceremonial* (London: Probsthain).

MICHAEL NYLAN

Yi li zhixue 義理之學
(Learning of meaning and principle)

Mengzi speaks of the heart/mind (*xin*) as enjoying principles and righteousness (*li yi* 理義) so that the heart/mind could develop moral principles of the human nature for moral choices and moral actions. Here we see a possible double meaning of *li yi*, namely the principles of reason and righteousness, which are the foundations of a human-nature-based morality and the principles and meanings of reason as we reflect on our understanding of texts and experiences. But the hidden grammars of these two are different: *li yi* is concerned with how to reach principles of righteousness by reason (from *li* to *yi*), whereas *yi li* 義理 (meanings and reasons/principles) is about how to reach principles of understanding by meanings (from *yi* to *li*). This latter dimension of implication is basically hidden in Mengzi's discourse and would only become explicit when one came to the study of the Neo-Confucian philosophy in the Song Period. This explicit meaning of *li yi* indicates that we can fully understand principles through their meaning, which is in contrast with the Qing Learning (*Qing xue* 清學) that emphasizes that right understanding must come from the study of historical facts and the philological study of texts. In the Qing era *yi li* becomes completely neutralised from moral understanding and acts as a medium for seeking moral and/or metaphysical understanding of truth. In other words, according to Qing scholars such as **Hui Dong** and **Dai Zhen**, we need to concentrate on the question of knowing meanings of words and sounds or philology/phonology of texts before seeking out their hidden meanings and principles. For exploring the meanings of words and sounds in texts we need historical comparison of texts and analysis and critique of past commentaries (such as those by Han scholars) and this is called the study of historical meanings of texts (*xun gu* 訓詁). Once we have a clear grasp of the word meanings of texts can we then reflect on, and explore, the philosophical meanings of the texts either within the tradition or independently of the tradition. This is what is meant by the study of meanings and principles. To make historical inquiries about the authenticity of texts in order to assess the authentic status of a text is called the study of historical evidence (*kao ju* 考據). It is clear that *kao ju* and *xun gu* compose the mainstay of *Qing xue*, which is often referred to in English as Textual Criticism. By comparison the study of *yi li* is philosophical and can be speculative whether based on *kao ju* and *xun gu* or not.

CHUNG-YING CHENG

Yi Ŏn-jŏk 李彥迪
1491–1553
(*zi* Pokgo 復古, *hao* Hwaechae 晦齋)

Yi is one of the representative **Zhu Xi** school scholars during the mid-Chosŏn dynasty (1392–1910). At the age of twenty-three he passed the civil service examination and took a government post. In 1530 he was dismissed from office due to his opposing the promotion of Kim An-ro 金安老 and returned to Gyungju to pursue his research in Neo-Confucian Learning (*Sŏngnihak* 性理學). By 1537, Kim's faction was politically ruined, and again Yi was appointed to government. The purges of scholars in 1545 (Kr. *sahwa* 士禍) and subsequent false charges directed at Yi led him to exile in Gang Gyae 江界, where he was thereby able to write and leave for posterity his many texts. Yi played an important role in the establishment of Zhu's principle (**li**, Kr. *i*) precedent (Kr. *Churironjŏk* 主理論的) views; Yi's debates on the concept of the Supreme Ultimate (**taiji**, Kr. *t'aegŭk*) are the first serious ones in the history of Chosŏn *Sŏngnihak*, and this led later to **Yi Hwang**'s establishment of the *Sŏngni* theory of the Yŏngnam School (**Yŏngnam Hakpa**).

His later years in exile enabled him to produce many important works that have been handed down to today. In his work the *Guinrok* 求仁錄, he systematised the concept of humaneness (**ren**, Kr. *In*) in the Confucian classics explored by Chinese Song dynasty scholars. In a work Yi presented to his king entitled *Ilgang Sipmokso* 一綱十目疏 (Commentaries to the One Principle and Ten articles), the Way of Heaven (**tian dao**, Kr. *Ch'ŏndo* 天道) is adapted to provide the fundamental concepts of the Way of the king (*wang dao*, Kr. *wangdo* 王道) to help rectify the people's minds (*ren xin*, Kr. *insim* 人心) and to cultivate the foundation of the nation. Yi's *Ilgang* 一綱 (fundamental principle) is the proper mind of the king (Kr. *injuji simsul* 人主之心術) and the ten articles are the concrete subjects which the king administers. In his *Five Precautions* (Kr. *Ogyul* 五箴) of revering Heaven, cultivating one's mind, preserving one's respectful mind, remedying one's mistakes and having sincere intentions, he takes Heaven and the heart/mind to be central to his method of self-cultivation.

JANG-TAE KEUM

Yi Sang-ŭn 李相殷
1905–1976
(*hao* Kyung'ro 卿輅)

A philosopher and educator, Yi learned the Chinese Classics from early childhood and studied abroad at various Chinese universities, returning to Korea upon graduation from the Department of Philosophy at Beijing University in 1931. From 1945 he founded the Korean–Chinese Cultural Society, and for the next twenty years he devoted his energy to education as a professor at Koryo University. In 1956 Yi was invited to the United States as an exchange professor at Harvard and Yale, during which time he worked on the problems surrounding East–West comparative philosophy. Upon his return to Korea, Yi assumed the head of the Asian Problems Institute, a post he made great contributions to over thirteen years. With respect to important social issues, Yi participated in the movement opposing the exclusive use of *hangul* (the native Korean script), and was a leading demonstrator of the Seoul professorate protesting the rigged general elections of 15 March 1960. His name was afterwards included on a government blacklist of participants.

Yi's scholarship tended towards Chinese philosophy, and he made great efforts to explore the modern meaning of Chinese philosophy. In 1960 Yi was elected to the National Academy of Sciences and in the same year became the President of the Korean Humanism Society. In 1962 he was awarded a Ph.D. from Koryo University. Yi's works include *Modernity and Asian Thought*

(1963), *Confucianism and Asian Culture* (1976), and articles such as *Mengzi's Theory of the Goodness of Human Nature* (1955), *Humanism in Confucian Thought* (1961), all of which are collected in the *Yi Sang-ŭn Junchip* 李相殷全集(*Collected Works of Yi Sang-ŭn*).

References: Yi Sang-ŭn, 1998, 1999.

NAM-JIN HUH

Yi Su-kwŏng 李晬光
1563–1628
(*zi* Yŏnkyung 潤卿, *hao* Chibong 芝峰)

Yi was a leading Practical Learning (*Sirhak*) scholar of the mid-Chosŏn dynasty (1392–1910). In particular he stressed the need for a new practical method of government and extensive social change, freeing oneself from traditional *Sirhak* after the traumatic shock the nation suffered at the hands of the Japanese invasion in 1592. Yi was less interested in Korean Neo-Confucian Learning of Nature and Principle (*Sŏngnihak* 性理學), and more inclined towards seeking solutions to the problems of cultivating human mind and human nature. Accordingly, the *Yudo* section of his major work entitled *Chibong Ryusŏr* (芝峰類說) is divided into five sections: Confucian scholarship (Kr. *hangmun* 學問), learning of the heart/mind (Kr. *simhak* 心學), overcoming desires (Kr. *Kwayok* 寡慾), primary education (Kr. *Chohak* 初學), and investigating words (Kr. *Gyŏk-ŏn* 格言). He set aside the great importance attached to **Zhu Xi**'s thought by Korean *Sŏngnihak*, promoting instead a unique theory of self-cultivation. In 1625 he presented to the king a memorial indicating the various causes for social disarray. He went on to show how a standard of sincerity (**cheng**, Kr. *sŏng*) should manage all affairs and that sincerity is none other than practicality in one's mind (Kr. *sirsim* 實心) and in government (*shizheng*, Kr. *sirchŏng* 實政), which in turn would have its proper practical effect (Kr. *sirhyo* 實效). He asserted the requirement of 'substantial effort' in every thought and action. At the same time, an ethical element is required. While he did not reject traditional ethics, he did seek to manifest the concrete and the practical in the spirit of Practical Learning. Meanwhile he also was one of the first to introduce the Chosŏn government to western Learning (**xi xue**, Kr. *sŏhak*) as found in late Ming China, and played a leading role in introducing Koreans to this knowledge.

Reference: Keum Jang-t'ae, 1987.

JANG-TAE KEUM

Yi zhuan 易傳
(*Commentary to the Book of Changes*)

The *Yi zhuan* refers to the seven canonical commentaries that are usually found together with the *jing* 經 or Classic portion, combined in the *Yi jing* 易經 (also known as the *Zhou Yi* 周易 or *the Changes of the Zhou*; note, however, that *Yi zhuan* 易傳 is also the title of a famous commentary to the text by **Cheng Yi**, which is generally differentiated from it by the title *Cheng Yi zhuan*). Because three of these seven distinct commentaries are usually divided into two parts, thus giving a total of ten chapters of commentarial material, they are also often referred to as the 'Ten Wings' (*shi yi* 十翼). The commentaries are the *Tuan* 彖 or Judgement (divided into two chapters, *Shang* 上 [Upper], covering hexagrams 1–30 in the received sequence, and *Xia* 下 [Lower], hexagrams 31–64), *Xiang* 象 or Image (divided into *Da* 大 [Greater] and *Xiao* 小 [Lesser]), *Wenyan* 文言 or Sayings of the Text, *Xici* 繫辭 or Appended Statements (divided into two chapters, *Shang* [Upper] and *Xia* [Lower]), *Shuo gua* 說卦 or Explanations of the Trigrams, *Xu gua* 序卦 or Sequence of the Hexagrams, and *Za gua* 雜卦 or Mixed-up Hexagrams.

The *Tuan* explains the hexagram statements of the sixty-four hexagrams. It is usually found immediately after them in most traditional editions of the *Yi jing*. It usually combines trigram symbolism and 'line position' (*yao wei* 爻位) theory with standard lexicographical explanations of the text.

The *Da xiang* or Greater Image also explains the hexagram statements, and is found immediately after the respective *Tuan* commentary; it almost always employs trigram symbolism and concludes with a moral maxim. The *Xiao Xiang* or Lesser Image, on the other hand, explains the line statements, and comes after the respective statement; it regularly uses notions of 'line position' and 'line virtue' (*yao de* 爻德) to explain the line.

The *Wenyan* is devoted to the first two hexagrams of the *Yi jing*, *Qian* 乾 and *Kun* 坤, the pure *yang* and pure *yin* hexagrams; it is usually found at the end of those hexagrams.

The *Xici*, also commonly known as the *Da zhuan* 大傳 or Great Commentary, is a lengthy theoretical statement of the significance of the *Changes*, its text, composition, function and meaning. Already in the Han dynasty (206 BCE–220 CE), if not before, the *Xici* began to be quoted and paraphrased extensively, and by the Song dynasty (960–1279) it had come to be recognised as perhaps the single most important essay in Chinese philosophy, at least in terms of metaphysics. A version of the *Xici* was included with the manuscript of the *Yi jing* discovered in 1973 at Mawangdui 馬王堆 in Changsha 長沙 (Hunan); although it differs from the received version of the text in certain significant respects, since the manuscript was copied about 190 BCE it demonstrates that the *Xici* must have been in circulation no later than the late Warring States period (475–221 BCE).

The *Shuo gua* begins with an account of the creation of the hexagrams, and then goes on to attribute each of the eight trigrams to such categories as personality, animal, body part, social status, etc. In the Mawangdui manuscript, the account of the creation of the hexagrams in the received *Shuo gua* is found instead as part of the *Xici*.

The *Xu gua* provides a moralistic explanation for the sequence of the sixty-four hexagrams in the received text of the *Yi jing*. The *Za gua* gives brief characterisations of the hexagrams, combined in pairs but in a different order from that of the received *Yi jing*.

The composition of the *Yi zhuan* has traditionally been attributed to Confucius. However, beginning with **Ouyang Xiu** in the Song dynasty, some scholars have doubted this attribution. Ouyang noted that the various texts of the *Yi zhuan* contain divergent and sometimes contradictory statements, that some of the statements are mundane or even nonsensical, and include frequent quotations of Confucius (in the form 'The Master said' [*zi yue* 子曰]). He concluded from this that the texts must have been authored by disciples of Confucius, rather than by the Master himself. During the twentieth century, many scholars have gone further to argue that at least some of the texts of the *Yi zhuan* were probably not written until the Han dynasty, while others have strenuously upheld the traditional attribution of authorship to Confucius – or at least to his immediate disciples. The recent discovery and publication of the Mawangdui manuscript provides evidence for both of these viewpoints. While the inclusion of the *Xici* together with the text of the *Yi jing* or sixty-four hexagrams proves that at least this one important commentary was extant by the beginning of the Han, and suggests that it was in circulation well before that, the absence of any of the other canonical commentaries would seem to suggest that by 190 BCE when the manuscript was copied, the various texts of the *Yi zhuan* had not yet been combined into their present form. On the other hand, the inclusion of other, heretofore unknown, commentaries with the Mawangdui manuscript suggests that these were but some of many commentaries that were in circulation. It remains to be determined when and by whom these seven texts were first written and then eventually edited together.

References: Legge, 1882: vol. XVI; Loewe, 1993: 216–28; Shaughnessy, 1996; Wilhelm, 1950.

EDWARD L. SHAUGHNESSY

Yin Chun 尹焞
1071–1142
(*zi* Yanming 彥明 or Dechong 德充, master Hejing 和靖先生)

Yin Chun came from a prominent family of Luoyang 洛陽 in present-day Henan, and was a leading disciple of **Cheng Yi**. Yin's grandfather Yin Yuan 尹源 (996–1045) and his great-uncle Yin Zhu 尹洙 (1001–1047) were both well-known scholars connected with the reformer **Fan Zhongyan**.

Life and career
Yin Chun was still young when his father Yin Lin 尹林 died. At the age of twenty, he became a student of Cheng Yi. He competed in the *jinshi* examination of 1094, and was given a question on the punishment of the 'Yuanyou faction' which included Cheng Yi. Yin considered this a malicious insult to his teacher and left without answering. Young and righteous, he vowed never to participate in the examinations again. Cheng Yi pointed out that Yin had financial responsibilities, since his mother was still living. For her part, though, Yin's mother *née* Chen said she understood about him being nurtured by goodness, but did not know of being nurtured by an official salary. As a result of these circumstances, Yin did not take office until late in life.

In 1107, Yin was attacked as one of Cheng Yi's accomplices; also in that year, he was one of only four people who dared attend Cheng's funeral. Having served and assisted Cheng Yi for twenty years, Yin took it upon himself to gather Cheng's followers in Luoyang. He committed himself to collecting Cheng Yi's books and advancing his teaching.

Yin survived into the Southern Song period and was recalled to court. In 1135, he was summoned to be lecturer in a subsection of the Hanlin Academy, tutoring the emperor Gaozong (r. 1127–1162) on classical texts. When the Jurchen Jin envoys from the North came to sue for peace, Yin submitted his resignation in protest against peace negotiations, and was transferred to a minor post.

Scholarly position

When Yin Chun first went to study with Cheng Yi, he waited half a year before being given the **Da xue** (Great Learning) and **Xi ming** (Western Inscription) to study. Patient and persevering, Yin was the disciple most seasoned in the teachings of Cheng Yi, particularly Cheng's commentary on the **Yi jing** (Book of Changes). Because of his long career, he influenced many later Confucians; his scholarly lineage included **Lü Benzhong** and **Lü Zuqian**. Yin kept strictly to the teachings of Cheng Yi; he commented on the Classics and preached to his many students. Yin wrote commentaries on the **Lunyu** (Analects) and **Mengzi** and his occasional writings are preserved in the **Hejing ji** 和靖集. Yin's lack of originality in developing **li xue** further was a corollary of his stalwart advocacy and application of Cheng Yi's views.

Some later commentators have criticised Yin Chun for being too pedantic and impractical while lecturing at court. Yet Yin was able to hold fast to his values in an uncertain political situation. He never gave up his didactic mission to the political order, insisting at the last, 'My commentary on *Mengzi* is my posthumous report to the emperor.'

References: Chan, Wing-tsit, 1967: 69–71; *Song–Yuan xuean*, 1966: 999–1023; Liu, 1988: 71–5; Mao, 1986.

                                    THOMAS SELOVER

Yin–Yang 陰陽

The Chinese terms yin and yang are known in contemporary western popular culture as complementary cosmic forces manifested in such phenomena as darkness and light, female and male, moisture and dryness and soft and hard, respectively. These associated meanings, however, are largely later accretions of correlative thinking and Five Phases (**Wu xing**) theory of late Warring States and early Han times. The original senses of yin and yang are more difficult to discern in pre-Han texts. The terms appear infrequently as a pair in such texts as the **Shang shu** (*Book of History*), **Shi jing** (*Book of Poetry*), or **Yi jing** (*Book of Changes*), although they are developed to some extent in the **Chunqiu Zuo zhuan**. Of pre-Han works that eventually were considered canonical literati texts, the **Xunzi** speaks of yin and yang most frequently, but the concepts are unimportant in the *Analects* (**Lunyu**), *Mengzi*, *Great Learning* (**Daxue**), or *Doctrine of the Mean* (**Zhongyong**).

In the *Shang shu* and *Shi jing*, yin means cloudiness, shade or the north side of a mountain, which receives little direct sunlight; yang is sunlight or the south side of a mountain. Yin and yang are occasionally paired with wind and rain. One of the responsibilities of a ruler was to survey the conditions of yin and yang, or shade and light, before establishing a new settlement. In these texts, then, yin and yang are observable, natural phenomena whose movements could be predicted with some regularity through the progressions of the seasons. They had little or none of the metaphysical import they later carried.

In the *Chunqiu Zuo zhuan*, a more complex, if unsystematic, association of external natural phenomena with the inner operations of the human body was established in a cosmology that combined yin and yang; **qi**, or vital energy; and numinous phenomena such as souls, spirits, hemological humours and essences. Yin and yang, along with wind and rain and darkness and light, were two of the six vital energies of Heaven. Humans were possessed of two 'souls', a **po** 魄 material soul and a **hun** 魂 cloudlike soul, the latter being associated with the force of yang. Somewhat later, in the *Xunzi*, yin and yang were understood more broadly as principles of transformation.

In the *Appended Statements* to the *Yi jing*, alternations of yin and yang were deemed the Way (*Dao*) itself, a path fulfilled by human nature, which was considered good and was manifested in humaneness and virtue. Here yang and yin were indirectly paired with other dyads such as Heaven and Earth, activity and tranquillity (*dong jing*) and hard and soft.

Correlations between yin and yang and other metaphysical principles were rendered more complex in a system of thought attributed to **Zou Yan**, an elusive figure of the third century BCE. Zou's writings are almost entirely lost and he was rarely mentioned by his contemporaries, but he was nonetheless posthumously credited by Han historians with synthesising late Warring States' thinking on yin and yang, Five Phases theory, the geography of Heaven (*tian*) and Earth (*di*), and human values. Early Han thinkers such as **Dong Zhongshu** synthesised yin and yang into a cosmology that privileged the person of the ruler: Dong observed Heaven and Earth operating through the movements of yang and yin, giving greater value to heaven and yang (which he associated with the ruler and humaneness) and lesser value to yin (which he associated with the earth, the people, and human desires).

It was the *Appended Statements*, however, that particularly influenced later Song understandings of yin and yang. **Zhou Dunyi** in his *Taijitu shuo* asserted that yin and yang were produced by the Supreme Ultimate (*tai ji*) in alternate states of tranquillity and activity; these in turn give rise to the Five Phases and eventually to all things. **Shao Yong** similarly described yin and yang in terms of tranquillity and activity, but as processes of heaven and earth. **Zhang Zai**, on the other hand, perceived yin and yang more as movements of vital energy or material force (*qi*). **Zhu Xi**, following Zhou, nonetheless saw the phases of yin and yang as the operations of the heavenly mandate and moreover distinguished the Supreme Ultimate, which was above form, from yin and yang, which were below form (*xingshang xingxia*). Also departing from the *Appended Statements*, Zhu believed yin and yang were vital energy (*qi*), not the Way (*dao*).

In the Ming, **Wang Shouren** critiqued Zhou Dunyi's views on yin and yang, believing that he had too strongly differentiated them; they were the same vital energy (*qi*), Wang claimed, and tranquillity and activity were of the same principle.

References: Chan, Wing-tsit, 1963a: 137–8 and 1963b: 244–50, 1996: 169–73; de Bary & Bloom, 1999: 292–310, 318–25, 667–754; Graham, 1986; Legge, 1985a: 580–1, 618, 1985b, ode 250; Knoblock, 1988–94; Li Zehou, 1986; Loewe & Shaughnessy, 1999: 860–6; Pang Pu, 1985; Raphals, 1998.

DEBORAH SOMMER

Yitai 以太
(Ether)

In the **Ren xue** (*Learning of Ren*), **Tan Sitong** uses the term *yitai* to transliterate the English word 'ether'. Just like what is meant by 'ether' in the physical sciences of the nineteenth century, *yitai* refers to the material substance that diffuses throughout the world. As the basic unit of the world, *yitai* never dies but transforms in different forms and shapes.

Tan's concept of *yitai* owes as much to western science as to **Neo-Confucianism**. Like the Song–Ming Neo-Confucian concept of *qi*, *yitai* is the driving force that allows the world to regenerate itself. It points to the fact that the world is an organic network of force. For Tan, understanding the world as a system of force is the first step towards achieving *ren* – a sense of togetherness with all things and beings in this world.

References: Chang Hao, 1997; Fung, 1952; Kwong, 1996; Li Zehou, 1979.

TZE-KI HON

Yokoi Shônan 横井小楠
1809–1869
(*azana*: Shisô 子操; *tsûshô*: Heishirô 平四郎)

Yokoi Shônan – an accomplished scholar, swordsman, and political reformer – is credited with being the Confucian thinker who worked out most completely the political theory by which the **Meiji Restoration** was actually carried out, though the theory was carried into action by more famous men: Takasugi Shinsaku 高杉晋作 in Chôshû and Ôkubo Toshimichi 大久保利通 in Satsuma. In H.D. Harootunian's words, Shônan 'was at once the most realistic and the most visionary of late Tokugawa thinkers, the most original and imaginative, and also the most consistent and persuasive'. The fact that he had no prominent students who glorified his memory in the Meiji period (except **Motoda Nagazane**, who did not really understand his thought) prevented him, however, from attaining the immortality achieved by other bakumatsu thinkers like **Sakuma Shôzan** and **Yoshida Shôin**. The new theory he worked out was born out of the strategic defeat of more idealistic conceptions of 'restoration' put forward by Shôzan, Shôin, Maki Izumi 真木和泉 and Kusaka Gensui – a defeat that, in retrospect, was due to their failure to recognise the tenacity of domainal claims and their blurring of the distinction between the domestic and foreign crises through their stress on expulsion (*jôi* 攘夷). The new theory, articulated against the bakufu's advocacy of *kôbu gattai* 公武合體 (unity of court and shogunate) was known as 'sectionalism' (*kakkyoron* 割據論), meaning the idea that the newly emerging political space of the entire realm centring on the emperor depended upon the strengthening of domainal power. This concept was expressed well by Kido Kôin 木戸孝允 who, at the time of the first bakufu punitive campaign against his domain of Chôshû in 1863, wrote in justifying Chôshû's defence that 'Chôshû is the best utensil for curing the illness of the imperial country'. The key to the success of this approach was its separation of the external problem from the domestic, the first to be dealt with by domainal military strength based on western technology and organisation, and the second by strengthening local authority and local fiscal autonomy.

Shônan was born the second son of a samurai of Kumamoto 熊本 domain in Kyushu. He studied at the domainal school, the Jishûkan 時習館, where he distinguished himself for his prose and poetry writings in classical Chinese. In 1839, two years after being selected as head of resident students (*kyoryôchô* 居寮長), he was allowed to go to Edo at domainal expense to further his studies. Here he sought out teachers of practical learning such as the gunnery expert Egawa Tarôzaemon, **Satô Issai**, and Fujita Tôko of Mito. His friendship with Fujita Tôko got him an invitation to teach at Mito, but at this time (1840.2) he was recalled to Kumamoto for discipline on a charge of using improper language while intoxicated after a banquet. The resulting house arrest and loss of status impelled him to begin a fundamental reexamination of the way he had been educated. In 1841 he formed a study group of young men interested in a practical, reformist approach to Neo-Confucian Learning aimed at the unification of learning and government, inspired particularly by **Kumazawa Banzan**'s *Shûgi washo* and Fujita Tôko's *Kôdôkanki jutsugi*. This group became the core of a domainal faction called the *Jitsugakutô* 實學黨 (Practical Studies Party), which investigated military technology, medicine and political and economic conditions in western nations, putting forth detailed proposals for domainal reform in 1844. Shônan also opened his own private school in 1843, where Tokutomi Itsukei, a later leader in domainal reform and father of the famous critic and historian, Tokutomi Sohô (1863–1957), was among his first disciples. At first he basically followed the expulsionist thought of the **Mito School**, but a six-month trip around western

Honshû in 1851 (including almost a month as an honoured guest in Fukui 福井 domain) helped propel his thinking in new directions. In 1854 he began to voice disagreements with the Mito School, and henceforth he made *makoto* 誠 (sincerity) his standard of conduct in place of the *meibun* 名分 (status order) ethic of Mito. In 1855 he condemned the Mito lord Nariaki for approving the opening of the country as a stopgap measure at the expense of his own most fundamental principles and for leaving the handling of the diplomatic crisis in the hands of bakufu elders, who could not even respond effectively to the Edo earthquake of that year. He put forth an activist interpretation of the *Great Learning* (**Da xue**) insisting that renovating the people must not wait until virtue is illuminated, as the conservatives argued, but is itself the means to that illumination. In 1856 he argued that western politics and religion were far closer than those of Japan to the ideal of Confucian government, using Russia as an example to claim that in Christian countries politics, religion and (scientific) education are united (*seikyô itchi* 政教一致). Because there were other countries besides Japan and China that possessed virtue and true principles, Japan should open relations with such countries – a sign of virtue, not barbarism. This discovery of the Way in countries traditionally regarded as 'barbarian' enabled Shônan to abandon the Sinocentric conceit typical of traditional East Asian thought and his later call for a 'return to the Three Dynasties', interpreted as the principle of innovation in response to the needs of the times, liberated him from Song learning's commitment to defending a specific socio-political order. Shônan's progressive ideas had no chance to be put into practice, however, until he was invited to move to Fukui as a guest teacher in 1858. The domainal lord, Matsudaira Yoshinaga 松平慶永, leader of the reformist daimyo, had been put into forced retirement by the Ansei Purge of that year, and Shônan took over the direction of domainal government. On the basis of a Confucian theory of enriching the people through trade, he promoted active participation of the peasants in increasing raw silk exports, bringing great profits to the domain. The guideline he followed for his policies was his 1860 work *Kokuze sanron* 國是三論 (Three treatises on government policy), consisting of essays on 'enriching the state' (*fukoku* 富國) through industry and trade, 'strengthening military power' (*kyôhei* 強兵) through building a modern navy, and promoting the 'Way of the statesman' (*shidô* 士道) by educating men through both civil and military arts to devote themselves totally and selflessly to the task of good government. After Yoshinaga was appointed a bakufu counsellor in 1862, Yokoi Shônan served as his adviser. When he was at the peak of his career, working as adviser for national policy in Kyoto in December 1862, a group of Higo 肥後 (Kumamoto) retainers with whom Shônan was drinking was attacked by radical loyalist assassins from Higo. The domainal government recalled him and, finding him guilty of improper conduct for fleeing the attack, stripped him of his stipend and his seniority. Between the ages of fifty and fifty-five, he was under house arrest and prevented from playing any role in the Restoration. Upon his release he was made a counsellor in the new government, but he was assassinated in Kyoto at the beginning of the second year of Meiji by a group of radical expulsionist *rônin*. The reason for his assassination, apparently, was the interest he had shown some years earlier in Christianity as the 'political learning' behind the success of western civilisation, even though he had since come to realise that western political and scientific achievements could not necessarily be identified with Christianity. Among the many East Asian thinkers who worked to make Confucianism compatible with modernity, Yokoi Shônan may be the one who most succeeded in seeing beyond the dualism of 'East' and 'West' and finding an essential, universal principle in ancient Confucianism that could accept and even justify the abandonment of the accrued institutions with which institutionalised Confucianism had become identified since the Han dynasty (206 BCE–220 CE).

BARRY D. STEBEN

Yômeigaku 陽明學
(Wang Yangming Learning in Japan)

Wang Yangming (**Wang Shouren**) Learning never really established itself in Japan as a lineage or school in the full sense, let alone as a social movement as it became in China. However, its teachings were studied and propagated by a number of great individual scholars whose teachings were quite influential, particularly among samurai of independent spirit who were dissatisfied with the more rationalistic and conventional forms of Confucian Learning. Although he cites no concrete evidence, Tetsuo Najita has even argued that, 'Although trained to become bureaucrats, all *samurai* were instructed in the Ôyômei principle of action'. 'This principle held', he explains, 'that at critical points in one's life (and by extension, of society's as well) conventional reason and perceptions may not be helpful guidelines to action and that in these moments, one must reach deeply into his spiritual self and commit himself decisively to a course of action because he believes that course to be right, not because it might be advantageous' (p. 53). The most famous of the figures who taught or were strongly influenced by Wang Yangming learning are **Nakae Tôju**, his students Fuchi Kôzan (1617–86) and especially **Kumazawa Banzan**, Miwa Shissai (1669–1744), **Satô Issai**, Miyake Sekian (1665–1730), Ôshio Chûsai (Heihachirô), Yoshimura Shûyô (1797–1866), Yamada Hôkoku (1805–1877), Hayashi Ryôsai (1807–1849), Yokoi Shônan (1809–1869), Kasuga Sen'an (1811–1878), Ikeda Sôan (1813–1878), Saigô Takamori (1827–1877), **Yoshida Shôin** and Kusaka

Genzui (1840–1864). None of these figures, with the possible exception of Miwa Shissai after his conversion from the 'external seeking' of Shushigaku (Ch. *Zhuxi xue*), were 'pure' followers of Wang Yangming's teachings, but were influenced also by other streams of Confucian Learning or, as in the case of Tôju, Chûsai and Shôin, by later developments in the Ming dynasty Wang Yangming School. This fact has led to much scholarly controversy, with Bitô Masahide, for instance, emphasising the gulf between Tôju's thought and Wang Yangming's teachings, Ogyû Shigehiro arguing that Chûsai was more a follower of the Ming dynasty **Donglin School** than of Yangming himself, and many pointing out the weakness of the evidence for identifying Yoshida and Saigô with Yômeigaku. In view of Wang Yangming's emphasis on finding one's own inborn light of ethical judgement within one's own mind, as opposed to following some outside authority regarding the truth, such arguments sometimes seem a little overwrought. When Yoshida Shôin, for instance, wrote in the year of his execution that 'I am not exclusively a practitioner of Yômeigaku; it is just that the truth in Yangming's teachings often happens to coincide with my own truth' (*Komi bunkô*), it may indicate a closer spiritual affinity with Yangming than that of a mere 'follower'. But it is certainly true that the different cultural, social and intellectual environment of Japan, as well as individual differences in life circumstances, led to considerably different emphases in Japanese Yômeigaku than we find in China.

No matter how much their thought differed from Yangming, and no matter how great were the individual differences in their thought, it appears that all the Japanese 'Yômeigakusha' regarded the essence of Yangming's teachings as the practice of turning one's attention back upon oneself to find the light within one's own mind – seen as an indwelling divine illumination equivalent to the ultimate source of both human life and the natural world – and continuing this practice in one's daily activites by extending this inner light into all the affairs of one's life. Tôju wrote, for instance, that 'Within all human beings there is a spiritual treasure with which nothing in the world can compare, known as the supreme virtue and the essential Way. The most important thing in life is to make use of this treasure, keeping it in our hearts and practising it with our bodies. Above, this treasure flows into the Way of Heaven; below, its luminosity shines over the four seas' (*Okina Mondô*, 1). Banzan wrote that 'Sincerity is the root [of human life] through [being the Way of] Heaven'. 'Heaven is without mind and without desire'. 'All actions should not be done from the self; rather, one should act on the basis of Heaven. To respond to affairs as if one has no choice in the matter, without personal likes and dislikes, that is called acting on the basis of Heaven' (*Shûgi washo*, fascicles 15 and 9). Shissai wrote that 'Although there is a bifurcation into good and evil at the point where thoughts become active, the spiritual light of the original substance of these thoughts remains always luminous. When that spiritual brightness manifests itself from Nature without crossing over to human will and is capable of illuminating the good and evil that has arisen, it is called the innate knowledge. It is the light of the God of Heaven or Divine Spirit . . . If people can just turn back on themselves to this innate knowledge and allow its light to shine forth in the midst of their interaction (*kannô*) with things and affairs, then the disordered movements of the mind will cease, and all interaction with things and affairs will become the functioning of the Original Mind itself' (*Shigenkyô kotogaki narabini uta*). Issai taught that 'Everyone knows that the great blue expanse above them is Heaven, and that the still and yielding thing that spreads out below them is the earth. But they do not know that our own body, with all its hair, skin, and bones is earth, and that the intelligent and luminous consciousness of their own minds is

Heaven' (*Genshibanroku*, item 7). Chûsai argued that 'Lu Xiangshan (**Lu Jiuyuan**) wrote, "If a sage appears in the Eastern Sea, this mind is the same, and this principle is the same." Who is worthy of being called the Sage of the Eastern Sea if not the Great Kami Amaterasu herself? . . . The spiritual radiance of the Great Goddess corresponds precisely to the "innate knowledge of the good" taught by Confucius, Mengzi and Wang Yangming' (*Hônô shoseki shûbatsu* 2).

Another idea that runs through Japanese Yômeigaku, though not prominent in Tôju, is the centrality of *kokorozashi* 志 will or resolution – as both the foundation and the totality of the Way, an emphasis directly related to the moral activism characteristic of Wang's original teachings and expressed in the doctrine of the oneness of knowledge and action. In regard to the fourth of Wang's Four Dicta, 'Doing good and eliminating evil is the investigation of things (*kakubutsu* 格物).' Shissai wrote, 'This dictum is the vow and the guideline by which one enters into the practice of the Way. One should receive and practice it only after purifying oneself mentally and physically. In becoming a disciple of Yao and Shun (see **Yao Shun**), one must understand that the original aspiration (*honbô* 本望) is to relinquish one's body and one's life. One should make a personal vow to the Original Mind to this effect. By means of this vow one will be able to plant firmly the root of one's nature and establish an unwavering resolution' (*Shigenkyô kôgi*). Issai wrote, 'The highest thing is to take Heaven as your teacher. The next is to take a person as your teacher. The next is to take the classics as your teacher.' 'A person who has firmly established this resolution finds learning even in carrying firewood and fetching water, let alone in reading books and seeking for principles. A person who has not established such a resolution will be idly engaged even if he gives his whole day to reading. Thus in the pursuit of learning, nothing is more exalted than establishing one's resolution' (*Genshiroku* 2 and 32).

In reference to Confucius' statement in *Analects* (**Lunyu**) 15: 8 that 'The resolute scholar (*shishi* 志士) and the humane person (*jinjin* 仁人) do not seek life at the expense of humaneness', Chûsai wrote that 'Life is something that can be annihilated. Humaneness is the virtue of the Great Vacuity, and it is never annihilated for all time. It is misguided to throw away what can never be annihilated to protect what is annihilated. Accordingly, it is truly reasonable that the resolute scholar and the humane person choose the former and give up the latter. This is not something that is understood by the ordinary person' (*Senshindô sakki*, 19). By establishing and renewing in daily meditation a profound resolution to achieve the Way, petty thoughts, distractions and worries are swallowed up and an independence of the will from the powers of the external world is established. Moroever, as the resolution itself, to be completely sincere, involves a readiness to give up one's physical life and a faith in the immortality of the spirit, it can give a person the courage to stand up against external forces of evil in the name of what one knows in one's heart is right. Such a teaching had much appeal in the context of samurai traditions of valour and resolute fearlessness, and it offered samurai frustrated by the Tokugawa bureaucratisation and pacification policies a way to redirect their energies from vengeance and violence toward Confucian ethical and political goals. Thus it is not surprising that many of the *shishi* active in the radical loyalist movements of the 1850s and 1860s were influenced by Yômeigaku teachings.

According to Uchimura Kanzô, when Takasugi Shinsaku (1839–1867) – a disciple of Yoshida Shôin who was to become one of the major radical strategists in Chôshû domain – first came in contact with the Christian Bible in Nagasaki, he exclaimed 'This is similar to Yômeigaku! Let the disintegration of our country begin with this!' Uchimura also quotes Saigô Takamori's dictum that, 'A person who does not need

life, fame, rank, or money is difficult to keep under control. Only with such an intractable person can one share the hardships and carry through to completion the great work of the nation' (*Nanshû ikun*, 30). Uchimura (1861–1930), a nationalistic Christian who founded the 'No Church' Japanese Christian movement, felt that among all East Asian teachings Yômeigaku came closest to Christianity. To this it would be added that with its rejection of elitism, contemplationism, scholasticism and institutional mediation between divinity and the individual, it is much closer to Protestantism than Catholicism. Yômeigaku was also promoted by other Meiji-period nationalistic intellectuals with varying positions on the political spectrum, including Miyake Setsurei (1860–1945), Tokutomi Sohô (1863–1957), Kuga Katsunan (1857–1907), and Inoue Tetsujirô, as a form of moral cultivation capable of arousing a vigorous, progressive spirit of self-respect and independence among the Japanese people. Ogyû Shigehiro has argued that it was these western-influenced intellectuals who created the conception that Yômeigaku played a major role in the Meiji Restoration's overthrow of the old order, and that their 'modern' conception of Yômeigaku is quite different from the Edo-period variety. This view is supported by Okada Takehiko's emphasis that the radical activism of rebels such as Ôshio Chûsai and Yoshida Shôin was very untypical of Yômeigaku followers in late Edo Japan, most of whom believed in the renewal of society through self-cultivation and the teaching of ethics, and sharply criticised such resorts to violence and heroic action. For Yamashita Ryûji, on the other hand, the most important distinction within Yômeigaku is between the anti-authoritarian, individualistic, religious version of men like Uchimura and the statist, Japanocentric, ethical version represented by Inoue Tetsujirô. However, Uchimura also wrote that the logical culmination of Yômeigaku was Saigô Takamori's belief in Japan as a unified empire under the restored monarchy and in Japan's mission to conquer East Asia. Mizoguchi Yûzô has emphasised the gulf between the rigorous, life-and-death transcending character of Japanese Yômeigaku – whether before or after the Restoration – and the desire-affirming, naturalistic trends within the influential left wing of the Yangming School in late Ming China, which ended up giving Yangming Learning a bad name among mainstream Chinese intellectuals even before the fall of the dynasty. He points out that the meaning of the word *kokoro* 心 in Japanese differs from the meaning of the same character in Chinese, giving different connotations to Yangming's teachings that 'the mind itself is principle'. I would add that the concept of *makoto* 誠 (Ch. ***cheng*** sincerity) – the pure, single, and self-less condition of the *kokoro* so emphasised by the Yômeigakusha – also has a long and distinctive history in Japanese moral thought that is ultimately rooted in Shinto. Ogyû Shigehiro argues that the revival of the prestige of Yangming Learning in China among late Qing reformist intellectuals like **Liang Qichao**, **Zhang Binglin** and Sun Yat-sen 孫中山 (1866–1925) was largely a result of their period of exile in Japan, where they picked up the vocabulary and symbolism of modern nationalism and 'reimported' the modern Japanese conception of Yangming Learning back to China, where it has continued to be promoted by scholars of East Asian intellectual history under Communist Party rule. As for the inheritance of Yômeigaku in postwar Japan, its most prominent advocates have been Yasuoka Masahiro (1898–1983), prolific scholar, adviser to several generations of LDP prime ministers and friend of Chiang Kai-shek, and the famous novelist, playwright and aesthete, Mishima Yukio (1925–1970). An international conference in Kyoto in 1997 entitled 'What does Wang Yangming Learning mean to humanity and the earth in the Twenty-First century?' attracted fifty-four scholars of Yômeigaku from Japan and ten other countries or regions, as well as a large number of Japanese professionals, writers and creative leaders who in some way or other consider themselves practitioners of Yômeigaku teachings.

Further reading: Uchimura Kanzô, *Representative Men of Japan* (Tokyo: Keiseisha Shoten, 1908, originally published 1894); Tetsuo Najita, *Japan: The Intellectual Foundations of Modern Japanese Politics* (University of Chicago Press, 1974), pp. 43–55; Takehiko Okada, 'Neo-Confucian Thinkers in Nineteenth Century Japan'. In Peter Nosco, ed., *Confucianism and Tokugawa Culture* (Princeton University Press, 1984), pp. 215–50.

BARRY D. STEBEN

Yong 勇
(Courage)

Yong is one of the three profound universal virtues (***dade***) which a noble man (***junzi***) must fundamentally and necessarily possess. In the *Doctrine of the Mean* (**Zhong yong**) 20: 7, where *yong* is the courage or strength to proceed with the proper course of action one recognises by one's humaneness (***ren***), and in the same chapter, *yong* is described as being near to having a sense of shame, meaning that to know what is wrong, one has the courage to avoid evil, whereas if one has already committed the indiscretion, then one would have the courage to admit to it and make amends. Thus, in the *Analects* 2: 24 Confucius says, 'Faced with what is right, to leave it undone shows a lack of courage.' Then in 14: 4 he points out that 'A benevolent person (仁者) is sure to possess courage, but a courageous person does not necessarily possess benevolence.'

In the ***Mengzi*** 1B: 3 there is a distinction made between the courage of a common person (*xiao yong* 小勇) which can control others individually, and great or broadened courage typical of a ruler as applied to the ruled. It is also stated that 'If, on looking within, one finds oneself to be in the wrong, then even though one's adversary be only a common fellow coarsely clad one is bound to tremble with fear. But if one is bound to the right, one goes forward even against men in the thousands . . .' (2A: 2).

Wang Shouren makes reference to *yong* as a determination to cultivate the heart/mind (*xin*). For example, in a letter to **Huang Wan**, Wang wrote: 'When one is about to elatedly speak, one is able to have the patience to remain silent; when one's will and energy are rising, one is able to bring them back to normal; when one's anger and desire are reaching boiling point, one is able to make them reduce them: only the person of great *yong* is able to do these.'

References: Lau, 1970, 1979; Morohashi, 1960.

TODD CAMERON THACKER

Yongjia xuepai 永嘉學派
(The Yongjia School)

The *Yongjia* School was one of the three major intellectual schools in the Southern Song period (1127–1279), distinguished from both **Zhu Xi**'s and **Lu Jiuyuan**'s schools. Since most influential thinkers and leading figures of the intellectual fellowship came from the Yongjia area, such as **Ye Shi**, **Xue Jixuan** and **Chen Fuliang**, the school was called the *Yongjia* School. Being a strong critic of *dao xue* fellowship, the school of thought advocated practical learning that focused on resolving practical problems of society from the perspectives of institutional changes, applications of historical experiences and personal involvement in practical governance in order to save the Southern Song from its internal and external crisis. Philosophically, the school emphasised the unity of polarities, such as *dao* and material embodiments, principle and material force, the Supreme Ultimate and concrete things, inner mind and outer world and integrity and utility.

The *Yongjia* School was the extension of the renaissance of classical studies in the eleventh century. *Yongjia* scholars were nurtured from the very beginning by the Cheng brothers' teaching and shared the goal with Cheng brothers' teachings to revive Chinese culture. When *Yongjia* scholars departed from the mainstream of the *dao xue* group eventually, they still believed that they carried on the true tradition of Confucianism.

The formation and development of the *Yongjia* School was also the response to the southern Song's social and political crisis highlighted by the Jurchen Jin's military threat from the North and the corrupt government. *Yongjia* scholars tried to identify the real issues and provided concrete solutions from institutional points of view.

If we examine the changes that happened within the Song intellectual community, we find that the emergence of the *Yongjia* School came about as a reaction against Zhu Xi and Lu Jiuyuan's efforts to establish their own authority over Confucian Classics and direct intellectual development. The exclusiveness from *dao xue* fellowship, particularly from Zhu Xi's school, actually stimulated the *Yongjia* scholars to develop more solid ground in order to contend with the changing intellectual climate.

The development of the *Yongjia* School experienced different stages. Its origins could be traced back to the Northern Song when Wang Kaizu 王開祖 introduced the Cheng brothers' teachings into the Yongjia area with more emphasis on the study of history. **Zhou Xingji** was another important figure at the initial stage of the *Yongjia* School, who posed a question about the *dao*'s transmission between **Mengzi** and the Cheng brothers, and showed great interest in real social issues such as financial management.

Xue Jixuan's contribution laid the foundations for the *Yongjia* teachings. He became the first person in the *Yongjia* School to advocate the use of Confucian Classics as historical records, and continued to question the succession and transmission of the *dao* in the *Dao xue* system. Philosophically, Xue Jixuan emphasised the understanding of concrete things and believed that this was the only way to understand the *dao*. Talking about integrity and utility, he pointed out that integrity and utility could not be separated from each other and a balance in between needed to be established. In practical governance, Xue Jixuan set up a good example by paying close attention to the details of government administration, from financial budgeting to the reform of institutions. The issues he touched and the positions he took were further developed by later *Yongjia* scholars.

As the direct student of Xue Jixuan and the mentor of Ye Shi, Chen Fuliang played an important role in the transmission of the *Yongjia* learning. Restoration of North China was the core issue in Chen Fuliang's practical teaching and he believed that the ultimate purpose of institutional reform was to regain the power for the country and recover the lands lost to the Jurchen Jin. In his system, all the major points of the *Yongjia* School were reinforced, and in particular, history clearly became the approach towards current social issues, not the object of ethical cultivation. He conducted extensive studies of history and evolution of institutions, in which he presented unique perspectives and suggestions on military systems, tax reduction, land reforms and government operations. Chen Fuliang established his status in the *Yongjia* School by his arguments and practices focusing on institutional changes and this becomes the most important contribution he made for the *Yongjia* School.

Ye Shi's life experience and theoretical synthesis on the *Yongjia* teaching raised the school up to the highest level it ever had been. Ye Shi developed and fulfilled *Yongjia* teachings from different aspects. The most important philosophical argument for Ye Shi was that material embodiments had priority over *Dao*. As an extension of the philosophical arguments,

Ye Shi pointed out that the Ultimate was not something mysterious but the general attribute of all material things and the perfect state that those all-material things could achieve. Investigating things was neither investigating principle nor investigating mind, as Zhu Xi and Lu Jiuyuan claimed. To Ye Shi, to investigate things was to realise, or reflect upon, external actual entities by using the human mind, and therefore, it was a gradual process. One of the important contributions Ye Shi made to the *Yongjia* School was his active involvement in practical governance. He served in different positions at both local and central levels of government administrations. He left us lengthy articles with extensive discussions on restoration plans against the Jurchen Jin in North China, military strategies, land systems, financial reform, tax collection, and bureaucratic operations. In these articles, he advocated institutional changes and applications of historical experiences. By doing so, his practice set a good example of how to implement the teachings of the *Yongjia* School.

Overall, the *Yongjia* School provided alternative approaches and practices toward statecraft issues and intellectual changes that were happening in the Southern Song. After Ye Shi died in 1223, the influence of the *Yongjia* School declined.

References: *Song–Yuan xuean*, 1966; Lo, 1974; Niu, 1998; Tian Hao 1996; Tillman, 1982, 1992a; Ye, 1959, 1977; Zhou Mengjiang 1992; Zhou Xuewu, 1988.

Pu Niu

Yongkang xuepai 永康學派
(The School of Chen Liang)

Chen Liang founded his academy of Confucian Learning in Wuzhou 婺州, Yongkang (modern-day Zhejiang), because he was a native of this region. The Yongkang School became better known in some circles as the Longchuan xuepai 龍川 學派 (Longchuan School), named for the honorific title granted to Chen Liang himself. During several unsuccessful attempts to pass the *jinshi* exam, the young Chen had submitted memorials to the Song court, encouraging reform and attacking Qin Gui's (1090–1155) 'Peace Party' policy of appeasement in dealings with the Jurchen Jin. When his advice went unheeded, Chen Liang eventually returned to his home region to devote his time to study and teaching.

The Yongkang School followed Chen Liang's particular brand of utilitarian Confucianism, focusing on Confucian teachings as they applied to military, economic and institutional affairs. *The Rites of Zhou* (*Zhou li*) and the *Spring and Autumn Annals* (*Chunqiu*) played important parts in supporting the central tenets of the school. Chen's influential students included Yu Nanqiang 喻南強 (?–?, *zi* Boqiang 伯強, *hao* Meiyin 梅隱), Chen Liang's son-in-law Wu Chen 吳深 (?–?), and Chen Gang 陳剛 (?–?, *zi* Zhengyi 正已), among others. Works by his students include Yu Nanqiang's *Meiyin bitan* 梅隱筆談 (*The Random Notes of Master Meiyin*), as well as Wu Chen's *Shangshu biaoshuo* 尚書標說 (*A Standardised Commentary on the Book of History*) and *Chunqiu shibian tu* 春秋世變圖 (*Diagram of Worldly Change in the Spring and Autumn Period*) and *Chunqiu zhuan shoupu* 春秋傳授譜 (*Index for the Spring and Autumn Annals*). Chen Gang would later follow **Lu Jiuyuan**, who challenged **Zhu Xi**'s teachings with his own Xiangshan 象山 School of the Learning of Heart/Mind. The Yongkang School also enjoyed support from such like-minded scholars as Lü Ziqian, **Xue Jixuan**, **Ye Shi**, **Chen Fuliang**, and Ni Pu 倪朴 (?–?, *zi* Wenqing 文卿, *hao* Shiling 石陵).

References: Tillman, 1992b: 150, 157; Wu & Song, 1992: 1475.

JAMES A. ANDERSON

Yŏngnam Hakpa 嶺南學派
(The Yŏngnam School)

The Yŏngnam School formed around the thought of **Yi Hwang** (T'oegye) and **Cho Sik**, both of whom lived in the Yŏngnam region in Southeast Korea (present-day Kyŏngsang province). Both focused on the Learning of the Way (**dao xue**, Kr. *Tohak*), although after the demise of Cho Sik's School of thought the remaining students merged with the T'oegye School of thought, so the Yŏngnam School is often also referred to as the T'oegye School. In any case, the focal point of the school is the Cheng–Zhu School as taught by **Chŏng Mong-ju**, who was killed for supporting the Koryo throne, and Kil Jae 吉再 (1353–1418) who refused government positions and returned to his hometown. The line of intellectual descent in the early period is: Chŏng Mong-ju, Kil Jae, Kim Suk-ja 金叔滋 (1389–1456), Kim Jiong-jik 金宗直 (1431–1492), Kim Gwing-pil 金宏弼 (1454–1504), and Chŏng Yŏ-ch'ang 鄭汝昌 (1449–1504). The scholars also made up the early *sarim* 士林 (lit. forest of literati) group. And, although many of the scholars perished in the literati purges in the late fifteenth and early sixteenth centuries, the Neo-Confucian (*Sŏngnihak* 性理學) consciousness of the *sarim* group deepened. In the first half of the sixteenth century **Yi Ŏn-jŏk**, who asserted the correct transmission of **Zhu Xi**'s philosophy of principle in a debate over the Supreme Ultimate (*taiji*), was a forerunner in influencing the Yŏngnam School.

The core of the school was formed in the middle of the sixteenth century by Yi Hwang and Cho Sik, following Yi Ŏn-jŏk's work. Most of the scholars were located near the Nakdong River, with Yi Hwang in Andong and Cho Sik in Sanch'ŏng. There were no theoretical disputes between these two scholars, although there was a difference in their respective attitude toward scholarship and assuming government posts. In particular, Cho Sik was careful not to be drawn into metaphysical disputes like the **Four-Seven Debate** that Yi Hwang was involved in; rather, the former concentrated on practice. Also, whereas Yi Hwang focused on the idea of attentiveness or reverence (*jing*) in self-cultivation, Cho Sik looked at the relation between reverence and righteousness (*yi*), focusing on practice in society. Some of these minor differences in the character of each scholar's thought carried over to their students. However, after the execution of Cho Sik's leading student in a purge, the remaining students affiliated with the T'oegye group. Moreover, given the number of prominent scholars among Yi Hwang's students and, in turn their students, it is easy to see why the Yŏngnam School is often seen as synonymous with the T'oegye School. Included among this group are: Yu Sŏng-yong 柳成龍 (1542–1607), Kim Sŏng-il 金成一 (1538–1598), Chŏng Ku 鄭逑 (1543–1620), and in later generations, Yi Hyŏn-il 李玄逸 (1617–1704), Chang Hyŏn-kwang 張顯光 (1554–1637), Hŏ Mok 許穆 (1592–1682), and **Yi Ik**.

In the seventeenth century students in the Yi Hwang lineage criticised the ideas of Yi I and his followers, thus giving rise to the two main schools of thought in later Chosŏn – the Yŏngnam and the Kiho Schools, respectively. But, even while the intellectual lineage of the school was being established there was starting to be increasing diversity within the group, centred around the villages of Andong 安東 and Sangju 尚州.

In the later Chosŏn period the T'oegye (Yŏngnam) School had five branches. The first branch included Kim Do-hwa 金道和 (?–?), Kim Hŭng-nak 金興洛 (1827–1899) and Yu P'il-yŏng 柳必永 (1841–1924) of Andong and was linked to Yu Chŏng-myŏng. Kim Hŭng-nak continued the T'oegye line on self-cultivation and the structure of academics. His student, Kwon Sang-ik 權相翊 criticised Yi Ik for excessively emphasising material force in thinking about the heart/mind (*xin*), and criticised

Yi Chu-sang 李雲相 (1818–1885) for over-emphasising principle (*li*), thus reaffirming T'oegye's concept of the heart/mind. The second branch included Yi Chin-sang of Sŏngchu who deviated from T'oegye's theory on the heart/mind combining principle and material force; and instead asserted the idea that the heart/mind is principle alone (Kr. *Shinjŭgisŏl* 心即理說). He systematised the principle only theory. The third branch included Chang Bok-ch'u 張福樞 (1815–1900) who criticised Yi Chin-sang's 'principle only' theory (Kr. *Chuiron* 主理論) and adhered to T'oegye's original idea. Chang also developed T'oegye's theory of self-cultivation through attentiveness/reverence. The fourth branch included Cho Kŭng-sŏp 曹兢燮 (1873–1933) who affirmed the theory that the heart/mind combines principle and material force but went a step further in saying it could not be broken down into these two concepts. Thus, he argued against Yi Chin-sang and Ch'ŏn-U 田愚 (1841–1922). The fifth branch included people from Kimhae 金海 who returned to the Yŏngnam region; this included Hŏ- Jŏn 許傳 (1797–1886) and the scholars connected to him – Yi Ik, An Chŏng-bok 安鼎福 (1712–1791), and Hwang Dŏk-kil 黃德吉 (1750–1827). This group, drawing from both the Practical Learning (**Sirhak**) School and the School of the Way, was more concerned with governing according to moral principles than they were with metaphysical theories.

In sum, the Yŏngnam School continued the earlier *sarim* tradition and established theories of self-cultivation and the predominance of principle on a solid textual foundation. They also promoted a theory of governance based on the School of the Way.

References: *Chosŏn Yuhakŭi Hakp'adul*, 1996; *Hanmar Yŏngnam Yuhak Kyeŭi Tongyang*, 1998.

JANG-TAE KEUM

Yoshida Shôin 吉田松陰

1830–1859

(*na*: Norikata 矩方; *azana*: 字義; *tsûshô*: Torajirô 寅次郎)

Yoshida Shôin is the most famous of the activist *shishi* 志士 (men of high purpose) who led the anti-Tokugawa movement that culminated in the **Meiji Restoration**. Since he was martyred for the cause, and since many of his disciples went on to become the core leaders of the Meiji government, Shôin came to be revered as a national hero and as a symbol of the independence of spirit and courageous commitment to reform needed in an age of revolutionary change. Shôin was born in Matsumoto 松本 village not far from the castle town of Hagi 荻 in the province of Nagato 長門 (Chôshû 長州), the second son of a low ranking samurai-farmer named Sugi Yurinosuke 杉百合之助 who served the daimyô house of Môri 毛利. His father was known in the village for his diligence, sincerity, and respect for learning, as well as for his devoutness in worshipping his ancestors and the Shinto gods. His mother was from a well-off family, but did not disdain the farm work and other demanding tasks required of her in the Sugi household. At the age of five Shôin was adopted as heir by his uncle, Yoshida Daisuke, becoming legal head of the Yoshida house when Daisuke died the next year. The Yoshida house had traditionally served the daimyô and his retainers as hereditary instructors in the **Yamaga Sokô** School of military studies, and a second uncle, Tamaki Bunnoshin 玉木文之進, took up the task of educating Shôin rigorously in both Confucianism and military studies. Shôin proved himself a precocious student, and at age ten he donned his Confucian robe and went up to the domainal academy, the Meirinkan 明倫館, as an apprentice instructor. Less than two years later, in 1839, he was appointed provisional instructor in Yamaga learning. The next year he delivered a lecture on military strategy to the daimyô, who was quite amazed at his skills. At sixteen, while studying under a teacher of another school of military learning, he first heard about what was going on in the world outside Japan, and began to become aware of the momentous forces of change that were at work in the modern world. At the age of nineteen he was appointed an independent instructor, and only nine months later he presented a lengthy paper to the domainal government expounding his ideas for the reform of the academy. Aware of the dangers that imperialism presented to Japan, he wrote a book on coastal defense strategy. But his eyes really began to be opened when he made a trip around Kyûshû in 1850, at age twenty-one. While staying for seventy-some days in Hirado 平戸 and Nagasaki 長崎 he devoured 106 books – about the Opium War, conditions in the West, gunnery and artillery, as well as various writings by reformist Japanese scholars, such as the *New Theses* of Aizawa Seishisai. Invited aboard a Dutch ship by some Dutch sailors and sampling their rum and bread, his mind was filled with curiosity about the mysterious world across the sea which Japanese were still prohibited from visiting. In the next year he was allowed to accompany his daimyô to Edo, where he called on the scholars Asaka Gonsai 安積艮齊, Yamaga Sosui 山鹿素水, and **Sakuma Shôzan**. The first two, he reported, recognised the value of western Learning, but only for defence purposes, while Sakuma had devoted great effort to mastering various fields of western knowledge and fully realised its great importance for Japan. While making regular visits to study under these scholars, Shôin also participated in reading circles on the Four Books organised by fellow samurai of Chôshû. Gradually he realised that he must devote himself to learning the Confucian Classics, rather than military studies, in spite of the undeniable importance of the latter for the nation. From Edo he took off on a trip to the northeast, too impatient to wait for the requisite permission from his domain.

Realising this would bring blame on his whole family, he later turned himself in, and his domain punished him by revoking his status as a domainal vassal. This cost him his stipend, but it also freed him from his restrictive duties as a military studies instructor. On his northward trip he had stopped for some days at Mito domain, and his discussions with Mito scholars greatly intensified his interest in studying Japanese history to discover the true foundations of the national polity. While he was confined as punishment for his desertion, he resolved to read all seventy fascicles of the **Nihon shoki** and the *Shoku Nihon shoki* – Japan's two most ancient national histories – followed by other national histories written in the Edo period. Through investigating the historic relation between the Môri and the Tokugawa houses, it eventually occurred to him that the shogunate was not a necessary intermediary in the fulfilment of the bushi's loyalty toward the imperial court. Two years after his desertion, he received permission to travel again to Edo, intending to resume his studies under Sakuma Shôzan. He arrived in Edo on the 4th of the 6th month, 1853, one day after the arrival of Perry's four 'black ships', which were steaming around Tokyo Bay at regular intervals firing their cannons. Hearing that Sakuma Shôzan had gone with some of his students to Uraga to inspect the ships, Shôin hastened after them, and the two stayed on the coast to observe the Americans for almost a week. When he heard that his other two teachers in Edo supported the bakufu policy of opening the country, he indignantly condemned them as conventional Confucians without the courage to stand up for principle. Sakuma applied to the bakufu for permission to send students abroad to study, but when he was refused he still encouraged Shôin to go, giving him money for the trip. Shôin headed in the 9th month 1853 for Nagasaki in hopes of stowing away on a Russian ship, but he arrived too late, and made his way back to Edo. When the American ships returned in

the 3rd month, 1854, he rowed out to Perry's flagship and boarded, begging to be allowed to go to America to study. Because of suspicions that he might be a spy, Perry refused, putting him ashore under cover of darkness. The next day, in order to force public discussion of the issue, Shôin turned himself in. The interrogators recommended execution, but a friend of Sakuma in the bakufu intervened, whereupon, after five months of imprisonment with Sakuma, he was handed over to the Chôshû authorities, who imprisoned him for over a year at the Noyama prison in Hagi. Determined more than ever to explore the fundamental questions of political theory, during his term of imprisonment he read 618 books, wrote numerous papers to other scholars, and left a large collection of essays as well as his famous work *Record from Prison* (*Yûshûroku* 幽囚録). He initiated classes in poetry and calligraphy for his fellow prisoners, and in time began to give regular lectures on the **Mengzi** in which he related passages from the text to current issues and events, and used Mengzi's principles to advocate far-reaching institutional reforms. His object was to have particular loyalties to feudal superiors replaced by a Mengzi's style of loyalty to an abstract ideal of righteous rule, the Will of Heaven, which for him was personified by the emperor. His lectures were even attended by the jailor and his son, the latter of whom later became a student at his school. After his release into domiciliary arrest in the 12th month 1855, Shôin took over the academy at which Tamaki had taught from 1842 to 1848. His maternal uncle had been teaching nearby at a school called the Shôka Sonjuku 松下村塾 the 'Academy of the Village Under the Pines' – and Shôin's academy gradually absorbed its functions as well and took over its name. Here he began a career as an educator that was to have an incalculable impact on Japan's future. Like Confucius himself, 'Shôin ignored samurai rank in the admission of students to his school and in the treatment of them after admisssion.

The sons of farmers and craftsmen attended as well as samurai of the lowest ranks' (Huber, p. 25). As the fame of his teaching spread, idealistic young samurai from all over Chôshû began to come to Hagi to study under him, and many of them went on to become leaders in Chôshû's radical *sonnô jôi* 尊王攘夷 movement. For Shôin, however, *jôi* meant actively opening the country to trade, information, and knowledge in order to strengthen the power of the nation, and radically opening the gates of national leadership to those with talent and new ideas. After the shogunate signed the commercial treaty with the United States in 1858 without the imperial seal, the *sonnô jôi* movement turned radically against the bakufu, and Ii Naosuke responded by placing activist daimyô and nobles under house arrest and imprisoning over a hundred activist *shishi*, including friends of Shôin. Convinced that the bakufu must be resisted, and informed of a plot to assassinate Ii Naosuke, Shôin devised a plot to assassinate the supervisory agent of the police repression in Kyoto. When he requested the Chôshû government for aid, the pragmatic faction had him reimprisoned. From jail he continued to plan strategies for building an alliance between the Chôshû government and the imperial court, but when they were opposed, he finally concluded that 'My trying to make a partner of the government was the error of a lifetime. In the future I would surely like to try again, relying on proposals that use ordinary, independent persons (*sômô* 草莽, students and unaffiliated activists not directly engaged in domainal service)'. Discouraged and wearied by his failures and by opposition to his radical tactics from among his students, Shôin even lost interest in reading and writing. Before he could rebuild his morale, he was extradited to Edo for interrogation. The interrogators recommended banishment, but Ii Naosuke intervened and changed the sentence to death. As he was led to the execution block on the 27th of the 10th month, 1859, he turned to the attendant who had escorted him and said politely, 'Thank you for your trouble.' The most outstanding of his seventy-some students were Kido Kôin (1833–1877), Kusaka Genzui (1840–1864), Takasugi Shinsaku (1839–1867), Itô Hirobumi (1841–1909), and Yamagata Aritomo (1838–1922). Kido, Itô, and Yamagata survived the struggles through which modern Japan was born and became core leaders of the new Meiji government, imprinting the indelible mark of Shôin's ideas on the institutional foundations of the modern Japanese state. Two poems that Shôin wrote the night before his death are often quoted in Japan even today, particularly *Kaku sureba / Kaku naru mono to / Shiri nagara / Yamu ni yamarenu / Yamato damashii*: That such an act would have such a result, I knew well enough. What made me do it anyhow, was the spirit of Yamato.

See also H.D. Harootunian, 1970. *Toward Restoration* (Berkeley: University of California Press), pp. 184–245.

BARRY D. STEBEN

You 友
(Friend)

You indicates either a friend or schoolmate, someone who would help, or be helped by, another without hesitation. In the *Rites of Zhou* (**Zhou Li**), one can find the following definition: 'Those with the same teacher are called *peng* 朋 (schoolmate, friend), those with the same intention or mind (*zhi* 志) *you*.' This is reminiscent of Confucius' statement in the *Analects* (**Lunyu**) 1: 8 '. . . Do not accept as a friend anyone who is not good as you . . .' or of brotherly love in 2: 21 'The *Book of Documents* says, "Oh! Simply by being a good son and friendly (*you*) to his brothers a man can exert an influence upon government . . ."' Similarly, *you* can imply a love or kindness in friendship.

The relationship between friends (*pengyou* 朋友) is the fifth fundamental human relation (see **wu lun**), where a similar outlook and trust are the key. *Pengyou* features prominently in the Classics, but *you* more so. *Peng* is said to have overtones of more an established fact, whereas *you* is closer to a future, free thought or intention. Therefore, in the **Mengzi** 5B: 3 it is said, 'In making friends with someone you do so because of his virtue, and you must not rely on any advantages you may possess.' The way of friendship is a pure, selfless approach. Thus in a continuation of 5B: 3, 'In making friends with others, do not rely on the advantage of age, position, or powerful relations.' In the *Analects*, 16: 4, Confucius speaks of three kinds of beneficial and injurous friendships, 'To make friends with the straight, the trustworthy in word and the well informed is to benefit. To make friends with the ingratiating in action, the pleasant in appearance and the plausible in speech is to lose.'

References: Lau, 1970, 1979; Morohashi, 1960.

TODD CAMERON THACKER

You Ruo 有若
518?–? BCE
(*zi* Ziyou 子有)

You Ruo was a native of Lu and a prominent disciple of Confucius. He received sacrifices in the temple in 739 when he was ennobled as Earl of Bian 卞伯. He was promoted to Marquis of Pingyin 平陰侯 in 1267. The Song court considered his promotion on grounds that, after Confucius' death, the disciples wanted to serve him because he bore a striking resemblance to the Master. In 1738 he was elevated to a Savant, the last to be so honoured, twenty-six years after Zhu Xi, finally constituting the Twelve Savants.

THOMAS A. WILSON

You–wu 有–無
(Being–nonbeing)

You behaves roughly like 'there is' in classical Chinese and *wu* like its negation. So '*you* X' says simply that X exists and '*wu* X' denies it. This use, however, is best treated in the context of their use as two-place predicates (transitive verbs). '[Subject] *you/wu* [Object]' says that [Subject] has/lacks [Object]. This analysis neatly generates the straightforward existential sentence because preverbal terms (e.g., topic or subject) are optional in ancient Chinese.

The *you–wu* duality features in the secondary literature questioning whether Chinese thought has a 'being' concept. The traditional Parmenidean puzzle about being is how we can speak of what is not. A word's meaning is what it refers to, so 'nothing' we cannot *intelligibly* utter it. Some argue that no similar problem occurs in China because it does not invite the confusion Aristotle identified between the 'is' of existence (being) and the 'is' of predication (properties of things that exist). The latter is conveyed by **shi–fei** (this–not this). The former is conveyed by *you–wu*. Thus the western notion of 'being' is bifurcated in China into its two *proper* parts.

However, a similar puzzle about *wu* does seem to grip some Daoist thinkers and for parallel reasons. Chinese thinkers tended to treat all words as *ming* 名 (names) and to understand names as coming in pairs with a single distinction. Thus the Daoist worry took this form – where could the *you–wu* distinction *be*? Wherever we draw it, it would imply separating something off into two and that implies the world *has* both sides of the distinction.

This puzzle produces a doctrine with interesting similarities and differences from Parmenides. **Guo Xiang**, in an early medieval commentary on the *Zhuangzi* avers that no passage from *wu* (non-being) to *you* (being) is possible since there is only *you* (being). Unlike Parmenides, however, he notes that *you* (being) is constantly changing and it is that which the dual role of 'to be' best explains. The bifurcation of 'being' into two distinctions (*you–wu* and *shi–fei*) thus does not rule out a concept of 'being' in China but it does helps to explain why there is no problem of change.

The contrasting pair, *you–wu*, and the paradox became the focus of the speculations of post-Han Neo-Daoists who professed Confucianism and argued for the compatibility of Confucianism and Daoism. Buddhists joined in their 'abstruse discussions' with their own paradox about the nature of Nirvana/Buddha nature. The consistent tendency was toward *you* in Buddhism, but not far enough for later Confucians who habitually contrast their 'positive' view with the non-being or emptiness of Daoism and Buddhism.

References: Graham,   1990:   322–59; Hansen, 1992.

CHAD HANSEN

You Zuo 游酢

1053–1123
(*zi* Dingfu 定夫, master Jianshan 廌山先生, master Guangping xiansheng 廣平先生)

You Zuo was one of the leading disciples of **Cheng Hao** and **Cheng Yi** in the mid-Song period Confucian revival called *dao xue* or *li xue*. He has been considered one of the three pillars of the Cheng School, along with **Xie Liangzuo** and **Yang Shi**.

You Zuo was a southerner from Jianyang 建陽 county in present-day Fujian. His father You Qian 游潛 (1030–1095) lost his own mother at an early age, and so strenuously served his father that he had a village-wide reputation for filial piety. You Qian's third cousin You Fu 游復 was a friend of the Cheng disciple **Yang Shi**, despite their difference in age. You Zuo's older brother You Chun 游醇 attained the *jinshi* degree in 1079, and You Zuo followed suit in 1083. His first appointment was as commandant of Xiaoshan 蕭山 in Zhejiang. Then he was called to the capital and made an erudite at the Imperial Academy (*taixue boshi* 太學博士). In succeeding years, he was appointed as district magistrate of Heqing 河清 in present-day Henan, then a *taixue boshi* again when his benefactor Fan Chunren 范純仁 was Chief Counsellor. This was followed by various appointments as magistrate, prefect and investigating censor (*jiancha yushi* 監察御史), interspersed with sinecure appointments as temple overseer. You Zuo died in 1123, just as the military situation in north China was worsening in the chaotic years before the fall of the Northern Song, and he did not live to see the Cheng School's influence reestablished in the Southern Song.

You Zuo studied with both Cheng Hao and Cheng Yi; even at their first meeting in the capital, Cheng Yi saw potential in him. In 1081, You went to study with Cheng Hao while he was magistrate of Fugou. Both Cheng brothers were teaching the local young people there, and they called You Zuo to come as an apprentice. He happily accepted, and they officially received him as a disciple. When he was given **Zhang Zai**'s *Xi ming* to reflect on, he immediately felt no opposition in his heart and mind. You Zuo and Xie Liangzuo received special direction from Cheng Hao to practice quiet-sitting (*jing zuo*). This is one of the few direct mentions of the important Neo-Confucian spiritual practice of quiet-sitting in the Chengs' sayings.

Once, when You Zuo and Yang Shi were standing in attendance on Cheng Yi, Cheng was resting (or meditating) with his eyes closed. When he woke up, Cheng looked at them and said, 'Are you gentlemen still here? It's late now, please go and rest.' When they went outside, a foot of snow had fallen in the meantime. This story is still told in schools to demonstrate an exemplary attitude of students towards their teacher.

You's most controversial opinion concerned the study of Buddhism. He advocated reading Buddhist sutras for oneself in order to understand the differences between Buddhist and Confucian theories, whereas Cheng Yi had advised his students not to read Buddhist texts, lest they become confused. For example, in a saying that You Zuo himself recorded, Cheng Yi said: 'What I attack is the external traces [of Buddhism]; as for their *dao*, I don't know about it. If their *dao* does not accord with the former kings, then I'm not willing to study it. If it does accord with the former kings, then seeking it in the Six Classics (*Liu jing*) is enough – why do we need the Buddha?' **Hu Hong** considered You to be a 'betrayer' of the Cheng school (*Chengmen zuiren* 程門罪人) because he was against criticising Buddhism without doing one's own research.

You was especially interested in the *Book of Changes* (*Yi jing*) because of its comprehensive applicability. In addition to his *Yishuo* 易說, he produced a *Zhongyong yi* 中庸義, a *Lunyu Mengzi zajie* 論語孟子雜解, and his literary collection, *Jianshan wenji* 廌山文集. He also recorded the Chengs' sayings found in the fourth chapter of the *Ercheng yishu* (see **Ercheng quanshu**). Though You's own publications did not circulate well, nor did he have many followers, he was one of the mentors of **Lü Benzhong** and shares part of the credit with Yang Shi for the spread of the Cheng School in the southeast. Yang Shi paid him high tribute as a friend and companion in the *Dao xue* fellowship.

References: Chan, Wing-tsit, 1967: 79, 304; Dong, 1995: 588; Huang & Quan, 1966: 993–8; Tsai, 1982: 458.

THOMAS SELOVER

Yu Hyŏng-wŏn 柳馨遠
1622–1673
(*zi* Tŏkbu 德夫, *hao* Pan'gye 磻溪)

Yu was a pioneer in late Chosŏn Practical Learning (**Sirhak**). He was born in Seoul, receiving his early schooling from his maternal uncle Yi Wŏn-jin 李元鎮, who was the cousin of prominent scholar **Yi Ik**. Yu's Practical Learning thus later came to be inherited by his relative Yi Ik. At the age of fourteen Yu and his family were forced to evacuate to Wonju due to the Manchu invasion of 1636, and at the age of thirty-one he devoted himself to his private investigation of stabilisation measures of the rural economy and the formulation of a national administrative infrastructure policy. His writings are said to have amounted to more than twenty titles on a vareity of subjects, including the explanation of the Confucian Learning of nature and principle (*Sŏngnihak* 性理學), history, geography, phonology, literature and military strategy; however only his *Pan'gye's Treatises* (**Pan'gye Surok**) is extant. In this work, not only did Yu systematically compose his theory of administration, but also elaborated profound knowledge of, and minutely argued for, metaphysical theory.

Yu's quest to bring power and prosperity to both the common people and the nation as a whole led him to advocate a reformation of the land system, to aid independant farmers, to bring peace to the common people and to improve the economy. On this fundamental political theme of land reform, Yu asserted that land reform as an objectively measurable basis of production is a standard of social reform. His principle of reform relied on the cultivation of land by the people themselves and thus he held that neither private nor centralised ownership of the land was adequate, but rather, that the land should be publicly owned and allotted to individual male citizens in a fixed, equal amount. The overall yield would then have a standard levy imposed upon it. Yu requested the simplification and rationalisation of the administrative system and the salaries of minor bureaucrats, and that the selection process for bureaucratic jobs rely not on the state examination system, which Yu thought should be abolished, but rather on a system of supporting the cultivation of talented individuals.

Moreover, he wished to see the social system based on hereditary slavery abolished, and a variety of internal contradictions in the system reformed.

Yu's methods of reform came to be the foundation of later social system reforms by scholars like Yi Ik and **Chŏng Yag-yong**. A century after Yu's death, his *Pan'gye Surok* received high praise. Eighteenth-century Practical Learning scholar Pak Chi-wŏn 朴趾源 (1737–1805, *zi* Chong Mi 仲美, *hao* Yun Am 燕巖) praised Yu for his ability to organise the nation for war (an essential ability in the light of Korea's relations with its neighbours); and in the early nineteenth century Yi Gyu-gyung 李圭景 (1788–?, *zi* Paekkyu 伯揆, *hao* Ochu 五州) ranked Yu as one of Korea's foremost pragmatic officials.

JANG-TAE KEUM

Yu Ji 虞集
1272–1348
(*zi* Bosheng 伯生, *hao* Shaoan 邵庵)

Yu was born in Hunan, but his family relocated to Jiangxi when his father, Yu Ji 虞汲, a Hanlin academician and an intimate of **Wu Cheng**, was stationed there. Yu Ji the son became a disciple of Wu Cheng but had a more active role in Beijing in official position than did his mentor and became one of the greatest literati of the fourteenth century.

During the first three decades of the fourteenth century, Yu served in the Directorate of Education (*Guozi jian* 國子監), the Hall of Worthies (*Jixian yuan* 集賢院), at the Classics Mat 經筵 colloquium (with Wu Cheng) during the reign of Yesün Temür (the Taiding 太定 emperor, r. 1323–1328), and in the Hanlin Academy. In 1329, Tugh Temür (the Wenzong 文宗 emperor, r. 1328–1332), appointed Yu to the Academy of Scholars in the Kuizhang Pavilion (*Kuizhangge xueshi yuan* 奎章閣學士院), where he served for a year. The Classics Mat and the Academy of Scholars in the Kuizhang Pavilion promoted classical Confucian Learning and the arts among the Mongolian official class, and Yu introduced Tugh Temür to Chinese calligraphy and painting, wrote essays supporting the emperor's legitimacy and was the prime mover behind the compilation of the *Great Canon Governing the World* (*Jingshi dadian* 經世大典). Throughout his career, Yu Ji also distinguished himself as a fine essayist and poet.

Yu Ji developed an interest in Daoism through the influence of Wu Cheng, whose penchant for the mind-oriented thought of **Lu Jiuyuan** blended well with Daoist ideas, especially among the southern literati. It was through Daoists that Yu gained access to the Mongol court, which then allowed him to promote the interests of Confucians there. As with Wu Cheng, he was close to Wu Quanjie 吳全節 (1269–1346), the Yuan Daoist who became the head of the *Xuanjiao* 玄教 sect in 1322, introduced Lu's writings at court, and became one of Wu's supporters there. Yu also was on close terms with Wu Quanjie's master Zhang Liusun 張留孫 (1248–1321).

Yu Ji contributed significantly to the Confucianisation of the Mongol establishment as he shed his typically Southern Song loyalist sentiments, promoted Mongol dynastic legitimacy on Confucian principles and used connections with Daoists and cultivation of his relationship with Tugh Temür to make inroads for Chinese scholars at the Mongol court. His follower, **Zhao Fang**, a late Yuan specialist on the *Spring and Autumn Annals*, was introduced by Yu Ji to Wu Cheng's approach to self-cultivation through classical study and Wu's efforts to synthesise the ideas of **Zhu Xi** and Lu Jiuyuan.

References: Chen Yuan, 1966: 114, 128, 151, 167, 201, 205; Franke & Twitchett, 1994: 539–40, 554–6; Fu, Marilyn Wong, 1981: 381; Gedalecia, 1981: 186, 194–7, 202–203; Langlois, 1978, 99–116; Liu Ts'un-yan, 1986: 523–6, 530–1, 534; *Song–Yuan xuean,*

1966: 92: 40a; Sun K'o-k'uan, 1981: 212–53; *Yuan shi,* 1976: 181.

DAVID GEDALECIA

Yuan dao 原道
(*On the Origins of the Way*)

This essay is one of the most celebrated compositions by the Confucian polemicist and anti-Buddhist **Han Yu**. Written in a rhythmic and eloquent style, it achieves its effect as much through stylistic elan as sound argument. Its attack on Daoism and Buddhism is mainly at the level of externals, their social effects, rather than their religious goals. In it, Han argues that Confucian values of goodness and righteousness were paramount, that Confucian social values were essential to stability, that heterodoxies had become widely accepted and threatened good order. The world had forgotten that it owed its civilisation to the sages of antiquity, and had set aside the truths that had been transmitted as far as Confucius and Mengzi. Society should be purged of the corrosive influences of Buddhism and Daoism and should revert to the hierarchical structure required by basic Confucian teaching. The essay concluded by calling for the laicisation of Buddhist and Daoist clergy, the burning of their scriptures and the demolition of their buildings, so that the traditional beneficiaries of Confucian social concern, the widowed, the orphaned, the rejected and ill should be nourished.

References: Hartman, 1986; McMullen, 1989.

DAVID MCMULLEN

Yuan Mei 袁枚
1716–1797
(*zi* Zicai 子才, *hao* Jianzhai 簡齋, Cunzhai 存齋, Suiyuan Laoren 隨園老人)

A native of Qiantang 錢塘 (Hangzhou 杭州), Zhejiang province, Yuan was a poet, essayist, literary critic and advocate of women's literacy. Yuan showed literary talent from childhood and passed the *jinshi* examination in 1739. He took various posts as district magistrate in Jiangsu 江蘇. In 1748 he resigned from his official career and led a life of learned ease in his residential garden named *Sui yuan* 隨園 (Garden of Contentment), located on a hill called Xiaocang Shan 小倉山 in Nanjing.

Yuan Mei in many ways broke with the Confucian tradition and inspired a liberation in the literary arena in the mid-Qing period. He did not recognise the authority of history and the Classics, asserting 'the Six Classics are all dregs' (*liu jing jin zao bo* 六經盡糟泊). He extensively attacked the Confucian literary criterion of *Shijiao* 詩教 (moral purpose in poetry) and *dao tong* 道統 (transmission of the Way), a doctrine initiated by **Han Yu** and promoted during the Qing period by Yuan's contemporary Shen Deqian 沈德潛 (1673–1769). Yuan advocated his theory of poetry, known as *Xingling shuo* 性靈說 ('*innate sensibility*'), which was mostly discussed in his collection of *Suiyuan Shihua* 隨園詩話 (*Poetry Critique from Suiyuan*), in which he emphasised that the function of poetry is to delight, and the important point for writing poetry is the poet's knowledge, genius and individuality. He valued spontaneous expression of natural emotions in life and affirmed that sexual love plays an important role. He was the first to point out that the encomia of states (*guo feng* 國風) in the **Shi jing** (*the Book of Poetry*) were mere folk love songs instead of allegorical poems, a view given by Mao Gong 毛公 (see **Mao Heng**) and accepted as authoritative commentary for over a thousand years. Yuan Mei's notion was supported and expounded in detail by the French Sinologist Marcel Granet (1884–1940). Yuan also protested that women should have an opportunity to have an education. He vigorously affirmed that women should have the right to write poetry, accepting them as students and publishing their works.

His various works were compiled as the *Xiaocangshan fang shiji* 小倉山房詩集;

Xiaocangshan fang wenji 小倉山房文集; *Xiaocangshan fang chidu* 小倉山房尺牘, a collection of his letters; a cookery book; and *Zibuyu* 子不語 (*Ghost Stories Censored by Confucius*). His writing, being full of humour and charm, has been popular with foreign readers as well as the Chinese.

References: Hummel, 1943–4; *Qing shi gao*, 1970.

REBEKAH X. ZHAO

Yuan qi 元氣
(Primal vital energy)

The term *yuan* here means 'primal', 'primordial' or 'original' and connotes a condition of pristine oneness or completeness that exists prior to later differentiation. *Qi* is the vital energy, material force or living breath that pervades individual creatures and the cosmos itself.

Although vital energy was described in many pre-Han texts, the compound 'primal vital energy' appears only around the early Han in the writings of such scholars as **Dong Zhongshu**, who in his *Chunqiu fanlu* posited the existence of a primal vital energy that pervaded Heaven and Earth. Without describing in detail the nature of this force, Dong asserted that its permutations within the seasons of the year and in meteorological phenomena were profoundly affected by the moral character of the ruler (*wang dao* 王道, the Way of the King). Primal vital energy was further elaborated in the later Han by such thinkers as **Yang Xiong** and Wang Chong (see *Lun heng*). In Wang's cosmological schema of this energy, in which the ruler has no privileged position, it was the refined essence of Heaven and Earth, and all things partake of it. When a woman gives birth to a child, the infant is born replete with this primal energy (chapter on *Si hui* 四諱).

Later thinkers developed various conceptualisations of primal vital energy: **Liu Zongyuan** understood it in terms of yin and yang; **Wang Anshi**, as the fundamental substance of the way; and **Wang Tingxiang**, as a pivotal matrix of generation and transformation.

References: Su Yu, 1992; Zhang Liwen, 1994.

DEBORAH SOMMER

Yuan ren 原人
(*On the Origins of Humanity*)

This short essay of **Han Yu** takes its place along with two others, entitled 'Yuan dao' 原道 and 'Yuan xing' 原性, as expositions of some of the author's basic ideas that lie within the Confucian tradition. He sets out the traditional scheme of the three realms of the universe, which comprise Heaven, earth and the living creatures, the latter being situated in an intermediate place between the other two. Heaven is the master of the sun, moon and constellations; earth that of vegetation, mountains and rivers; and civilised man that of the living creatures, including human beings who are not assimilated to a Chinese way of life and the animal world. Should Heaven, earth and civilised man fail to maintain their correct order, the normal operations and regular movements of the heavenly bodies, of the natural features of earth and of members of the living world would be forfeited. It is the responsibility of the three masters to refrain from treating the individual elements within their realms with violence. Against such an eventuality, the true sage (*sheng ren* 聖人) practises his humanity universally.

M.H. KIM

Yuan Xie 袁燮
1144–1224
(*zi* Heshu 和叔, *hao* Xiezhai 絜齋)

Yuan Xie, one of the Four Masters from Ming Prefecture (*Mingzhou si xiansheng*), belonged to the important students of **Lu Jiuyuan**. He passed the palace examination in 1181 and began a political career which was, however, interrupted when chancellor Zhao Ruyu 趙汝愚 (1140–1196) and **Zhu Xi** had to leave their offices in the nineties of the twelfth century due to Han Tuozhou 韓侂冑 (1152–1207) starting his campaign to recover the northern central plain. After the fall of Han Tuozhou, Yuan Xie rose step by step to the office of a vice-director in the Ministry of Rites. Later he was removed from this position because he protested against the peace policies of the regent Shi Miyuan 史彌遠 (1164–1233) even though he could count some members of the Shi family among his students.

Yuan Xie is said to have added to the teachings of Lu Jiuyuan, which was focused on the term 'heart/mind' (**xin**) having both a socio-political and also a moral component. He said that the famous dictum of Lu Jiuyuan that the 'heart/mind is principle' (*xin ji li* 心即理) also implied that Heaven and Earth shared one and the same heart/mind and that, furthermore, this meant that princes and people had the same substance. A ruler was, according to Yuan Xie, not allowed to think of himself as elevated and of the people as mean, because this would have implied that for him the heart/mind was not one anymore. Thus, despite the seemingly abstract content of the philosophy of Lu Jiuyuan and his followers, Yuan Xie was very interested in social and political matters. It is for this reason that Quan Zuwang says that **Yang Jian** and Yuan Xie should be discussed in two separate chapters.

Among the works of Yuan Xie which have come down to us there are his collected literary writings (*Xiezhai ji* 絜齋集) in twenty-four chapters (*juan*), a commentary to the **Mao shi** as expounded in the imperial seminar (*Xiezhai Mao shi jingyan jiangyi* 絜齋毛詩經筵講義) and a commentary to the *Book of History* under the title of *Xiezhai jiashu shu chao* 絜齋家塾書抄. Besides Yuan Xie himself, his son Yuan Fu 袁甫 (*jinshi*,

1214) also became famous as a teacher. Yuan Fu wrote a discussion of some important passages from the **Zhongyong**, transmitting the family teachings to his son Yuan Xi 袁㴤 (?–?) and his grandson Yuan Pou 袁裒 (?–?). According to Quan Zuwang, except for the Hu family from Hunan (**Hu Anguo**, **Hu Hong**, **Hu Dashi** *et al.*, who successfully spread the fame of Hu Anguo's commentary to the *Spring and Autumn Annals*) there was no other family during the Song that could claim to have established a teaching of its own and transmitted it for more than two generations within the family. The Yuans can therefore be seen as belonging to the founders of the tradition of family academies.

HANS VAN ESS

Yuan xing 原性
(*On the Origins of the Nature*)

The second in **Han Yu**'s series of polemical essays on aspects of contemporary mores, the *Yuan xing* is addressed to the debate on the moral nature of human beings that took place at the end of the eighth century and the beginning of the ninth. The essay attempts to reassert the basic Confucian doctrine of human nature as an endowment at birth that was in one of three grades. In this, Han's ultimate authority was the *Analects* 17: 2, 'By nature men are close to one another; by practice they grow far apart. It is only the very wise and very stupid who do not change.' Han was confronted by Buddhist and Daoist concepts of human nature that saw it as a universal value to be realised by a process of contemplation leading to an enlightened state. These concepts in turn required taking a negative view of the emotions, as forces that obstructed enlightenment. In this essay and elsewhere, Han appears to have been reluctant to adopt a negative view of the emotions. He was by temperament an extravert, committed to anti-Buddhism at the level mainly of practical administrative action, and disinclined to explore the problematic of quietism and its role in an exclusively Confucian religious system. It was for this reason that he fell back on early formulations of the nature, which took little account of the experiences of either Buddhists or Daoists.

References: Barrett, 1992; Hartman, 1986; McMullen, 1989.

DAVID MCMULLEN

Yuanling yizhu 元陵儀注
(*Ritual Directives for the Yuanling Mausoleum*)

The *Yuanling yizhu* are a set of detailed ritual directives for the funeral of the Tang emperor Daizong 代宗 (r. 763–779). They were almost certainly compiled immediately after the emperor's death by the ritual commissioner, Yan Zhenqing 顔真卿 (709–785), a collateral descendant of **Yan Shigu**. They prescribe the rituals from the moment of the emperor's death until his burial, some five months later, at the Yuanling mausoleum, to the north-east of Chang'an. The death of an emperor had always been politically sensitive, and up to this time directives had been destroyed after use. The Yuanling directives, the earliest to have survived in China, were copied into the early ninth-century *Tong dian* 通典 (*Comprehensive Compendium*) by **Du You**. They show that the medieval emperors of China were buried according to rites based on canonical prescriptions contained in the **Yi li**, the **Zhou li** and the **Li ji** and on historical practice since the Former Han dynasty (206 BCE–8 CE). The imperial funeral sequence was also a grander version of the sequence prescribed for officials in the **Da Tang Kaiyuan li**. It moves through a series of rites, from the 'Calling back of the soul' (*Fu* 復) and the various rites for dressing the body (*Da xiao lian* 大小斂) to the rites for divining the final resting place (*Jiang zang*

shi zhai 將葬筮宅), for moving the coffin to the burial site, and for the rituals up to the end of the prescribed period of mourning. This was, for emperors, a period of twenty-seven days rather than the twenty-seven months prescribed by canonical sources for non-imperial individuals. The *Yuanling yizhu* and the anecdotal evidence that survives for the funeral show that the new emperor Dezong 德宗 (r. 779–805) used the rites to show commitment to correct political values, while Yan Zhenqing stressed the canonical qualities of austerity and filial piety, and kept the Confucian sequence from any taint by Buddhist and Daoist funerary practices.

References: Zhang Changtai, 1990; McMullen, 1999.

DAVID MCMULLEN

Yue ji 樂記
(*The Record of Music*)

The *Yue ji* is a chapter on music consisting of eleven sections and numbered nineteenth in **Dai Sheng**'s arrangement of the **Li ji**, and is recognised as the earliest fully elaborated musical thesis in the Chinese (or Confucian) Classics. It is believed to have been compiled by the Ruists (or Confucians) no later than the middle of the Former Han dynasty (206 BCE–8 CE) from various sources. Much of it dates from the Warring States period (475–221 BCE). To some extent overlapping with the **Yue lun**, the *Yue ji* explores the significance of music and the relationship between music, moral cultivation, governance and natural phenomena. It, however, rarely deals with musical theory.

References: Cook, 1995a: 1–96; DeWoskin, 1982: 85–98; Hong, 1976: 20–3; Liang Mingyue, 1985: 14–16; Zhang Hui-hui, 1991: 139–213.

HUI-SHAN CHEN

Yue jing 樂經
(*The Book of Music*)

The *Yue jing* (or *Book of Music*), also known simply as *Yue* 樂 (music), is one of the *Liu jing* (Six Classics) of the pre-Qin era (770–221 BCE). This text on music was considered as important as the *Li jing* 禮經 (*Book of Rites*), being regarded as the primary source of ancient Chinese musical thinking. However, there is no extant book, either because it was lost (perhaps in the Burning of Books in 213 BCE) or because its ideas are contained in the *Shi jing* (*Book of Poetry*) and the *Li ji* (*Book of Rites*).

References: Chen Wan-nai, 1982: 35–57; Kaufmann, 1976; Wang Jing-zhi, 1971: 1–14.

HUI-SHAN CHEN

Yue lun 樂論
(*The Discourse on Music*)

The *Yue lun* is a chapter on music numbered twentieth in the *Xunzi* and one of the earliest systematic musical theses identified with the Confucian school. It provides a theoretical basis for the Confucian concepts of ritual and music, indicating the important educational and reformational functions of music in a feudal society. It is written as a refutation of the denunciation of music by Mozi 墨子 (478?–392? BCE; Modi 墨翟, see **Confucianism and Moism**). Believing that music is indispensable to human life and has the power to influence military matters, the *Yue lun* presents descriptions of different kinds of music for ceremonies and classes.

References: Cook, S.B., 1995a: 1–96, 1995b: 372–456; DeWoskin, 1982: 53, 85–98; Wu Wen-zhang, 1994; Zhang Hui-hui, 1991: 83–107.

HUI-SHAN CHEN

Yuelu xuepai 嶽麓學派
(The School of Yuelu)

In 1147 the philosopher **Hu Hong** asked the regent Qin Gui to be appointed the head of the old Yuelu Academy, which had been deserted a long time ago. Although his request was not granted, the Yuelu Academy at Mount Heng nevertheless later became the centre of the scholarly tradition which Hu Hong had founded. 'Yuelu School' was the name for the group of students of **Zhang Shi** who had remained at Hunan. The most important representatives of this group were **Hu Dashi**, the son of Hu Hong, Peng Guinian 彭龜年 (1142–1206, *zi* Zishou 子壽, *hao* Zhitang 止堂), Wu Lie 吳獵 (1143–1213, *zi* Defu 德夫, *hao* Weizhai 畏齋) and descendants of **You Zuo** or You Jiuyan 游九言 (*zi* Mianzhi 勉之 and Yucheng 禹成) and You Jiugong 游九功 (1142–1206, *zi* Chengzhi 誠之, *hao* Mozhai xiansheng 默齋先生). Zhong Ruyu 鍾如愚 (*zi* Shiyan 師顏), one of Zhang Shi's followers and a member of the Yuelu group, even managed to become employed as the head of the academy.

After the death of Zhang Shi the Yuelu group studied with **Chen Fuliang**. They were also influenced by the teachings of **Lu Jiuyuan**, and furthermore, they were also close to the philosophy of **Zhu Xi**. However, some remarks which the latter made on the Yuelu scholars show that the old split between the Hunan and the Fujian schools persisted. For example, Zhu Xi said that trusting their natural ability the students of Hu Hong were not willing to read and to make their minds empty before they approached important practical matters. This reflects the different attitudes of Hu Hong and Zhang Shi on the one hand and Zhu Xi on the other concerning meditation and other mental exercises rejected by the Hunan group.

These differences are the rationale behind Quan Zuwang's rhetorical question in his introduction to the chapter on the

Yuelu scholars: 'Who says that after Master Zhang they were weaker than Zhu Xi?'

References: Chen & Zhu, 1992; Yang Shenchu, 1986; Zhu Hanmin, 1991.

HANS VAN ESS

Yun Hyu 尹鑴
1617–1680
(*zi* Hŭich'ŭng 希仲, *hao* Paekho 白湖)

Yun was a leading Confucian scholar who departed from the traditional **Zhu Xi** doctrine, to interpret the Classics in a unique way. He was born in Kyungju, and while living in Seoul as a boy, he repeatedly had to flee to the countryside on account of foreign invasions. He already had an academic reputation by the age of twenty, and two years later he moved to Kongju (公州) where he was to befriend many young scholars who would later become great Confucians of the **Kiho** School. At this time, Yun was not inclined to either one or the other views of the great Korean philosophers **Yi Hwang** and **Yi I**, but developed his original theories independently of Zhu Xi's works in his *Commentaries on the Grand Norms* (*Hongpŏmsŏr* 洪範說), *Commentaries on the Rites of Zhou* (*Juyaesŏr* 周禮說) and *Commentaries on the Doctrine of the Mean* (*Chung'yongsŏr* 中庸說).

Yun's views on Zhu's scholarship were respectful but he sharply contrasted with those of **Song Si-yŏl**, who held Zhu Xi to be the utmost authority. Yun's unrestrained, new interpretation of the Classics even led Song to call him 'the disruptive thief of Confucian tradition'.

These two scholars again clashed over the matter of funeral clothing of the king (who died in 1659) and after many years of power struggles in 1680 Yun was accused of perpetrating conspiracies, and was exiled and ordered to take his own life by poison.

The earnest attention and interpretation which Yun gave to the Classics is recorded in his *Toksŏki* 讀書記. One of the

characteristics of this work is his illumination of faith in the Lord on High (**Shang Di**, Kr. *sangje*) in the Classics, and its function in one's method of self-cultivation. When he was twenty-four, Yun stated in his diary, 'In everything there is but one: my adoration for the Lord on High; it fills everything', thus indicating that in all things, the Lord's orders and prohibitions are to be the standards by which humans behave.

Yi Ik's student Kwŏn Ch'ŏl-sin 權哲身 (1736–1801, *zi* Ki Myung 既明, *hao* Nok Am 鹿庵) draws the lineage of Yi Hwang's thought through Yun, to **Yi Ik** and then to himself. Next in line, **Chŏng Yag-yong** confirmed Yun's important place in Korean thought by taking up many of Yun's ethical interpretations of filial piety (*xiao*, Kr. *hyo*), fraternal love (*ti*, Kr. *jae*) and paternal affection (*ci*, Kr. *cha*) and his theory of self-cultivation by 'holding Heaven in awe and serving Heaven' (Kr. *wich'ŏn sach'ŏn* 畏天, 事天).

JANG-TAE KEUM

Yushan xuepai 玉山學派
(The School of Wang Yingchen)

The school founded by **Wang Yingchen** had as its most famous pupil the scholar **Lü Zujian**. Wang received the posthumous name Wending 文定, but he was known to his students as Master Yushan 玉山. The collected writings of this school are known by the title *Record of Yushan Learning* 玉山學案. Wang's most important students include You Bao 尤裒 (1124–1193, *zi* Yanzhi 延之), Lü Zuqian, Zhang Ying 章穎 (1140–1217, *zi* Maoxian 茂獻), Zhang Jie 張杰 (?–?, *zi* Mengyuan 孟遠), Zhao Zhuo 趙焯 (?–?, *zi* Jingzhao 景昭), Wang Jie 王介 (1185–1213, *zi* Yuanshi 元石, *hao* Hunchi jushi 渾尺居士), Zheng Qiao 鄭僑 (?–?, *zi* Huishu 惠叔, *hao* Huixi 回溪), as well as his sons Wang Boshi 汪伯時 (?–?) and Wang Kui 汪逵 (?–?, *zi* Jilu 季路). This school maintained that while their mentors **Zhang Jiucheng** and **Lü Benzhong** were both overly sympathetic to Buddhist thought, they had followed Zhang and Lü without showing any appreciation for Buddhism in general. Wang's teaching combined several different schools of Confucianism. At the core of his teachings, however, was the ability to control one's own desire through one's study of the *Book of Changes* (*Yi jing*), as well as the ability to restrict one's vices and indulgences through study of the *Book of History* (*Shang shu*). The school was formed around the concept of 'considering sincerity as one's foundation (*yizhicheng weiben* 以至誠為本)'.

Wang Yingchen adopted the teachings of the Cheng brothers' Yi Luo 伊洛 School, and studied the Wu Yi 武夷 School from **Hu Anguo** and the ZiWei 紫微 School from Lü Benzhong. Wang had heard that Zhang Jiucheng's Hengpu 橫浦 School was well established, and so Wang went to Zhang to study from him. Later, when Wang was demoted in the aftermath of court disagreement with Qin Gui and his followers, Wang continued to teach a small group of disciples. Friends and associates of Wang included Lü Da-tong 呂大同 (?-?), Zhao Ruyu 趙汝愚 (1140–1196), **Zhu Xi**, and **Lu Jiuling**.

Reference: *Song–Yuan xuean*, 1966: 1451–5.

JAMES A. ANDERSON

Yuzhang xuepai 豫章學派
(The School of Luo Congyan)

The Confucian scholar **Luo Congyan**, known also by his *hao*, Yuzhang, founded this school in the late Northern Song. However, the school of learning may be traced directly to the Song scholar **Yang Shi**, who had been Luo's principal teacher. This school has also been called the Fujian School, given the fact that its three main proponents were all natives of Fujian's Nanjian County. The Yuzhang School did not ultimately have a strong impact on the development of *dao xue* (the Learning of the Way). However, figures associated with this school included the teacher and the father of *dao xue*'s greatest promoter **Zhu Xi**. The Yuzhang School emphasised *guayu* 寡欲 (limiting one's desires) and *zhujing*.

According to the *Song–Yuan xuean*, Luo Congyan's teaching, through his student **Li Tong**, had a direct bearing on the *dao xue* learning espoused by the famous Southern Song thinker Zhu Xi. In fact, Luo, and later Li, had adopted the practice of 'quiet-sitting' to reach a clearer understanding of the unmanifested mind. Zhu Xi would, in turn, study 'quiet-sitting' from an elderly Li Tong. However, Zhu Xi would modify the practice to accommodate his belief that the manifested mind (the state of thinking after one's feelings were aroused), as well as the unmanifested mind, deserved equal consideration. Therefore, 'quite-sitting' as practised in the teaching of the Yuzhang School closely followed the practice advocated by **Cheng Hao**, while Zhu Xi's modifications of the practice incorporates the teachings of **Cheng Yi** as well. This school included Luo Congyan, Li Tong, Luo Bowen 羅博文, Liu Jiayu 劉嘉譽 and **Zhu Song**, among others.

References: *Song–Yuan xuean*, 1966: 1269; Ts'ai Jen-hou, 1986: 466; Wu & Song, 1992: 1467.

JAMES A. ANDERSON

Z

Zai Wo 宰我

or Zai Yu 宰予; 522–458 BCE
(*zi* Ziwo 子我)

Zai Wo was a native of Qufu and a prominent disciple of Confucius known for his oral and diplomatic talents. He received sacrifices in the temple as one of the **Ten Savants** in 712, was ennobled as Marquis of Qi 子我齊候 in 739, promoted to duke in 1009, given the title of Duke of Linzi 臨淄公宰予 in 1113, and called Master Zai Yu 宰子予 in 1530, when everyone enshrined in the temple was stripped of their noble titles.

THOMAS A. WILSON

Zeng Guofan 曾國藩

1811–1872
(*zi* Baihan 伯涵, *hao* Disheng 滌生)

Native of Xiangxiang 湘鄉 in Hunan, Zeng Guofan was a major figure in suppressing the Taiping Rebellion and a leader of the Self-Strengthening Movement. He was the first one in his farmer–gentry family to win an important post in the Qing government. Having earned a *jinshi* degree in 1838, he became a member of the Hanlin Academy. Before he was appointed to provincial posts, he served in the Board of Rites and the Board of Punishments. While he was in Beijing, he befriended the leading Neo-Confucian scholars of the Cheng-Zhu School (**Cheng–Zhu xuepai**).

Zeng's career in the Qing government would have been uneventful, had there not been the Taiping Rebellion (1850–1864). In 1852, after the regular army had failed to defeat the Taiping rebels, the Qing government decided to commission the important gentry families to organise local militia forces (*tuanlian* 團練). While Zeng was still mourning his mother's death, he was called upon to form the Hunan Army (*Xiangjun* 湘軍) to defend his native province. Combining his Confucian Learning with his military skills, he developed a private army based on friendship, local ties, personal allegiance and Confucian ethics. In the name of defending the Confucian social order against the Taiping utopianism, he succeeded in gaining widespread support from the gentry families to expand his campaign against the Taiping rebels beyond the Hunan borders. Because of the success of the Hunan Army, the Qing agreed to allow another capable scholar–official, Li Hongzhang 李鴻章 (1823–1901), to form the Huai Army (*huaijun* 淮軍) in Anhui. Appointed the president of the Board of War and the imperial commissioner for military operation in Jiangnan 江南, Zeng led a decisive campaign to crush the Taiping rebels in 1864.

Before his death, Zeng was a leader in the early phase of the Self-Strengthening Movement (1860–1894). Along with Li Hongzhang and Zuo Zongtang 左宗棠 (1812–1885), he introduced western military technology into China. Among his many westernising projects was the establishment of the Jiangnan Arsenal at Shanghai in 1895. Through Rong Hong (Yung Wing, 1828–1912), he bought machines from the United States to make guns and ships. In the arsenal, he set up a translation bureau to produce ninety-eight titles of western works in ten years.

Despite his interest in western military technology, Zeng was a Confucian reformer. Influenced by his early exposure to the Tongcheng (桐城) School (**Tongcheng pai**) of Confucianism, he was critical of the early Qing's philological learning for the lack of concern with moral cultivation. For him, personal ethics and family rituals were the two foundations of the Confucian social and political order. Among his writings, he revealed his moralistic concern most clearly in a collection of his family letters written while he was on tour of duty from 1856 to 1870. Known as the *Zeng Guofan jiaxun* 曾國藩家訓 (*Family Teaching of Zeng Guofan*), he reiterated the Cheng–Zhu teaching of building a social and political order based on personal ethics.

References: Porter, 1972; Qian Mu, 1937; Liu Kwang-ching, 1994.

TZE-KI HON

Zhan Ruoshui 湛若水
1466–1560
(*zi* Minze 民澤, Yuanming 元明, *hao* Ganquan 甘泉)

Zhan was from Zengcheng 增城 in Guangdong. After failing the palace exam in Beijing in 1493, he became discouraged and returned to Guangdong. In 1494 he became a student of **Chen Xianzhang**, who had already established a reputation for independence of mind by emphasising the importance of the heart/mind (*xin*), rather than relying exclusively on learning in achieving sagehood. The six years that he studied with Chen before Chen's death in 1500 had a profound effect on Zhan's entire life and thought, and his affection for his teacher was reciprocal – Chen referred to Zhan as his most accomplished student.

In 1505 Zhan again took the palace exam in Beijing, this time passing with a high score (ranking sixth that year) and receiving the coveted *jinshi* degree. During his time in Beijing Zhan met **Wang Shouren** (Wang Yangming), six years younger than Zhan, for the first time and they became close friends for the rest of their lives. In those early years he served in the Hanlin Academy, as an examiner for the palace examinations, and travelled as far as Annam 安南 (Vietnam) as a representative of the Ming court. In 1517 he built a school on Mt Xiqiao 西樵 near Guangzhou, where students came in large numbers to study under his tutelage. In 1522 he returned to Beijing to resume his official posts, and in 1524 became head of the Directorate of Education (**Guozi jian**) in Nanjing. In 1529 he served in the Ministry of Rites in Beijing, only to return in 1533 to Nanjing, where he was put in charge, successively, of the Ministry of Rites, the Ministry of Personnel and the Ministry of War. In 1540 he incurred the displeasure of the emperor through the publication of a work on the ancient *Book of Rites* (the **Li ji**) that apparently contained passages implying criticism of the emperor's policies regarding certain rituals. He was ordered to retire, which he did, returning to his home in Guangdong. From that time until his death on 16 May 1560, at the age of ninety-three, Zhan occupied himself with scholarly projects. He continued to found academies in several provinces, some thirty-six in all. He remained vigorous and sharp until the last, conversing with students frequently and taking an active role in their education.

The major intellectual influence on Zhan's early development was his teacher

Chen Xianzhang, to whose memory Zhan remained intensely loyal throughout his life. It was from Chen that Zhan acquired his emphasis on the importance of the mind in apprehending the true nature of reality, on the fundamental unity of all things, on the balance of the subjective and the objective worlds, and on self-reliance. Zhan Juoshui's own thought was centred around the concept of heavenly principle, *tian li* 天理, which he identified with the essence of the heart/mind (*xin*) before it was disturbed by the action of human desires. By disciplining the heart/mind a person could purify and restore one's own authentic nature, and reestablish the natural connections between the inner and the outer worlds. It was this focus on the power of the heart/mind that formed the connecting link between Zhan Ruoshui and Wang Yangming, and the basis of their intellectual discourse over the years. They both gave credence to the indispensable role of the individual heart/mind in cultivating moral character. Zhan, however, was unwilling to go as far as Wang did in setting aside the importance of Classical Learning. Although Zhan defined *gewu*, the 'investigation of things', as a process of realising heavenly principle, *tian li*, he strongly believed that Classical Learning provided a balance and standard of understanding necessary to prevent a potential tendency to subjectivism.

There is little doubt that Zhan exercised considerable influence on the philosophical development of his friend Wang Yangming. It seems reasonable to suppose that he played a role in diverting Wang from an early preoccupation with Daoist meditation practices and sitting in quiet meditation (see *jing zuo*). On the issue of the extension of innate knowledge, Zhan placed more importance than Wang on the need to cultivate knowledge of the objective world through the disciplined study of the Confucian Classics. In the formulation of Wang Yangming's notion of Heaven, Earth and all things in them as forming one unified body, Zhan appears, once again, to have had considerable influence on Wang Yangming.

References: Chan Wing-tsit, 1973: 9–30; Fang, Chaoying, 1976.

ALAN T. WOOD

Zhang Binglin 章炳麟
1869–1936
(*zi* Meishu 枚叔, *hao* Taiyan 太炎)

Zhang Binglin, a native of Yuyao (Zhejiang), was originally named Xuecheng 學乘. Later his admiration for **Gu Yanwu** prompted him to change his name to Jiang 絳. Zhang was among a few Chinese intellectuals whose influence was far and wide in both the academic circles and in politics. Few matched the breadth and profundity of his thought in the late Qing and early Republican period. Given his intellectual breadth and the complexity of his thought and experience, the term 'Confucian' is hardly adequate to characterise his ideological affiliation.

Zhang began his education by studying Confucian texts. In 1890 Zhang began his rigorous training in classical studies and philology at the Gujing jingshe 詁經精社 under the towering classical scholar Yu Yue 俞樾 (1821–1906). The next year, he began writing notes on various topics, which were later published under the title *Gaolanshi zaji* 膏蘭室扎記. The notes showed clearly that Zhang was reading extensively in Classics, history, literature and Chinese philosophy. In addition, he was reading books on western knowledge. The notes attested to his attempt to explain some passages and issues in ancient texts in terms of knowledge of natural sciences he obtained from translated books (*Gaolanshi zaji* 243–65).

After the Sino-Japanese war, Zhang joined the 'Society for the Learning of Power' (*Qiangxue hui* 強學會) and was actively involved in the campaign for reform under the leadership of **Kang Youwei** and **Liang Qichao**. After the abortive Hundred

Days Reform in 1898, he fled to Taiwan and then to Japan. He became committed to overthrowing the Manchu regime and engaged in heated debate with the reformists like Kang Youwei and Liang Qichao. Zhang contributed significantly to the revolutionary propaganda against the Manchu regime and the reformists. He advocated anti-Manchu revolution in the *National Gazette* (*Guomin bao* 國民報) and later in the *Jiangsu Gazette* (*Subao* 蘇報). He wrote a preface for the revolutionary pamphlet 'Revolutionary Army' (*Geming jun* 革命軍) by Zou Rong 鄒容 (1885–1905). He was arrested for his anti-Manchu writings with Zou Rong who died in prison. After Zhang was released, he went to Japan and became the editor of *People's Gazette* (*Minbao* 民報), the mouthpiece of the revolutionaries under the leadership of Sun Yat-sen in Japan.

Zhang's greatest contribution to the 1911 Revolution was his powerful rhetoric, which helped promote the cause of the revolution and to undermine the legitimacy of the Manchu regime through debate with the reformists. The fashioning of a revolutionary rhetoric was no easy task. Before 1900, under the influence of Social Darwinism, Zhang Binglin's perspective in his political writings was dominated by the issue of the struggle between the 'yellow race' and the 'white race.' The idea of a 'war of the races' put the Manchus and the Chinese in the same category of 'yellow race' and an internal strife between the Manchus and the Han Chinese would jeopardise the fight against the invading 'white race.' In his debate with the revolutionaries, Kang Youwei pointed out that the Manchus belonged to the same 'race' (*zhong* 種) as the Han Chinese. To drive a wedge between the Han Chinese and the Manchus, Zhang came to formulate the term '*Hanzu*' (漢族) or 'Han lineage', a concept combining indigenous lineage terminology with the imported notion of 'race.' The *Hanzu* Zhang narrated in his writing descended from Huangdi 黃帝 and was bound by a common language and history. He therefore

also referred to the *Hanzu* as a 'historical race' (*lishi di minzu* 歷史的民族). To differentiate the Manchus from the Han Chinese was critical to the revolutionary cause. Since culturally, the Manchus had become undifferentiated from the Han Chinese, Zhang stressed the tracing of surnames (*bian shi* 辨氏) as a reliable method to track the distinction. In his eulogy commemorating the anniversary of the founding of the Minbao, Zhang hailed: 'Long live Minbao! Long Live Hanzu!' If both the Manchus and the Han Chinese belonged to the same 'yellow race,' they were nonetheless different branches with initially different languages and histories.

To heighten consciousness of the oppression of the Chinese under the Manchu regime, Zhang underscored the need to study history and 'national essence' (**guo cui**). He strove to promote the study of 'national essence' which was crucial to the cultivation of nationalistic sentiment. Zhang explicitly stated that to promote national essence was anything but to encourage the worship of Confucius. By national essence, Zhang meant three things: language and writing, institutions and documents, and historical personages and their stories. The study of language and writing (*xiao xue* 小學) and history was the cornerstone of national culture, without which no nation would be able to survive.

As an exponent of Old Text Classicism (**guwen jingxue**, 古文經學), Zhang regarded Confucius as a historian and the Six Classics (**Liu jing**) history. After the abortive Hundred Days Reform, Zhang's disagreement with Kang Youwei was intensified as his dissatisfaction with the New Text Classicism deepened, and Zhang's disagreement with Kang was much more than just the result of his training in Old Text Classicism. His notion of national essence was much more inclusive than Confucianism, which Kang sought to make the national religion of China. For Zhang, Confucianism was hardly adequate in providing a cultural basis for the new nation.

With all the leading intellectuals of his time, Zhang believed that a unified language was crucial to the forging of a strong nation. He was aware of the problem for arguing a homogenous language because there was indeed a great variety of dialects. In tackling the problems of the lack of a unified spoken language and the disparity between speech and writing, Zhang argued that the critical condition for building a national language was already present. He sought to show in a few essays in the *Qiushu* 訄書 that the nine major dialects he identified developed originally from the same writing system. Marshalling evidences from different dialects and bringing them to his aid, Zhang sought to argue that there was a common spoken language that predated the writing system. Change in pronunciation had obscured their origin. By culling examples from various dialects and placing his extensive knowledge of phonology and Classical Learning at his service, Zhang argued that it was possible to show links of new characters and words to earlier states of the archaic language through identifying phonetic family resemblance and ideographic form. Zhang's formidable knowledge of philology and phonology helped to provide hope for a unified language based on a commonly shared writing system.

Given the critical role of the Chinese writing system in his political thought, Zhang was compelled to criticise and debate with those who called for the abolition of the Chinese writings. Wu Zhihui 吳稚暉 (1865–1953), member of an anarchist group in Paris criticised the Chinese writings as primitive and not suitable for educating the people. He called for replacing it with Esperanto. In response to such a radical proposal, Zhang made it unequivocal how important it was to preserve Chinese writing. He explained: 'when it comes to differentiation between nations, the individual distinction cannot be manifested without language'.

Despite his achievements in philology, phonology, and classical studies, Zhang was not a Confucian by his own reckoning. What linked him with Confucianism was his scholarship on Confucian texts. His interest and knowledge of Old Text Classicism were not meant to promote Confucianism, which was but one of several intellectual traditions he drew upon to fashion a broad cultural basis for the new Chinese nation.

References: Chang Hao, 1997; Chow Kai-wing, 1997.

KAI-WING CHOW

Zhang Jiucheng 張九成
1092–1159
(*zi* Zishao 子韶)

Zhang Jiucheng was a native of Qiantang 錢塘 in Zhejiang, although his family allegedly came from the Kaifeng region. While he was later known by the *hao Hengpu jushi* 橫浦居士 (The Retired Scholar of Hengpu), he adopted for himself the title *Wugou jushi* 無垢居士 (The Retired Scholar Without Blemish). Zhang received his *jinshi* degree in 1132, at which time he was ranked first among the successful candidates. Zhang's first political appointment was as vice-director of the Ministry of Rites (*libu shilang* 禮部侍郎). Political trouble soon followed Zhang, however, and he was forced to resign from his post. Zhang had received his position on the strong recommendation of Zhao Ding 趙鼎 (1085–1147), but through this association with Zhao he also made enemies, particularly among the supporters of Chancellor Qin Gui 秦檜 (1090–1155), who wished to appease the Jurchen threat from the North. Specifically, Qin Gui accused Zhang of fraternising with a well-known Buddhist monk Zong Guo 宗果 (?–?) from Jingshan 徑山 (modern-day Zhejiang), and this association brought Zhang difficulties at court. Zhang was eventually demoted to serve in the Nan-an Military Prefecture 南安軍 (in the southwest corner of modern-day Jiangxi), where he lived for the next fourteen years. Following

Qin's death, Zhang received another political appointment as prefect of Wenzhou 溫州. Zhang died of an illness at the age of sixty-eight. The Southern Song court under Emperor Lizong 理宗 (r. 1225–1264) granted Zhang the nominal ranks of Grand Preceptor 太師 and Duke of Chongguo 崇國公, along with the posthumous title Wenzong 文忠. His writings were later compiled in the collection *Hengpu ji* 橫浦集 (*The Collected Works of Master Hengpu*).

Although his reputation has fallen somewhat in Neo-Confucian scholarship since his day, Zhang is still credited with furthering the development of *dao xue* (the Learning of the Way). He had begun his studies under the renowned scholar **Yang Shi**. During his banishment to Nan-an, Zhang spent much of his time compiling his own commentaries on the Confucian Classics. He also produced a biography of the ancient Confucian philosopher **Mengzi**. As Hoyt Tillman notes, Zhang, as with fellow scholar **Hu Hong**, regarded human virtues to be closely tied to the 'mind of Heaven (*tian xin* 天心)', as revealed in the doctrines of ancient sage rulers. It was the 'mind of Heaven' that one sought with self-cultivation.

Zhang's teachings introduced more room for the accommodation of the basic tenets of Buddhism. Zhang himself was known to associate with students of Buddhist studies, and Buddhist thought exerted an influence on his own work. Qin Gui had, among other things, accused Zhang of having in his youth attended public lectures conducted by Zong Guo on Chan Buddhist ethics. Perhaps for this reason, the famous Southern Song thinker **Zhu Xi** was highly critical of Zhang's work, likening its Buddhist-tinged impact on Confucian thought to the cataclysmic floods of the Sage–King Yao's legendary age. In the mid-Ming the scholar **Luo Qinshun** would use Zhu Xi's criticism of Zhang's use of Buddhist terms to explain Confucian concepts as evidence that the Song thinker had wished to 'deceive the eyes and ears of the world'.

References: Bloom, 1987: 109; Tillman, 1992b: 7, 122; *Song shi*, 1977.

JAMES A. ANDERSON

Zhang Junmai 張君勱
1886–1969
(*zi* Shilin 士林, *hao* Lizhai 立齋)

Zhang Junmai was the most politically involved and internationally recognised figure among **Modern New Confucians** during the Republican period, known outside China as Carsun Chang. He was a multifaceted scholar deeply concerned about Chinese cultural renewal in posttraditional China. Due to his various roles in government, politics and teaching at Beijing University, Zhang was also a much sought after public speaker and made several world tours during his later life. Chosen as chairman of the Chinese Social Democratic Party in 1946, he intended to form a 'third force' political alternative to the Nationalists and Communists. Philosophically committed by 1921 to idealism which strongly opposed any form of materialism, Zhang was later noted for his consistent publicly expressed opposition to communism in general and the Chinese Communist Party in particular.

Born as Zhang Jiasen 張嘉森 into a large Shanghai-based family, he was trained at home in classical Chinese history, but educated in a church school which equipped him with English, Latin and exposure to studies in European philosophy and history. Later he studied law, economics, politics and German at Waseda University 早稻田大學 in Tokyo, earning a degree in political studies there in 1909. While in Japan he worked with **Liang Qichao** for constitutional reform before the 1911 Revolution, and so entered into Chinese political life. After serving in the Republican government for a few years, Zhang travelled to Germany and studied briefly at Berlin University. After the World War he returned to Europe, becoming influenced by two philosophers there, Rudolf Eucken (1846–1926) and Henri Bergson (1859–1941). Eucken's perspective on life philosophies (*rensheng guan* 人生觀) informed Zhang for wide-ranging public debates in 1923 about the values and limits inherent in science and life philosophies; Bergson's dualistic vitalism paralleled themes in 'Oriental' philosophy, prompting Zhang to study epistemology and metaphysics in a comparative philosophical manner.

Tensions between empirical knowledge and intuitive moral understanding Zhang found not only in European idealist philosophy but also in Song–Ming Confucianism, specifically in writings of **Zhu Xi** and **Wang Shouren** (Wang Yangming). At first approaching these from a dualistic metaphysical perspective, Zhang later argued they were resolved in an all-embracing moral heart/mind. This philosophical idealism Zhang found in the earlier teachings of **Mengzi**, noting its later development in both China and Japan by disciples of Wang Yangming. Because it confirms the reality of the material world, Confucian idealism is different from Indian idealism, but shares with all idealisms that the ultimate source of the external world is the mind. It was this moral-minded Confucian perspective that Zhang promoted as the basis for Chinese cultural revival along with other modern New Confucians in Hong Kong in the 1958 'Confucian Manifesto', adding the lengthy document to the end of his two-volume work on the history of Neo-Confucianism in order to emphasise their continuity with Neo-Confucianism.

Writing often about constitutional law, international affairs and political problems, Zhang provided intellectual and political support for the New Confucian scholars-in-exile, and was a major participant in debates between **Confucianism and Marxism**.

References: Carsun Chang, 1957, 1962; Fang & Li, 1995: vol. I, 199–428; Fang & Zheng, 1995: 24–63; Li Yi, 1994.

LAUREN PFISTER

Zhang Shi 張栻
(1133–1180)
(*zi* Jingfu 敬夫, *hao* Nanxuan 南軒)

Born as the son of the general Zhang Jun 張浚 (1097–1164) who had – with poor success – defended the Sichuan and Shaanxi border against the invading Jurchen troops after 1127 and who had held the highest state office during the so-called 'small Yuanyou period' (1134–1137), Zhang Shi grew up near Mount Heng where his father had been banished due to his opposition to the peace policy of Qin Hui 秦檜 (1090–1155). When Zhang Jun was recalled from his banishment in Hunan to supervise bureaucratic affairs in Jiankang 建康 (Nanjing) in 1161, his son went to study with the philosopher **Hu Hong** who lived nearby in Hunan. Although Hu Hong died only a few months later, Zhang Shi later was to emerge as his most influential student. During the sixties of the twelfth century he was regarded by many as the greatest living philosopher. He followed his father to the capital and stayed there until 1164 when he had to return to Hunan because he belonged to the war faction which was ousted by the supporters of peace. In 1171 Emperor Xiaozong (r. 1162–1189) of the Southern Song recalled Zhang Shi to court but a year later he again had to leave. Between 1174 and 1180 Zhang Shi served as pacification commissioner responsible for all military affairs first in Jingjiang 靜江 (Guilin 桂林) and then in Hubei. He is known to have destroyed heterodox cults in Jingjiang and to have successfully reestablished military order in Hubei which as a border province housed large contingents of unruly garrison-troops.

After his first meeting with Hu Hong, Zhang Shi wrote a letter about humaneness (*ren*). Hu Hong is said to have been so excited about the capacities of his student that he exclaimed: 'The school of the sages has such a person; how fortunate, how fortunate for this Dao of ours!' Later, Zhang Shi wrote a second essay about humaneness, and this term was also the main topic of his treatise on *Admiring Yanzi* (*Xi Yan lu* 希顏錄). Besides these short pieces he produced commentaries to the *Book of Changes* (**Yi jing**) (*Nanxuan Yi shuo* 南軒易說), to the *Confucian Analects* (**Lunyu**) (*Nanxuan xiansheng Lunyu jie* 南軒先生論語解) and to the **Mengzi** (*Nanxuan xiansheng Mengzi jie* 南軒先生孟子解). Finally, under the influence of the historiographic tradition of the Hu family he produced a biography of Zhuge Liang 諸葛亮 (181–234), the famous counsellor of the state of Shu during the period of the Three Kingdoms (220–265). His *Collected Works* are composed of forty-four chapters altogether. They were published after his death by **Zhu Xi** who, however, omitted some earlier texts. This fact has led some scholars to speculate that Zhu Xi intentionally edited out of the collection those pieces which did not agree with his own philosophical ideas.

Though Zhang Shi departed from Hu Hong's thesis that human nature (**xing**) was beyond good and evil, his thought still remained firmly rooted in the teachings of his master. This can best be seen by looking at the theoretical differences between Zhang Shi and Zhu Xi. Against the opinion of Zhu Xi that quiet-sitting and meditation should come before practice, Zhang Shi stressed that heavenly principle could best be found in daily affairs. Furthermore, although according to his thinking human nature was good, he, like Hu Hong, argued that the emotions and evil also belonged to it, an opinion which was directed against the Buddhist theory of the illusionary nature of the passions. Also like Hu Hong, he associated the term 'nature' with the tranquil state mentioned in the **Zhongyong** when the feelings are not yet expressed, and the term 'mind' with the active, already-expressed state. The famous Four Beginnings (**si duan**) which *Mengzi* had ascribed to human nature in Zhang Shi's philosophy became a component of the mind. Thus it seems that, as was the case for Hu Hong, for Zhang Shi human nature

and the state before the feelings are expressed were only abstract terms serving as a theoretical basis for a practical purpose, namely the successful accomplishment of daily affairs and one's living with one's environment in harmony.

References: Tillman, 1992a; Takahata, 1976, 1996.

HANS VAN ESS

Zhang Xuecheng 章學誠
1738–1801
(*zi* Shizhai 實齋, *hao* Shaoyan 少巖)

Zhang Xuecheng, a native of Yuyao 餘姚, was one of the original and most systematic thinkers in the eighteenth century. He was most well known for his defence of the value of history relative to the Confucian Classics with his catch phrase: 'the Six Classics are nothing but history' (*liujing jieshiye* 六經皆史也). His reason was simply that they were the records and documents of rulers in high antiquity. They were not written as works to theorise about abstract principles independently of human experience (*lishi er yan li* 離事而言理). Zhang's statement was clearly a protest against the current trend of putting the classical studies above other types of learning. To remind his contemporaries like the renowned polymath **Dai Zhen** of the historical origin of the Classics, he meant to elevate his own status as a historian and to justify his contribution to both historiography and historical writing.

Zhang distinguished history as a product of historians or as a 'work' (*zhushu* 著述; *zhuanshu* 撰述) and history as documents. Among the Six Classics, the only 'work' was the *Spring and Autumn Annals* (**Chunqiu**) by Confucius. For Zhang, the *Chunqiu* was the first historical work by a private scholar (*jiaxue* 家學). The significance of Confucius in Zhang's thought was his contribution to the creation of the first historical work, whose didactic function helped to 'manage the world' (***jing shi*** 經世). Zhang's new thesis about *Chunqiu* as the first historical work served to substantiate another central thesis of his thought – 'to manage the world with scholarship' (*xueshu jingshi* 學術經世). This idea was scattered in the major essays in his *Wenshi tongyi* 文史通義 (*General Meaning of Literature and History*). He argued that a scholar without political office could still contribute to social order.

Zhang took pride in his innovative approach to writing history, especially local history. He was exceptional in his reflection on the problems a historian faces: how to write history and the theoretical issues of using different genres to organise his information. Zhang took a multiple approach, arguing that no single literary genre was adequate in registering the past. The complexity and multifaceted nature of human society required a great variety of genres, be it chronology, biography, or sweeping narratives of events. A historian by virtue of his training and talents needed to select a combination of genres to present his topic of study.

The only genre in which Zhang had put into practice his ideas regarding history writing was local gazetteers (*fang zhi* 方志). He had written extensively on issues related to the compilation of gazetteers. His view of history was still state-centred in the sense that he regarded the writing of local histories as complementary to the writing of dynastic history. However, Zhang differed significantly from his precursors in that he allowed more local conditions to be included and thought that this was a legitimate concern for local historians. His notion of local history expanded far beyond convention. He recommended the establishment of a regular office in each local government to keep records, which would be used to compile its gazetteer. This amounted to a proposal for building local archives.

Consistent with his idea of 'managing the world with scholarship', Zhang was involved in lineage reform, which included a reconceptualisation of the role of genealogy in his thought on writing local history. Zhang theorised about the functions of genealogy as a historian. He regarded genealogies as a genre of historical writing crucial to local history. For him genealogies were both historical records and didactic writings. Zhang argued that genealogies should be inclusive in its recording of members. Biographies of kinsmen in the genealogies provided examples of moral examplars. The signicance of Zhang's writings was not discovered until the early twentieth century.

References: Chow Kai-wing, 1984, 1994.

KAI-WING CHOW

Zhang you 長幼
(Senior–junior relationship)

This relationship usually refers to that between villagers who share an equivalent social status, but who, based on age, arrange themselves hierarchically. The ***Xunzi*** states that, 'When one chances upon someone from one's hometown, one cultivates the obligations of the senior and junior (*zhangyou*)' (*Xunzi*, 6: 10). These obligations are that one shows respect to an older fellow villager and solicitude to a younger one.

The senior–junior relationship copies that between elder and younger brothers. In other words, it is an outgrowth of the virtue of brotherly conduct (*ti*). The ***Mengzi*** states that, 'To walk slowly and behind one's senior is called 'brotherliness' (*di* 第). To walk quickly and be ahead of one's senior is called being unbrotherliness' (*Mengzi*, 6B: 2). The ***Li ji*** states this even more explicitly, 'One respects his or her seniors because they are similar to one's elder brother; one is kind to juniors because they are similar to one's sons' (*Li ji*, 25: 15). Since the two relationships of senior–junior and younger brother–older brother were nearly equivalent, early Confucian lists of significant relationships usually include one or the other, but not both.

The effects of this virtue go beyond the village because one's respect for seniors and solicitude towards juniors should be extended to one's superiors and subordinates. According to the **Da xue**, 'Thus, without leaving his home, the gentleman perfects teachings for the entire country: by means of filial piety one can serve his lord, by means of brotherliness one can serve his superiors, by means of kindness, one can employ the multitude' (*Li ji*, 43.2).

References: Hung, William, 1972b; Lau & Chen, 1992, 1996.

KEITH KNAPP

Zhang Yu 張禹
d. 5 BCE

In his youth, Zhang Yu received a training in the interpretations of the *Book of Changes* (*Yi jing*) by Liangqiu He 梁丘賀 and Shi Chou 施讎, and in the Qi 齊 version of the *Analects* (**Lunyu**). Appointed an academician (*boshi*), in 48–44 BCE he was engaged in giving instruction in the *Analects* to the Heir Apparent, the future Han Chengdi 成帝 (r. 33–7 BCE).

As a scholar who enjoyed Chengdi's admiration, Zhang Yu held several appointments before becoming chancellor (*Cheng xiang* 丞相) in 25 BCE. As such, he sent a subordinate official to study local customs in different parts of the empire, and the resulting work was used as the basis for part of Chapter 28 of the *Han shu*, which concerns the administrative and geographical divisions of the Han empire. Some of Zhang Yu's actions were subject to criticism, but he was allowed to retire honourably on the grounds of ill health and old age in 20 BCE.

Zhang Yu's contribution to Confucian Learning was of considerably greater importance than the part that he played in politics. To assist his pupil the Heir Apparent he wrote an exegetical commentary (*Zhang ju* 章句) for the *Analects*, choosing as he thought fit from the teachings of his own mentors. The Han imperial library possessed a copy of his written exposition of the Lu 魯 version of that work and it was this text, modified by reference to the Qi version, that was approved for inscription on stone in 175 CE. Zhang Yu's work may well have formed a landmark in the transmission and interpretation of this highly influential book which affected the training and outlook of officials throughout imperial times.

Reference: Cheng, Anne, 1993: 316.

MICHAEL LOEWE

Zhang Zai 張載
1020–1077
(*zi* Zihou 子厚, *hao* Hengqu Xiansheng 橫渠先生)

Although his forebears had resided in Daliang 大梁 (near Kaifeng 開封, the Song-dynasty capital) for generations, upon the death of his father, Zhang Zai moved as a child with his family to Hengqu 橫渠 (in modern Mei 郿 county, Shanxi 陝西). As a youth, he revelled in the study of military affairs, such that, upon the incursions into the North by the Tangut 唐古忒 western Xia dynasty (1038–1227), he set about organising a militia force, with the aspiring aim of seizing enemy territory west of the Tao 洮 River (in modern Gansu 甘肅). In 1040, Zhang corresponded with **Fan Zhongyan** and subsequently met with him while Fan was stationed in Zhang's home area. Impressed by Zhang Zai's talents for scholarship, Fan Zhongyan counselled him against pursuing a military career and presented him with a gift of the **Zhongyong** (*Doctrine of the Mean*). However, this encounter hardly dissuaded Zhang from forays into Daoist and Buddhist learning before ultimately returning to Confucianism.

Zhang Zai appeared at the imperial capital in 1056 and regaled large audiences with his lectures on the **Yi jing** (*Book of*

Changes), thus coming to the attention of many scholars of eminence, such as **Sima Guang**. At that time, Zhang Zai, who was a young brother-in-law of Cheng Xiang 程珦 (1006–1090; *zi* Bowen 伯溫), also met his two youthful nephews **Cheng Hao** and **Cheng Yi** and he thereafter desisted in public lecturing because he felt their knowledge of the *Yi jing* surpassed his own. Under their influence, Zhang became more committed than ever to Confucian Learning; he no longer sought knowledge that was beyond the pale of the Confucian tradition so vigorously as in the past.

Together with Cheng Hao, Zhang Zai obtained the *jinshi* degree in the metropolitan civil service examination of 1057 and he, thereupon, embarked upon a promising official career. Beginning as an administrator in charge of laws (*sifa canjun shi* 司法參軍事), Zhang served ably in a variety of provincial positions for more than a decade. In 1069, upon the recommendation of Lü Gongzhu 呂公著 (1018–1089; *zi* Huishu 晦叔), Zhang Zai was summoned to the capital for an audience with the newly ascended Shenzong emperor (r. 1067–1085). Pleased with Zhang's answers concerning the best way to govern the empire, Shenzong requested that he participate in the deliberations on the New Policies (*xinfa* 新法) of **Wang Anshi**. For his part, Zhang, having served exclusively in the provinces, asked for time to inform himself about Wang's programme and Shenzong granted his request by having him appointed an editing clerk (*jiao shu* 校書) in the Institute for the Veneration of Literature (*chongwen yuan* 崇文院). When Wang Anshi later sought to recruit him as a participant in implementing the New Policies, Zhang Zai responded that if Wang were to conduct himself properly, all in the empire would rush to participate. However, if he continued to insist on pursuing a strategy of micro-management – presuming to 'teach jade cutters how to cut jade', he was doomed to fail (*Songshi* 宋史, 1977: 36: 12723). Displeased by his response and even more outraged by the

much more confrontational attitude displayed by his younger brother Zhang Jian 張戩 (1030–1076; *zi* Tianqi 天祺), Wang pressed Zhang Zai back into the provinces with demotions and eventually drove him to the verge of quitting office altogether. Finally, following Zhang Jian's death, Zhang Zai voluntarily resigned from all official duties and – apart from a brief re-entry into the bureaucracy for only a few months – devoted his own remaining year of life to study and teaching.

Thought and works

While it was inspired by the *Yi jing* and was well within the contours of the **dao xue** (Learning of the Way) movement, Zhang Zai's philosophy manifested features that distinguished it from the occultism practised by his older contemporaries **Zhou Dunyi** and **Shao Yong**. In fact, in conception, his philosophy was highly materialist. Basing himself on what have been called rationalist premises, Zhang Zai formulated a naturalistic model of universal evolution, in which neither an anthropomorphised **tian** (Heaven) nor the spirits of the dead played any part. Zhang Zai further surmised that the most elemental substance in the universe was **qi**, the psychic material of which everything – animate and inanimate, sentient and insentient – is composed. Zhang then proceeded to identify his primordial *qi* with the **tai ji** or Supreme Ultimate itself, with the former in fact supplanting the latter as the chief generative force in the universe. For Zhang Zai, it was not the Supreme Ultimate but rather the condensation and dispersion of *qi* that both produced and constituted the myriad things in the world. Moreover, the dyadic opposites **yin–yang** that were so crucial in the systems of Zhou Dunyi and Shao Yong became nothing more than dissimilar (either condensed or dispersed) manifestations of a unified *qi*.

The naturalistic foundation of Zhang Zai's philosophy enabled him to meet specific challenges posed by Daoism and Buddhism that had formerly been beyond the capacity of the *dao xue* movement either to match or to refute. His dynamic view of *qi* alternating between its congealed and rarified states enabled him to offer a positivist alternative to such concepts as the Buddhist emptiness (*kong* 空) and the Daoist non-being (*wu*). There could never be a case of true emptiness or non-being but, instead, only instances of *qi* in its most extremely attenuated state. Moreover, Zhang Zai was convinced of the ubiquitous nature of *qi* – believing that it is everywhere and that everything in existence is composed of it. This conviction permitted him to create a bond or linkage between the individual's **xin** (heart/mind) and *shen* 身 (body) and those of the universe that compared favourably with the established schemas of the Daoists and Buddhists. He thus was able to justify the extension of the cardinal virtue of **ren** well beyond the particularised realm of humankind to the universe as a whole. This view subsequently drew criticism from some quarters because of its approximation of the maligned doctrine of universal love (*jian ai* 兼愛) that is ascribed to the ancient philosopher Mozi 墨子 (see **Confucianism and Moism**). Nevertheless, we can infer from this expansion of *ren* how fully convinced Zhang was that the **cheng** or sincerity of humanity upholds and sustains the natural order, just as assuredly as he believed it to bolster the entire sphere of social relations. Finally, given the fact that *qi* is omnipresent in his system, Zhang Zai was able to caution confidently against withdrawal from the world in the manner of Buddhist clerics. Zhang maintained that the sage lives normally, in this world but, nevertheless, in a kind of enlightened synchronicity with the universe. All of the foregoing ideas are expounded in depth in Zhang Zai's two most famous works – the **Zheng meng** (*Correcting the Unenlightened*) and the **Xi ming** (*Western Inscription*).

Influence

The importance of Zhang Zai lies primarily in the moderating position he assumed within the *Dao xue* fold – one that stands at the midpoint on the Confucian intellectual spectrum between two extremes. His rationalist standpoint made him more mainstream than the occultists who exhibited affinities especially for philosophical Daoism but more creative in confronting such rival doctrines as Buddhism than were the orthodox (and largely ossified) classical Confucian purists. Meeting the Buddhists on their own terms, Zhang argued compellingly, for example, that absolute nothingness is an illogical supposition because such a condition can never be anything more than *qi* dispersed and suspended in its most ethereal state.

Yet another dimension of Zhang's importance involves his belief that – if ever achieved – the actual practice of sagaciousness is a simple affair. One example drawn from his own relatively short time spent as an official fully demonstrates the spirit of this principle. Early in his career, while serving as a magistrate *xianling* 縣令 in Yunyan 雲巖 (modern Yichuan 宜川 county, Shanxi), Zhang Zai – out of courtesy – inaugurated a practice of inviting district elders to monthly banquets. In this setting, while personally pouring wine for them, he solicited their views on government, with the goal of bringing whatever future decisions he would make into alignment with local norms and expectations. Zhang Zai recognised these mundane and routinised acts as indispensable. For him, these acts represented the practicable but ennobling essence of the road to sagehood, as perhaps best captured in the salient final sentence of the *Western Inscription*: 'While living, I will serve without resistance; upon death, I will be at peace' (*Zhangzi quanshu*, 1: 6b).

Zhang Zai, together with his wife *née* Guo 郭, had one son – Zhang Shang 張尚, who died as a youth. Zhang's teachings became known as the School of the Teachings from Within the Passes (*Guanxue xuepai* 關學學派), which signified his own geographical base in the Shanxi corridor region, and best known among his disciples was **Lü Dalin** – a younger brother of **Lü**

Dajun. In 1220, Zhang Zai received the posthumous title (*shi*) of Ming 明. In 1241, he was honoured as Earl of Mei (Mei Bo 郿伯) and the regularised conduction of sacrifices in his behalf were commenced within the **Kong miao** (Temple of Confucius).

References: Balazs & Hervouet, 1978: 3, 11, 29, 30, 218–19, 220, 222, 223, 224, 296, 391, 396, 411; Bol, 1992: 28, 30, 202, 300, 338, 415n. 56, 421n. 161; Chan, Wing-tsit, 1976: 39–43; Chen Junmin, 1986; Collins, 1998: 5, 63, 75, 301–2, 304, 308, 309, 312, 314, 973n. 12; He Zhaowu, 1991: 298, 305–10, 313, 346, 368, 372, 393, 399; Huang Siu-chi, 1999: 57–84; Jiang Guozhu, 1982: 3, 20, 73–84, 251, 279, 280, 308, 369, 371, 375, 376, 381, 389, 392, 430, 435; Kasoff, 1984; Wyatt, 1996: 3, 4, 98–9, 157–9, 217, 218, 291n. 41, 305n. 25, 309n. 3.

DON J. WYATT

Zhang Zhidong 張之洞
1837–1909
(*zi* Xiaoda 孝達)

Leader of the late Qing reform, Zhang Zhidong was a main force in introducing western technology and methods to improve Chinese economy, national defence and education system. During his tenure as the governor-general of Guangdong and Guangxi (1884–1889) and of Hunan and Hubei (1890–1907), he enlisted support from local merchants to build arsenals, coal mines, iron and steel works, cotton mills, silk factories, tanneries, railroads and dykes. In 1905, he supported the establishment of a nationwide school system to replace the civil service examinations as the new ladder of success.

On the other hand, as a scholar–official, Zhang was committed to reviving Confucianism. From his first assignment as the director of education in Sichuan (1873–1877) to his last post as the Grand Counsellor (1907–1909), he made a tremendous effort to build Confucian academies, revise the Confucian curriculum and reprint classical texts. Among the academies that he helped to build were the *Zunjing shuyuan* 尊經書院 (Academy of Revered Classics) in Chengdu, the *Guangya shuyuan* 廣雅書院 (Academy of Extended Refinement) in Guangzhou, and the *Lianghu shuyuan* 兩湖書院 (Academy of Hunan and Hubei) in Wuchang. One of his best known works as a Confucian scholar was *Shumu dawen* 書目答問 (*Answers to Bibliographical Questions*) which he compiled with Miao Quansun 繆荃孫 (1844–1919). An annotated bibliography of major works published in China, *Shumu dawen* offered guidance to beginners on the scope of Confucian Learning as well as the best versions of texts available.

Attempting to strive a balance between the need for modernisation and the need for preserving Confucianism as the heart of Chinese civilisation, Zhang wrote *Quanxue pian* 勸學篇 (*Exhortation to Learning*) in 1898. Dividing the work into the 'inner' and 'outer' chapters, he gave full expression to what he considered to be a **ti-yong** (substance and function) relationship between Chinese learning and western learning. In the 'inner chapters', he argued that the attempts to modernise the country should not challenge the three premises of Qing China – the legitimacy of the Qing rule, the authority of Confucian Classics, and the hierarchical structure based on the Three Cardinal Guides (**san gang**). Equating Confucian Learning with Chinese learning, he called on his readers to employ Confucian Learning as the 'fundamental principles' (*ti* 體) to regulate their private and public behaviour. In the 'outer chapters', he urged his readers to adopt drastic social and economic reforms to ensure China's survival in the global competition for wealth and power. He reminded them that without such western 'practical applications' (*yong* 用) as a nationwide school system and a dynamic economy, China would have difficulty in protecting her autonomy in the age of colonialism.

Zhang's dual commitment to modernisation and Confucian revival has made him a controversial figure. For some, he was a reformer who brought substantial changes to Chinese economy and education. For others, he was a conservative who employed the rhetoric of reform to perpetuate the Confucian social and political order. Nevertheless, he raised the question 'What role does Confucianism play in Chinese modernisation?' that later became a central issue of twentieth-century Chinese thought.

References: Ayers, 1971; Bays, 1978.

TZE-KI HON

Zhangzi quanshu 張子全書
(*Complete Works of Master Zhang*)

This collection – in fourteen chapters (*juan*), with a one-chapter supplement (*fulu* 附錄) – comprises the complete philosophical and literary production of the philosopher **Zhang Zai**. Featured foremost in the collection is the text of the *Xi ming* which constitutes the first chapter, as well as that of the lengthier *Zheng meng* which constitutes chapters 2 and 3. Chapters 4–8 consist of Zhang Zai's commentaries on various Classics; chapters 9–11 are commentaries specifically on the *Yi jing*; and chapter 12 is a sampling drawn from his recorded sayings (*yulu* 語錄). The miscellaneous material of chapter 13 and another set of sayings (also preserved in the fifteenth-century collection *Xingli daquan* 性理大全) complete Zhang's contributions to his *Complete Works*. A final appended fifteenth chapter contains remarks about Zhang Zai by contemporaries and a biography by his faithful disciple **Lü Dalin**.

References: Balazs & Hervouet, 1978: 3, 218–19, 220.

DON J. WYATT

Zhao Fang 趙汸
1319–1369
(*zi* Zichang 子常, *hao* Dongshan 東山)

Zhao hailed from Anhui, where his grandfather had joined the Mongol invaders in the 1270s in order to save the citizenry from slaughter. Zhao aspired to be a Confucian scholar from a young age, and at nineteen he became the disciple of **Huang Ze**, with whom he studied the Classics. Huang encouraged him to develop his own point of view and to focus on the *Spring and Autumn Annals* (**Chunqiu**). Zhao also studied with **Yu Ji**, a disciple of **Wu Cheng** who became an important official in the 1320s. Yu introduced Zhao to Wu's thinking on self-cultivation and moral enlightenment and the necessity to reconcile the teachings of **Zhu Xi** and **Lu Jiuyuan** in order to fully grasp the Confucian scholarship of the Song dynasty (960–1279). Zhao also was associated with Wu's student Yuan Mingshan 元明善 (1269–1322), who was conversant with Wu's views on the Four Books. Zhao refused many requests to serve the Mongol regime, but during the last year of his life, he did participate in compiling the *History of the Yuan* (*Yuanshi* 元史) under the first Ming emperor.

In his work on the *Spring and Autumn Annals*, Zhao at first followed Huang Ze's emphasis on the *Zuo* commentary and the interpretations of the Jin 晉 scholar Du Yu 杜預 (222–284), but as he developed his own viewpoint, he came to feel that the *Zuo* seriously under-emphasised Confucius' 'praise and blame' approach to the *Annals*, in which the aim was to elucidate moral principles in history. Zhao also felt that even though the *Gongyang* and *Guliang* commentaries emphasised this didactic approach, they fell short on the historical side, and he sought a balanced interpretation.

Zhao is known for his attempts to reconcile the teachings of Zhu and Lu by balancing cultivation and study, which derived from his association with Yu Ji's mentor Wu Cheng, and, according to the Qing scholar **Gu Yanwu**, for influencing Cheng Minzheng 程敏政 (1445–1499) (in his *Compendium on the Unity of Dao, Daoyi bian* 道一編), **Wang Shouren** (in his *Final Theory of Zhu Xi in His Later Years, Zhuzi wan'nian dinglun* 朱子晚年定論), and Li Fu 李紱 (1675–1750) in the idea that Zhu Xi and Lu Jiuyuan differed in their early years but were in agreement later in life. Zhao is therefore an important link between Wu Cheng and later Ming and Qing thinkers.

References: Gedalecia, 1999: 144–5, 155–6; Goodrich & Fang, 1976: I, 125–8; Huang Jinxing, 1995: 107–17; *Ming shi*: 1974: 282; *Song–Yuan xuean*, 1966: 92; Wilson, 1995: 304.

DAVID GEDALECIA

Zhao Fu 趙復

c. 1206–1299

(*zi* Renpu 仁甫, *hao* Jianghan 江漢)

Zhao is most famous for being the patriarch of Neo-Confucian studies in North China from the time of the Mongol conquest of that region in the 1230s. Prior to this time, under the Jin 金 dynasty (1115–1234), the works of **Zhu Xi** were known among scholars in North China, such as Yuan Haowen 元好問 (1190–1257) and Wang Yun 王惲 (1227–1304), but his philosophy was not widely propagated. After Zhao was captured in 1235 during the invasion of Hubei, a region where Zhu's ideas had become popular among Zhao's many disciples, he helped reestablish scholarly contact between North and South after a century of separation and disseminate the Neo-Confucianism of Southern Song. He transcribed the Cheng–Zhu commentaries on the Classics that he had committed to memory and taught Neo-Confucian thought to hundreds of students at the Academy of the Great Ultimate (*Tai ji shuyuan* 太極書院) in Yanjing (Beijing), which was founded in 1238 by **Yao Shu**, who had convinced Zhao not to commit suicide upon his capture, and Yang Weizhong 楊惟中 (1205/6–1260),

who became a high official under Emperor Ögödei 太宗窩闊臺 (r. 1229–1241) and a principal patron of Zhao at court. While in Yanjing, Zhao discussed Neo-Confucian philosophy with the scholar and future adviser of Khubilai (r. 1260–1294), **Hao Jing**.

In his *Diagram of the Transmission of the Way* (*Chuandao tu* 傳道圖), Zhao traced the continuity of Confucian thought, the **daotong**, from the sage–kings Yao and Shun (see **Yao Shun**), through Confucius and **Mengzi**, and on down through the Song Neo-Confucians, **Zhou Dunyi**, the Cheng brothers (**Cheng Hao** and **Cheng Yi**), **Zhang Zai**, and Zhu Xi. He composed the *Guide to Emulate the Sages* (*Xixian lu* 希賢錄) to encourage students to cultivate themselves in the pursuit of sage-learning, and he also compiled lists of the primary Neo-Confucian works in order to overcome the lack of basic knowledge of Neo-Confucian thought in the North. Rather than on cosmology and metaphysics, however, Zhao's emphasis in these works was on the practical application of Zhu's ethical and social philosophy.

Zhao introduced Song philosophy to the well-known early Yuan scholars **Xu Heng** and **Liu Yin** and founded the Jianghan 江漢 School. In this regard, he is important for having amplified the legacy of Song thought in the North under the Mongols and setting in motion the process of Confucianisation based on the ideas of Zhu Xi, which eventually drew together intellectuals from north and south under the patronage of Khubilai and his immediate successors. This process culminated in the reinstitutionalisation of the civil service examination system on a Four Books (*Si shu*)-Zhu Xi basis in the early fourteenth century.

References: Chan, Wing-tsit, 1982: 197–9, 203–4, 217–18; Liu Ts'un-yan and Judith Berling, 1982: 485–7; Mao Huaixin, 1986: 514, 522–3, 530, 542; *Song–Yuan xuean*, 1966: 90: 1a–2a; *Yuanshi*: 1976: 189.

DAVID GEDALECIA

Zhao Qi 趙岐
108?–201
(*zi* Binqing 邠卿)

Zhao Qi's outstanding contribution was his editing of, and commentary on, *The Book of Mengzi* (**Mengzi**). Originally named Zhao Jia 趙嘉, *zi* Taiqing 臺卿, he became known by the pseudonyms that he adopted in flight from persecution. He married a niece of **Ma Rong** but, despising the Ma clan, he refrained from associating with that famous classics scholar. Zhao Qi lived to be a nonagenarian only after having narrowly escaped death time and again. In 158, for instance, having offended Tang Xuan 唐琓, the governor of Jingzhao (Jingzhao *yin* 京兆尹), he fled certain execution; in his stead his family and many members of his kin were killed.

Zhao Qi served three emperors in positions that included inspector (*Cishi* 刺史) of Bingzhou 并州 (on the northern frontier) and Superintendent of Transport (*Taipu* 太僕, one of the Nine Ministers). He was appointed, but did not serve, as governor (*Taishou* 太守) of Dunhuang 敦煌 and, before he died, Superintendent of Ceremonial (*Taichang* 太常). Zhao Qi's two most important monographs were *Sanfu juelu* 三輔決錄 (*Evaluative Records of the Sanfu Area*), no longer extant, and *Mengzi zhangju* 孟子章句 (*Chapter and Verse Exegesis of the Mengzi*), the earliest surviving commentary on the *Mengzi*. Zhao Qi also edited the text, eliminating four 'outer' chapters (*pian*) – which he considered spurious accretions – and retaining the seven 'inner' ones. These seven he divided into two sections apiece; this is the fourteen-*juan* arrangement of most received versions today.

References: Ebrey, 1986; Lau, 1993.

MARK L. ASSELIN

Zhao Qian 趙謙
1351–1396
(*zi* Weiqian 為謙, *hao* Qiongtai waishi 瓊臺外史)

Zhao Qian, whose original name was Guze 古則, was a native of Yuyao 余姚 (near modern-day Shaoxing, Zhejiang). Orphaned at a young age, Zhao was raised by monks of the Congshan 崇山 Buddhist temple. At the age of seventeen or eighteen, Zhao travelled east to study with Zheng Sibiao 鄭四表 (?–?) in Tiantai 天台 (eastern Zhejiang). When Zhao eventually took a court appointment, he came into conflict with Song Lian 宋濂 (1310–1381) and other officials in Nanjing. Zhao chose instead to retire from official service, and he returned home to continue his studies. He would become best known in his day for his studies of phonetics, including *Shengyin wenzi tong* 聲音文字通 (*The Correlation Between Speech and Writing*). In 1389, the court appointed Zhao as *jiaoyu* 教諭 (instructor) for the region near Qiongshan 瓊山 at Qionghai 瓊海. Zhao died seven years later on New Year's Day in Guangcheng 廣成 at the age of forty-five.

Zhao was deeply interested in the nature of creativity found within the heart/mind of ancient sages and worthies. Furthermore, he contended that the heart/mind held within it the **tai ji** (Supreme Ultimate), following a line of Confucian thinking that would culminate in the school of thought promoted by the late Ming thinker **Wang Shouren**. Zhao maintained that if one nourished the heart/mind, one could then strengthen one's nature to counter the influences of base desires. To expound upon these ideas, Zhao wrote the 12-*juan Liushu benyi* 六書本義 (*Essential Principles of the Six Books*). Another significant work on this subject was Zhao's *Kaogu wenji* 考古文集 (*A Collection of Observations of the Ancient World*).

References: Goodrich & Fang, 1976: 124–215.

JAMES A. ANDERSON

Zhedong xuepai 浙東學派
(The School of the East Zhejiang area)

The notion of a Zhedong School of thought arises from the particularly strong statecraft (*jingshi*) concerns among many thinkers – in the area of Zhejiang province from Song through Qing times – to use classical, historical and institutional studies to address practical issues in society and government. This rubric highlights such concerns throughout the province although there was considerable distinctiveness in approaches within particular areas, such as Jinhua and Yongjia. He Bingsong claimed in the 1930s that a distinct Zhedong School had since the Song been the most faithful to **Cheng Yi**'s intellectual legacy. Although he pointed to significant links between Cheng Yi's learning and the ideas of **Chen Liang** and others, He's criticisms of **Zhu Xi**'s deviations from Cheng Yi have led many modern scholars to discount entirely the notion of a Zhedong School. It is true that friendships and shared orientations among Zhedong thinkers did not culminate in a school of thought as well defined as Zhu Xi's. Zhedong never developed one authoritative voice to delineate a particular tradition. Still, the academy established by **Lü Zuqian** in Jinhua and his writings could be seen as crucial in establishing classical, historical, institutional and statecraft studies as characteristically Zhedong concerns. Despite diverse interests, Lü had remained a leading figure within *Dao xue*; however, Chen Liang and **Ye Shi** eventually broke with *Dao xue* as it became less tolerant of their Zhedong obsessions with pragmatic statecraft and historical studies. Similarly without being constrained by any narrowly conceived school, later Zhedong historical and statecraft studies responded primarily to compelling sociopolitical issues of the era.

References: He Bingsong, 1932; Tillman, 1982, 1992a, and 1994.

HOYT TILLMAN

Zhen 貞
(Steadfast, chaste)

Early Confucian philosophical works rarely mention the minor virtue of *zhen*. When they do, it means something like being unwavering in one's conduct. The **Xunzi** says, 'Someone whose words cannot always be trusted and whose conduct is not always steadfast (*zhen*) . . . can be called a petty person' (*Xunzi*, 3.11).

In Confucian works about women, though, *zhen* is one of the most important female virtues. **Liu Xiang**'s *Lienü zhuan* dedicates an entire chapter (out of seven) to women who embodied this virtue. In regard to women, *zhen* is commonly translated as 'chastity' and is associated with a widow refusing to remarry. (I prefer to translate *zhen* as steadfast because it applies equally well to the actions of men and women.) In fact, the compound *zhen nü* 貞女 'steadfast woman' means a woman who throughout her life only has one husband. Liu Xiang's *Shuoyuan* 說苑 declares that, 'a loyal retainer does not serve two lords; a chaste woman (*zhen nü*) does not switch to a second husband' (*Shuoyuan*, 4.21).

Nevertheless, *zhen* did not only mean being steadfast in marriage. Steadfast (*zhen*) women were also ones who faultlessly adhered to Confucian propriety. The *Lienü zhuan* tells of Steadfast Jiang 貞姜 (fifteenth century BCE) who chose to drown rather than be saved by an official who lacked the proper credentials. Upon hearing of her death, her husband proclaimed, 'To reside by her agreement and maintain her faithfulness (*xin*), [she died] to perfect her steadfastness (*zhen*)' (*Lienü zhuan*, 4.10).

References: Lau & Chen, 1992c, 1994, 1996a.

KEITH KNAPP

Zhen Dexiu 真德秀
1178–1235
(*zi* Jingyuan 景元, Xishan 西山)

Zhen Dexiu, like **Zhu Xi** and **Chen Chun**, was from Fujian. Poor and fatherless at fourteen, he owed his education to a local scholar–official who recognised his talents. After obtaining the highest civil service examination degree, the *jinshi*, in 1199 at the early age of twenty-one, Zhen achieved further distinction in 1205 by passing the infrequently given examination for *Erudite Literatus* (*boxue hongci* 博學宏辭). That same year he was introduced to the thought of Zhu Xi and was soon convinced by Zhu's teachings. Zhen went on to play a major role in the political as well as intellectual life of his time and was influential in getting the court to recognise and officially accept **dao xue**. His political career included service both in the capital and in provinces and even an aborted mission to the Jin court. He submitted numerous memorials on foreign policy as well as domestic issues and persistently stressed the need for the dynasty to strengthen itself through internal reform.

Somewhat similarly, Zhen Dexiu insisted that the reform of the state depended on the reform of the emperor which in turn depended on the reform of the emperor's own heart/mind. He followed Zhu Xi in urging this on the emperor by employing *The Great Learning* (**Daxue**), the canonical text which most clearly links personal rectification and transformation of the world. Zhen asserts that it is a text which every ruler and minister needs to study. Zhen's treatment of this text is consistent with that of Zhu Xi but his *Extended Explanation of the Great Learning* (*Daxue yanyi* 大學衍義) goes beyond Zhu in specifying how a reformed emperor would conduct himself in selecting officials, informing himself about people's feelings and life in the countryside, controlling the inner and outer courts, and settling succession. Zhen's own emperor paid little heed, but his *Extended Explanation* remained very influential.

To deal with local government Zhen also authored a shorter text, *The Classic on Governance* (*Zheng jing* 政經). Here too he combines discussion of general moral principles with attention to education, granaries, the administration of justice and fiscal matters. The principles he extols and attempts to implement are in line with the teachings of Zhu Xi, but he was unusual in celebrating the extraordinary filial piety of acts of self-mutilation performed to cure an ailing parent including two cases of men who 'plucked out' their livers.

Such 'heroic' acts are of course made possible only by curbing of selfish desire, a theme that runs through the selections Zhen assembled in the *Xin jing* 心經 *Classic of the Heart/Mind*, not to be confused with the Buddhist sutra of the same name (*The Heart Sutra*). Indeed, Zhen's text, which draws on the writings of Zhu Xi and his predecessors, constitutes a Confucian alternative to that sutra although Zhen himself did not show particular animosity toward Buddhism. It is a work that greatly influenced the great Korean Confucian scholar **Yi Hwang** and was also widely read in China where it was later supplemented and annotated by Chen Minzheng (陳敏政 1445–1499). Like the *Extended Meaning* it highlights the centrality of the heart/mind and the urgent need for Heaven's principle to overcome selfish human desires, both present in all people, and was influential in how the teachings of Zhu Xi and his school were perceived in later times.

A negative attitude toward human feelings reminiscent of **Zhou Dunyi** along with a strict moral rigorism is forcefully expressed in Zhen's essay, 'Dedication to the Way' (*Zhihdao* 志道), the name he gave to his son. The goal is to attain *dao*, 'a general term for all principle' and **ren**, 'the entire virtue of the heart/mind'. This requires a struggle between *li* (principle), and the desires 'which wound more grievously than a double-edged sword and burn more fiercely than the hottest fire'. The desires must be attacked and vanquished as in war. (*Wenji* 33, last passage as trans. in de Bary, 1981: 762.)

A persistent theme in Zhen's writings is the importance of *jing* 敬: 'If we look to remote antiquity, we can see that in the one expression "reverent seriousness (*jing*)" as passed down through a hundred sages, is represented their real method of the heart/mind' (*Wenji* 26, tr. de Bary, 1993: 46). It is whereby the *Mean* is attained and the prerequisite to sincerity (**cheng**). 'The violence of the passions is like runaway horses, reverence is like reigning them in. The wildness of the feelings is like a river in flood; reverent seriousness is like the dikes to hold it back' (*Wenji* 26, in de Bary, 1981: 762). It is demanded both in **jing** 靜 (quiescence) and in *dong* 動 (activity). It is of the utmost seriousness in that it calls for total concentration, and it is reverent in that the object of such concentration are the principles that are not only found in the heart/mind but also extend beyond the self in time and space.

References: de Bary, 1993: 349–79, 1981, 1989, 1999: 755–64; Tillman 1992b.

CONRAD SCHIROKAUER

Zheng 政
(Governance)

Zheng means 'governance', 'administration' or 'affairs of state' and can also mean participating in that governance or taking office in its administration. The realms of human activity subject to administration are suggested by the 'eight governmental offices' (*ba zheng* 八政 ennumerated in the 'Great Norms' chapter of the **Shang shu**, a chapter whose perhaps idealistic descriptions of early governmental structure nonetheless greatly influenced the shape of imperial administration until modern times. These eight were the offices that managed foodstuffs, goods and commodities, sacrifices, public works, education, punishments, the reception of guests and military affairs, respectively.

Thinkers such as Confucius, however, discussed governance not so much in terms of structure as of content and moral direction. Whereas for him governance also required managing the procurement of foodstuffs and arms, the trust the people had for leaders who provided such resources was more important than the material goods themselves. If pressed by straightened circumstances, Confucius advised, one might do without arms or even food, but trust could not be eliminated without the inevitable destruction of the community.

When asked what governance (*zheng*) was, Confucius defined it not in terms of administrative structure but as what was upright, proper or correct (*zheng* 正). One of the optimal operational forces for sustaining governance was **de**, virtue or inner power, a compelling, axial energy whose strength to draw things ineluctably toward itself was likened to the Pole Star and its perceived capacity to attract the homage of the stars encircling it. The enigmatic potency of virtue, combined with the proprieties of ritual behaviour, was considered more likely to instil in the people the internal moral qualities requisite to an ordered society than was a system based instead largely on external punishments, harsh executions, or administrative measures. The virtue of the noble person was like the wind; that of a petty person was like the grass. When the wind blew, the grass would surely bend.

It would bend, ideally, in the direction of the moral qualities exemplified by figures of leadership. According to the *Analects* (**Lunyu**), taking office in government required magnanimity, dignity, consideration for others and a striving toward humaneness, and it precluded cruelty, oppression and stinginess. Those in office led by example and could not demand anything of others that they did not demand of themselves.

Confucius' expanded notion of governance, however, required the participation of everyone, regardless of rank or position, and was ultimately based upon the proper maintenance of relationships within the family. Fulfilment of familial obligations was so important that it was paralleled to the maintenance of obligations between the highest-ranking leaders of state. Once, when asked about governance, Confucius remarked that when rulers acted as rulers, then ministers acted as ministers should; when parents acted as parents, then children acted as children should. Without the proper development of these relationships, society would not otherwise function. Moreover, simply by being filial toward one's parents and amicable toward one's siblings, one was already participating in governance.

References: Ames & Rosemont, 1998: 2: 1, 2: 3, 2: 21, 6: 6, 12: 7, 12: 11, 12: 14, 12: 17, 12: 19, 13: 13, 20: 2; Brooks & Brooks, 1998; Legge, 1985c: 327.

DEBORAH SOMMER

Zheng meng 正蒙
(*Correcting the Unenlightened*)

The *Zheng meng* is conventionally regarded as the first book we should encounter in attempting to comprehend the teachings of **Zhang Zai**. In 1076 (a year prior to his death), purportedly stimulated by a strange dream that he had had, Zhang Zai hastily composed what became the *Zheng meng* – in two chapters (*juan*), divided into seventeen sections. Thus, we can infer that – by the time he bequeathed it to his students – Zhang himself regarded this treatise as the summation of his illustrious career as a philosopher. Statements indirectly attributed to him and his disciples as well as history itself have shown this to be precisely the case.

But, as much as any other indicator, even a cursory analysis of the title of the *Zheng meng* sheds much light on the purpose, content and importance of this work. *Meng* 蒙 denotes the kind of ignorance or naïveté, often associated with youth; *zheng* 正, in this instance, carries the verbal implications of corrective adjustment in comportment or thinking that naturally ensues upon receiving proper instruction. Hence, in many respects, *Correcting the Unenlightened*

represents a sort of primer for students at the beginning of intellectual life.

While the work touches upon many subjects, the main focus throughout *Correcting the Unenlightened* is on the theme of the cosmological. All of Zhang Zai's signature concepts surface in the sections of this protean work – *qi* (material force), the *tai he* (Supreme Harmony), the *tai xu* (Supreme Void), etc. Also contained in *Correcting the Unenlightened* are Zhang Zai's personal reflections on what emerged over time as stock constructs within the newly revitalising Confucian tradition, such as the interplay between the cosmic dyads yin and yang (**yin–yang**), *tian dao* (the Way of Heaven), and the capacities of the *xin* (heart/mind). Zhang, furthermore, discusses many concepts more thoroughly propounded by other contemporaries, such as **Zhou Dunyi**'s *cheng* (sincerity), as well as such venerable classical concepts as **li** (rites) and *yue* 樂 (music). *Correcting the Unenlightened* is indeed one of the richest and most replete compendiums of its kind.

References: Balazs & Hervouet, 1978: 3, 218; Chan, Wing-tsit, 1963d: 500–14; Fung, 1952: 478–91.

DON J. WYATT

Zheng ming 正名
(Rectification of names)

The *locus classicus* of the term *zheng ming* is *Analects* (*Lunyu*), 13: 3. *Zheng ming* ('*On the Correct Use of Names*') is also the title of a chapter in **Xunzi**. What Confucius meant by the 'correction of names' continues to be a subject of interpretative controversy, with some scholars contending that the term's occurrence in the *Analects* is a later interpolation, a problem exacerbated by the difficulty of dating most of the disparate contents of the *Analects*. Historically, **Sima Qian**'s interpretation has been the most influential. Interpreting the passage against the background of a succession issue in the state of Wei 衛 from 493 to 489 BCE, for Sima Qian the main referents of *ming* in Confucius' *zheng ming* programme were the role types, 'father' and 'son'. The conventional modern interpretation is that names of various social, political and ethical institutions were rectified so as to accord or conform with certain immutable standards inherited from tradition. The Confucius who emerges from this interpretation is a conservative figure. Other modern commentators (assuming an early date for the passage) have focused on *zheng ming* to argue for a non-conservative interpretation of Confucius' philosophy. According to them, for Confucius the real value of names was to prescribe, and not simply describe socio-political distinctions. Principally it was 'ruler', 'minister', 'father' and 'son' that were selected by Confucius for this task in the belief that if these key role types could be successfully established, all other pertinent social change would be realised as a corollary.

References: Hall & Ames, 1987: 268–75; Makeham, 1994: 35–47, 163–5.

JOHN MAKEHAM

Zheng xian 正獻
(Principal Consecration)

The Principal Consecration refers to the sacrifices to the main god or spirit of imperial sacrifices, as distinct from correlates and other secondary spirits invoked during the ceremony. The Principal Consecration consists of the full feast, as prescribed by the liturgy, and is offered by the principal consecration officer – usually the highest ranking official present – before the Separate Consecration (**Fen xian**), which consists of a reduced amount of the feast. In the Temple of Confucius the Principal Consecration is offered to the spirit of Confucius alone.

THOMAS A. WILSON

Zheng Xuan 鄭玄
127–200
(*zi* Kangcheng 康成)

'Zheng Xuan had bagged the great canons, and netted the numerous schools; he excised the many errors and repaired the lacunae, and from this point on scholars generally knew where to turn'. (*Hou Hanshu* 35) This judgement by Fan Ye 范曄 (398–446, *zi* Weizong 蔚宗) reflects the consensus that Zheng Xuan, whose textual scholarship reconciled competing versions of Confucian scriptures, was the most important classics scholar towards the end of the Later Han (25–220 CE). His methodology became the model for Northern Learning's (*Bei xue*, see **Nanbei xue**) textual criticism, and his contributions have had an inestimable impact on classical studies.

Zheng Xuan was born into a relatively poor family from Gaomi 高密, located on the Shandong peninsula. In his youth, he worked as a district bailiff (*Xiang sefu* 鄉嗇夫). He eventually entered the Imperial Academy (**Tai xue**) and taking for his master a certain Diwu Yuan 第五元 (?–?), became versed in the *Book of Changes* (**Yi jing**) of **Jing Fang the Younger** 京房 (77–37 BCE, *zi* Junming 君明), *the Spring and Autumn Annals with the Gongyang's Commentary* (**Chunqiu Gongyang zhuan**), the *Calendar of the Three Sequences* (*San tong li* 三統歷; see **San tong**), and the *Nine Essays on the Art of Calculations* (*Jiu zhang suan shu* 九章筭術).

Subsequently, he studied under Zhang Gongzu 張恭祖 (?–?) *The Rites of the Zhou* (**Zhou li**), *The Book of Rites* (**Li ji**), *the Spring and Autumn Annals with Zuo's Commentary* (**Chunqiu Zuo zhuan**), the Han version of *The Book of Poetry* (**Han Shi**), and the *Guwen* version of *The Book of History* (**Guwen Shangshu**). Finally, obtaining the support of Lu Zhi 盧植 (*ob.* 192, *zi* Zigan 子幹), he went to study in the household of Lu's teacher, the renowned classics scholar, **Ma Rong**. The famously arrogant litterateur kept Zheng Xuan at bay for over three years, but when he finally deigned to receive him, he was duly impressed by the young scholar's ability to resolve difficult problems of interpretation.

After returning home some ten years later, and having been proscribed from office, Zheng Xuan remained sequestered in his house studying the Classics. His students are said to have numbered in the thousands. At this time, he wrote three trenchant criticisms of the work of the *Gongyang* scholar and proponent **He Xiu**. He Xiu reportedly said of these critiques, 'Kangcheng entered my home, grasped my lance, and attacked me with it!' When the proscription was lifted, General-in-Chief (*Da jiangjun* 大將軍) He Jin 何進 (*ob.* 190, *zi* Suigao 遂高) summoned him and received him with great honours, but Zheng Xuan fled the court rather than be invested with office. This was followed by a series of attempts to appoint him to various posts, including superintendent of agriculture (*Da sinong* 大司農), but in each case he found a reason to decline the offer. Also, Chancellor of State (*Guo xiang* 國相) **Kong Rong** honoured Zheng Xuan with the special establishment of a township, Zheng Gong Township 鄭公鄉, in the district of Gaomi. Before his death, Zheng Xuan dreamt of Confucius exclaiming, 'Rise! Rise! This year is *Chen* 辰, and the next year is *Si* 巳.' Consulting the prognostication texts, he concluded that he was soon to die, and shortly after became bedridden with an illness from which he never recovered.

Zheng Xuan produced commentaries on, and studies of, all of what would later be known as the Thirteen Classics (**Shisan jing**), and on various other works such as prognostication and aprocryphal texts (**Chen wei**). Only the commentaries to *The Book of Poetry* and the three ritual classics are yet extant, and with respect to his entire corpus, only six of some sixty to sixty-five works attributed to him survive.

Zheng Xuan's methodology was to edit a recension based on available texts, and in his commentaries add glosses to difficult words, provide historical context and other information as needed, and offer some interpretation. A good example is his work on *The Book of Poetry*, for which he wrote both explanatory notes (*Mao shi jian* 毛詩箋) and a chronological record (*Shi pu* 詩譜). Though he began with the Mao version of the text (**Mao shi**), he incorporated some readings from the Three Schools on the *Poetry*; the new redaction in time completely replaced the other versions. His commentary, though consistent with the Mao tradition in holding that the songs represented political events of the Zhou and Chunqiu periods and contained warnings about improper behaviour, sometimes expressed independent views. A similar pattern can be seen in his editing of *The Rites of Literati* (**Yi li**). His recension is based on the *Guwen* version of fifty-six *pian* and the seventeen-*pian Jinwen* version. Using his best judgement, he selected from the two versions as he saw fit, and noted the variants. His redaction of *The Rites of Literati* is the one that was transmitted to later generations; unfortunately, Zheng Xuan's premier scholarship had the effect of leaving the earlier versions to the dustbin of history. Nonetheless, his recensions did not always attain the status of primacy. In the case of *The Analects of Confucius* (**Lunyu**), for example, the primary received tradition was that of **He Yan**, though he used Zheng Xuan's recension for his base text.

Zheng Xuan's greatest contribution to the study of the Classics was his reconciling various versions of the Confucian scriptures, including *Guwen* and *Jinwen* texts, and creating a new synthesis using his prodigious knowledge of the canon to sort out what was true and what was spurious. In the Northern and Southern Dynasties period (317–581), scholarship was broadly conceived, particularly in the subsequent Tang dynasty (618–907), to have comprised a Northern (*Bei xue*) and a Southern (*Nan xue*) tradition. Northern Learning's philologically rigorous exegesis combined with an eisegesis based on historical memory, took as its exemplar Zheng Xuan.

References: Boltz, 1993; Cheng, 1993; Kunstler, 1962; Loewe, 1993; van Zoeren, 1991.

MARK L. ASSELIN

Zheng Yu 鄭玉
1298–1358
(*zi* Zimei 子美, *hao* Shishan 師山)

Zheng, from Anhui, was one of many Confucian scholars who maintained loyalty to the Yuan during the Ming conquest. In his youth he studied the Six Classics (*Liu jing*), concentrating on the *Spring and Autumn Annals* (*Chunqiu*). He dedicated himself to teaching, founded an academy, and educated many students, thereby keeping Song thought alive in Anhui. In 1344, he was appointed to the Hanlin Academy but declined to serve. During the Red Turban uprising in the 1350s, which led to the ascendancy of Zhu Yuanzhang 朱元璋 (Ming Taizu 明太祖, r. 1368–1398), Zheng was in seclusion, teaching with the classical scholar Wang Kekuan 汪克寬 (1304–1372). As the Ming armies advanced into Anhui, Zheng hanged himself, feeling that he was unable to serve two regimes.

Zheng wrote commentaries on the *Book of Changes* (*Yi jing*) and the *Spring and Autumn Annals*, but he is best known for his attempt to reconcile the philosophies of **Zhu Xi** and **Lu Jiuyuan**, continuing the work of **Wu Cheng**, whose ideas Zheng probably absorbed from Jie Xisi 揭傒斯 (1274–1344), a follower of Wu with whom Zheng was acquainted. The Qing thinker **Quan Zuwang**, in his emendations on the *Records of Song and Yuan Scholars* (*Song–Yuan xuean*), claims that while Wu tended toward Lu in his synthesis, Zheng tended more toward Zhu, even though Zheng felt that Zhu and Lu both embraced the *dao* and that the supposed division between them was created by later scholar–partisans. Zheng

criticised Lu's students for veering off into Buddhist mysticism and, like Wu, chided Zhu's followers for carrying exegesis to extremes; he sought a creative balance between moral improvement and skill in literary expression. As with **Zhao Fang**, Zheng Yu kept Lu's ideas alive in Yuan times in the synthetic context introduced by Wu Cheng, and this became important in the rise of the Learning of the Heart/Mind (*xin xue*) in the Ming era.

References: Bol, 1997: 48–9; Chen Gaohua, 1983: 283–5; Gedalecia, 1999: 143–5; Goodrich & Fang, 1976: vol. II, 1386; Han Rulin, 1986: vol. II, 327; Liu Ts'un-yan, 1986: 531, 535–6, 541; *Song–Yuan xuean*, 94; Tang Yuyuan, 1982: 5–10; *Yuan shi*, 1976: 196.

DAVID GEDALECIA

Zhenyuan liu shu 貞元六書
(*Purity Descends, Primacy Ascends: Six Books*)

Purity Descends, Primacy Ascends: Six Books is the English title given to **Fung Yu-lan**'s modern Chinese philosophical system published in six tomes between 1939 to 1946. The system itself, following the title of the first book, Fung called *Xin lixue* 新理學, 'New Principle-centred Learning'. It was self-consciously conceived by him as a critically received and creatively extrapolated modern expression (*jiezhe jiang* 接著講) of Song-dynasty Confucian teachings, particularly those of **Zhu Xi**, as well as American New Realist philosophy following William P. Montague (1873–1953) and the early Bertrand Russell (1872–1970).

Each volume's title began with *xin* 新 'new', promoting its revisionary intentions. They appeared as follows:

Xin Li xue 新理學 (*New Principle-centered Learning*) (1939)
Xin shilun 新事論 (*New Treatise on Practical Affairs*) (1940)

Xinshi xun 新世訓 (*Teachings for a New Age*) (1940)
Xin yuanren 新原人 (*New Treatise on the Nature of Humans*) (1943)
Xin yuandao 新原道 (*New Treatise on the Nature of the Way*) (1944)
Xin zhiyan 新知言 (*Speaking about New Knowledge*) (1946)

In the first volume, Fung set forth a 'formal' analytical system based on two levels of knowledge, the actual (*shiji* 實際) and the true (*zhenji* 真際). From this he extrapolated a modern metaphysics responsive to both Song Confucian terminology and Euro-American metaphysical analysis and criticism. The next two volumes applied general philosophical principles to institutions and values needed in everyday life, at times manifestly displaying Chinese patriotism. New philosophical developments appeared in his *New Treatise on the Nature of Humans*, where Fung presented a hierarchy of 'intellectual/spiritual realms' (*jingshen jingjie* 精神境界) in order to distinguish the truly philosophical mindset from ignorant, utilitarian and moral realms. It is this philosophical achievement, at its height a cosmic consciousness achieved through comprehensive analytic thinking in both 'positive' and 'negative' modes, which Fung employed as a standard for philosophical acumen in his last two volumes. In the fifth volume he recapitulated major moments in Chinese philosophical traditions, and crowned its development by proclaiming his own New Principle-centred Learning to be the new modern philosophy for China, simultaneously a synthesis and critique of the best Chinese traditions in philosophy. In a similar way, but using very different emphases, Fung summarised in the last volume major 'western' philosophical systems from Plato to the Vienna Circle, and claimed that by following the New Realist approach he had provided a modern Chinese answer to their major methodological and metaphysical problems.

In his concern to provide an analytical foundation for a modern Chinese philosophy, Fung privileged intellectual thinking based on 'principles' (*li*), which he redefined as 'concepts' within the 'true world' in opposition to 'things' in the 'actual world'. Both concepts and things exist in reality, but exist in different modes; philosophers pursue knowledge of subsistent concepts, while scientists only accrue knowledge about actual things. Highest forms of knowledge for Fung were constituted by comprehensive mental understanding of the flowing movement of all existing things, the 'embodiment of the Way' (*daoti* 道體), and the totality made up of all that is actual and true, the 'great whole' (*daquan* 大全).

References: Cai Zhongde, 1974: 294–312; Cheng Weili, 1994; Fang & Zheng, 1995: 104–30; Fung 1939–46, 1947, 1992, 1996, 2000; Masson 1985; Möller 1998; Obenchain ed. 1994: 263–396, 431–49; Pfister 2002; Tian 1990; Wang & Gao, 1995: 82–98, 135–53, 163–75; Yan 1991; Zheng 1995: 141–70.

LAUREN PFISTER

Zhi 祇
(Terrestrial divinity or power)

In early texts such as the **Zhou li**, the cosmology of human and suprahuman beings is sometimes described as a tertiary division of heavenly spirits (*tian shen* 天神), human ghosts (*ren gui* 人鬼), and terrestrial divinities (*di zhi* 地祇). The importance of Heaven in Chinese culture is widely known, but the religious significance of the earth, with which Heaven is usually paired, is less widely appreciated. Heaven's spirits abided in a realm above and could be invoked to descend, human ghosts inhabited the surface of the land, but the terrestrial divinities abided below within the earth and could be invoked to emerge. These latter phenomena were the authochthonous powers of the earth and soil that supported agriculture and the activities of terrestrial formations. Early texts described a bureaucracy of officials who supervised these realms and ministered to the needs of their respective spiritual inhabitants. During sacrificial offerings, terrestrial divinities received reports about such events as the ascension of a new ruler or of military expeditions; supplications invoked their assistance in the event of floods, landslides or famine.

In later times, terrestrial divinities were understood to be the same as the *tu di* 土地, or earth gods, or sometimes the *sheji* 社稷, the spirits of the altars of the land and grain. Throughout Chinese history, maintaining these altars at state, regional and local levels was one of the most important responsibilities of the imperial ritual system.

References: Qin Huitian, 1994: *juan* 37–45; Sun Yirang, 1987.

DEBORAH SOMMER

Zhi 智
(Wisdom, understanding)

Zhi is variously translated as 'wisdom', 'understanding', 'knowledge', 'knowing' or 'realisation'; in early texts the character is often used interchangeably with *zhi* 知, 'to know', 'to understand' or 'to realize'. The precise content of wisdom or understanding is rarely articulated; wisdom is not revealed through a textual canon, body of technical lore, or suprahuman realm but is realised through lived human relationships as one strand of a larger web of such values as humaneness (*xing*), rightness (*yi*), courage (*yong*), humility, and filial piety (*xiao*).

In the *Analects* (*Lunyu*), for example, wisdom was manifested not in a familiarity with discrete items of information but in the ability to interact effectively with others. When asked about wisdom, or understanding, Confucius replied that it consisted of understanding other people. Wisdom was intimately connected to humaneness and was wanting without it; if one did not socialise with humane people, one could not be considered wise. Those who were wise but not humane were considered ill-equipped to lead others effectively, and wisdom in part consisted of serving the people according to the principle of rightness (*yi*). True wisdom moreover required a measure of humility and necessitated admitting when one did or did not know something.

For Confucius, wisdom was a quality bestowed at birth (but bestowed unequally on different people) that nonetheless required development throughout one's life through learning. Ranking types of people by their powers of understanding, he once remarked that people who are possessed of understanding at birth are the highest type, followed, in descending order, by those who understand through learning, who understand only with difficulty, and who struggle but never understand at all.

Whereas Confucius emphasised how people are different, **Mengzi** emphasised their commonality: all people, he asserted, are endowed with an incipient tendency toward wisdom, which he considered the ability to distinguish between right and wrong. All people are possessed of four minds (also understood as germs, beginnings or incipient qualities) of compassion, shame and disgrace, reverence and respect and the ability to distinguish right and wrong (see *si duan*). These are associated with the values of humaneness, rightness/righteousness, ritual/propriety and wisdom, respectively. Human nature being endowed with such tendencies, people can become good. Wisdom moreover was expressed in one's ability to nourish family relationships.

By Han times, these four values came to be called the Four Cardinal Virtues or Four Constant Virtues, to which a fifth, *xin* or trustworthiness, was sometimes added, to make the Five Constant Virtues (*Wu chang*). In his biography in the *History of the Han Dynasty* (*Han shu*), **Dong Zhongshu** is attributed with developing these associations. In the Han, the virtues were moreover correlated with the Five Phases (*Wu xing*), the seasons, and the directions. In later centuries, wisdom was discussed in the context of its relationships with the other three or four virtues.

Song scholars built upon Mengzi's notion that the Four Beginnings of humaneness, rightness/righteousness, ritual/propriety and wisdom are inherent to the human condition, and they synthesised these with the Five Phases, principle, and human nature. **Zhou Dunyi** called these the 'five natures' (adding the quality of trustworthiness as the fifth) in the cosmology he developed in his *Taijitu shuo*, correlating them with the Five Phases. Those who were able to develop their five natures, he asserted, could become sages.

Zhu Xi described the five virtues in his commentary on the *Doctrine of the Mean* (*Zhongyong*), a text that described wisdom as the ability to discern a mean between two extremes, a fragile and easily lost capacity that could be honed by a love of learning. Zhu associated the five virtues with a human nature possessed of principle (*li*), a nature bestowed by Heaven as it produced things through the permutations of yin and yang and the Five Phases. Elsewhere he spoke of four cardinal virtues, privileging humaneness and wisdom. Later in life, he associated these four with processual metaphors of the *Book of Changes* (*Yi jing*) and developed a theory of wisdom that is both hidden and stored. This latter idea influenced the thinking of Japanese Confucian scholar **Yamazaki Ansai**. Zhu's notions of the Four Cardinal Virtues were also influential in the **Four–Seven Debates** in Korea concerning the relationships of the Four Virtues to the Seven Emotions.

Chen Chun outlined the main characteristics of wisdom in his discussion of the interrelatedness of the Five Constant Virtues in his *Beixi ziyi*, concisely condensing the views of Song thinkers on these concepts.

References: Ames & Rosemont, 1998: 2: 17, 4: 1, 4: 2, 12: 22, 6: 20, 6: 22, 15: 33, 16: 9, 17: 3, 17: 8; Chan, Wing-tsit, 1986b: 69–85, 1989: 96–7; de Bary & Bloom, 1999: 672–8, 704–5, 735; Kalton, 1994; Lau, 1984, 2A: 6, 6A: 6, 7A: 21, 4A: 27; Legge, 1966: *Doctrine of the Mean* 4, 6, 7, 20:8, 20:10, 25:3; Okada, 1986; Shun, 1997a: 66–71.

DEBORAH SOMMER

Zhi guo 治國
(Ordering the state)

In keeping with the fundamental Confucian emphasis on dedicating one's own capacities to the higher aim of maintaining order in human society, the chain of phases of self-cultivation enumerated in the so-called 'eight specific points' (*ba tiaomu*) in the opening section of the **Daxue** culminates in the ideals of 'ordering the state' (*zhi guo*) and 'bringing peace to the entire world' (*ping tianxia*). The supreme value of instilling order at different levels of human interaction runs through most of the objective spheres of cultivation set forth in this canonic passage, from 'setting straight one's mental faculties' (*zheng xin*) and 'cultivating the individual self' (*xiu shen*), to 'stabilising the family' (*qi jia*) and finally ordering the state and the world. At each of these levels the act of ordering can be understood as the antithesis, or the corrective, of the greatest anathema of Confucian thought: disorder (*luan*).

The ordering of the state is thus the natural extension of rectifying the individual mind and its outward manifestations in interpersonal behaviour, both in the personal and the social dimensions. In this sense, the ordering of the state emerges as the broadest possible sphere for concrete human action, short of the more abstract realm of the 'entire world', and so the 'expansion chapters' that constitute the remainder of the text pointedly refrain from discussing the latter sphere in specific detail. In the 'expansion chapter' devoted to 'ordering the state' (Chapter 10), the initial emphasis is placed less on practical techniques of statecraft and more on the central concept of cultivating a solid foundation of moral judgement, grounded in one's own essential humanity, before turning to the fulfilment of one's role in the larger structures of social and political order. This idea is expressed here in the striking metaphor of measuring by the 'carpenter's square' (*xie ju* 絜矩), used in the sense of determining one's proper function in the outer world according to the measure of one's own inner moral self.

ANDREW PLAKS

Zhi liangzhi 致良知
(Extending the Innate Knowledge of the Good)

Zhi liangzhi means extension (*zhi* 致) of 'radically good knowledge' or 'innate knowledge of the good'. In the thought and practice of **Wang Shouren** (Wang Yangming) and his followers, *zhi liangzhi* represents a breakthrough synthesis of two ideas: *liangzhi* as found in *Mengzi* 7A: 15 (see *liangzhi liangneng*) and *zhi zhi* 致知 (extension of knowledge), the second of the eight steps (*ba tiaomu*) of cultivation practice in the *Daxue* (Great Learning). Mengzi defines *liangzhi* as that which a person knows without deliberation (*lü* 慮); using 'radically good' for *liang* 良 indicates both fundamental rootedness and far-reaching implications.

In the context of the *Daxue*, **Zhu Xi** had taught that extension of knowledge was a gradual accumulation based on 'investigation of things' (*gewu* 格物, see *gewu zhizhi*). Wang presents a different conclusion in his commentary on the *Daxue*; in his view, genuine knowledge is not something gathered from outside, but an extension of one's own conscientious consciousness. The starting point is the distinction of heavenly principle and human desire (*tianli renyu*). 'Extension' means to apply this innate good knowing with regard to particular affairs, in order to 'correct them'

(also *gewu* 格物). *Zhi liangzhi* became the foundation for Wang's dynamic idealistic epistemology; he remarked that all learning is the extension of *liangzhi* (see **Chuanxi lu**). Wang's teaching of *zhi liangzhi* was criticised by many, such as **Luo Qinshun** and **Wang Fuzhi**. Nevertheless, it remains a significant development of Mengzi's thought and a fruitful resource for contemporary Confucian thinkers such as **Cheng Zhongying**, **Liu Shuxian** and **Tu Wei-ming**.

References: Chan, Wing-tsit, 1963d: 654–67, and 1963c; Ching, 1976: 104–24; Dong, 1995: 303–5, 472; Nivison, 1996: 220–31; Tu, 1976; Zhong, 1993: 79–98.

THOMAS SELOVER

Zhi ren 至人
(Supreme humans)

Zhi ren is originally a Daoist ideal where a human can fulfil the ultimate Way (**dao**). In chapter 1 and chapter 22 of the *Zhuangzi* 庄子, it is said that a *zhiren* has no self (*wuji* 無己) and practises non-action (*wu wei*). Following this line of thought, **Xunzi** described a *zhiren* as the one who has understood the distinction between Heaven and humanity (*Tian lun* 天論 chapter). It is also stated that 'Not to act, yet to bring to completion; not to seek, yet to obtain – this indeed may be described as the work of Nature.' In such a situation, the *zhi ren*, however profound, does not apply any thought to the work of Nature . . . 'Heaven has its seasons; Earth its resources; and humans their government.' This, of course, is why it is said that they 'can form a triad'. As John Knoblock indicates, 'Following the course of Nature makes life easy; contravening its principles makes life impossible . . . The *zhiren*, thus, takes care to assure that everything is controlled and ordered because he "knows Nature" in this sense.'

Reference: Knoblock, 1988, vol. III.

TODD CAMERON THACKER

Zhi shan 至善
(The fullest attainment of the good)

The third of the 'three basic principles' (**san gangling**) enumerated at the start of the opening chapter of the **Daxue** canon presents a challenge to interpretation, in that the term **shan** (善) used here is far less common than its western equivalent ('goodness') in the vocabulary of Confucian ethics, where the term *ren* ('humaneness') covers some of the same semantic ground. The expression *zhi shan*, literally something like 'supreme goodness', is even more problematic, since it seems to bespeak a notion of the absolute good that is largely foreign to Confucian philosophical discourse.

In the 'expansion chapter' devoted to an elucidation of this concept (chapter 3), we learn from a variety of proof texts and attached commentaries that the point at issue here is, in fact, precisely the sort of self-cultivation that is exemplified in its most perfect form by the ancient sages, and attainable by other men of noble character through the practice of the Confucian virtues. The apparently paradoxical injunction that the man of noble character must 'come to rest' (*zhi* 止) in the 'fullest attainment of the good' is here clarified as a process of reaching a state of stable equilibrium in one's exercise of virtuous behaviour that is understood to be not a final end of cultivation, but rather just the first stage in an ongoing process of self-perfection.

Andrew Plaks

Zhi sheng 至聖
(Supreme Sage)

The term 'supreme sage' appears in the *Doctrine of the Mean* (**Zhongyong**), where it refers to the only man in the world with the ability and brilliant insight to rule properly. **Sima Qian** calls Confucius (*Fuzi*) a Supreme sage because he correctly embodies the Six Arts (**Liu yi**). The term 'Supreme Sage' was first added to Confucius' posthumous title in 1013, when he was called Supreme Sage, Exalted King of Culture (*Zhi sheng Wenxuan Wang* 至聖文宣王). A few years earlier he had been given the title **Xuan sheng Wenxuan Wang** (Dark Sage, Exalted King of Culture), but the word 'dark' was changed to 'supreme' to avoid an imperial taboo.

Thomas A. Wilson

Zhi sheng xianshi 至聖先師
(Supreme Sage, First Teacher)

Confucius, who held the posthumous title of king since the eight century (see **Wenxuan Wang**, Exalted King of Culture), was stripped of this rank in 1530 and given the title 'Supreme Sage, First Teacher' during a series of fundamental temple changes. The titles of all gods and spirits of the imperial pantheon were eliminated in 1370, except that of Confucius, who held on to his royal status. The 1530 reforms necessitated changes in the liturgy of sacrifices such as the reduction in the number of sacrificial vessels and ritual dancers. The reforms were vehemently opposed by many court officials – who endured severe punishments as a result – in part because of claims by some that the changes signified Confucius' declining status *vis-à-vis* the throne. The changes did not, however, affect Confucius' status in the imperial pantheon – rather, it brought his cult in line with those of other gods and spirits – and by no means signalled a decline in the importance of Confucianism at court or in Chinese culture generally.

Thomas A. Wilson

Zhi tian shi tian 知天事天
(To know Heaven and to serve Heaven)

Zhi means to know or to understand; *shi* means to serve (see **shi tian**); and **tian** is Heaven. The relationship between understanding and serving Heaven is stated in **Mengzi** 7A: 1, where knowing heaven is premised upon knowing the nature (**xing**), which in turn is premised upon the development of the mind or heart (**xin**). By sustaining the mind and nourishing the nature, one thereby serves Heaven. Hence, inward cultivation, which is accessible to anyone regardless of social status, is itself tantamount to maintaining obligations to the larger cosmos.

The *Mengzi* interpretation of knowing or serving Heaven differs from others in several ways. Elsewhere, serving Heaven consists of ritualised offerings (also known as *shi*, or services) to Heaven and its spirits (**shen**) performed only by those whose rank permitted them direct access to Heaven. And the **Zhongyong** associates understanding Heaven not with knowing oneself but with understanding ghosts and spirits (**gui shen**; *Zhongyong* 29.4). Before the *Mengzi*, knowing Heaven was largely within the purview of sages and sovereigns. The sage Confucius claims to have understood the Mandate of Heaven (**Tian ming**), but only when he reached the age of fifty (*Lunyu* 2: 4). The *Zhongyong* asserts that sovereigns must first understand Heaven in order to understand human beings, serve their parents and cultivate themselves, but it does not present a similar imperative for ordinary people.

The *Xunzi*, moreover, asserts the seemingly contrarian notion that the sage does not seek to know Heaven – yet devotes an entire chapter to a discussion of Heaven's operations.

References: Ames & Rosemont, 1998: 2:4; Knoblock, 1988–94: vol. III, pp. 9–10, 15; Lau, 1984, 7A: 1; Wang Xianqian, 1988: vol. II, p. 309.

DEBORAH SOMMER

Zhi xing 知行
(Knowing and acting)

Zhi means 'knowing', 'understanding', or even 'knowledge'. 'Knowing', however, better evokes the sense of an active process than 'knowledge', which suggests cognitive acquaintance with a body of lore or information. Knowing, particularly when it is paired with the term '*xing*', which means acting, implies an awareness that is truly validated only when it is brought into living practice. *Zhi* can also mean 'to know', 'to understand' or 'to be wise'. It is sometimes used interchangeably with **zhi** 智, 'wisdom' or 'understanding'. *Xing* means 'to act', 'to enact', 'to put into action' and 'to put into practice'; it also literally means 'to walk'. Hence, *xing dao* means both to walk on the way and to enact the Way.

Most early thinkers spoke of the relationship between knowing and acting in a general sense without necessarily using both the terms *zhi* and *xing*. Confucius, for example, described the relationship between humaneness and action, defining the former as the putting into practice of such values as trustworthiness, respect and magnanimity. He moreover described the relationship between learning (rather than knowing) and the performance of ritual. **Mengzi**, on the other hand, said that what people are able to do (*neng* 能) *without* study is what they are truly capable of doing (*liang neng* 良能); what they know without reflection is what they truly know (*liang zhi* 良知). The spontaneity of Mengzi's sense of truly knowing was later to influence greatly the thought of **Wang Shouren**.

The **Chunqiu Zuo zhuan** (Duke Zhao 10th Year) and the **Shang shu** (*Book of History*), however, refer specifically to the relationship between *zhi* and *xing*. Describing the difficulties of implementing wise political counsel, a brief passage from the *Shang shu* asserts that it is not knowing what to do but actually putting that understanding into practice that is difficult.

Xunzi explored these difficulties and was one of the first thinkers to articulate the relationship between *zhi* and *xing* at some length. In a chapter on the teachings of the **Ru**, or Confucians, he defined the ideal behaviour of the *Ru* in part as the ability to put into practice what one knew. Simply knowing something was not as good as enacting it, for the epitome of learning was action; the accumulated efforts to implement what one knew transformed the self, facilitated sagehood and allowed one to form a ternion with Heaven and Earth. To ascertain what one should know, one required the guidance of a teacher.

The *Doctrine of the Mean* (**Zhongyong**) and the *Great Learning* (**Daxue**), however, were more influential in later understandings of knowing and acting than was the **Xunzi**. The *Doctrine of the Mean* described the access people had to the Way, which was at once vast and hidden: ordinary men and women could know it and enact it, but there were aspects of the Way that even sages could neither know nor put into practice (Chapter 12). The *Great Learning*, on the other hand, outlined an eight-step programme for self-development that expanded to encompass the development of the entire world. One of the first of these steps was the extension of one's knowing or understanding (*zhi zhi* 致知), a stage that then led to such activities (albeit not specifically called *xing*) as regulating the family and ordering the state.

These two chapters of the *Book of Rites* (*Li ji*) were much later elevated to the status of independent texts and greatly influenced the thought of such Song scholars as **Zhu Xi**. Knowing, for Zhu, was localised in the mind or heart (**xin**), and was premised upon investigating the things and events of this world and comprehending principle (**li**). Knowing and acting were like two wheels of a cart or two wings of a bird; one could not have one without the other, although knowing took precedence in terms of order and acting took precedence in terms of importance. Knowing something without acting upon it was superficial; great effort was moreover necessary for extending one's understanding of things and events to the utmost. He followed **Cheng Yi**'s belief that the development of

knowing and acting might eventually lead to sagehood.

The interrelatedness of knowing and acting reached a high point in the writings of Wang Shouren, who asserted that knowing and acting were one (*zhixing heyi*). One did not need to wait to know something before enacting it; knowing was already implied in the doing. People who claimed to know what filiality was, for example, but did not act filially, simply did not yet really know what filiality was. The perceived distinction between knowing and acting was an obfuscation, Wang asserted, caused by selfish human desires.

References: Ames & Rosemont, 1998: 6: 27, 17: 6; Chan, Wing-tsit, 1963a: 9–12, 201, 1963b: 609–12, 1989: 235–54, 1996: 117–122; de Bary & Bloom, 1999: 721–37; Knoblock, 1988–94: vol. I: 205, vol. II: 81–3; Lau, 1984, 7A: 15; Legge, 1985c: 258; Wang Shouren, 1992: 1–6; Wang Xianqian, 1988: 77, 142.

DEBORAH SOMMER

Zhi xing heyi 知行合一
(Unity of knowing and acting)

This notion was developed by the fifteenth-century thinker **Wang Shouren**, who asserted that such unity was simply the fundamental substance (*ben ti* 本體) of knowing and acting. Knowing was the conceptual focus (*zhu yi* 主意) for acting, and acting was the effort (*gongfu* 功夫) of knowing. Knowing was the beginning of acting, and acting was knowing's completion – and yet, he emphasised, they were not two separate things. In his **Chuanxi lu**, Wang, using an analogy from the ancient text of the *Great Learning*, claimed that knowing was like 'seeing beautiful colours' whereas acting was like 'loving beautiful colours'; the immediate and uncalculated response of 'loving' demonstrated that a seamless unity prevailed between knowing (seeing) and acting (loving).

Even though one's powers of knowing inherently tended toward the good (*liang zhi* 良知), the unity between knowing and acting could be marred, nonetheless, by the interference of selfish desires, which one needed to overcome in order to return to the fundamental substance and potentially become a sage. Because knowing was already acting, Wang urged the removal of even evil thoughts, for they already constituted evil actions.

Wang believed that much human discord and moral languor was caused by inappropriate distinctions (some of which he attributed to Song thinkers) between such things as mind and principle, knowledge and action. The remedy for the inertia of such divisiveness, which produced people who neither acted nor understood, was his 'medicine' of the unity of knowing and acting.

References: Chan, Wing-tsit, 1963c: 9–12, 201; Wang Shouren, 1992: 1–6.

DEBORAH SOMMER

Zhi zhong he 致中和
(The fullest realisation of balance and harmony)

This expression from the opening chapter of the canonic *Zhongyong* text describes the combined fulfilment of the two supreme ideals delineated in that passage: 'balance and harmony' (*zhong he*). Since this passage is at pains to differentiate these two seemingly synonymous terms as related to the realm of cosmic totality, on the one hand, and the world of concrete existence, on the other, the notion of their maximum fulfilment at one and the same time indicates a degree of attainment attributable only to the most perfect sages, and entailing consequences of a metaphysical character. These latter implications are further elucidated in the discussions of the 'supreme sage' or 'perfect sagehood' (*zhi sheng*) and 'supreme sin-

cerity' or 'perfect self-completion' (*zhicheng* 至誠) in chapters 26 to 33.

ANDREW PLAKS

Zhizhai xuepai 止齋學派
(The School of Chen Fuliang)

The Zhizai School, founded by **Chen Fuliang** and his students, was located in the Zhedong 浙東 region (modern Zhejiang). Chen's leading students included Cai Youxue 蔡幼學 (1154–1217, *zi* Xingzhi 行之), Cao Shuyuan 曹叔遠 (?–?, *zi* Qiyuan 器遠), Lü Shengzhi 呂聲之 (?–?, *zi* Daheng 大亨), Zhou Duanchao 周端朝 (1172–1234, *zi* Zijing 子靜, *hao* Xili 西麗), Li Yuanbai 李元白 (?–?, *zi* Jingping 景平, *hao* Sanjiang 三江), among others. The Zhizai School further developed the pragmatic style of Confucianism advocated by **Xue Jixuan**. However, followers of the school would eventually come into conflict with scholars associated with **Zhu Xi**'s Hui-an 晦庵 School over matters involving the Zhizai School's 'utilitarian' 功利 orientation.

Hoyt Tillman has noted that Chen followed fellow Zhedong scholars **Lü Zuqian** and **Chen Liang** in maintaining that virtue was the foundation of proper government and that it would be a suitable role for government to enforce strong laws to encourage such virtue. Therefore, Chen Fuliang may be counted among the utilitarian Confucians of twelfth-century Zhejiang. Many of the school's teachings focused on the ancient text of the *Rites of Zhou* (**Zhou li**) in seeking roots for an ideal social blueprint, and followers of this school searched ancient texts for evidence describing the ideal balance of civil and military powers. Moreover, scholars of this group criticised their own court's overwhelming preference for civil authority even in matters that should have been the prerogative of military officials. However, Tillman qualified the label 'utilitarian' by noting that it was an approach to Confucian thinking that included an 'understanding of the Way (*Dao*) in terms of what was appropriate to meet the ends of the time and circumstance'. In this case, the criticism of *dao xue* (the Learning of the Way) scholars that the Zhizai School leaned dangerously close to Legalism seems erroneous.

References: *Song–Yuan xuean*, 1966: 1707–10; Tillman, 1992a: 95, 156; Wu & Song, 1992a: 1474.

JAMES A. ANDERSON

Zhong 忠
(Devotion to duty, loyalty)

In many contexts in classical and colloquial Chinese this word functions as the simple equivalent of the English word 'loyalty'. In a number of seminal texts of the Confucian canon, however, it can be glossed, and translated, in the sense of 'doing one's best', or 'doing the utmost', in accordance with the demands of a given set of interpersonal relations or ritual obligations. This meaning is particularly striking in a key passage in the *Analects* (**Lunyu** 4: 15), also paraphrased in Chapter 13 of the *Zhongyong* (*Doctrine of the Mean*), where it is singled out, along with the related term *shu*, as constituting the 'central thread' of the Way of Confucius. On the basis of its *locus classicus* in the *Analects*, in which this formulation is attributed to the disciple Zeng Shen 曾參 (505 BCE?–435 BCE?), as well as certain other writings also traditionally ascribed to his name, the concept of *zhong* is frequently cited as the particular preoccupation of Zeng Shen as a thinker.

The more abstract meaning of the term *zhong* as the fulfilment of one's role in interpersonal relations, rather than in the narrow sense of political or personal 'loyalty', parallels the deeper construal of the word *xiao* as a more profound ideal than

simply filial 'obedience'. And so, these two terms are frequently paired in both their narrower and their broader senses.

Reference: Nivison, 1996.

ANDREW PLAKS

Zhong dao 中道
(The middle way)

While this is not a fixed term of Confucian philosophical discourse, it is quite current as a common expression for the 'middle way' of moderation and temperance that is implicit in much of Confucian thinking. In this popular sense it is more or less synonymous with the colloquial usage of the expression *zhongyong*. It can also be understood literally as the 'Way' (*Dao*) governed by the principle of 'the mean' (*zhong*), and in this sense it can also refer to the more profound and nuanced meaning of this latter term as elaborated in the *Zhongyong* treatise.

ANDREW PLAKS

Zhong he 中和
(Balance and harmony)

These two terms for states of equilibrium are often virtually synonymous in common speech, but when they are brought together in the opening chapter of the *Zhongyong*, they are significantly distinguished from one another. Whereas the former ideal is posited there as the primary attribute of a hypothetical state of being 'prior to the emergence of the experiential markers of the world of concrete existence' (*xi nu ai le zhi weifa* 喜怒哀樂之未發), later (in Chapter 20) identified with the 'Way of Heaven' (*tian zhi dao*), the latter term is ascribed specifically to the compensatory restoration of equilibrium in the existential world, that in which the parameters of human experience have already 'emerged' into reality (*yifa* 已發).

ANDREW PLAKS

Zhong jing 中經
(The Medium Classics)

The usage of the term of *Zhong jing*, the Medium Classics, first appeared in the Wei (220–265) period by Zheng Mo 鄭默. He collected the books and kept them in Mishu-Sheng Zhongwai Ge 秘書省中外三閣 for the purpose of their safety (*Sui shu* 隋書, ch. 32). In the Sui and Tang periods, classical texts were divided into three categories: the *Da jing* (Great Classics), *Zhong jing* (Medium Classics) and *Xiao jing* (Minor Classics) according to their length and complexity. The Medium Classics consisted of the **Shi jing**, **Zhou li** and **Yi li**. This tradition started with the **civil service examinations**. The Song dynasty continued to implement the civil service examinations, and as a result, the Medium Classics were expanded and rearranged as five canons: the **Shang shu**, **Zhou yi**, (**Chunqiu**) **Gongyang zhuan**, (**Chunqiu**) **Guliang zhuan** and **Yi li**.

References: Fung Yu-lan, 1952; *Song shi*, 1977; *Tang Huiyao*, 1955.

M.H. KIM

Zhong lun 中論
(*Balanced Discourses*)

Balanced Discourses is the representative writing of the late Han philosopher–literatus, **Xu Gan**, and a collection of essays which embraces topics ranging from Confucian cultivation to calendrical calculation. Taken as a whole, the collection constitutes a wide-ranging polemical inquiry into the causes of political and social breakdown, while also proposing various remedies. Xu Gan's argumentation frequently appeals to the authority of classical Confucian

ethical values; indeed, the work is classified under *ru jia* 儒家 in all bibliographical lists of the standard histories, except for that of *Song shi* 宋史, where it is listed among miscellaneous writers. Xu Gan lived at a nodal point in the history of Chinese thought, when Han (206 BCE–220 CE) scholasticism had become ossified and the creative and independent thinking that characterised Wei–Jin (220–420) thought was just emerging. The *Balanced Discourses* offers modern historians of Chinese thought a unique contemporary account of a range of social, intellectual and cosmological factors that Xu Gan identified as having precipitated the demise of the Han order. His perspectives on these issues are also of philosophical interest as they reveal his belief in a special correlative bond that should obtain between names (*ming* 名) and actualities (*shi* 實), and his understanding of the consequences of that bond being broken. In naming the collection '*Balanced Discourses*', the author/editor may have been suggesting that the particular mode of expression common to the individual essays was itself ordered in accordance with the mode of ordering which the collection as a whole expounded. In other words, he understood these essays to display that same quality of 'balance' which motivated Xu Gan to write them in the first place: as catalysts to restore the point of balance, or centred equilibrium, of the Way.

References: Makeham, 1994; Makeham, tr., 2002.

JOHN MAKEHAM

Zhong You 仲由
542–480 BCE
(*zi* Zilu 子路, *aka* Jilu 季路)

Zhong You, a native of Sishui 泗水 county (twenty-five kilometres west of Qufu), was a prominent disciple of Confucius known for his oratory. He received sacrifices in the temple as one of the **Ten Savants** in 712, was ennobled as Marquis of Wei 子路衛侯 in 739, promoted to duke in 1009, given the title of Duke of Henei 河內公仲由 in 1113, and called Master Zhong You 仲子由 in 1530, when everyone enshrined in the temple was stripped of their noble titles. A temple 仲子廟 was built for him in Sishui in 1591.

THOMAS A. WILSON

Zhongchang Tong 仲長統
c. 180–220
(*zi* Gongli 公理)

Zhongchang Tong was a leading political thinker in the twilight of the Han dynasty. The scholar and Wei official Miao Xi 繆襲 (186?–245, *zi* Xibo 熙伯) praised his talent as heir to **Dong Zhongshu**, **Jia Yi**, **Liu Xiang**, and **Yang Xiong**. As a youth, Zhongchang Tong threw himself into his studies; in his twenties, he took to the road, travelling throughout the North as an itinerant scholar. Called the 'Madman' (Kuangsheng 狂生) by some, Zhongchang Tong was uncompromisingly straightforward in criticisms, and was rarely reticent. He defied entreaties by local officials to join their administrations, and his reproach of those who curried favour to obtain office was unrelenting. Eventually, he served the central court, first as a gentleman of the secretariat (*Shangshu lang* 尚書郎), and then as an adviser to Cao Cao 曹操 (155–220, *zi* Mengde 孟德). His seminal work, *Chang yan* 昌言 (*Frank Remarks*; *c.* 206), was a monograph in thirty-four sections; only three sections and some fragments survive. *Chang yan* advocates strong, authoritarian leadership and a severe penal code, attacks the disproportionate power wielded by the great landowners and consort clans, and champions the destitute yet talented *shi*. Zhongchang Tong discourses on the inevitability of dynastic decline, and on the downward spiral of cyclical history, in which upheavals were growing ever more malicious and brutal. His extreme pessim-

ism reflects the times; the year of his death coincides with that of the last Han ruler's abdication.

References: Balazs, 1964; Hsiao, 1979.

MARK L. ASSELIN

Zhongguo Kongzi Jijinhui
中國孔子基金會
(Chinese Confucius Foundation)

The *Zhongguo Kongzi Jijinhui* was established in September 1984, as a national academic organisation for encouraging studies of Confucianism and Chinese traditional cultures and exchanges between scholars and academic institutes both in China and abroad. The honorary president of the Foundation was Gu Mu 谷牧, its chief adviser was Zhou Gucheng 周谷城, and the first president was Kuang Yaming 匡亞明. A good number of well-known academics and intellectuals from a wide range of areas joined the foundation as advisers, associate presidents, and directors. The Foundation is composed of five subcommittees covering academics, funding, information, publication and the research institute of Confucius and Confucianism. The contents of the academic studies and exchanges of the Foundation are engaged on five levels or in five aspects: Confucius, the different schools of Confucianism, traditional Chinese culture based on Confucianism, East Asian cultures and the comparison between eastern and western cultures. Methodologically, the Foundation sets out to encourage independent thinking and free discussion among people of differing viewpoints, in order to prompt Chinese Socialist construction and to further the progress of human civilisation. The main activities of the Foundation are such as follows. Firstly, it launched in March 1986 a quarterly journal of *Confucius Studies* (*Kongzi yanjiu* 孔子研究) that has since published a great number of high quality academic papers. Secondly, it has so far organised or co-organised five important and influential international conferences on Confucianism, of which three were held on the anniversary of Confucius' 2540th, 2545th, and 2550th birthdays. Thirdly, the foundation published a series of books on topics such as Research of Traditional Chinese Culture and proceedings of conferences. Fourthly, it established connections of various kinds with the main Institutes of Confucius Studies abroad and co-founded the *International Confucian Studies Association* (*Guoji Ruxue Lianhehui* 國際儒學聯合會). The positive activities of the CCF has successfully enhanced the level of research in Confucianism and helped correct misunderstandings of Confucianism, while promoting academic relationships and exchanges between Chinese scholars and those abroad. It has helped to raise the social position of Confucian studies, and provided Confucianism with a more positive role to play in contemporary China and in the world.

Reference: Wu & Song, 1992.

OUYANG KANG

Zhongguo renwen jingsheng zhi fazhan 中國人文精神之發展

(*The Development of Humane-and-Literary Spirit in China*)

A Confucian humanist response to crises putatively caused by Sino-western cultural conflicts, this book, originally published in 1957 by **Tang Junyi**, is a detailed comparative philosophical and cross-cultural apologetic for the contemporary relevance of major Confucian teachings. It focuses on the human heart/mind (*xin* 心) and human nature (*xing* 性) addressed in the *Mengzi* and developed by the Song dynasty Principle-Centred Learning (*li xue*). Tang emphasises their role in moral effort (*gong fu* 功夫) expressed in 'looking for the causes of affairs in oneself' (*fan qiu zhu ji* 反求諸己). Arguing historically and philo-

sophically in Hegelian style, Tang believes Sino-western cultural conflicts need to be resolved in a new cultural synthesis – based on a modern 'humane-and-literary spirit' (*renwen jingshen* 人文精神) – which sublates past shortcomings in humanist traditions and transformatively advances their strengths.

While recognising that aspects from both the scientific or 'non-humane-and-literary' spirit (*fei renwen* 非人文) and religious or 'trans-humane-and-literary' spirit (*chao renwen* 超人文) can support this development, Tang also argues that 'anti-humane-and-literary' ideologies (*fan renwen* 反人文), and especially Chinese Communism, must be properly opposed and humanely overcome through this development. Consequently he supports humane development of scientific and technological enterprises as well as democratic political associations supported by objective law, and generally appreciates the value of major world religions. These all help to develop the modern humanistic self-consciousness Tang promotes. This book anticipates and justifies the major themes expressed in the 1958 Confucian Manifesto written by Tang and four other New Confucians.

References: Cheng & Bunnin, 2002; Fang & Li, 1995: vol. I: 242–331; Fang & Zheng, 1995: 238–42; Pfister 1985.

LAUREN PFISTER

Zhongguo renxinglun shi 中國人性論史

(*The History of Chinese Theories of Human Nature*)

By studing the origin and development of theories of human nature in the preimperial period, **Xu Fuguan** proved in this book of 1963 that questions about human nature were central to both early Chinese philosophical history and the overall development of a humane-and-literate spirit (*renwen jingshen* 人文精神) in China. While most of the book was devoted to Confucian texts and figures, ranging from the early Zhou period to **Xunzi** and the **Daxue** (*Great Learning*) Xu also included chapters on Moist and Daoist traditions. Scholarly comments assessing later Song and Ming Confucian reflections on problems in the **Zhongyong** and the *Great Learning* add to the book's value. Rich in critical textual scholarship and historical reconstruction, Xu argues that a major transformation from early transcendent religious world-views to a morality expressed in inwardly focused humane culture occurred in early Confucian writings. The pivotal transition in ancient Zhou texts relates to an anxious consciousness (*youhuan yishi* 憂患意識) about proper government, traditions which Confucius later developed through practices of 'moral effort' (*gong fu* 工夫) and teachings related to humaneness (**ren**). Highpoints of theoretical development came in Mengzi's arguments for the goodness of human nature and the aesthetic application of Daoist theories in Zhuangzi's 莊子 teachings. A final reflective summary of the mainline Confucian tradition appeared later in the section on the *Great Learning*.

Setting forth a revised account of the origins of Chinese philosophical history and the character of Chinese culture, Xu's study became a standard work in modern New Confucian studies.

References: Huang Chün-chieh, 1995; Fang & Li, 1995: vol. III: 612–16; Fang & Zheng, 1995: 306–9.

LAUREN PFISTER

Zhongti xiyong 中體西用
(Chinese   substance   and   western applications)

This was one of the main arguments used by some leading Confucian scholars to deal with the relationship between western and Chinese culture in the later nineteeth and

early twentieth century. In China, Korea and Japan, the argument was couched in such slogans as: 'The spirit of Confucianism as substance and western culture as applications', 'Chinese learning for the essential principle, while western Learning (*xi xue*) for the practical application', 'eastern morality and western technology', or 'eastern ethics and western science'. Some of the scholars involved in this debate include **Feng Guifen** and **Wang Tao**, among others, who based on the traditional perception of **dao qi** (the Way is constant while the arte-facts are changing), emphasised Chinese traditional thought as a foundation on which to receive western scientific knowledge and techniques. After the Qing–Japanese war (894–95) there was a gradual decline in its favour, until **Zhang Zhidong**'s *Quan Xue Pian* 勸學篇. From Zhang's critical stand-point, the proper course of action was to pro-ceed with Chinese learning (*zhong xue* 中學) as the substance and western learning (*xi xue* 西學) as the process or use. This proposal would thereby facilitate and mediate the importation of western culture, and in the process empower and thereby protect the nation from detrimental western influence by, so to speak, fighting 'fire with fire'. For Zhang, Chinese learning is inner learning (*nei xue* 內學), in which the body and soul is trained, while Western Learning is outer learning (*wai xue* 外學), that which cor-responds to worldly affairs (*shi shi* 世事). Thus underlying this new method, tradi-tional culture and the national spirit of the people would be the foundation of learning, while the new training, knowledge and technical innovations from outside would go overtop this, supplementing and modern-ising China in a controlled fashion. Above all, traditional culture was not to be affected. Naturally, two main camps emerged: those who sought to enrich and empower China, modernising it through reforming the con-stitution as rapidly as possible, hence the reformers (*Bian Fa Pai* 變法派), and those who sought this goal through gradual improvement, hence the conservatives (*Bao

Shou Pai 保守派). Modern western philosophy was not introduced to China until 1898, with **Yan Fu**'s translation of Huxley's *Evolution and Ethics.*

References: Yao, 2000.

TODD CAMERON THACKER

Zhongyong 中庸
(*Doctrine of the Mean*)

The canonical text **Zhongyong** has been consistently paired with the **Daxue** through its entire textual history, from its inclusion as a chapter in the *Book of Rites* (*Li ji*) compendium in the Han period to its incorporation into the Four Books (*Si shu*) in the restructuring of the canon in the time of **Zhu Xi** in the Song period. It, too, is of uncertain provenance. Its traditional attribution to Confucius' grandson, the second-generation disciple Zisi (子思, see **Kong Ji**), is generally discounted by modern scholars, but in this case a body of other writings in the *Li ji* corpus ascribed to this same figure, plus certain other listings in early bibliographical sources, lend a greater degree of significance to the claim. In this light, Zisi is also viewed as a transitional figure in the orthodox chain of transmission (*dao tong*), linking the first-generation disciples of the Master to the first full exposition of Confucian thought in the writings of **Mengzi** 150 years later. Even more than the *Daxue*, however, the *Zhongyong* is tied by a dense network of intertextual borrowings and allusions to a variety of philosophical writings dating from both before and after its first attested recension in the early Han. Of particular interest to scholars is the presence in the text of strong echoes, in some cases direct paraphrases, of important passages in the **Mengzi**, on the one hand, and **Xunzi**, on the other, since these have provided the grounds for ongoing controversies regarding the intellectual orientation of the original author. Despite the uncertainties of its date and authorship, the text of the *Zhongyong* has remained remarkably stable over the course of its development, with no major variants to speak of in its canonic recension.

An initial perusal of the *Zhongyong* shows a structural arrangement identical to that found in the *Daxue*: an opening section presenting a programmatic overview of the core message of the text (similarly termed the 'canon,' or *jing*) and a series of 'expansion chapters' referred to as 'commentarial traditions' (*zhuan*) developing in detail the ideas presented at the outset. In this case, however, the expansion chapters are not keyed to specific terms or lines in the opening section, but rather take up the central threads of the argument and probe their meaning through a patchwork of proof texts, interpretive comments and philosophical argumentation. These thirty-two chapters fall neatly into three distinct sections. The first (Chapters 2 to 11) consists of a series of actual or fabricated quotations from the Master dealing with the supreme difficulty of realising the ideal of the mean in common practice. The following section (Chapter 12 through Chapter 20) explores a variety of concrete expressions of Confucian cultivation, notably in matters of filiality and other ritual obligations and in the exercise of statecraft. The final section (end of Chapter 20 through Chapter 33) introduces a new definition of the ideal of perfect cultivation, the concept of 'self-completion' (*cheng*), and, with this as its central focus, proceeds to explore the substance and significance of the highest degree of self-cultivation, that of 'sagehood'.

The sharp division in language and focus between these three sections has led many scholars, from as early as the Song period down to modern times, to speculate about the possibility that the *Zhongyong* may in fact be a composite text rather than a single unitary work, perhaps even reflecting formal disputation between competing philosophical schools, or at least divergent views regarding some of the central issues of Confucian thought. A close reading and analysis of the text, however, reveals a coherent central thread of conception running through the different phases of the argument. In order to follow this argument, one must immediately note that the term constituting the traditional title of the treatise: *zhongyong* cannot be read here in the simple sense of moderation, or mediocrity, as it is used in a passage in the *Analects* (*Lunyu*). Nor can the text be understood as a mere restatement of the 'doctrine of the mean', as it has been often rendered in western translations, since, after introducing the conception of equilibrium in the opening chapter, the remainder of the text then turns its entire attention to other issues. One is therefore forced to reinterpret the words *zhongyong* here, in line with the major commentaries, as referring to the application of the ideal of equilibrium in the concrete context of Confucian moral practice. The exploration of this theme in the text takes us, after an initial exposition of the major themes and concepts, from a series of statements on the virtual impossibility, for all but sages, of fully attaining this ideal, through a discussion of varying forms and degrees of putting it into practice, and finally to a lofty contemplation of the human and cosmic implications of its highest conceivable realization.

The central thread of the argument of the *Zhongyong* can also be grasped more clearly when one recognises the rhetorical method of the text, whereby certain statements are used primarily to set the groundwork, or to lead up to, its primary propositions. This is seen immediately in the loaded opening line of the work, where two difficult clauses on the 'nature of things' (*xing*) ordained by Heaven and on the abstract relation between this 'nature' and the 'Way' are used to set the ontological grounding for the following clause, in which the primary focus of the text is turned to the 'cultivation of the Way' in the concrete human realm. The same method of rhetorical analysis must be applied in the best-known passage in the opening section, where the notion of a hypothetical state of perfect equilibrium (*zhong* 中), posited as temporally or logically 'prior' to the emergence of the world of concrete existence (*xi nu ai le zhi weifa* 喜怒哀樂之未發, see **Zhong he**), is introduced to provide the logical underpinning for the main point at issue in this text: the process of seeking a degree of harmonious balance (**he**) in the real world, which is subject to the parameters of human experience in concrete existence (*yifa* 已發). When the text is read in this way, the crucial passage in Chapter 12: 'The Way is not far from humanity' takes on its full meaning, as does the passage marking the transition to the final section of the text in Chapter 20, where the 'Way of Man', as opposed to the spontaneous wholeness of the 'Way of Heaven', is distinguished by the need for unceasing, concerted effort in order to strive toward a less cosmic level of moral self-completeness. Finally, this human ideal of wholeness is linked, by way of the common ground of being shared by the individual with all other men and all existing things, to a notion of the perfect cultivation of the sage that takes on its fullest significance within the cosmic scheme of things.

The profound metaphysical implications attached to the process of human cultivation in the *Zhongyong*, especially in the opening chapter and in the final expansion chapters, help to explain why it became a primary focus of Confucian philosophical debate. Not only were the expressions *weifa* 未發 and *yifa* 已發 later extracted from the text and used as shorthand indicators for the metaphysical and existential realms, respectively, but the deeper meanings of such terms as 'nature (*xing*)' 'equilibrium and harmony' (*zhong he*) and 'self-completeness' as developed here came to provide the core concepts for a large portion of the intellectual discourse of the Neo-Confucian period.

References: Graham, 1989; Pang Pu, 1980; Riegel, 1978; Tang Junyi, 1966; Xu Fuguan, 1963.

ANDREW PLAKS

Zhongyong 中庸
(The mean in common practice)

The expression *zhongyong*, literally meaning 'balanced and common', is often used in everyday speech in the simple sense of a golden mean of moderation, or sometimes to describe 'mediocre' human qualities. As a term of Confucian discourse, however, it is usually charged with far more profound layers of meaning. Its earliest appearance in classic Confucian texts is found in the *Analects* (**Lunyu** 6: 29), where it still seems to refer to something like the 'common run' of humanity. But this is very significantly revised and expanded in the later Confucian canonic text taking this two-character expression as its traditional title: the **Zhongyong**, where it is glossed in most orthodox commentaries as the 'putting into common practice' (*yong* 庸) of the ideal of perfect equilibrium (*zhong* 中). As developed in the chain of arguments composing that text, this comes to mean not an *a priori* state of immutable balance, such as that attributed to the cosmic sphere of 'Heaven' alone, but rather a compensatory restoration of equilibrium within the shifting circumstances of concrete human existence. The 'common practice' by which this is to be achieved is illustrated in the *Zhongyong* in terms of the paradigmatic acts of Confucian self-cultivation: primarily filiality, mourning ritual, and the exercise of benevolent rulership. The conventional translation of this term as the 'doctrine of the mean' suggests a fruitful comparison to Aristotle's conception of flexible standards of ethical balance, but the Chinese term, with its explication in the canonic text, clearly shifts its focus to the concrete application of this ideal in the *praxis* of Confucian life.

ANDREW PLAKS

Zhou Dunyi 周敦頤
1017–1073
(*zi* Maoshu 茂叔, *hao* Lianqi Xiansheng 濂溪先生)

Zhou Dunyi was originally named Zhou Dunshi 周敦實. But, in avoiding the taboo associated with the personal name of the Yingzong emperor (r. 1064–1067), he changed his given name to the one by which we recognise him today. There is no evidence that Zhou Dunyi either participated in or passed the civil service examinations. Nevertheless, he did secure an official post as a keeper of records (*zhubu* 主簿) in 1036. This appointment probably resulted partially from the strength of the records of service of two immediate relatives. Dunyi's father Zhou Fucheng 周輔成 (*fl.* 1020), a 1013 recipient of the *jinshi* degree by examination, and his maternal uncle Zheng Xiang 鄭向 (*fl.* 1030; *zi* Gongming 公明), a first-rank examination *jinshi* degree holder and prominent official who reared the younger Zhou following his father's early death. Zhou Dunyi's 1036 marriage to the daughter of Lu Can 陸參 (*fl.* 1040) – a director of the Bureau of Operations (*zhifang langzhong* 職方郎中), an agency of the Ministry of War (*qibing* 七兵) – also very likely played some role in his procuring this first appointment.

Zhou Dunyi deferred assuming his initial post until 1040 because of the death of his mother in 1037. However, once he commenced in it, he immediately distinguished himself as an excellent adjudicator of legal disputes and an erudite scholar of Confucianism. During the 1040s, Zhou Dunyi attracted a growing coterie of students and included within this group were the adolescent brothers **Cheng Hao** and **Cheng Yi**. By order of their father Cheng Xiang 程珦 (1006–1090; *zi* Bowen 伯溫), the two youths briefly came under Zhou's tutelage in 1046–1047. The actual depth of Zhou Dunyi's influence upon the young Chengs has been subject to considerable debate. To be sure, the infrequent and insubstantial manner in which they mention Zhou in their mature writings elicits suspicion. Moreover, their singularly unflattering reference to him as 'decrepit Chan stranger' (*qiongchan ke* 窮禪客) certainly militates against what we would even call a relationship of mutual respect, not to mention, veneration (*Henan Chengshi yishu* 河南程氏遺書, 6.4). Nonetheless, tradition holds that through his brief rendering of instruction to them, Zhou Dunyi forged an auspicious and fruitful intellectual association with the Cheng brothers – one that was fated to determine the main directions and emphases of Confucian Learning over the course of the eleventh and twelfth centuries.

By earning and amassing successive promotions, Zhou Dunyi continued to enjoy an effective bureaucratic career until the end of his life. His career concluded with stints as an assistant fiscal commissioner (*zhuanyun panguan* 轉運判官), which began in 1068, and a judicial commissioner (*tidian xingyu gongshi* 提點刑獄公事), which began in 1071. However, the respect that Zhou garnered for his successes as an official was preempted by the acclaim that he received simply for his incremental emergence as a learned man. In 1060, he reputedly met and spent several days in the company of **Wang Anshi**, on whom he made an indelibly favourable impression. While journeying through Lushan 盧山 in northern Jiangxi 江西 in 1061, he found the terrain so alluring in its resemblance to his native village of Lianqi 濂溪 (modern Dao 道 county in Hunan 湖南) that he declared his intention of ultimately residing there by constructing a study bearing that name beside a stream. He returned to Lushan upon his resignation and retirement from office at the end of 1072. He died in the summer of the following year at the age of fifty-seven *sui* 歲.

Thought and works

The immense respect that Chinese have traditionally accorded Zhou Dunyi stems primarily from his status as the founder of the ***dao xue*** (Learning of the Way) movement – one stream of the complicated matrix of intellectual currents that westerners typically subsume under the broad, amorphous, and imprecise heading of '**Neo-Confucianism**'. Zhou did not consciously seek to establish himself in this position as the head of a movement. On the contrary, he was elevated to it posthumously by his preeminent successor Zhu Xi, who exercised his prerogative of inserting Zhou into an essential spot in his particular version of the ***dao tong*** or 'genealogy of the Way'. According to Zhu, Zhou was the vital and definitive personage who linked the line of classical patriarchs of Confucianism – which ended abruptly with **Mengzi** – with that of later times. In Zhu Xi's view, prior to Zhou Dunyi, the true Confucian tradition had already – centuries before – lapsed into extinction.

Zhu Xi's manipulations notwithstanding, Zhou Dunyi's conscious, imaginative and timely efforts to revivify and also expand the scope of Confucian Learning do in fact contribute enormously to the singularity of his thought. Zhou Dunyi no doubt drew upon and synthesised the various divination conventions that had preceded him. But Zhou is noteworthy as perhaps the first in a long series of Song-period thinkers to use the ***Yi jing*** (*Book of Change*) foremost as the catalyst for his entire philosophy.

In seeking to shore up the metaphysical foundations of Confucianism in its protracted confrontation with Buddhism, Zhou Dunyi took the lead. He selected an obscure construct from the iconographic arsenal of religious Daoism – the ***tai ji*** or Supreme Ultimate – and made it pivotal to the Confucian tradition through his ***Taijitu shuo*** (*Diagram of the Supreme Ultimate Explained*). Zhou maintained that this Supreme Ultimate is the progenitor of the cosmos itself and everything in it. The normative state of the Supreme Ultimate is one of benign quiescence or tranquillity (*jing*). Nevertheless, through a single, spontaneous motion, the Supreme Ultimate manifests its boundless capacity; surging, it thereby produces the dyadic opposites yin–yang and these – through a process of evolutionary succession – give rise to the multiplicity of all existence. Writing about the dynamism of the Supreme Ultimate, Zhou remarked, 'Through alternation, movement and quiescence become the root of each other, giving rise to the distinction between yin and yang, and these two modes thus become established' (*Taijitu shuo*, 1: 2).

Within this unified entity of the Supreme Ultimate, the cosmogonic **dao** or Way and the ethical **li** or principle are united by the sublime virtue of **cheng** (sincerity, authenticity or genuineness). Zhou Dunyi stressed that by cultivating sincerity, humans emulate the Supreme Ultimate itself and they thereby position themselves to reap unparalleled rewards. 'Sincerity', Zhou insisted, 'is the foundation of the sage' (*Tong shu*, 1: 1) and 'sagehood is nothing more than sincerity' (*Tong shu*, 2: 2). The deliberation on and the promotion of the cultivation of *cheng* are the central foci particularly of the latter of Zhou Dunyi's two principal works – the **Tong shu** (*Explanatory Text*, or *Penetrating the Book of Change*).

Influence

It is difficult to overestimate the importance of Zhou Dunyi in the formation and subsequent history of the 'Learning of the Way', for it was no accident that it was he who was chosen to define the dominant contours of the movement. Zhu Xi doubtless chose Zhou out of a sense that the combination of the thought he espoused and the life he led commented constructively on all the major aspects of Confucian Learning that would merit the deliberations of posterity. Through his exemplary (if inconspicuous) official career, he epitomised the Confucian dedication to public-minded service. His emphasis on the value of compassion became legendary. It was Zhou Dunyi who, by his example, reputedly led the young Cheng brothers (**Chen Hao** and **Chen Yi**) to abandon the sport of hunting game and when once asked why he allowed the grass to grow unchecked outside his

window, Zhou replied that his feelings were as one with that of the grass. But we are perhaps intended to remember Zhou Dunyi most of all as a staunch and unyielding defender of Confucian values at the expense of all others. This lifelong resolve is well indicated by such examples as his 1071 visit to the Zhejiang 浙江 temple honouring the cleric Dadian 大顛 (of the ninth century), to whom the Confucian **Han Yu** had once given a gift of friendship. Therein, Zhou Dunyi inscribed a poem denigrating the gift and deriding Han Yu's gesture, thus leaving behind a tangible and unequivocal indication for future generations that he potentially surpassed even the polemicist Han Yu in his antipathy toward Buddhism.

Zhou Dunyi received the posthumous title (*shi*) of Yuan 元 in 1200. In 1241, Zhou was honoured as Earl of Runan (Runan Bo 汝南伯) – for the county in modern Henan province to which he traced his ancestry – and the regularised conduction of sacrifices in his behalf were commenced within the **Kong miao** (Temple of Confucius).

References: Balazs and Hervouet, 1978: 393–4; Bol, 1992: 28, 30, 110, 300, 303, 307, 328, 338, 415n. 66, 421n. 158; Chan, Wing-tsit, 1976: 277–81; Collins, 1998: 5, 63, 75, 301–2, 307, 308, 312, 314, 973n. 12; He Zhaowu, 1991: 255, 297–9, 301, 316; Hsieh, 1979: 5, 104n. 1; Huang Siu-chi, 1999: 19–36; Jiang Guanghui, 1994: 49–52, 112, 117, 153, 278, 289, 290, 293, 300, 307, 325, 340, 389; Wyatt, 1996: 3, 4, 82, 102, 235, 274n. 29.

DON J. WYATT

Zhou Gong 周公
(The Duke of Zhou)

'Zhou' is the name of a culture, a dynasty and a region; 'gong' is a title of rank usually translated 'duke'. The Duke of Zhou (*fl.* eleventh century BCE) was one of the sons of King Wen and a younger brother of King Wu, two founding figures of the Zhou dynasty (1945?–256 BCE). King Wu upon his death was to have been succeeded by his son, who was later known as King Cheng, but the Duke of Zhou claimed Cheng was too young and established himself as regent in his stead. After pursuing a fratricidal civil war and consolidating the sovereignty of Zhou culture established by Kings Wen and Wu, the duke eventually stepped down in favour of King Cheng.

In later texts, the Duke of Zhou is described not as a usurper but as a virtuous and talented guardian figure. The 'Metal-bound Coffer' section of the *Book of History* (***Shang shu***), for example, testifies piously to the duke's unrecognised concern for the young ruler's health – the duke had sworn, he claimed, to have offered his own life to the spirits as a substitute for the king's life, which had been threatened by illness. The duke came to be perceived of as a sage possessed of great personal integrity, governing skills, and learning, and key architect of the Zhou culture, especially its traditions of rites and music. Until modern times, he was attributed the authorship or editorship of many early texts such as the Zhou version of the *Book of Changes* (***Yi jing***) and *The Rites of the Zhou* (***Zhou li***).

References: Legge, 1985c; Lewis, 1999; Loewe & Shaughnessy, 1999.

DEBORAH SOMMER

Zhou li 周禮
(*The Rites of the Zhou*)

The *Zhou li* (also called the *Zhou guan* 周官, *Officers of Zhou*) *guwen* text purportedly reconstructs the entire bureaucratic structure of the administration led by the Duke of Zhou (**Zhou Gong**), the powerful regent whom legend credits with establishing peace and prosperity in early western Zhou. First attributed to the Duke of Zhou (eleventh century BCE) in Former Han, the *Zhou li* was thereafter denounced regularly as a late compilation, possibly even a forgery

by **Liu Xin**. The *Zhou li* text is certainly later than the western Zhou (1100?–771 BCE) and earlier than Liu Xin. Most scholars now date it to late Eastern Zhou (770–256 BCE), though some scholars such as Zhu Qianzhi 朱謙之 believe it to be 'no later than' the reign of King Hui of the Zhou (r. 676–652 BCE). **Pi Xirui**, Gu Jiegang 顧詰剛 (1893–1980), and Guo Muoro 郭沫若 (1892–1978) all thought it a product of the Warring States period (475–221 BCE); Gu and Guo went so far as to speculate on the identity and provenance of its Warring States author. Some have even argued for a date of the Qin (221–206 BCE) or the early Former Han (206 BCE–8 CE).

The book was originally organised into six sections, named after Heaven, Earth and the four seasons. Five of the six list various governmental officials at every level from the highest to the lowest, arranged in hierarchical order. The book was to give descriptions for some 360 main posts, one for each day of the lunar year. More than 2,000 offices are assigned by the central government, who are then to be in charge of altogether about 330,000 petty officers and menial functionaries. From the time of its first appearance during the reign of **Han Wudi**, the section on 'Winter Officers' has been lost in its entirety, and replaced by the *Kaogongji* 考功記 devoted to the technical arts and crafts, including architecture and mining. Some passages in the Earth Offices, Summer Offices and Autumn Offices sections are also missing. Each section begins with the same phrase: 'It is only the king who establishes the domain, who regulates the official ranks, who apportions the domain and demarcates the outlying areas, who establishes the bureaucratic offices and divides their responsibilities, so as to become to ultimate standard of morality for the common people.' Nonetheless, it is clear that the model king delegates great powers to his officers: Heaven's Officers, being those under the direction of the prime minister; Earth's Officers, those under the *situ* 司徒, or Minister over the

Masses; Spring's Officers, those under the *zongbo* 宗伯, ritual master; Summer's Officers, being under the direction of the *sima* 司馬, commander; autumn's masters, under the *sikou* 司寇, minister of justice.

As the *Zhou li* takes a pro-active approach to government, promoting agriculture, comprehensive education, social welfare programmes and price controls, it is hardly surprising that it inspired major political reformers in imperial China, including the 'usurper' **Wang Mang** 王莽 (r. 9–23 CE); Yu Wentai 宇文泰 (in 556) under the Northern Zhou; and such men evidently thought it to be their duty to promote agriculture, education and social welfare programmes, offering outright grants to the poor. Probably because of its association with Wang Mang, the text received imperial sponsorship only briefly under the Han. According to some accounts, Yu Wentai was the first to try to deliberately institute a government that fully reflected the administrative structure of the book. By Tang times, in any case, with the publication of the *Wu jing zhengyi* (653) under the nominal editorship of **Kong Yingda**, the *Zhouli* came to be regarded by many as more authoritative than the other two canonical ritual texts, the *Yi li* and the *Li ji*. Given its exhaustive bureaucratic accounts, the *Zhou li* represented a veritable treasurehouse for antiquarians intent upon tracing the history of early ritual practices or utensils and for linguists hoping to reconstitute the archaic Chinese language (since the *Zhou li* is the only Rites Classic to include a few pre-Han characters). It was consulted also by reformers intent upon recreating its structural perfection in a reorganised government and society.

As with the *Yi li*, we rely on **Zheng Xuan**'s commentary; Jia Gongyan's 賈公彦 subcommentary (*Zhou li Yishu* 周禮義疏); and **Ruan Yuan**'s *Shisan jing zhushu* edition for a preliminary understanding of the text. **Sun Yirang**'s *Zhou li zhengyi* 周禮正義 (*Correct Meaning of the Zhou li*) is also helpful. There is only one translation of the *Zhou li* into a western language, that by Édouard Biot in 1851: *Le Tscheou-li ou Rites des Tscheou*, 3 vols. Paris: Imprimerie Nationale; rpt, Taipei: Chengwen, 1975.

MICHAEL NYLAN

Zhou Xingji 周行己

1067–c.1120

(*zi* Gongshu 恭叔, *hao* Fuzhi xiansheng 浮沚先生)

Although Zhou eventually passed the *jinshi* examination in 1091, he made the unusual decision to go first to Luoyang and secure **Cheng Yi** as his teacher. He and eight other men from Yongjia 永嘉 in the prefecture of Wenzhou 溫州 (Zhejiang) travelled to the Imperial Academy (*Tai xue* 太學) in Luoyang where Zhou personally met Cheng. At this time, he apparently devoted his attention to understanding the *Zhongyong* (*Doctrine of the Mean*) (Li Jingyuan, 1989: 287). His return to his home district has been seen as the conduit by which Cheng's learning entered Yongjia (Tillman, 1992: 86).

Despite this focus on moral development and his role in the spread of *dao xue* in Southern China, his own moral life generated some controversy in his time. He was particularly praised by Cheng Yi for his integrity in marrying one of his maternal relatives despite the fact that the girl was blind. Nevertheless, he was later criticised by Cheng and other figures in the *Dao xue* movement for a tryst with a lower-class singing girl (Li Youwu, 1967: 9.14 (1991–2)).

His surviving writings are contained in his *Fuzhi ji* 浮沚集 in nine *juan*. These compositions testify to Zhou's interest in the issues that engaged *dao xue* thinkers. They contain, for example, his glosses on important lines from the Classics as well as less formal discussions of the behaviour of the scholar–officials (*shi* 士). He also discussed the core issues of human nature (**xing**), the

Supreme Ultimate (*Tai ji*), and the 'investigation of things' (*gewu*).

Zhou's later follower, Zheng Boxiong
鄭伯熊 (1127?–1181), took up his teachings
and ensured the continuation of *Dao xue* in
Yongjia. By the end of his life, Zhou seems
to have made a comeback, yet his teachings
were ultimately rejected as unreliable by
Zhu Xi (*Song–Yuan xuean*, 1966: 32.2a).

References: *Song–Yuan xuean*, 1966; Li
Jingyuan, 1989; Li Youwu, 1967; Tillman,
1992a.

ANTHONY DEBLASI

Zhou Yutong 周予同
1898–1981
(*zi* Yu Tong 予同)

Originally named Zhou Yumao 周毓懋,
Zhou Yutong has been known as a historian,
educator and scholar of Confucian Classics
in modern China. He graduated from
Beijing Normal University in 1921 where he
studied Chinese history and the history of
Confucian Classics. He then served successively as a lecturer at Xiamen 廈門 University, an editor of Shangwu Press (*Shangwu
yinshu guan* 商務印書館) and after 1932 as
a professor at Anhui University, Jinan 暨南
University and Fudan 复旦 University. After
1949, he worked as a professor and the
Dean of the History Department, Fudan
University, as well as the vice director of
the Institute of History at the Shanghai
Academy of Social Sciences. As a student
of Qian Xuantong 錢玄同 (1887–1939), a
great master of Chinese culture, Zhou
Yutong spent about half a century studying
the history of Confucian Classics and transformed the traditional Classical Learning
(*jingxue*) into a historical study of Classics.
Qunjing gailun 群經概論 (*A General Discussion of Various Classics*) is one of his most
important works in the area. He observed
that although there were many works
which put together various materials and textual researches of the Confucian Classics, no

systematic research had so far been done
concerning the nature and changing laws
of Confucian Classics. He divided different
schools of traditional Classical Learning
into four groups: the New Text School of
the Former Han dynasty (*Xi Han Jinwen
jingxue* 西漢今文經學); the Old Text School
of the Later Han dynasty (*Dong Han Guwen
jingxue* 東漢古文經學); the School of Song
learning (*Song xue* 宋學); and the New
School of History (*Xin shi xuepai* 新史學派).
He held Confucius as the central figure in
Confucian studies, whose influence extends
not only to all areas of China, but also
through to East Asia and other areas. Thus
there is a necessity for Confucian studies not
only to understand the changes of Chinese
philosophy and cultures, but also to understand other countries and areas influenced
by Confucius and his ideas.

References: Wu & Song, 1992; *Zhongguo
ruxue baike quanshu*, 1997.

OUYANG KANG

Zhouzi quanshu 周子全書
(*Complete Works of Master Zhou*)

This collection – in twenty-two chapters
(*juan*) – comprises the complete philosophical and literary production of the
philosopher **Zhou Dunyi**. Featured foremost in the collection is the text (together
with its accompanying diagram) of the
Taijitu shuo, which constitutes the first six
chapters as well as that of the *Tong shu*,
which constitutes chapters 7 through 10.
Chapters 11–16 contain approximately seventy commentaries and essays on either of
these works by subsequent authors, including **Zhu Xi**. The remainder of the collection
contains examples of Zhou's literary writings,
the most influential of which is his famed
essay *Ailian shuo* 愛蓮說 (*Explaining the Love
of the Lotus*).

Reference: Balazs & Hervouet, 1978: 216–
17, 218.

DON J. WYATT

Zhu 注
(Commentary on Classics)

Zhu, literally meaning 'to flow', was a form of commentary introduced in the second century CE by scholars like **Zheng Xuan** (writing *zhu* for the ritual canons *Zhou li*, *Yi li*, and *Li ji*) and **Zhao Qi** (writing *zhu* on the *Mengzi*). This new form represented a departure from earlier commentarial genres like those of the *zhuan* (tradition, commentary) and its related forms *ji* 記 (records) and *shuo* 說 (explanations) in that it was physically integrated directly into the text of the canon, providing inter-linear exegetical notes that were 'flowing around' individual words and phrases of the main text. After this model had been established in Later Han times, scholars in Wei and Jin times wrote *zhu* commentaries for an increasing number of texts, among them the *Yi jing* (Wang Bi, 226–249), *Laozi* (Wang Bi), (*Chunqui*) *Zuo zhuan* (Du Yu 杜預 222–284) and *Er ya* (Guo Pu 郭璞 276–324); for most canonical works, two or three competing *zhu* commentaries were produced. In later times, *zhu* became a standard designation for interlinear commentaries; in the Song dynasty compilation of the Thirteen Classics under the title *Shisan jing zhushu*, *zhu* denotes the early (Han through Jin) layer of commentaries, while *shu* refers to the Tang and Song subcommentaries.

References: Nylan, 2001; Wang Baoxuan, 1994: 20–8.

MARTIN KERN

Zhu hou 諸侯
(Feudal lords)

Zhu hou refers to the lords of the states enfeoffed by the King or 'Son of Heaven' (*tian zi*). A *hou* 侯 is the third of the five ranks in the Zhou dynasty (1045?–256 BCE), and their importance in shaping Confucianism should not be understated. Since the Zhou was founded on a feudalistic system, the King exerted control over all states and was able to preserve peace. As this power declined, the entire kingdom was thrown into chaos. Confucius, **Mengzi**, and many others developed their doctrines in the midst of this disarray. For example, a quote in the *Mengzi* (5B: 2) is revealing. When asked what the system of rank and income was under the House of Zhou, Mengzi replies with 'This cannot be known in detail, for the feudal lords destroyed the records, considering the system to be detrimental to themselves'; and he continues, 'But I have heard a brief outline of it. The King, the duke (*gong* 公), the marquis (*hou* 侯), and the earl (*bo* 伯) each constituted one rank, while the viscount (*zi* 子) and the baron (*nan* 男) shared the same rank, thus totalling five grades.'

References: Lau, 1970; Morohashi, 1960.

TODD CAMERON THACKER

Zhu jing 主靜
(Concentrating on quiescence)

'Concentrating on quiescence' in the attempt to achieve mastery of it was the methodological approach most favoured by **Zhou Dunyi** in the quest for the attainment of *cheng* – his supreme virtue of sincerity or authenticity. In Zhou's view, attaining *cheng* could only occur by emulating the placid qualities obtaining to the virtue itself. He claimed that 'sincerity engages in no activity' and, incorporating a phrase from the *Yi jing* to underscore the point, he stated that ' "total quiet and inactivity" is sincerity' (*Tong shu*, 3, 4). Many critics construed Zhou's persistent advocacy of quiescence as coming at the expense of activity and they maintained that it strongly suggested the sort of quietism promoted by Daoism. However, Zhou Dunyi's defenders countered that he had never intended for his emphasis on quiescence to preclude activity. Their opinion has subsequently held sway.

Reference: Chan, Wing-tsit, 1963d: 464–5.

DON J. WYATT

Zhu Song 朱松

1097–1143

(*zi* Qiaonian 喬年, *hao* Weizhai 韋齋)

Zhu Song was the father of **Zhu Xi**, and a native of Wuyuan 婺源 in modern-day Anhui. Zhu received his *jinshi* degree in 1118. In 1134 Zhu received an appointment as Proofreader (*Zhengzi* 正字) in the Palace Library. Eventually Zhu Song achieved the honorific official position of secretary in the Bureau of Merit Titles (*Sixun* 司勳) of the Ministry of Personnel. However, due to his opposition to the appeasement policies of Qin Hui 秦檜 (1090–1155), Zhu was criticised at court and subsequently demoted to the position of Raozhou 饒州 prefect (in modern Fujian). He was demoted even further, soon thereafter, and finally chose early retirement to excuse himself from the political turmoil. Zhu Song died at the relatively young age of forty-seven.

Zhu Song provided Zhu Xi with his earliest Confucian training, although he would have a less lasting effect on his son's mature philosophical writings. Zhu Song had been a student of **Yang Shi** and an associate of **Luo Congyan**, both of whom influenced his thinking and that of his son in the early years. One of Zhu's main philosophical concerns was the investigation of *yi li* (righteousness and profit) and its application to public life. Before he died Zhu Song made certain that his son would learn the important tenets of the Cheng brothers' teachings. Zhu asked his friend Luo Congyan's student **Li Tong** to perform this task. However, Zhu Xi would later deny that he had been strongly influenced by Li Tong's brand of Confucianism. Zhu Song's collected works were first compiled as *Wei zhai ji* 韋齋集 and later as *Huiweng xuean* 晦翁學案 (*Records of an Obscure Old Man's Teachings*).

References: Giles, H., 1898: 185; *Song–Yuan xuean*, 1966: 1294–6; Tillman, 1992b: 40.

JAMES A. ANDERSON

Zhu wen 祝文

(Text of Prayer)

The Text of Prayer is written on boards and read at the beginning of the ceremony after the preliminary libation offering to inform the spirit of the ceremony. The invocator (*yin zan* 引贊) reads the prayer announcing the circumstances of the ceremony (i.e., the date, location and bureaucratic authority responsible for the rite) and the names of the consecration officers, then invokes the spirits that receive the sacrifice by intoning or chanting their names and praising the virtues of the principal recipient. For example, a prayer at the sacrifice to Confucius in the early Ming typically began with 'On this date, magistrate X dares to make known to the First Sage, Exalted King of Culture, whose virtue matches Heaven and Earth, whose **Dao** permeates all time, who edited and composed the Six Classics that bequeathed the founding charter to the ten thousand generations, now the appointed time has come to respectfully offer up this victim and silk damask, this wine, bowls of grain and sundry offerings all lined up in rows. Correlate sacrifices are offered to the Returning Sage Master Yan, the Ancestral Sage Master Zeng, the Following Sage Master Zisi and the Second Sage Master Meng.' The prayer is followed by the three offerings (*san xian*).

THOMAS A. WILSON

Zhu Xi 朱熹

1130–1200

(*zi* Yuanhui 元晦, *hao* Huian 晦庵)

Zhu Xi was born in Fujian after his father, **Zhu Song**, was demoted to serve as a county sheriff there. After his father lost even this lowly post just before Zhu's birth, he became the focus of his father's attention. On his father's deathbed, Zhu's education was entrusted to three local friends. Losing his father when Zhu was about thirteen had a profound and lasting impact on his personality and thinking; moreover, this impact deepened during his teens as he lost two of the three designated mentors and his two brothers. Firstly, his mother's example gave him a model for promoting not only widow's chastity but also wife's management of household finances for the good of her husband's family, so men could pursue education and the cultivation of generosity unencumbered by worries about household stringencies. In devoting herself to the Zhu family's economic welfare, Zhu's widowed mother was such a striking model because her conduct went against the dominant Song trend for widows to take their dowry property into second marriages arranged by their natal families. Zhu's praise of a wife's absolute devotion to the husband's patriline influenced his followers to advocate tighter rules of female chastity and legal subordination of a wife's property rights to the interests of the husband's family.

Secondly, Zhu's three designated mentors were faithful to their charge, but his education did not lead to the levels of career success for which most literati of his day aimed. Still, their efforts bore fruit when Zhu passed the national civil service examinations about six years later at nineteen (which was about half the median age for successful candidates during that era). No doubt his mentors deserve some credit for Zhu's success in the examinations at such an early age. While most literati had to focus on examinations for twenty or more years longer than Zhu, he was free to pursue other avenues of learning and to devote himself to scholarship. With such an early start, Zhu had a marked advantage in the length of his intellectual career of teaching and research. Moreover, passage of the examinations meant that Zhu could enter the governmental bureaucracy at an earlier age and have a longer official career. Nevertheless, he held only a few posts as a local official and spent only about forty-six days in an official capacity at the emperor's court. Although he would have had additional opportunities if he had not declined appointments to several offices, his limited official career was not particularly noteworthy, so he had to look elsewhere for validation of his worth and status as a scholar. He would ultimately present personal morality, instead of government degrees and officers, as the criterion for literati class status.

Thirdly, during the intellectually formative years of his youth, Zhu was left without a definitively authoritative mentor; moreover, without the influence of one dominant teacher, Zhu was compelled into an independent quest for certainty. When his father died, the thirteen-year-old Zhu was no longer under the ultimate authority figure for young men in his culture. His three mentors exposed him to a range of thought beyond his own father's focus on the Learning of the Way (**dao xue**) and especially the writings of the Cheng brothers (**Cheng Hao** and **Cheng Yi**) and **Sima Guang**. Most significantly, they did not discourage his exploration of Daoism and Buddhism, especially Chan discipline of silent meditation. When in his mid-twenties he finally returned to Confucian teachings under the influence of **Li Tong**, Zhu apparently had something of a conversion experience and accepted Li Tong's fundamentalist zeal for orthodoxy. By his mid-thirties, Zhu had become so hostile to the prevailing trend toward greater common ground between the Three Teachings (**san jiao jiu liu**) that he wrote his 'Critique of Adulterated Learning' to condemn those Song Confucian scholars whose commentaries corrupted the Classics with ideas drawn from Daoism and Buddhism. Zhu's own series of commentaries on the classical Four Books (**Si shu**) illustrates his continuing quest for authority. In his early thirties to late forties, he wrote three sets of commentaries through which he progressively worked back to the views of the Cheng brothers; moreover, he gradually rejected most of the distinct views expressed by their disciples. After his late forties, he grew increasingly critical in his reading, even of the *Book of Changes*; moreover, he became more independent in developing his own readings of the Classics, particularly in his last set of commentaries on the Four Books.

As he made progress in projecting himself as the authoritative reader of the tradition, he developed the concept of the *dao tong*, i.e., the transmission and succession of the Way from the ancient sages, through **Zhou Dunyi** and the Chengs, and ultimately to himself. Although he articulated the idea in his early fifties, it attained full philosophical expression in his 1189 preface to the *Doctrine of the Mean* (**Zhongyong**), in which he outlined how the oral transmission from one ancient sage to another had been transferred to the Classics as the textual carrier of the Way. Especially the *Doctrine of the Mean* and the *Great Learning* (**Daxue**) provided a thread for later generations to grasp the sages' true Way. Nevertheless, although the Classics were essential in ensuring that the Way would not be lost, the texts alone had failed to ensure the transmission of the Way, for the Way was not transmitted for about twelve centuries between **Mengzi**'s death and Zhou Dunyi's recovery of the Way. While Zhu was elaborating on this textual linkage to the ancient sages and the doctrine of the transmission of the Way, he was also developing a personal connection to the spirit of Confucius. Leading his students in burning incense and offering sacrificial foods to the ancient sages and recent worthies, as well as in making prayerful reports to Confucius, Zhu's actions and words at shrines mirrored rituals reserved strictly for one's own ancestors. Indeed, he appropriated the concept of the most direct lineage decent (*zong* 宗) within the patrilineal kinship system to present himself as the imagined heir of Confucius. Thus, his prayers and intercessions in the presence of his disciples seemingly conveyed an image of Zhu as spiritually linked directly to the Sage and thus empowered with an authoritative

voice to speak for the Way. Even though it was **Zhang Shi** who drew Zhu's attention to shrine building, Zhang had disagreed with Zhu's embrace of popular religious rituals, not in accord with the Classics, like offering food to departed relatives at their gravesites and selecting gravesites through geomancy (*feng shui* 風水). Perhaps Zhu's early loss of his father and his search for approval from an authority figure influenced his unprecedented claims to a direct lineage connection to Confucius' spirit. In any event, his documented invocation of Confucius' spirit adds a dimension to his other efforts to project himself as the authoritative voice of tradition and reader of the Classics.

Zhu's self-confidence in his particular readings is evident in his special attention to elaborating rules for reading texts. He emphasised that the purpose of reading was to improve one's self as a person, rather than to enhance one's erudition or advance one's welfare, career and status. Therefore, he streamlined traditional culture in his curriculum focused resolutely on the Four Books, so that the principles he identified therein would serve as the guide for any and all other reading, which was quite secondary in importance. After memorising and internalising the Four Books, one could understand and communicate with the ancient sages. Thereafter, one would not lose one's focus on what was primary or lose one's Way amidst the details of the Five Classics (**Wu jing**), the histories or literature. In his rules for reading texts, Zhu urged students to approach texts reverently and diligently; however, his own stewardship of texts fell short of the ideals he championed. For example, he interjected a section into the *Great Learning*, purged objectionable passages from **Hu Hong**'s *Zhi yan* 知言 (*Understanding Words*), and omitted key letters and essays while entrusted with editing Zhang Shi's collected works. For instance, it is only a passing comment in a letter Zhu later wrote to **Lü Zuqian**'s brother that reveals that it was actually Zhang who initiated the first half of the definition of **ren** (humaneness) which has traditionally been credited to Zhu alone. Zhu is renowned for characterising humaneness as 'the virtue of the heart/mind' (*xin zhi de* 心之德) and 'the principle of love' (*ai zhi li* 愛之理).

Zhu is also famous for his synthesis of ideas advanced by Zhou Dunyi, Cheng Hao, Cheng Yi, **Zhang Zai**, and others. For instance, seizing upon Zhou's isolated postulation that the **wu ji** (Non-Ultimate) was also the **tai ji** (Supreme Ultimate), Zhu incorporated it into his refutation of Buddhist philosophical teachings about the essential emptiness of all things and moral principles. Further equating the Supreme Ultimate with the Chengs' concept of **li** (principle) as the origin and manifestation of all things in Heaven and Earth, Zhu constructed a philosophical system in which *li* and *qi* (material force) formed all things. The *li*, with which Heaven endowed humans at birth, was human nature (*xing*). Even though *qi*, in itself, was not evil, it easily became clouded and obscured perception of innate goodness because *qi* was in flux and usually turbid. Hence, Zhu advanced both a philosophical defence of Mengzi's claims regarding innate goodness in all people and an explanation for the ethical gap in actual human behaviour. Because the heart/mind (*xin*) was the purest *qi*, the mind enclosed principle, and Zhu entrusted the mind with the responsibility for self-cultivation so that one's physical *qi* nature would be transformed to reflect and accord with the goodness of the *li* inherent within one's moral nature. Another way Zhu articulated this ethical task was: the wayward human mind (*ren xin*) had to be restrained and transformed to conform to the moral mind or the mind of the Way (*dao xin*), which existed as a subtle spark within us. Scholars have debated for centuries whether or not Zhu was monistic (based on the primacy of *li*) or dualistic (based on the interaction between *li* and *qi*). Most of Zhu's philosophical statements suggest a monistic view of 'principle being one and

its manifestations being manifold' (*liyi fenshu*); for instance, *li* and *qi* could not exist independently, and *li* only had a logical priority. However, when he turned his attention to the real world of history and politics, a gulf opened between *li* and *qi* because of his obsession with the ethical gap prevalent in human actions. For instance, in his debates with **Chen Liang**, Zhu claimed that the Way (*dao*) had been lost or absent for centuries of human history. Zhu's critics have often quoted such statements to prove that he was dualistic. However, such claims ignore the context of Zhu's debate with Chen, for both men were dealing with the *dao* as cultural values, not as speculative (metaphysical) philosophy. Nonetheless, since *dao* and *li* were synonymous in Zhu's system, the debate does demonstrate the dualistic strains within Zhu's larger holistic philosophy. Scholarly perception of this tension has been eclipsed by a rigid assumption among mainstream scholars that Zhu was the most systematic Chinese philosopher and that his philosophy was completely rationalistic and coherent. However, striving for a fuller understanding of this gifted and conflicted human being, recent work has highlighted the tensions and inconsistencies within Zhu's thought and actions, as well as the relevance of his communion with Confucius' ghost.

The principal obstacle to comprehending Zhu both as a person and as a philosopher has been his elevation as the central figure of what became intellectual and state orthodoxy in East Asia. Although Zhu died under a government ban against his teaching, the Four Books and his commentaries thereupon soon became the core curriculum of the civil service examinations, and he was enshrined in the Confucian Temple in 1241. In the first half of the fourteenth century, the Yuan dynasty recommitted the examination system to Zhu's commentaries and officially endorsed a narrow version of Learning of the Way focused on Zhu. Later dynasties further enhanced Zhu's status in the Temple of Confucius and in official culture; moreover, his writings became orthodoxy in Korea and Japan, too.

References: Birge, 1999; Bol, 1992; Gardner, 1986; Neskar, 1993; Tillman, 1982, 1992a, 1992b, 2004.

HOYT TILLMAN

Zhu Yixin 朱一新
1846–1894
(*zi* Rong Sheng 容生)

Born in Yiwu (Zhejiang), Zhu Yixin became a successful candidate in the civil service examinations at the provincial level (*ju ren* 舉人) in 1870 and at the higher level (*jinshi*) in 1876. After that for some years he served as *Neige Zhongshu* 內閣中書 and *Shu jishi* 庶吉士, becoming one of the chief examiners of Hubei province and later the supervisor of Shanxi province. For exposing the affairs of personnel matters in the navy and impeaching the imperial eunuch Li Lianying 李蓮英 (1848–1911), Zhu Yixin was demoted to *Zhushi* 主事. Then he was invited by **Zhang Zhidong** to serve as the president of Duanxi Academy 端溪書院 in Zhaoqing 肇慶 and Guangya Academy 廣雅書院 in Guangzhou. His basic political attitude was to protect the social system of the Qing dynasty and its related ideology. He criticised **Kang Youwei**'s reformation ideas and his textual research of the Six Classics (*Liu jing*). He thought that Kang's textual criticism of the Confucian Classics was unnecessary and would lead to scepticism about the ancients and abandonment of historical property. He opposed the reform movement led by Kang Youwei and **Liang Qizhao**, characterising it as an unnecessary borrowing from abroad. He respected Song–Ming **Neo-Confucianism** and took it as the main trend of Chinese cultures. He agreed with the idea that principle is prior to material force (*li zai qi xian* 理在氣先) and controls material force. For Zhu, if there is no principle, there is no material force. He insisted on the necessity and rationality of the permanent existence of the traditional ethical code and Confucian values. He suggested that since there are matters, then there are laws, since there is nature, then there are principles, since there are fathers and sons, then there is love, since there are monarchs and their subjects, so it is necessary to have Confucian ethics. He thought that the society of his time was changeable, so it was better to do more study than administration of society. He studied history and wrote some books on the subject, including the *Wuxie tang dawen* 無邪堂答問, *Zou shu* 奏疏, *Shi guwen ci za zhu* 詩古文詞雜著, *Jingshi fangxiang kao* 京師方巷考, *Han shu guanjian* 漢書管見, among others.

Reference: Wu & Song, 1992.

OUYANG KANG

Zhu Zhen 朱震
1072–1138
(*zi* Zifa 子發, master Hanshang 漢上先生, *shi* Wending 文定)

Zhu Zhen was a native of Jingmen commandery 荊門軍 in present-day Hubei province. A specialist in *Yi jing* studies, Zhu was one of the followers of the Cheng School (*Luo xue*) who rose to prominent position at court during the early part of the Southern Song dynasty.

Zhu attained the *jinshi* degree during the Zhenghe period (1111–1118) and subsequently was appointed to local office. **Hu Anguo** considered him a person with great potential and recommended him as Vice Director of the Bureau of Merit Titles in the Ministry of Personnel (*sixun yuanwailang* 司勳員外郎). Zhao Ding 趙鼎 (1085–1147, *zi* Yuanzhen 元鎮, *wen* Zhongjian 忠簡), who became Chief Counsellor from 1134 to 1138, also recommended him. Zhu's most influential position was as an academician at the Hanlin Academy and tutor to the heir apparent. He had been slated to head the *jinshi* examinations of 1138 but he was never appointed, for the winds of political fortune turned against the Cheng followers.

Zhu Zhen was a leading disciple of **Xie Liangzuo**, and thus a second-generation follower of the Cheng brothers. His approach to learning combined the *Luoxue* of the Cheng school with **Xiangshu xue** (numerological cosmology), including ideas from **Shao Yong** and **Zhou Dunyi**. Zhu's chief written work is the *Hanshang Yizhuan* 漢上易傳 (Zhu Zhen's commentary on the *Yi jing*, also called *Zhouyi Jizhuan* 周易集傳) in 11 *juan* with appended charts, completed in 1134. In this work, Zhu collected and sifted various theories concerning the *Yi jing* from the Han dynasty to his own time, taking **Cheng Yi**'s *Yichuan Yizhuan* 伊川易傳 as the central interpretive line, supplemented by ideas from Shao Yong and **Zhang Zai**. Due to the conceptual difficulty of Zhu's theories, the editors of the *Song–Yuan xuean* comment that few have understood them.

As part of his work on the *Yi jing*, Zhu traced the path of transmission of the 'Anterior Heaven Diagram' (*Xiantian tu* 先天圖) from the Daoist practitioner Chen Tuan 陳摶 (?–989) to Shao Yong, the 'River chart' (*Hetu* 河圖) and 'Luo scripts' (*Luoshu* 洛書) to Liu Mu 劉牧 (1011–1064), and the 'Diagram of the Supreme Ultimate' (see *Taijitu shuo*) to Zhou Dunyi. There was considerable controversy in Northern Song over the transmission of these esoteric diagrams, particularly the 'River chart' and 'Luo scripts'. It was Zhu Zhen who first placed the 'River chart' and 'Luo scripts' in the context of *Yi jing* studies, in his '*Zhouyi tu*' 周易圖 presented to Emperor Gaozong (r. 1127–1162) in 1136.

Also in 1136, Zhu Zhen submitted a memorial to Emperor Gaozong that was to have far-reaching implications for the later history of Neo-Confucianism. In this memorial, Zhu set forth the authentic line of transmission of the Confucian *Dao*, in the following words: 'Your servant humbly states that the Dao of Confucius was transmitted to Zeng Zi (see *Li ji*, *Lunyu*), Zeng Zi transmitted it to Zi Si (**Kong Ji**), and Zi Si transmitted it to **Mengzi**. After Mengzi there was no transmission. Coming to our dynasty, **Cheng Hao** and **Cheng Yi** of Luoyang transmitted this *Dao* more than a thousand years afterwards. Those engaged in learning shouldered satchels and hiked up their garments [in hurrying] to personally receive their instruction, spreading it to the four directions. Some in secret and some openly – none can exhaust the record.'

This fateful memorial, included by Li Xinchuan 李心傳 (1167–1244) in his *Daoming lu* 道命錄 (Record of the Destiny of the Dao, 3/2a–b) was the first official statement at court of the claim that *Luo xue* was the sole authentic transmission since the time of Mengzi. This claim set off a firestorm of criticism that labelled the Cheng School as 'spurious learning' (*wei xue* 偽學). Nevertheless, after numerous vicissitudes, the *Dao xue* fellowship eventually saw its claim to orthodoxy recognised by the court (in 1313) and sustained for nearly six hundred years.

Though Zhu Zhen was the first to make the authentic transmission claim at court, he was left out of **Zhu Xi**'s *Yiluo yuanyuanlu* 伊洛淵源錄 (Records of the Origins of the Chengs' School) and received only minor attention in later Neo-Confucian transmission accounts. One factor may have been his focus on numerological cosmology; after all, Shao Yong's cosmological system was considered abstruse by the Cheng brothers themselves. Ironically, in focusing his transmission account exclusively on the Chengs, Zhu Zhen may have contributed to later lack of attention to the element of the Neo-Confucian revival which most fascinated him, numerological cosmology.

References: Chang, 1986; Dong, 1995; Selover, 2002; Tillman, 1992b: 20–1.

THOMAS SELOVER

Zhu Zhiyu 朱之瑜
1600–1682
(*zi* Luyu 魯嶼, *hao* Shunshui 舜水)

Better known by his alternative name Shunshui, Zhu represents one of the rare cases in Japanese history of the sustained and direct influence of Chinese thought and the ideals of the Chinese literati through the person of a Chinese scholar living in Japan. Born as the son of a Ming official in Yuyao 余姚 (Zhejiang), Shunshui became a political refugee after the fall of the Ming in 1644, wandering between southern China, Nagasaki, and Annam seeking support for the Ming cause before finally being granted permission to stay in Japan in 1659, his seventh trip to that land. After repeated invitations from Tokugawa Mitsukuni 德川光國 (1628–1700), daimyo of Mito domain, he took up residence in Edo in 1665 to serve on Mitsukuni's historiographical commission. Zhu Shunshui was an uncompromising loyalist devoted to what gradually revealed itself to be a hopeless cause – the restoration of the Ming dynasty. He himself wrote in Japan of the many faults of Ming dynasty rule and the lack of concern for practical problems of government on the part of Ming scholar–officials that accounted for the loss of the Empire, as well as the lack of discipline and firm command among the loyalist forces of Coxinga 國姓爺 (Zheng Chenggong 鄭成功 1624–1662) and other Ming pretenders that doomed their restoration attempts. However, he put much of the blame for the loss of the dynasty on the corruption of high officials rather than on the Ming emperors themselves. It was possible for him to write about the dynasty's deficiencies in 'virtue' and failure in maintaining popular support (*min xin* 民心) – two factors that are always brought forth to account for a dynasty's loss of the Mandate – without it affecting at all his loyalty to the Ming throne, which was something that transcended any failings on the part of the dynasty or its individual emperors. This unconditional loyalty was interwoven with a long tradition of Chinese loyalist thought intertwined with the concept of an absolute distinction (*ming fen* 名分) between civilisation (Jn. *chûka* 中華) and barbarism (*iteki* 夷狄). Accordingly, even after the collapse of his cause in China, the spirit of his Ming loyalism refused to die, becoming transferred instead to his Confucianising mission in Mito domain. Zhu Shunshui's thought is generally identified loosely with **Zhu Xi** Learning, and he retained much respect for the Cheng–Zhu tradition of self-cultivation. But what his Confucianising mission in Mito domain focused upon was not philosophy or cosmology – he refused to discuss *tai ji* or *li* and *qi*, citing Confucius' refusal to discuss the Way of Heaven, and even ridiculed the idea of a transmission of the Way of the sages from mind to mind (without reliance on the transmission of concrete ritual practices). What he focused on, rather, was the teaching of the concrete rituals and institutions prescribed by the Confucian Classics, as well as the realisation of benevolent government – government that truly provided for the material needs and livelihood of the people. This included, for example, giving instruction in the proper rituals for burying parents and for honoring the domainal ancestors; teaching the meaning and ranks of the various official positions in the Ming government; the designing of the Confucian temple and school compound in Mito (which was later reproduced in Edo at the Yushima Seidô); the teaching of the ancient Zhou dynasty rituals for performance at the Confucian temple (including the production of the proper sacrificial vessels); and the designing of the great Kôrakuen 後樂園 garden in Edo for spiritual relaxation *after* concerning oneself with the problems of the world (*kôraku*). In short, Zhu was in many ways already an 'ancient learning' scholar of independent mind who rejected the Song to Ming turn of Confucianism toward abstract philosophising and introspection in favour of the study and practical realisation of the institutions of the ancient kings. He seems to have had no significant influence, however, on the beginnings of what is known as the Ancient Learning movement in Japan, writing for instance that Itô Jinsai's scholarship was 'useless to the service of the world'. Through his influence on Mitsukuni and on Mito historians such as **Asaka Tanpaku**, however, he exerted a tremendous influence on the development of Japanese imperial loyalist historiography. Tanpaku studied under Zhu in his youth, and as a protégé of Mitsukuni, entered the Shôkôkan in 1683, becoming a director (*sôsai* 總裁) in 1693. Between 1716 and 1720, he took up the task of writing Appraisals (*ronsan* 論贊) on both the chronological accounts and the biographies of the *Dai Nihonshi*. Although these appraisals were later expurgated from the history on the grounds that they represented the judgements of a private individual regarding individual emperors, they were published separately and exerted much influence on later private historians such as **Rai San'yô**. Some of Tanpaku's Appraisals read as if they have superimposed Zhu's experience in seeking the restoration of a fallen dynasty upon the similar experience of Emperor Go-Daigo and his loyal vassals in the fourteenth century. At the end of the Appraisal on Go-Daigo, for instance, he writes, 'The thought of restoration only grows more intense when it is frustrated. Facing death he took hold of his sword and braced himself for battle. Thus he was able to keep the regalia safe among deep mountain crags, and lay down the foundation for a court that held out for more than fifty years. The place where the legitimate line dwells shines bright like the sun and the moon! Was this not a great accomplishment?'

At his death, Zhu left all of his wealth to be used in efforts to restore the Ming. Zhu was granted the posthumous name Bunkyo Sensei 文恭先生, and Mitsukuni had his writings compiled in the twenty-eight-*juan* collection *Zhu Shunshui xiansheng wenji*

朱舜水先生文集 (*The Literary Collection of Master Zhu Shunshui*). This collection stressed as very pragmatic style of Confucian Learning, which eventually would appeal to Japan's Meiji reform generation after 1868. Zhu would also become popular among anti-Manchu Chinese activists at the turn of the century. His anti-Qing tract *Yangjiu shulue* 陽九述略 became particularly popular. A Chinese edition of Zhu's collected writings was published after the fall of the Qing in 1913 as *Shunshui yishu* 舜水遺書 (*The Extant Works of Zhu Shunshui*).

References: Asaku Tanpaku, *Dai Nihon shi sansô*, in *Kinsei shiron shû*, NST, vol. 48 (Tokyo: Iwanami Shoten, 1974), pp. 12–319 (quotation from p. 67); Ching, in de Bary & Bloom, 1979: 189–229; Hummel, A., 1943–1944: 179–80.

BARRY D. STEBEN, JAMES A. ANDERSON

Zhuan 傳
(Tradition or commentary)

The genre of the *zhuan* is among the earliest forms of Chinese exegetical literature on canonical texts (*jing*). By the Former Han times (206 BCE–8 CE), all Five Classics (**Wu jing**) had attracted texts that either carried the word *zhuan* in their title or were generically considered as *zhuan* in the contemporaneous literature. Important examples are the *Xici zhuan* and others of the 'ten wings' (*shi yi* 十翼) of the *Yi jing*; the **Shang shu** *dazhuan*; the *Mao shi guxun zhuan* (also including philological *guxun* glosses); the **Zuo zhuan**, **Guliang zhuan**, and **Gongyang zhuan** of the **Chunqiu**; and the **Li ji** as a *zhuan* of either the **Yi li** or the **Zhou li**. The genre continued to exist in the later tradition through works like **Cheng Yi**'s *Yi zhuan* 易傳 (*Commentary on the Changes*). In generic terms, a *zhuan* commentary served as an exposition of the principles and overall significance of a Classic. As a relatively independent work in its own right, a *zhuan* was circulated and read separately from the *jing* Classic to which it was related; only towards the end of the Later Han (25–220), through the new textual arrangements of Classics and commentaries by scholars like **Zheng Xuan** and **Ma Rong**, were *jing* and *zhuan* physically combined. Because of their significance and self-contained nature, expository writings that were at some time considered *zhuan* could over time assume the status of a canonical text and receive their own commentaries, like the three *zhuan* to the *Chunqiu* or works like the **Lun yu** or the **Xiao jing**.

References: Henderson, 1991: 62–88; Nylan, 2001; Wang Baoxuan, 1994: 20–8.

MARTIN KERN

Zhuansun Shi 顓孫師
503–? BCE
(*zi* Zizhang 子張)

Better known by his style name *Zizhang* in the *Analects*, Zhuansun Shi is said in the *Records of the Historian* (**Shi ji**) to be a native the state of Chen 陳 near Kaifeng, but his immediate ancestors had resettled in Lu 魯 (modern Shandong). Zhuansun was a prominent disciple of Confucius but was not distinguished from the others as a savant until 1267. He received sacrifices in the temple in 739 when he was ennobled as Earl of Chen 陳伯. He was promoted to Marquis of Wanqiu 宛丘侯 in 1009. This title was changed to Marquis of Yingchuan 潁川侯 and he was promoted to Duke of Chen 陳國公 in 1267, when he was elevated to a Savant.

THOMAS A. WILSON

Zhulin Qixian 竹林七賢
(The Seven Sages of the Bamboo Grove)

The Seven Sages of the Bamboo Grove were a group of men who are said to have gathered together towards the middle of the third century CE in a bamboo grove located some eighty kilometres to the northeast of the capital Luoyang. Their supposed meetings there became legendary at least as early as the fourth century when they became models of free living, engaging in metaphysical conversations far from the trammels of the court and with little concern for Confucian ritual and commitment to their duties as servants of the state and society.

It is said in a work about the group that dates from the end of the fourth century quoted the commentary to the **Shishuo xinyu** (17: 2), that the anecdotes about them and their reunions 'under the bamboos' began at the earliest only after the fall of Luoyang in 311, and it is possible, perhaps probable, that the stories told about the meetings of these seven men are apocryphal, fabricated when the northern aristocrats, exiled in the south, were attempting to reimagine the history of their ancestors so that they could find in them models who lived the kind of life they themselves would like to live a century later when the intellectual atmosphere had changed enormously.

In any case, it can be shown from historical sources that the seven men knew one another. One of the leaders of the group, **Ji Kang**, on whose estate the meetings are said to have taken place, speaks of the other supposed leader, **Ruan Ji**, in one of his letters, and there are other texts linking the other members of the group together. Their characters, however, and their intellectual orientations do not seem to have destined most of them to make fast friends of one another. Ji Kang was indeed truly enamoured of Daoist philosophy and the research for Long Life. This could make him the only member of the group who could be imagined to have embodied the life of a man completely freed of all social and political bonds such as those in the descriptions given of the Seven Sages. Liu Ling 劉伶 and Ruan Xian 阮咸, a nephew of Ruan Ji, have left us no authentic works that might enable us to ascertain their intellectual tendencies and the little we know of their lives was in all probability written after the legend of the Sages had been formed. Of Wang Rong 王戎 (234–305) and Shan Tao 山濤 (205–283) we know mainly that they were very successful government officials whose intellectual interests seem to have been far different from Ji Kang's. Xiang Xiu 向秀 and Ji Kang seem to have been good friends, but the essays they exchanged and that are still extant reveal their strong differences of opinion and show that Xiang Xiu was at heart a firm supporter of Confucian ideals and was far from being a free-thinking 'Daoist' libertarian. Ruan Ji has bared his tortured soul to us in his poetry where he shows himself to be anything but a man indifferent to social morality.

The discovery in 1960 of a tomb datable to the end of the fourth century that contains representations of the Seven Sages on its walls shows us that the group had already become icons of individual liberty a century or so after they had supposedly lived together. Whether they actually existed as a group is secondary: their legend has kept alive an ideal of personal freedom that has been very rare in the history of Confucian China.

References: Holzman,   1957;   Xu Kangsheng, 1989.

Donald Holzman

Zhushu jinian 竹書記年
(*Bamboo Annals Chronicle*)

The *Bamboo Annals* chronicle was discovered *c.* 281 CE, when a tomb at Jixian 汲縣 that reportedly belonged to King Ai 哀 (or Xiang 襄 or Anxi 安釐) of the State of Wei 魏 (403–225 BCE) was plundered by thieves. Three separate versions of the chronicle must be distinguished for scholarly purposes: (1) the original text(s), which would have been written in pre-

Qin script (almost certainly lost), (2) the 'Modern' edition (*jin ben* 今本) in two *juan* (which may be based on the original); and (3) the so-called 'Archaic' edition (*gu ben* 古本), a collection of quoted fragments presumed by many to be the remnants of the original text. Many reputable classical scholars (including **Wang Mingsheng**, **Qian Daxin** and **Wang Guowei**) have argued that the Modern edition is a late forgery, possibly of Ming date. But more recent research argues that the Modern edition is not a fabrication, though it departs at points from the original.

The original text, after its discovery in a cache of texts, was deciphered and then transcribed by at least three court scholars: Shu Xi 束皙, Xun Xu 荀勖 and He Qiao 和嶠. Apparently, there was disagreement on some of the transcriptions, since both the earliest commentary to the *Shi ji* by Pei Yin (fifth century CE) and the commentary to the Modern edition by Shen Yue 沈約 (441–513), author of the *Song shu* 宋書 (comp. 489 CE), make reference to other versions. Du Yu 杜預 (222–284), the famous commentator on the *Chunqiu Zuo zhuan*, reports in his Postface (*houxu* 後序) to the *Zuo zhuan* that the *Zhushu jinian* was relatively complete. Du makes three important observations about the original, which distinguish it from the Modern edition: (1) that it began with Xia, rather than with the Yellow Emperor (see below); (2) that it used the Xia calendar, which began the new year with the lunar month prior to the spring equinox; (3) that only the Zhou royal calendar was used for dates prior to 784 BCE, after which the calendars of Jin 晉 and Wei were used. Tang-dynasty texts talk of a *Bamboo Annals* in 12 *juan*, with 1 *juan* of variants, which suggests that the original was considerably longer than either of the two versions known today. Chapter 47 of the *Yu hai* 玉海 (published 1343–1351) describes three chapters that were already lost, including a *juan* 6 on '*Decrees and Responses*'. In any case, the earliest extant editions of the Modern edition date from the Ming dynasty.

The Modern edition begins with the reign of the Yellow Emperor and ends in 299 BCE, which corresponds to the last year of the reign of King Ai of Wei. The first *juan* covers events until the downfall of the Shang 商 (with exact dates given from 2145 BCE, in the reign of the legendary sage–emperor Yao 堯). The second covers the Zhou down to 299 BCE, largely from the perspective of the vassal state of Jin and later its successor state of Wei. Material on portents appears quite often in the first half of *juan* 2 (perhaps as a commentary interpolated into the text); the second half of the same *juan* provides a greater number of realistic details about historical events. Occasional commentary by Shen Yue accompanies the received text. Notable is the fact that from 784 BCE on, the text is increasingly careful to correlate the Zhou royal calendar with the reign dates of the local rulers.

The 'Archaic' edition appears to represent fragments or loose paraphrases of phrases drawn from the original or Modern editions and culled from early commentaries, encyclopedias and such. In some sense, there is no separate 'Archaic' edition though that sobriquet provides a convenient term for the important materials therein.

To scholars of early China, the importance of the Modern edition can hardly be overestimated. The *Bamboo Annals* not only provides a fairly detailed chronology stretching back to pre-Shang times; it also provides a wealth of information on the affairs of Jin and its successor state, Wei. And though discrepancies between the Modern edition and quotations from the *Bamboo Annals* in other texts once caused scholars to denounce it as a late forgery perpetrated either by Shu Xi 束皙 of the Jin 晉 dynasty or by a forger living centuries later, David Nivison has verified the authenticity of the Modern edition, showing its chronology to be (1) correct and (2) not based on the Archaic edition, which includes almost no dated entries.

Two translations are currently available in western languages. The first by Édouard Biot (in *Journal Asiatique*, third series, vols. XII–XIII) omits the portent texts. The second by James **Legge** (in vol. III of *The Chinese Classics, The Shoo King or Book of Historical Documents*) provides a complete translation, which is generally reliable except for its dates, which are usually one year late.

References: Nivison, 1990: 87–95; Shao, 1998.

MICHAEL NYLAN

Zhuzi wenji 朱子文集
(*Collection of Literary Works by Master Zhu*)

The formal title of this collection uses Zhu Xi's honorific names: *Hui'an xiansheng Zhu Wengong wenji* 晦庵先生朱文公文集 (*Collection of Literary Works by the Duke of Culture, Zhu, Master of Hui'an*). The main collection in 100 chapters (*juan*) was compiled by Zhu's third son, Zhu Zai 朱在 (b. 1169), and first published in 1245. Within the next twenty years, both a supplementary collection (*xuji* 續集) in 11 chapters and a separate collection (*bieji* 別集) in 10 chapters were added. Besides memorials, petitions, lectures to the emperor, other official documents, poems, essays, prefaces, postscripts, commemorative records, funeral addresses, tomb inscriptions, biographies, prayers, invocations, etc., the collections include almost 2,000 letters to about 500 people. Zhu's literary works, especially his letters, are the most important source for studying his personal life and thought; however, modern scholars have often relied more heavily on conversations recorded by his students in the *Zhuzi yulei*. There are several twentieth-century editions of the *Wenji*. In the year 2000, a new edition of Zhu literary works was published by the Asian Culture Company (*Yunchen wenhua gongsi*) in Taipei. This new edition is the culmination of cooperative efforts by scholars in mainland China and Taiwan to compile the most complete and authoritative text of Zhu's literary works. There is a prefatory volume, *Zhu Xi de lishi shijie* 朱熹的历史世界 (*Zhu Xi's Historical World*) written by Princeton Professor Yu Ying-shih 余英時, setting forth the importance of Zhu's life and works in the context of the Song era and society. The publication of the new edition marked the 800th anniversary of Zhu Xi's death and should significantly advance the study of Zhu's thought.

Reference: Balazs & Hervouet, 1978: 420.

HOYT TILLMAN

Zhuzi xin xuean 朱子新學案
(*A New Account of the Learning of Master Zhu*)

A five-volume set, completed in 1970 by the elderly Confucian historian and educator, **Qian Mu** 錢穆, it claims to be a 'new systematic account' of the teachings of the influential Neo-Confucian master, **Zhu Xi**. The newness of the study is manifest in its methodology, content and suggested results. Methodologically, to avoid partisan accounts, Qian allowed 'Master Zhu to explain himself'. This he accomplished by reorganising selected passages taken mainly from Zhu Xi's extensive collected literary essays (*wenji* 文集) and classified conversations (*yulei* 語類), into nearly sixty minor themes. These were further arranged into general units, dealing first with metaphysics, then with studies of self-cultivation, followed by his discussions with and about various scholars and schools. This was followed by guidance for reading and interpreting books, leading to lengthier discussions about the Confucian Classics, their commentaries, and readings in history, literature, textual criticism and other arts. While Qian himself linked passages together with his own narration, always indicating their sources and occasionally adding brief biographical cues, the main ideas flow from Zhu's own statements. To the whole Qian added a lengthy summarising essay.

Overall results of this study emphasise Zhu's balanced vision and synthetic comprehensiveness. While arguing for two distinct metaphysical realms – principle (*li* 理) and material force (*qi* 氣) – Zhu insisted that they exist in unity. Unexpectedly, he relates heart/mind (*xin* 心) to principle more than emphasising their differences. Finally, though engaged in many discussions, Zhu sought creatively to synthesise ideas in order to overcome sectarian views.

References: Fang & Zheng, 1995: 182–5; Qian Mu, 1989.

LAUREN PFISTER

Zhuzi yulei 朱子語類
(*Classified Conversations of Master Zhu*)

Consolidating and correcting passages from seven earlier editions of **Zhu Xi**'s recorded conversations, Li Jingde 黎靖德 produced the definitive edition in 1270. Although recorded by his students and compiled after his death, instead of being written by Zhu himself, this collection has long been regarded by philosophically oriented scholars as 'the primary source on' Zhu's thought because its topical organisation and conversational style facilitate its use. No one would question the importance of using the recorded conversations; however, some modern historians have sought to give greater attention to Zhu's own writings in the *Zhuzi wenji*. Whereas the *Zhuzi wenji* includes Zhu's writings from 1153 to 1200, the *Zhuzi yulei* records conversations from 1170 to 1200. Since most of these conversations occurred within the last sixteen years of Zhu's life when he attracted large numbers of students, philosophers have confidently taken the *Yulei* as Zhu's most mature and systematic views. As statements made to his closest disciples and edited by them while propagating his school of thought, Zhu's voice in the *Yulei* is generally unchallenged and reverently received as authoritative. Hence, scholars within this tradition have looked to the *Yulei* for Zhu's philosophical coherence and system.

The work's 140 chapters (*juan*) contain about 14,200 sections classified by topic; moreover, an effort was made to organise the topics in a logical sequence following the principles of Zhu's philosophy and educational curriculum. The preface, written by Hu Shi 胡適 (1891–1962), to the 1962 Taibei edition provides the history of the compilation. Noteworthy is Daniel Gardner's translation of chapters 7 through 13 on learning and reading.

References: Balazs & Hervouet, 1978: 225; Chan, Wing-tsit, 1989: 374–8.

HOYT TILLMAN

Zi 子
(Son or daughter)

Zi can refer to both sons and daughters. The **Baihu tong** defines it as 'to multiply, to work tirelessly'. Therefore, the **Xiao jing** states, 'If a father has a remonstrating son then his embodied self will neither fall into danger nor be unrighteousness' (*Baihu tong*, 29: 54). A son (*zi*), then, is someone who unstintingly enhances, both materially and morally, the lives of his parents. He does so because they are the source of everything he possesses, including his body. Hence, 'A father is his son's Heaven (*tian*)' (*Yi li* 11: 66). A son, thus, 'respects and loves [his father], and exhausts his reverence towards him' (*Xunzi*, 12: 57).

References: Lau & Chen, 1995, 1996a, 1996b.

KEITH KNAPP

Zi xue 子學
(Teachings of philosophers)

The character *zi* 子 in classical Chinese represents a number of different meanings:

firstly, it indicates a fine man; secondly, a person who knows the moral value of humanity; thirdly, it denotes a teacher, in particular, a sage teacher (*shi*). The word *zi* was attached to names such as Laozi 老子, Kongzi 孔子 (Confucius), Mozi 墨子, Yangzi 楊子, **Mengzi** 孟子, Zhuangzi 莊子 and they were generally regarded as the *Zhuzi* 諸子 (various masters of philosophy) and their scholarship and teachings as the *Zixue* 子學.

In Fung Yu-lan's *A History of Chinese Philosophies*, the age extending from Confucius down to the Prince of Huai-nan 淮南 王 (d. 122 BCE) is counted as the Period of Teachings of the Philosophers (*Zixue shidai* 子學時代), or the Age of Various Philosophers and Hundred Schools (*Zhuzi baijia shidai* 諸子百家時代). In other words, the rise of the Confucian School marked the beginning of the Period of the Philosophers, while its supremacy over all other schools marked the Close of the Period.

During the age from the *Chunqiu* period (770–476 BCE) to the beginning of the Han (206 BCE–220 CE), political institutions, social organisations, and economic structures all underwent fundamental changes. In particular, along with the feudal system's gradual collapse, the earlier rigid social system was beginning to change, and the result was described as follows: 'with the decline of the house of Zhou, the rites (**li**) and laws fell into decay' (**Han shu**, 91). This gradual collapse of the old institutions influenced the development of philosophical writings and scholarship, and thus began the Period of the Philosophers, especially with the appearance of Confucius.

Up to the time of Confucius, there appears to have been no one who wrote books under his own name expressing his own ideas or opinions. **Zhang Xuecheng** of the Qing pointed out that there were no instances of (private) writing of books during this early period.

From the time of Confucius onward, there were men who criticised the establishment of new institutions or who were opposed to any institutions whatsoever. This age was one of transition, during which the institutions of the past had lost their authority, and those of the new age had not yet been definitely formulated. It was inevitable that it should also be one of uncertainty and divergence.

Thus when Confucians advanced their arguments for the preservation of the past, other philosophers, holding divergent views, were forced to explain in turn the reasons why they considered their own doctrines superior.

Literally thousands of scholars, belonging to every school of thought, travelled about from state to state offering their advice to the different rulers. The Confucian philosopher, **Xunzi**, refers to this situation as follows: 'what they support (all) seems resonable; their teachings are (all) plausible' (*Xunzi*).

In chapter 30 of the *Han shu* it is stated that 'The various philosophers belonged to ten schools, but there are only nine worthy of notice. They differed widely in what they preferred and disliked. Just so the differing practices of the nine schools swarmed forth and developed side by side. Each school picked a single point which was exalted as the good and was discussed so as to win the favour of the feudal lords [*zhu hou*].'

There are, mainly, two different opinions concerning the numbers of the schools; one was 'the Six Schools' put forward by Sima Tan 司馬談 (?–501 BCE), the father of **Sima Qian**, the chief author of the famous *Shi ji*, and the other 'Ten Schools' by **Liu Xin** (?–23 CE). According to Sima Tan, there had been six main schools of thought, namely, the *Yin–yang jia* 陰陽家, the Literati or Confucians (*Ru jia* 儒家), the Moists (*Mo jia* 墨家), the school of Names (*Ming jia* 名家), the Legalists (*Fa jia* 法家) and the Daoists (*Daode jia* 道德家). To them, Liu Xin added those of Political Strategists (*Zongheng jia* 縱橫家), Miscellaneous (*Za jia* 雜家), Agriculturalists (*Nong jia* 農家) and Story-tellers (*Xiao-shuo jia* 小說家).

Although the thinkers of the Period of the Philosophers deliberated on metaphysics, ethics, epistemology and logic, their special emphasis on human affairs prevented them from delving profoundly enough into each subject. For example, logic is a requirement for dialectic discussion and yet only the School of Names was interested in examining the processes and methods of thinking.

Dong Zhongshu advised the Han emperor to dismiss the Hundred Schools and venerate only Confucian arts. When this policy took effect, the Period of the Philosophers came to an end, and that of the Study of the Classics commenced. Influenced by the New Text School's teachings, Confucius was venerated, no longer simply as a teacher, but as a divine being who was commissioned by Heaven to save the world. It was not until the rise of the so-called 'Old Text School' at the end of the Former Han dynasty (206 BCE–8 CE) that Confucianism returned to the school of literati.

Reference: Fung Yu-Lan, 1952.

M.H. KIM

Zi zi 子子
(Sonly son)

The idea of a 'sonly son' is related to the concept of the rectification of names (*zheng ming*). One can only earn the name of son if one acts like a son. A 'sonly son' fulfils all the duties inherent in his role, which are embodied in the virtue of filial piety (*xiao*). The *Analects* (*Lunyu*) provides this idea's *locus classicus*. When a duke asked Confucius about governance, he replied 'A lord must be lordly, a retainer loyal, a father fatherly, and a son sonly'. (*Analects*, 12: 11) The result of a son not being sonly is chaos.

Reference: Hung, 1972a.

KEITH KNAPP

Ziwei xuepai 紫微學派
(The School of Lü Benzhong)

The family of **Lü Benzhong** originated from Donglai (Shandong) but early on had moved to Shouzhou (Anhui) and then later, during the first half of the eleventh century, to Kaifeng. Two famous family members, namely Lü Benzhong and **Lü Zuqian**, are known as Masters of Donglai. Lü Benzhong is referred to as the Elder Donglai (Da Donglai 大東萊) and Lü Zuqian the Lesser Donglai (Xiao Donglai 小東萊). In order to avoid confusion Lü Benzhong is often called Ziwei xiansheng (Master from Ziwei) after a famous grotto near Wuzhou 婺州 (present-day Jinhua 金華 in Zhejiang 浙江) where Lü Haowen, the father of Lü Benzhong had settled down after the Jurchen invasion. As Lü Haowen died shortly afterwards, Lü Benzhong was the first of the Lü family to actually live in Wuzhou. Therefore, Ziwei School is the name for the group associated with his teachings.

Except for Lü Zuqian, a grandnephew of Lü Benzhong, there are no famous names linked to his school. His nephews Lü Daqi 呂大器 (*zi* Zhixian 治先), the father of Lü Zuqian, Lü Dalun 呂大倫 (*zi* Shixu 時敘), Lü Dayou 呂大猷 (*zi* Yunsheng 允升) and Lü Datong 呂大同 (*zi* Fengji 逢吉) should be mentioned although none of them produced written texts, which could help to further define the Ziwei school. Of some importance are Lin Zhiqi 林之奇 (1112–1176, *zi* Shaoying 少穎 or Zhuozhai 拙齋, *hao* Sanshan xiansheng 三山先生), a student of Lü Benzhong who became one of the teachers of Lü Zuqian, Li Nan 李楠 (1111–1147, *zi* Hebo 和伯) and his brother Li Shu 李樗 (*zi* Yuzhong 迂仲), and Fang Chou 方疇 (*zi* Gengdao 耕道, *hao* Kunzhai Xiansheng 困齋先生), who also studied with **Zhang Jiucheng** and **Hu Anguo** and his sons, a fact which shows that he was interested in the *Spring and Autumn Annals'* (**Chunqiu**) teachings of all three schools.

HANS VAN ESS

Zizhi tongjian 資治通鑑
(*Comprehensive Mirror for the Aid of Government*)

At the very end of his life, after almost two decades spent in its composition, **Sima Guang** presented the world with his majestic *Zizhi tongjian*. Consisting of nearly 300 chapters (*juan*), the work is a monumental narrative history of China. Its chronology spans from the year of the formal beginning of the Warring States (403 BCE) to the year just prior to the founding of the Song dynasty (959 CE) – a period of more than one and a third millennia. While Sima Guang is customarily ascribed sole authorship of this influential work, three erudite contemporaries are mentioned in the text itself as his collaborators – the best known of whom today is **Fan Zuyu**.

Certainly with imperial knowledge and consent and perhaps even under an imperial directive, Sima Guang began writing the *Comprehensive Mirror* in 1067 – the last year of the reign of the Yingzong emperor (r. 1064–1067). It was the emperor who supplied the title for the book and, upon its completion in 1084, the then-reigning Shenzong emperor (r. 1067–1085) contributed the admiring imperial preface that all new printings still bear today. Sources contemporary with the time as well as somewhat later ones – stating that it 'remained unfinished for a long time' – suggest that the completion of the *Comprehensive Mirror* was delayed not by the scope of the project but by Sima Guang's own dilatoriness. Nevertheless, once it was finally completed, the book was quickly published in 1086 – the year of Sima Guang's death and, as he himself had written in his own preface to the work, 'in preparing this book, I have expended all my energies'.

Much of the seminal mystique of the *Comprehensive Mirror* derives from the fact that present-day scholars regard it much in the same manner as Song literati scholars tended to regard it in their own time – as an exemplary articulation of an emerging postclassical Confucian conception of history. Sima Guang contended that an appreciation for and understanding of history is prerequisite for becoming a Confucian (**Ru**). Sima Guang so argued because he believed history, more effectively than any other discipline, teaches us to accept and value both the constancy of a universal Way (**Dao**) or way as well as the primacy of hierarchy in all political affairs. As a book, the *Comprehensive Mirror* exemplifies Sima's theory that the forces that determine the success or failure of governments have been invariant throughout history, thus enabling the past to be always instructive regarding the present. Moreover, every device that Sima employs in the *Comprehensive Mirror* – from his detached descriptions of dynasties rising and falling in succession to his balanced and even-handed scrutiny of the motives and behaviour of past actors – adumbrates a political vision in which hierarchy is both natural and necessary. Hierarchy is natural because the ancient sages, who were themselves the architects of culture, subscribed to it. Hierarchy is necessary because only through the act of subordination to persons and principles higher than oneself does civilisation become at all possible. For Sima Guang, history itself was as much the preserve of hierarchy in the world as it was the primary illustration of its inherent order.

While its insistence on a constant *dao* and on hierarchy is preeminent, the *Comprehensive Mirror* exhibits a number of additional features that all contribute to the construction and promotion of Sima Guang's particular latter-day Confucianist historical sensibility. The importance of individuals maintaining the proper distinction in names or titles (*ming* 名) is certainly one corollary of hierarchy. Moreover, in a manner eerily suggestive of Legalist thinking, such distinctions were for the ruler to make, and he was not to relinquish his authority to do so for any reason. Another discrete but significant theme is the conscious and conspicuous minimising of the

role of fate or destiny (**ming**) in human affairs. At the same time that he attempted to accommodate metaphysical speculation, Sima Guang stresses that humankind makes its own history. But, ultimately, perhaps the greatest mark of the ingeniousness of the *Comprehensive Mirror* is the way that it seems to have been calculated to solicit the upholding of moral responsibility and to induce the outpouring of genuine pangs of accountability on the part of any subsequent ruler who read it. In this as well as numerous other respects, the *Comprehensive Mirror* remains, by any measure and in any time, nothing less than a most remarkable and singular work of scholarship.

References: Balazs & Hervouet, 1978: 61, 64, 65, 68, 69–70, 71, 72, 73, 75, 76, 77, 78, 85, 90, 92, 113, 210, 211, 273, 297, 298, 315, 321, 349, 350, 392, 394, 400, 485; Bol, 1992: 224, 233–46, 300, 339; Wyatt, 1996: 62, 173, 287n. 120.

DON J. WYATT

Zong sheng 宗聖
(The Ancestral Sage)

Zong sheng is the title of Zeng Shen 曾參 (505?–435? BCE, aka Zengzi 曾子, *zi* Ziyu 子輿) in temple sacrifices to Confucius. The title is to give credit to Zeng Shen for his part in carrying on the lineage of Confucius by supposedly having as his disciple **Kong Ji** (Zisi, 子思), the grandson of the Master. Reputedly one of the most prolific writers of Confucius' followers, Zeng Shen is commonly regarded as the founder of several canonical traditions, such as that of the *Book of Filial Piety*, the *Great Learning* and several other chapters in the *Book of Rites* and the *Elder Dai's Book of Rites* 大戴禮記. Also probably for his role in educating the young Kong Ji, Zeng was posthumously dubbed Junior Guardian of the Heir Apparent (*Taizi shaobao* 太子少保) in 669, and promoted to Grand Guardian of the Heir Apparent (*Taizi taishi* 太子太師),

which carried a status equivalent to a feudal lord, in 712, when he received secondary sacrifices, although he was not a Correlate at the time. In 739 Zeng was ennobled as Earl of Cheng 郕伯. He was promoted to Marquis of Xiaqiu 瑕丘侯 in 1009 and to Duke of Cheng 郕國公 in 1267, when he was installed as a Correlate. In 1333 he was given the title of the Lineage Sage Duke of Cheng 郕國宗聖公.

THOMAS A. WILSON

Zou Yan 鄒衍
305?–240 BCE

No writings attributable to Zou Yan are extant, and his presence was scarcely noted by his contemporaries, yet he was considered by Han scholars to be one of the most significant Warring States' thinkers. In the *Han Fei zi* (Section 19, 飾邪, 'Pretensions and heresies'), for example, Zou Yan is noted in passing as an example of an ineffective minister. In a brief entry in the *Zhanguo ce* 戰國策, however, he is mentioned more positively as a gifted adviser from Qi 齊 who was attracted to the court of King Zhao of Yan 燕昭王. Zou is not mentioned in such texts as the *Xunzi* that otherwise devote considerable space to praising or maligning rival thinkers.

It is only in the Han that Zou Yan is otherwise noted in the historical record. **Sima Qian**'s *Shi ji* devotes more attention to Zou Yan's biography (section 74) than to that of either Xunzi or **Mengzi**, and Sima Qian believes Zou compares very favourably to both **Confucius** and **Mengzi** in terms of the respect shown by the rulers they advised. According to this account, Zou Yan was a noted cosmologist who compiled lengthy treatises titled *Ends and Beginnings* 終始 and *The Great Sage* 大聖, which totalled tens of thousands of words. Zou was versed in the mysteries of yin and yang, prodigies, and the Five Powers or Virtues (**wu de** 五德, later known as the Five Phases, or **wu xing** 五行). His cosmogonic vision traced human history

to the time of the mythic Yellow Emperor, and in an expansive vision of the geography of the cosmos that incorporated all terrestrial phenomena and living things, he posited that the area then known as the Central Kingdom (*Zhongguo* 中國) was not the totality of all under heaven but was only a small fraction of it; the Central Kingdom was but one of the nine continents. The human dimensions of this cosmos were guided by principles of humaneness and rightness.

Ideas developed by Zou Yan and his followers are also incidentally mentioned in section 28 of the *Shi ji*, where Sima Qian describes the Feng and Shan sacrifices and numerous other religious practices. Within this discussion of ritual theory and praxis and their significance for governance, Sima notes that Zou was well known among the ruling elite for his ideas on the fluctuations of yin and yang. Zou also elaborated the theory of the cyclical succession of the Five Powers (**wude zhongshi**), which later captured the attention of Qin Shihuang 秦始皇, the First Emperor of the Qin (r. 221–210 BCE). Some of Zou's followers engaged in techniques to liberate themselves from their mortal coils and transform themselves into spirits. Adepts (*fang shi* 方士) of the Yan 燕 and Qi regions tried to implement the Zou arts, but with little success.

Two lost works attributed to Zou Yan are listed in the bibliographic section of the *Han Shu* (*juan* 30), where they are included under the section on Yin–yang traditions. Recorded here is a text in fifty-six sections titled (as in the *Shi ji*) *Ends and Beginnings* and another untitled work in forty-nine sections.

References: Chan, Wing-tsit, 1963d: 244–8; Crump, 1970: 523–5; Fung Yu-lan, 1952: 159–69; Liao, 1959: vol. I, p. 156; Loewe & Shaughnessy, 1999: 822–5; Watson, 1993: 14; Yang & Yang, 1979: 70–5; Yang Jialuo, 1997: 1368–9, 2344–5; Zhang & Wang, 1993: 777–80.

DEBORAH SOMMER

Bibliography

Abe Takeo 阿部建夫, 1972. '*Gendai chishikijin to kakyo* 元代知識人と科舉', in Abe Takeo, *Gendaishi no kenkyu* 元代史の研究. Tokyo: Sobunsha 創文社.

Acker, William R.B., 1954 and 1974. *Some T'ang and Pre-T'ang Texts on Chinese Painting*, vol. I and vol. II part 1. Leiden: E.J. Brill.

Adler, Joseph Alan, 1984. 'Divination and Philosophy. Chu Hsi's Understanding of the I-Ching', Ph.D. dissertation. University of California.

—— 2002. 'Varieties of Spiritual Experience: Shen in Neo-Confucian Discourse', in Mary Evelyn Tucker and Tu Wei-ming, eds., *Confucian Spirituality*, vol. II. New York: Crossroads.

Ahern, Emily M., 1973. *The Cult of the Dead in a Chinese Village*. Stanford University Press.

Almond, Brenda, 1998. *Exploring Ethics*. Oxford: Blackwell Publishers.

Ames, Roger T., 1991. 'The Mencian Conception of Ren xing: Does it Mean "Human Nature"?', in Henry Rosemont, Jr., ed., *Chinese Texts and Philosophical Contexts. Essays Dedicated to Angus C. Graham*. La Salle (IL): Open Court, pp. 143–75.

—— and Henry Rosemont, 1998. *The Analects of Confucius: A Philosophical Translation*. New York: Ballantine Books.

An Mengsong 安夢松, comp. 1599. *Kongsheng quanshu* 孔聖全書 (Complete Writings of the Sage Confucius). Jianyang, Fujian: Zongwen shushe 宗文書社.

Aoki Kazuo, ed., 1982. *Kojiki*. Tokyo: Iwanami Shoten.

Araki Kengo, 1970. 'Shushigaku no tetsugakuteki seikaku – Nihon Jugaku kaimei no tame no shiten settei', in Araki Kengo & Inoue Tadashi, comps., *Kaibara Ekiken – Muro Kyûsô*, pp. 445–66. (*NST* 34, Tokyo: Iwanami Shoten.

Araki, T., 1976. 'Liu An-shih', in Herbert Franke, ed., *Sung Biographies: volume I A–M*, pp. 616–19. Wiesbaden: Franz Steiner Verlag GMBH.

Ariel, Yoav, 1986. 'The *K'ung-Family-Masters' Anthology* and Third-Century Confucianism', in Irene Eber, ed., *Confucianism: The Dynamics of Tradition*, pp. 39–59. New York: Macmillan.

—— 1989. *K'ung-ts'ung-tzu: The K'ung Family Masters' Anthology*. Princeton University Press.

—— 1996. *K'ung-ts'ung-tzu: A Study and Translation of Chapters 15–23 with a Reconstruction of the* Hsiao Erh-ya *Dictionary*. Leiden: E.J. Brill.

Asselin, Mark Laurent, 1991. *The Hou Han shu Biography of Cai Yong (A.D. 132/133–192)*, M.A. thesis. University of Washington.

—— 1997. 'A Significant Season, Literature in a Time of Endings: Cai Yong and a Few Contemporaries', Ph.D. dissertation. University of Washington.

Aston, W.G., tr., 1972. *Nihongi: Chronicles of Japan from the Earliest Times to A.D. 697*. Tokyo: C.E. Tuttle Co.

Aubin, Françoise, 1990. 'En Islam Chinois: Quels Naqshbandis?' in Marc Gaborieau, Alexandre Popovic and Thierry Zarcone, eds., *Naqshbandis: Cheminements et situation actuelle d'un ordre mystique musulman, Varia Turkica* XVIII. Institut Francais d'Etudes Anatoliennes d'Istanbul, Istanbul.

Ayers, William, 1971. *Chang Chih-tung and Educational Reform in China*. Cambridge, MA: Harvard University Press.

Baba Harukichi 馬場春吉, 1934. *Koshi Seiseki Shi* 孔子聖蹟志 (Annals of the Sage Confucius' Traces). Tokyo: Daito Bunka Kyokai 大同文化協會.

—— 1940. *Ko Mo Seiseki Zukan* 孔孟聖蹟圖鑑 (Reflection in Pictures of the Traces of the Sages Confucius and Mengzi). Tokyo: Zendo Bunka Kenkyukai 山東文化研究會.

Bäcker, Jorg, 1982. *'Prinzip der Natur' und 'Sein Selbst Vergessen': Theorie und Praxis des Neo-konfuzianismus anhand der 'Aufgezeichneten Aussprüche des Hsieh Liang-tso (1050–1121)'*, Ph.D. dissertation. Bonn: Rheinische Friedrich-Wilhelms-Universität.

Bai Juyi 白居易, 1988, in Zhu Jincheng 朱金城, ed., *Bai Juyi ji jian jiao* 白居易集箋校 (Annotated and Collated Edition of Bai Juyi's Collected Works). Shanghai guji chubanshe.

Bai Shouyi 白壽彝, 1982. *Zhongguo Yisilanjiao shi cungao* 中國伊斯蘭教史存稿 (Collected Papers on Chinese Islam). Yinchuan: Ningxia renmin chubanshe.

Balazs, Etienne, 1964, in H.M. Wright, trans. and Arthur F. Wright, ed., *Chinese Civilization and Bureaucracy: Variations on a Theme*. New Haven: Yale University Press.

Balazs, E. and Hervouet, Y. 1978, in Yves Hervouet, ed., initiated by Etienne Balazs *A Sung Bibliography (Bibliographie des Sung)*. Hong Kong: The Chinese University Press.

Barrett, T.H., 1992. *Li Ao: Buddhist, Taoist, or Neo-Confucian?* Oxford University Press.

Bays, Daniel H., 1978. *Enters the Twentieth Century: Chang Chih-tung and the Issues of a New Age, 1895–1909*. Ann Arbor: University of Michigan Press.

Beasley, W.G., and E.G. Pulleyblank, 1961. *Historians of China and Japan*. London: Oxford University Press.

Beck, B.J. Mansvelt, 1990. *The Treatises of Later Han: Their Author, Sources, Contents and Place in Chinese Historiography*, Sinica Leidensia Edidit Institutum Sinologicum Lugduno Batavum, vol. XXI. Leiden: E.J. Brill.

Befu, Harumi, ed., 1993. *Cultural Nationalism in East Asia: Representation and Identity*. Berkeley: University of California Press.

Beijing Library, comp., 1993. *Beijing Tushuguan Cang Huaxiang Taben Huibian* 北京圖書館藏畫像拓本匯編 (Compilation of Rubbings of Pictorial Stelae Housed in the Beijing Library vol. I). Beijing: Shumu wenxian chubanshe 書目文獻出版社.

Bell, Catherine, 1997. *Ritual: Perspectives and Dimensions*. New York: Oxford University Press.

Bellah, Robert N., 1970. 'Father and Son in Christianity and Confucianism', in his *Beyond Belief: Essays on Religion in a Post-Traditionalist World*, pp. 76–99. Berkeley: University of California Press.

Bernal, Martin, 1976. 'Liu Shih-p'ei and National Essence', in Charlotte Furth, ed., *The Limits of Change: Essays on Conservative Alternatives in Republican China*, pp. 90–112. Cambridge, MA: Harvard University Press.

Bernard-Maitre, Henri, 1935. *Sagesse chinoise et philosophie chretienne*. Leiden: E.J. Brill.

Berthrong, John H. 1998. *Transformations of the Confucian Way*. Boulder, CO: Westview Press.

Bettray, Johannes, 1955. *Die Akkommodationsmethode des P. Matteo Ricci in China*. Romae: Universitatis Gregorianae.

Bian Xiaoxuan 卞孝萱, 1963. *Liu Yuxi nianpu* 劉禹錫年譜 (Chronological Biography of Liu Yuxi). Beijing: Zhonghua shuju.

Bian Xiaoxuan and Wu Ruyu 吳汝煜, 1980. *Liu Yuxi* 劉禹錫, Shanghai guji chubanshe.

Bieg, Lutz, 1976. 'Huang T'ing-chien', in Herbert Franke, ed., *Sung Biographies: vol. I A–M*, pp. 454–61. Wiesbaden: Franz Steiner Verlag GMBH.

Bielenstein, Hans, 1976. 'Loyang in Later Han Times', *BMFEA* 48, pp. 1–142.

Bilsky, Lester James, 1975. *The State Religion of Ancient China*. 2 vols. Taipei: The Chinese Association for Folklore.

Birdwhistell, Anne D., 1989. *Transition to Neo-Confucianism: Shao Yung on Knowledge and Symbols of Reality*. Stanford University Press.

Birge, Bettine, 1999. *Women, Property, and Confucian Reaction in Sung and Yuan China (960–1368)*. Cambridge University Press.

Bitô Masahide, 1961. *Nihon hôken shisôshi kenkyû*. Tokyo: Aoki Shoten.

Black, Alison H., 1989. 'Gender and Cosmology in Chinese Correlative Thinking', in Caroline Walker Bynum, Stevan Harrell, & Paula Richman, eds., *Gender and Religion: On the Complexity of Symbols*. Boston: Beacon Press.

Bloom, Irene, 1979. 'On the "Abstraction" of Ming thought: Some Concrete Evidence from the Philosophy of Lo Ch'in-shun', in de Bary, William Theodore and Irene

Bloom, eds., *Principle and Practicality, Essays in Neo-Confucianism and Practical Learning*, pp. 69–125. New York: Columbia University Press.

—— 1987. *Knowledge Painfully Acquired: The K'un-chih chi by Lo Ch'in-shun*. New York: Columbia University Press.

—— 1994. 'Mencian Arguments on Human Nature (Jen-hsing)', *Philosophy East and West*, 44, 1: 19–53.

—— 1997a. 'Human Nature and Biological Nature in Mencius', *Philosophy East and West*, 47, 1: 21–32.

—— 1997b. 'Three Visions of *Jen*', in Irene Bloom and Joshua A. Fogel, eds., *Meeting of Minds: Intellectual and Religious Interaction in East Asian Traditions of Thought*, pp. 8–42. New York: Columbia University Press.

Bloom, Irene and Wm. Theodore de Bary, eds., 1979. *Principle and Practicality: Essays in Neo-Confucianism and Practical Learning*. New York: Columbia University Press.

Bloom, Irene and Joshua A. Fogel, eds., 1997. *Meeting of Minds: Intellectual and Religious Interaction in East Asian Traditions of Thought: Essays in Honor of Wing-tsit Chan and Wm. Theodore de Bary*. New York: Columbia University Press.

Bloom, Irene, J. Paul Martin, and Wayne L. Proudfoot, eds., 1996. *Religious Diversity and Human Rights*. New York: Columbia University Press.

Bodde, Derk, 1991. *Chinese Thought, Society, and Science: The Intellectual and Social Background of Science and Technology in Pre-Modern China*. Honolulu: University of Hawaii Press.

Bodde, Derk and Clarence Morris, 1967. *Law in Imperial China*. Cambridge, MA: Harvard University Press.

Bohn, Hermann G., 1998. *Die Rezeption des Zhouyi in der Chinesischen Philosophie von den Anfangen bis zur Song-Dynastie*. Munich: Herbert Utz Verlag.

Bol, Peter K., 1982. 'Ch'in Kuan (1049–1100)', in *Culture and the Way in Eleventh Century China*, pp. 276–343. Ph.D. dissertation. Princeton University.

—— 1989. 'Chu Hsi's Redefinition of Literati Learning', in Wm. Theodore de Bary and John W. Chaffee, eds., *Neo-Confucian Educa-tion: The Formative Stage*. Berkeley: University of California Press.

—— 1992. *'This Culture of Ours': Intellectual Transitions in T'ang and Sung China*. Stanford University Press.

—— 1997. 'Examinations and Orthodoxies: 1070 and 1313 Compared', in Theodore Huters, Wong, R. Bin and Pauline Yu, eds., *Culture and State in Chinese History*. Stanford Unversity Press, pp. 29–57.

Boltz, William G., 1990. 'Notes on the Textual Relationship between the Kuo Yu and the Tso Chuan', *BSOAS* 53, pp. 491–502.

—— 1993. 'Chou li', 'Hsiao ching', 'I li', in Michael Loewe, ed., *Early Chinese Texts: A Bibliographical Guide*, pp. 24–32, 141–53, 234–43, Early China Special Monograph Series No. 2. Berkeley: The Society for the Study of Early China, and The Institute of East Asian Studies. University of California, Berkeley.

Bonner, Joey, 1986. *Wang Guowei: An Intellectual Biography*. Cambridge, MA: Harvard University Press.

Bouilliard, G. 1923. 'La Temple du Terre', *La Chine* (January–March).

Bresciani, Umberto, 1992. 'Il filosofo Xiong Shili (1885–1968)' ('The Philosopher Xiong Shili (1885–1968'), *Mondo Cinese (The Chinese World)* 79 (Settembre 1992): 25–46.

Brodsgaard, Kjeld Erik and David Strand, eds., 1998. *Reconstructing Twentieth Century China*. Oxford: Clarendon Press.

Brook, Timothy and B. Michael Frolic, eds., 1997. *Civil Society in China*. London: M.E. Sharpe.

Brooks, E. Bruce and A. Taeko, 1998. *The Original Analects. Sayings of Confucius and His Successors. A New Translation and Commentary*. New York: Columbia University Press.

Brown, William Andreas, 1986. *Wen T'ien-hsiang: A Biographical Study of a Sung Patriot*. San Francisco: Chinese Materials Center.

Bruce, Joseph Percy, 1922. *The Philosophy of Human Nature by Chu Hsi*. London: Probsthain & Co.

—— 1923. *Chu Hsi and His Masters: An Introduction to Chu Hsi and the Sung School of Chinese Philosophy*. London: Probsthain & Co.

Bujard, Marianne, 1992. 'La vie de Dong Zhongshu: enigmes et hypotheses'; *Journal asiatique* 280: 1–2, 142–217.

Busch, Heinrich, 1955. 'The Tung-lin shuyuan and its Philosophical Significance'. In *Monumenta Serica*, 14: 163.

Bush, Susan H., 1978. *The Chinese Literati on Painting: Su Shih (1037–1101) to Tung Ch'ich'ang (1555–1636)*, 2nd edn. Cambridge, MA: Harvard University Press.

Bush, Susan H. and Christian F. Murck, eds., 1983. *Theories of the Arts in China*. Princeton: The Art Museum, Princeton University.

Bush, Susan H. and Shih Hsio-yen, eds., 1985. *Early Chinese Texts on Painting*. Cambridge, MA: Harvard University Press.

Cady, Lyman Van Law, 1939. *The Philosophy of Lu Hsiang-shan: A Neo-Confucian Monistic Idealist*. Shanghai: Pacific Cultural Foundation.

Cahill, James F., 1960. 'Confucian Elements in the Theory of Painting', in Arthur F. Wright, ed., *The Confucian Persuasion*, pp. 115–40. Stanford University Press.

Cai De'an 蔡德安, 1973. *Kangjie Xiantian Yixue Pingyi* 康節先天易學平議 (Deliberations on the Before-Heaven Book of Change Learning of (Master) Kangjie). Taipei: Dragon Springs Press.

Cai Fanglu 蔡方鹿, 1996. *Cheng Hao Cheng Yi yu Zhongguo Wenhua* 程顥程頤與中國文化 (Cheng Hao, Cheng Yi, and Chinese Culture). Guiyang: Guizhou renmin chubanshe.

Cai Renhou (Tsai Jen-hou 蔡仁厚), 1980. *Song–Ming lixue: Nan Song Pian.* 宋明理學: 南宋篇. Taipei: Xuesheng shuju.

—— 1998. Kongzi de shengming jingjie – Ruxue de fansi yu kaizhan 孔子的生命境界 – 儒學的反思與開展. Taipei: Xuesheng shuju.

—— 1999. 'Mou Zongsan Xiansheng Dui Zhcxuc Huiming De Shutong Yu Kaifa – Mou Xiansheng Zhuzao Xueshu Xice Zhi Yihan Shujie' 牟宗三先生對哲學慧命的疏通與開發 – 牟先生鑄造學術新詞之意涵述解 (Mou Zongsan's Dredging through and Opening up Philosophical Wisdom and its Propositions: Explanations of the Meaning of the New Academic Terminology Coined by Mou Zongsan', *Kongzi Yanjiu* 孔子研究 (Studies of Confucius), 53: 4–14.

Cai Zhongdao 蔡仲道, 2000. *Wei-Jin Ru Dao hubu zhi yanjiu* 魏晉儒道互補之研究. Taipei: Wenjin chubanshe 文津出版社.

Cai Zhongde 蔡仲德, 1994. *Fung Yu-lan xiansheng nianpu chubian.* 馮友蘭先生年譜初編 (Initial Draft of a Chronology of Fung Yu-lan's Life). Zhengzhou: Henan renmin chubanshe.

—— 1995. 'Lun Fung Yu-lan de sixiang licheng' 論馮友蘭的思想歷程 ('On the Historical Development of Fung Yu-lan's Ideas'), *Tsing Hua Journal of Chinese Studies*, 25: 237–72.

Campany, Robert Ford, 1996. *Strange Writing: Anomaly Accounts in Early Medieval China*. Albany: State University of New York Press.

Carlitz, Katherine, 1991. 'The Social Uses of Female Virtue in Late Ming Editions of the *Lienü zhuan*'. *Late Imperial China*, vol. 12, no. 2: 117–48.

—— 1994. 'Desire, Danger, and the Body: Stories of Women's Virtue in Late Ming China', in Christine K. Gilmartin, Gail Hershatter, Lisa Rofel, and Tyrene White, eds., *Engendering China: Women, Culture, and the State*, pp. 101–24. Cambridge, MA: Harvard University Press.

Chaffee, John W., 1995. *The Thorny Gates of Learning in Sung China*, new edn. Albany: State University of New York Press.

Chamberlain, B.H., tr., 1982. *The Kojiki: Records of Ancient Matters*. Tokyo: C.E. Tuttle Co.

—— 1993. 'On the Search for Civil Society in China'. *Modern China*, 19, 2: 199–215.

Chan Hok-lam, 1976. 'Hao Ching' (pp. 503–504), 'Liu Chi' (pp. 932–938) in L. Carrington Goodrich and Fang Chao-ying eds., *Dictionary of Ming Biography*, vol. II. New York: Columbia University Press.

—— 1981. 'Chinese Official Historiography at the Yuan Court: The Composition of the Liao, Chin, and Sung Histories', in J.D. Langlois, ed., *China Under Mongol Rule*. Princeton University Press, pp. 56–106.

—— 1982. '"Comprehensiveness" (T'ung) and "Change" (Pien) in Ma Tuan-lin's Historical Thought', in W.T. de Bary and Chan Hok-lam. *Yuan Thought*. New York: Columbia University Press.

Chan, Sin-wai. 1984. *An Explanation of Benevolence: The* Jen-hsüeh *of T'an Ssu-t'ung*. Hong Kong: The Chinese University Press.

Chan, Wing-tsit (Chen Rongjie 陳榮捷), 1953. *Religious Trends in Modern China*. New York: Columbia University Press.

—— 1955. 'The Evolution of the Confucian Concept *Jen*', *Philosophy East and West* 4 (January): 295–319.

—— 1963a. *The Platform Scripture*. New York: St. John's University Press.

—— 1963b. *The Way of Lao Tzu*. Indianapolis: Bobbs-Merrill.

—— 1963c. *Instructions for Practical Living and Other Neo-Confucian Writings by Wang Yangming*, trans. Wing-tsit Chan. New York: Columbia University Press.

—— 1963d. *A Source Book in Chinese Philosophy*. Princeton University Press and London: Oxford University Press.

—— 1964. 'The Evolution of the Neo-Confucian Concept *Li* 理 as Principle', *Tsing Hua Journal of Chinese Studies*, n.s. 4/2 (Feb. 1964): 123–48.

—— 1967. *Reflections on Things at Hand: The Neo-Confucian Anthology*. New York: Columbia University Press.

—— 1969. *Neo-Confucianism, etc.: Essays by Wing-tsit Chan*, Comp. by Charles K.H. Chen. Hanover, NH: Oriental Society.

—— 1972. 'Wang Yang-ming: a biography', *Philosophy East and West* 22, 1 (January 1972): 63–92.

—— 1973. 'Chan Jo-shui's Influence on Wang Yang-ming', in *Philosophy East and West* 23 (January–April 1973): 9–30.

—— 1975. 'The *Hsing-li ching-i* and the Ch'eng-Chu School of the Seventeenth Century', in W.T. de Bary, ed., *The Unfolding of Neo-Confucianism*. New York: Columbia University Press, pp. 543–79.

—— 1976. 'Chang Tsai' (pp. 39–43), 'Chou Tun-I' (pp. 39–43) in Herbert Franke, ed., *Sung Biographies*, pp. 39–43. Weisbaden: Franz Steiner Verlag.

—— 1979. *Commentary on the Lao Tzu*. Honolulu: University Press of Hawaii.

—— 1982. 'Chu Hsi and Yuan Neo-Confucianism in Chan', in Hok-lam and Wm. Theodore de Bary eds., *Yuan Thought: Chinese Thought and Religion Under the Mongols*. New York: Columbia University Press.

—— 1986a. *Chu Hsi and Neo-Confucianism*. Honolulu: University of Hawaii Press.

—— 1986b. *Neo-Confucian Terms Explained*. New York: Columbia University Press.

—— 1987. *Chu Hsi: Life and Thought*. Hong Kong: Chinese University Press.

—— 1989. *Chu Hsi: New Studies*. Honolulu: University of Hawaii Press.

—— 1996. *Song Ming lixue zhi gainian yu lishi* 宋明理學之概念與歷史 (Concepts and History of the Song–Ming Schools of Principle). Taipei: Academia Sinica.

Chang, Carson, 1957. *The Development of Neo-Confucian Thought*, vol. I. New York: Bookman Associates.

—— 1962. *The Development of Neo-Confucian Thought*, vol. II. New York: Bookman Associates.

Chang Hao, 1976. 'New Confucianism and the Intellectual Crisis of Contemporary China', in Charlotte Furth, ed., *The Limits of Change: Essays on Conservative Alternatives in Republican China*. Cambridge, MA: Harvard University Press.

—— 1997. *Chinese Intellectuals in Crisis: Search for Order and Meaning (1890–1911)*. Berkeley: University of California Press.

Chang I-jen 張以仁, 1962. '*Lun Guoyu yu Zuozhuan de guanxi*', *Academia Sinica*, Taipei, *Bulletin of the Institute of History and Philology*, 33: 233–86.

—— 1993. '*Kuo Yu*', in Michael Loewe, ed., *Early Chinese Texts: A Bibliographical Guide*, The Society for the Study of Early China and the Institute of East Asian Studies. University of California, Berkeley.

Chang Liwen (Zhang Liwen 張立文), 1986. 'An Analysis of Chu Hsi's System of Thought of *I*', in Wing-tsit Chan, ed., *Chu Hsi and Neo-Confucianism*. Honolulu: University of Hawaii Press.

Chang Myŏng-suk, 1994. *Tamhŏn Ŭisanmundapŭi Ch'eggye Jŏgyŏngu*. Seoul: Sŏnggyungwan University.

Chang Yung-chün, 1988. *Er Chengxue guanjian* 二程學管見 (Humble Views on the Learning of the Two Chengs). Taipei: Dongda tushu.

Chao Yuezhi 晁說之. *Ru yan* 儒言 (Statements of the Classicists). Congshu jicheng edition.

—— *Jingyu sheng ji* 景迂生集 (The Student of Jingyu's Collected Works). Siku quanshu edition.

—— *Chao shih keyu* 晁氏客語 (Polite Remarks of Mr Chao). Congshu jicheng edition.

—— *Zhongyong zhuan* 中庸傳 (Commentary on the Doctrine of the Mean). Congshu jicheng edition.

Chavannes, Edouard, 1910. *Le T'ai chan: Essai de monographie d'un culte chinois*. Reprinted 1970. Taipei.

—— 1969. *Les memoires historiques de Se-ma Ts'ien*, vols. I–V. Paris: Ernest Leroux, 1895–1905; rpt with vol. VI. Paris: Adrien Maisonneuve.

Chen Chi-yun, 1968. 'A Confucian Magnate's Idea of Political Violence: Hsun Shuang's Interpretation of the Book of Changes'. *T'oung Pao* 54: 73–115.

—— 1975. *Hsun Yueh (A.D. 148–209): The Life and Reflections of an Early Medieval Confucian*. Cambridge University Press.

—— 1980. *Hsun Yueh and the Mind of Late Han China, A Translation of the 'Shen-chien' with Introduction and Annotations*. Princeton University Press.

—— 1986. 'Confucian, Legalist, and Taoist Thought in Later Han', in Denis Twitchett and Michael Loewe, eds., *The Cambridge History of China, vol. I, The Ch'in and Han Empires*, pp. 608–48. Cambridge University Press.

—— 1993. 'Shen chien', in Michael Loewe, ed., *Early Chinese Texts: A Bibliographical Guide*, pp. 390–3, Early China Special Monograph Series No. 2. Berkeley: The Society for the Study of Early China, and The Institute of East Asian Studies, University of California, Berkeley.

Chen Chun 陳淳, 1986. *Neo-Confucian Terms Explained: The Pei-Hsi Tzu-I*. Trans., ed. and with an intro. by Wing-tsit Chan. New York: Columbia University Press.

—— *Beixi Daquanji* 北溪大全集 (Collected Works of Chen Chun). Siku chuanshu edition.

Chen Dasheng 陳大生, 1984. *Quanzhou Yisilanjiao shike* 泉州伊斯蘭教石刻. Fuzhou: Fujian renmin chubanshe.

Chen, Dehe 陳德和, ed., 1997 *Dangdai Xinruxue de Guanhuai yu Chaoyue* (Concern

and Transcendence in Contemporary New Confucianism) 當代新儒學的關懷與超越. Taipei: Wenjin Chubanshe 文津出版社.

Chen Dongyuan, 1936. *Zhongguo jiaoyushi*. Shanghai: Shangwu yinshuguan.

Chen Gaohua 陳高華, 1983. Luxue zai Yuandai 陸學在元代 (The Lu School in the Yuan Era), in *Zhongguo zhexue* 中國哲學, 9: 270–85.

Chen Guan 陳瓘, 1995. *Song Zhongsu Chen Liaozhai Siming Zun Yao ji* 宋忠肅陳了齋四明尊堯集 (Chen Guan's Collection Honouring Yao). Shanghai guji chubanshe.

—— *Liao weng Yi shuo* 了翁易說 (The Satisfied Old Man's Explanation of the Yijing). Siku quanshu edition.

Chen Gujia 陳谷嘉 and Zhu Hanmin 朱漢民, 1992. *Huxiang Xuepai Yuanliu* 湖湘學派源流 (The Story of the Hunan School). Changsha: Hunan Educational Press.

Chen Hao 陳鎬, 1505. *Queli zhi* 闕里誌. Kangxi 康熙 (*c.* 1700) edn.

Chen, Ivan, 1908. *Hsiao Ching: The Book of Filial Piety*, reprinted 1968, London: John Murray.

Chen, Jo-shui, 1992. *Liu Tsung-Yuan and Intellectual Change in T'ang China 773–819*. Cambridge University Press.

Chen Junmin 陳俊民, 1986. *Zhang Zai Zhexue Sixiang ji Guanxue Xuepai* 張載哲學思想及關學學派 (The Philosophical Thought of Zhang Zai and the School of the Teachings from Within the Passes). Beijing: People's Press.

Chen Lai 陳來, 1993. *Song Ming Lixue* 宋明理學 (Neo-Confucianism of the Song and Ming periods). Taipei: Hongye wenhua.

—— 1996. *Gudai zongjiao yu lunli – rujia sixiang de genyuan* (古代宗教與倫理 – 儒家思想的根源). Beijing: Sanlian shudian.

—— 1997. 'Lun Fung Yu-lan zhexue zhong de shenmizhuyi' 論馮友蘭哲學中的神秘主義 (On the Mysticism within Fung Yu-lan's Philosophy), in Cai Zhongde 蔡仲德, ed., *Fung Yu-lan yanjiu* 馮友蘭研究 (Studies on Fung Yu-lan), vol. I, pp. 294–312. Beijing: Peking University Press.

Chen Pan, 1972. *Chunqiu de jiaoyu* 春秋的教育 in *Zhongyang yanjiuyuan Lishi yuyan yanjiusuo jikan* 中央研究院歷史語言研究所輯刊, vol. 45. Taipei: Zhongyang yanjiuyuan lishisuo.

Chen Qizhu 陳祺助, 1986. *Hu Wufeng zhi xinxinglun yanjiu* 胡五峰之心性論研究. Taipei: Guoli gaoxiong shifan xueyuan 國立高雄師範學院.

Chen Shaoming 陳少明, 1992. *Ruxue de Xiandai Zhuanzhe* 儒學的現代轉折 (The Modern Transition of Confucianism). Shenyang: Liaoning University Press.

Chen Wan-nai 陳萬鼐, 1982. *Zhongguo Shanggu Shiqi de Yinyue Zhidu: Shishi Guyuejing de Hanyi* 中國上古時期的音樂制度: 試釋[古樂經]的涵義 (The Chinese Music System in Prehistoric Times: A Tentative Interpretation of the Meanings of the *Ancient Book of Music*), *Academic Journal on literature and history of Soochow University*, 4.

Chen Yinke 陳寅恪, 1927 (1968). 'Wang Guantang xiansheng wanci bingxu' 王觀堂先生挽辭并序 (An Elegiac Poem, with a Prose Preface, on Mr Wang Guantang (Guowei), in Wang Xiansheng Guantang chuanji 王先生觀堂全集 (The Collected Works of Mr Wang Guantang), 16: 7120–1. Taipei: Wenhua chubenshe.

Chen Yuan, 1966. *Western and Central Asians in China Under the Mongols*, trans. Ch'ien Hsing-hai and L. Carrington Goodrich. Los Angeles: Monumenta Serica at the University of California.

Chen Zhengyan 陳正焱 and Lin Qitan 林其錟, 1988. *Zhongguo Gudai Datong Sixiang Yanjiu* 中國古代大同思想研究 (Studies on the Ancient Idea of the Great Unity in China). Hong Kong: Chinese Bookstore.

Cheng, Anne 程艾藍, 1985a. *Entretiens de Confucius*, 2nd rev. edn. Paris: Editions du Seuil.

—— 1985b. *Etude sur le Confucianisme Han: l'elaboration d'une tradition exegetique sur les classiques*. Paris: College de France et Institut des Hautes Etudes Chinoises.

—— 1993. 'Ch'un ch'iu, Kung yang, Ku liang and Tso chuan', 'Lun yu', in Michael Loewe, ed., *Early Chinese Texts: A Bibliographical Guide*, pp. 67–76. Early China Special Monograph Series No. 2, Berkeley: The Society for the Study of Early China and the Institute of East Asian Studies, No. 2.

—— 1997. 'Nationalism, Citizenship, and the Old Text/New Text Controversy in Late 19th Century China', in Joshua A. Fogel and Peter G. Zarrow, eds., *Imagining the People: Chinese Intellectuals and the Concept of Citizenship, 1890–1920*. Armonk and London: M.E. Sharpe.

—— 1999. 'Un classique qui n'en finit pas de faire parler de lui: les Entretiens de Confucius. Un aperçu des traductions du XXe siècle en langues européennes', *Revue Bibliographique de Sinologie*, 471–9.

Cheng, Chung-ying (Cheng Zhongying 成中英), 1971. *Tai Chen's Inquiry Into Goodness: A Translation of the Yuan shan*. Honolulu: East–West Center Press.

—— ed., 1975. *Philosophical Aspects of the Mind–Body Problem*. Honolulu: University Press of Hawaii.

—— 1986. 'Chu Hsi's Methodology and Theory of Understanding', in Wing-tsit Chan, ed., *Chu Hsi and Neo-Confucianism*, pp. 169–96. Honolulu: University of Hawaii Press.

—— 1991. *New Dimensions of Confucian and Neo-Confucian Philosophy*. Albany: State University of New York Press.

—— and James C. Hsiung, eds., 1991. *Distribution of Power and Rewards: Proceedings of the International Conference on Democracy and Social Justice East and West*. Lanham: University Press of America.

—— and Nicolas Bunnin, eds., 2002. *Blackwell Guide to Contemporary Chinese Philosophy*. Oxford: Blackwell Publishers.

Cheng Hao 程顥 and Cheng Yi 程頤, 1981. *Er Cheng ji* 二程集 (Collected Writings of the Two Chengs). Beijing: Zhonghua shuju.

—— 1992. *Er Cheng yi shu* 二程遺書 (Writings Handed Down from the Two Chengs). Shanghai guji chubanshe.

Cheng Weili 程偉禮, 1994. *Xinnian de lucheng – Fung Yu-lan zhuan.* 信念的旅程 – 馮友蘭傳 (Journey of Convictions – A Biography of Fung Yu-lan), Shanghai: Literary Arts Press.

Chiang I-pin 蔣義斌, 1997. *Songru yu Fojiao* 宋儒與佛教 (Song Dynasty Confucians and Buddhism). Hong Kong: Haixiao 海嘯 chubanshiye.

Ch'ien, Edward T., 1986. *Chiao Hung and the Restructuring of Neo-Confucianism in the Late Ming*. New York: Columbia University Press.

Chin Ann-ping and Mansfield Freeman, 1990. *Tai Chen on Mencius*. New Haven: Yale University Press.

Ching, Julia, 1972. *The Philosophical Letters of Wang Yang-ming*. Columbia: University of South Carolina Press.

—— 1976a. 'Shao Po-wen', in *Sung Biographies*, ed. Herbert Franke, pp. 846–9. Wiesbaden: Franz Steiner Verlag.

—— 1976b. *To Acquire Wisdom: The Way of Wang Yang-ming*. New York: Columbia University.

—— 1976c. 'Yang Shih', in Herbert Franke, ed., *Sung Biographies*. 2 vols., pp. 1226–8. Wiesbaden: Steiner Verlag.

—— 1977. *Confucianism and Christianity: A Comparative Study*. New York: Kodansha International.

—— 1986. 'Chu Hsi on Personal Cultivation', in Wing-tsit Chan, ed., *Chu Hsi and Neo-Confucianism*, pp. 273–91. Honolulu: University of Hawaii Press.

—— 1993. *Chinese Religions*. Maryknoll, NY: Orbis Books.

—— 1994. 'Sung Philosophers on Women', *Monumenta Serica*, 42: 259–74.

—— 1997. *Mysticism and Kingship in China: The Sage–King Paradigm*. New York: Cambridge University Press.

Ching, Julia and Chaoying Fang, eds., 1987. *The Records of Ming Scholars*. Honolulu: University of Hawaii Press.

Ching, Julia and Willard G. Oxtoby, eds., 1992. *Discovering China: European Interpretations in the Enlightenment*. Rochester, NY: University of Rochester Press.

Ching, Julia and Willard G. Oxtoby, eds., 1992. *Moral Enlightenment: Leibniz and Wolff on China*. Nettetal: Steyler.

Chiu Hansheng, 1986. 'Zhu Xi's Doctrine of Principle', in Wing-tsit Chan, ed., *Chu Hsi and Neo-Confucianism*, pp. 116–37. Honolulu: University of Hawaii Press.

Cho, Haejoang, 1998. 'Male Dominance and Mother Power: The Two Sides of Confucian Patriarchy in Korea', in Walter H. Slote and George A. DeVos, eds., *Confucianism and the Family*, pp. 187–208. Albany: State University of New York Press.

Cho Nam-ho, 1994. *Kim Ch'ang-hyŏp*. Seoul: Hanguk Ch'ŏlhakhoe.

Ch'oe Dong-hui, 1980. *Tonghakŭi Sasanggwa Undong*. Seoul: Sŏnggyungwan Ch'ulp'ansa.

Ch'oe Han-gi, 1978. *Kich'ŭk Ch'eŭi*. Seoul: Minjong Munhwa Ch'ujinhoe.

—— 1979. *Injung*. Seoul: Minjong Munhwa Ch'ujinhoe.

Ch'oe Yŏng-jin, 2000. *Ch'oe Han-giŭi Ch'ŏlhakkwa Sasang*. Seoul: Ch'ŏlhakkwa Hyŏnshilsa.

Ch'oe Yŏng-sŏng, 1997. *Hanguk Yuhak Sasangsa*. Seoul: Aseamunhwasa.

Chŏng Byŏng-nyŏn, 1998. *Kobong Ki Daesŭngŭi Saeng-aewa hangmun*. Seoul: Chŏnnamedaehakkyo Ch'ulp'anbu.

Chŏng To-jŏn, 1977. *Sambongjip*. Seoul: Minjong Munhwa Ch'ujinhoe.

Chosŏn Hugiŭi Hakp'adŭl, 1996. *Hanguk Sasang Sayŏngguhoe*. Seoul: Yemunsŏwon.

Chosŏn Yuhakŭi Hakp'adul, 1996. *Hanguk Sasang Yŏn-guhoe*. Seoul: Yemunsŏgwan.

Chou, Eva Shan, 1995. *Reconsidering Tu Fu: Literary Greatness and Cultural Context*. Cambridge University Press.

Chow Kai-wing 周啟榮, 1984. *Cong kuangyan dao weiyan – lun Gong Zizhen de jingshi sixiang yu jing jinwen xue* 從狂言到微言 – 論龔自珍的經世思想與經今文學 (From Frivolous Talk to Profound Metaphoric Message: A Study of Gong Zizhen's Statecraft Thinking and his New Text School of Confucianism), in *Jinshi Zhongguo jingshi sixiang yantaohui lunwenji* 近世中國經世思想研討會論文集 (Proceedings of the Conference on the Theory of Statecraft of Modern China). Taipei: The Institute of Modern History, Academia Sinica.

—— 1994. *The Rise of Confucian Ritualism in Late Imperial China: Ethics, Classics, and Lineage Discourse*. Stanford University Press.

—— 1997. 'Imagining Boundaries of Blood: Zhang Binglin and the Invention of the Han "Race" in Modern China', in Frank Dikotter, ed., *The Construction of Racial Identities in China and Japan*, pp. 34–52. London: Hurst and Co.

Chow, Rey 1991. *Women and Chinese Modernity: The Politics of Reading between East and West*. Minneapolis: University of Minesota.

Chu, Hung-lam, 1998. 'The Debate over Recognition of Wang Yang-ming', *Harvard Journal of Asiatic Studies* 48, no. 1.

Chu, Ron Guey 朱榮貴, tr., forthcoming. *Shang-ts'ai Yü-lu* (Recorded Sayings of Hsieh Liang-tso). Binghampton, NY: Global Publications.

Ch'u T'ung-tsu, 1961. *Law and Society in Traditional China*. Paris and The Hague: Mouton.

Chung, Edward Y.J., 1995. *The Korean Neo-Confucianism of Yi T'oegye and Yi Yulgok*. Albany: State University of New York Press.

Chunqiu Gongyang zhuan 春秋公羊傳, 1982. Taipei: Xinxing shuju.

Chuxue ji 初學記, 1962. By Xu Jian (659–729). 2 vols. Beijing: Zhonghua shuju.

Ci Xiaofang, 1998. *Zhongguo gudai xiaoxue jiaoyu yanjiu* 中國古代小學教育研究 Shanghai: Jiaoyu chubanshe 教育出版社.

Clart, Philip, 1992. 'The Protestant Ethic Analogy in the Study of Chinese History: On Yü Ying-shih's *Zhongguo jinshi zongjiao lunli yu shangren jinshen*', *British Columbia Asian Review* 6 (1992): 6–31.

Cohen, Alvin, 1982. *Tales of Vengeful Souls: A Sixth Century Collection of Chinese Avenging Ghost Stories*. Taipei: Institut Ricci.

Cohen, Paul A., 1974. *Between Tradition and Modernity: Wang T'ao and Reform in Late Ch'ing China*. Cambridge, MA: Harvard University Press.

Cohen, Paul A., and John E. Schreckers, eds., 1976. *Reform in Nineteenth Century China*. Cambridge, MA: Harvard University Press.

Collani, Claudia von, 1981. *Die Figuristen in der Chinamission*. Bern: Peter Lang.

Collie, David, tr., 1828. *The Chinese Classical Work Commonly Called the Four Books*. Malacca: Mission Press.

Collins, Randall, 1998. *The Sociology of Philosophies: A Global Theory of Intellectual Change*. Cambridge, MA/London: Harvard University Press.

Cook, S.B., 1995a. 'Unity and Diversity in the Musical Thought of Warring States China', Ph.D. dissertation. University of Michigan.

—— 1995b. '*Yue Ji* 樂記 – Record of Music: Introduction, Translation, Notes, and Commentary', *Asian Music*, 26, 2: 1–96.

Couplet, Philippe, *et al.*, trans., 1687. *Confucius sinarum philosophus, sive Scientia Sinensis Latine Exposita*. Parisiis: Danielem Horthemels.

Couvreur, Séraphin, 1895. *Entretiens de Confucius et de ses disciples*, in *Les Quatre Livres*.

Ho Kien Fou, Imprimerie de la Mission Catholique, rept Paris, Cathasia, 1950.

—— 1895. *Œuvres de Meng Tzeu*, in *Les Quatre Livres*. Ho Kien Fou, Mission catholique, 2nd edn, 1910.

—— 1951. *Tch'ouen ts'iou et Tso tchouan. La chronique de la principaut de Lou*, 1914, rept Paris: Cathasia.

Covell, Ralph R., 1986. *Confucius, the Buddha, and Christ: A History of the Gospel in Chinese*. Maryknoll: Orbis.

Creel, H.G., 1951. *Confucius: The Man and the Myth*. London: Routledge & Kegan Paul.

—— 1960. *Confucius and the Chinese Way*. New York: Harper Paperback.

—— 1970. *The Origins of Statecraft in China*. University of Chicago Press.

—— 1980. 'Legal Institutions and Procedures during the Chou Dynasty', in Jerome A. Cohen, R. Randle Edwards, and Fu-mei Chang Chen, eds., *Essays on China's Legal Tradition*. Princeton University Press.

Crump, J.I., trans. 1970. *Chan-Kuo Ts'e*. Oxford: Clarendon Press.

Cua, A.S., 1982. *The Unity of Knowledge and Action: A Study in Wang Yang-ming's Moral Psychology*. Honolulu: University of Hawaii Press.

—— 1993. 'Between Commitment and Realization: Wang Yang-ming's Vision of the Universe as a Moral Community', *Philosophy East and West* 43, 4 (Oct 1993): 611–47.

—— 1998. *Moral Vision and Tradition: Essays in Chinese Ethics*. Washington, DC: Catholic University of America Press.

Da Ming huidian 大明會典, 1976. 5 vols., Wanli 萬曆 (1587) edn comp. Li Dongyang 李東陽 and Shen Shixing 申時行. Taipei: Xinwen feng chuban gongsi 新文豐出版公司.

Da Ming jili 大明集禮. 40 vols. Jiajing 嘉靖 (1530) edn comp. Xu Yi-kui 徐一夔. Harvard–Yenching Library.

Da Qing huidian 大清匯典 (Assembled Canon of the Qing), 1899. 1763/Qianlong edn. Beijing: Guangxu edition.

Da Qing tongli 大清通禮 (Comprehensive rites of the Qing) 1756. Comp. Lai Bao. Beijing: Qianlong edition.

Da zai Kongzi 大哉孔子, 1991. Ed. Zhang Zuoyao 張作耀, *et al.* Hong Kong: Heping tushu youxian gongsi 和平圖書有限公司.

Davis, A.R., 1983. *T'ao Yuan-ming* 2 vols. Cambridge University Press.

Dawson, Raymond, 1993. *Confucius, The Analects.* Oxford and New York: Oxford University Press.

de Bary, Wm. Theodore, 1953. 'A Reappraisal of Neo-Confucianism', in Arthur F. Wright, ed., *Studies in Chinese Thought*, pp. 81–111. The University of Chicago Press.

—— 1958. *Sources of Indian Tradition.* New York: Columbia University Press.

—— 1969. *The Buddhist Tradition in India, China, and Japan.* New York: Vintage Books.

—— 1975. *The Unfolding of Neo-Confucianism.* New York: Columbia University Press.

—— 1981. *Neo-Confucian Orthodoxy and the Learning of the Mind-and-Heart.* New York: Columbia University Press.

—— 1983. *The Liberal Tradition in China.* Hong Kong: Chinese University Press.

—— 1988. *East Asian Civilizations: A Dialogue in Five Stages.* Cambridge, MA: Harvard University Press.

—— 1989. *The Message of the Mind in Neo-Confucianism.* New York: Columbia University Press.

—— 1991a. *Learning for One's Self: Essays on the Individual in Neo-Confucian Thought.* New York: Columbia University Press.

—— 1991b. *The Trouble with Confucianism.* Cambridge, MA: Harvard University Press.

—— 1993a. 'Chen Te-hsiu and Statecraft', in Robert P. Hymes and Conrad Schirokauer, eds., *Ordering the World: Approaches to State and Society in Sung Dynasty China.* Berkeley: University of California Press.

—— 1993b. *Waiting for the Dawn: A Plan for the Prince: Huang Tsung-hsi's Ming-i-tai-fang lu.* New York: Columbia University Press.

—— 1998. *Asian Values and Human Rights.* Cambridge, MA: Harvard University Press.

de Bary, Wm. Theodore and Irene Bloom, eds., 1979. *Principle and Practicality: Essays in Neo-Confucianism and Practical Learning.* New York: Columbia University Press.

de Bary, Wm. Theodore and Irene Bloom, eds., 1999. *Sources of Chinese Tradition*, 2nd edn, vol. I. New York: Columbia University Press.

de Bary, Wm. Theodore and Chaffee, John W., eds., 1989. *Neo-Confucian Education: The Formative Stage.* Berkeley: University of California Press.

de Bary, Wm. Theodore and Chan, Hok-lam, eds., 1982. *Yuan Thought: Chinese Thought and Religion Under the Mongols.* New York: Columbia University Press.

de Bary, Wm. Theodore and the Conference on Ming Thought, eds., 1970. *Self and Society in Ming Thought.* New York: Columbia University Press.

de Bary, Wm. Theodore and the Conference on Seventeenth-Century Chinese Thought, eds., 1975. *The Unfolding of Neo-Confucianism.* New York: Columbia University Press.

de Bary, Wm. Theodore and JaHyun Kim Haboush, eds., 1985. *The Rise of Neo-Confucianism in Korea.* New York: Columbia University Press.

de Bary, Wm. Theodore and Richard Lufrano, eds., 2000. *Sources of Chinese Tradition*, 2nd edn, vol. II. New York: Columbia University Press.

de Bary, Wm. Theodore, Ryusaku Tsunoda and Donald Keene, eds., 1958. *Sources of Japanese Civilization.* New York: Columbia University Press.

de Bary, Wm. Theodore and Tu Wei-ming, eds. 1997. *Confucianism and Human Rights.* New York, NY: Columbia University Press.

de Bary, Wm. Theodore, Wing-tsit Chan and Burton Watson, eds., 1960. *Sources of Chinese Tradition.* New York: Columbia University Press.

de Groot, J.J.M., 1892–1910. *The Religious System of China*, 6 vols. Leiden: Brill.

de Rachewiltz, Igor, ed., 1993. *In the Service of the Khan.* Wiesbaden: O. Harrassowitz Verlag.

De Weerdt, Hilde, 1999. 'Canon Formation and Examination Culture: The Construction of *Guwen* and *Daoxue* Canons', *Journal of Sung-Yuan Studies*, vol. 29: 91–134.

Demieville, Paul, 1986. 'Philosophy and Religion from Han to Sui', in Denis Twitchett and Michael Loewe, eds., *The Cambridge History of China*, vol. I, *The Ch'in and Han Empires*, pp. 808–72. Cambridge University Press.

Deng Xiaonan, 1999. 'Women in Turfan during the Sixth to Eighth Centuries: A Look at their Activities Outside the Home', *Journal of Asian Studies*, 58, 1: 85–103.

Deuchler, Martina, 1977. 'The Tradition: Women during the Yi Dynasty', In Sandra Mattielli, ed., *Virtues in Conflict: Tradition and the Korean Woman Today*. Seoul: The Royal Asiatic Society Korean Branch.

Deuchler, Martina, 1992. *The Confucian Transformation of Korea: A Study in Society and Ideology*. Cambridge, MA: Harvard University Press.

Dewey, John, 1973. *Lectures in China, 1919–1920*, eds. Robert W. Clopton and Tsuin-chen Ou. Honolulu, HI: University Press of Hawaii.

DeWoskin, K.J., 1982. *A Song for One or Two: Music and the Concept of Art in Early China*. Michigan Papers in Chinese Studies, Nr. 42. Ann Arbor: Center for Chinese Studies, The University of Michigan.

—— 1983. 'Early Chinese Music and the Origins of Aesthetic Terminology', in Susan Bush and Christian Murck, eds., *Theories of the Arts in China*. Princeton University Press.

—— 1985. 'Philosophers on Music in Early China', *The World of Music*, 27, 1: 33–45.

d'Hormon, Andre, Guoyu, 1985. *Propos sur les principauts: I – Zhouyu (complements par Remi Mathieu)*. Paris: College de France, Institut des Hautes Etudes Chinoises.

Dien, Albert E., 1962. 'Yen Chih-t'ui (531–591+), a Buddho-Confucian', in Arthur F. Wright and Denis Twitchett, eds., *Confucian Personalities*. Stanford University Press.

—— 1976. *Pei-Ch'i shu 45: Biography of Yen Chih-t'ui*. Frankfurt: Peter Lang.

Dillon, Michael, 1996. *China's Muslims*. Hong Kong: Oxford University Press 1996.

—— 1999. *China's Muslim Hui Community: Migrations, Settlements and Sects*. London: Curzon Press.

Dimberg, Ronald G., 1974. *The Sage and Society: The Life and Thought of Ho Hsin-Yin*, Monographs of the Society for Asian and Comparative Philosophy, no. 1. Honolulu: University Press of Hawaii.

Ding Weixiang 丁為祥, 1999. *Xiong Shili Xueshu Sixiang Pingzhuan* 熊十力學術思想評傳 (A Critical Biography of Xiong Shili's Academic Thought). Beijing Library Press.

Dittmer, Lowell and Samuel S. Kim, eds., 1993. *China's Quest for National Identity*. Ithaca: Cornell University Press.

Dobson, W.A.C.H., 1963. *Mengzi, a New Translation Arranged and Annotated for the General Reader*. Toronto University Press, London: Oxford University Press.

Dong Gao 董誥, *et al.*, 1983. *Quan Tang wen* 全唐文 (Complete Tang Prose). Beijing: Zhonghua shuju edition.

Dong Yuzheng 董玉整, 1995. Zhongguo Lixue Dacidian 中國理學大辭典 (Dictionary of Neo-Confucianism in China). Jinan Daxue chubanshe.

Dore, Henri, 1918. *Recherches sur les superstitions en Chine*, part 3, vol. 13. Shanghai: Mission Catholique.

Dreyer, Edward, 1976. 'Chao Ch'ien', in L. Carrington Goodrich and Fang Chao-ying, eds., *Dictionary of Ming Biography*, vol. 1, pp. 124–5. New York: Columbia.

Dubs, Homer H., 1927. *Hsuntze . . . the Moulder of Ancient Confucianism*. London: A. Probsthain.

—— 1928. *The Works of Hsüntze*. London: A. Probsthain.

Ducornet, Etienne, 1992. *Matteo Ricci: Le Lettre d'Occident*. Paris: Editions du Cerf.

Duke, Michael S., 1986. '*Huang T'ing-chien*', in William H. Nienhauser, ed., *The Indiana Companion to Traditional Chinese Literature*, pp. 447–8. Bloomington: Indian University Press.

Dull, Jack L., 1966. 'A Historical Introduction to the Apocryphal (Ch'an-wei) Texts of the Han Dynasty', Ph.D. dissertation. University of Washington.

Duncan, John, 1998. 'The Korean Adoption of Neo-Confucianism', in Walter H. Slote and George A. DeVos, eds., *Confucianism and the Family*, pp. 75–91. Albany: State University of New York Press.

Durrant, Stephen, 1981. 'On Translating Lun yu', *Chinese Literature: Essays, Articles, Reviews*, 3, 1: 109–19.

Eber, Irene, Sze-kar Wan and Knut Walf, eds., 1999. *Bible in Modern China: The Literary and Intellectual Impact*, Monumenta Serica Monograph Series, XLIV. Nettetal: Steyler Verlag.

Ebrey, Patricia Buckley, 1986. 'Early Stages in the Development of Descent Group Organization', in Patrician Buckley Ebrey, and James L. Watson, eds., *Kinship Organization in Imperial China, 1000–1940.* Berkeley: University of California Press.

—— 1986. 'The Economic and Social History of Later Han', in Denis Twitchett and Michael Loewe, eds., *The Cambridge History of China*, vol. I, *The Ch'in and Han Empires*, pp. 608–48. Cambridge University Press.

—— 1990a. 'Women, Marriage, and the Family in Chinese History', in Paul S. Ropp, ed., *Heritage of China: Contemporary Perspectives on Chinese Civilization*, pp. 197–223. Berkeley: University of California Press.

—— 1990b. 'Cremation in Sung China', *American Historical Review*, 95: 406–28.

—— 1991a, trans., *Confucianism and Family Rituals in Imperial China: A Social History of Writing about Rites.* Princeton University Press.

—— 1991b. *Chu Hsi's Family Rituals: A Twelfth-Century Chinese Manual for the Performance of Cappings, Weddings, Funerals, and Ancestral Rites.* Princeton University Press.

—— 1993. *The Inner Quarters: Marriage and the Lives of Chinese Women in the Sung Period.* Berkeley: University of California Press.

—— ed., 1993. *Chinese Civilization: A Sourcebook.* 2nd edn., revised and expanded. New York: Free Press, Princeton University Press.

—— 1995. 'Liturgies for Ancestral Rites in Successive Versions of the Family Rituals', in David Johnson, ed., *Ritual and Scripture in Chinese Popular Religion: Five Studies*, pp. 104–36. University of California Center for Chinese Studies.

—— 1997a. 'Portrait Sculptures in Imperial Ancestral Rites in Song China', *T'oung Pao* 83: 42–92.

—— 1997b. 'Sung Neo-Confucian Views on Geomancy', in Irene Bloom and Joshua A. Fogel, eds., *Meeting Of Minds: Intellectual And Religious Interaction In East Asian Traditions Of Thought: Essays In Honor Of Wing-Tsit Chan and William Theodore De Bary*, pp. 75–107. New York: Columbia University Press.

Egan, Ronald C., 1977. 'Narratives in Tso chuan', *Harvard Journal of Asiatic Studies* 37, 2 (Dec.): 323–52.

Elia, Pasquale M. d' (ed.), 1942–1949. *Fonti Ricciane*, 3 vols. Roma: La Libreria dello Stato.

Elman, Benjamin A., 1984. *From Philosophy to Philology.* Cambridge, MA: Harvard University Press.

—— 1990. *Classicism, Politics, and Kinship: The Chang-Chou School of New Text Confucianism in Late Imperial China.* Berkeley: University of California Press.

—— 2000. *A Cultural History of Civil Service Examinations in Late Imperial China.* Berkeley: University of California Press.

Emmerich, Reinhard, 1987. *Li Ao: Ein chinesische Gelehrtenleben.* Wiesbaden: Harrassowitz.

Eno, Robert, 1990. *The Confucian Creation of Heaven: Philosophy and the Defense of Ritual Mastery.* Albany: State University of New York.

Ershiwu shi 二十五史, 1986. 12 vols. Shanghai: Guji chubanshe.

Fairbank, John K., *et al.*, 1973. *East Asia: Traditional and Transformation.* Boston: Houghton Mifflin Company.

Fan Jun 范浚. *Xiangxi ji* 香溪集 (Fragrant Brook Collection). Siku quanshu edition.

Fang, Chaoying, 1976. 'Chan Jo-shui', and 'Wang Shu', in L. Carrington Goodrich and Fang Chao-ying, eds., *Dictionary of Ming Biography*, vol. II. New York: Columbia University Press.

—— 1976. 'Chan Jo-shui', *Dictionary of Ming Biography.* New York: Columbia University Press.

Fang Hao 方豪, 1966. Li Zhizao yanjiu 李之藻研究. Taipei: Commercial Press.

Fang Keli 方克立 and Zheng Jiadong 鄭家棟 eds. 1995. *Xiandai xinrujia renwu yu zhuzuo* 現代新儒家人物與著作 (*Contemporary New Confucians: The People and Their Works*). Tianjin: Nankai University Press.

—— and Li Jinquan 李錦全, eds., 1995. *Xiandai Xinrujia Xue'an (Shang)* 現代新儒家學案 (*Systematic Accounts of Contemporary New Confucians*), 3 vols. Beijing: Chinese Social Sciences Press.

Fang Xing, 1989. 'Why the Sprouts of Capitalism were Delayed in China', *Late Imperial China*, 10: 2 (December 1989): 106–38.

Fang Xuanling 房玄齡, *et al.*, eds., 1974. *Jinshu* 晉書. Beijing: Zhonghua shuju.

Fang Xuanling 房玄齡 and Liu Ji 劉績, eds., 1989. *Guanzi.* Shanghai guji chubanshe.

Feifel, Eugene, 1961. *Po Chu-i as a Censor: His Memorials Presented to the Emperor Hsien-Tsung During the Years 808–810.* The Hague: Mouton.

Fingarette, Herbert, 1972. *Confucius: The Secular as Sacred.* New York: Harper and Row.

Fisher, Carney T. 1987. 'The Ritual Dispute of Sung Ying-Tsung', *Papers on Far Eastern History,* 36: 109–38.

—— 1990. *The Chosen One: Succession and Adoption in the Court of Ming Shizong.* Sydney: Allen and Unwin.

Fogel, Joshua A. and Peter G. Zarrow, eds., 1997. *Imagining the People: Chinese Intellectuals and the Concept of Citizenship, 1890–1920.* Armonk, New York: M.E. Sharpe.

Forke, Alfred, tr., 1907. *Lunheng: Part I, Philosophical essays of Wang Ch'ung; Part II, Miscellaneous essays of Wang Ch'ung,* 2 vols. Shanghai: Kelly and Walsh; rpt., New York: Paragon, 1962.

—— 1938. *Geschichte der neueren chinesischen Philosophie.* Hamburg: De Gruyter and Co.

Franke, Herbert, ed., 1976. *Sung Biographies.* Wiesbaden: Franz Steiner Verlag.

—— 1982. 'Wang Yun (1227–1304): A Transmitter of Chinese Values', in de Bary, W.T. and Chan Hok-lam, eds., *Yuan Thought.* New York: Columbia University Press.

—— and Denis Twitchett, eds., 1994. *Cambridge History of China: Alien Regimes and Border States, 907–1368.* Cambridge University Press.

Franke, Wolfgang, 1968. *An Introduction to the Sources of Ming History.* Kuala Lumpur: University of Malaya Press.

Fu, Marilyn Wong, 1981. 'The Impact of the Re-unification: Northern Elements in the Life and Art of Hsien-Yu Shu (1257?–1302) and Their Relation to Early Yuan Literati Culture', in J.D. Langlois, ed., *China Under Mongol Rule,* pp. 371–433. Princeton University Press.

Fu Sinian 傅斯年, 1952. Xingming gu xun bianzheng 性命古訓辯証, in *Fu Mengzhen xiansheng ji* 傅孟真先生集. Taipei: 國立台灣大學出版社.

Fu Weixun 傅偉勳, 1996. 'Foxue, Xixue yu Dangdai Xinrujia – Hongguan de Zhexue Kaocha' 佛學, 西學與當代新儒家 – 宏觀的哲學考察 ('Buddhist Learning, Western Learning and Contemporary New Confucians – A Macroscopic Philosophical Investigation'), *Ershiyi Shiji* 二十一世紀 (*Twenty-First Century*) 38 (December 1996): 68–79.

Führer, Bernhard, 1995. *Chinas erste Poetik: Das Shipin (Kriterion Poietikon) des Zhong Hong,* Dortmund: projekt verlag.

Fung, Yu-lan 馮友蘭, 1924. 'A Comparative Study of Life Ideals', Ph.D dissertation. Columbia University, in Fung Yu-lan, 1991. *Selected Philosophical Writings of Fung, Yu-lan,* pp. 1–189. Beijing: Foreign Languages Press.

—— 1934. *Zhongguo zhexueshi (shang, xia).* 中國哲學史 (A History of Chinese Philosophies, 2 Volumes). Shanghai: Commercial Press.

—— 1939. *Xin Lixue* 新理學 (*New Principle-centered Learning*). Shanghai: Commercial Press.

—— 1940a. *Xin shilun* 新事論 (*New Treatise on Practical Affairs*). Shanghai: Commercial Press.

—— 1940b. *Xinshi xun* 新世訓 (*Teachings for a New Age*). Shanghai: Kaiming Bookstore.

—— 1943. *Xin yuanren* 新原人 (*New Treatise on the Nature of Humans*). Chongqing: Commercial Press.

—— 1944. *Xin yuandao* 新原道 (*New Treatise on the Nature of the Way*). Chongqing: Commercial Press.

—— 1946. *Xinzhi yan* 新知言 (*Words about New Knowledge*). Shanghai: Commercial Press.

—— 1947. *The Spirit of Chinese Philosophy* (English translation of *Xin yuandao*). E.R. Hughes, tr. London: Kegan Paul, Trench, Trubner & Co., Ltd.

—— 1952. *A History of Chinese Philosophy: Vol. II – The Period of Classical Learning (from the Second Century B.C. to the Twentieth Century A.D.),* tr., Derk Bodde. Princeton University Press.

—— 1964–89. *Zhongguo zhexueshi xinpian (di yi zhi liu ce)* 中國哲學史新編 (第一至六冊) (A New Edition of the History of Chinese Philosophies (vols. I to VI)). Beijing: Renmin chubanshe.

—— 1992. *Zhongguo xiandai zhexueshi* 中國現代哲學史 (A History of Contemporary Philosophies in China). Hong Kong: Zhonghua Bookstore.

—— 1996. *Zhen yuan liu shu (shang xia)* 貞元六書 (上下) (Purity Descends, Primacy Ascends: Six Books). Shanghai: Huadong Normal University Press.

—— 1997. *A New Treatise on the Methodology of Metaphysics* (English translation of *Xin zhiyan*), C.I. Wang trans. Beijing: Foreign Languages Press.

—— 2000. *Die Philosophischste Philosophie. Feng Youlans Neue Metaphysik* (German translation of *Xin zhiyan* with annotations), Hans-Georg Muller, tr. Wiesbaden: Harrassowitz.

Gale, Esson M., 1931. *Discourses on Salt and Iron.* Leyden: E.J. Brill.

Gale, Esson, Peter A. Boodberg and T.C. Lin, 1934. 'Discourses on Salt and Iron Yen T'ieh lun: Chs.: XX–XXVIII', *Journal of the North China Branch of the Royal Asiatic Society*, 65: 73–110.

Gao Lingyin 高令印 and Chen Qifang 陳其芳 1986. *Fujian Zhu zi xue* 福建朱子學 (The Learning of Zhu Xi in Fujian). Fuzhou: Fujian People's Press.

Gao Mingshi 高明士, 1980. '*Tangdai de shidianli zhi ji qi zai jiaoyu shang de yiyi* 唐代的祀奠制及其意義, in *Dalu zazhi* 大陸雜誌, vol. 61: 5.

—— 1984. *Tangdai dongya jiaoyuquan de xingcheng* 唐代東亞教育圈的形成. Taipei: Guoli bianyiguan 國立編譯館.

Gao Panlong 高攀龍, 1876. *Gaozi yishu* 高子遺書. Siku quanshu edition.

Gao Xiuchang 高秀昌, 1995. 'Fung, Yu-lan de Kongzi yanjiu pingshu' 馮友蘭的孔子研究評述 (Description and Evaluation of Fung, Yu-lan's Studies on Master Kong), in Wang Zhongjiang 王中江 and Gao Xiuchang 高秀昌, eds., *Fung Yu-lan xueji* 馮友蘭學記 (Notes from Studies on Fung Yu-lan), pp. 187–205. Beijing: Three Connections Bookstore.

Gao Zhanfu, 1991. *Xibei Musilin shehui wenti yanjiu* 西北穆斯林社會問題研究 (Research on Social Issues in Northwestern Muslim society). Lanzhou: Gansu renmin chubanshe.

Gardner, Daniel, 1986. *Chu Hsi and the Ta-hsüeh, Neo-Confucian Reflection on the Confucian Canon.* Cambridge: Harvard Council on East Asian Studies.

—— 1995. 'Ghosts and Spirits in the Sung Neo-Confucian World: Chu Hsi on Kuei-shen', *Journal of the American Oriental Society* 115.4: 598–611.

—— 1996. 'Zhu Xi on Spirit Beings', in Donald S. Lopez, ed., *Religions of China in Practice.* Princeton University Press.

Gedalecia, David, 1981. 'Wu Ch'eng and the Perpetuation of the Classical Heritage in the Yuan', in J.D. Langlois, ed., *China Under Mongol Rule*, pp. 186–211. Princeton University Press.

—— 1982. 'Wu Ch'eng's Approach to Internal Self-Cultivation and External Knowledge-Seeking', in de Bary, W.T. Chan and Chan Hok-lam, eds. *Yuan Thought*, pp. 279–326. New York: Columbia University Press.

—— 1999. *The Philosophy of Wu Ch'eng: A Neo-Confucian of the Yuan Dynasty.* Bloomington: Indiana University.

—— 2000. *A Solitary Crane in a Spring Grove: The Confucian Scholar Wu Ch'eng in Mongol China.* Wiesbaden: O. Harrassowitz Verlag.

Gerhart, Karen M., 1997. 'Tokugawa Authority and Chinese Exemplars: The Teikan Zusetsu Murals of Nagoya Castle', *Monumenta Nipponica*, 52: 1–34.

Gernet, Jacques, 1982. *Chine et christianisme: Action et reaction.* Paris: Gallimard.

—— 1986. *A History of Chinese Civilization*, second edn. Cambridge University Press.

Giles, Herbert A., 1898. *A Chinese Biographical Dictionary.* Shanghai: Kelly and Walsh.

—— tr., 1910. *San tzu ching.* Shanghai: Kelly and Walsh, Ltd.

Giles, Lionel, 1942. *The Book of Mengzi* (abridged). London: John Murray/New York, Dutton.

Gong Yanxing 宮衍興 and Wang Zhiyu 王致玉. 1994. *Kongmiao zhushen kao* 孔廟諸神考 (On the various spirits in the Confucian temple). Jinan: Shandong youyi chubanshe.

Goodrich, L. Carrington and Fang Chao-ying, eds., 1976. *Dictionary of Ming Biography*, 2 vols. New York: Columbia University Press.

Graham, A.C., 1958. *Two Chinese Philosophers: Ch'eng Ming-tao and Ch'eng Yi-ch'uan.* London: Lund Humphries.

—— 1969. 'Chuang-tzu's Essay on Seeing Things as Equal', *History of Religions* v. n.: pp. 137–59.

—— 1978. *Later Mohist Logic, Ethics and Science.* Hong Kong and London: Chinese University Press.

Graham, A.C., 1981. *Chuang-tzu: The Seven Inner Chapters and Other Writings from the Book Chuang-tzu.* London: George Allen & Unwin.

—— 1983. 'Daoist Spontaneity and the Dichotomy of "Is" and "Ought"', in Victor Mair, ed., *Experimental Essays on Chuang-tzu*, pp. 3–23. Honolulu: University of Hawaii Press.

—— 1986a. *Yin-Yang and the Nature of Correlative Thinking.* Singapore: National University of Singapore, Institute of East Asian Philosophies.

—— 1986b. 'The Background of the Mencian Theory of Human Nature', repr. in *Studies in Chinese Philosophy and Philosophical Literature*, pp. 7–68. Singapore.

—— 1989. *Disputers of the Tao: Philosophical Argument in Ancient China.* La Salle, IL: Open Court.

—— 1990. ' "Being" in Western Philosophy Compared with shih-fei and yu-wu in Chinese Philosophy', in A.C. Graham, ed., *Studies in Chinese Philosophy and Philosophical Literature.* Albany: State University of New York Press.

—— 1992. *Two Chinese Philosophers: The Metaphysics of the Brothers Ch'êng*, second edn. La Salle, IL: Open Court.

Granet, Marcel, 1932. *Fetes et chansons anciennes de la Chine*, Paris: E. Leroux, 1919; tr. by E.D. Edwards as *Festivals and Songs of Ancient China.* London: George Routledge.

Grant, Beata, 1994. *Mount Lu Revisited: Buddhism in the Life and Writings of Su Shih.* Honolulu: Hawaii University Press.

Gregory, Peter, 1991. *Tsung-mi and the Sinification of Buddhism.* Princeton University Press.

Gu Jiegang 顧詰剛, ed., 1987. *Gushibian* 古史辨. Shanghai Guji chubanshe.

Guarino, Marie, tr., 1999. 'Fan Zuyu: The Learning of the Emperors' in Wm. Theodore de Bary and Irene Bloom, eds., *Sources of Chinese Tradition*, vol. I, 2nd edn. New York: Columbia University Press.

Guo Jianyu 郭建宇 and Zhang Wenru 張文儒, eds., 2001. *Zhongguo Xiandai Zhexue* 中國現代哲學 (Contemporary Chinese Philosophy). Beijing University Press.

Guo Qiyong 郭齊勇, 1990. *Xiong Shili yu Zhongguo Chuantong Wenhua* 熊十力與中國傳統文化 (*Xiong Shili and Traditional Chinese Culture*). Taipei: Yuanliu Press Company.

—— 1993. *Xiong Shili Sixiang Yanjiu* 熊十力思想研究 (Studies of Xiong Shil's Thought). Tianjin People's Press.

Guo Yong 郭雍, *Guo shi chuanjia Yi shuo* 郭氏傳家易說 (Explanations of the Yijing Transmitted in the Guo Family). Siku quanshu edition.

Guodian Chumu zhujian 郭店楚木竹簡, 1998. *Jingmenshi bowuguan* 荊門市博物館. Beijing: Wenwu chubanshe.

Guy, Kent, 1994. 'Fang Bao and the Ch'int'ing Ss shu-wen, in Benjamin Elman and Alexander Woodside, eds., *Education and Society Late Imperial China*, 1600–1900, pp. 150–82. Berkeley: University of California Press.

Haboush, JaHyun Kim, 1991. 'The Confucianization of Korean Society', in Gilbert Romzman, ed., *The East Asian Region: Confucian Heritage and its Modern Adaption*, pp. 84–110. Princeton University Press.

Haeger, John Winthrop, 1972. 'The Intellectual Context of Neo-Confucian Syncretism', in *The Journal of Asian Studies* 31, 3: 499–513.

Hall, David L. and Roger T. Ames, 1987. *Thinking Through Confucius.* Albany: State University of New York Press.

—— 1999. *Democracy of the Dead.* La Salle, IL: Open Court.

Halperin, Mark Robert, 1997. 'Pieties and Responsibilities: Buddhism and the Chinese Literati, 780–1280'. Ph.D. dissertation. University of California, Berkeley.

Han Dong-il, 1972. *Chosŏn Shidaeŭi Hyanggyo Gyoyuk Chŏng Ch'aegŭi Yŏn-gu.* Seoul: Sŏnggyungwan Daehakkyo Nonmunjip 16.

Han Jing 韓敬, 1992. *Fayan zhu* 法言注 (Notes on the Model Sayings). Beijing: Zhonghua shuju.

Han Rulin 韓儒林,.1986. *Yuanchao shi* 元朝史, in 2 vols. Beijing: Renmin chubanshe.

Han shu 漢書, 1962. Beijing: Zhonghua shuju.

Han U-gŭn, 1980. *Sŏnghoikyŏn-gu.* Seoul: Taech'ulp'anbu.

Han Won-jin, 1741. *Chujaŏllongdong-igo.* Seoul: Namdangjip.

Han Won-jin, 1987. *Namdang Sŏnsaeng Munjip.* Seoul: Kyŏng Inch'ulp'ansa.

Han Yŏng-u, 1999. *Wangjoŭi Sŏlgyeja: Chŏngdojŏn*. Seoul: Chishiksanŏpsa.

Han Zhongwen, 1998. *Zhongguo ruxue shi: Song Yuan juan* 中國儒學史: 宋元卷 (History of Chinese Confucianism: Song–Yuan Volume). Guangzhou: Guangdong Jiaoyu chubanshe.

Hanabusa Hideki 花房英樹, 1971. *Haku Kyoi kenkyu* 白居易研究 (Studies on Bai Juyi). Kyoto: Sekkai shisoha.

Hanguk Inmur Yuhaksa, 1996. Nambaek Ch'oegŭn Dŏksŏnsaeng Hwagapkinyŏm Nonch'ong Ganhaeng-wi Wonheo.

Hanmar Yŏngnam Yuhak Kyeŭi Tongyang, 1998. Seoul: Yŏngnametae ch'ulp'anbu.

Hansen, Chad, 1983. 'A Tao of Tao in Chuang Tzu', in Victor Mair, ed., *Experimental Essays on Chuang-tzu*. Honolulu: University of Hawaii Press.

—— 1985. 'Chinese Language, Chinese Philosophy, and "Truth"', *Journal of Asian Studies*, 44, 3: 491–519.

—— 1989. 'Mozi: Language Utilitarianism: The Structure of Ethics in Classical China' *Journal of Chinese Philosophy*, 16, 1: 355–380.

—— 1992. *A Daoist Theory of Chinese Thought*. New York: Oxford University Press.

—— 1995. 'Qing (Emotions) in Pre-Buddhist Chinese Thought', in Joel Marks and Roger T. Ames, eds. *Emotions in Asian Thought*. Buffalo: State University of New York Press.

Hao Wanzhang 郝萬章, 1993. *Cheng Hao yu DaCheng shuyuan* 程顥與大程書院 (Cheng Hao and the Elder Cheng Academy). Zhengzhou: Zhongzhou guji 中州古籍 chubanshe.

Harper, Donald, 1987. 'Wang Yen-shou's Nightmare Poem', *Harvard Journal of Asiatic Studies* 47, 1 (June), pp. 239–83.

Hartman, Charles, 1986. *Han Yu and the Tang Search for Unity*. Princeton University Press.

Hartwell, Robert M., 1971. 'Historical Analogism, Public Policy, and Social Science in Eleventh- and Twelfth-Century China', *American Historical Review*, 76: 690–727.

Hatch, George, 1976. '*Su Shih*'. In Herbert Franke, ed., *Sung Biographies*, pp. 900–68. Wiesbaden: Franz Steiner Verlag GMBH.

Hawkes, David, 1985. *The Songs of the South*. Harmondsworth: Penguin.

—— 1989. 'The Heirs of Gaoyang', in John Minford and Siu-kit Wong, eds., *David Hawkes: Classical, Modern and Humane: Essays in Chinese Literature*, pp. 205–28. Hong Kong University Press.

He Bingsong, 1932. *Zhedong xuepai suoyuan* 浙東學派朔源 (Tracing the Sources of the Zhedong School), Shanghai: Shangwu yinshuguan.

He Xinyin 何心隱, 1960. *He Xinyin ji* 何心隱集 (Collected Works of He Xinyin) ed. by Rong Zhaozu 容肇祖. Beijing: Zhonghua shuju.

He Zeheng 何澤恆, 1981. *Wang Yinglin zhi jingshixue* 王應麟之經史學 (The Studies of the Classics and the History by Wang Yinglin), Ph.D. dissertation. Taipei: Taiwan University.

He Zhaowu, *et al.*, 1991. *An Intellectual History of China*. Beijing: Foreign Languages Press.

Hegel, Georg Wilhelm Frederich, 1892. *Hegel's Lectures on the History of Philosophy*, tr., E.S. Haldane and Frances H. Simson. London: Kegan Paul, Trench, Trubner & Co., Ltd.

Helman, Isidore-Stanislas, 1788. *Abrege historique des principaux traits de la vie de Confucius*. Paris: Helman.

Henderson, John B., 1991. *Scripture, Canon, and Commentary: A Comparison of Confucian and Western Exegesis*. Princeton University Press.

Henricks, Robert, 1983. *Philosophy and Argumentation in Third-Century China*. Princeton University Press.

Henry, Eric, 1999. 'Junzi yue vs. Zhongni yue in Zuozhuan', *HJAS* 59, 1 (June): 125–61.

Hervouet, Yves, 1964. *Un poete de cour sous les Han: Sseu-ma Siang-jou*. Paris: Presses Universitaires de France.

—— ed., 1978. *A Sung Bibliography (Bibliographie des Sung)*. Hong Kong: The Chinese University Press.

Heyndrickx, Jerome, 1990. *Philippe Couplet, S.J. (1623–1693): The Man Who Brought China to Europe*. Nettetal: Steyler-Verlag.

Hightower, James Robert, 1952. *Han Shih Wai Chuan: Han Ying's Illustrations of the Didactic Application of the Classic of Songs: An Annotated Translation*. Cambridge, MA: Harvard University Press.

Hinsch, Bret, 1998. 'Women, Kinship, and Property as Seen in a Han Dynasty Will', *T'oung Pao* 1998, 84: 1–20.

Hirose Yutaka, ed., 1940–2. *Yamaga Sokô zenshû*. Tokyo: Iwanami shoten.

Holzman, Donald, 1957. *La vie et la pensée de Hi Kang*, Leiden: E.J. Brill.

—— 1974. 'Literary Criticism in China in the Early Third Century A.D.', *Asiatische Studien, Etudes Asiatiques* 28: 113–49.

—— 1976. *Poetry and Politics: The Life and Works of Juan Chi*, Cambridge: Cambridge University Press, 1976.

—— 1998. *Chinese Literature in Transition from Antiquity to the Middle Ages*, Aldershot: Ashgate/Variorum.

Hon, Tze-ki, 1999. 'Military Governance versus Civil Governance: A Comparison of the Old History and the New History of the Five Dynasties', in Kai wing Chow, On-cho Ng and John B. Henderson, eds., *Imagining Boundaries: Changing Confucian Doctrines, Texts, and Hermeneutics*, pp. 85–106. Albany: State University of New York Press.

Hong Tae-yong, 1984. *Ŭisan mundap*. Kŏngukdaehakkyo Ch'ulp'anbu.

Hong, Wei-zhu 洪惟岱, 1976. 'Lun Liji Yueji de Yinyue Sixiang' 論禮記樂記的音樂思想 (On the Musical Thoughts of the Yue Ji in the Li Ji), *Monthly Periodical on Confucius and Mencius*, 1976, 14, 10: 20–3.

Hook, Brian ed., 1996. *The Individual and the State in China*. Oxford University Press.

Hori Isao, 1959. *Yamaga Sokô*. Jinbutsu sôsho, vol. 33. Tokyo: Yoshikawa Kôbunkan.

—— 1964. *Hayashi Razan*. Tokyo: Yoshikawa Kôbunkan.

Hou Han shu 後漢書, 1965. By Fan Ye 范曄 (398–446). Beijing: Zhonghua shuju.

Hou Wailu, Qiu Hansheng and Chang Qizhi, 1984. *Song Ming Lixue shi* 宋明理學史 (History of Song–Ming Li Learning). Beijing: Renmin chubanshe.

Hsiao, Harry Hsin-i, 1978. 'Filial Piety in Ancient China: A Study of the Hsiao-ching', Ph.D. dissertation. Harvard University.

Hsiao Kung-chuan, 1960. *Rural China, Imperial Control in the Nineteenth Century*. Seattle: University of Washington Press.

—— 1979. *A History of Chinese Political Thought. Vol. 1, From the Beginnings to the Sixth Century A.D.*, tr. Frederick W. Mote. Princeton University Press.

Hsieh Shan-yuan, 1979. *Life and Thought of Li Kou, 1009–1059*, Asian Library Series, 14. San Francisco: Chinese Materials Center, Inc.

Hsu Cho-yun and Katheryn M. Linduff, 1988. *Western Chou Civilization*. New Haven: Yale University Press.

Hsu Dau-Lin, 1970–1. 'The Myth of the "Five Human Relations" of Confucius', *Monumenta Serica*, 39: 27–37.

Hsu, Francis, 1948. *Under the Ancestors' Shadow*, rev. edn. Stanford University Press, 1971.

Hu Fangping 胡方平, 1990. *Yixue Qimeng Tongshi* 易學啟蒙通志 (Comprehensive Interpretation of the Yixue Qimeng), reprint of the Tongzhitang 通志堂 edition. Taipei: Wooling Publishing Co.

Hu Meiqi 胡美琦, 1978. *Zhongguo jiaoyushi* 中國教育史. Taipei: Sanmin 三民.

Hu Qing 胡青, 1996. *Wu Cheng jiaoyu sixiang yanjiu* 吳澄教育思想研究. Nanchang: Jiangxi renmin chubanshe.

Hu Shih, 1931. 'What I Believe', *Forum* 85, 2: 114–22.

Hu Zhikui 胡志奎, 1978. *Lunyu bianzheng* 論語辨證. Taipei: Lianjing chuban shiye gongsi.

Hu Zhikui, 1984. *Xue Yong bianzheng* (Studies on the *Daxue* and *Zhongyong*). Taipei: Lianjing.

Huang Bingtai 黃秉泰, 1995. *Ruxue yu xiandaihua: Zhong Han Ri Ruxue bijiao yanjiu* 儒學與現代化: 中韓日儒學比較研究 (Confucianism and Modernization: Comparative Studies of Chinese, Korean, and Japanese Contexts). Beijing: Social Sciences Literature Press.

Huang Chin-shing 黃進興, 1994. *You ru sheng yu: quanli, xinyang, yu zhengdangxing* 優入聖域: 權力, 信仰, 與正當性 (Entering the Master's Sanctuary: Power, Belief, and Legitimacy in Traditional China). Taipei: Yunchen wenhua chubanshe.

Huang Chin-shing 黃進興, 1994. *Youru shengyu quanli xinyang yu zhengdangxing* 優入聖域權力信仰與正當性. Taipei: Yunchen.

Huang Chin-Shing, 2002. 'The Cultural Politics of Autocracy: The Confucian Temple and the Formation of Ming Despotism, 1368–1530', In Thomas A. Wilson, ed., *On Sacred Grounds: Culture, Society, Politics, and the Formation of the Cult of Confucius*. Institute for East Asian Studies, Harvard University.

Huang Chün-chieh 黃俊傑, 1995. 'Three Contemporary Interpretations of Mencius: T'ang Chün-i, Hsü Fu-kuan, and Mou Tsung-san', *Zhongyang Yanjiuyuan Zhongguo Wenzhe Yanjiusuo Zhongguo Wenzhe Yanjiu Jikan* 中央研究院中國文哲研究院中國文哲研究集刊 (Bulletin of the Institute of Chinese Literature and Philosophy, Academia Sinica) 6 (March 1995): 221–56.

Huang Hui 黃暉, 1990. *Lunheng jiaoshi* 論衡校釋. Beijing: Zhonghua shuju.

Huang Jinxing, 1995. *Philosophy, Philology, and Politics in Eighteenth-Century China: Li Fu and the Lu–Wang School Under the Ch'ing.* New York: Cambridge University Press.

Huang Siu-Chi, 1976. *Lu Hsiang-shan: A Twelfth Century Chinese Idealist Philosopher.* Westport, CT: Hyperion Press.

—— 1999. *Essentials of Neo-Confucianism: Eight Major Philosophers of the Song and Ming Periods.* Westport, CT: Greenwood Publishing Group.

Huang Tingjian 黃庭堅. *Shan'gu nei ji* 山谷內集 (The Inner Collection of Mr. Shan'gu), *waiji* 外集 (The Outer Collection of Mr. Shan'gu), and *bieji* 別集 (The Supplementary Collection of Mr. Shan'gu). Siku quanshu editions.

—— *Shan'gu ci* 山谷詞 (The Song Lyrics of Mr. Shan'gu). Siku quanshu edition.

Huang Tsung-hsi (Huang Zongxi 黃宗羲), 1987. *The Records of Ming Scholars* 明儒學案, tr. Julia Ching, *et al.* Honolulu: University of Hawaii Press.

—— 1993. *Ming Yi Dai Fang Lu* (Waiting for the Dawn: A Plan for the Prince), tr. W.T. de Bary. New York: Columbia University Press.

[Huang Zongxi] 黃宗羲, 1985. *Mingru xuean* 明儒學案 (The Writing of Ming Confucians). Beijing: Zhonghua Shuju.

[Huang Zongxi] and Quan Zuwan 全祖望, 1966 reprint. *Song–Yuan xuean* 宋元學案 (Records of Song–Yuan Scholars). Beijing: Zhonghua shuju.

Huang Zuo 黃佐, 1976 (1544). *Nanyong zhi* 南雝志. Taipei: Wei wen chubanshe 偉文出版社.

Huh Nam-jin, 1981. *Yulgok Sŏng-ihagŭi Hyŏngsŏnggwa Jŏnggwa Kibon-gujo*, MA thesis. Seoul National University.

—— 1999. *Ch'oe Han-giŭi Kihakkwa Hanguk Ch'ŏlhakŭi Chŏllip*, Ch'ŏlhak 58. Seoul: Hanguk Ch'ŏlhakhoe.

Huker, Charles O., 1975. *China's Imperial Past.* Stanford University Press.

Hulsewé, A.F.P., 1985. *Remnants of Ch'in Law.* Leiden: Brill.

—— 1993. 'Han chi', in Michael Loewe, ed., *Early Chinese Texts: A Bibliographical Guide,* pp. 113–14, Early China Special Monograph Series No. 2, Berkeley: The Society for the Study of Early China, and The Institute of East Asian Studies, University of California, Berkeley.

Hummel, Arthur W., 1943–4. *Eminent Chinese of the Ch'ing Period,* 2 vols. Washington: United States Government Printing House.

Hung, William, 1952. *Tu Fu China's Greatest Poet.* Cambridge, MA: Harvard University Press.

—— 1969. 'A T'ang Historiographer's Letter of Resignation', *Harvard Journal of Asiatic Studies* 29: 5–52.

—— ed., 1972a. *A Concordance to the Analects of Confucius,* Harvard–Yenching Institute Sinological Series, supplement no. 16. Taipei: Ch'eng-wen.

—— 1972b. *A Concordance to the Mencius.* Harvard–Yenching Institute Sinological Series, supplement no. 17. Taipei: Ch'eng-wen.

Huters, Theodore, Wong, R. Bin and Yu, Pauline, eds., 1997. *Culture and State in Chinese History: Conventions, Accommodations, and Critiques.* Stanford University Press.

Hutton, Eric, 2000. 'Xunzi' in Philip J. Ivanhoe and Bryan W. Van Norden, eds., *A Reader in Classical Chinese Philosophy.* New York: Seven Bridges Press.

Hwang Jun-yŏn, 1995. *Yulgok Ch'ŏlhakŭi Ihae.* Seoul: Sŏgwangsa.

Hymes, Robert and Conrad Schirokauer, eds., 1993. *Ordering the World: Approaches to State and Society in Sung Dynasty China.* Berkeley: University of California Press.

Idano Shôhachi 板野長八, 1995. *Jukyo seiritsu shi kenkyû* 儒教成立史研究. Tokyo: Iwanami shoten.

Ihm Sŏng-ju, 1976. *Rokmunjip.* Seoul: Kyŏngmunsa.

Ihm Won-bin, 1994. *Namdang Han Won-jin Ch'ŏlhagŭi iekwanhan yŏn-gu.* Yonsei University Ph.D. dissertation.

Im Hanyŏng, 1974. *Chŏnguk Hyanggyo Hyŏnhwangjosa.* Seoul: Sŏnggyungwan Daehakkyo Nonmunjip.

Inoue Tetsujirô, 1902. *Nippon kogakuha no tetsugaku.* Tokyo: Fuzanbo.

Inoue Tetsujirô and Karie Yoshimaru, eds. 1903. *Nihon rinri ihen,* Ikuseikai, vol. IX. Tokyo.

Intorcetta, Prospero, tr., 1691. *The Morals of Confucius, A Chinese Philosopher.* London: Randal Taylor.

Itô Jinsai, 1926. *Rongo kogi,* in Sekigi Ichirô (general editor), *Nihon meika, Shisho chûshaku zensho, Rongo bu,* vol. I. Tokyo: Tôyô tosho.

—— 1970. *Gomô jigi,* in Kimura Eiichi, ed., *Itô Jinsai shû,* Nihon no shisô, vol. XI. Tokyo: Chikuma shobô.

—— 1972. *Rongo kogi,* in Kaizuka Shigeki, ed., *Itô Jinsai, Nihon no meicho,* vol. XIII. Tokyo: Chûô kôron.

—— 1985. *Gomô jigi,* in Shimizu Shigeru and Yoshikawa Kôjirô, eds., *Itô Jinsai/Itô Tôgai,* Nihon shisô taikei, vol. XXXIII. Tokyo: Iwanami shoten.

Ito Shigehiko 伊東倫原, 1976. 'Wei Heshan' in *Shushigaku Taikei* 朱學大系. Tokyo: Meitoku Shupansha.

Ivanhoe, Philip J., ed. 1996. *Chinese Language, Thought, and Culture.* Chicago and La Salle, IL: Open Court.

Jameson, Melanie Alison, 1990. 'South-Returning Wings: Yang Shih and the New Sung Metaphysics', Ph.D. dissertation. University of Arizona.

Jamieson, Neil, 1993. *Understanding Vietnam.* Berkeley: University of California Press.

Janousch, Andreas E., 1991. 'The Religious Policies of Emperor Wu of the Liang Dynasty: Ideological and Social Background', M. Phil. dissertation. Cambridge University.

—— 1998. 'The Reform of Imperial Ritual during the Reign of Emperor Wu of the Liang Dynasty (502–549)', Ph.D. dissertation, Cambridge University.

Jen Yu-wen, 1970. 'Ch'en Hsien-chang's Philosophy of the Natural', in Wm. Theodore de Bary, ed., *Self and Society in Ming Thought.* New York: Columbia University Press.

Jenner, W.J.F., 1992. *Tyrannies of History: The Roots of China's Crisis.* Middlesex, UK: Penguin.

Jensen, Lionel M., 1997. *Manufacturing Confucianism – Chinese Traditions and Universal Civilization.* Durham and London: Duke University Press.

—— forthcoming in 2004. *When Words Move Stones: Figures, Fictions, and the Chinese Past.* Durham: Duke University Press.

Ji Tian si Kong 祭天祀孔. *Zhengfu gongbao fenlei huibian* 政府公報分類會編, vol. XXI. Shanghai: Saoye shanfang 掃葉山房, 1915.

Jian Boxian 簡博賢, 1986. *Jincun Sanguo liang Jin jingxue yiji kao* 今存三國兩晉經學遺籍考, Taipei: Sanmin shuju.

Jiang Guanghui 姜廣輝, 1994. *Lixue yu Zhongguo Wenhua* 理學與中國文化 (The Study of Principle and Chinese Culture). Shanghai People's Press.

Jiang, Guozhu 姜國柱. 1982. *Zhang zai de zhexue sixiang* 張載的哲學思想. Shenyang: Liaoning renmin chubanshe.

—— 2001. *Zhang Zai guanxue* 張載關學. Xian: Shaanxi renmin chubanshe.

Jiang, Paul Yun-Ming, 1980. *The Search for Mind: Ch'en Pai-sha, Philosopher, Poet.* Singapore University Press.

—— 1983. 'Some Reflections on Ch'en Pai-sha's Experience of Enlightenment', *Journal of Chinese Philosophy* 10, 3 (Sep): 229–50.

Jin Guantao, 1998. '"On Practice" and the Confucianization of Marxism-Leninism', *The Stockholm Journal of East Asian Studies*, 9: 1–16.

Jin shu 晉書 (*A History of The Jin Dynasty*), 1974. Beijing: Zhonghua Shuju.

Jing Haifeng 景海峰, ed., 1992. *Rujia sixiang yu xiandaihua: Liu Shuxian xin ruxue lunzhu jiyao* 儒家思想與現代化: 劉述先新儒學論著輯要 (Confucian Thought and Modernization: Summarized Essays on New Confucian Studies by Liu Shu-hsien). Beijing: China Broadcasting and Television Publishing Company.

Jiu Tang shu 舊唐書 (An Old History of The Tang Dynasty), 1997. Beijing: Zhonghua Shuju.

Joachim, Christian, 1992. 'Confucius and Capitalism: Views of Confucianism in Works on Confucianism and Economic Development', *Journal of Chinese Religions*, 20 (Fall 1992): 135–71.

Johnson, Wallace, 1979. *The T'ang Code. Volume I General Provisions.* Princeton University Press.

—— 1997. *The T'ang Code. Volume II Specific Articles.* Princeton University Press.

Johnston, Reginald Fleming, 1935. *Confucianism and Modern China: The Lewis Fry Memorial Lectures, 1933–34.* New York: D. Appleton-Century.

Jordan, David K., 1972. *Gods, Ghosts, and Ancestors.* Berkeley: University of California Press.

—— 1986. 'Folk Filial Piety in Taiwan: The "Twenty-Four Filial Exemplars"', in Walter H. Slote, ed., *The Psycho-Cultural Dynamics of the Confucian Family: Past and Present,* pp. 47–105. Seoul: International Cultural Society of Korea.

Kaizuka Shigeki, ed., 1972. *Itô Jinsai, Niô n no meichô,* vol. 13. Tokyo: Chûyô ron.

Kaji Nobuyuki 加地伸行, 1991. Koshi Gaden 孔子畫傳 (Pictorial Biography of Confucius). Tokyo: Shueisha.

Kalinowski, Marc, 1999. 'La Rhetorique oraculaire dans les chroniques anciennes de la Chine. Une etude des discours predictifs dans le Zuozhuan', *EOEO* 21: 37–65.

Kalton, Michael C., 1994. *The Four–Seven Debate.* Albany: State University of New York Press.

Kam, Louie, 1980. *Critiques of Confucius in Contemporary China.* Hong Kong: The Chinese University Press.

—— 1986. *Inheriting Tradition: Interpretations of the Classical Philosophers in Communist China, 1949–1966.* Hong Kong: Oxford University Press.

Kanaya Osamu, 1962. *Junshi.* Kyoto: Heirakuji Shoten.

Kang Youwei, 1992. *Kang Youwei quanji* (The Complete Works by Kang Youwei). Shanghai guji chubanshe.

Kano Naoki, 1923. 'Yô Yû to Hôgen' 揚雄と法言 ('Yang Xiong and the Fayan'), *Shinagaku* 1923, vol. 3: 6: 399–420.

—— 1968. *Gi Shin gakujutsu kô* 魏晉學術考, Tokyo: Chikuma shobô.

Karlgren, Bernhard, 1926. 'On the authenticity and nature of the Tso chuan', Goteborg, Elanders (Goteborgs Hogskolas Arsskrift XXXII); rept 1968. Taipei, Chengwen Publishing Co.

—— 1926. *Philology and Ancient China.* Oslo: H. Aschehoug & Co.

—— 1931. *The Early History of the Chou-li and Tso chuan Texts.* Stockholm: A.-B. Hasse W. Tullbergs Boktr.

—— 1950. 'The Book of Documents', *BMFEA* 22 (1950): 1–81; re-issued as *The Book of Documents.* Gotebord: Elanders.

—— 1964. *Glosses on the Book of Odes.* Stockholm: Museum of Far Eastern Antiquities.

Kasoff, Ira E., 1984. *The Thought of Chang Tsai (1020–1077).* Cambridge University Press.

Katô Nihei, 1940. *Itô Jinsai no gakumon to kyôiku: Kogidô sunawachi Horikawa juku no kyôiku shiteki kenkyu.* Tokyo: Meguro shoten.

Kaufmann, W., 1976. *Musical References in the Chinese Classics.* Detroit Monographs in Musicology Number Five Information Coordinators, Inc.

Keightley, David N., 1984. 'Late Shang Divination: The Magico-Religious Legacy', in Henry Rosemont, Jr, ed., *Explorations in Early Chinese Cosmology.* Chicago: Scholars Press.

Kelleher, M. Theresa., 1987. 'Confucianism', in Arvind Sharma, ed., *Women in World Religions.* Albany: State University of New York Press.

—— 1989. 'Back to Basics: Chu Hsi's Elementary Learning (Hsiao-hsh)', in Wm. Theodore de Bary, and John W. Chaffee, eds., *Neo-Confucian Education: The Formative Stage.* Berkeley: University of California Press.

Kern, Iso, 1998. 'Die Vermittlung chinesischer Philosophie in Europa', Grundriss der Geschichte der Philosophie (begrundet von Friedrich Ueberweg, vollig neubearbeitete Ausgabe): Die Philosophie des 17. Jahrhunderts, Band 1 (Jean-Pierre Schobinger ed.; Allgemeine Themen; Iberische Halbinsel; Italien), Basel: Schwabe.

Kern, Martin, 2000. *The Stele Inscriptions of Ch'in Shih-huang: Text and Ritual in Early Chinese Imperial Representation.* New Haven: American Oriental Society.

—— 2001. 'Ritual, Text, and the Formation of the Canon: Historical Transitions of *wen* in Early China', *T'ung Pao*, 86.

Keum Jang-t'ae, 1984. *Tongsŏgyosŏpkwa Kŭndaehanguksasang.* Seoul: Sŏnggyungwan Ch'ulp'ansa.

—— 1987. *Hanguk Sirhak Sasang Yŏngu,* Seoul: Chipmundang.

—— 1997. *Chosŏn Jŏgiŭi Yuhaksasang,* Seoul: Taech'ulp'anbu.

—— 1998a. *Chosŏn Hugiŭi Yuhaksasang,* Seoul: Taech'ulp'anbu.

—— 1998b. *T'oegyeŭi Samgwa Ch'ŏlhak,* Seoul: Taech'ulp'anbu.

—— 1999. *Hanguk Hyŏndaeŭi Yuhak Munhwa,* Seoul: Taech'ulp'anbu.

—— 2000. *T'oegye Hakp'a Ich'ŏlhagŭi Chŏn-gae.* Seoul: Taech'ulp'anbu.

Ki Chŏng-jin, 1987. *Nosa Sŏnsaeng Munjip.* Seoul: Kyŏng-Inmunhwasa.

Ki Tae-sŭng, 1997. *Kobongjip.* Seoul: Minjongmunhwa Ch'ujinhoe Pŏnyŏk Kugyŏk.

Kiho Hakpaŭi Ch'ŏlhak Sasang, 1995. Seoul: Yemun Sŭwŏn.

Kihohakp'aŭi Ch'ŏlhak Sasang, 1995. Seoul: Ch'ungnamedae Yuhagyŏnguso.

Kim Ch'ang-hyŏp, 1996. *Nongamjip.* Seoul: Minjong Munhwa Ch'ujinhoe.

Kim Chŏng-hŭi, 1976. *Ch'usajip.* Seoul: Hyŏnamsa.

—— 1997. *Wandang Jŏnjip.* Seoul: Hyŏnamsa.

Kim Ch'ung-yŏl, 1988. *Ugye Sach'il Lonbyŏn p'yongŭi Sŏng Ugye, Sasaeng- Yŏn-gunonch'ong iljip.* Seoul: Ugyemunhwajaedan.

Kim Hyŏn, 1995. *Ihm Sŏng-juŭi Saeng-ŭi Ch'ŏlhak.* Seoul: Hangilsa.

Kim Hyŏng-ch'an, 1988. *Ki-Nonsaŭi Ich'ŏlhage Kwanhan Yŏn-gu.* Ph.D. dissertation. Tongguk University.

Kim Myong-gŏl, 1989. *Sŏnghoik Ŭi Ch'ulhak Sasang Yŏngu.* Seoul: Sŏnggyungwan Ch'ulp'ansa.

Kim Sang-gi, 1947. *Tonghakkwa Tonghaknan.* Seoul: Taesŏng Ch'ulp'ansa.

Kim Si-sŭp, 1995. *Maewoldangjip.* Seoul: Aseamunhwasa.

Kimura Eiichi, 1970. *Itô Jinsai shû,* Nihon no shisô, vol. XI. Tokyo: Chikuma shobô.

—— 1971. *Koshi to Rongo* 孔子と論語, Tokyo: Sobunsha.

Kinney, Anne B. 1990. *The Art of the Han Essay: Wang Fu's Ch'ien-fu lun.* Tempe: Center for Asian Studies, Arizona State University Press.

Kleeman, Terry F., 1994. 'Licentious Cults and Bloody Victuals: Sacrifice, Reciprocity, and Violence in Traditional China', *Asia Major* 7, 1: 185–211.

Kline, T.C. and Philip J. Ivanhoe, eds., 2000. *Virtue, Nature and, Moral Agency in the Xunzi.* Indianapolis: Hackett Publishing.

Knapp, Keith N., 1996. 'Accounts of Filial Sons: *Ru* Ideology in Early Medieval China', Ph.D. dissertation. University of California, Berkeley.

Knechtges, David R. trans. and annot., 1996. *Wen xuan or Selections of Refined Literature,* compiled by Xiao Tong (501–531). Vol. III, *Rhapsodies on Natural Phenomena, Birds and Animals, Aspirations and Feelings, Sorrowful Laments, Literature, Music, and Passions.* Princeton University Press.

Knoblock, John, 1988–94. *Xunzi: A Translation and Study of the Complete Works* (in three volumes). Stanford University Press.

Knoblock, John and Jeffrey Riegel, 2000. *The Annals of Lü Buwei.* Stanford University Press.

Ko, Dorothy, 1992. 'Pursuing Talent and Virtue: Education and Women's Culture in Seventeenth- and Eighteenth-Century China', *Late Imperial China,* 13.1 (June): 9–39.

—— 1994. *Teachers of the Inner Chambers: Women and Culture in Seventeenth-Century China.* Stanford University Press.

Kohn, Livia, 1992. *Early Chinese Mysticism.* Princeton University Press.

Kong Chuan 孔傳 (1134), 1967. *Dongjia Zaji* 東家雜記 (Miscellaneous Records of the Eastern House), rpt. Taipei: Guangwen shuju 廣文書局.

Kong Decheng 孔德成, 1937. *Kongzi shijia pu* 孔子世家譜, in *Kongzi wenhua daquan* 孔子文化大全. Jinan: Shandong youyi chubanshe 山東友宜出版社.

Kong Jifen 孔繼汾 (1762), 1967. *Queli wenxian kao* 闕里文獻考. Taipei: Zhongding wenhua gongsi.

Kong Yuancuo 孔元措 (1227), 1967. *Kongshi Zuting Guangji* 孔氏祖庭廣記 (An Expanded Record of the Kong Lineage, rpt.) Taipei: Guangwen shuju 廣文書局.

—— 1227. *Kongshi zuting guangji* 孔氏祖庭廣記. Sibu congkan 四部叢刊 edition.

Kong Yuqi 孔毓圻 (1717), 1990. *Kong Zhai Zhi* 孔宅志 (Gazetteer of Kong Zhai), rpt. in *Kongzi Wenhua Daquan* 孔子文化大全 (Complete Works of Confucianism). Jinan: Shandong youyi chubanshe 山東友宜出版社.

Kong Zhaozhen 孔昭楨, 1918. *Kongshi zongpu: nanzong shipu* 孔氏宗譜南宗世譜. Shili tang 詩禮堂.

Kong Zhencong 孔貞叢, 1609. *Queli zhi* 闕里誌. Wanli 萬曆 edition.

Kongzi Jiayu 孔子家語 (Sayings of Confucius' Family), (3rd c.), 1962. ed. Wang Su 王肅, rpt. Taipei: Shijie shuju 世界書局.

Kongzi Shengji Tu 孔子聖蹟圖, *c.* 1506 (1934) *c.* 1984/1988. (Pictures of the Traces of the Sage Confucius), Beiping minshe 北平民社 ed., rpt. Taipei: Wensi/Jinan: Shandong meishu chubanshe 山東美術出版社.

Kono Tatsu 今野達, 1954. *Yomei bunko koshi den to nihon setsuwa bungaku no kosho*, 陽明文庫孝子傳と日本文學の考證 (The Yomei Library's Accounts of Filial Offspring and Japanese Literature). Kokugo Kokubun 國語國文, 22.5: 19–36.

Köster, Hermann, 1967. *Hsün Tzu ins Deutsche übertragen*. Kaldenkirchen: Steyer Verlag.

Koyasu, Nobukuni, 1982. *Itô Jinsai jinrinteki sekai no shishu*. Tokyo daigaku shuppansha.

—— 1990. *Jiken to shite no Sorai gaku*. Tokyo: Seidôsha.

Kôzen Hiroshi 興膳宏, 1970. *Bunshi chôryû* 文心雕龍, Sekai koten bungaku zenshû, Vol. 25, Tokyo: Chikuma shobô.

Kramers, R.P., 1950. *K'ung Tzû Chia Yü*, (The School Sayings of Confucius), Sinica Leidensia, vol. VII. Leiden: E.J. Brill.

—— 1986. 'The Development of the Confucian Schools', in Twitchett and Loewe eds., *Cambridge History of China*, vol. I, pp. 747–765. Cambridge University Press.

Krieger, Silke and Rolf Trauzettel, eds., 1991. *Confucianism and the Modernization of China*. Mainz: Hase und Koehler Verlag.

Küng, Hans and Julia Ching, eds., 1989. *Christianity and Chinese Religions*. New York: Doubleday.

Kunstler, Mieczyslaw Jerzy, 1962. 'Deux biographies de Tcheng Hiuan', *Rocznik Orientalistyczny*, 26: 23–64.

—— 1969. *Ma Jong vie et oeuvre. 35 Dissertationes Universitatis Varsoviensis.* Warszawa: Panstwowe wydawnictwo naukowe.

Kurata, Nobuyasu, 1984. *Inoue Kinga*. Tokyo: Meitoku Shuppansha.

Kutcher, Norman. 1999. *Mourning in Late Imperial China.* Cambridge University Press.

Kwan, Peter, 1996. 'The Dimension of Objectivity of Liang-Chih: A Critical Study of Mou Tsung-San's Theory of Liang-Chih', *Journal of Chinese Philosophy* 23, 4: 415–52.

Kwong, Luke S.K., 1996. *T'an Ssu-t'ung, 1865–1898: Life and Thought of a Reformer.* Leiden: E.J. Brill.

Lai, T.C. and Mok, R., 1985. *Jade Flute: The Story of Chinese Music.* New York: Schocken Books.

Laidlaw, James, 1999. 'On Theatre and Theory: Reflections on Ritual in Imperial Chinese Politics', in Joseph P. McDermott, ed., *State and Court Ritual in China.* Cambridge University Press.

Lam Kit-chen 林浩珍 and Dennis McCann, 1999. 'Shichang Daode: Qianxiandai Xifang Zhexue he Ruxue de Duibi Yanjiu ji qi dui Shangye Daode de Qishi' 市場道德: 前現代西方哲學和儒學的對比研究及其對商業道德的啟示 ('Marketplace Morality: A Comparative Study of Premodern Western Philosophy and Confucianism and their Insights into Business Morality'), *Sichuan Shifan Xueyuan Zhexue Shehui Kexue Ban* 四川師範學院哲學社會科學版, *Journal of the Philosophy and Social Sciences in Sichuan Teacher's College*, 4 (July 1999): 77–88.

Lamont, H.G., 1973. 'An Early Ninth Century Debate on Heaven: Liu Tsung-yuan's T'ien Shuo and Liu Yu-hsi's T'ien Lun, An Annotated Translation and Introduction', Part I, *Asia Major*, n.s. 18, 2: 181–208.

—— 1974. 'An Early Ninth Century Debate on Heaven: Liu Tsung-yuan's T'ien Shuo and Liu Yu-hsi's T'ien Lun, An Annotated Translation and Introduction', Part II, *Asia Major*, n.s. 19, 1: 37–85.

Lan Zhongrui 藍種瑞 (1845), 1989. *Wenmiao dingji pu* 文廟丁祭譜, in *Kongzi wenhua daquan* 孔子文化大全. Jinan: Shandong youyi chubanshe 山東友宜出版社.

Langley, Charles Bradford, 1986. *Wang Yinglin (1223–1296) – A Study in the Political and Intellectual History of the Demise of*

Song, Ann Arbor, MI: University Microfilm International.

Langlois, John D., 1978. 'Yu Ji and his Mongol Sovereign: The Scholar as Apologist', *Journal of Asian Studies* (JAS), 38: 99–116.

—— ed., 1981. *China Under Mongol Rule*. Princeton University Press.

Lao Yan-shuan, 1981. 'Southern Chinese Scholars and Educational Institutions in Early Yuan: Some Preliminary Remarks', in J.D. Langlois, ed., *China Under Mongol Rule*, pp. 107–33. Princeton University Press.

Lau, D.C., 1953. 'Theories of Human Nature in Mencius and Shyuntzyy (Xunzi)', *BSOAS* 15: 541–65.

—— 1963. *Lao Tzu: Tao Te Ching*. Harmondsworth: Penguin Books.

—— 1967. 'A Note on Gewu', in *Bulletin of the School of Oriental and African Studies* 30: 353–57.

—— 1970. *Mencius*. Harmondsworth: Penguin Books.

—— 1979. *Confucius: The Analects*. Harmondsworth: Penguin Books.

—— 1984. *Mencius*. 2 vols. Hong Kong: The Chinese University Press.

—— 1993. 'Meng tzu', in Michael Loewe, ed., *Early Chinese Texts: A Bibliographical Guide*, The Society for the Study of Early China and the Institute of East Asian Studies. University of California, Berkeley.

Lau, D.C. and Chen Fong Ching, eds., 1992a. *A Concordance to the Liji*. ICS series. Hong Kong: The Commercial Press.

—— 1992b. *A Concordance to the Xinxu*, ICS series. Hong Kong: The Commercial Press.

—— 1992c. *A Concordance to the Shouyuan*. ICS series. Hong Kong: The Commercial Press.

—— 1994. *A Concordance to the Lien zhuan*. ICS series. Hong Kong: The Commercial Press.

—— 1995. *A Concordance to the Baihutong*. ICS series. Hong Kong: The Commercial Press.

—— 1996a. *A Concordance to the Xunzi*. ICS series. Hong Kong: The Commercial Press.

—— 1996b. *A Concordance to the Yili*. ICS series. Hong Kong: The Commercial Press.

Le Blanc, Charles, 1985. *Huai-nan Tzu: Philosophical Synthesis in Early Han Thought*. Hong Kong University Press.

Lee, Peter H., ed., 1993. *Sourcebook of Korean Civilization*, vol. I. New York: Columbia University Press; Paris, UNESCO publishing.

Lee, Thomas H.C., 1985. *Government Education and Examinations in Sung China*. Hong Kong: The Chinese University Press.

—— 2000. *Education in Traditional China*. Leiden: E.J. Brill.

Legge, James, 1850. *Letters on the Rendering of the Name God in the Chinese Language*, Hong Kong: Hong Kong Register Office.

—— 1852. *The Notions of the Chinese Concerning God and Spirits*. Hong Kong Register Office.

—— 1861. *Analects*, 1st edn. in vol. I of The Chinese Classics, 2nd edn. Oxford: Clarendon Press (1893).

—— 1877. *Confucianism in Relation to Christianity*. Shanghai: Kelly and Walsh.

—— 1879. *The Sacred Books of China: The Texts of Confucianism*. Oxford: Clarendon Press.

—— 1880. *The Religions of China: Confucianism and Taoism Described and Compared with Christianity*. London: Hodder and Stoughton.

—— 1882. *The Yi King*, vol. XVI of The Sacred Books of the East, Oxford: Clarendon Press.

—— 1893–4a. *The Ch'un Ts'ew with the Tso Chuen*, in The Chinese Classics, vol. V, 2nd edn. Oxford: Clarendon Press.

—— 1893–4b. *The Works of Mengzi*, in The Chinese Classics, vol. II, 2nd edn. Oxford: Clarendon Press.

—— 1966. *The Four Books: Confucian Analects, The Great Learning, The Doctrine of the Mean, and The Works of Mencius*. New York: Paragon Book Reprint Corp.

—— tr., Chai, Chu, ed., Chai, Winberg, joint ed., 1967. *Li chi: Book of Rites. An Encyclopedia of Ancient Ceremonial Usages, Religious Creeds, and Social Institutions*. New Hyde Park, NY: University Books.

—— (reprint) 1985a. *The Ch'un Ts'ew*. Taipei: Southern Materials Center, Inc.

—— (reprint) 1985b. *The She King*. Taipei: Southern Materials Center, Inc.

—— (reprint) 1985c. *The Shoo King*. Taipei: Southern Materials Center, Inc.

—— (reprint) 1986. *The Li Ji*. 2 vols. Vols. XXVII–XXVIII of F. Max Müller, ed., *The Sacred Books of the East*. Delhi: Motilal Banarsidass.

Leonard, Jane Kate, 1984. *Wei Yuan and China's Discovery of Maritime World*. Cambridge, MA: Harvard University Press.

Leslie, Daniel, 1961. 'Notes on the Analects, Appendixed by a Select Bibliography for the Analects', *T'oung Pao*, 49: 54–63.

Leslie, Donald, 1956. 'Contribution to a New Translation of the Lunheng', *T'oung pao* 1956, 44: 100–49.

Levenson, Joseph Richmond, 1953. *Liang Ch'i-ch'ao and the Mind of Modern China*. Cambridge, MA: Harvard University Press.

—— 1958. *Confucian China and its Modern Fate, vol. 1: The Problem of Intellectual Continuity*. Berkeley: University of California Press.

—— 1965. *Confucian China and Its Modern Fate – Volume Three: The Problem of Historical Significance*. London: Routledge & Kegan Paul.

Lewis, Mark Edward, 1999. *Writing and Authority in Early China*. Albany: State University of New York Press.

Leys, Simon, 1997. *The Analects of Confucius*. New York: W.W. Norton.

Li Hongyan, 1997. 'Developments in the Study of Confucianism on the Mainland of China in Recent Years', *Social Sciences in China* 1997: 2, pp. 17–30.

Li Jingyuan 李經元, 1989. '*Zhou Xingji*' 周行己. In Zhang Qizhi 張豈之, *et al.*, *Zhongguo lishi da cidian: sixiang shi juan* 中國歷史大辭典思想史卷 (A Chinese Historical Dictionary: Intellectual History Volume), p. 287. Shanghai cishu chubanshe.

Li Rizhang 李日章, 1986. *Cheng Hao Cheng Yi* 程顥程頤. Taipei: Dongda 東大 chubanshe.

Li Tiangang 李天綱, 1998. *Zhongguo liyi zhi zheng: Lishi, wenxian he yiyi* 中國禮儀之爭: 歷史, 文獻和意義, Shanghai guji chubanshe.

Li Xinchuan 李心傳, 1935a. *Dao Ming Lu* 道命錄 (Record of the Destiny of the Way). Congshu jicheng edition.

—— 1935b, *Jianyan Yilai Chaoye Zaji* 建炎以來朝野雜記 (Various Records of Affairs at the Court and from the Country Since the Beginning of the Jianyan-Period). Congshu jicheng edition.

Li Xinlin 李新霖, 1989. *Chunqiu Gongyang zhuan yao yi* 春秋公羊傳要義 (Essential Meaning of the Gongyang Traditions to the Chunqiu), Part V. Taipei: Wenjin chubanshe.

Li Yi 李毅, 1994. *Zhongguo Makesizhuyi Yu Xiandai Xinruxue* 中國馬克思主義與現代新儒學 (Chinese Marxism and Contemporary New Confucianism). Shenyang: Liaoning University Press.

Li Youwu 李幼武, 1967. *Huangchao Daoxue mingchen yanxing wailu* 皇朝道學名臣言行外錄 (Supplementary Record of the Words and Deeds of Illustrious Dao Xue Ministers During the Song), in *Song mingchen yanxinglu wuji* 宋名臣言行錄五集 (Five Collections of the Records of the Words and Deeds of Illustrious Song Ministers). Taipei: Wenhai chubanshe edition.

Li Zehou 李澤厚, 1979. *Zhongguo jindai sixiang shilun* 中國近代思想史論 (A Study of Modern Chinese Thought). Beijing: Renmin chubanshe.

—— 1986. 'Confucian Cosmology in the Han Dynasty', *Social Sciences in China* 7.1, pp. 81–116.

Li Zhizao 李之藻, 1970. *Pan'gong liyue shu* 頖宮禮樂疏. 2 vols. 1618. Taipei: Guoli zhongyang tushuguan 國立中央圖書館.

Liang Mingyue 梁銘越, 1985. *Music of the Billion: An Introduction to Chinese Musical Culture*. New York: Heinrichshofen Edition.

Liang Qichao 梁啟超, 1920. *Qing dai xueshu gailun* 清代學術概論 (An Intellectual History of the Qing). In Yinbingshi heji 飲冰室合集 (Collected Writings from the Ice-Drinker's Studio), vol. VIII. Beijing: Zhonghua shuju.

—— 1957. *Zhongguo jin sanbai nian xueshu shi* 中國近三百年學術史 (History of Scholarship during the Last Three Hundred Years). Taipei: Shangwu yinshu guan.

—— 1959. *Intellectual Trends in the Ch'ing Period*, Cambridge, MA: Harvard University Press.

Liang Shuming 梁漱銘, 1989. *Liang Shuming Quanji* 梁漱銘全集 (Complete Works by Liang Shuming). Jinan: Shandong renmin chubanshe.

Liang Yuansheng 梁元生, 1988. 'Qiusuo dongxi tiandijian: Li Zhizao youru ruye de daolu' 求索東西天地間: 李之藻由儒入耶的道路, *Jiuzhou xuekan* 九州學刊 3, 1 (1988), pp. 1–14.

—— 1990–1. 'Towards a Hyphenated Identity: Li Zhizao's Search for a Confucian-Christian Synthesis', *Monumenta Serica* 39 (1990–1): 115–30.

Liao Ping 廖平, 1886. *Jingu xuekao* 今古學考. Chengdu.

Liao, W.K. 1959. *The Complete Works of Han Fei Tzu*, 2 vols. London: Arthur Probsthain.

Lidin, Olof G., 1970. *Ogyû Sorai's 'Distinguishing the Way'*. Tokyo: Sophia University Press.

—— 1973. *The Life of Ogyû Sorai: A Tokugawa Confucian Philosopher*, Scandinavian Institute of Asian Studies Monograph Series, No. 19. Lund, Sweden: Studentlitteratur.

Liji yinde 禮記引得, 1936. Beijing, Harvard–Yenjing Institute, Index no. 27.

Lin Tongqi, Henry Rosemont, Jr, and Roger T. Ames, 1995. 'Chinese Philosophy: A Philosophical Essay on the "State-of-the-Art"', *Journal of Asian Studies* 54, 3: 727–58.

Lin Xiyi, 1997. *Zhuangzi Juanzhai kouyi jiaozhu* 莊子鬳齊口義校注 (Juanzhai's Annotated Oral Interpretation of the *Zhuangzi*). Beijing: Zhonghua shuju.

Lin Yelian 林葉連, 1993. *Zhongguo lidai Shi jing xue* 中國歷代詩經學. Taipei: Xuesheng shuju.

Lin Zhenghua 林政華, 1976. *Huang Zhen ji qi zhuzi xue* 黃震及其諸子學 (Huang Zhen and his Studies of the Philosophers). Taipei: Chia Hsin Foun-dation.

Liu Anshi 劉安世, 1782. *Jinyan ji* 盡言集 (Collection of Candid Words). Siku quanshu edition.

Liu, I-ching, 1976. *Shih-shuo hsin-yu: A New Account of Tales of the World*, tr. by Richard B. Mather. Minneapolis: University of Minesota Press.

Liu, James T.C. (Liu Zijian 劉子健), 1957. 'An Early Sung Reformer: Fan Chung-yen', in John King Fairbank, ed., *Chinese Thought and Institutions*, pp. 105–31. University of Chicago Press.

—— 1959. *Reform in Sung China*. Cambridge: Harvard University Press.

—— 1967. *Ou-yang Hsiu: An Eleventh-Century Neo-Confucian*. Stanford University Press.

—— 1988. *China Turning Inward: Intellectual-Political Changes in the Early Twelfth Century*. Cambridge, MA: Harvard University Press.

—— 1993a. 'Some Reflections on Fan Chung-yen (989–1052)', in *A Festschrift in Honor of Professor Jao Tsung-i on the Occasion of His Seventy-fifth Anniversary*, pp. 293–300. Chinese University of Hong Kong Press.

—— 1993b. 'Wei Liao-weng's Thwarted Statecraft', in Robert P. Hymes and Conrad Schirokauer, eds. *Ordering the World: Approaches to State and Society in Sung Dynasty China*. Berkeley: University of California Press.

Liu Kwang-ching, 1990. *Orthodoxy in Late Imperial China*. Berkeley: University of California Press.

—— 1994. 'Education for Its Own Sake: Notes on Tseng Kuo-fan's Family Letters', in Benjamin A. Elman and Alexander Woodside, eds., *Education and Society in Late Imperial China, 1600–1900*, pp. 76–108. Berkeley, CA: University of California Press.

Liu Qiyu 劉起釪, 1989. *Shang shu xue shi* 尚書學史. Beijing: Zhonghua shuju.

Liu Shu-hsien (Liu Shuxian) 劉述先, 1971. 'The Religious Import of Confucian Philosophy: Its Traditional Outlook and Contemporary Significance', *Philosophy East and West* 1971, 21: 157–75.

—— 1972. 'The Confucian Approach to the Problem of Transcendence and Immanence', *Philosophy East and West* 1972, 22, 1: 45–52.

—— 1978. 'The Function of Mind in Chu Hsi's Philosophy', *Journal of Chinese Philosophy* 1978, 5: 195–208.

—— 1982. *Chu-tzu che hsueh ssu hsiang ti fa chan yu wan cheng* (The Development and Completion of Chu Hsi's Philosophical Thought). Taipei: Hsueh-sheng shu-chu.

—— 1984. *Zhuzi zhexue sixiang de fazhan yu wancheng* 朱子哲學思想的發展與完成 (The Development and Completion of Zhu Xi's Philosophical Thought), Revised and enlarged 3rd edition, 1995. Taipei: Student Book Company.

—— 1986a. *Huang Zongxi xinxue de dingwei* 黃宗羲心學的定位 (The Orientation of Huang Zongxi's Heart–mind Centered Learning). Taipei: Asian Culture Company.

—— 1986b. 'The Problem of Orthodoxy in Chu Hsi's Philosophy', in Wing-tsit Chan, ed., *Chu Hsi and Neo-Confucianism*, pp. 437–60. Honolulu: University of Hawaii Press.

—— 1988a. *Harmony and Strife: Contemporary Perspectives, East & West*. Hong Kong: Chinese University Press.

—— 1988b. 'On the Confucian Ideal of "Sageliness Within and Kingliness Without",' in Confucius–Mencius Society, ed.,

International Symposium on Confucianism and the Modern World. Taipei, Ministry of Education.

—— 1989. 'Postwar Neo-Confucian Philosophy: Its Development and Issues', in Charles W.H. Fu and Gerhard E. Spiegler, ed., *Religious Issues and Interreligious Dialogues*, pp. 277–302. New York: Greenwood Press.

—— 1992. *Rujia Sixiang yu Xiandaihua* (Confucian Thought and Modernisation) 儒家思想與現代化 – 劉述先新儒學論著輯要. Beijing: Zhongguo Guangbo Dianshi Chubanshe 中國廣播電視出版社.

—— 1994. *Chuantong yu xiandai de tansuo* 傳統與現代的探索 (The Search for Tradition and Modernity (– An Intellectual Biography)). Taipei: Zhengzhong Publishers.

—— 1996. 'Confucian Ideals and the Real World: A Critical Review of Contemporary Neo-Confucian Thought', in Tu Wei-ming 杜維明 ed., *Confucian Traditions in East Asian Modernity: Moral Education and Economic Culture in Japan and the Four Mini-Dragons*. Cambridge, MA: Harvard University Press.

—— 1998. *Understanding Confucian Philosophy: Classical and Sung-Ming*, Westport, CT: Greenwood Press.

—— 2000a. *Li yi fen shu* 理一分殊(Principle is One, but its Manifestations are Many), Jing, Haifeng 景海峰 ed., Shanghai Literary and Arts Press.

—— 2000b. *Rujia sixiang yihan zhi xiandai chanshi lunji* 儒家思想意涵之現代闡釋論集 (Collected Essays on Contemporary Explanations of the Significance of Confucian Thought). Taipei: Academia Sinica.

Liu Shu-hsien and Robert E. Allinson, 1988. *Harmony and Strife: Contemporary Perspectives – East and West*. Hong Kong: The Chinese University of Hong Kong Press.

Liu Ts'un-yan 1986. 'Chu Hsi's Influence in Yuan Times', in Wing-tsit Chan, ed., *Chu Hsi and Neo-Confucianism*, pp. 521–50. Honolulu: University of Hawaii Press.

Liu Ts'un-yan and Berling, Judith, 1982. 'The "Three Teachings" in the Mongol-Yuan Period', in W.T. de Bary, and Hok-Lam Chan, eds., *Yuan Thought*, pp. 479–512. New York: Columbia University Press.

Liu Wu-chi, 1955. *A Short History of Confucian Philosophy*. New York: Hyperion Press.

Liu Xiangbin 劉象彬, 1987. *Ercheng Lixue Jiben Fanchou Yanjiu* 二程理學基本範疇研究 (Researches on the Fundamental Categories of the Two Chengs' Neo-Confucianism). Kaifeng: Henan Daxue chubanshe.

Liu Xu 劉昫, 1975. *Jiu Tang shu* 舊唐書 (The Old Tang History). Beijing: Zhonghua shuju edition.

Liu Yuxi 劉禹錫, 1989. *Liu Yuxi ji jian zheng* 劉禹錫集箋證 (Annotated Edition of Liu Yuxi's Collected Works), ed. Qu Tuiyuan 瞿蛻園, 3 volumes. Shanghai guji chubanshe.

Lo, Winston W., 1974. *The Life and Thought of Yeh Shih*. Hong Kong: The Chinese University Press.

—— 1976. 'Wang An-shih and the Confucian Ideal of "Inner Sageliness"', *Philosophy East and West* 1976, 26: 41–53.

Loden, Torbjorn, 1992. 'Traditions Reconsidered: Marxism and Confucianism in Post-Mao China' in *Zhongguoren De Jiazhiguan Guoji Yantaohui Lunwenji (Xia Ce)* 中國人的價值觀國際研討會論文集 (下冊) (Collected Essays from the International Conference on the Value Systems of Chinese Persons – Volume Two), pp. 577–608. Taipei: Sinology Research Center.

Loewe, Michael, 1974. *Crisis and Conflict in Han China 104 BC to AD 9*. London: George Allen and Unwin.

—— 1982. *Chinese Ideas of Life and Death*, London: George Allen and Unwin.

—— 1993. ed. *Early Chinese Texts: A Bibliographical Guide*, 415–23, 467–70, Early China Special Monograph Series No. 2, Berkeley: The Society for the Study of Early China, and The Institute of East Asian Studies, University of California, Berkeley.

—— 1994. *Divination, mythology and monarchy in Han China*. Cambridge University Press.

—— 2000. *A Biographical Dictionary of the Qin, Former Han and Xin Periods*. Leiden: Brill.

Loewe, Michael and Edward L. Shaughnessy, eds., 1999. *The Cambridge History of Ancient China: From the Origins of Civilization to 221 B.C.* Cambridge University Press.

Lokuang, Stanislaus, 1986. 'Chu Hsi's Theory of Metaphysical Structure', in Wing-tsit Chan, ed., *Chu Hsi and Neo-Confucianism*. Honolulu: University of Hawaii Press.

Longobardo, Niccolo, 1676. *Respuesta Breve, sobre las Controversias de el Xang Ti, Tien Xin, y Ling Hoen, y otros* nombres y terminos Chinicos . . . , i.e. ch. V of D.F. Navarette, *Tratados historicos, politicos, ethicos y religiosos de la monarchia de China*. Madrid.

—— 1701. *De Confucio Ejusque Doctrina Tractatus: Traite sur quelques points de la religion des Chinois*. Paris.

Lu Dian 陸佃, 1995. *Er ya xinyi* 爾雅新義 (New Meanings of the Erya). Shanghai guji chubanshe.

—— 1782a. *Pi ya* 埤雅 (Collection of Refined Usage). Siku quanshu edition.

—— 1782b. *Taoshan ji* 陶山集 (Literary Collection from Taoshan). Siku quanshu edition.

Lu Guimeng and Pi Rixiu, 1782. *Songling ji* 松陵集 (Poetry Collection from Songling). Siku quanshu edition.

Lu Jiuyuan, 陸九淵, 1980. *Lu Jiuyuan ji* 陸九淵集 (Collected Works of Lu Jiuyuan). Beijing: Zhonghua shuju.

Lü Qinli, 1979. *Tao Yuanming ji*. Beijing: Zhonghua shuju.

Lu Wenchao 盧文弨, 1784. *Baojing tang congshu* 抱經堂叢書, facsimile reproduction in Congshu jicheng 叢書集成 no. 238.

Lü Yuanshan 呂元善, 1937. *Shengmen zhi* 聖門志. 1613. Congshu jicheng 叢書集成 edition.

Luo Guojie, 1997. 'Theoretical and Methodological Principles for the Critical Inheritance of Traditional Ethics', *Social Sciences in China*, 1997: 2, pp. 41–4.

Luo Yijun 羅義俊, ed. 1994. *Lixing yu Shengming – Dangdai Xin Ruxue Wencui* (Rationality and Life (1) – A Collection of Contemporary New Confucian Essays) 理性與生命 (1) – 當代新儒學文萃. Shanghai Shudian 上海書店.

Ma Tong 馬通, 1983. *Zhonguo Yisilan jiaopai yu menhuan zhidu shilue* 中國伊斯蘭教派與門宦制度史略 (Brief History of Sects and the Sufi Pathway System in China's Islam) Yinchuan: Ningxia renmin chubanshe.

MacIntyre, Alasdair, 1981. *After Virtue*. London: Duckworth.

Mackerras, Colin, 1989. *Western Images of China*. New York: Oxford University Press.

Mair, Victor, tr., 1990. *Tao Te Ching: The Classic Book of Integrity and the Way*. New York: Bantam Books.

—— 1994. *Wandering on the Way: Early Taoist Tales and Parables of Chuang Tzu*. Honolulu: University of Hawaii Press.

Major, John S., 1987. 'The Meaning of Hsing-te', in Charles Le Blanc and Susan Blader, eds., *Chinese Ideas about Nature and Society*. Hong Kong University Press.

Makeham, John, 1994. *Name and Actuality in Early Chinese Thought*, Albany: SUNY Press.

—— 1996. 'The formation of Lunyu as a book', *Monumenta Serica* 44.

—— tr., 2002. *Balanced Discourses: An Annotated Translation of Xu Gan's Zhong lun*. New Haven: Yale University Press.

Malm, W.P., 1977. *Music Cultures of the Pacific, the Near East, and Asia*. Englewood Cliffs: Prentice-Hall, Inc.

—— 1990. *Japanese Music & Musical Instruments*. Tokyo: Charles E. Tuttle Co, Inc.

Malmqvist, Goran, 1971. 'Studies on the Gongyang and Guliang Commentaries', *BMFEA* 43 (1971): 67–222; 47 (1975): 19–69; and 49 (1977): 33–215.

Mann, Susan, 1997. *Precious Records: Women in China's Long Eighteenth Century*. Stanford University Press.

Mao Huaixin 冒懷辛, 1986. 'The Establishment of the School of Chu Hsi and Its Propagation in Fukien', in Wing-tsit Chan, ed., *Chu Hsi and Neo-Confucianism*. Honolulu: University of Hawaii Press.

Marshman, Joshua, tr., 1809. *The Works of Confucius, Containing the Original Text with a Translation*. Serampore: Mission Press.

Maruyama Masao, 1974. *Nihon seiji shisôshi kenkyû* (Tokyo Daigaku Shuppankai, 1952), trans. Mikiso Hane as *Studies in the Intellectual History of Tokugawa Japan*. University of Tokyo Press and Princeton University Press.

Masao Yaku, 1969. *The Kojiki in the Life of Japan*, trans. G.W. Robinson. Tokyo, Center for East Asian Cultural Studies.

Mason, Mary Gertrude, 1939. *Western Concepts of China and the Chinese, 1840–1876*. London: Russell & Russell.

Maspero, Henri, 1931–2. 'La composition et la date du Tso tchouan', *Melanges chinois et bouddhiques*, 1: 137–215.

—— 1939. 'Les instruments astronomiques des chinois au temps du Han', *Melanges chinois et bouddhiques*, 6: 183–370.

Masson, Michel C., 1985. *Philosophy and Tradition: The Interpretation of China's Philosophic Past, Fung Yu-lan 1939–1949*. Taipei: Ricci Institute.

Mather, Richard, 1969/70. 'The Controversy over Conformity and Naturalness during the Six Dynasties', *History of Religions* 9.2 and 3: 160–80.

—— 1976. *Shih-shuo hsin-yu: A New Account of Tales of the World*. Minneapolis: University of Minnesota Press.

McAleavy, Henry, 1953. *Wang T'ao: The Life and Writings of A Displaced Person*. London: The China Society.

McDermott, Joseph P., ed., 1999. *State and Court Ritual in China*. Cambridge University Press.

McEwan, J.R., 1962. *The Political Writings of Ogyû Sorai*. Cambridge University Press.

McMullen, David, 1987. 'Bureaucrats and Cosmology: The Ritual Code of T'ang China', in David Cannadine and Simon Price eds., *Rituals of Royalty: Power and Ceremonial in Traditional Societies*. Cambridge University Press, 181–236.

—— 1988. *State and Scholars in Tang China*. New York: Cambridge University Press.

—— 1989. 'Han Yu an Alternative Picture', *Harvard Journal of Asiatic Studies*, 49, 2: 603–57.

—— 1999. 'The Death Rites of Tang Daizong', in Joseph P. McDermott, ed., *State and Court Ritual in China*, pp. 150–96. Cambridge University Press.

Meng Wentong 蒙文通, 1995. *Jingshi jueyuan 經史抉原 (A Study of Classics and Histories)*. Chengdu: Bashu chubanshe.

Meskill, John, 1963. *Wang An-shih: Practical Reformer?* Boston: D.C. Heath and Company.

—— 1982. *Academies in Ming China: A Historical Essay*. University of Arizona Press.

Meyer, Jeffrey, 1991. *The Dragons of Tiananmen: Beijing as a Sacred City*. Columbia: University of South Carolina Press.

Miao, Ronald, 1972. 'Literary Criticism at the End of the Eastern Han', *Literature East and West*, 16: 1013–34.

Miller, Roy Andrew, 1977–78. 'The Wu-ching i-i of Hsu Shen', *Monumenta Serica* 33 (1977–8): 1–21.

Minear, Richard H., 1976. 'Ogyû Sorai's Instructions for Students: A Translation and Commentary', *Harvard Journal of Asiatic Studies*, 36.

Ming hui yao 明會要, in 2 vols., (Nineteenth century) 1956, ed. Long Wenbin 龍文彬. Taipei: Shijie shuju 世界書局.

Ming shi 明史 (1739), 1974, in 14 vols. Zhang Tingyu 張廷玉. Beijing: Zhonghua shuju.

Mingru xuean 明儒學案, 1985, by Huang Zongxi 黃宗羲. Beijing: Zhonghua Shuju.

Misra, Kalpana, 1998. *From Post-Maoism to Post-Marxism: The Erosion of Official Ideology in Deng's China*, London: Routledge.

Mitchell, Peter, 1972. 'The Limits of Reformism: Wei Yuan's Reaction to Western Intrusion', *Modern Asian Studies*, 6, 2: 175–204.

Miyake Masahiko, 1987. *Kyôto machishû. Itô Jinsai no shisô keisei*, Kyoto: Shibunkaku shuppansha.

Mo Lifeng, 1984. '*An Analysis of Huang Tingjian's Metamorphosis*', *Social Sciences in China*. Beijing: 3: 170–90.

Möller, Hans-Georg, 1998. 'Eine philosophische Standortbestimmung des Neukonfuzianismus am Beispiel der *Neuen Metaphysik Feng Yu-lans*' ('Feng Youlan's New Metaphysics: An Example of the Determination of a Philosophical Orientation for Neoconfucianism'), in Ralf Moritz and Lee Ming-huei, eds., *Der Konfuzianismus: Ursprunge – Entwicklungen – Perspektiven* (Confucianism: Origins – Developments – Perspectives), pp. 190–5. Leipzig: Universitätsverlag.

Morgan, Carole, 1990–1. 'Tang Geomancy: The Wu hsing ('Five Names') Theory and its Legacy', in *T'ang Studies* 8–9: 45–76.

Mori Mikisaburo, 1971. *Joko yori Kandai ni itaru seimeikan no tenkai*. Tokyo: Sobunsha.

Morohashi Tetsuji, ed., 1960. *Dai Kan-Wa jiten*. Tokyo: Taishukan shoten.

Mote, Frederick W., 1960. 'Confucian Eremitism in the Yuan Period', in Arthur Wright, ed., *The Confucian Persuasion*. Stanford University Press.

—— 1976. 'The Arts and the "Theorizing Mode" of the Civilization', in Christian F.

Murck, ed., *Artists and Traditions: Uses of the Past in Chinese Culture*, pp. 3–8. The Art Museum, Princeton University.

Mou, Sherry J., ed., 1999. *Presence and Presentation: Women in the Chinese Literati Tradition*. New York: St. Martin's Press.

Mou Zongsan (Mou Tsung-san) 牟宗三, 1963. *Xinti yu Xingti* 心體與性體 (Substance of the Heart/Mind and Substance of Human Nature). Taipei: Zhengzhong shuju.

—— 1971. *Zhi de Zhijue yu Zhongguo Zhexue* 智之直觀與中國哲學 (Intellectual Intuition and Chinese Philosophy). Taipei: Commercial Press.

—— 1982. *Zhongguo Zhexue de Tezhi* 中國哲學的特質 (*The Essential Characteristics of Chinese Philosophy*). Taipei: Student Bookstore.

—— 1984. *Zhongguo Zhexue Shijiu Jiang* 中國哲學十九講 (Nineteen Lectures on Chinese Philosophy). Taipei: Student Bookstore.

—— 1985. *Yuan Shan Lun* 圓善論 (*The Theory of Perfected Goodness*). Taipei: Taiwan Student Bookstore.

—— 1990. *Cong Lu Xiangshan dao Liu Jishan* 從陸象山到劉蕺山 (*From Lu Xiangshan to Liu Jishan*). Taipei: Taiwan Student Bookstore.

—— 1991. *Xinti yu Xingti (San Ce)* 心體與性體 (三冊) (The Essence of Heart–Mind and the Essence of Human Nature in three volumes). Taipei: Zhengzhong.

—— 1997. *Zhongguo Zhexue Shijiujiang* 中國哲學十九講 (Nineteen Lectures in Chinese Philosophy). Shanghai: Ancient Books Publisher.

Mungello, David E., 1977. *Leibniz and Confucianism: The Search for Accord*. Honolulu: University Press of Hawaii.

—— 1985. *Curious Land: Jesuit Accommodation and the Origins of Sinology*, Studia Leibnitiana Supplementa, XXV. Wiesbaden: Steiner Verlag.

—— 1989. *Curious Land: Jesuit Accommodation and the Origins of Sinology*. Honolulu: University of Hawaii Press.

—— ed., 1994. *The Chinese Rites Controversy: Its History and Meaning*, Monumenta Serica Monograph Series, XXXIII. Nettetal: Steyler Verlag.

Munro, Donald J., 1969. *The Concept of Man in Early China*. Stanford University Press.

Murray, Julia K., 1992. 'The Hangzhou Portraits of Confucius and Seventy-Two Disciples (*Sheng xian tu*): Art in the Service of Politics', *Art Bulletin*, 74: 7–18.

—— 1996. 'The Temple of Confucius and Pictorial Biographies of the Sage', *Journal of Asian Studies*, 55.2: 269–300.

—— 1997. 'Illustrations of the Life of Confucius: Their Evolution, Functions, and Significance in Late Ming China', *Artibus Asiae*, 57: 73–134.

—— 2002. 'Varied Views of the Sage: Illustrated Narratives of the Life of Confucius'. in Thomas A. Wilson, ed., *On Sacred Ground: Culture, Society, Politics, and the Formation of the Temple of Confucius*, pp. 222–64. Cambridge, MA: Harvard University Press.

Najita Tetsuo, 1987. *Visions of Virtue in Tokugawa Japan*. Chicago, London: University of Chicago Press.

Nakamura Shûsaku, 1986. *Minakawa Kien, Ôta Kinjô*. Meitoku.

Nan Qi shu 南齊書, 1972, in 3 vols. Xiao Zixian 蕭子顯. Beijing: Zhonghua shuju.

Nan shi 南史, 1975, in 6 vols. Li Yanshou 李延壽. Beijing: Zhonghua shuju.

Nathan, Andrew J., 1986. *Chinese Democracy*. Berkeley: California University Press.

Needham, Joseph, 1956, 1959. *Science and Civilization in China*. Cambridge University Press.

Neininger, Ulrich, 1983. 'Burying the Scholars Alive: On the Origin of a Confucian Martyr's Legend', in Wolfram Eberhard *et al.*, eds., *East Asian Civilizations: New Attempts at Understanding Traditions*, vol. II: *National and Mythology*, pp. 121–36. Munich: Simon and Magiera.

Neskar, Ellen G. 1993. 'The Cult of Worthies: A Study of Shrines Honoring Local Confucian Worthies in the Sung Dynasty (960–1279)', Ph.D. dissertation. Columbia University.

Ng Wai-ming, 2000. *The I Ching in Tokugawa Thought and Culture*. Honolulu: University of Hawaii Press.

Nienhauser, William H., ed., 1973. *Liu Tsung-yuan*. New York: Twayne Publishers Inc.

—— 1979. *P'i Jih-hsiu*, Boston: Twayne Publishers.

—— ed., 1986. *The Indiana Companion to Traditional Chinese Literature*. Bloomington: Indian University Press.

—— ed., 1994. *The Grand Scribe's Records, vols. I, VII*. Bloomington and Indianapolis: Indiana University Press.

Niu Pu, 1998. 'Confucian Statecraft in Song China: Ye Shi and the Yongjia School', Ph.D. dissertation. Arizona State University.

Niu Sengru 牛僧孺, 1982. *Youguai lu* 幽怪錄 (A Record of Mysterious and Strange Occurances). Congshu jicheng chubian weichufen edition. Beijing: Zhonghua shuju.

Nivison, David S., 1953. 'The Problem of 'Knowledge' and 'Action' in Chinese Thought Since Wang Yang-ming', in Arthur F. Wright, ed., *Studies in Chinese Thought*. University of Chicago Press.

—— 1980. 'On Translating Mengzi', *Philosophy East and West*, 30: 93–121.

—— 1990. 'Astronomical Evidence for the Bamboo Annals' Chronicle of Early Xia', *Early China*, 15: 87–95.

—— 1996. *The Ways of Confucianism*, ed. and intro. by Bryan W. van Norden. Chicago, Open Court.

Nosco, Peter, ed. 1984. *Confucianism and Tokugawa Culture*. Princeton University Press.

—— 1997. 'Confucianism and Nativism in Tokugawa Japan', in Irene Bloom and Joshua A. Fogel, eds., *Meeting of Minds: Intellectual and Religious Interaction in East Asian Traditions of Thought*. New York: Columbia University Press.

—— ed., 1997. *Confucianism and Tokugawa Culture*. Honolulu: University of Hawaii Press.

Nuyen, A.T., 1999. 'Chinese Philosophy and Western Capitalism', *Asian Philosophy*, 9: 1 (1999): 71–9.

Nylan, Michael, 1992. *The Shifting Center. The Original 'Great Plan' and Later Readings*. Nettetal: Steyler Verlag. Monumenta Serica Monograph Series; 24.

—— tr., 1993. *The Canon of Supreme Mystery, a Translation with Commentary of the T'ai hsuan ching*. Albany: State University of New York.

—— 1994a. *The Elemental Changes*. Albany: State University of New York Press.

—— 1994b. 'The chin wen/ku wen (New Text/Old Text) Controversy in Han', *T'oung pao*, 80: 83–145.

—— 1995. 'The ku wen Documents in Han Times', *T'oung pao*, 81: 1–27.

—— 1996. 'Confucian Piety and Individualism in Han China', *Journal of the American Oriental Society*, 116, 1.

—— 2001. *The Five 'Confucian' Classics*, New Haven: Yale University Press.

Nylan, Michael and Nathan Sivin, 1987. 'The First Neo-Confucianism: An Introduction to Yang Hsiung's 'Canon of Supreme Mystery' (T'ai hsuen ching), *c.* 4 B.C', in Charles Le Blanc and Susan Blader, eds., *Chinese Ideas about Nature and Society: Studies in Honour of Derk Bodde*, pp. 41–99. Hong Kong University Press.

Obenchain, Diane B., ed. and tr., 1994. *Feng Youlan: Something Exists – Selected Papers of the International Research Seminar on the Thought of Feng Youlan, Journal of Chinese Philosophy*. 21: i–cxii: 229–574.

Ogyû Sorai, 1978. *Rongo chô*, in Imanaka Kanji and Naramoto Tatsuya, eds., *Ogyû Sorai zenshû*, vol. II. Tokyo: Kawade shobô.

Okada Takahiko 岡田武彦, 1965. 'Ko Go-ho' 胡五峰, in *Toyobunka* 東洋文化, 10: 23–33.

—— 1970. 'Wang Chi and the Rise of Existentialism', in Wm. Theodore de Bary, ed., *Self and Society in Ming Thought*, pp. 121–44. New York: Columbia University Press.

—— 1986. 'Chu Hsi and Wisdom as Hidden and Stored', in Wing-tsit Chan, ed., *Chu Hsi and Neo-Confucianism*, pp. 197–211. Honolulu: University of Hawaii Press.

Ooms, Herman, 1985. *Tokugawa Ideology: Early Constructs, 1570–1680*. Princeton University Press.

Ouyang Jiong 歐陽炯, 1992. Lu Benzhong yanjiu 呂本中研究. Taipei: 文史哲出版社.

Pae Jong-ho, 1974. *Hanguk Yugyosa*. Seoul: Yonsei Taech'ul P'anbu.

—— 1985. *Hanguk Yuhakŭi Ch'ŏlhakjuk Chŏkkae*. Seoul: Yonsei Taech'ul P'anbu.

Pae Sang-hyŏn, 1996. *Chosŏncho Kiho Hakpaŭi Yehak Sasange Kwanhan Yŏn-gu*. Seoul: Koryo University Minjong Munhwa Ch'ujinhoe.

Pak Chong-hon, 1998. *Pak Chong-honjip*. Seoul: Minŭmsa.

Pak Sae-dang, 1975. *Sabyŏl-lok*. Seoul: Minjong Munhwa Ch'ujinhoe.

Palais, James B., 1996. *Confucian Statecraft and Korean Institutions: Yu Hyongwon and the*

Late Choson Dynasty. Seattle: University of Washington Press.

Palumbo-Liu, David, 1993. *The Poetics of Appropriation: The Literary Theory and Practice of Huang Tingjian*. Stanford University Press.

Pang Pu 龐朴, 1980. *Zhongyong pingyi* 中庸評義 (On the Meaning of the *Zhongyong*), in *Zhongguo shehui kexue* 中國社會科學.

—— 1985. 'Origins of the Yin-Yang and Five Elements Concepts', *Social Sciences in China*, 6.1: 81–131.

—— 1997. *Zhongguo ruxue* 中國儒學. Shanghai: 東方版中心.

Pang Zhonglu 龐鍾璐, 1988. *Wenmiao sidian kao* 文廟祀典考. 1865. Taipei: Zhongguo liyue xuehui 中國禮樂學會.

Paper, Jordan, tr., 1987. *The Fu-tzu: A Post-Han Confucian Text*. Leiden: E.J. Brill.

Pearson, Margaret J., 1989. *Wang Fu and the Comments of a Recluse: A Study with Translations*. Tempe, Arizona: Center for Asian Studies, Arizona State University Press.

Pelliot, Paul, 1916. 'Le *Chou king* en caractères anciens et le *Chang chou che wen*'; in *Memoires concernant l'Asie Orientale*, vol. II. Paris.

Peng Dingqiu 彭定求, *et al.*, comp., 1960. *Quan Tang shi* 全唐詩 (Complete Tang Poetry). Beijing: Zhonghua shuju edition.

Peng Ruli 彭汝礪, 1782. *Poyang ji* 鄱陽集 (Literary Collection from Poyang). Siku quanshu edition.

Penny, Benjamin, 1996. 'The Text and Authorship of the Shenxian zhuan', *Journal of Oriental Studies*, 34.2: 164–209.

Petersen, Jens Ostergard, 1995. 'Which Books Did the First Emperor of Ch'in Burn? On the Meaning of Pai Chia in early Chinese Sources', *Monumenta Serica*, 43: 1–52.

Petersen, Willard J., 1986. 'Another Look at Li', *Bulletin of Sung and Yuan Studies*, 18: 13–32.

—— 1998. 'Why Did They Become Christians? Yang T'ing-yun, Li Chih-tsao, and Hsu Kuang-ch'i', in Charles Ronan and Bonnie Oh, eds., *East Meets West: The Jesuits in China, 1582–1773*, pp. 129–52. Chicago: Loyola University Press.

Pfister, Lauren F., 1995. 'The Different Faces of Contemporary Religious Confucianism: An Account of the Diverse Approaches of Some Major Twentieth Century Chinese Confucian Scholars', *Journal of Chinese Philosophy*, 22: 5–79.

—— 1998. 'The Legacy of James Legge', *International Bulletin of Missionary Research*, 22: 2 (April): 77–82.

—— 2002. 'Feng Youlan', in Chung-ying Cheng and Nicholas Bunnin, eds., *Blackwell Guide to Contemporary Chinese Philosophy*. Oxford: Blackwell Publishers.

Pi Mingju 皮名舉, 1959. 'Pi lumen xianshang zhuanlue' 皮鹿門先生傳略 (A Brief Biography of Mr. Pi Lumen (Pi Xirui))', in Pi Xirui 皮錫瑞, *Jingxue lishi* 經學歷史 (History of Confucian Learning). Beijing: Zhonghua shuju.

Pi Rixiu 皮日休, 1999. *Pizi wensou* 皮子文藪 (Literary Marsh of Master Pi). Siku quanshu edition.

Pi Xirui 皮錫瑞 (1923), 1954. *Jingxue tonglun* 經學通論. Beijing: Zhonghua shuju.

—— 1959. *Jingxue lishi* 經學歷史. Beijing: Zhonghua shuju.

Pian, Rulan Chao, 1967. *Song Dynasty Musical Sources and Their Interpretation*. Cambridge, MA: Harvard University Press. Harvard–Yenching Institute Monograph Series, no. 16.

Pines, Yuri, 1997a. *Aspects of Intellectual Developments in the Chunqiu Period (722–453 B.C.)*, Ph.D. dissertation. Hebrew University, Jerusalem.

—— 1997b. 'Intellectual Change in the Chunqiu Period: The Reliability of the Speeches in the Zuozhuan as Sources of Chunqiu Intellectual History', *Early China*, 22: 77–132.

Pinot, Virgile, 1932. *La Chine et la formation de l'esprit philosophique en France (1640–1740)*. Paris: Geuthner.

Pokora, Timoteus. 1963. 'The Life of Huan T'an', *Archiv Orientální*, 31: 1–79, 521–76.

—— 1975. *Hsin-lun (New Treatises) and Other Writings by Huan Tan (43 B.C.–28 A.D.)*. Ann Arbor: University of Michigan.

—— 1981. 'Ch'u Shao-sun 褚少孫 – the Narrator of Stories in the *Shih-chi*', Istituto Orientale di Napoli: Annali 41, 4: 403–30.

Pollack, David, 1986. *The Fracture of Meaning*. Princeton University Press.

Porter, Jonathan, 1972. *Tseng Kuo-fan's Private Bureaucracy*. Berkeley: University of California Press.

Pratt, K., 1987. *Korean Music: Its History and Its Performance*. London: Faber Music Ltd Press.

Pulleyblank, Edwin G., 1961. 'Chinese Historical Criticism: Liu Chih-chi and Ssu-ma Kuang' in W.G. Beasley and E.G. Pulleyblank eds., *Historians of China and Japan*. London: Oxford University Press.

—— 1994. *Middle Chinese: A Study in Historical Phonology*. Vancouver: University of British Columbia Press.

Pye, Lucian, 1985. *Asian Power and Politics: The Cultural Dimensions of Authority*. Cambridge, MA: Belknap Press.

Qian Daxin 錢大昕, 1937. *Shijiazhai Yangxinlu* 十駕齋養新錄. Shanghai: Commercial Press.

Qian Mu 錢穆, 1937. *Zhongguo jin sanbainian xueshu shi* 中國近三百年學術史 (A History of Intellectual Development in the last Three Hundred Years). Shanghai: Commercial Press.

—— 1953. *Song Ming lixue gaishu* 宋明理學概述 (A General Survey of the Confucian Philosophers of the Song and Ming Periods). Taipei: Zhonghua wenhua.

—— 1974. 'Wang Shenning xueshu' 王深寧學術 (The Scholarship of Wang Shen-ning), *Dongfang zazhi fukan* 東方雜志副刊, 8, 5, 1974: 10–15.

—— 1977. *Song Ming lixue gaishu* 宋明理學概述 (A Brief Survey of Song–Ming Neo-Confucianism). Taipei: Xuesheng shuju.

—— 1989. *Xinya yiduo* 新亞遺鐸 (Musical Tones of New Asia's Inheritance). Taipei: Great Eastern Press.

Qin Guan 秦觀, 1782. *Huaihai ji* 淮海集 (Literary Collection from Huaihai). Siku quanshu edition.

Qin Huitian 秦蕙田 (1761), 1994. *Wuli tongkao* 五禮通考 (Conspectus of the Five Categories of Ritual). Taipei: Shenghuan tushu gongsi.

Qing shi gao 清史稿 (1927), 1985, in 48 vols. Zhao Erxun 趙爾巽 *et al.* Beijing: Zhonghua shuju.

Qiu Jun 邱濬 (1487), 1779. *Daxue yanyi bu* 大學衍義補. Wenyuange Siku quanshu 文淵閣四庫全書 edition.

Qu Jiusi 瞿九思, 1609. *Kongmiao liyue kao* 孔廟禮樂考. Naikaku Bunko 內閣文庫 edition.

Qu Wanli 屈萬里, 1961. *Han shi jing Zhou Yi canzi jizheng* 漢石經周易殘字集證. Nangang: Academia Sinica.

Queen, Sarah A., 1996. *From Chronicle to Canon. The Hermeneutics of the Spring and Autumn, According to Tung Chung-shu*. Cambridge University Press.

Qufu Administrative Commission of the Cultural Relics of Shandong, 1987. *Kongzi xiang Yansheng gong ji furen xiaoxiang* 孔子像衍聖公及夫人肖像 (Portraits of Confucius, Portraits of the Dukes of Yansheng and their Wives). Shandong: Youyi shushe.

Quzhou fuzhi 衢州府志 (1711), 1882. Yang Jingru 楊兢如, rev. edn Liu Guoguang 劉國光.

Rao Zongyi 饒宗頤, 1977. *Zhongguo shixueshang zhi zhengtong lun* 中國史學上之正統論. Hong Kong: Longmen shudian.

Raphals, Lisa, 1998. *Sharing the Light: Representations of Women and Virtue in Early China*. Albany: State University of New York Press.

Rawski, Evelyn Sakakida, 1979. *Education and Popular Literacy in Ch'ing China*. Ann Arbor: University of Michigan.

Ri Sang-ho, ed., 1960. *Samguk Yusa*. Seoul: Puk'an Kwahagwon Ch'ulp'ansa.

Ricci, Matteo, 1953. *China in the Sixteenth Century: The Journals of Matthew Ricci, 1583–1610*. New York: Random House.

—— 1981. *Imperatori e mandarini: estratti dalla Storia dell'introduzione del cristianesimo in Cina*. Torino: Societe editrice internazionale.

—— 1985. *The True Meaning of the Lord of Heaven* (T'ien-chu shih-i); trans. Douglas Lancashire and Peter Hu Kuo-chen; ed. E. Malatesta. St. Louis: The Institute of Jesuit Sources/Taipei: Ricci Institute.

Rickett, Adele A., 1978. 'Method and Intuition: The Poetic Theories of Huang T'ing-chien', in Adele Rickett, ed., *Chinese Approaches to Literature from Confucius to Liang Ch'i-ch'ao*, pp. 97–119. Princeton. University Press.

Rickett, W. Allyn, 1965. *Kuan-tzu: A Repository of Early Chinese Thought*. Hong Kong University Press.

Riegel, Jeffrey, 1978. 'The Four Tzu Ssu Chapters of the Li Chi: An Analysis and Translation of the Fang Chi, Chung Yung, Piao Chi and Tzu I', Ph.D. dissertation. Stanford University.

Riegel, Jeffrey, 1979. 'Reflections on an Unmoved Mind: An Analysis of Mencius 2A2', *Journal of the American Academy of Religions*, 47, 3 (September): 433–58.

—— 1993. 'Li chi' in Michael Loewe, ed., *Early Chinese Texts: A Bibliographical Guide*. The Society for the Study of Early China and the Institute of East Asian Studies, University of California, Berkeley.

Robinet, Isabelle, 1997. *Taoism: Growth of a Religion*. Stanford University Press.

Roetz, Heiner, 1993. *Confucian Ethics of the Axial Age: A Reconstruction under the Aspect of the Breakthrough Toward Postconventional Thinking*. Albany. State University of New York Press.

Ropp, Paul S., 1976. 'The Seeds of Change: Reflections on the Condition of Women in the Early and Mid Ch'ing', *Signs: Journal of Women in Culture and Society*, 2, 1: 5–23.

Rosemont, Henry, Jr, 1989. 'Rights-Bearing Individuals and Role-Bearing Persons', in Mary I. Bockover, ed., *Rules, Rituals and Responsibility*, pp. 71–101. La Salle, IL: Open Court.

—— and Daniel J. Cook, trs., 1977. *Discourse on the Natural Theology of the Chinese*. Honolulu: University of Hawaii Press.

Rossabi, Morris, 1981. 'The Muslims in the Early Yuan Dynasty', in Langlois, J.D., ed. *China Under Mongol Rule*, pp. 257–95. Princeton University Press.

Roth, Harold, 1999. *Original Tao: Inward Training (Nei-yeh) and the Foundations of Taoist Mysticism*. New York: Columbia University Press.

Ruan Yuan 阮元, *et al.*, 1980. *Shisanjing zhushu* 十三經注疏 (The Thirteen Classics with Commentaries and Sub-Commentaries). Beijing: Zhonghua shuju.

Rule, Paul A., 1986. *K'ung-tzu or Confucius? The Jesuit Interpretation of Confucianism*. Sydney: Allen & Unwin.

Russell, Bertrand, 1922. *The Problem of China*. London: George Allen & Unwin.

Rutt, Richard, 1996. *The Book of Changes (Zhouyi): A Bronze Age Document Translated with Introduction and Notes*. Richmond: Curzon Press.

Ryckmans, Pierre, 1987. *Les Entretiens de Confucius*, Paris, Gallimard (an adaptation in English has been published under the pseudonym of Simon Leys, *The Analects of Confucius*. Translation and Notes, New York and London: W.W. Norton & Company, 1997.

Sadan Ch'iljŏng Non Minjokkwa Sasang Yŏnguhoe. 1992. Seoul: Sŏgwangsa.

Sagara Tôru, 1999. *Itô Jinsai*. Tokyo: Perikansha.

Sagye Shindokchaeyang Sŏnsaeng Ginnŏm Saŏp'oe, 1991. Seoul: Sagyesasang Yŏngu.

Sailey, Jay, 1978. *The Master Who Embraces Simplicity: A Study of the Philosopher Ko Hung, A.D. 283–343*. San Francisco: CMC.

Sakamoto Tarô, ed., 1980. *Nihon shoki*. Tokyo: Iwanami shoten.

Samguk Sagi, 1959. *Puk'an Kwahagwon Ch'ulp'ansa*.

Sanguo zhi 三國志 (A History of Three Kingdoms), 1997, in 二十四史, vol. III. Beijing: Zhonghua Shuju.

Sariti, Anthony William, 1972. 'Monarchy, Bureaucracy, and Absolutism in the Thought of Ssu-Ma Kuang', *Journal of Asian Studies*, 32: 53–76.

Sato Hitoshi, 1986. 'Chu Hsi's "Treatise on Jen"', in Wing-tsit Chan, ed., *Chu Hsi and Neo-Confucianism*. Honolulu: University of Hawaii Press.

—— 1996. *Shushigaku no kihon yogo: Beiji Ziyi yakkai* 朱子學的基本佣語: 北溪字義譯解 (Basic Terminology of Zhu Xi Thought: An Annotated Translation of Beiji Ziyi). Tokyo: Yenbun Shupan.

Sato Kazuyoshi 佐藤一好, 1991–2. 'Cho Ki no Shogai to Shisaku to Seiseki Zu' 張楷の生涯と詩作と聖蹟圖 (Zhang Kai's Life, Poetry, and Pictures of the Sage's Traces). *Gakuda kokubun* 學大國文, 34: 79–98.

Sawada, Janine, 1993. *Confucian Values and Popular Zen: Sekimon Shingaku in Eighteenth-Century Japan*. Honolulu: University of Hawaii Press.

Sawyer, Ralph D., and Mei-chun Lee, 1995. *Ling Ch'i ching: A Classic Chinese Oracle*. Boston: Shambhala.

Scarpari, Maurizio, 1998. 'Mencius and Xunzi on Human Nature: The Concept of Moral Autonomy in the Early Confucian Tradition', *Annali di Ca' Foscari* (Venice) XXXVII, 3: 467–500.

Schaberg, David, 1996. 'Foundations of Chinese Historiography: Literary Representation in Zuozhuan and Guoyu', Ph.D. dissertation. Harvard University.

—— 1997. 'Remonstrance in Eastern Zhou Historiography', *Early China*, 22: 133–79.

Schak, David C., 1995. 'The Spirit of Chinese Capitalism: A Critique', *The Tsing Hua Journal of Chinese Studies*, New Series, 25, 1 (March 1995): 87–113.

Schilling, Dennis, 1998. *Spruch und Zahl. Die chinesischen Orakelbucher 'Kanon des Hochsten Geheimen' (Taixuanjing) und 'Wald der Wandlungen' (Yilin) aus der Han-Zeit.* Aalen: Scientia Verlag.

Schirokauer, Conrad, 1975. 'Neo-Confucians Under Attack: The Condemnation of Weihsueh', in John W. Haeger, ed., *Crisis and Prosperity in Song China.* Tucson: University of Arizona Press.

—— 1986. 'Chu Hsi and Hu Hung', in Wing-tsit Chan, ed. *Chu Hsi and Neo-Confucianism.* Honolulu: University of Hawaii Press.

—— 1993. 'Hu Yin's "Recounting the Past in a Thousand Words": A Little History Primer Praised by Chu Hsi', in *Guoji Zhu zi xue huiyi lunwen ji* 國際朱子學會議論文集, pp. 1049–82. Taipei.

Schmidt, J.D., 1976. *Yang Wanli.* Boston: Twayne.

—— 1986. '*Chiang-hsi shih-p'ai*', in William H. Nienhauser, ed., *The Indiana Companion to Traditional Chinese Literature.* Bloomington: Indian University Press.

Schwartz, Benjamin I., 1951. *Chinese Communism and the Rise of Mao.* Cambridge, MA: Harvard University Press.

—— 1964. *In Search of Wealth and Power: Yen Fu and the West.* Cambridge, MA: Harvard University Press.

—— 1985. *The World of Thought in Ancient China.* Cambridge, MA: Harvard University Press.

—— 1996. *China and Other Matters.* Cambridge, MA: Harvard University Press.

Selover, Thomas W., 2001. 'The Cheng Brothers and their Circle' in Tu Wei-ming and Mary Evelyn Tucker, eds., *Confucian Spirituality*, vol. II. New York: Crossroad Press.

—— 2002. *Hsieh Liang-tso and the Analects.* New York: Oxford University Press.

Shao Dongfang 邵東方, 1998. *Cui Shu yu Zhongguo xueshu shi yanjiu* 崔述與中國學術史研究 (Research on Cui Shu and the History of Chinese Scholarship), pp. 293–385. Beijing: Renmin chubanshe.

Shaughnessy, Edward, 1996. *I Ching: The Classic of Changes: The First English Translation of the Newly Discovered Second-Century B.C. Mawangdui Texts.* New York: Ballantine Books.

Shengji zhi Tu 聖蹟之圖 (Pictures of the Sage's Traces) (1548, 1592) 1988, reproduction of late Ming painted album. Jinan: Shandong General Press.

Shi ji 史記, 1962. 10 vols., by Sima Qian 司馬遷. Beijing: Zhonghua shuju.

Shi Jie 石介, 1984. *Culai Shixiansheng wenji* 徂徠石先生文集 (Collected Writings of Master Shi Culai). Beijing: Zhonghua shuju.

Shi Ke 石可, 1987. *Kongzi Shiji Tu, Lunyu Zhenyan Yin* 孔子事蹟圖，論語真言印. (Pictures of the Deeds of Confucius, and Seal-Impressions of True Sayings from the Analects of Confucius). Jinan: Qi Lu shushe 齊魯書社.

Shiba Yoshinobu and Herbert Franke, 1976. '*Su Ch'e*', in Herbert Franke, ed., *Sung Biographies*, pp. 882–85. Wiesbaden: Franz Steiner Verlag GMBH.

Shibunkai 斯文會 comp., 1938. *Shisei Bunsen'o* 至聖文宣王 (Foremost Sage and King of Propagating Culture). Tokyo: Shibunkai.

Shisan jing zhushu 十三經注疏 (1816), 1980, 2 vols., ed. by Ruan Yuan 阮元. Beijing: Zhonghua shuju.

Shryock, John K., 1937. *The Study of Human Abilities: the Jen wu chih of Liu Shao.* New Haven: American Oriental Society.

—— 1966. *The Origin and Development of the State Cult of Confucius.* New York: American Historical Association, 1932. Rpt, New York: Paragon Book Reprint Corp.

Shun Kwong-loi, 1997a. *Mencius and Early Chinese Thought.* Stanford University Press.

—— 1997b. 'Mencius on Jen-hsing', *Philosophy East and West*, 47, 1 (Jan.): 1–20.

Sima Guang 司馬光, 1966. *Zizhi tongjian* 資治通鑑. Beijing: Zhonghua shuju.

Sima Qian 司馬遷, 1962. *Shi Ji* 史記 (The Records of the Historian). Beijing: Zhonghua shuju.

Sirhakŭi Ch'ŏlhak, 1996. Seoul: Yemun Sŭwŏn.

Sivin, Nathan, 1969a. *Cosmos and Computation in Early Chinese Mathematical Astronomy.* Leiden: E.J. Brill.

—— 1969b. 'On the Pao p'u tzu neip'ien and the Life of Ko Hung (283–343), *Isis*, 60: 388–91.

Smith, Kidder, Jr., Peter K. Bol, Joseph A. Adler, and Don J. Wyatt, 1990. *Sung Dynasty Uses of the* I Ching. Princeton University Press.

Smith, Warren W., 1959. *Confucianism in Modern Japan: A Study in Conservatism in Japanese Intellectual History.* Tokyo: Hokuseido Press.

Sommer, Deborah, 1993. 'Ch'iu Chun (1421–1495) 'On the Conduct of Sacrificial Offerings', Ph.D. disseration. Columbia University.

—— 1994. 'Images into Words: Ming Confucian Iconoclasm', *National Palace Museum Bulletin*, 14: 1–24.

—— 2002. 'Destroying Confucius: Iconoclasm in the Confucian Temple', in Thomas A. Wilson, ed., *On Sacred Grounds: Culture, Society, Politics, and the Formation of the Cult of Confucius.* Harvard University Press.

—— 2003. 'Ritual and Sacrifice in Early Confucianism: Contacts with the Spirit World', in Mary Evelyn Tucker and Tu Wei-ming, eds., *Confucian Spirituality*, vol. I, pp. 199–221. New York: Crossroad.

Song, Cze-tong and Julia Ching, 1976. 'Hsueh Hsuan', in L. Carrington Goodrich and Fang Chao-ying, *Dictionary of Ming Biography*, vol. II, pp. 616–19. New York: Columbia.

Song Dingzong 宋鼎宗, 1979. *Chunqiu Hu shi xue* 春秋胡氏學. Taipei: 文史哲出版社.

Sŏng Hon, 1976. *Ugye Sŏngsaeng Munjip.* Seoul: Kyŏng-inmunhwasa.

Song shi 宋史, 1977 (1345), by Toghto (Tuotuo 脫脫) *et al.* Beijing: Zhonghua shuju.

Song Yŏng-ah, 1995. *Pulssi chappyŏn ŭl Chungshimŭro.* Sŏnggyungwan University MA Thesis.

Song–Yuan xuean 宋元學案 (Records of Song-Yuan Scholars), 1966 reprint., by Huang Zongxi 黃宗羲 and Quan Zuwan 全祖望. Beijing: Zhonghua Shuju.

Soothill, William Edward, 1910. *The Analects of Confucius.* Edinburgh: Oliphant, Anderson, Ferrier.

—— 1923. *The Three Religions of China.* London: Oxford University Press.

—— 1927. *A History of China.* London: Ernest Benn Limited.

—— 1930. *The Lotus of the Wonderful Law.* Oxford: Clarendon Press.

—— 1937. *A Dictionary of Chinese Buddhist Terms.* London: K. Paul, Trench, Trubner & Co., Ltd.

Spade, Beatrice, 1979. 'The Education of Women in China during the Southern Dynasties', *Journal of Asian History*, 13, 1 (1979): 15–41.

Spae, Joseph John, 1948. *Itô Jinsai: A Philosopher, Educator, and Sinologist of the Tokugawa Period.* Monumenta Serica Monograph XII. Peiping: The Catholic University of Peking edition.

Spence, Jonathan D., 1990. *The Search for Modern China.* New York: W.W. Norton.

Spiro, Audrey, 1990. *Contemplating the Ancients: Aesthetic and Social Issues in Early Chinese Portraiture.* Berkeley: University of California Press.

Standaert, Nicolas, 1988. *Yang Tingyun, Confucian and Christian in Late Ming China: His Life and Thought.* Leiden: E.J. Brill.

—— 1995. 'The Discovery of the Center through the Periphery: A Preliminary Study of Feng Youlan's *History of Chinese Philosophy* (New Version)', *Philosophy East and West*, 45: 569–89.

Steele, John., tr. 1917. *The I-li, or Book of Etiquette and Ceremonial.* London: Probsthain.

—— 1966. *The I-Li.* (rpt) 2 vols. Taipei, Ch'eng-wen Publishing Company.

Su Tianjueh 蘇天爵, 1970. *Zixi wengao* 滋溪文稿. National Central Library reprint of Yuan edition. Taipei.

Su Yu 蘇輿, 1992. *Chunqiu fanlu yizheng* 春秋繁露義證 (Commentary on the Luxuriant Dew of the Spring and Autumn Annals). Beijing: Zhonghua shuju.

Sui shu 隋書 (636) 1973, in 6 vols, by Wei Zheng 魏徵. Beijing: Zhonghua shuju.

Sun Kekuan 孫克寬, 1968. *Yuandai Hanwenhua zhi huodong* 元代漢文化之活動. Taipei: Zhonghua shuju.

—— 1976. *Yuandai Jinhua xueshu* 元代金華學述. Taizhong: 東海大學出版社.

—— 1981. 'Yu Chi and Southern Taoism during the Yuan period', in J.D. Langlois, ed., *China Under Mongol Rule*, pp. 212–53. Princeton University Press.

Sun Qifeng 孫奇逢, 1880. *Lixue zongchuan* 理學宗傳.

Sun Shangyang 孫尚揚, 1994. *Mingmo tianzhujiao yu ruxue de jiaoliu he chongtu* 明末天主教與儒學的交流和衝突. Taipei: Wenjin.

Sun Yirang 孫詒讓, 1987. *Zhou li zhengyi* 周禮正義 (The meaning of the Rites of Zhou). Beijing: Zhonghua shuju.

Swann, Nancy Lee, 1932. *Pan Chao: Foremost Woman Scholar of China.* New York: Russell & Russell.

Taam Cheuk-woon, 1953. 'On Studies of Confucius', *Philosophy East and West*, 3: 147–65.

Tahara Tsuguo, 1991. *Soraigaku no sekai.* Tokyo daigaku shuppansha.

Tahara Tsugho and Morimoto Junichirô, comp., 1970. *Yamaga Sokô, Nihon shisô taikei*, vol. XXXII. Tokyo: Iwanami shoten.

Takahata Tsunenobu 高洠常信, 1976. *Cho Nanken shu jinmei sakui* 張南軒集人名索引, Nagoya: 采華書林.

—— 1996. *Sodai konangaku no kenkyu* 宋代湖南學の研究. Tokyo: 武藏野, 秋山書店.

Takeuchi Yoshio 武內義雄, 1979. *Rongo no kenkyu* 論語之研究 (1st edn 1939), in *Takeuchi Yoshio zenshu* 武內義雄全集, 10 vols. Tokyo: 岩波書店, vol. I.

Tang Chun-i, 1970. 'The Development of the Concept of Moral Mind from Wang Yang-ming to Wang Chi', In *Self and Society in Ming Thought*. New York: Columbia University Press.

Tang huiyao 唐會要 (961), 1955. 2 vols. ed. by Wang Fu 王溥 *et al.* Beijing: Zhonghua shujiu.

Tang Junyi, 1966. 'Zhong Yong zhi chengdao' 中庸之誠道 (The Way of Self-completion in the Zhongyong), in *Zhongguo zhexue yuanlun* 中國哲學原論 (A Fundamental Discussion of Chinese Philosophy). Hong Kong: Rensheng chubanshe.

Tang Kailin 唐凱麟 and Cao Gang 曹剛, 2000. *Chongshi Chuangtong: Rujia Sixiang de Xiandai Jiazhi Pinggu* 重釋傳統: 儒家思想的現代價值評估 (Reinterpreting Tradition:

Evaluating the Contemporary Value of Confucian Thought). Shanghai: China Eastern Normal University Press.

Tang Yijie 湯一介, 1983. *Guo Xiang yu Wei-Jin xuanxue* 郭象與魏晉玄學. Wuhan: Hubei renmin chubanshe.

Tang Yongtong 湯用彤, 1957. *Wei-Jin Xuan xue lungao* 魏晉玄學論稿. Beijing: *Renmin chubanshe*.

Tang Yuyuan 唐宇元, 1982. *Yuandaide Zhu Lu heliu yu Yuandaide lixue* 元代的朱陸合流與元代的理學 (The Unification of Chu and Lu and Neo-Confucianism in the Yuan Period). *Wenshi zhe* 文史哲, 3 (1982): 3–12.

Tang Zhijun 湯志鈞, 1995. Jingxueshi lunji 經學史論集 (Collected Essays on History of Confucian Learning). Taipei: Daan chubenshe.

Taylor, Rodney Leon, 1978. *The Cultivation of Sagehood As A Religious Goal in Neo-Confucianism: A Study of Selected Writings of Kao P'an-lung (1562–1626)*. Missoula, Mont.: Scholars Press.

—— 1986. *The Way of Heaven: An Introduction to the Confucian Religious Life*. Leiden: E.J. Brill.

—— 1988. *The Confucian Way of Contemplation: Okada Takehiko and the Tradition of Quiet-Sitting*. Columbia, S.C.: University of South Carolina Press.

—— 1990a. 'Official and Popular Religion and the Political Organization of Chinese Society in the Ming', in Kwang-ching Liu, ed., *Orthodoxy in Late Imperial China*, pp. 126–57. Berkeley: University of California Press.

—— 1990b. *The Religious Dimension of Confucianism*. Albany, N.Y.: State University of New York Press.

—— 1997. 'Chu Hsi and Meditation', in Irene Bloom & Joshua A. Fogel, eds., *Meeting Of Minds: Intellectual and Religious Interaction in East Asian Traditions of Thought: Essays in Honor of Wing-Tsit Chan and William Theodore De Bary*. New York: Columbia University Press.

Teng, Ai-min, 1986. 'On Chu Hsi's Theory of the Great Ultimate', in Wing-tsit Chan, ed., *Chu Hsi and Neo-Confucianism*. Honolulu: University of Hawaii Press.

Teng Ssu-yu, 1968. *Family Instructions for the Yen Clan*. Leiden: E.J. Brill.

Teng Ssu-yu and Knight Biggerstaff, 1971. *An Annotated Bibliography of Selected Chinese Reference Works*, 3rd edn. Cambridge, MA: Harvard University Press.

Thomsen, Rudi, 1988. *Ambition and Confucianism: A Biography of Wang Mang*. Aarhus University Press.

Thrasher, A.R., 1985. 'The Role of Music in Chinese Culture'. *The World of Music*, 27, 1: 3–17.

Tian Hao 田浩, 1996. *Zhu Xi de siwei shijie* 朱熹的思維世界 (Chu Hsi's World of Thought). Taipei: Yunchen.

Tian Wenjun 田文軍, 1990. *Fung, Yu-lan xinlixue yanjiu* 馮友蘭新理學研究 (Studies in Fung, Yu-lan's New Principle-Centered Learning). Wuhan Press.

Tillman, Hoyt C., 1982. *Utilitarian Confucianism: Ch'en Liang's Challenge to Chu Hsi*. Cambridge, MA: Harvard University, Council on East Asian Studies.

—— 1992a. 'A New Direction in Confucian Scholarship: Approaches to Examining the Differences between Neo-Confucianism and Tao-hsueh', *Philosophy East and West*, 42.3 July: 455–74.

—— 1992b. *Confucian Discourse and Chu Hsi's Ascendancy*. Honolulu: University of Hawaii Press.

—— 1994. *Ch'en Liang on Public Interest and the Law*. Honolulu: University of Hawaii Press.

—— 2000. 'Reflections on Classifying "Confucian" Lineages With Special Reference to Sung Reinventions of Tradition', in Benjamin Elman, Herman Ooms, John Duncan, and Alexander Woodside, eds., *Rethinking Confucianism: Past and Present in China, Japan, Korea, and Vietnam*. Los Angles: Asia Pacific Center Monograph Series.

—— 2001. 'Translator's Epilogue: Controversy over Confucian Ethics in East Asian Economic Development' in *Business as a Vocation: The Autobiography of Mr. Wu Ho-su, by Huang chin-shing*. Cambridge, MA: Harvard University Press and the East Asian Monograph Series of the Harvard Law School.

—— 2004. 'Zhu Xi's Prayers to the Spirit of Confucius and Claim to the Transformation of the Way', *Philosophy East and West*, Volume 54, No. 4.

Tjan Tjoe Som, 1949. *Po Hu T'ung* 白虎通. *The Comprehensive Discussions in the White Tiger Hall*. Vol. 1, *Introduction; Translation of Chapters I, II, XVIII, XL; Notes. A Contribution to the History of Classical Studies in the Han Period*. Sinica Leidensia Edidit Institutum Sinologicum Lugduno Batavum, vol. 6. Leiden: E.J. Brill.

Tokuda Susumu 德田進, 1963. *Koshi setsuwashu no kenkyu – nijuyoko chushin ni* 孝子說話集の研究 – 二十四孝を中心に (Studies on Filial Offspring Tales, with a Special Emphasis on the Twenty-Four Filial Exemplars). 3 vols. Tokyo: Inoue shobo.

Tong dian 通典 (801), 1936, by Du You 杜佑. Shitong 十通 edition. Shanghai: Shangwu yinshu guan 商務印書館.

Ts'ai Jen-hou (Cai Renhou 蔡仁厚), 1982. *Song Ming Lixue: Beisongpian* 宋明理學: 北宋篇 (Song–Ming Neo-Confucianism, Northern Song volume), 3rd edn. Taipei: Xuesheng shuju.

—— 1986. 'A Reappraisal of Chu Hsi's Philosophy', in Wing-tsit Chan, ed., *Chu Hsi and Neo-Confucianism*, pp. 461–79. Honolulu: University of Hawaii Press.

Tsien Tsuen-hsuin, 1962. *Written on Bamboo and Silk: The Beginnings of Chinese Books and Inscriptions*. Chicago and London: the University of Chicago Press.

Tu Wei-ming 杜維明 1976a. *Centrality and Commonality: An Essay on Chung-yung*. Honolulu: University Press of Hawaii.

—— 1976b. *Neo-Confucian Thought in Action: Wang Yang-ming's Youth (1472–1509)*. Berkeley: University of California Press.

—— 1978. *Humanity and Self-Cultivation: Essays in Confucian Thought*. Berkeley: Asian Humanities Press.

—— 1982. 'Towards an Understanding of Liu Yin's Confucian Eremitism', in W.T. de Bary, and Chan Hok-lam, eds., *Yuan Thought*. New York: Columbia University Press.

—— 1984. *Confucian Ethics Today: The Singapore Challenge*. Singapore: Curriculum Development Institute of Singapore, Federal Publications.

—— 1985. *Confucian Thought: Selfhood as Creative Transformation*. New York: State University of New York Press.

—— 1986. 'Toward a Third Epoch of Confucian Humanism: A Background Understanding', in Irene Eber, ed., *Confucianism: The Dynamics of Tradition*. New York: Macmillan.

—— 1989. *Centrality and Commonality: An Essay on Confucian Religiousness*. Albany, N.Y.: State University of New York Press.

—— 1991. *The Triadic Chord: Confucian Ethics, Industrial East Asia, and Max Weber: Proceedings of the 1987 Singapore Conference on Confucian Ethics and the Modernisation of Industrial East Asia*. Singapore: Institute of East Asian Philosophies.

—— 1993a. 'Confucianism', in Arvind Sharma, ed., *Our Religions*. Harper Collins Publishers.

—— 1993b. *Way, Learning, and Politics: Essays on the Confucian Intellectual*. Albany: State University of New York Press.

—— 1994. *China in Transformation*. Cambridge, MA: Harvard University Press.

Tu Wei-ming, ed., 1994. *The Living Tree: The Changing Meaning of Being Chinese Today*. Stanford University Press.

—— 1995. 'Confucius and Confucianism', in *The New Encyclopaedia Britannica*, ed. R. McHenry, pp. 653–62. Chicago: Encyclopaedia Britannica, Inc.

—— ed., 1996. *Confucian Traditions in East Asian Modernity: Moral Education and Economic Culture in Japan and the Four Mini-Dragons*. Cambridge, MA: Harvard University Press.

—— 1998. 'Probing the "Three Bonds" and "Five Relationships" in Confucian Humanism', in Walter H. Slote and George A. DeVos, eds., *Confucianism and the Family*, pp. 121–36. Albany: State University Press of New York.

Tu Wei-ming and W.T. de Bary, eds., 1997. *Confucianism and Human Rights*. New York: Columbia University Press.

Tu Wei-ming, Milan Hejtmanek and Alan Wachman, eds., 1992. *The Confucian World Observed: A Contemporary Discussion of Confucian Humanism in East Asia*. Honolulu: The East-West Center.

Tucker, John Allen, 1989. *Moral and Spiritual Cultivation in Japanese Confucianism: The Life and Thought of Kaibara Ekken (1630–*1714)*. Albany: State University of New York Press.

—— 1998. *Itô Jinsai's Gomô jigi and the Philosophical Definition of Early Modern Japan*. Leiden: E.J. Brill.

Tuo Tuo 脫脫, *et al.*, 1977. *Song shi* 宋史. Beijing: Zhonghua shuju.

Twitchett, Denis and Michael Loewe, eds., 1986. *The Cambridge History of China, volume I: The Ch'in and Han Empires, 221 B.C.–A.D. 220*. Cambridge University Press

Ubelhor, Monika, 1968, 1969. 'Hsu Kuang-ch'i und seine Einstellung zum Christentum', *Oriens Extremus* 15 (1968): 191–257 (I); 16 (1969): 41–74 (II).

Uno Tetsuto 宇野哲人, 1924. *Zhûgaku shi* 儒學史, Vol. 1, Tokyo: Hôbunkan.

Unschuld, Paul U., 1985. *Medicine in China: A History of Ideas*. Berkeley: University of California Press.

van der Loon, P., 1952. 'On the Transmission of Kuan-tzu'; *T'oung Pao*, 41: 4–5: 357–93.

van Ess, Hans, 1993. *Politik und Gelehrsamkeit in der Zeit der Han – Die Alttext/Neutext-Kontroverse*, Wiesbaden: Otto Harrassowitz.

—— 1994. 'The Old Text/New Text Controversy: Has the 20th Century Got it Wrong?', *T'oung pao*, 80: 146–70.

van Norden, Bryan W., 1992. 'Mengzi and Xunzi: Two Views of Human Agency', *International Philosophical Quarterly*, 32: 161–84.

van Zoeren, Steven, 1991. *Poetry and Personality: Reading, Exegesis, and Hermeneutics in Traditional China*. Stanford University Press.

Veith, Ilza, 1966. *Huang Ti Nei Ching Su Wên: The Yellow Emperor's Classic of Internal Medicine*. Berkeley: University of California Press.

von Falkenhausen, Lothar, 1996. 'The Concept of Wen in the Ancient Chinese Ancestral Cult' in *Chinese Literature: Essays, Articles, Reviews*, 18: 1–22.

von Zach, Erwin, tr., 1939. *Yang Hsiung's Fa-Yen (Worte strenger Ermahnung)*. Batavian: Drukkerij Lux.

Waley, Arthur, 1937. *The Book of Songs: The Ancient Chinese Classic of Poetry*. London: Allen & Unwin.

—— 1938. *The Analects of Confucius*. London, George Allen and Unwin. rpt Vintage, 1989.

—— 1939. *Three Ways of Thought in Ancient China*. London: George Allen & Unwin.

Waley, Arthur, 1949. *The Life and Times of Po Chu-i*. London: George Allen and Unwin.

Wallacker, Benjamin. 1972. 'Liu An, Second King of Huai-nan (180?–122 B.C.). *Journal of the American Oriental Society*, 92: 36–49.

—— 1978. 'Han Confucianism and Confucius in Han', in David T. Roy and Tsuen-hsuin Tsien eds., *Ancient China: Studies in Early Civilization*, pp. 215–28. Hong Kong: The Chinese University Press.

Waltner, Ann, 1990. *Getting an Heir: Adoption and the Construction of Kinship in Late Imperial China*. Honolulu: University of Hawaii Press.

Wang Aihe, 2000. *Cosmology and Political Culture in Early China*. Cambridge University Press.

Wang Baoxuan 王葆玹, 1994, *Xi Han jingxue yuanliu* 西漢經學源流 (*Origin and Development of Canonical Studies in Western Han Times*), Taipei: Dongda tushu gongsi.

Wang Cheng 王偁, 1782. *Dongdu shilue* 東都事略 (Anecdotes from the Eastern Capital). Siku quanshu edition.

Wang Chong 王充, 1994. Lun Heng 論衡 (Balanced Discussions), rpt. Beijing: Zhonghua shuju.

Wang Fu 王溥 (961), 1955. *Tang Huiyao* 唐會要. Beijing: Zhonghua shuju.

Wang Fuzhi 王夫之, 1962. *Shang Shu Yinyi* 尚書引義 (Elaborations on the Book of Documents). Beijing: Zhonghua Shuju.

Wang Gen 王艮, 1912. *Mingru wang Xinzhai xiansheng yiji* 明儒王心齋先生遺集 (Bequeathed Works of the Ming Confucian Wang Gen). Shanghai: Guocui xuebao guan.

Wang Guowei 王國維, 1956. 'Han Wei boshi kao' 漢魏博士考, in *Guantang jilin* 觀堂集林, vol. IV, pp. 43–55. Taipei: Yiwen 藝文, 1956 rpt.

Wang Jin 王進, Yang Jianghua 揚江華, eds., 1989. *Zhongguo Dangpai Shituan Cidian* 中國黨派社團辭典. Beijing: Zhonggong Dangshi Ziliao Chubanshe 中共黨史出版社 (Press of the Materials of the Chinese Communist Party).

Wang Jing-zhi 王靜芝, 1971. 'Kongzi yu Liujing zhong de Yue' 孔子與六經中的樂 (Confucius and the Yue in the Six Classics), *Academic Journal on Confucius and Mencius*, vol. 21: 1–14.

Wang Kaifu 王開府, 1978. *Hu Wufeng de xinxue* 胡五峰的心學. Taipei: Xuesheng shuju.

Wang Liqi, 1980. *Yanshi jiaxun jijie*. Shanghai guji chubanshe.

Wang Maohong 王懋竑, 1973. *Zhu Zi Nianpu* 朱子年譜 (Year by Year Chronicle of Master Zhu). Taipei: Shijie.

Wang Meng'o 王夢鷗, 1984. *Li Ji Jinzhu Jinyi* 禮記今註今譯 (Modern Commentary and Translation of The Book of Rites). Taipei: Commercial Press.

Wang Ming 王明, 1983. *Baopuzi neipian jiaoshi* 抱扑子內篇校釋 Beijing: Zhonghua, second edn.

Wang Pin 王蘋 (1782). *Wang Zhuzuo ji* 王著作集 (The Literary Collection of Editorial Director Wang). Siku quanshu edition.

Wang Shiyi 王拾遺, 1983. *Bai Juyi zhuan* 白居易傳 (A Biography of Bai Juyi). Xi'an: Shaanxi renmin chubanshe.

Wang Shouren, 1992. *Wang Yangming quanji* 王陽明全集 2 vols. Shanghai guji chubanshe.

Wang, Simon Man-Ho and Lloyd Sciban, 1999. 'Liu Zongzhou's Criticism of Wang Yangming's Teachings' *Journal of Chinese Philosophy* 26: 2 (June).

Wang Su 王肅, 1990. *Kongzi jiayu* 孔子家語. Shanghai Guji chubanshe.

Wang Tingxiang 王廷相, 1989. *Wang Tingxiang ji* 王廷相集 (Collected Writings of Wang Tingxiang). Beijing: Zhonghua shuju.

Wang Xianqian 王先謙, 1988. *Xunzi jijie* 荀子集解 (Collected Commentaries on the Xunzi). 2 vols. Beijing: Zhonghua shuju.

Wang Xianshen 王先慎. 1998. *Han Fei zi jijie* 韓非子集解 (Collected Commentaries on the *Hanfeizi*). Beijing: Zhonghua shuju.

Wang Ying Zhi 王英志, ed., 1993. *Yuan mei quan ji, Nan jing: Jiang su gu ji chu ban she* 袁枚全集. Nanjing: Jiangsu guji chubanshe 江蘇古籍出社.

Wang Yu 王煜, 1987. 'Li Gang sixiang yanjiu' 李綱思想研究 (Research on the Thought of Li Gang), *Zhongguo wenhua yuekan* 中國文化月刊, 1987, 10: 73–95.

Wang Zhongjiang 王中江 and Gao Xiuchang 高秀昌, eds., 1995. *Fung, Yu-lan xueji* 馮友蘭學記 (Notes from Studies on Fung, Yu-lan). Beijing: Three Connections Bookstore.

Wang Zicai 王梓才 and Feng Yunhao, 1962. *Song Yuan xuean buyi* 宋元學案補遺 (Supplement to the Schools of Song and Yuan Learning). Taipei: Shijie shuju edition.

Ware, James, 1960. *The Sayings of Mengzi*. New York, Mentor Books.

—— 1967. *Alchemy, Medicine and Religion in the China of A.D. 320: The Nei-p'ien of Ko Hung.* Cambridge, MA: MIT Press.

Watanabe Hiroshi, 1985. *Kinsei Nihon shakai to Sôgaku.* Tokyô: Daigaku Shuppankai.

Watson, Burton, 1958. *Ssu-ma Ch'ien, Grand Historian of China.* New York, Columbia University Press.

—— tr. 1963. *Hsun Tzu: Basic Writings.* New York: Columbia University Press.

—— tr. 1964. *Han Fei Tzu, Basic Writings.* New York: Columbia University Press.

—— tr. 1968. *The Book of Chuang Tzu.* New York: Columbia University Press.

—— tr. 1974. *Courtier and Commoner in Ancient China: Selections from the* History of the Former Han *by Pan Ku.* New York: Columbia University Press.

—— tr. 1989. *The Tso chuan. Selections from China's Oldest Narrative History.* New York, Columbia University Press.

—— tr. 1993a. *Records of the Grand Historian: Qin Dynasty.* The Chinese University of Hong Kong and Columbia University Press.

—— tr. 1993b. *Records of the Grand Historian: Han Dynasty II*, rev. edn. New York: Columbia University Press.

Watson, James L., and Evelyn S. Rawski, eds. 1988. *Death Ritual in Late Imperial and Modern China. Studies on China*, 8. Berkeley: University of California Press.

Weber, Max, 1951. *The Religion of China: Confucianism and Taoism* (Konfuzianismus und Taoismus, 1922), tr., Hans H. Gerth. New York: Free Press.

Wechsler, Harold, 1974. *Mirror to the Son of Heaven: Wei Cheng at the Court of T'ang T'ai-tsung.* New Haven and London: Yale University Press.

—— 1985. *Offerings of Jade and Silk: Ritual and Symbol in the Legitimation of the T'ang Dynasty.* New Haven: Yale University Press.

Wei Jichang 魏際昌, 1988. *Tongcheng guwne xuepai xiaoshi* 桐城古文學派小史. Shijiazhuang: Xinhua Shudian.

Wen Yiduo 聞一多, 1984. *Gu dian xin yi* 古典新義, in *Wen Yiduo quanji* 聞一多全集 1948, rpt. Shanghai Guji chubanshe, 1984, vol. 2.

Wenxian tongkao 文獻通考 (1322) 1936, by Ma Duanlin 馬端臨. Shitong 十通 ed. Shanghai: Shangwu yinshu guan 商務印書館.

Whyte, Martin King, 1974. *Small Groups and Political Rituals in China.* Berkeley: University of California.

Wilhelm, Richard (1910), 1955. *Kungfutse, Gesprache (Lun Yu).* Jena: Eugen Diederichs Verlag; repr. Eugen Diederichs Verlag, Dusseldorf-Koln.

—— 1916. *Mong Dsi (Mong Ko).* Jena: Eugen Diederichs.

—— 1950. *The I Ching or Book of Changes*, trans. Cary F. Baynes, Bollingen Series 19. New York: Princeton University Press.

—— 1959. 'I-ching Oracles in the Tso-chuan and the Kuo-yu', *JAOS* 79, 4, pp. 275–80.

Wilkinson, Endymion, 1998. *Chinese History: A Manual.* Cambridge, MA: Harvard University Press.

Williams, E.T., 1936. 'Agricultural rites in China', *Journal of the North China Branch, Royal Asiatic Society*, 57.

Williamson, H.R., 1935–7. *Wang An Shih: A Chinese Statesman and Educationalist of the Sung Dynasty*, 2 vols., London: A. Probsthain.

Wilson, Thomas A., 1995. *Genealogy of the Way: The Construction and Uses of the Confucian Tradition in Late Imperial China.* Stanford University Press.

—— 1996. 'The Ritual Formation of Confucian Orthodoxy and the Descendants of the Sage', *The Journal of Asian Studies*, 55.3 (Aug.): 559–84.

—— 2002. 'Ritualizing Confucius (Kongzi): The Family and State Cults of the Sage of Culture in Imperial China', in Thomas A. Wilson, ed., *On Sacred Grounds: Culture, Society, Politics, and the Formation of the Cult of Confucius.* Harvard University Press.

Wong, David, 1989. 'Universalism versus Love with Distinctions', *Journal of Chinese Philosophy*, 16: 252–72.

—— 1991. 'Is There a Distinction between Reason and Emotion in Mencius? And a reply to a commentary by Craig Ihara' *Philosophy East and West*, 41: 31–58.

Wood, Alan T., 1995. *Limits to Autocracy: From Sung Neo-Confucianism to a Doctrine of Political Rights*. Honolulu: University of Hawaii Press.

Wright, Mary Clabaugh, 1957. *The Last Stand of Chinese Conservatism: The Tung-chih Restoration, 1862–1874*. Stanford University Press.

Wu Feng and Song Yifu, eds., 1992. *Zhonghua Ruxue Tongdian* 中華儒學通典 (Dictionary of Chinese Confucianism). Haikou: Nanhai chubanshe.

Wu Hung, 1989. *The Wu Liang Shrine: The Ideology of Early Chinese Pictorial Art*. Stanford University Press.

—— 1995. *Monumentality in Early Chinese Art and Architecture*. Stanford University Press.

Wu Jiamo 吳嘉謨, 1589. *Kongsheng Jiayu Tu* 孔聖家語圖 (Illustrated Sayings of the Sage Confucius' Family). Hangzhou: Wu Jiamo.

Wu Wen-zhang 吳文璋, 1994. *Xunzi de Yinyue Zhexue* 荀子的音樂哲學 (Xunzi's Philosophy of Music). Taipei: Wenjin Press.

Wu Yi, 1986. *Chinese Philosophical Terms*. Lanham, MD: University Press of America.

Wu Yu 吳虞, 1922. Wu Yu wenlu 吳虞文錄 (Collected Works of Wu Yu). Shanghai: Oriental Book.

Wyatt, Don J., 1996. *The Recluse of Loyang: Shao Yung and the Moral Evolution of Early Sung Thought*. Honolulu: University of Hawaii Press.

—— 1999. 'Bonds of Certain Consequence: The Personal Responses to Concubinage of Wang Anshi and Sima Guang', in Sherry J. Mou, ed., *Presence and Presentation: Women in the Chinese Literati Tradition*. New York: St. Martin's Press.

Xi Zezong 席澤宗 and Wu Deduo 吳德鐸, eds., 1986. *Xu Guangqi yanjiu lunwenji* 徐光啟研究論文集. Shanghai: Xuelin chubanshe.

Xia Nairu 夏乃儒, 2000. 'Kongzi de Yiliguan yu Dangdai de Wenhua Jianshe' '孔子的義利觀與當代的文化建設' ('Confucius' View of (the Relationship between) Rightness and Benefit and (its Value for) Contemporary Cultural Construction', in Zhu Ruikai 祝瑞開, ed., *Ruxue yu Ershiyi Shiji Zhongguo – Goujian, Fazhan 'Dangdai Xinruxue'* 儒學與二十一世紀中國 – 構建, 發展 '當代新儒學' (*Confucianism and 21st Century China – Constructing and Advancing 'Contemporary New Confucianism'*). Shanghai: Xuelin Press.

Xin Sanzijing 新三字經, 1995. ed. Huang Huahua, *et al.* Canton: Guangdong Provincial Editorial Committee; foreign edn. Hong Kong: Joint Publishing Committee.

Xin Tang shu 新唐書 (1060), 1975. 20 vols., by Ouyang Xiu 歐陽修. Beijing: Zhonghua shuju.

Xinya yanjiusuo 新亞研究所 (New Asia Research Center), ed. 1981. *Xinya jiaoyu* 新亞教育 (*New Asia Education*). Hong Kong: New Asia Research Center.

Xiong Shili 熊十力, 1985. *Xin weishi lun* 新唯識論 (*New Doctrine of Mere Consciousnessi*). Beijing: Zhonghua Bookstore.

—— 1988a. *Lun Liu Jing* 論六經 (*On the Six Scriptures*). Taiwan: Ming Wen Book Company.

—— 1988b. *Yuan Ru* 原儒 (*On the Ru*). Taiwan: Ming Wen Book Company.

—— 1989. *Shili yuyao* 十力語要 (*Important Discussions of (Xiong) Shili*). Taipei: Mingwen Bookstore.

Xu Duanrong 許端容, 1981. 'Ershisixiao yanjiu' 二十四孝研究. M.A. thesis, Zhongguo wenhua daxue.

Xu Fuguan, 徐復觀, 1963. *Zhongguo renxing lunshi* 中國人性論史 (A History of the Concept of Human Nature in China). Taizhong: Donghai daxue chubanshe.

Xu Guangqi ji 徐光啟集, 1984. ed. by Wang Zhongmin 王重民. Shanghai: Shanghai guji chubanshe.

Xu Jijun 徐吉軍, He Yunao 賀雲翱, 1991. *Zhongguo sangzang lisu* 中國喪葬禮俗 (Chinese Funerary and Burial Customs). Hangzhou: Zhejiang People's Press.

Xu Kangsheng 許康生, ed., 1989. *Wei Jin xuanxue shi* 魏晉玄學史, Xi'an: Shaanxi shifan daxue chubanshe.

Xu Song 徐松, 1984. *Dengke jikao* 登科記考 (A Study of the Record of Examination Graduates). Beijing: Zhonghua shuju.

Xu Tianlin 徐天麟 (1226), 1980. *Dong Han huiyao* 東漢會要. Taipei: Shijie shuju.

Xu Yingpu 徐映璞, 1989. *Kongzhi nanzong kaolue* 孔氏南宗考略. 1946. In *Nanzong shengdi: Quzhou Kongshi jiamiao* 南宗聖地衢州孔氏家廟, Quzhou: Internal documents 內部資料.

Xu Zhen'e 徐震堮, 1984. *Shishuo xinyu jiaojian* 世說新語校箋. Beijing: Zhonghua shuju.

Xu zizhi tongjian 續資治通鑑 (1801), 1957, by Bi Yuan 畢沅. Beijing: Zhonghua shuju.

Xue Jixuan 薛季宣. *Lang yu ji* 浪語集 (Collected words of Xue Jixuan). Congshu jicheng edition.

Yamashita, Samuel Hideo, 1994. *Master Sorai's Responsals: An Annotated Translation of Sorai Sensei Tômonsho*. Honolulu: University of Hawaii.

Yan Binggang 顏炳罡, 1995. *Zhenghe Yu Chongzhu: Dangdai Da Ru Mou Zongsan Xiansheng Sixiang Yanjiu* 整合與重鑄: 當代大儒牟宗三先生思想研究 (*Conformity and Recasting: Studies in the Ideas of the Great Contemporary Confucian, Mou Zongsan*). Taipei: Student Bookstore.

Yan Ding 殷鼎, 1991. *Fung Yu-lan* 馮友蘭. Taipei: Great Eastern Library.

Yang Bojun 楊伯峻, 1960. *Mengzi yizhu* 孟子譯注, 2 vols. Beijing, Zhonghua shuju.

—— 1980. *Lunyu yizhu* 論語譯注. Beijing: Zhonghua shuju.

Yang Hongnian 楊鴻年, 1982. *Han Wei zhidu congkao* 漢魏制度叢考. Wuhan daxue 武漢大學.

Yang Hsien-yi and Gladys Yang, trans. 1979. *Selections from* Records of the Historian. Beijing: Foreign Languages Press.

Yang Jialuo 楊家駱, ed. 1997. *Xinjiaoben Shiji sanjia zhu bing fubian erzhong* 新校本史記三家注並附編二種 (New edition of the *Records of the Historian* with the Commentaries of Three Schools and Two Supplements). Taipei: Dingwen shuju.

Yang, Mayfair, 1994. *Gifts, Favors, and Banquets: The Art of Social Relationships in China*. Ithaca: Cornell University.

Yang Mingzhao 楊明照, 1991. *Baopuzi waipian jiaojian* 抱扑子外篇校箋. Beijing: Zhonghua shuju.

Yang Rubin, 1996. *Rujia shenti guan* 儒家身體觀 (Literati Perspectives on the Body). Taipei: Academia Sinica, Institute of Literature and Philosophy.

Yang Shenchu 楊慎初, 1986. *Yuelu shuyuan shilüe* 岳麓書院史略. Changsha 長沙: Yuelu shushe 岳麓書社.

Yang Shi 楊適, 1965. *Yang Guishan Ji* 楊龜山集, Zongshu jicheng jianpian edition. Taipei: Taiwan Shangwu.

Yang Zhen'e 楊振鶚, 1944. *Yang Qiyuan xiansheng nianpu* 楊淇園先生年譜. Chongqing: Shangwu yinshuguan; Shanghai Shangwu yinshuguan, 1946 (2nd edn).

Yao Xinzhong, 1996. *Confucianism and Christianity – A Comparative Study of Jen and Agape*. Brighton: Sussex Academic Press.

—— 2000. *An Introduction to Confucianism*. Cambridge University Press.

—— 2001. 'Who is a Confucian Today? – A Critical Reflection on the Issues Concerning Confucian Identity in Modern times', *Journal of Contemporary Religion*, 16, 3 (2001): 313–28.

Ye Shi 葉適, 1959. *Ye Shi ji* 葉適集 (Collected Writings of Ye Shi). 1230. Zhonghua shuju ed. Rpt. Beijing: Zhonghua.

—— 1977. *Xixue jiyan xumu* 習學記言序目 (An Orderly Presentation of Words Jotted Down while Studying). Beijing: Zhonghua shuju.

Yi Ae-hǔi, 1990. *Chosŏnhugi Insŏngwa Mulsŏng-e Taehan Chaengnonǔi Yŏn-gu*, Ph.D. dissertation. Koryo University.

Yi Byŏng-do, ed., 1947. *Samguk Sagi*. Seoul: Pagmunsa.

—— ed., 1956. *Samguk Yusa*. Seoul: Tongungmunhwasa.

—— 1972. *Hanguksa Taegwon*. Seoul: Pomungak.

—— 1987. *Hanguk Yuhaksa*. Seoul: Aseamunhwasa.

Yi Gan, *Oeamjip*. Seoul: Psalhaeng Sahang Pulmyŏng.

Yi Ga-won, 1989. *T'oegye Hakkǔp Kigyebo Jǒgyŏn-gu*. Seoul: T'oegyehak Yŏnguwon.

Yi I, 1968. *Yulgokjip*. Seoul: Minjong Munhwa Ch'ujinhoe.

—— 1985. *Yulgokjǔnjip: Sŏnghak chibyo*. Seoul: Hanguk Chŏngshin Munhwayŏnguwon.

Yi Jin-sang, 1980. *Ihakchong-yo*. Seoul: Hanguk Munhŏnyŏn-guso Aseamunhwasa.

—— 1982. *Hanjusŏnsŏ*. Seoul: Kyŏnginminsa.

Yi Jŏng-ho, 1976. *Chŏng Yŏk Yŏn-gu*. Kukchedaehak Inmunsahoegwa Gwahagyŏnguso.

—— 1998. *Hwadam-Sŏgyŏngdŏk*. Seoul: Iljisa.

Yi Nam-yŏng, 1987. *Sŏgyŏngdŏkǔi Kich'ŏlhaksa*. Seoul: Hanguk Ch'ŏlhakhwae – Tongmyŏngsa.

Yi Sang-ŭn, 1998. *Isang-ŭn Sŏnsaeng jŏnjip.* Seoul: Yemunsŏwon.

Yi Sang-ŭn, 1999. *T'oegyeŭi Saeng-aewa hangmun.* Seoul: Yemunsŏwon.

Yi Sŏng-mu, 1967. *Chosŏnŭi Sŏnggyun'gwan Yŏn-gu.* Seoul: Yŏksa Hakpu 35.36.

Yonezawa Yoshiho, 1974. *Japanese Painting in the Literati Style,* tr. Betty Iverson Monroe. New York: Weatherhill/Heibonsha.

Yoshikawa Kôjirô, 1983. *Jinsai, Sorai, Norinaga: Three Classical Philologists of Mid-Tokugawa Japan.* Tokyo: Tôhô Gakkai.

—— *et al.,* 1987. *Ogyû Sorai,* Nihon shisô taikei, vol. XXXVI. Tokyo: Iwanami shoten.

Yoshikawa Kôjirô and Shimizu Shigeru, 1971. *Itô Jinsai/Itô Tôgai,* Nihon shisô taikei, vol. XXXIII. Tokyo: Iwanami shoten.

Young, John D., 1980. *East–West Synthesis: Matteo Ricci and Confucianism.* Centre of Asian Studies, University of Hong Kong.

Yu, Yamanoi, 1986. 'The Great Ultimate and Heaven in Chu Hsi's Philosophy', in Wing-tsit Chan, ed., *Chu Hsi and Neo-Confucianism.* Honolulu: University of Hawaii Press.

Yu Ying-shih, 1986. 'Morality and Knowledge in Chu Hsi's Philosophical System', in Chan, Wing-tsit, ed. *Chu Hsi and Neo-Confucianism,* pp. 228–54. Honolulu: University of Hawaii Press.

Yu Yŏng-jong, 1987. *T'oegyewa Yulgokŭi Ch'ŏlhak.* Tong-ah Dae Ch'ul p'anbu.

Yu Zhengui 余振貴, 1986. *Wang Daiyu* 王岱與. Yinchuan: Ninxia renmin chubanshe.

Yuan Ji 袁冀, 1972. *Yuan Xu Luzhai pingshu* 元許魯齋評述 Taipei: Shangwu yinshuguan.

—— 1978. *Yuan Wu Caolu pingshu* 元吳草盧評述. Taipei: Shangwu yinshuguan.

Yuan shi 元史 (1370), 1976, in 15 vols., by Song Lian 宋濂. Beijing: Zhonghua shuju 中華書局.

Yuan Yingguang 袁英光 and Liu Yinsheng 劉寅生, 1996. *Wang Guowei nianpu changbian* 王國維年譜長編 (Expanded Version of the Chronological Biography of Wang Guowei). Tianjin renmin chubenshe.

Yugyo Sajon Pyonchan Wiwonhoe ed., 1990. *Yugyo taesajon.* Seoul: Tukpyolsi Pagyongsa (Chopan).

Yun Sa-sun, 1982. *Hanguk Yuhak Yŏngu.* Seoul: Hyŏnamsa.

Yuzo Mizoguchi and Leon Vandermeersch, eds., 1991. *Confucianisme et Societes Asiatiques.* Paris, Tokyo: L'Harmattan, Sophia University.

Zarrow, Peter, 1990. *Anarchism and Chinese Political Culture.* New York: Columbia University Press.

Zhang Bingnan, 1991. *Jixia gouchen* 稷下鉤沈. Shanghai guji chubanshe.

Zhang Boxing 張伯行 (1710), 1968. *Lianluo Guanmin shu* 濂洛關閩書 (Book of the (Neo-Confucian Learning of) Lianxi, Loyang, Guanzhong, and Fujian). Taipei: Commercial Press.

Zhang Changtai 張長臺, 1990. *Tangdai sanli yanjiu* 唐代喪禮研究. Taipei: Soochow University Press.

Zhang Chaorui 張朝瑞, 1594. *Kongmen chuandao lu* 孔門傳道錄, Yao Lixuan 姚履旋, *et al.* eds., 1598.

Zhang Delin 張德麟, 1986. *Cheng Mingdao Sixiang Yanjiu* 程明道思想研究 (Researches on Cheng Hao's Thought). Taipei: Student Books.

Zhang Hui-hui 張蕙慧, 1991. *Zhongguo Gudai Yuejiao Sixiang Lunji* 中國古代樂教思想論集 (A Collection of Treatises of Chinese Ancient Thought on Musical Disciplines). Taipei: Wenjin Press.

Zhang Liwen 張立文, 1994. *Qi* 氣. Taipei: Hanxing shuju.

—— 1996. *Hehe xue gailun* 和合學概論, vols. I–II. Beijing: Shoudu Shifan chubanshe.

Zhang Qingchang 張清常 and Wang Yandong 王延棟, 1993. *Zhanguoce jianzhu* 戰國策箋注 (The Annotated Annals of the Warring States). Tianjin: Nankai daxue chubanshe.

Zhang Shimin 張世敏 and Zhao Junliang 趙軍良, 1999. *Guanxue zongshi Zhang Hengqu* 關學宗師張橫渠. Meixian wenhua guangbo dianshiju.

Zhang Shuangdi 張雙棣, Yin Guoguang 殷國光 and Chen Tao 陳濤, eds. 1993. *Lüshi chunqiu cidian* 呂氏春秋詞典 (A Dictionary of Lü's Annals of Spring and Autumn). Ji'nan: Shandong jiaoyu chuban she.

Zhang Wei-an 張維安, 1993. 'Wei Ba Yiti yu Dongya Jingqi Huodong Buzheng ji qi Fanxing' 韋伯議題與東亞經濟活動補正及其反省 (Criticisms of the Weberian Thesis on China and East Asian Develoment and

Subsequent Reflections), *Zhongyang Yanjiu Yuan Minzuxue Yanjiu Suo Jikan* 中央研究院民族學研究所集刊 (*Bulletin of the Institute of Ethnology, Academia Sinica*), 76 (Autumn 1993): 137–67.

Zhang Yanyuan 張彥遠, 1974. *Li Dai Ming Hua Ji* 歷代名畫記 (Record of Famous Painters Through the Ages), rpt. Taipei: Wenshizhe chubanshe 文史哲出版社.

Zhang Zai 張載, 1985. *Zhang Zai Ji* 張載集 (Collected Writings of Zhang Zai). Beijing: Zhonghua shuju.

Zhao Jihui 趙吉惠, Guo Houan 郭厚安, eds., 1989. *Zhongguo Ruxue Cidian* 中國儒學辭典. Shenyang: Liaoning Renmin Chubanshe.

Zhao, Lingling 趙玲玲, 1973. *Shao Kangjie Guanwu Neipian di Yanjiu* 邵康節觀物內篇的研究 (Research on Shao Kangjie's Inner Chapters on Observing Things). Jiaxin, Taiwan: Jiaxin Cement Company.

Zhao Zhiyang 趙制陽, 1984. '*Wang Bo Shiyi pingjie*' 王柏《詩疑》評介 (Review of Wang Bo's 'Doubts about The Book of Poetry'), Zhonghua wenhua fuxing yuekan 中華文化復興月刊, 5: 33–46.

Zheng Acai 鄭阿財, 1982. *Dunhuang xiaodao wenxue yanjiu* 敦煌孝道文學研究. Taipei: Shimen tushu gongsi.

Zheng Jiadong 鄭家棟, 1995. *Dangdai xinruxue lunheng* 當代新儒學論衡 (Evaluative Discussions of Contemporary New Confucian Learning). Taipei: Osmanthus Crown Library.

—— 2000. *Mou Zong San* 牟宗三. Taipei: Great Eastern Library Press.

Zheng Wangeng 鄭萬耕, 1989. *Taixuan jiaoshi* 太玄校釋 (Annotations to the Taixuan). Beijing: Shifan daxue chubanshe.

Zheng Xiaojiang 鄭曉江, 1996. *Yang Jian* 楊簡. Taipei: Dongda tushu gongsi.

Zheng Xuan 鄭玄, 1990. 'Sang fu' 喪服, in *Yili Zheng zhu* 儀禮鄭注 (Zheng's Commentary on the Ceremonial and Ritual). Taipei: Xinxing shuju.

Zheng Zhenduo 鄭振鐸, 1958. *Zhongguo Gudai Banhua Congkan* 中國古代書畫圖目 (Compendium of Traditional Chinese Printed Pictures). Shanghai: Gudian wenxue chubanshe 古典文學出版社.

Zhong Caijun 鍾彩鈞, 1993. *Wang Yangming sixiang zhi jinzhan* 王陽明思想之進展 (The Progress of Wang Yangming's Thought). Taipei: Wenshizhe.

Zhong Youmin, 1985. *Xielingyun Lungao* 謝靈運論稿. Jinan: Qilu Shushe.

Zhongguo ruxue baike quanshu 中國儒學百科全書 (Encyclopedia of Confucianism in China), 1997. ed. Confucius Foundation of China. Beijing: China Great Encyclopedia Press 中國大百科全書出版社.

Zhongguo zhexueshi tonglan 中國哲學史通覽, 1994. (A Comprehensive History of Chinese Philosophy). Shanghai: Zhongguo baike jinshu.

Zhonghua Ruxue Tongdian 中華儒學通典 (*Dictionary of Chinese Confucianism*) 1992, ed. Wu Feng and Song Yifu. Haikou: Nanhai chubanshe.

Zhou Mengjiang, 1992. *Ye Shi yu Yongjia xuepai* 葉適與永嘉學派 (Ye Shi and the Yongjia School). Hangzhou: Zhejiang guji chubanshe.

Zhou Xingji 周行己. *Fuzhi ji* 浮沚集 (Literary Collection from Fuzhi). Congshu jicheng edition.

Zhou Xuewu, 1988. *Ye Shuixin xiansheng nianpu* 葉水心先生年譜 (Chronological Record of Ye Shi). Taipei: Da'an.

Zhou Yangshan 周陽山 and Yang Su 楊肅, ed., 1981. *Jindai Zhongguo sixiang renwu lun – wanqing sixiang* 近代中國思想人物論: 晚清思想 (Studies of Modern Chinese Thinkers – Late Qing Period). Taipei: Shibao chuban gongsi.

Zhou Yutong 周予同, 1996. *Zhou Yutong jingxueshi lunzhu xuanji* 周予同經學史論著選集 (Collected Essays of Zhou Yutong on History of Classical Learning). Expanded edn. Shanghai renmin chubanshe.

Zhu Bin 朱彬, 1996. *Liji xunzuan* 禮記訓纂. Beijing: Zhonghua shuju.

Zhu Bokun 朱伯崑, 1991. *Yixue Zhexueshi* 易學哲學史 (The Philosophy of the Studies of the Book of Changes). Taipei: Landeng Wenhua Shiye Gufen Youxian Gongsi.

Zhu Hanmin 朱漢民, 1991. *Huxiang xuepai yu yuelu shuyuan* 湖湘學派與嶽麓書院. Changsha, Hunan jiaoyu chubanshe.

Zhu Heng 朱衡, *Dao nan yuanwei lu* 道南源委錄 (The Development of the Way in the South), contained in *Zhengyitang quanshu* 正一堂全書. Baibu congshu 百部叢書 edition.

Zhu Xi 朱熹, 1782. *Yi Luo yuanyuan lu* 伊洛淵源錄 (Records of the Origins of the Yi–Luo School). Siku quanshu edition.

—— 1975. *Huian Xiansheng Zhu Wen Gong Wenji* 晦庵先生朱文公文集 (Collected Works by Zhu Xi). Shanghai: Shangwu yinshuguan reprint.

—— 1983. *Sishu zhangju jizhu* 四書章句集注. Beijing: Zhonghua shuju.

—— *Sanchao mingchen yanxing lu* 三朝名臣言行錄 (Records of the Words and Deeds of Famous Ministers during Three Reigns). Sibu congkan edition.

—— 1996. *Lunyu jizhu* 論語集注 (Collected Commentaries on the *Analects*). In his *Sishu wujing* 四書五經 (The Four Books and the Five Classics). Shanghai Guji chubanshe.

Zito, Angela, 1997. *Of Body and Brush: Grand Sacrifice as Text/Performance in 18th c. China.* University of Chicago Press.

Zufferey, Nicholas, 1995. *Wang Chong (27–97?): connaissance, politique, et verité en Chine ancienne.* Bern: Peter Lang.

Name index

Subject index

Text index